DEVELOPING FOR THE
INTERNET
WITH
Winsock

Publisher	*Keith Weiskamp*
Editor	*Diane Green Cook*
Proofreader	*Jenni Aloi*
Interior Design	*Michelle Stroup*
Cover Design	*Bradley O. Grannis*
Layout Production	*Michelle Stroup*
Indexer	*Diane Green Cook*

Distributed to the book trade by IDG Books Worldwide, Inc.

Library of Congress Cataloging-in-Publication Data

Roberts, Dave
    Developing for the Internet with Winsock / Dave Roberts
       p. cm.
    Includes Index
    ISBN 1-883577-42-X : $39.99

Printed in the United States of America

10 9 8 7 6 5 4 3 2 1

DEVELOPING FOR THE
INTERNET WITH
Winsock

Dave Roberts

CORIOLIS GROUP BOOKS

Table of Contents

Chapter 5   The Windows Sockets API 57

Chapter 7   A First Winsock Programming Project 163

Chapter 8   Internet Message Format: RFC 822 205

Chapter 9   Sending Mail: SMTP 215

Chapter 11   Encoding Binary Data: UUENCODE 375

Chapter 12   Mail Extensions: MIME 395

Chapter 13   Network News Transport Protocol: NNTP 453

Chapter 14   File Transfer Protocol: FTP 545

CHAPTER 1

Introduction

An understanding of networking technology and the ability to build network applications are skills that will be in significant demand in the coming years.

Epiphanies are wonderful. One minute you are going about your life, performing the mundane, routine acts of daily living, and the next minute, everything falls into place and the world suddenly looks very changed. In an instant, chaos is tamed and order reigns.

So it was with Archimedes, the Greek mathematician, physicist, and inventor. Archimedes experienced an epiphany as he stepped into a bath. Previously, his king had asked him to determine whether the royal crown was made of pure gold or a silver alloy. In a flash of insight, Archimedes realized that an alloy crown would displace more water than pure gold of an equivalent weight, an application of what is now known as Archimedes' principle. In response to this discovery, Archimedes is said to have run home naked from the bath house shouting, "Eureka!"

Eureka!

Some years ago, I had a college summer job working for Hewlett-Packard Company. Although I had worked with personal computers for quite a while before that, I had never dealt with workstations or the Unix operating system. I was hired to program a database system that HP was using to store production test results. In my off hours, I would fiddle with the operating system, familiarizing myself with the commands and trying to understand Unix's capabilities. Clearly, it was capable of much more than the simple DOS systems with which I had worked.

The feature that interested me the most was the ability of Unix to network. From my machine, I could copy files to other computers and log in to them remotely. As a major workstation vendor and one of the first companies to embrace Unix for commercial applications, HP had one of the largest private internetworks in the world at that time, most of it based on the TCP/IP protocol suite. All HP locations were on the internal network and that network was in turn connected to the global Internet itself.

One day, I was snooping around the Unix file system and found a file named *hosts*. The hosts file contained the names and addresses of all the computers on HP's network. For those already familiar with TCP/IP, this took place before the Domain Name System (DNS) was in common use; host name to address mappings were looked up in a local file on each machine. HP's system administrators generated a host file for the computers in their particular area of responsibility. All of the hosts files generated in this way were automatically combined into one large file every few days and distributed on the network to all the connected computers.

In the hosts file, I found the name of a computer in Germany. I knew it was in Germany because HP named machines using a bit of geographic information to avoid name clashes between different sites (again, this was before the DNS was in use). Until then, my networking experience was limited to machines at the site where I worked. As an experiment, I decided to see if I could access the machine in Germany.

I typed in a *Telnet* command and waited a few seconds for the link to become active. "Login:" the foreign computer demanded. I typed a few characters and waited for them to be echoed back to me. And that's when it happened—my epiphany.

"This networking stuff," I thought to myself. "Wow!" ("Eureka!" isn't exactly the kind of word that a California college student thinks when having an epiphany. "Wow!" is as close as it gets.) There was terrible lag on the link (the characters took about a second to echo back to me) and I didn't have an account on the machine—so I couldn't log in—but these things were unimportant. I could reach out from my desktop in California and touch something in Germany!

Just like Archimedes, my whole world changed in an instant. I finally started to grasp some of the possibilities of this technology. You could do much more than simply copy files. You could control a distant computer; you could distribute information automatically; you could access resources wherever they were located, whether across the room, a campus, or the world. The network was much more than a fancy serial cable!

Since then I've spent a lot of time using, experimenting with, and developing networking products in both my professional and private lives. I've watched as the Internet has grown up from an experimental curiosity to a world-wide avenue for commerce and recreation. I've seen governments proclaim the virtues of the information revolution and declare the value of a global network. Although I take little stock in the plans of politicians, I do believe that we'll see the Internet continue to evolve into a global network upon which many future services will be built. The future is clear: Networking and the Internet will become a greater and greater part of everyday life. We haven't even begun to glimpse the possibilities.

What's in It for You?

The next question is, who will develop those services? Clearly, a need exists for programmers who understand networking protocols and programming. New applications must be developed and challenges must be overcome—challenges for programmers like you and me.

Now that many programmers have mastered the Windows API, C++, and graphics, networking is the new frontier. It's programming for the next century. No longer are applications being written to run solely on a single machine. Rather, new programs embrace the pervasive connectivity that is rapidly being put into place. An understanding of networking technology and the ability to build network applications are skills that will be in significant demand in the coming years.

A Look Ahead

This book is your introduction to network programming. It introduces how to program TCP/IP-based applications in a Microsoft Windows environment using the Windows Sockets, or *Winsock*, Application Programming Interface (API).

If you want to write an application for tomorrow's information superhighway, however, you must understand what sort of traffic is running on that highway today. We won't discuss just the Winsock API. We'll also learn a bit of the history of the Internet. We'll see how a small research network grew up to become a media headline and household word. We'll take a look at some of the application level protocols that are used on the Internet to get real work done. We'll see how to interface with electronic mail protocols and how to browse network newsgroups, all from the application's point of view.

Other network protocols and operating environments still exist, however. Why not learn to program them instead? Why TCP/IP and why Windows? Simply put, TCP/IP and Windows represent the future. The TCP/IP protocols link the very heterogeneous elements of the Internet. No other protocol suite has the ability to scale up to global proportions and deal with the complexities of such growth. It's safe to say that TCP/IP and its direct descendants will be running on the Internet for a long time.

Although many of the current Internet hosts are Unix-based, this fact stems from the historical inclusion of TCP/IP protocols as standard components of Unix distributions. Windows is the most popular desktop computing environment, however, and is poised to take the Internet by storm. Microsoft is including TCP/IP support as a standard feature of future Windows versions.

Chapter by Chapter

Okay, here's a quick summary of each of the chapters in the book.

Chapter 2 takes a short look at the history of the Internet. You'll learn who developed the network and how it grew into what it is today. This chapter contains some interesting lessons about developing systems that will last a long time. Some of the original decisions made about Internet protocols were very forward-looking; others were short-sighted. Those who don't know history are doomed to repeat it!

Chapter 3 introduces you to basic networking and TCP/IP concepts. If you aren't a networking guru, it will prepare you for the chapters that follow and make sure that the vocabulary and concepts are not too foreign. If you *are* a networking guru, you can skip this chapter and get right to the meat of the book.

Chapter 4 is an introduction to socket programming. It explains what sockets are and the basic mechanisms for manipulating them. Even if you're familiar with network programming on Unix machines using the Berkeley Sockets API, you still may want to read this chapter because it describes some differences between the Windows Sockets API and Berkeley Sockets API.

Chapter 5 is a reference chapter on the Windows Sockets API. It describes each of the functions in the API and can serve as a companion to the official Windows Sockets Specification (provided on the companion CD-ROM).

Chapter 6 describes some basic C++ classes that encapsulate Winsock functionality, including such concepts as Internet addresses and sockets. We'll use these classes as building blocks in later chapters to implement each of the sample programs.

Chapter 7 is the first programming example—a simple client for the Finger protocol. The Finger protocol allows a user to get information about another remote user. The Finger client project developed in this chapter introduces an application that uses the asynchronous Winsock extension API.

Chapter 8 describes the format of Internet text messages, as defined in RFC 822. The Internet uses the RFC 822 format as the basic message format for mail and news services.

Chapter 9 looks at the SMTP protocol and portions of an Internet mail client example. The SMTP protocol allows a program to send mail to remote hosts. We'll use the mail client program (cleverly named "Mail Client") for the next several chapters. Chapter 9 describes the portions of the program that allow mail to be composed and sent.

Chapter 10 describes the POP3 protocol. The POP3 protocol allows a client machine to retrieve mail stored on a remote server machine. Chapter 10 describes the portions of the Mail Client application that implement the message retrieval and viewing capabilities.

Chapter 11 examines the UUENCODE encoding format. This format was one of the first solutions to the problem of sending binary data through the Internet mail system. The UUENCODE format is still in active use today.

Chapter 12 describes the new Internet standard for complex mail messages: MIME. The MIME standard allows mail messages to contain textual data, binary attachments, images, video, and other complex data types. Chapter 12 describes the portions of the Mail Client application that implement MIME functionality.

Chapter 13 looks at the NNTP standard. NNTP is the protocol used by network news client applications to browse network news articles. We'll develop a simple browser application, News Client, to demonstrate the concepts.

Finally, Chapter 14 examines the FTP protocol. FTP allows users to transfer files between hosts over the network. Since the early days of the Internet, FTP has been one of the most-used protocols running on the Internet.

The Code

If you've already peeked ahead, you'll see that we're going to use C++ as the programming language for our explorations. We'll use C++'s power to encapsulate Winsock's complexity into some easy-to-use objects. We'll reuse those objects in our projects as we delve into some of the most popular Internet application protocols.

Although we're using C++ to encapsulate the Winsock API, we won't use any application framework to encapsulate the Windows API. Unfortunately, most application frameworks are specific to a given compiler vendor or are not widely used. To keep the code usable for a broad audience, I've forgone the luxuries of window and dialog classes and written directly to the API. In some cases, though, I've whipped up smaller, less industrial strength versions of framework-like classes to increase our code reuse. Both Borland and Microsoft compiler users should find that the code works well. All differences in libraries and compilers are hidden in header files using compiler defined symbols to control the conditional portions of the source text.

The code was compiled on both Windows 3.11 and Windows NT 3.5 (x86). The code runs under Windows 95 and should also work under versions of Windows NT running on processors other than the x86 family. I can't promise any of these other platforms work because I don't use them as my standard development environment, however.

> *Note: Each of the sample programs uses the Microsoft 3D controls library. If you don't have CTL3DV2.DLL and CTL3D32.DLL in your /WINDOWS/ SYSTEM directory, you should copy these files (supplied on the companion CD-ROM) into this directory.*

Although the Windows Sockets API is supposed to be a standard specification, various vendors' implementations often contain subtle differences and sometimes outright bugs. Although I've tested the applications on two or three different Winsock implementations, it's possible that you'll find an implementation that has problems with the code in this book. If you do find a problem, you're on your own because I don't have the time, energy, or financial resources to acquire and test every Winsock implementation. I would appreciate hearing about it, however, and if possible, I'll try to help you.

Before reporting problems, make sure that you've configured your Winsock implementation correctly and it works with many other applications. Most often, the cause of problems is simply operator error.

The Sample Applications

Like most programming books, this book is meant to teach. You'll find that the applications aren't as robust as they could be. Rather, they were written to get their point across as quickly as possible without obscuring that point with all of the source necessary to make them production worthy. I'm not saying that the applications are simplistic, only that their interfaces are somewhat crude and their error checking and error recovery procedures lack some elegance.

Many of the examples build from chapter to chapter. You'll find that code from earlier chapters is reused in later ones. If you like to jump into the middle of a book at whatever location looks appealing, you may find that things do not stand on their own. Simply search back a few chapters and you'll find the explanation you need.

Setting Up a Development Environment

To do network programming, you need a network on which to test. If you're working for a corporation and this is part of your job, a network probably won't be a problem. If you're working from home, you can put together a simple setup relatively easily.

I've got a simple three-node network in my house that I use for my own development and testing. My main development machine is a high-end Am486-based system. I have another Am486 system and an Am386DX-40 connected using Ethernet cards. You don't need a very high-end machine to help you test. I use my older machines as nodes on my network. Whenever I buy a new machine, I attach it to the network and simply leave the old machine connected as well.

Beware of testing your early prototype applications with real Internet hosts. Although it may seem harmless, buggy applications can cause problems with remote servers, problems that remote system administrators don't like. Theoretically, the remote server applications should be written to be robust in the case of network failures and buggy clients, but you never know. In any case, it isn't nice to foist your problems on system administrators you don't even know. Test your applications in an environment you can control before you jump onto the global Internet. Once you've removed most of the bugs, try your applications across the global Internet.

Note that I can't help you diagnose problems with your test configuration. You'll have to learn how to set up Ethernet cards, configure interrupts, install Winsock stacks, and generally get your network up and running yourself.

The Companion CD-ROM

The companion CD-ROM contains a bunch of stuff! First, you'll find all the source code to the demonstration applications. This code will save you a lot of typing. I've included IDE project and make files for a number of compilers. You should be able to find something that will import into your compiler.

Second, you'll find all the RFCs published before this book went to press. The RFCs serve as the definitive references to the protocols described in this book and to many other protocols. You can find other RFCs as they are published on various Internet FTP servers. Use the instructions in the *References* section to download other RFCs.

Finally, you'll find a lot of Winsock applications, servers, and other utilities that you can use to test your applications or just for fun. Some may be more useful than others. I found all the applications on public FTP sites on the Internet. Some are shareware, and you should abide by the usage and distribution restrictions placed on them. Some may contain source code and may serve as good examples of other protocol implementations. Some may work; others may not. If you find a problem, please report it to the original author of the program.

Things Unsaid

Although this book is about the Internet and the various application-level protocols used to get work done with it, you won't learn everything here. This book is written for application developers, not low-level protocol developers. You won't, for instance, find a grand discussion of Internet routing protocols or a detailed analysis of the sliding window scheme TCP uses to keep a stream connection up and running. These topics are research issues, and as application writers, we'll simply take some things for granted. We'll assume, for example, that routing protocols work and that TCP provides us with an error free, stream-like connection. Exactly how those things are done is not our concern.

Unfortunately, we also won't cover every popular application protocol. The book only has only so much space and thousands of Internet RFCs exist to describe numerous protocols. Some are trivial, while others are very complex. I've tried to choose popular protocols that are in daily use and aren't exceedingly simple or too complex. Once you're familiar with these protocols, you should have no trouble picking up the official RFC describing any other protocol and implementing it yourself.

If any of the topics missing from this book interest you (they certainly interest me!), look at the *References* section at the end of the book. Many books, RFCs, and Internet drafts are listed there; the RFCs can be found on the companion CD-ROM.

Contacting Me

I'm always interested in receiving comments on my work. If you have a comment on or question about the material in this book, please send me email at: dave@droberts.com. I want to hear about bug reports for the sample applications. Unfortunately, bugs are a fact of life, and I'm sure that I won't catch every one before the book goes to press.

If you don't have email connectivity to the Internet (note that every online service like Compuserve or America Online is connected to the Internet), you can always reach me through the Coriolis Group using good old paper mail. Then again, if you aren't connected to the Internet, what were you planning to do with the knowledge in this book?

#include <disclaimer.h>

Now that I've invited you to contact me, please be considerate. Note that I can't (won't) answer questions about how to configure Ethernet cards or why a given shareware application provided on the companion CD-ROM won't work with a given Winsock implementation. *Networking systems are very complex* and you're likely to find things that don't work quite right. I can take responsibility only for the work that I have done, not the work of others. Please direct these sorts of questions to the people supporting the hardware or software involved with the problem.

I won't be able to respond to every comment or question I receive. I'm an email junkie, but sometimes I just get buried and can't keep up. Don't worry if you don't receive a reply. I'm probably just swamped. Don't associate the lack of a reply with any lack of caring about your comments on my part. I do appreciate the feedback!

Thanks!

A book never appears by itself. You're looking at the work of many talented people. I'd like to thank the crew at The Coriolis Group for putting together another great product. Thanks, also, to Katie Hafner who directed me to much of the material in Chapter 2. My wife, Dawn, as always, deserves a medal for her editing input and her ability to put up with my high stress level. Finally, I'd like to thank Brian Hook, who helped get me started writing books. There are probably others that I'll remember right as the book goes to press, as is always the case. Thanks one and all!

Internet History

The Internet has recently been thrust to the front of public attention, but the seeds of the network were sown long ago. This chapter describes where the network started and how it has changed and grown.

Although the Internet was recently on the front cover of *Time* magazine and many major newspapers, had its merits debated in the U.S. Congress, and is an icon of popular culture, things weren't always that way. Like many systems that end up being ubiquitous, the Internet began with a simple idea that grew beyond anyone's imagination because it was simply too useful to be abandoned.

In this chapter, we'll examine the history of the Internet. We'll find out where it came from, how it was developed, and how it has evolved and grown to meet the changing needs of the population it serves.

The history presented here is not comprehensive. Only the highlights are provided, and we do not mention the people who actually did the initial work. This omission is not meant to imply that these details are unnecessary or irrelevant; on the contrary, the description of the technologies and personalities involved with the early network development effort is fascinating. If you're interested in reading more, consult the *References* section of this book for other sources.

In the Beginning...

Computers have become appliances. Not only do we have personal computers that sit on desktops in major corporations, a significant number of homes have one or more computers. The microprocessor has become the fundamental component of many other complex systems in our environment. Microprocessors control the front panel of your microwave oven and the fuel injection system of your car. There seems to be no end in sight. With increasing technology development comes the promise of falling technology costs. It's clear that microprocessors and computer technology will be absorbed into almost every facet of modern life at one level or another. We've come a long way in 30 years.

In the 1960s, things were very different. Computers were not the fundamental building blocks of society's appliances; in fact, they were downright scarce by today's standards. Of course, from the perspective at the time, the computer revolution had already begun and things were growing by leaps and bounds. Tens of thousands of computers were in use throughout the world.

In the 1960s, most computer manufacturers produced several different computer models. There were few standards in the computer industry, however. Operating systems tended to be developed by each manufacturer specifically for each computer model. Different models from the same manufacturer were frequently incompatible. The standards that did exist were at a very low level—the format of characters on magnetic tape, for instance—and were driven less by agreement than by who had the most market share and developed the technology first.

This lack of standards made it difficult for computers to communicate. The movement of data and programs between systems was usually limited to computers of the same manufacturer and model, and the transport medium was usually physical rather than electronic—a person transporting magnetic tape, paper tape, or punched cards. Electronic communication was frequently used to attach a number of interactive terminals to a central computer system rather than to transfer data between two systems.

In 1967, the Information Processing Techniques Office (IPTO) of the Advanced Research Projects Agency of the U.S. Department of Defense began serious work on the ARPA network, or ARPANET. The goals of the ARPANET project were to develop experience in computer communications and to improve the productivity of computer research through the sharing of computers and data. By sharing resources, the project's designers reasoned, computer sites would not need to replicate programs, software, or equipment. When needed, data could be moved to a different site and researchers could use the hardware of distant sites without having to buy their own or travel to a far-away location. The design of the ARPA network progressed throughout 1967 and the first half of 1968.

The ARPANET researchers wanted to develop methods of sharing resources between dissimilar computer systems. But because the various computer models and operating systems were so diverse, few of the hoped-for productivity gains could be realized; communicating only with other sites that shared the same hardware and software combinations limited the research significantly.

ARPANET

By mid-1968, the network architecture was basically complete. The ARPA researchers had devised a packet-switched architecture, as shown in Figure 2.1. Each computer, or host, in the network was connected to an Interface Message Processor (IMP) that performed all the communications functions: switching of messages, error checking, and retransmission. The IMP was connected to the host using a serial connection and to one or more IMPs using high-speed leased phone lines operating at 56 Kbps. The IMP would accept messages of up to 8192 bits from the host, fragment the message into packets of not more than 1024 bits, compute a 24-bit Cyclic Redundancy Check (CRC) over the packet for error detection purposes, and route the packets to their final destination. The IMP provided storage for buffering messages. This scheme allowed different line speeds to be used in different parts of the network and enabled an IMP to absorb a transient burst of traffic routed through it to another host.

Figure 2.1

The initial
ARPANET
architecture.

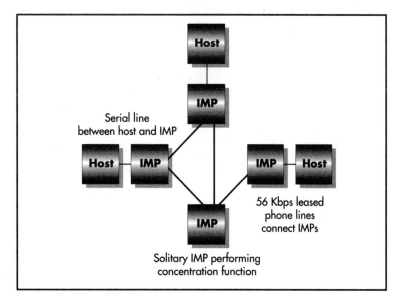

The IMP was a full-fledged computer, which presented advantages as well as disadvantages. Among the advantages:

- IMPs could all be constructed from the same computer model, allowing a common set of hardware and software to be built. As the network was upgraded, changes could be made much faster to the IMPs than to all the various hardware and software combinations that made up the hosts.
- IMPs would relieve the hosts of the network communications burden. An IMP would switch traffic passing through it that was not destined for the host attached to it. Separating the network tasks from the host tasks allowed the IMP and the host to concentrate on their respective duties.
- IMPs did not need to have hosts attached to them. If necessary, a solitary IMP could be located at a strategic point in the network to concentrate traffic from other IMPs.

The main disadvantage was the need for a separate computer next to each host, which was expensive. In spite of the cost, however, the decision to use IMPs was finalized, and in mid-1968 a Request For Quotation (RFQ) was mailed to 140 potential bidders who had indicated interest in the project.

Building the ARPANET

In response the ARPANET RFQ, IPTO received 12 large proposals toward the end of 1968. The field was narrowed to four candidates, then two. Finally, one week before Christmas, 1968, the contract was awarded to Bolt Beranek and Newman, Inc. (BBN), located in Cambridge, MA.

BBN started work in January 1969, and the equipment for an initial four-node network was in place and operating before the end of the year. The four nodes were located at the University of CA at Los Angeles (UCLA), the Stanford Research Institute (SRI) in Menlo Park, California, the University of California at Santa Barbara (UCSB), and the University of Utah in Salt Lake City. Each site was connected to the others using 56 Kbps leased phone circuits, as shown in Figure 2.2.

The network expanded rapidly after the initial deployment. By June 1970, five more sites had been added, bringing the total to nine. The additional sites included the RAND Corporation, located in Santa Monica, CA, System Development Corporation, also in Santa Monica, the Massachusetts Institute of Technology (MIT), Harvard University, and BBN itself, all three in MA. As shown in Figure 2.3, the new sites necessitated the use of two long-haul lines, from RAND to BBN and from University of Utah to MIT.

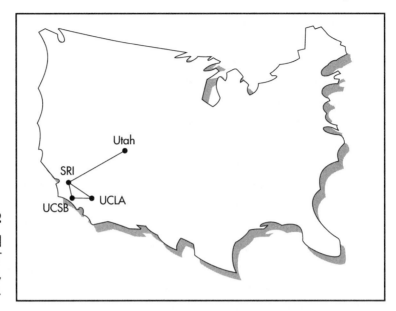

Figure 2.2

The initial
ARPANET
deployment,
December 1969.

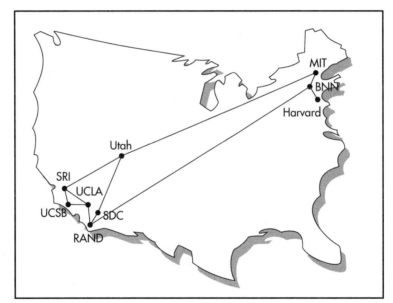

Figure 2.3

The ARPANET
in June 1970.

ARPANET Protocols

Today's Internet runs on different protocols than the ARPANET, although many
of the current protocols have their roots in those of the original ARPANET.

Initially, the message format used in the ARPANET allowed four hosts to be connected to a single IMP, with a total of 64 IMPs in the network. By today's standards, this sounds pitifully small, dwarfed even by some local area networks, let alone wide area networks. Today's Internet has millions of hosts. These figures were simply outside the realm of comprehension of the early researchers, however. When you start from a base of zero, 64 IMPs and a total of 256 hosts seems like a very large number.

The original design called for the IMPs to do all character-set, word size, and operating system conversions. This design would allow the hosts to be ignorant of the fact that they were communicating with incompatible computer systems. However, the IMPs were never given this ability. Hosts did the conversions themselves.

Early on, the conversions used a set of ad-hoc protocols that were developed as needed when sites wished to communicate. Representatives from the initial ARPANET sites formed a group called the Network Working Group (NWG) to develop a set of standard host-to-host protocols. In October 1971, general agreement was finally reached on the set of protocols to be used, and implementation of the protocols began soon after.

Several protocols were developed using a layered approach. This approach was the best way to do things, given the equipment and network topology of the time. We now know that layered network protocols provide many advantages. We'll describe some of the advantages in the next chapter.

The bottom layer of the ARPANET protocols connected the hosts to the IMPs. The second layer established connections between hosts and managed buffer space at each end of the connection. The third layer was the Initial Connection Protocol (ICP), which was used when a remote user or process wanted to gain the attention of a network host.

The fourth layer was the Telecommunications Network (Telnet) protocol, which was designed to support network terminal access to remote hosts. At the time, terminals from different manufacturers provided many different features to be used with a host computer made by the same manufacturer. The early Telnet protocol provided a specification for both a generic network terminal (an abstract entity) and the communications protocols to allow it to be "connected" to a remote host. This early Telnet protocol provided the model for the newer Telnet protocol in use on the Internet today.

Other protocols developed for the ARPANET included a File Transfer Protocol (FTP) and a Remote Job Entry protocol (RJE).

Many of the ideas embodied in today's Transmission Control Protocol (TCP) were first pioneered in a host-to-host protocol called the Network Control Protocol (NCP). The NCP was used to set up a virtual circuit connection between two hosts at the beginning of a session or transaction and to take it down at the end. The NCP provided flow control and defined an abstraction called a "socket" as the endpoint of the virtual circuits.

The Internet

In October 1972, Washington D.C. was host to the First International Conference on Computer Communications. Researchers from around the world were brought together to discuss their individual research projects on computer communications. The researchers agreed that it was time to start considering the eventual connection of the various world wide projects. Clearly, new protocols would be needed for communication over the disparate networks.

The InterNetwork Working Group (INWG) was formed to consider such problems. The INWG began work on the protocols and systems that would be necessary to support a mesh of interconnected networks acting as a global internetwork. The immediate vision was a set of autonomous networks connected by gateways. Like the ARPANET's IMPs, the gateways would switch messages from network to network according to the destination addresses contained in the messages.

In 1974, the first revision of the Transmission Control Protocol (TCP) was published. At that time, TCP included many functions that are no longer present in the modern protocol. The early version of TCP was expanded by a group of U.S. researchers from ARPA sites who formed the Internet Engineering Group. The original TCP protocol was split into two protocols: a new TCP with the functionality of today's TCP and the Internet Protocol (IP), which dealt with the issues of addressing and fragmentation of packets on networks with different maximum packet size constraints.

The early versions of TCP and IP were developed steadily for the next several years. In 1981, the networking community had gained enough experience with the protocols to warrant an official transition from the old NCP to TCP/IP. In November, an official announcement was made: NCP would be phased out in favor of TCP/IP, with the conversion process to be complete by January 1, 1983. During the transition, several systems would provide translations services between the old and new protocols to keep the network running.

Several surveys were taken between December 1982 and February 1983. By that point the ARPANET had swelled to 320 hosts, 285 of which were general-purpose systems. Of these hosts, one-third were using the new TCP/IP protocol by December 1982, about half had made the conversion by early January 1983, and more than two-thirds by February 1983. Although the initial goal of January 1, 1983 was not met, the Internet, based on the TCP/IP protocol, was up and running early in 1983.

While the conversion process was underway, the Defense Communication Agency (DCA) split the ARPANET into two separate networks, one to support research and one for non-classified military communication. The research network retained the original ARPANET name, while the new military communication network was named MILNET.

ARPA actively encouraged the use of the new protocols among university researchers. At the time the protocols were developed, many universities were using the University of California's Berkeley Software Distribution Unix, or BSD Unix. ARPA funded BBN to create a version of the TCP/IP protocol that would work with Unix and funded Berkeley to integrate the protocol with BSD Unix. Concurrently, many university computer science departments were acquiring their second or third computer and wanted to network them using local area networks. The TCP/IP protocol integrated with BSD Unix provided an excellent solution when there were few other choices. As a result, the use of the TCP/IP protocol spread quickly among universities. As we'll see in Chapter 4, BSD Unix was very important in the development of the Internet. It not only spread the TCP/IP protocol with it, but also provided the Application Programming Interface (API) that came to be known as Berkeley Sockets.

As the Internet grew, the connection pace accelerated. It was more productive for researchers to join the existing network than to try to start one of their own. As the network became a more important part of general scientific research of all kinds, the National Science Foundation accepted the task of expanding the network to as much of the scientific community as possible. It established a set of regional networks connected to a new wide area backbone named NSFNET.

Within seven years, the Internet had grown tremendously. It connected hundreds of individual networks across the United States and Europe. Nearly 20,000 hosts in universities, government offices, and corporate research laboratories were connected. In 1987, the growth rate was 15 percent per month and showed no signs of slowing down. By 1990, there were 3,000 networks connected, encompassing 200,000 computers.

Here and Now

Although the ARPANET is no longer the center of the Internet, its place in networking history is secure. If nothing else, it was a shining example of the way government money should be spent—that is, on projects that are creative, dynamic, and necessary. With the assistance of government funding, the ARPANET researchers designed, built, and nourished a global network. They started with little more than an idea—there were few examples of computer networks at the time—and the journey still has not ended.

Many follow-on protocol design and standardization efforts used the work of the early ARPANET researchers as a pool of knowledge from which to draw. The design of the OSI 7-layer Reference Model was based on knowledge derived from the first ARPANET. The CCITT's (now ITU) X.25 packet network standard bears a striking resemblance to some ARPANET concepts.

Today the Internet is the world's largest research network. New ideas and protocols are put into use frequently. Some end their lives as historical anachronisms, labeled with the most feared word in networking circles—*deprecated*. Others prove themselves as reliable and useful staples of Internet daily life. The Hypertext Transport Protocol (HTTP) protocol, used to control the transmission of hypertext documents of the World Wide Web, did not exist only a few years ago. Now the World Wide Web is one of the most popular Internet services.

The current size of the Internet is not known. Estimates place it at several million hosts connected all over the world. The growth rate continues to be astronomical and unstoppable. Clearly, if there is anything likely to resemble the fabled *information superhighway* of political rhetoric, the Internet is it. Many of the applications that will be in daily use on that superhighway have yet to be written.

And that's where you, the network software developer, come in.

Internet Internals

To master Internet programming, you'll need a good working knowledge of the TCP/IP protocol suite—the foundation of Internet communications.

Before we learn how to program applications for the Internet, we'll review the operation of some basic Internet protocols. In this chapter, we'll introduce some of the terms and concepts that appear in later chapters. Note that this chapter is *not* meant to be a complete, precise description of each protocol in the TCP/IP suite. Rather, this is a quick, high-level introduction. If you're interested in more detail, consult one of the many books covering this subject, some of which are listed in the *References* section of this book.

OSI 7-Layer Reference Model

The Open System Interconnection (OSI) Reference Model provides a basis for describing the TCP/IP protocol suite. The OSI model was developed by the International Standards Organization (ISO) to document the separation of networking functions into a set of layered services. Figure 3.1 illustrates the OSI model.

Each layer in the model provides distinct services to the layers above it and encapsulates its services within itself. Upper layers do not need to know how a given layer provides its services; they only need a description of the service contract it provides.

Conceptually, each layer of the model communicates with its peer in a remote network entity. The communication path is virtual, however. Lower layers provide communication services for upper layers to use for their communications. Only the lowest layer, the physical layer, makes a true direct connection between peers.

The peer-to-peer communication relationship keeps the layering abstraction intact. A given layer does not depend on the mechanics of lower layers, and it doesn't even need to know the upper layer's purpose in using its services. Data

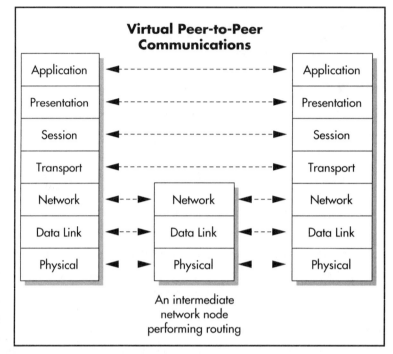

Figure 3.1

The OSI 7-layer Reference Model.

from the upper layer enters the top of a given layer, where it is communicated to the remote peer using lower layers. When the data reaches the peer layer at the remote entity, the data is handed back to the upper layer.

The OSI model describes seven distinct layers: physical, data link, network, transport, session, presentation, and application.

The *physical* layer is responsible for the physical communication between entities. It carries raw bits between devices. The physical layer typically uses an electrical signal like voltage to represent a given bit value on the physical medium (typically some sort of wire). The physical layer defines the way individual bits are represented by the electrical signals, so that they have a high chance of being received correctly by the peer physical layer entity. It makes no guarantees, however. Note that the physical layer is not limited to wires. Radio- and microwaves can be used to carry bits through the air just as easily as voltages carry them on a wire.

The *data link* layer adds framing and reliability to the raw bit stream that is sent between physical layers. The data link layer recognizes the starts and ends of frames within the bit stream and detects when frames have been corrupted by the physical layer. Some data link layers provide retransmission of frames that are detected to be in error. Others, usually built on top of more reliable physical layers, do not. IEEE 802 networks (802.3 Ethernet and 802.5 Token Ring) are examples of data links.

The *network* layer routes data between different data links. Using the network layer, a large internetwork can be built of many heterogeneous data link types (Ethernet, Token Ring, and FDDI, for example). The network layer provides a uniform addressing system in which the individual addressing mechanisms of a given data link type are hidden from higher layers.

The *transport* layer takes data from the session layer and divides it into smaller units, which are then passed to the network layer. The transport layer keeps track of many different connections at the same time and ensures that data for a given session is delivered to the correct session layer entity. The transport layer is the first end-to-end layer. In a large internetwork, the network, data link, and physical layers are all used to communicate between immediate neighbors in the internetwork topology. The transport layer actually carries on a dialog with the remote peer.

The *session* layer manages connections between different applications. The session layer can provide such features as checkpointing and recovery in the event of a failure.

The *presentation* layer is concerned with the representation of data types. In a heterogeneous internetwork, it's quite conceivable that two computers might not even use the same character set encoding. The presentation layer provides such services as ASCII to EBCDIC conversion and encryption.

The session and presentation layers typically are not as well-defined as the transport and lower layers. The session and presentation layers were designed to standardize the mechanisms that control connections and provide application services. In truth, most applications take on the roles of the session and presentation layers themselves. Rather than standardize a specific ASCII to EBCDIC conversion layer function, for instance, many applications simply perform the conversion themselves.

The *application* layer is, well, the application layer. Users typically interact with these programs. An email user agent or network news browser are examples of application layer entities.

TCP/IP and the OSI Reference Model

Although the OSI Reference Model is often used to describe the functioning of the TCP/IP protocol suite, it really should be the other way around. Many of the concepts that are embodied in the OSI model were discovered and tested during the development of the TCP/IP protocol suite. After these concepts were proven in working TCP/IP implementations, the OSI model was developed to codify and communicate the knowledge.

Because TCP/IP predates the OSI model, the TCP/IP layer does not fit precisely into the OSI model. Protocols within the TCP/IP suite often cross the boundaries that define layers in the OSI model. For example, many of the functions in TCP would be considered session layer functionality in the OSI model, and applications frequently deal with presentation layer issues themselves. Figure 3.2 compares the strict OSI model with TCP/IP's protocol layering.

Many developers of the TCP/IP protocol suite would argue that TCP/IP's layering is as it should be. The OSI model, they say, is too rigid. It artificially constrains protocol implementation boundaries that should not be constrained. Whether they are correct or not is a matter of opinion, but no one can deny that TCP/IP has enjoyed much greater market success than any official ISO protocol conforming to the OSI Reference Model.

Internet RFCs

Rigorous standards are required to keep the Internet functioning. These standards define the various application level protocols such as email and network

Figure 3.2

Comparing the OSI Reference Model to the TCP/IP protocol suite.

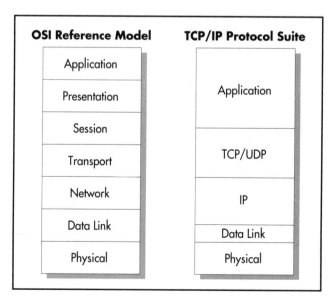

news. Standards also describe the formats of individual data packets and the algorithms to route those packets through the network, a vital job, indeed!

Internet standards are defined in documents called Request For Comments, or RFCs. Not all RFCs define standards but all standards are defined by RFCs. Some RFCs contain informational commentary or experimental protocols that were never adopted as standards.

Originally, RFCs were just what the term "request for comments" implies—documents that described protocols and requested feedback from others interested in standardizing the particular functionality described. Initially, there wasn't much rigor in the system. If you wanted to exchange electronic mail with somebody, you simply implemented the appropriate RFC that described the email system and you were up and running. If you found a particular piece of functionality that you wanted to define, you implemented it and then wrote an RFC to document it. Others could then implement your functionality if they found it useful. Today, RFCs have taken on more of an official standards role. Some RFCs define standards while others are still informational.

RFCs are published in electronic form on the Internet itself. Several official sites are maintained to distribute the authoritative versions of these RFCs to anybody who's willing to come get them.

> The companion CD-ROM contains all the RFCs available at the time of this book's publication. The RFCs are named RFCxxxx.txt, where *xxxx* is the RFC's number, which can be found in the RFC subdirectory. As new RFCs appear, you can get them from the official distribution sites using FTP. See the *References* section for more information about official RFC distribution sites and how to FTP RFCs from them.

Every published RFC is assigned a document number. Document numbers are issued in sequential order. Table 3.1 lists the number, title, and acronym for the more important RFCs. We'll examine some of these RFCs in detail in later chapters.

RFCs are updated to reflect changes in the standards they define or to clarify an ambiguity. Unfortunately, RFCs don't have version numbers attached to them. When a revised RFC is published, it is given a new number, just as if it were a new RFC. This process can be quite confusing. You cannot tell immediately if the version you have is the most recent.

Table 3.1	RFC numbers and titles	
Number RFC	**Title**	**Acronym**
742	Finger Protocol	FINGER
768	User Datagram Protocol	UDP
791	The Internet Protocol	IP
793	Transmission Control Protocol	TCP
821	Simple Mail Transport Protocol	SMTP
822	Format for Internet Messages	MAIL
959	File Transfer Protocol	FTP
977	Network News Transfer Protocol	NNTP
1460	Post Office Protocol, Version 3	POP3

The best way to tell if you have the most recent copy of the standard is to look at the index of RFCs. The index informs you if an RFC is obsolete, and directs you to a more recent version. Of course, that second RFC may also be obsolete, so you'll have to check the second RFC with the index. The most recent version of the RFC index is always named rfc-index.txt and is located in the same directory as the other RFCs at the Internet distribution sites.

IP: The Internet Protocol

The Internet Protocol, or IP, is defined by RFC 791. IP provides the most basic level of service in the Internet, routing a datagram through the Internet switching fabric. IP is the basis upon which the other familiar protocols stand, as shown in Figure 3.3. Let's take a short look at IP, the services it provides, and the addressing scheme upon which the Internet is based.

Figure 3.3

IP is the basis of all other Internet protocols.

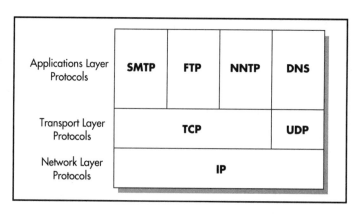

Best Effort Service

IP provides the protocols above it with a very simple service model. IP is similar to the public postal service. Given a bit of data, a packet, and an address, IP tries to route the packet through the network until it reaches its destination. Like most public postal services, however, IP doesn't promise great service. It does its best to see that the packet is delivered, but sometimes that just is not possible.

For instance, IP may lose the packet somewhere in the network. This event is usually caused by some sort of network fault. IP may also deliver the packet corrupted. Although IP never intentionally corrupts data en route, it does not check to ensure that the data is not corrupted. If corruption does occur, IP will not notice it and will deliver the data anyway. You might imagine this as a mail carrier who doesn't notice that your package was damaged on the way to your house.

Given a set of packets, IP does not guarantee that they'll arrive in the same order that they were sent. IP may choose to send different messages on different paths to the destination, sometimes for the purpose of load balancing and sometimes to avoid a network fault. Because the separate paths may have different delays associated with them, the messages can arrive out of order at the final destination. In all of these cases, IP does nothing to inform either the source or destination of the packet that anything has gone wrong. You might imagine this scenario as the post office receiving two letters on two successive days, both with the same destination. The second letter might be sent via air mail and the first on a truck. The second letter will probably arrive before the first.

In summary, IP makes a *best effort* delivery guarantee. It doesn't promise that everything will go well, only that it will do its best to see that things are delivered to their ultimate destination in a somewhat timely fashion, most of the time, if possible.

The shortcomings in IP's service guarantee are unacceptable when dealing with computer data, however. Users want their file transfers to be error-free (imagine that!). To guarantee users that everything will work correctly *most of the time*, on sunny days when there wasn't a full moon the previous night, is not at all comforting. To compensate for IP's shortcomings, the Internet uses two transport protocols, TCP and UDP, which are discussed later in this chapter.

IP Addresses

One of the key parameters given to IP along with a packet of data is the destination address for the packet. Before a packet is sent, IP prepends it with a header that contains both the source and destination address for the packet. On the path to the destination, the address is examined at each router to decide how to handle the packet.

An IP address is independent of a data-link address like an Ethernet or FDDI address. IP imposes a standard address format over all the individual data links that comprise the Internet, making it independent of each data link's individual peculiarities.

IP addresses are 32-bit quantities. Within each address, a variable number of bits is allocated between a network portion and host portion, as shown in Figure 3.4. The network portion of the address is used to route a packet to the individual network that contains the host. An example of an individual network is an Ethernet segment. The host portion is used to distinguish among hosts connected to that specific network. Using the public postal system analogy again, the network portion of the address is similar to a street name and the host portion is similar to the address number of a building on that street.

The number of bits allocated to the network and host portions of the address varies. Network administrators can choose the number of bits according to the number of hosts that are located on a network. An application cannot assume much about the structure of IP addresses. As far as the application is concerned, IP addresses are just 32-bit numbers.[1]

Every entity in the Internet that can be communicated with has one or more IP addresses. An IP address is associated with and identifies an interface to the net-

Figure 3.4

IP address format.

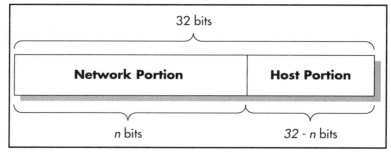

---

[1]   Note that most textbooks describing IP would mention class A, B, and C address formats here. I'm deliberately not because these older classes are more of an address allocation administration issue today than anything else. Applications don't have to deal with address classes, and so I'm not covering them here.

work. A router always has two or more network interfaces. A host system typically has one network interface, but may have more than one. Sometimes a host is given two interfaces to ensure its availability in the face of a failure of the interface. For instance, a corporate-wide mail server may want to be able to provide service even if its network interface fails. If it has two interfaces and one fails, the other can be used to reach the system.

When writing an IP address in human readable form, the address is written in *dotted decimal* notation, not binary or hexadecimal format. Each of the four bytes representing the 32-bit address is converted to a decimal number and is written with a period separating each number. For instance, the address 0x0F000001 is written as 15.0.0.1 in dotted decimal notation.

IP Routing

Routing is the primary function that IP performs. Given an internetwork of network segments connected by routers, as shown in Figure 3.5, IP makes the forwarding decision in each of the routers. Every packet gets from its source to its destination according to IP's best effort delivery service guarantee.

Figure 3.5

An internetwork of hosts connected by routers.

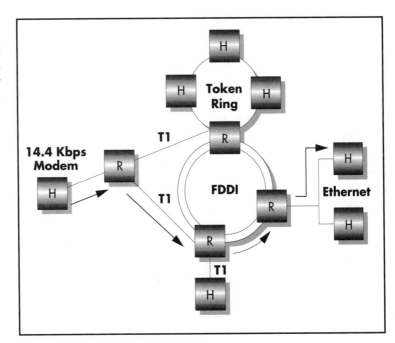

To route an IP packet, each router along the path from the source to the destination inspects the IP destination address contained in the packet header. The routers look up information stored in the router, using the network portion of the destination address as a key. The information keyed by the destination address tells the router which of its interfaces to use to forward the packet to its destination. If the router cannot deliver the packet directly, it forwards the packet to the next router in the chain, until the last router finally delivers it to the destination.

Routing protocols are used to exchange the routing information between routers. The information exchanged includes the status of the links to which each router is connected, whether operational or not, and the distance to reach a given network segment over a certain path. In general, routing protocols are very complex. They are the subject of much research, and many different protocols have been invented. Different parts of the Internet use different routing protocols, depending on the needs of a particular administrative domain.

We won't say any more about how routing gets done. If you're interested in the various routing protocols, see the books in the *References* section of this book. For our purposes, simply keep in mind that routing is performed in a store-and-forward manner by routers along the path to the destination and that it's IP's responsibility to choose the next router based on the information exchanged between routers.

TCP and UDP: Streams vs. Datagrams

Computers typically have two different types of communication needs: bulk data transfer and quick messages. The Transmission Control Protocol (TCP) and User Datagram Protocol (UDP) are designed to provide these services to application programs. TCP and UDP use IP to route datagrams through the Internet.

TCP

TCP is designed for error-free bulk data transfer and provides error detection, recovery, and sequencing information to make up for IP's best effort delivery service. TCP sets up a connection between two hosts before data transmission begins. The connection models a reliable, bi-directional circuit, as shown in Figure 3.6. Data sent to the other node is guaranteed to arrive error-free and in order.

TCP breaks the data provided to it into chunks, checksums each chunk, adds sequencing information, and then encapsulates the chunks in IP packets. IP is

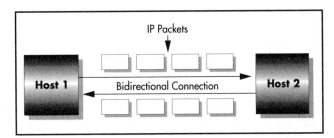

Figure 3.6

TCP provides a reliable, bi-directional connection between two hosts using IP's best-effort datagram service as a base.

used to route each chunk of data through the Internet to the destination. The checksum and sequencing information is used by the receiver to detect corrupted or misordered data. When IP loses or corrupts a packet, TCP notices that a problem has occurred and retransmits the data as appropriate. Although hiccups may occur in the data stream as the error recovery processes kick in, the receiving application always sees that the data chunks arrive in order, error free.

TCP also provides demultiplexing services using ports. The demultiplexing process is described in a following section.

Because TCP requires a few packets of information to be exchanged between the two hosts to set up the connection, it is better suited to applications where a lot of data will be exchanged and the connection setup cost can be amortized over a longer transmission time.

UDP

UDP is designed for lightweight application messaging. UDP is little more than a thin error detection and demultiplexing layer over raw IP. UDP is inherently unidirectional and does not require that a connection between two nodes be established before data transfer can begin, as shown in Figure 3.7. Nodes simply send data to the intended destination. Because UDP eliminates the time TCP

Figure 3.7

UDP is a slightly higher-level datagram service based on IP's service.

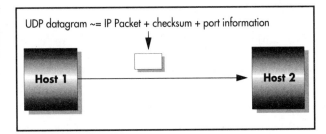

takes to set up a connection, UDP is better suited to single message request-response applications.

UDP uses a simple checksum to check for data corruption of received packets. UDP does not provide for retransmission of lost or corrupted data or resequencing of misordered packets. When an error is discovered, a UDP datagram is simply thrown away. If IP loses a UDP datagram on the way to the destination, UDP does not detect that it was lost.

If an application needs to ensure that a UDP packet arrives error-free at the destination, a simple error-control protocol should be used. For example, the receiver of the packet should send a positive acknowledgment to the source to indicate that a packet has been received. If the source does not receive the acknowledgment in a given amount of time, it should assume that the packet was lost and retransmit it. The receiver should be able to deal with duplicate data in the case that the original data was received correctly but the acknowledgment packet was delayed or lost in the network.

UDP also provides demultiplexing services using the concept of a port. Ports are described in the next section.

If applications require reliable, sequenced data transfer, TCP should be used or a simple error-control protocol such as the one described previously should be built on top of UDP. Typically, the engineering of anything but simple error-control protocols is better left for the experts, however, and so TCP is often the best choice when things start to get complicated.

Ports

Both TCP and UDP provide demultiplexing services to different, concurrently running applications. Although IP routes packets through the Internet using the destination address, its work is done once the packet reaches the destination host. More information is needed to identify which application on that host should receive the information once it arrives. Ports provide this capability, as shown in Figure 3.8.

A port is a small integer number. Both the sending and receiving applications are assigned port numbers to send and receive data (either with TCP or UDP). Coupled with the source and destination IP addresses, the source and destination port numbers uniquely identify which applications on hosts are associated with any given data transfer.

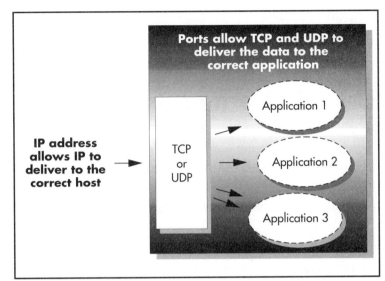

Figure 3.8

Ports specify the application that should receive the data on a given host.

A good analogy of the port concept is the name portion of a standard postal address. The postal service routes a letter based on the street address. Once the postal service (IP) delivers a letter to your house, its work is done. Somebody at your house (TCP or UDP) still has to look at the name on the letter to determine which of your roommates, Bob, Mary, Joan, or you, is the intended recipient.

Well-Known Ports

To make a TCP connection or send a UDP datagram, the sender must know the port number associated with the intended receiver on the destination host. If two hosts are participating in a special communication, humans can manually exchange and enter the correct port numbers, but generally this is not the case. More often, the port number is known before the communication starts.

For example, I may want to send an email message using a TCP connection to an unknown computer in another company. To set up the connection, my mail program must know the destination port number associated with the mail program on the receiving machine. I don't want to have to telephone a system administrator at the other company to learn the port number associated with the mail program every time I want to send a mail message.

To resolve this problem, certain port numbers are assigned to popular application programs. By convention, an SMTP email server always waits for connections on port 25. If I want to send mail to a given host, the mail program on my machine connects to port 25 of the remote host. There are many other well-known ports assigned for such services as network news (NNTP, port 119), network terminals (Telnet, TCP port 23) , file transfer (FTP, TCP port 21), and so on.

Domain Names

People hate identification numbers. How often have you ever heard a friend lamenting that she recently dealt with a government agency or local utility company and felt "like just another number?" People like to express themselves with the names they give objects and each other. To simply exist as a number is to be plain vanilla, without any personality or character whatsoever.

Imagine if everything around you had a number in place of a name. I'd be #4, that book on the table would be #704, your car would be #13. It would be a bland world, don't you think? Further, it would be hard to keep things straight. In general, people don't remember random strings of digits very well. Was my car #13 or #704? Were you #37, or was that me?

Well, this is just the situation that IP confronts. Everything in IP's world is a number—a 32-bit IP address to be exact. IP deals with nothing else, but because it's a computer protocol, it has no trouble keeping all the numbers straight. Humans have to interact with IP, however, at least indirectly. When I want to make a connection from my computer to your computer, I need a way to tell IP which computer I want. I could type the IP address of your computer each time, but because humans are so poor at keeping track of those addresses, I'm likely to make a mistake. It would be much nicer if you could give your computer a name that I could then use. Fortunately, the Domain Name System (DNS) was created to resolve this issue.

DNS is a distributed database of name-to-IP-address mappings. Give DNS the name of a computer and it returns its address. Your system no longer has to be 193.47.23.5. Rather, it can be *rick*, *superman*, *netsurfer*, or something equally creative and personal.

Names in the DNS are arranged in a tree-structured hierarchy of administrative domains. When writing a domain name, each individual subdomain is separated from its neighbors by a period. You know what domain names look like. You've seen them in email addresses following the at-sign ("@"). Given a domain name of *foo.bar.com*, *com* is the first level of hierarchy, followed by *bar*, and finally *foo*. In this

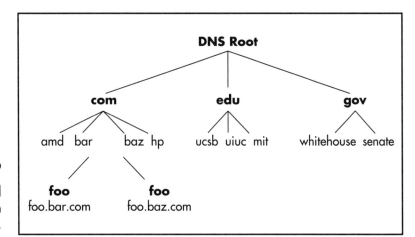

Figure 3.9

Hierarchical domain names.

case, *bar.com* is the domain name assigned to a company, and *foo* is an individual computer in that company. Figure 3.9 shows some other domain names in the hierarchical name space. The *edu* domain is used by educational institutions like universities and colleges. The *gov* domain is used by the U.S. government. There are many other top-level domains, some based on functional classification (network providers like *net*) and some based on geographical boundaries (country names).

The hierarchical name space helps prevent clashes between names and allows the naming of individual hosts to be carried out in a distributed fashion. For instance, if my company has a domain name of *bar.com* and I want to name my computer *foo*, I only have to check with my own network administrator to make sure there is no other computer named *foo* in the *bar.com* domain. There can be many other computers named *foo*, as long as they are in different domains. For instance, an organization with the *baz.com* domain name can name its machine *foo* as well.

The DNS database is distributed. To look up a given name, your computer sends a request to a remote domain name server (unless the server happens to be running on your machine). A domain name server can answer queries about a portion of the domain name space; it also knows of other servers that can help it answer the queries it cannot answer directly. Typically, a given organization runs a domain name server for its portion of the domain name hierarchy. If my company domain were *bar.com*, the domain name server for my company would answer directly any queries for names of *bar.com* computers. If I ask the server to look up *whitehouse.gov*, it won't be able to give me the answer—it doesn't know the information itself. However, it will go get the answer.

When a server can't answer a query directly, it forwards the query to another server that *might* know the answer. The other server may not know the answer either, and may reforward the query. This procedure might occur several times until we finally reach a server that can answer the question. The next server consulted is always supposed to be "closer" to a server that does know the answer. In general, requests propagate up the hierarchy and then back down again to a server that can answer the question.

For instance, if I ask DNS to look up *whitehouse.gov* from my *foo.bar.com* machine, my request might propagate to the *bar.com* server, the *com* server, the root server, and back down to the *gov* server, which is able to answer my query. This process is shown in Figure 3.10. Most of the time, an intermediate server will short-circuit the path at some point on the way to the top of the hierarchy. The intermediate server will know about other branches of the tree and forward the request to one of the other branches directly. For instance, in our example, the *bar.com* server may know about the *gov* server and forward the request directly to it without going to the *com* server or root server.

That is our introduction to the TCP/IP protocol suite. In the next chapter we'll learn about sockets!

Figure 3.10

The DNS forwards queries through the hierarchy but sometimes is able to use a shortcut.

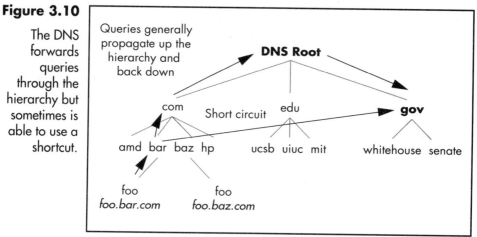

Socket Overview

Sockets: the key to Internet network programming. In this chapter, you'll learn where sockets came from and what you can do with them.

When I hear the word "socket," I think of those old telephone switchboards that AT&T used before electronic switches were developed. An operator (usually an old busybody who listened in on every phone call, if old movies are to be believed) would make connections between phones via a patch cord with plugs on the ends. When you dialed the operator, she would ask you what party you wanted. After you told her, she'd ring the other party and install a patch cord between your socket and the other party's socket on the switchboard. Your connection was then established and you could talk. Electronic switches now do the work in a fraction of the time and without human intervention, but that old telephone patch panel with all those sockets still has some modern analogies.

Sockets are the key to network programming in a TCP/IP environment. In this chapter, we'll examine where sockets came from, what they are, and how we can use them to write network applications. In addition, we'll learn the differences between Windows Sockets and previous sockets implementations. In the last chapter, we used a series of postal service analogies to describe the operation of some of the protocols in the TCP/IP protocol suite. In this chapter, we'll use a series of analogies based on the telephone switchboard. Keep that old operator and her patch panel in mind as we dig through socket operation.

The Origin of Sockets

The sockets interface originated with Berkeley Unix as the API to the TCP/IP network stack. It was a simple interface that allowed network applications to be written easily. As the popularity of Unix soared, so did the popularity of the sockets API. In fact, many people would claim that one of the reasons for Unix's popularity was its standard networking features, based on the Berkeley Sockets API. More and more commercial versions of Unix were based on the Berkeley Software Distribution (BSD) Unix source code, and the sockets API became a virtually universal network programming API. This universal acceptance allowed network applications to be quickly ported from one Unix variant to another with very few changes to the networking code. As a result, many networked applications have been written for the Unix environment.

Theoretically, the BSD Sockets interface is independent of the underlying network protocols. Sockets can be created for other non-TCP/IP protocol families, and these sockets can be used at the same time as sockets from other protocol families. In practice, however, the BSD Sockets interface is used primarily with the TCP/IP protocol family, and a number of API functions are specific to TCP/IP.

Windows Sockets, or Winsock, allows standard TCP/IP-based applications to be written for the Microsoft Windows environment. Before Winsock, various TCP/IP implementations for Windows used different APIs. Although most implementations included an API based on the familiar Berkeley Sockets API, there were subtle differences among the products that kept socket applications from being portable across implementations. As a result there were very few network applications for Windows. The applications that were written were custom crafted to run on a single vendor's stack, or at most a small handful of different implementations.

In reaction to this situation, the Windows TCP/IP community came together to develop a standard API—Winsock. Winsock is based on the Berkeley Sockets API. The Winsock API includes most of the standard BSD API functions as well as some extensions. The use of standard BSD functions allows older socket-based Unix programs to be ported to Windows more easily. Although changes may have to be made to the Unix code in some areas, the changes are smaller and more localized than if a whole new network API had been created. In spite of the similarities, Windows has some fundamental differences from Unix, and these are reflected in the Winsock API.

The Winsock API is implemented in a standard DLL named WINSOCK.DLL (WSOCK32.DLL in Win32). The actual underlying TCP/IP protocol implementation may be implemented in a number of ways—a DLL or VxD is typical. Each vendor ships a custom version of WINSOCK.DLL that interfaces with the vendor's TCP/IP implementation. The interface between the shipped WINSOCK.DLL and the protocol implementation is proprietary. You can't take any old WINSOCK.DLL and use it with any other vendor's protocol implementation. Some TCP/IP implementations put much of the protocol implementation into WINSOCK.DLL. In other cases, WINSOCK.DLL is little more than a thin dispatch layer, simply mapping Winsock function calls down into the actual protocol implementation. Figure 4.1 shows how WINSOCK.DLL relates to the protocol implementation.

Socket Concepts

A socket is similar to a file descriptor. A socket identifies an endpoint for communication and is implemented as a small positive integer. A socket is not a TCP or UDP port; it is a handle that is associated with a larger set of data stored in the network protocol implementation. The data associated with a socket includes things like the IP addresses and ports for both sides of a TCP connection and the current connection state. As data is received from the network, the TCP and UDP protocol implementations demultiplex it according to the port number included in the packet headers. The buffered data can then be retrieved from the protocol implementation using the socket descriptor as a key.

Figure 4.1

The relationship between entities in a Winsock environment.

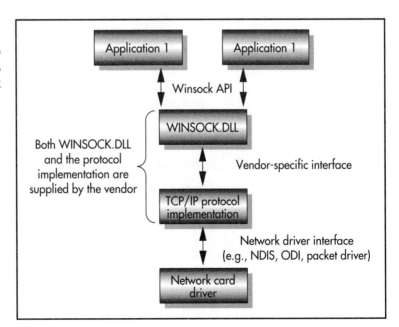

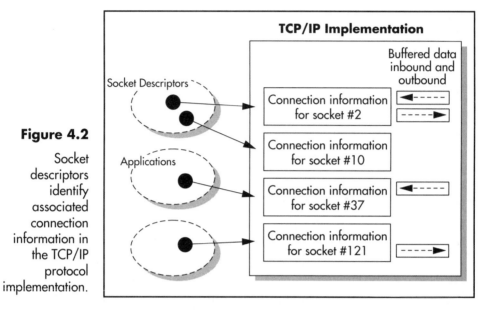

Figure 4.2

Socket
descriptors
identify
associated
connection
information in
the TCP/IP
protocol
implementation.

Like a file handle, a socket has a state associated with it. A file handle, for instance, can be used to open or close a file. After the file is opened, the file handle can be used to read or write data associated with the file. After the file is closed, the file handle can no longer be used to read or write. A socket has a similar state associated with it, but because a network connection is more complex than a simple disk file, there are additional functions to manipulate the state of a socket, as shown in Figure 4.2. Unlike a simple file handle, you cannot simply "open" a socket and use it immediately.

Exactly what must occur before you can use a socket depends on whether the socket will be used for datagram or stream communication and whether it acts as a client or server.

Datagrams and Streams

Sockets come in two primary flavors: datagram and stream. The type is designated when the socket is created and cannot change for the lifetime of the socket. Datagram sockets use UDP datagrams to carry the data written to them; stream sockets use TCP.

You'll remember from Chapter 3 that UDP guarantees that when data is delivered it will be correct, but it doesn't guarantee delivery in all cases. In particular, UDP datagrams may be lost, found to be corrupted and discarded, or misordered upon delivery. UDP does not respond to any of these events. Applications that use datagram service must therefore be prepared to deal with these problems. Because of this design, datagram service is most applicable to simple application protocols and a quick transactional model, where the cost of setting up a stream connection is too high. The design of reliable error-control protocols is better left to protocol experts. The TCP error-control protocols are very complex and have been developed and fine-tuned over a number of years of operational experience. Trying to duplicate TCP's functionality in an application using datagram service is unwise.

A Protocol that Uses UDP

An example of a protocol that uses datagram service is the Domain Name System, or DNS (RFC 1034 and RFC 1035). As described in Chapter 3, the DNS is a distributed database system that is used to map host names to their IP addresses. DNS uses a simple transactional model. A host that wants to look up a host name formats a query and sends it to a DNS server using a UDP datagram. As the query is sent, the host starts a timer. When the server receives the query, it formats a response and returns it via a UDP datagram. The requesting host's timer serves as the error-control mechanism. If either the query or response is lost or corrupted, the timer on the requesting host expires, and the host sends another query and restarts the timer. UDP is better suited to the quick transactional nature of the DNS protocol than TCP. UDP eliminates the overhead of setting up a reliable TCP connection for the relatively small amount of data exchanged in a typical domain name lookup. This approach allows a heavily used DNS server to respond to many more requests in a given amount of time than it could if the DNS protocol used TCP to carry the requests and responses.

Stream sockets are used to set up bi-directional TCP connections. TCP ensures that data written to the socket will be error-free and will appear at the destination in the same order as it was written. If individual IP packets carrying portions of the data stream are corrupted in transit, misordered, or lost completely, TCP will recognize that a problem has occurred and compensate by retransmitting or reordering the data as appropriate. Because TCP guarantees a reliable data connection, it is well-suited to protocols that require the error-free exchange of a large amount of data. All the application protocols discussed in this book use stream services to exchange their data.

Clients and Servers

Sockets can be used as clients or servers. Unfortunately, the terms "client" and "server" are very overused in networking and have different meanings depending on the context. Frequently, the terms client and server are used to refer to a type of operating system software or to the machine that runs that software.

For instance, many people call the machine that runs Novell's Netware or Microsoft's Windows NT operating systems a "server." In this context a server is typically a dedicated, high-powered machine that sits apart from the clients and provides file sharing, print sharing, email, and perhaps database services to desktop clients. This configuration contrasts with *peer-to-peer* operating systems like Windows for Workgroups. Peer-to-peer operating systems typically provide a subset of services (usually just file and print sharing) and are designed to be run on all users' desks. Although users can share files and printers, there is no single server in the "back room." This definition of client and server is *not* the definition that is used for network programming.

In the context of network programming, a *server* is a program that provides a service and waits for clients to contact it. The program that initiates contact is the *client.* That is, given that two programs have to connect, one program has to initiate the contact and the other has to wait at a well-known location (address and port) to receive contact. This process has nothing to do with which program is running on the big machine that sits in the corner and which is on the machines that sit on people's desktops. Any machine could be running both client programs and server programs at the same time. A program may even have multiple connections open at once and act as both a client and server at the same time!

Most of the time, server programs run continuously. They typically are started by the operating system at boot time and continue to provide the given service while the machine is running. Clients are more transitory. Let's look at an example of a file transfer service like FTP. The server typically waits for clients to connect at all times. The FTP client program generally is launched at the request of the user when a given file needs to be moved between machines. The client program provides a nice interface to the human user to allow the selection and transfer of files. The server program operates in the background with little or no user interface.

Socket Programming

The difference between clients and servers is apparent in the operations that must be performed on a socket to initiate contact compared to waiting for contact to occur. Figure 4.3 shows the state transitions of a stream socket being used in a client role. Figure 4.4 shows a similar set of transitions for a stream socket being used to implement a server.

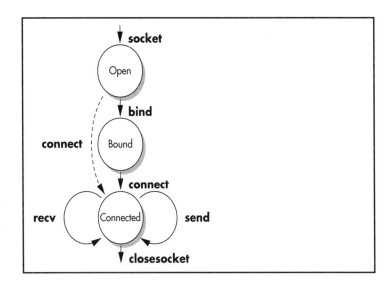

Figure 4.3

State transitions of a client stream socket.

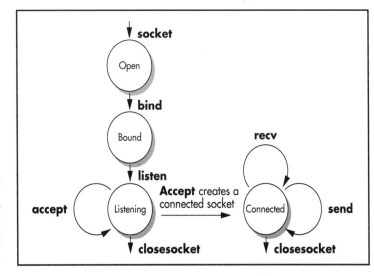

Figure 4.4

State transitions of a server stream socket.

All sockets are allocated using the **socket** function. At the time the socket is allocated, the program specifies whether it wants a stream socket or datagram socket. The program does not explicitly specify whether it wants to use the socket in a client or server role, however. Whether a socket is used as a client or server is established by subsequent operations.

Stream Socket Programming

In the case of a stream socket (for both client and server usage), after a socket is created, it must be bound to a local address using the **bind** function. See Figures 4.3 and 4.4. Binding a local address to the socket associates an interface and a port number with the local side of the connection. Although most hosts have only one network interface, they are allowed to have multiple interfaces. Binding a socket to an address associates the socket descriptor with the particular interface that has been assigned the address.

In a client program, the address and port numbers are typically irrelevant to the operation of the program. Most client programs specify "don't care" values for the address and port numbers, which causes the socket implementation to choose them for the program. A server program typically specifies a "don't care" address but a specific port number. This procedure allows it to accept connections from all the attached interfaces using the specified port number. Note that a server should always specify a well-known port number so a client knows how to contact it. As you'll see when we examine the various Internet protocols, the servers for each protocol wait on different well-known ports that are published as a part of the protocol specifications.

Binding is analogous to sitting by a particular phone in your house. Binding announces that you intend to use a particular phone line for a future call. In the case of receiving calls, binding specifies which phone you're sitting by and intending to answer when somebody calls you.

The programming for clients and servers diverges after the socket is created and bound to a local address. In the client case, the next step is to make a connection with the remote host. This step is accomplished using the **connect** function. A parameter of the **connect** function is the address and port number of the remote host. If the **connect** function returns with success, the socket is connected to the remote host and data can be sent and received using the socket.

Using the **connect** function is similar to dialing a phone. You specify the ID of the destination party, the IP address and port, and, like the switchboard operator, TCP tries to set up the connection.

When a stream socket operates as a server, after the socket is bound to a local address, the program must indicate that it wants to listen for connections to arrive on that socket, using the **listen** function. Connections are then accepted using the **accept** function. **accept** returns a new socket with the same local endpoint as the original socket but with a remote address and port number of the remote host that is initiating the connection. Data transfer can then proceed using the new socket descriptor and the **send** and **recv** functions. Additional new connections can be accepted on the original socket at any time.

The **listen** and **accept** functions equate to listening for the phone to ring and answering it, respectively. **listen** tells TCP that you want to be notified of arriving connections, and **accept** tells TCP that you want to establish the connection. If an application is set up to **listen** on a given socket but never **accepts** a connection, the client application will see behavior similar to the phone system. The phone will ring and ring, and after a while TCP will return from the **connect** system call with a failure result code—nobody answered.

Note that **accept** does not conform exactly to the phone system analogy. When **accept** returns, it creates a new socket descriptor that can be used for communication. The original socket is still in the listen state, and more connections can be received on it while the second socket descriptor is active. In the phone analogy, this scenario would be like listening for your phone to ring, answering the call, and having another phone magically appear, over which you actually conduct a conversation. The original phone would still exist and when it rang again, another magic phone would be created. Who knows what the old switchboard lady would think of all these magic phones!

Some simple server programs are designed to serve only one connection at a time. Before the server accepts another connection, it must close the connected socket. This method works well for simple application protocols that don't stay connected too long or in low-demand situations. More sophisticated servers that must support a higher demand will want to accept many more connections and manage them simultaneously. This requirement raises the complexity of the server application but may result in faster service for the waiting clients. TCP identifies connections by both the local and remote IP addresses and port numbers. Thus, multiple connections can be active on the same server address and port number simultaneously as long as the clients have different IP address numbers and ports.

Once a socket is connected, either because a client initiated a connection or a server accepted one, the **send** and **recv** functions can be used to send and receive data. This process corresponds to a voice conversation in the phone system analogy.

When the program finishes with a socket, it closes it with the **closesocket** function. It frees the state information associated with the socket descriptor and releases it. No functions should be used to operate on the socket descriptor after it is closed. Closing a socket corresponds to hanging up the phone at the end of a conversation.

Datagram Socket Programming

Datagram socket programming uses many of the same socket functions as stream socket programming. The two are fundamentally different, however. In the case of stream sockets, many of the socket functions are designed to set up connections with the remote host. Datagrams are inherently connectionless. There is no long-lived context shared between parties using datagrams. Data is simply sent to a remote host, which then receives it.

In the case of datagrams, a socket identifies the IP address and port number pair used as the source and destination of UDP datagrams. As with stream sockets, a socket is created using the **socket** function. A parameter to the **socket** function allows us to specify that we want a datagram socket rather than a stream socket. The socket is then bound to a local interface address and assigned a port number using the **bind** function. Figure 4.5 shows the sequence of state transitions that can be performed on a datagram socket.

Figure 4.5

State transitions of a datagram socket.

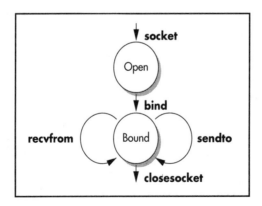

So far the sequence of events is similar to stream socket programming. The sequence diverges at this point, however. As soon as a datagram socket is bound to an address, it can be used. There is no need to connect it. Data is written to or read from the socket using the **sendto** and **recvfrom** socket functions. **sendto** and **recvfrom** are similar to the **send** and **recv** functions used to transmit and receive data on a stream socket. **sendto** has an additional parameter, however, that allows the program to specify the destination for the datagram. Because datagram sockets are not connected, the destination address must be supplied with each bit of data sent. The data handed to the socket is sent in a single UDP packet. **recvfrom** is used to receive data from the socket. In addition to data, **recvfrom** also returns the address and port number of the remote source.

sendto and **recvfrom** work with whole datagrams. There is no concept of a partial datagram. All the data you want to send in a particular datagram must be handed to **sendto** at one time. Similarly, there is no way to tell **recvfrom** to return only a bit of an incoming datagram. You must retrieve the whole datagram at one time. Each socket's implementation supports a maximum datagram size that must not be exceeded. If you pass too much data to the **sendto** function, it is ignored and an error is returned. The maximum datagram size supported by a Winsock implementation can be determined by looking at the **iMaxUdpDg** element in the structure returned by the **WSAStartup** function.(See Chapter 5 for more information.)

If an application needs to exchange a series of datagrams with another single host, it can be inconvenient to keep specifying the same destination address. A datagram socket can be "connected" using the **connect** function to streamline the transmission of multiple datagrams. When used on a datagram socket, **connect** sets a default destination (address and port) for datagrams transmitted using that socket. No actual connection is established with the other host as occurs with a stream socket. After a datagram socket is connected, **send** and **recv** function calls can be used on it to send and receive datagrams. **sendto** and **recvfrom** will still work on a connected datagram socket; they simply override the default address. Figure 4.6 shows the alternate sequence of states through which a datagram socket can progress.

As with stream sockets, **connect** can be used before a socket has been bound. In this case the local interface address and port number are chosen by Winsock itself. This procedure allows client sockets that don't have to be bound to well-known port numbers or a particular interface to save a step. Server sockets should always use **bind** to specify a particular protocol port number.

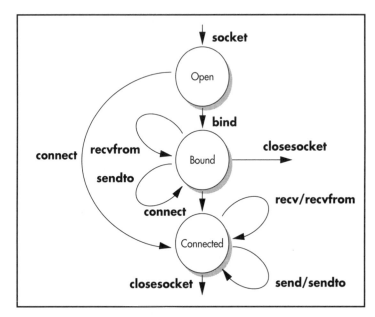

Figure 4.6

Alternate state transitions of a datagram socket.

When an application is done with a datagram socket, it should call **closesocket** to signal to Winsock that it is finished. All buffered incoming datagrams and all context associated with the socket will then be discarded.

Database Functions

Many databases are used to store information about the network. These databases are accessed by Winsock programs to find the addresses of remote hosts and the appropriate well-known port numbers for a given service.

Host Name Lookup

Every well-written Winsock program will be a heavy user of the host name database. The host name database stores mappings between host names and their associated addresses. The functions **gethostbyaddr** and **gethostbyname** are used to access the database and retrieve the information about the host. The information retrieved includes the host name, any aliases, and the network addresses for each of its interfaces. **gethostbyaddr** uses the host IP address as a key to the database, while **gethostbyname** uses the host name. **gethostbyname** is the most frequently used database function. Each time the user specifies a host name for a program for connection, **gethostbyname** must be invoked to determine the host's network address to be used by the socket functions.

As the previous chapter described, the actual host database may be the Domain Name System and the information may be spread all over the world. Invoking **gethostbyname** or **gethostbyaddr** may generate many network connections and messages to fulfill the lookup request.

Service Lookup

The service database is the second most frequently used database. The service database stores mappings between Internet service names and their associated well-known port numbers. **getservbyname** and **getservbyport** are used to retrieve the information associated with a given service. Given a service name, "smtp" for example, **getservbyname** returns the default port number to use. **getservbyport** returns the service name using the port number as the lookup key.

Why use a database to store well-known port numbers for services? A network manager might want to assign a different well-known port number for a service within the administrative area, sometimes for security reasons. In other cases, the service database can be used to store the port number for a service that is under development. The service typically is assigned a random port number during development and testing, and an Internet-wide official port number is assigned later by the Internet Assigned Numbers Authority (IANA). By using the service database, a port number can be changed easily without recompiling the code that implements the service.

Use of the service database is not strictly necessary if you are implementing a well-known protocol like SMTP or NNTP. The port numbers for these services never (in practice) change. Even when they do, a good program will still allow the user to specify a port to use for connections to override the hard-coded default value.

Protocol Lookup

The protocol database is the least often used database in Winsock programming. The protocol database stores mappings between protocol names ("tcp" or "udp," for instance) and their associated integer constant values. The protocol integer constant can be used in the protocol parameter position in the **socket** function. **getprotobyname** and **getprotobynumber** access the database using either the name of the protocol or its integer constant, respectively.

Many most programs never use the protocol database. The **socket** function allows the caller to set the protocol parameter to 0, which specifies that **socket** should use the default protocol based on the address family and socket type parameters that are specified in the function call. In the case of the Internet address family, stream sockets default to using TCP; datagram sockets default to using UDP. Specifying a protocol number as retrieved by **getprotobyname** is redundant in this case.

Winsock Extensions

Although Windows Sockets is based on the Berkeley Sockets model, there are some changes that were required because of the differences between Windows and BSD Unix. In particular, Winsock includes changes to start up network services and work more efficiently in Windows' cooperative multitasking environment.

Winsock Startup and Closure

In Unix, the network protocol implementation is typically compiled directly into the operating system kernel. Network services are initialized as the kernel boots and are available from that moment on. Applications are not required to start the network explicitly or initialize any networking parameters—they simply use network services when they want.

Under Windows, no standard exists for the implementation of network services. Some protocol implementations can be implemented as DLLs. Others can be implemented as VxDs. Some implementations need to be initialized before they can be used by an application. To provide the needs of the implementations that must be initialized, Winsock requires that applications register their intent to use Winsock services by calling the **WSAStartup** function before calling other Winsock APIs.

WSAStartup also allows applications and the WINSOCK.DLL to negotiate the particular version of Winsock that each supports. This process is described in more detail in the next chapter.

Winsock also requires that applications call the **WSACleanup** function when done using Winsock services. This function allows the underlying protocol implementation to free any resources that may have been assigned to the application while it was running. Any open sockets are closed, and any waiting data is destroyed.

Blocking and Non-Blocking Functions

Although Windows 3.1 and Unix both allow multiple programs to operate simultaneously, they differ in a fundamental way. Unix is a pre-emptive multitasking operating system, while Windows 3.1 is a cooperative multitasking operating environment. (We'll examine Windows NT later in this chapter.) This difference has a profound impact on the way that networking operations are processed.

Windows 3.1 applications multitask using an event-dispatch loop, which consists of calls to **GetMessage** and **DispatchMessage**. **GetMessage** retrieves the next window message from the system queue, and **DispatchMessage** calls the window procedure setup to handle the message. If there are no messages for the program, **GetMessage** causes a task switch to another task that has waiting messages. If the current task does not call **GetMessage** for a substantial amount of time, other tasks in the system won't be given a chance to run.

In Unix, the multitasking is pre-emptive. The operating system kernel schedules a timer interrupt to occur at a given rate. Each task is given one timer interval to run. When the timer interrupt occurs, the kernel causes a task switch, and the next task is allowed to run for a while. In this case, no one program can seize the system for longer than a timer interval.

These two multitasking styles affect the way that programs are written. In Unix, user I/O is similar to that in MS-DOS. If a program wants to get a keystroke from the user, it simply calls an OS function that blocks until the user hits a key and then returns with the ASCII code. This approach works in Unix because of the pre-emptive multitasking. The system doesn't grind to a halt when one program requires user input, because task switching occurs as timer interrupts are generated.

In Windows 3.1, calling a blocking operating system function causes the whole system to lock up until the function returns. As a result, Windows 3.1 uses a message-based, event-driven programming style. Rather than calling a function when a program wants user input, Windows generates event messages whenever a notable user event occurs. If a given program wants to respond to the event, it does; otherwise, it is ignored. In the case of keystrokes, Windows generates a message whenever the user types on the keyboard. If responding to a keystroke doesn't make sense to the program at a given moment, it simply ignores the keystroke message. This programming style has the effect of never forcing programs to call blocking operating system functions.

Unfortunately, many networking operations frequently block. When the program calls the **recv** function to read data from a socket, it may be the case that no data is immediately available. If the program calls **gethostbyname** to look up an address from a host name, many DNS servers may have to be consulted, which may take a minute or longer. Many other sockets functions can block or delay for a long period of time. The question is, what should be done when a networking call takes more than a moment to complete? Under Berkeley Sockets and Unix, the call simply will block. Multitasking continues because of Unix's pre-emptive multitasking operation. Eventually, network data will arrive, the **recv** function will return, and the program will continue.

Under Windows 3.1, a blocking **recv** function is clearly unacceptable. If the **recv** function blocked in a Windows 3.1 program, the system would lock up until network data arrives. During this time, no programs would progress at all, and the user could not type or move the mouse. It could take minutes for network data to arrive at the socket to allow the **recv** function to return. If it takes more than a few moments, the user would likely conclude that the machine had crashed and would reboot.

To allow the Windows 3.1 environment to progress in a blocking situation, each of the functions in the Winsock API that could block waiting for a network event performs pseudo-blocking. Instead of actually blocking, the Winsock call enters polling loop, waiting for the network event to complete. The basic loop structure looks like the following:

```
for(;;) {
    /* flush messages for good user response */
    while(BlockingHook())
      ;
    /* check for WSACancelBlockingCall() */
    if(operation_cancelled())
      break;
    /* check to see if operation completed */
    if(operation_complete())
      break;   /* normal completion */
}
```

The loop calls **BlockingHook** at least once on each iteration. If the blocking operation is canceled or completes, the loop exits. **BlockingHook** can be a user-supplied function or a default function that Winsock supplies. The default **BlockingHook** looks like the following:

```
BOOL DefaultBlockingHook(void) {
    MSG msg;
    BOOL ret;
    /* get the next message if any */
    ret = (BOOL)PeekMessage(&msg,NULL,0,0,PM_REMOVE);
    /* if we got one, process it */
    if (ret) {
        TranslateMessage(&msg);
        DispatchMessage(&msg);
```

```
    }
    /* TRUE if we got a message */
    return ret;
}
```

Each call to **BlockingHook** causes one message to be removed from the queue and dispatched. The **while** loop surrounding the call to **BlockingHook** in the polling loop causes **BlockingHook** to be called repeatedly until there are no more messages in the queue. The blocking hook calls **PeekMessage**, which allows Windows to switch tasks if needed. This method keeps Windows events flowing so that tasks can continue to run.

An application can install its own blocking hook function using the **WSASetBlockingHook** function. A custom blocking hook function can be used to update a status bar or perform background processing that should progress while the application is in a blocking state. However, user-defined blocking hooks should be functionally equivalent to **DefaultBlockingHook** to work correctly with the polling loop. In general, it's safe to add code to the **DefaultBlockingHook** function to create a custom blocking hook, but code should not be removed.

Note that under the Berkeley Sockets API an individual socket can be marked *non-blocking*. In this case, a call that would block will return with an error code saying that the call could not be completed immediately, and no action is performed. It might be tempting to put a socket into non-blocking mode and simply poll, as shown in the following code:

```
while (recv(...) == SOCKET_ERROR &&
  WSAGetLastError() == WSAEWOULDBLOCK) {
    while (BlockingHook())
      ;
}
```

Unfortunately, this technique won't work in all cases; for instance, it won't work with the database functions. The lookup of a given host name might always take a long time (the name server for that host might be on the other side of the world), and the database functions always block.

Don't create your own polling loops! Let Winsock do it for you. If you need to modify the default blocking hook functionality, provide your own blocking hook in the same style as Winsock's **DefaultBlockingHook**.

Event-Driven Winsock Programming

Although the blocking hook solution works correctly and allows Windows 3.1 to continue to process messages, it isn't necessarily the best solution in the Windows environment. This approach allows older Unix code to be ported to Windows 3.1, but it really doesn't conform to the Windows event-driven model.

Further, Winsock only allows one blocking call to be in effect at once. Your program must take special steps to ensure that the user doesn't start another network function while your program is sitting in a blocking hook. Because the event-dispatch function in the blocking hook can cause user menu choices and keystrokes to be delivered to your program, you'll have to disable all menu items and keyboard accelerators that can cause network calls to be generated. The simplest way to do this is to capture all mouse and keyboard input and put up an hourglass cursor while your program is performing a networking function. This method is unappealing from a user-interface standpoint, however. The whole point of Windows' multitasking environment is to allow the user to do more than one task at a time. Limiting an application to one network activity at a time is a step backwards. A user might want to send an email to several people and then collect his or her own mail at the same time. Forcing the user to wait for the first task to finish before starting the second is not good user-interface design.

Luckily, the Winsock designers thought these restrictions were a step backwards as well. In keeping with the Windows event-driven model, the Winsock designers created an alternative way to handle blocking network calls. Sockets can be marked non-blocking, as mentioned previously. Rather than invoking the Winsock polling loop with a blocking hook, the network call returns immediately with a status code indicating that it would have blocked. Later, Winsock sends the program a standard Windows message indicating that the blocking call may be attempted again and that this time it (probably) won't block. (There are still some situations where things might block again, so a program should be prepared for these events. The next chapter will describe some of these situations). Using the **WSAAsyncSelect** Winsock-specific function, the program can specify the types of socket events for which it wants to be notified.

We'll use event-driven Winsock programming throughout the example code in this book.

Windows NT

The previous discussion contrasted Unix with Windows 3.1. We've seen that Windows 3.1's cooperative multitasking model is not well-suited to the standard Berkeley Sockets API blocking calls. The Windows Sockets API can also be used with Windows NT, however. Windows NT is an advanced, 32-bit, pre-emptive multitasking operating system. Does it suffer from the same limitations as Windows 3.1 and does it require the same solutions? Well, no, and yes. Because Windows NT is a pre-emptive multitasking system, it does not suffer the same blocking problems as Windows 3.1, but there still are some reasons to use the extended non-blocking Winsock functionality.

Like Unix, when a process calls a blocking function under Windows NT, the operating system continues to pre-emptively switch tasks and the system continues to run. Under Windows NT, there is no default blocking hook. When a blocking Winsock function is called, the operating system suspends the current thread and task switches to another. If a program wants to install a custom blocking hook, it can do so. This functionality is retained to remain compatible with Windows 3.1 and to allow a single program to compile and run under both environments.

Does this mean that a Windows NT program has no need of the **WSAAsyncSelect** function and non-blocking sockets? No, a Windows NT program might still want to use non-blocking sockets. Although Windows NT uses pre-emptive multitasking to keep the system running, the current thread is suspended until the blocking task completes. If this thread is the only thread in the process, all user input is halted for that process until the thread unblocks and can continue to dispatch window messages to the process. There are two ways around this problem: use multiple threads or the extended, event-driven Winsock API.

If a program is designed exclusively for Windows NT, the use of multiple threads is a realistic alternative. One thread is dedicated to servicing the user interface and never invokes a blocking Winsock function. Each time a network task is started by the user as the result of a menu selection or some other action, a separate thread is created to handle the network operation. If the network thread blocks, it is not a problem because the user interface task continues to execute and respond to the user.

Using multiple threads is not an option if the program is being designed to compile and run under both Windows NT and Windows 3.1. Since Windows 3.1

does not support independent threads, the code will have to be designed to run without them. The equivalent Windows NT program will probably only create a single thread for the entire process, using it to service both the user interface and operate the network. In this case, the program should use the extended, event-driven Winsock API.

Database Functions

As described in previous sections, lookups to the Winsock databases may require a node to access a networked, distributed database like the DNS (a common example in the case of host name resolution). A lookup of a host or service name could be a potentially lengthy operation. Just as Winsock provides asynchronous extensions to overcome problems with blocking operations related to sockets themselves, Winsock also provides asynchronous extensions to the standard database functions.

Each of the standard database functions has a similar extension function that performs the same operation but uses window messages to inform the application when the operation is complete. The extension functions use the same names as the standard database functions but with "WSAAsync" prepended and capitalization changed to reflect Windows' typical capitalization style. For instance, **gethostbyname** is changed to **WSAAsyncGetHostByName**.

In this chapter, we've had a quick introduction to sockets programming and some of the differences between the Berkeley Sockets API and Windows Sockets API. In the next chapter, we'll take a detailed look at the functions that make up the Windows Sockets API.

The Windows Sockets API

The Windows Sockets API consists of 44 functions. In this chapter, we'll take a look at each one.

The Windows Sockets API is not very complicated. It consists of 44 functions, only a few of which are used frequently. In this chapter, we'll examine these functions, their parameters, and the data structures that are used in concert with them.

The functions can be grouped into four main categories: conversion, database, socket, and Winsock extensions. The conversion functions assist with the conversion of integer quantities between host and network byte orders and the conversion of IP addresses between string and numeric formats. The database functions allow a program to retrieve information about hosts, network services, and protocols from the network databases. In particular, the database functions allow a program to determine the address of a remote host given its name as entered by a user. The socket functions are used to create and connect sockets, send and receive data using them, and finally destroy them when they are no longer needed. We introduced socket functions in Chapter 4. The Winsock extension functions are unique to the Windows Sockets API. They are designed to allow a Winsock program to better integrate with the Windows cooperative multitasking environment. The Winsock extension functions use Windows messages to signal the completion of asynchronous network tasks to prevent programs from blocking.

Although this chapter presents a much more detailed view of these functions than the previous chapters, it is not the definitive reference to Winsock. For the last word on the behavior of all Winsock functions, consult the *Windows Sockets Specification, version 1.1* or later. Copies of the Winsock specification in both Microsoft

Word for Windows and Windows Help format are included on the companion CD-ROM.

Yes, this is the dry, boring chapter. It's filled with lots of tables and descriptions of functions and not much in the way of fun stuff. In spite of this, it's likely to be the chapter to which you most often refer. Even if you don't read it in detail, be sure to skim it to familiarize yourself with the way that I've grouped the functions so that you can find things later when you're looking for them.

Winsock Programming Overview

Before we examine each Winsock function, we need to cover some general concepts that apply to Winsock programming.

Network Byte Order

TCP/IP runs on an amazingly diverse set of hardware platforms. This flexibility is one of the reasons for its success. A problem that must be confronted when developing communications protocols designed to operate between heterogeneous systems is the difference in byte order. Some systems use little-endian byte order, in which the least significant byte of a multibyte integer is stored in memory before the more significant bytes. Others use big-endian byte order, in which the most significant byte of a multibyte integer is stored before the less significant bytes. The x86 family of processors use little-endian byte order, but many other processors (notably the Motorola 68000 series) use big-endian byte order.

When communicating multibyte quantities between hosts on a network, standards must exist to deal with mismatches between the hosts' byte orderings. By convention, TCP/IP (and many other network protocols) use big-endian byte order, which is often termed *network byte order*. In particular, the IP addresses and port numbers are transmitted in network byte order.

By convention, wherever IP addresses and port numbers appear in the Winsock (as well as in the Berkeley Sockets) API, they must be in network byte order. Functions are provided by the API to swap bytes from host byte order to network byte order and back again. On x86 platforms these functions *must* be used for programs to run correctly. In general, it's always wise to use these functions even when programming on a big-endian machine under Berkeley Sockets. You never know when you might want to port things to a little-endian machine, and you won't want to spend time finding all those places where you should have included them the first time.

Out-of-Band Data

The stream socket abstraction includes the concept of *out-of-band data*. Out-of-band data is associated with a particular stream connection but is not conceptually part of the same data stream. Generally, out-of-band data is used to indicate an exceptional error condition that must be processed immediately, before any data pending in the receive queue. Generally, the error condition will make the data in the receive queue obsolete for some reason, so it should be processed before any pending data to save time or prevent some action from taking effect.

An application has the choice of processing out-of-band data "inline" or "out-of-line." When processed inline, the out-of-band data is put at the front of the receive queue when it arrives and is processed through normal calls to **recv**. When there is out-of-band data in the receive queue, the next call to **recv** will retrieve it. Even if normal data is in the queue and room will be left in the buffer supplied by the application after the out-of-band data has been retrieved, only out-of-band data is retrieved.

When out-of-band data is processed out-of-line, the application has the option of receiving normal data or out-of-band data. The **recv** function includes a flag to indicate that any out-of-band data should be returned rather than normal data.

> *Note: The description of out-of-band data in RFC 793 has generated two conflicting interpretations. The implementation of out-of-band data in the Berkeley Software Distribution differs from the interpretation presented in RFC 1122. Windows Sockets implementations are free to implement either interpretation. Before using out-of-band signaling, an application developer should understand the differences between interpretations and know the interpretation that a particular Windows Sockets implementation uses.*

Berkeley Sockets Compared to Winsock

If you're used to programming Berkeley Sockets, you'll have little trouble adapting to Winsock. The hardest jump to make is from the blocking Berkeley Sockets API to the newer event-driven Winsock extensions. Though not large, there are some other differences from the Berkeley Sockets API that you might confront.

SOCKET Type

In the Berkeley Sockets API, a socket descriptor is a simple integer, and most programs simply define a socket variable as:

```
int sock;
```

When using the Windows Sockets API, a socket should be defined using the new type name, **SOCKET**:

```
SOCKET sock;
```

Currently, the definition of **SOCKET** is simply

```
typedef u_int SOCKET;
```

so it's little more than a different name for virtually the same thing.

The new definition allows the alteration of the socket descriptor type when future versions of the Windows Sockets API are developed. In future versions of Windows Sockets, possibly under different operating environments, the definition of **SOCKET** might change to bring added capabilities. Programs written to use **SOCKET** instead of **int** or **u_int** will be able to operate in these enhanced environments without major surgery and recompilation.

Error Values

When an error occurs in the Berkeley Sockets API, the global variables **errno** and **h_errno** are set to the specific error code. In the Windows Sockets API, these variables are not used. Instead, the function **WSAGetLastError** issued to retrieve the specific error code. For compatibility with older code that might be ported to Windows Sockets from the Berkeley Sockets environment, macros are provided to define **errno** and **h_errno** as a call to **WSAGetLastError**. All new Windows Sockets programs should use **WSAGetLastError**.

Many Berkeley Sockets functions return the value -1 in place of a positive-valued socket descriptor to signal an error condition. Much of the code written for the Berkeley Sockets environment directly tests the return values from such functions to see if they are less than zero or contain a hard-coded -1 constant. For example:

```
int s;
s = socket(...);
if (s == -1) {
  /* error */
}
```

In Windows Sockets, the **SOCKET** type is defined to be an unsigned integer value. A **SOCKET** variable can never be less than 0, and compiler warning messages will be generated if a **SOCKET** variable is tested against -1. The only value of the **SOCKET** type that is guaranteed not to be a legal socket descriptor value is defined by the constant **INVALID_SOCKET**. All Windows Sockets code should be written to use **INVALID_SOCKET** instead of testing for -1. The above code should be rewritten as:

```
SOCKET s;
s = socket(...);
if (s == INVALID_SOCKET) {
  /* error */
}
```

Structure Names

In Winsock, the Berkeley Sockets data structures have been given duplicate names more in line with Windows naming conventions. Old names still exist and can be used, but the new names will eliminate the style clash between typical Windows code and typical BSD Unix code. The new names are uppercase versions of the Berkeley names and are defined equivalently to the original structure names.

For instance, the Berkeley Sockets **struct sockaddr_in** type has been given the duplicate name **SOCKADDR_IN**. Further, in typical Windows style, a pair of companion pointer types have been defined as **PSOCKADDR_IN** and **LPSOCKADDR_IN**. Using either set of names for the same structure is acceptable; it's nothing more than an issue of style.

Error Names

Integer constants used for error values have also been given duplicate names. When Winsock was created, some new network error values were needed. To distinguish Winsock error values from other error values (DOS or Windows NT errors, for instance), a naming convention was adopted where the standard Berkeley error names are prefixed with "WSA". To make the set of Winsock error names consistent, Berkeley errors were given duplicate names beginning with "WSA".

For instance, the Berkeley Sockets error **ENETDOWN** is also named **WSAENETDOWN**. In general, the Windows Sockets names should be used unless you are porting older Berkeley Sockets code into the Winsock environment. Under Windows NT, some of the original Berkeley Sockets names conflict with Windows NT error names, so the Berkeley Sockets names are not available.

Compiling and Linking

All the function declarations, constant definitions, and data structure declarations used in the Winsock API are included in the WINSOCK.H header file. This same header file is used whether you are programming for Win16 or Win32. The actual DLLs containing the Winsock interface code are named WINSOCK.DLL and WSOCK32.DLL for Win16 and Win32, respectively. To access functions in the Winsock DLLs, link your program with an import library named WINSOCK.DLL or WSOCK32.DLL. For more information about import libraries and their creation, see your compiler and linker documentation.

Note: Each WINSOCK.DLL is a proprietary module shipped with your particular TCP/IP stack. Although the Winsock interface implemented by the WINSOCK.DLL is standard, the interface between WINSOCK.DLL and your particular TCP/IP implementation is proprietary. Because of its proprietary nature, WINSOCK.DLL is not included on the companion CD-ROM.

Conversion Functions

The Winsock API provides six functions that provide conversion between different data formats. Four of the functions convert 16-bit and 32-bit integers between host and network byte order; the previous two functions convert an IP address between 32-bit format and a dotted-decimal character string. Table 5.1 gives a summary of the Winsock conversion functions.

htonl

The **htonl** function converts a 32-bit integer between host and network byte order. This function frequently is used to convert an IP address being manipu-

Table 5.1 Conversion functions	
Function	**Description**
htonl	Converts a long (32-bit) quantity from host to network byte order
htons	Converts a short (16-bit) quantity from host to network byte order
inet_addr	Converts an address string in dotted-decimal format to a 32-bit IP address
inet_ntoa	Converts a 32-bit IP address to a dotted-decimal string
ntohl	Converts a long (32-bit) quantity from network to host byte order
ntohs	Converts a short (16-bit) quantity from network to host byte order

lated as a 32-bit quantity to network byte order before storage in a **sockaddr_in** structure. The **htonl** function is prototyped as:

```
u_long PASCAL FAR htonl (u_long hostlong);
```

htons

The **htons** function converts a 16-bit integer between host and network byte order. This function frequently is used to convert a port number to network byte order before storing it in a **sockaddr_in** structure. The **htons** function is prototyped as:

```
u_short PASCAL FAR htons (u_short hostshort);
```

inet_addr

The **inet_addr** function converts a character string containing a dotted-decimal IP address to a 32-bit integer representing the IP address. The address is returned in network byte order. The **inet_addr** function is prototyped as:

```
unsigned long PASCAL FAR inet_addr (const char FAR * cp);
```

inet_ntoa

The **inet_ntoa** function formats an IP address as a dotted-decimal character string. The IP address is provided to the function in the form of an **in_addr** structure. By definition the IP address in the **in_addr** structure is already in network byte order. The string returned by **inet_ntoa** resides in memory local to the Windows Sockets implementation. An application must not try to free this memory. The string is guaranteed to be valid until the next Windows Sockets call; the application should make a copy of the string, if needed. The **inet_ntoa** function is prototyped as:

```
char FAR * PASCAL FAR inet_ntoa (struct in_addr in);
```

ntohl

The **ntohl** function converts a 32-bit integer in network byte order to host byte order. The **ntohl** function is prototyped as:

```
u_long PASCAL FAR ntohl (u_long netlong);
```

ntohs

The **ntohs** function converts a 16-bit integer in network byte order to host byte order. The **ntohs** function is prototyped as:

```
u_short PASCAL FAR ntohs (u_short netshort);
```

Database Functions

Winsock provides seven database functions for retrieving information about hosts, protocols, and services. The **gethostbyaddr** and **gethostbyname** functions access host information using the host address and name as keys, respectively; **getprotobyname** and **getprotobynumber** access protocol information by protocol name and number; and **getservbyname** and **getservbyport** access service information by service name and port number. Finally, the **gethostname** function allows a program to retrieve the name of the local host. The databse functions are listed in Table 5.2.

gethostbyaddr

The gethostbyaddr function retrieves information about a host for the host's database (perhaps implemented with DNS) using its IP address as a key. The **gethostbyaddr** function is prototyped as:

```
struct hostent FAR * PASCAL FAR gethostbyaddr(const char FAR * addr, int len, int type);
```

The **addr** parameter points to an address in network byte order. The **len** parameter specifies the length of the address (which is always 4 for 32-bit IP addresses). The **type** parameter must be the constant **PF_INET**.

gethostbyaddr returns a pointer to a **hostent** structure. This structure contains the following information about the specified host:

```
struct hostent {
  char FAR *      h_name;
  char FAR * FAR * h_aliases;
  short           h_addrtype;
  short           h_length;
  char FAR * FAR * h_addr_list;
};
```

The **h_name** member contains the official name of the host. The **h_aliases** member contains a null-terminated array of pointers to aliases. The **h_addrtype** mem-

Table 5.2 Database functions

Function	Description
gethostbyaddr	Retrieves host information according to the host IP address
gethostbyname	Retrieves host information according to the host name
gethostname	Retrieves the name of the local host
getprotobyname	Retrieves protocol information according to a familiar protocol name
getprotobynumber	Retrieves protocol information according to the specified protocol number
getservbyname	Retrieves service information according to a familiar service name
getservbyport	Retrieves service information according to the service port number

ber specifies the address type and is always **PF_INET** in Winsock. The **h_length** parameter specifies the length of each individual address and is always 4 for **PF_INET** addresses. The **h_addr_list** parameter points to a null-terminated array of pointers to addresses. *The addresses are in network byte order.*

The returned pointer points to a **hostent** structure allocated within the Winsock implementation. It should not be freed or altered by the application program. It is guaranteed to be valid only until the next Winsock call; the application should make a copy of the data, if needed.

If an error occurs, **gethostbyaddr** returns **NULL**. The specific error can be retrieved by calling **WSAGetLastError**.

gethostbyname

The **gethostbyname** function is analogous to **gethostbyaddr** except it uses the name of the host as the lookup key rather than the address. The **gethostbyname** function is prototyped as:

```
struct hostent FAR * PASCAL FAR gethostbyname(const char FAR * name);
```

The **name** parameter points to a null-terminated string containing the host name to look up.

As with **gethostbyaddr**, **gethostbyname** returns a pointer to a **hostent** structure or **NULL** if an error occurs. The structure is allocated within the Winsock implementation and should not be freed or altered by the application. It is guaranteed to be valid only until the next Winsock call; the application should make a copy of the structure if necessary.

If an error occurs, **gethostbyname** returns **NULL**. The specific error can be retrieved by calling **WSAGetLastError**.

gethostname

The **gethostname** function allows a program to determine the name of the host on which it is running. The **gethostname** function is prototyped as:

```
int PASCAL FAR gethostname (char FAR * name, int namelen);
```

gethostname takes a pointer to a buffer that will receive the host name. The **namelen** parameter should be set to the length of the buffer to keep Winsock from writing past the end of the buffer.

If **gethostname** is successful, it returns 0; otherwise, it returns the constant **SOCKET_ERROR**. The specific error may be determined by calling **WSAGetLastError**.

*Note: Although every host should have a name, some Winsock stacks do not require it. **gethostname** can return a null string in those cases and still not generate an error. Do not assume that the string returned by **gethostname** is a valid host name or that the host information is configured correctly. If you require **gethostname** to be a valid name, be sure to check the returned string to avoid problems.*

A Missing API Function: gethostaddr

If you examine the list of database functions, you might notice that one function seems to be missing. Although there are two methods to look up information about hosts, protocols, and services, only one function gets information about the local host: **gethostname**. A program might need to know the network address of the local host in addition to its name. Alas, there is no **gethostaddr** function in the Winsock (or Berkeley Sockets) API.

It's easy to create your own **gethostaddr** function, however. For instance, you might define it as:

```
char FAR * FAR * gethostaddr(void)
{
   char szHostName[40];
   // Get the local host name.
   int iResult = gethostname(szHostName, sizeof(szHostName));
```

```
   if (iResult != 0)
     return NULL;
   // Make sure the host name is somewhat valid.
   if (lstrcmp(szHostName, "") == 0)
     return NULL;
   // Look up the information about this host using the local
   // host name.
   HOSTENT FAR * lphostent = gethostbyname(szHostName);
   if (lphostent == NULL)
     return NULL;
   else
      return lphostent->h_addr_list;
}
```

In this example, **gethostaddr** returns a pointer to the **h_addr_list** field of the **HOSTENT** structure retrieved using the name returned by **gethostname**. If anything goes wrong along the way, **gethostaddr** returns **NULL**. Note that **gethostaddr** does not return a single address as a **u_long** value. A host may have several network interfaces, each with its own network address. Rather than choose a single address to return, **gethostaddr** returns a pointer to all the addresses.

getprotobyname

The **getprotobyname** function returns information about a protocol using the name of the protocol as the database key. The **getprotobyname** function is prototyped as:

```
struct protoent FAR * PASCAL FAR getprotobyname(const char FAR * name);
```

getprotobyname returns a pointer to a **protoent** structure, defined as:

```
struct protoent {
  char FAR *      p_name;
  char FAR * FAR * p_aliases;
  short           p_proto;
};
```

The **p_name** field is the official name of the protocol and **p_aliases** is a pointer to a null-terminated set of aliases. The **p_proto** field gives the protocol identification constant suitable for use in a call to **socket**. *The protocol number is returned in host byte order.* The returned pointer points to a structure allocated within the Windows Sockets implementation itself. The application must not free this memory or modify its contents. The data stored in the structure is guaranteed to be valid only until the next Windows Sockets call; the application should make a copy of the data, if needed.

If an error occurs, **getprotobyname** returns **NULL**, and the specific error code can be retrieved by calling **WSAGetLastError**.

getprotobynumber

The **getprotobynumber** function retrieves information about a protocol using the protocol identification number as a key to the database. The **getprotobynumber** function is prototyped as:

```
struct protoent FAR * PASCAL FAR getprotobynumber(int proto);
```

Like **getprotobyname**, **getprotobynumber** returns **NULL** if an error occurs, and the specific error code can be retrieved using **WSAGetLastError**.

This is one of the least-used functions in the Winsock API.

getservbyname

The **getservbyname** function retrieves information about a particular network service. This function uses the name of the service as a key to the service database. The **getservbyname** function is prototyped as:

```
struct servent FAR * PASCAL FAR getservbyname(const char FAR * name, const char
   FAR * proto);
```

The **name** parameter is the official name of the service or a registered alias. The **proto** parameter is an optional protocol name. If **proto** is **NULL**, the **getservbyname** function returns the first entry in the service database that matches the service name. If **proto** is non-**NULL**, the **getservbyname** function attempts to find an entry that matches both the service and protocol names.

The **getservbyname** function returns a pointer to a **servent** structure defined as:

```
struct servent {
  char FAR *     s_name;
  char FAR * FAR * s_aliases;
  short         s_port;
  char FAR *     s_proto;
};
```

The **s_name** field of this structure points to the official name of the service; **s_aliases** is a null-terminated list of aliases. The **s_port** field specifies the well-known port number on which the service can be contacted. *The port number is returned in network byte order.* The **s_proto** field specifies the protocol that should be used to make contact with the service.

The returned pointer points to a structure allocated within the Windows Sockets implementation itself. The application should neither free the structure nor alter its contents. The data in the structure is guaranteed to be valid only until the next Windows Sockets call; the application should make a copy of the data, if needed.

If an error occurs, **getservbyname** returns **NULL**, and the specific error code can be retrieved by calling **WSAGetLastError**.

getservbyport

The **getservbyport** function accesses the service database using the service's well-known port number as a key. The **getservbyport** function is prototyped as:

```
struct servent FAR * PASCAL FAR getservbyport(int port, const char FAR * proto);
```

The **getservbyport** function takes the service port number as its first parameter. *The port number is given in network byte order.* As with the **getservbyname** function, the **proto** parameter specifies an optional protocol string to use when searching the service database. If **proto** is **NULL**, **getservbyport** returns the first entry that matches the port parameter. If **proto** is specified, **getservbyport** attempts to match both the service port number and the protocol name.

If an error occurs, **getservbyport** returns **NULL**, and the specific error code can be retrieved by calling **WSAGetLastError**.

Socket Functions

The socket group contains those functions responsible for the creation, manipulation, and destruction of sockets. There are 17 functions in the socket group, as shown in Table 5.3. We introduced some of these functions in the previous chapter. In this section, we'll examine the socket functions in more detail.

Table 5.3 Socket functions	
Function	**Description**
accept	Accepts a connection on a listening socket and returns a newly created, connected socket
bind	Binds a local interface address and port number to a socket
closesocket	Closes a socket and releases the socket descriptor
connect	Establishes a connection with a remote host
getpeername	Gets the address and port information of the remote host to which a socket is connected
getsockname	Gets the local interface address and port information for a socket
getsockopt	Gets the value of a local socket option
ioctlsocket	Gets or sets the operating parameters of a socket
listen	Indicates a socket that should listen for incoming connections
recv	Receives data from a socket
recvfrom	Receives data from a socket and returns the remote host addressing information
select	Determines the readability, writability, and error status for one or more sockets
send	Sends data using a connected socket
sendto	Sends data to a specific remote host address and port number
setsockopt	Sets the value of a local socket option
shutdown	Disables the sending or receiving of data on a socket
socket	Creates a socket

Socket Data Structures

Many socket functions accept or return the Internet address and port number of the local or remote end of a connection. The **sockaddr** structure holds these values. A pointer to a **sockaddr** structure is passed into the functions that require an address parameter. The **sockaddr** structure is defined as:

```
struct sockaddr {
    u_short sa_family;
    char    sa_data[14];
};
```

The **sockaddr** structure reflects Berkeley Sockets' original goal of supporting multiple protocols. The **sockaddr** structure does not contain any TCP/IP-specific information. The first field of the structure, **sa_family**, identifies the type of address that the structure data contains. Windows Sockets defines the constant **AF_INET** to represent TCP/IP address information. Other protocols define their own address family constant; ISO address information is identified by the constant **AF_ISO**. The remainder of the **sockaddr** structure is 14 bytes of information whose structure depends on the value of the **sa_family** field.

To make manipulation of a **sockaddr** structure easier, Windows Sockets also defines an equivalent structure to be used when working with TCP/IP addresses—**sockaddr_in**. The **sockaddr_in** structure is defined as:

```
struct sockaddr_in {
    short   sin_family;
    u_short sin_port;
    struct in_addr sin_addr;
    char    sin_zero[8];
};
```

The length of the **sockaddr_in** structure is the same as that of the **sockaddr** structure, but the fields in the data portion of the **sockaddr** structure have been explicitly defined so that a program can manipulate them. A program typically defines a variable as a **sockaddr_in** structure and then casts a pointer to the variable to a **sockaddr** structure in function calls.

The **sin_family** field of a **sockaddr_in** structure must always be **AF_INET**. The **sin_port** field stores the port number *in network byte order*. The **sin_addr** field stores the IP address *in network byte order*. The remainder of the structure is unused and should be set to 0.

The **sin_addr** field is another structure of type **in_addr**. The **in_addr** structure allows a program to access individual portions of the IP address and is defined as:

```
struct in_addr {
    union {
        struct { u_char s_b1,s_b2,s_b3,s_b4; } S_un_b;
        struct { u_short s_w1,s_w2; } S_un_w;
        u_long S_addr;
    } S_un;
};
```

The **in_addr** structure allows access to an IP address as a set of bytes, a pair of 16-bit words, or a single 32-bit word. Although the flexibility of the **in_addr** structure is sometimes helpful, it's often an annoyance. Most programs only need to access an IP address as a single 32-bit word. The structure definition of **in_addr** requires that many levels of structure addressing syntax must be entered in order to access the IP address. Fortunately, Winsock defines a few macros that eliminate one level of addressing syntax. In particular, Winsock defines the following:

```
#define s_addr S_un.S_addr
```

This allows a program to write

```
sockaddr_in sin;
sin.sin_addr.s_addr = ...
```

to access the address portion of the structure. Eliminating one level of structure addressing may not seem like a lot, but it's a big help when confronted with this alternative:

```
sockaddr_in sin;
sin.sin_addr.S_un.S_addr = ...
```

accept

The **accept** function accepts a connection on a specified socket. The **accept** function is declared as:

```
SOCKET PASCAL FAR accept (SOCKET s, struct sockaddr FAR *addr, int FAR *addrlen);
```

As connection requests arrive on a listening socket, they are queued in the Windows Sockets implementation. The **accept** function gets the first connection request on the queue for the specified socket, creates a new socket with the same parameters as the specified socket, and returns a socket descriptor for it. The socket returned to the caller is connected and may be used immediately to send or receive data.

The **addr** parameter points to a **sockaddr** structure that indicates the address of the remote host at the other end of the connection. On entry, the **addrlen** parameter points to an integer that indicates the length of the buffer pointed to by **addr**. On exit, the integer pointed to by **addrlen** receives the length of the data returned in the structure pointed to by **addr**. The **addr** parameter is optional. If **addr** or **addrlen** is set to **NULL**, no address information is returned.

bind

The **bind** function is used to associate a specific interface address and port number with a socket. The **bind** function is declared as:

```
int PASCAL FAR bind (SOCKET s, const struct sockaddr FAR *addr, int namelen);
```

When a socket is first created, it does not have a local address associated with it. The **bind** function specifies the local interface address and port number to be associated with the socket. The **addr** parameter is a pointer to a **sockaddr** structure containing the address and port information. The **namelen** parameter specifies the length of the buffer pointed to by **addr**; normally **namelen** is set to **sizeof(sockaddr)**.

Within the **sockaddr** structure, the address may be the address assigned to a network interface on the host or **INADDR_ANY**. The port number can be specified or set to 0. Using **INADDR_ANY** causes Windows Sockets to use any appropriate network interface address. Using a port number of 0 causes a unique port number to be assigned.

Most programs use **INADDR_ANY** for the interface address. Specifying one interface address over another offers no advantages. Server programs usually specify their own well-known port number, while client programs typically specify port 0 to allow the Winsock implementation to choose any unused descriptor value.

A function is not required to bind a socket to an address before calling **connect**. If **connect** is called before a socket has been bound, the socket is automatically bound as if the **bind** function had been called for the socket using an address of **INADDR_ANY** and a port number of 0. Because many client applications have no need to specify either a local interface address or a particular port value, calling **connect** before calling **bind** can save a step for those applications. Server applications typically have to create a socket bound to a well-known port, so the **bind** function must be explicitly invoked for most servers.

The **bind** function returns 0 if it is successful. If an error occurs, it returns **SOCKET_ERROR**, and the specific error code can be retrieved by calling **WSAGetLastError**.

At first, it might seem obvious that a program will want to bind a socket to an address immediately after creating it. If it's such a frequent operation, why can't the **socket** function simply create a pre-bound socket? Remember that a host may have more than one network interface, each with its own network address. If **socket** created a pre-bound socket on a machine with multiple interfaces, to which interface would it bind the socket? The **bind** function eliminates this problem by allowing the user to specify the interface address.

closesocket

The **closesocket** call frees the resources associated with a socket descriptor when a program is done using the socket. The **closesocket** function is declared as:

```
int PASCAL FAR closesocket (SOCKET s);
```

After the **closesocket** function returns, the socket descriptor is no longer valid. An error will result if socket functions are invoked on a closed socket descriptor.

The **closesocket** function may return immediately or not, depending on the value of the **SO_LINGER** and **SO_DONTLINER** socket options. Table 5.4 summarizes the combinations and actions taken in each instance.

When **SO_DONTLINGER** is set, the **closesocket** function returns immediately. If possible, data that is queued on the socket for transmission is sent before the socket is actually closed. This closure method is called a *graceful close* or disconnect.

When **SO_LINGER** is set with a non-zero value, the **closesocket** function will not return until all data queued on the socket for transmission is sent or until the timeout period has expired. This method is also a graceful close. If the socket was set to non-blocking, **closesocket** returns immediately with a **WSAEWOULDBLOCK** error code.

Table 5.4   Effect of linger options on the closesocket function

Option	Timeout	Type of Close	Wait for Close?
SO_DONTLINGER		Graceful	No
SO_LINGER	Non-zero	Graceful	Yes
SO_LINGER	Zero	Hard	No

When **SO_LINGER** is set to a value of zero, the **closesocket** function returns immediately. All remaining data queued on the socket for transmission is discarded immediately. If a **recv** is attempted on the remote end of the connection, it returns with an error of **WSAECONNRESET**. This type of closure is called a *hard close*.

For more information about the **SO_LINGER** and **SO_DONTLINGER** socket options, see **getsocketopt** and **setsocketopt**.

If no error occurs, **closesocket** returns 0. If an error occurs, it returns **SOCKET_ERROR**, and the specific error code can be retrieved by calling **WSAGetLastError**.

connect

The **connect** function establishes a connection with a remote host. The **connect** function is declared as:

```
int PASCAL FAR connect (SOCKET s, const struct sockaddr FAR *name, int namelen);
```

The **connect** function takes the specified socket, **s**, and pointer to a **sockaddr** structure containing the network address and port number of the remote endpoint, **name**, as inputs. The **namelen** parameter is set to the size of the buffer pointed to by **name** and is set to **sizeof(sockaddr)**.

s designates the socket type. If **s** designates a stream socket, a connection is established; if **s** designates a datagram socket, the addressing information indicated by the **name** parameter is associated with the socket and is used for the destination address of datagrams sent using the **send** function.

If **s** is unbound at the time the **connect** function is invoked upon it, Windows Sockets will bind the socket to an interface address and port number as if the **bind** function had been called on the socket, specifying **INADDR_ANY** and 0 as the interface address and port number, respectively.

The **connect** function returns 0 to signal that no errors occurred. It returns **SOCKET_ERROR** to signal an error; the specific error code can be retrieved using **WSAGetLastError**.

When **s** has been designated a non-blocking socket, the **connect** function might return with an error. If the error code returned by **WSAGetLastError** is **WSAEWOULDBLOCK**, Windows Sockets is simply indicating that the request did not complete immediately and is in progress. If your program is using the asynchronous Windows Sockets extension functions (discussed in detail later in this chapter), you will receive an **FD_CONNECT** message if you have enabled such messages for the socket using **WSAAsyncSelect**. If not, your program can use the **select** function to determine that the socket is connected by testing if the socket is writable.

getpeername

The **getpeername** function gets the interface address and port number of the remote connection endpoint. The **getpeername** function is declared as:

```
int PASCAL FAR getpeername (SOCKET s, struct sockaddr FAR *name, int FAR * namelen);
```

The **getpeername** function takes the socket of interest, **s**, and a pointer to a buffer in which to return the remote endpoint information, **name**, as inputs. The **namelen** parameter is a pointer to an integer that, on entry, indicates the maximum size of the buffer pointer by name and, on exit, indicates the amount of buffer space actually used. Most programs simply set the integer to **sizeof(sockaddr)** before calling the function, then ignore the return value.

The **getpeername** function must be used on a connected stream or datagram socket. It will return an error if the socket is unconnected.

The **getpeername** function returns 0 to signal that no errors occurred. It returns **SOCKET_ERROR** to signal an error; the specific error code can be retrieved using **WSAGetLastError**.

getsockname

The **getsockname** function is similar to the **getpeername** function, but it returns the local address and port number bound to a socket instead of the remote address and port number. The **getsockname** function is declared as:

```
int PASCAL FAR getsockname (SOCKET s, struct sockaddr FAR *name, int FAR * namelen);
```

The parameters for **getsockname** are the same as those for **getpeername** and are used in the same manner.

The **getsockname** function retrieves the local address and port information for the specified bound or connected socket. It is an error to use **getsockname** on an unbound socket. The **getsockname** function is often used to return the address and port information of a socket that was connected without being bound first.

If **getsockname** is invoked on a socket that was bound to the address **INADDR_ANY** but has not yet been connected, the address returned by **getsockname** could be the actual address to which the socket is bound or **INADDR_ANY**. On a host with multiple network interfaces, Windows Sockets will not bind the socket to a specific network interface until it is connected. The interface selected will be best suited to communicating with the specified end-point of the connection request. Until the socket is connected, a Windows Sockets application should not assume that the address returned by **getsockname** is anything other than **INADDR_ANY**.

The **getsockname** function returns 0 to signal that no errors occurred. It returns **SOCKET_ERROR** to signal an error; the specific error code can be retrieved using **WSAGetLastError**.

getsockopt

The **getsockopt** function retrieves the values of socket option. The **getsockopt** function is declared as:

```
int PASCAL FAR getsockopt (SOCKET s, int level, int optname, char FAR * optval, int
FAR *optlen);
```

The socket on which to operate is specified by the **s** parameter. Socket options can be defined for multiple layers of the protocol stack, and all are accessed through the **getsockopt** function. The **level** parameter indicates the level at which the socket option is defined and can take one of two values: **SOL_SOCKET** or **IPPROTO_TCP**. The **optname** parameter indicates the option that is being retrieved. The **optval** parameter points to a buffer to receive the value of the option. The **optlen** parameter points to an integer that indicates the size of the **optval** buffer on entry and the size of the data returned in the buffer upon return.

Table 5.5 lists the various standard socket options, their type, and the interpretation of the value returned by **getsockopt**. The **TCP_NODELAY** option is accessed at the **IPPROTO_TCP** level; all other socket options are accessed at the **SOL_SOCKET** level.

The linger structure used for the **SO_LINGER** option is defined as:

```
struct linger {
  u_short l_onoff;
  u_short l_linger;
};
```

Table 5.5	Socket options	
Option	**Option Type**	**Interpretation**
SO_ACCEPTCONN	BOOL	If true, the socket is listening
SO_BROADCAST	BOOL	If true, the socket is configured for the transmission of broadcast messages
SO_DEBUG	BOOL	If true, debugging is enabled
SO_DONTLINGER	BOOL	If true, the SO_LINGER option is disabled
SO_DONTROUTE	BOOL	If true, routing is disabled
SO_ERROR	int	Retrieves error status and clears
SO_KEEPALIVE	BOOL	If true, keepalives are being sent
SO_LINGER	struct linger FAR *	Returns the current linger options
SO_OOBINLINE	BOOL	If true, out-of-band data is being received in the normal data stream
SO_RCVBUF	int	Contains the buffer size for receives
SO_REUSEADDR	BOOL	If true, the socket can be bound to an address that is already in use
SO_SNDBUF	int	Contains the buffer size for sends
SO_TYPE	int	The type of the socket (for example, SOCK_STREAM or SOCK_DGRAM)
TCP_NODELAY	BOOL	Disables the Nagle algorithm for send coalescing

The **l_onoff** field of the **linger** structure is a Boolean value that determines whether the option will be turned on or off. If **l_onoff** is non-zero, **SO_LINGER** will be turned on and the **l_linger** field specifies the amount of time to wait when a connection is closed. (See the section on **closesocket** for more information about the behavior of **SO_LINGER**.) If **l_onoff** is zero, **SO_DONTLINGER** is turned on and the **l_linger** value is ignored.

The **getsockopt** function returns 0 to signal that no errors occurred. It returns **SOCKET_ERROR** to signal an error; the specific error code can be retrieved using **WSAGetLastError**. If **getsockopt** is called to retrieve an unknown socket option, **SOCKET_ERROR** is returned and **WSAGetLastError** indicates **WSAENOPROTOOPT**.

ioctlsocket

The **ioctlsocket** function is used to control the mode of a socket. It is declared as:

```
int PASCAL FAR ioctlsocket (SOCKET s, long cmd, u_long FAR *argp);
```

The **s** parameter indicates the socket on which to invoke the command. The **cmd** parameter indicates the command to perform on the socket and **argp** is used as a parameter for the command.

Windows Sockets supports three **ioctlsocket** commands, which are summarized in Table 5.6.

The **ioctlsocket** function returns 0 to signal that no errors occurred. It returns **SOCKET_ERROR** to signal an error; the specific error code can be retrieved using **WSAGetLastError**.

listen

The **listen** function informs Windows Sockets that a particular socket will be used to listen for incoming connections and to establish the incoming connection queue length. The **listen** function is declared as:

```
int PASCAL FAR listen (SOCKET s, int backlog);
```

The **s** parameter identifies the socket that will be used for listening. The **backlog** parameter indicates the maximum length of the queue for incoming connections.

As connection requests are received, they are acknowledged and queued on the listening socket. The **accept** function is invoked on the listening socket to create

Table 5.6 Commands supported by **ioctlsocket**	
Command	**Description**
FIONBIO	Enables or disables non-blocking mode on the specified socket. The argp command parameter points to an unsigned long that, if non-zero, enables non-blocking mode. If the parameter value is zero, blocking mode is restored.
	Note that WSAAsyncSelect forces a socket into non-blocking mode. Any attempt to change the socket to blocking mode while WSAAsyncSelect is still operating on the socket will fail.
FIONREAD	Determines the amount of data that can be read from the socket. The argp command parameter points to a unsigned long, which is used to store the returned value.
	If the socket is of type SOCK_STREAM, the return value indicates the amount of data that can be read by a single call to recv. If the socket is of type SOCK_DGRAM, the return value indicates the size of the first queued datagram.
SIOCATMARK	Determines whether or not all out-of-band data has been read from the socket. The argp parameter points to a BOOL into which the returned value is stored. TRUE is returned if there is no out-of-band data waiting to be read; FALSE is returned otherwise.
	This command is applicable only to sockets of type SOCK_STREAM that have been configured for inline reception of out-of-band data using the SO_OOBINLINE socket option.

a second socket that can be used to communicate. If many connection requests arrive in a short period of time and the application is unable to service them fast enough, the incoming connection queue will reach its maximum value. A remote station initiating subsequent requests will receive a **WSAECONNREFUSED** error.

The **listen** function returns 0 to signal that no errors occurred. It returns **SOCKET_ERROR** to signal an error; the specific error code can be retrieved using **WSAGetLastError**.

recv

The **recv** function receives data from a socket. The **recv** function is declared as:

```
int PASCAL FAR recv (SOCKET s, char FAR * buf, int len, int flags);
```

The **s** parameter indicates the socket from which to receive the data. The **buf** parameter points to a buffer into which the received data should be stored and **len** indicates the size of the buffer. The **flags** parameter is used to slightly alter the standard behavior. See Table 5.7 for a description of values for the **flags** parameter.

If the socket is of type **SOCK_STREAM**, as much data as is queued and that fits into the buffer is returned. Subsequent calls to **recv** will return data that follows in the stream. If the socket has been configured for inline reception of out-of-band data using the **SO_OOBINLINE** socket option and there is out-of-band data to be read, only out-of-band data will be read.

> *Note: There is no concept of a boundary for a TCP stream socket. If a remote application used three calls to the **send** function to transmit data to the local host, a local application might need to use one, two, three, or more calls with **recv** to retreive the data. There is no one-to-one correspondence between the data in calls to **send** and the data returned by calls to **recv**. The number of calls required depends on the timing of the data arrival and size of the buffer that the receiving application is using relative to the size of the received data.*

Table 5.7	Recv function flags
Flag	**Description**
MSG_PEEK	The MSG_PEEK flag is used to peek at the incoming data. The data at the head of the queue is copied to the return buffer but the data is not removed from the queue.
MSG_OOB	The MSG_OOB flag is used to process out-of-band data.

If an application needs to preserve any sort of record boundary, it must use a private protocol within the data stream to indicate the presence of the boundaries to the receiver.

If the socket is of type **SOCK_DGRAM**, as much data as will fit in the buffer from the first datagram in the queue is returned. Any data from the first datagram that will not fit in the buffer is discarded. In this case, **recv** will signal the **WSEMSGSIZE** error. The **flags** parameter alters the standard behavior of the **recv** function. Two flags options may be or-ed together to create the **flags** parameter, as shown in Table 5.7.

The **recv** function returns the number of bytes read. If the connection has been closed, **recv** returns 0. If there is no data to be read and the socket is in blocking mode, **recv** blocks, waiting for data to arrive. If there is no data to be read and the socket is in non-blocking mode, **recv** returns **SOCKET_ERROR** and the code returned by **WSAGetLastError** is **WSAEWOULDBLOCK**. An application can determine when data arrives using the **select** and **WSAAsyncSelect** functions.

If an error occurs, **recv** returns **SOCKET_ERROR**; the specific error code can be retrieved using **WSAGetLastError**.

recvfrom

The **recvfrom** function is similar to the **recv** function. It retrieves data from a socket and also returns the address and port number associated with the sender. The **recvfrom** function is declared as:

```
int PASCAL FAR recvfrom (SOCKET s, char FAR * buf, int len, int flags, struct
sockaddr FAR *from, int FAR * fromlen);
```

The first few parameters, **s, buf, len,** and **flags** are used identically as in the **recv** function.

If **s** is a **SOCK_DGRAM** and **from** is non-**NULL**, the **from** and **fromlen** parameters return the address of the sender of the datagram. On entry to the **recvfrom** function, **fromlen** should be initialized with the size of the buffer pointed to by **from**. On return, **fromlen** will be set to the size of the actual data returned.

If **s** is a **SOCK_STREAM**, the **from** and **fromlen** parameters are ignored. No address is returned. The address of the remote peer of a stream connection can be found using the **getpeername** function.

If an error occurs, **recv** returns **SOCKET_ERROR**; the specific error code can be retrieved using **WSAGetLastError**.

> The **recvfrom** function is used for protocols based on UDP datagrams. Using the **recvfrom** function, the receiver of a datagram can easily determine who sent the datagram. No space should be allocated in the datagram itself to store the sender's return address. When implementing a simple request-response client server protocol, a server can capture the address of the client using **recvfrom** and use the same **sockaddr** structure holding the information in the return call to **sendto**. Often, the server does not even have to look at the address of the client.

select

The **select** function is used to determine the status of one or more sockets. The **select** function is declared as:

```
int PASCAL FAR select (int nfds, fd_set FAR *readfds, fd_set FAR *writefds, fd_set
    FAR *exceptfds, const struct timeval FAR *timeout);
```

The **nfds** parameter was used in the original Berkeley Sockets API. It is included in the Windows Sockets version of the **select** function to be compatible with the Berkeley Sockets function of the same name, but it is ignored in Windows Sockets.

The **readfds**, **writefds**, and **exceptfds** parameters identify a set of sockets for which read, write, or error status is of interest. On return from the function, Windows Sockets updates the set of descriptors with the subset for which the condition is true. For instance, if a program wants to find out whether data is waiting in the queues of three sockets, it will specify those socket descriptors in the **readfds** set. If only one of the sockets specified is readable at the time of the call to **select**, Windows Sockets removes the other socket descriptors from the **readfds** set, leaving only the readable socket.

The **timeout** parameter establishes a maximum time that **select** should wait until at least one descriptor from the sets meets the specified criteria.

The **readfds** parameter identifies those sockets that should be checked for readability. Sockets that are listening are identified as readable if an incoming connection request was received and the **accept** function will not block when invoked on the socket. Otherwise, sockets are identified as readable if data is queued on them. Stream sockets are also marked readable if they were closed. In this case, the next call to **recv** will return 0 bytes, as described in **recv**. If the socket experienced a hard close, **recv** indicates **WSAECONNRESET**. **select** indicates readability for out-of-band data if the **SO_OOBINLINE** socket option was enabled on the socket.

The **writefds** parameter identifies those sockets that should be checked for writability. A socket can be written to if a call to **send** or **sendto** will complete without blocking. If the **connect** function was invoked on a non-blocking socket, the **select** function considers the socket as writable as soon as the connection is established.

The **exceptfds** parameter indicates those sockets that should be checked for error conditions or for the presence of out-of-band data. The **exceptfds** set notes two exception conditions. First, if a stream socket connection that is using "keepalives" closes, the event is noted here. Second, if the **connect** function is called on a non-blocking socket and later fails, the event is noted here. The presence of out-of-band data is signaled in the **exceptfds** set if the **SO_OOBINLINE** socket option is *not* enabled for the socket (otherwise, out-of-band data is indicated in the **readfds** set).

Any of the **readfds**, **writefds**, or **exceptfds** parameters may be set to **NULL** to indicate that the particular set is empty.

The actual implementation of the **fd_set** data structure is unimportant. In fact, the Windows Sockets implementation of the data structure differs from the Berkeley Sockets implementation. The **fd_set** data structure should be accessed using a set of macros that hides the underlying implementation. Four macros are defined, as shown in Table 5.8. The socket descriptor values should be of type **SOCKET**, and the **set** parameter should be a pointer to an **fd_set** structure.

Table 5.8 Descriptor set manipulation macros

Macro	Description
FD_CLR(SOCKET s, fd_set FAR * set)	Removes the specified socket descriptor from the set
FD_ISSET(SOCKET s, fd_set FAR * set)	Returns non-zero if the socket descriptor is present in the set
FD_SET(SOCKET s, fd_set FAR * set)	Adds the specified socket descriptor to the set
FD_ZERO(fd_set FAR * set)	Removes all socket descriptors from the set

By default, the **fd_set** structure is sized to handle a maximum of 64 socket descriptors. If a program needs more than 64 descriptors for each set, **#define** the FD_SETSIZE constant before including the WINSOCK.H header file.

The **timeout** parameter limits the amount of time that the **select** function waits for a socket to become readable, to be writable to, or to have an exception occur. The **timeout** parameter is a pointer to a **timeval** structure, which is defined as:

```
struct timeval {
   long  tv_sec;       /* seconds */
   long  tv_usec;      /* and microseconds */
};
```

If the **timeout** parameter is **NULL**, the **select** function blocks indefinitely until one more socket is readable, is writable to, or has an exception occur. Otherwise, the **select** function waits until one or more sockets meet the specified criteria or the **timeout** value expires. If **timeout** points to a **timeval** structure containing {0, 0}, the **select** function returns immediately, indicating which sockets met the specified criteria at the time the function was called. This procedure can be used to poll the status of one or more descriptors.

The **select** function directly returns the number of sockets that met the specified criteria or returns zero if the timeout value expired. In the case of an error, the function returns **SOCKET_ERROR**; the specific error code can be retrieved by calling **WSAGetLastError**.

send

The **send** function sends data to a remote host using a connected socket. The **send** function is declared as:

```
int PASCAL FAR send (SOCKET s, const char FAR * buf, int len, int flags);
```

The **s** parameter specifies the socket on which the data should be queued for transmission. The **buf** pointer points to the data, and the **len** parameter specifies the length of the buffer. The **flags** parameter modifies the standard behavior of the **send** function, depending on the optional flags set.

The **send** function must be used on a connected socket. If the socket is a datagram socket, the **connect** function must have been invoked on the socket previously to specify a remote destination for the data. The maximum datagram size of the current network, as specified in the **iMaxUdpDg** member of the **WSAData** structure returned from **WSAStartup**, must not be exceeded.

Upon return from the **send** function, the data is queued for transmission. Note that actual delivery of the data may not have occurred. If no buffer space is available for the data, the **send** function blocks unless the socket was put into non-blocking mode. If the socket is a stream socket and is non-blocking, the **send** function accepts as much of the buffer as it can. The number of bytes accepted will be returned as the function result. The application should send the remaining bytes at a later time, as determined using the **select** or **WSAAsyncSelect** functions.

The **flags** parameter alters the behavior of the **send** function beyond the various socket options that may have been set for the socket. The **flags** parameter is constructed by or-ing together the constant values described in Table 5.9.

The **send** function returns the number of bytes queued for transmission. If an error occurs, the function returns **SOCKET_ERROR**. The specific error code can be retrieved by calling **WSAGetLastError**.

sendto

The **sendto** function, similar to the **send** function is declared as:

```
int PASCAL FAR sendto (SOCKET s, const char FAR * buf, int len, int flags, const
   struct sockaddr FAR *to, int tolen);
```

The **sendto** function's first four parameters, **s**, **buf**, **len**, and **flags**, function identically to the same parameters in the **send** function. The **to** and **tolen** parameters are used to indicate a remote host address to which the data should be sent.

The **sendto** function typically is used on an unconnected datagram socket. When used on a stream socket the **to** and **tolen** parameters are ignored, making the function identical to the **send** function.

Table 5.9	Send function flags
Flags	**Description**
MSG_DONTROUTE	Indicates that the data should not be routed. Windows Sockets implementations may ignore this value as well as the corresponding socket option.
MSG_OOB	The data should be sent as out-of-band data. This flag should be used only with stream sockets.

A datagram socket may specify that a datagram be broadcast to all stations on the local subnet. To send a broadcast datagram, the special address **INADDR_BROADCAST** and an appropriate port number should be used as the destination address.

The **sendto** function returns the number of bytes queued for transmission. If an error occurs, the function returns **SOCKET_ERROR**. The specific error code can be retrieved by calling **WSAGetLastError**.

setsockopt

The **setsockopt** function allows an application to set the value of an option associated with a socket. The **setsockopt** function is declared as:

```
int PASCAL FAR setsockopt (SOCKET s, int level, int optname, const char FAR * optval,
   int optlen);
```

The socket on which to operate is specified by the **s** parameter. Socket options can be defined for multiple layers of the protocol stack, and all are accessed through the **setsockopt** function. The **level** parameter indicates the level at which the socket option is defined and can take one of two values: **SOL_SOCKET** or **IPPROTO_TCP**. The **optname** parameter indicates the option that is being retrieved. The **optval** parameter points to a buffer to receive the value of the option. The **optlen** parameter indicates the size of the **optval** buffer.

The various socket options are described in the **getsockopt** section. The **setsockopt** function returns 0 if no errors occur. If an error occurs, **setsockopt** returns **SOCKET_ERROR**; the specific error code can be retrieved by calling **WSAGetLastError**.

shutdown

The **shutdown** function is used to disable sends or receives on a socket. The **shutdown** function is declared as:

```
int PASCAL FAR shutdown (SOCKET s, int how);
```

The **s** parameter specifies the socket on which to shut down transmission or reception. The **how** parameter specifies which operation to shut down. If **how** is 0, all receives on the socket are disabled. If **how** is 1, all sends are disabled. If **how** is 2, both receives and sends are disabled.

The **shutdown** function does not close a socket, and no resources are freed until the **closesocket** function is invoked on the socket.

The **shutdown** function returns 0 if no errors occur. If an error occurs, **shutdown** returns SOCKET_ERROR; the specific error code can be retrieved by calling **WSAGetLastError**.

socket

The **socket** function creates a socket and returns the descriptor to the application. The **socket** function is declared as:

```
SOCKET PASCAL FAR socket (int af, int type, int protocol);
```

The **af** parameter determines the address family that the socket will use. The **type** parameter determines whether the socket will support stream or datagram communication. The **protocol** parameter specifies which protocol will be used with the socket. In general, only two of the three parameters are needed to determine all the details of the socket.

The **af** parameter can be **AF_INET** for Internet addresses or **AF_UNSPEC** if the socket specification is based on the other two parameters. If the **af** parameter is **AF_UNSPEC**, the **protocol** parameter must be specified.

The **type** parameter can be **SOCK_DGRAM** for datagram sockets or **SOCK_STREAM** for stream sockets. In the Internet address family, **SOCK_DGRAM** corresponds to UDP and **SOCK_STREAM** corresponds to TCP.

The **protocol** parameter can be the constant assigned to the protocol, such as **IPPROTO_TCP** or **IPPROTO_UDP**, a protocol value returned by **getprotobyX**, or zero if the application does not wish to specify a protocol. If the **protocol** parameter is zero, the **af** parameter must be specified as **AF_INET**.

The newly created socket is unbound and unconnected. The **closesocket** function must be used to release the resources associated with the socket and to close the connection with a remote host (in the case of a stream socket).

If no error occurs, the **socket** function returns the valid socket descriptor for the newly created socket. If an error occurs, the **socket** function returns **INVALID_SOCKET** (not **SOCKET_ERROR**); the specific error code can be retrieved using **WSAGetLastError**.

Winsock Extension Functions

The Windows Sockets API provides several extensions to the Berkeley Sockets API. In general, the extensions provide asynchronous, message-based notification of database lookup completion or socket status changes. Other functions provide control of asynchronous operations, the ability to manage the blocking hook loop for traditional Berkeley Sockets functions, and Windows Sockets startup and shutdown. Table 5.10 shows the Windows Sockets extension functions.

General Functionality of Asynchronous Database Functions

Windows Sockets provides six extension functions for asynchronous database lookup. These functions perform the same tasks as their traditional counterparts,

Table 5.10 Windows Sockets extensions

Function	Description
WSAAsyncGetHostByAddr	Asynchronously retrieves host information using the host address as a key
WSAAsyncGetHostByName	Asynchronously retrieves host information using the host name as a key
WSAAsyncGetProtoByName	Asynchronously retrieves protocol information using the name of the protocol as a key
WSAAsyncGetProtoByNumber	Asynchronously retrieves protocol information using the number of the protocol as a key
WSAAsyncGetServByName	Asynchronously retrieves service information using the name of the service as a key
WSAAsyncGetServByPort	Asynchronously retrieves service information using the port number of the service as a key
WSAAsyncSelect	Requests notification of events pertaining to a given socket
WSACancelAsyncRequest	Cancels an in-progress asynchronous database operation
WSACancelBlockingCall	Cancels an in-progress function that is blocked in a blocking hook loop
WSACleanup	Terminates the use of Windows Sockets
WSAGetLastError	Gets the specific error code of the last Winsock error generated by this thread
WSAIsBlocking	Returns TRUE if a blocking operation is in progress
WSASetBlockingHook	Installs an application-specific blocking hook
WSASetLastError	Sets the error code that will be retrieved by WSAGetLastError
WSAStartup	Initiates startup of Windows Sockets
WSAUnhookBlockingHook	Restores the blocking hook to the Windows Sockets default blocking hook

but they do so asynchronously. Where the traditional function is named **getXbyY**, the corresponding asynchronous function is named **WSAAsyncGetXByY**.

In general, the asynchronous database functions all operate in a similar manner. The first two parameters of each function are **hWnd** and **wMsg**. The **hWnd** parameter identifies a window that should receive a window message when the database operation is complete. The **wMsg** parameter is the window message that should be sent to the window identified by **hWnd**. Typically, **wMsg** indicates an application-defined window message indexed from **WM_USER**.

The last two parameters of each function are **buf** and **buflen**. The **buf** parameter is a pointer to a buffer into which the database information should be placed. Unlike the traditional database functions, the asynchronous database functions require the caller to supply the buffer into which to place the data. The **buflen** parameter indicates the length of the buffer pointed to by **buf**. If the supplied buffer is too short to receive all the data resulting from the database lookup, an error will be returned. To avoid generating an error message, an application should supply a buffer of at least **MAXGETHOSTSTRUCT** bytes in length.

If the asynchronous database lookup was successfully initiated, the functions return a non-zero asynchronous task handle. The handle can be used to cancel the operation at a later time, before it completes, or to match up the completion messages with the corresponding asynchronous operation. If the lookup could not be successfully initiated, the functions return zero. The specific error code can then be retrieved by calling **WSAGetLastError**. Note that a non-zero value does not indicate that the database lookup is complete, only that it has been started.

When the asynchronous lookup is complete, Windows Sockets sends a window message to the application window that was specified in the initiating database lookup function. The window message will be the window message that was specified in the initiating database lookup function. The **wParam** value contains the asynchronous task handle returned to the application by the database function. The high-word of **lParam** indicates any error that may have occurred during the lookup or zero if the lookup completed with no errors. If the lookup completes with no errors, the appropriate data is contained in the buffer supplied by the application.

If the **lParam** error code is **WSAENOBUFS**, the application-supplied buffer was too small to contain all the data. The buffer contains all the data that could fit, and the low-word of **lParam** indicates the buffer length that would be required to contain all the data. At this point the application can choose what to do. If the partial data is adequate, the application can simply proceed. If the application needs all the database data, it should reissue the asynchronous database function and provide a buffer of the size indicated in the low-word of **lParam**.

The following macros can be used to access the buffer length and error code from **lParam**. Use of these macros will enhance the portability of Windows Sockets code.

```
#define  WSAGETASYNCBUFLEN(lParam)       LOWORD(lParam)
#define  WSAGETASYNCERROR(lParam)        HIWORD(lParam)
```

The following sections regarding the asynchronous database functions describe only the differences of the function from the general behavior presented previously.

WSAAsyncGetHostByAddr

The **WSAAsyncGetHostByAddr** function asynchronously retrieves host information using the host address as the database key. The **WSAAsyncGetHostByAddr** function is declared as:

```
HANDLE PASCAL FAR WSAAsyncGetHostByAddr(HWND hWnd, u_int wMsg, const char FAR *
    addr, int len, int type, char FAR * buf, int buflen);
```

The **addr** parameter points to an Internet address *in network byte order*. Note that **addr** does *not* point to a **sockaddr** structure. The **len** parameter specifies the length of the address pointed to by **addr**; its value is always 4 for Internet addresses. The **type** parameter indicates the type of address specified by **addr** and must be **PF_INET** for Internet addresses. The **buf** pointer should point to a **hostent** structure that is at least **MAXGETHOSTSTRUCT** bytes in length.

WSAAsyncGetHostByName

The **WSAAsyncGetHostByName** function asynchronously retrieves host information using the host name as the database key. The **WSAAsyncGetHostByName** function is declared as:

```
HANDLE PASCAL FAR WSAAsyncGetHostByName(HWND hWnd, u_int wMsg, const char FAR *
    name, char FAR * buf, int buflen);
```

The **name** parameter points to a null-terminated host name. The **buf** pointer should point to a **hostent** structure that is at least **MAXGETHOSTSTRUCT** bytes in length.

WSAAsyncGetProtoByName

The **WSAAsyncGetProtoByName** function asynchronously retrieves protocol information using the protocol name as the database key. The **WSAAsyncGetProtoByName** function is declared as:

```
HANDLE PASCAL FAR WSAAsyncGetProtoByName(HWND hWnd, u_int wMsg, const char
    FAR *name, char FAR * buf, int buflen);
```

The **name** parameter points to a null-terminated protocol name such as "tcp" or "udp." The **buf** pointer should point to a **protoent** structure that is at least MAXGETHOSTSTRUCT bytes in length.

WSAAsyncGetProtoByNumber

The **WSAAsyncGetProtoByNumber** function asynchronously retrieves protocol information using the protocol number as the database key. The **WSAAsyncGetProtoByNumber** function is declared as:

```
HANDLE PASCAL FAR WSAAsyncGetProtoByNumber(HWND hWnd, u_int wMsg, int number, char
    FAR * buf, int buflen);
```

The **number** parameter indicates the constant assigned to a given protocol *in host byte order*. The **buf** pointer should point to a **protoent** structure that is at least MAXGETHOSTSTRUCT bytes in length.

WSAAsyncGetServByName

The **WSAAsyncGetServByName** function asynchronously retrieves service information using the service name as the database key. The **WSAAsyncGetServByName** function is declared as:

```
HANDLE PASCAL FAR WSAAsyncGetServByName(HWND hWnd, u_int wMsg, const char FAR *
    name, const char FAR * proto, char FAR * buf, int buflen);
```

The **name** parameter points to a null-terminated service name, such as "smtp." The **proto** parameter points to a null-terminated protocol name, such as "tcp." If **proto** is NULL, the first entry in the service database that matches the name parameter is returned as the lookup result. If **proto** is non-**NULL**, an entry matching both the name and protocol is returned. Note that some services may be accessed using either TCP or UDP (the "echo" or "daytime" services, for example) and so, in general, it is wise to specify the protocol for those services to avoid inconsistent lookup results when the application runs in different environments. The **buf** pointer should point to a **servent** structure that is at least MAXGETHOSTSTRUCT bytes in length.

WSAAsyncGetServByPort

The **WSAAsyncGetServByPort** function asynchronously retrieves service information using the service port number as the database key. The **WSAAsyncGetServByPort** function is declared as:

```
HANDLE PASCAL FAR WSAAsyncGetServByPort(HWND hWnd, u_int wMsg, int port, const char
    FAR * proto, char FAR * buf, int buflen);
```

The **port** parameter specifies the port number of the service *in network byte order*. The **proto** parameter points to a null-terminated protocol name, such as "tcp." If **proto** is non-NULL, both the port number and protocol name are used as keys for the lookup. If **proto** is NULL, the first database entry matching **port** is returned. The **buf** pointer should point to a **servent** structure that is at least MAXGETHOSTSTRUCT bytes in length.

WSAAsyncSelect

The **WSAAsyncSelect** function is used to inform an application about changes in a socket's state. The **WSAAsyncSelect** function is declared as:

```
int PASCAL FAR WSAAsyncSelect(SOCKET s, HWND hWnd, u_int wMsg, long lEvent);
```

The **s** parameter is the socket of interest. The **hWnd** parameter is the window handle of the window to which a message should be sent when the socket state changes. The **wMsg** parameter is the message to send to the window as the window message. The **lEvent** parameter identifies the state changes that are of interest to the application for the specified socket. The **lEvent** parameter is created by or-ing together the constants listed in Table 5.11.

The Windows Sockets implementation stores an event mask for every socket. Invoking the **WSAAsyncSelect** function on the socket sets the event mask to the new value indicated by the **lEvent** parameter. All the events of interest at a given point in time must be set in a single call to **WSAAsyncSelect**. To cancel all event notification, call the **WSAAsyncSelect** function with **lEvent** set to 0.

Table 5.11	WSAAsyncSelect events
Event	**Description**
FD_ACCEPT	Sends a message when the socket has an incoming connection and **accept** can be called on the socket without blocking
FD_CLOSE	Sends a message when the socket has been closed
FD_CONNECT	Sends a message when the socket has completed its connection
FD_OOB	Sends a message when out-of-band data is available to be read
FD_READ	Sends a message when there is data available to be read
FD_WRITE	Sends a message when the socket is ready for writing

Note that setting a new event mask using **WSAAsyncSelect** only affects the delivery of *future* status changes. Status change messages already might have been posted to the message queue. Additionally, invoking **closesocket** on a socket will stop all future status change messages but will not cancel any messages already in the message queue. An application should be prepared to handle messages for events that recently have been masked and for sockets that recently have been closed.

When the **accept** function is called on a listening socket, a socket is created for the new connection with the same properties as the listening socket. This behavior applies to the event mask of the listening socket as well. The newly created socket resulting from a call to the **accept** function will inherit the same event mask as the listening socket. The application should call **WSAAsyncSelect** on the new socket to change the event mask if needed. Typically, an application should only enable **FD_ACCEPT** events on a listening socket. After a connection has been accepted, the application should enable other events on the new socket.

When one of the events indicated by the event mask occurs, the **hWnd** window is sent the **wMsg** message. The **wParam** parameter of the message is set to the appropriate socket descriptor. The low-word of **lParam** identifies the network event using the same constants as **lEvent** in the call to **WSAAsyncSelect**. Only one event will be signaled in each window message (that is, only one bit of the low-word of **lParam** will be set at a time). The high-word of **lParam** contains any error code associated with the event.

The WINSOCK.H file defines two macros for the extraction of the event and the error code. Use of these macros will enhance the portability of Windows Sockets code.

```
#define WSAGETSELECTEVENT(1Param)        LOWORD(1Param)
#define WSAGETSELECTERROR(1Param)        HIWORD(1Param)
```

Windows Sockets sends only a single message for a given event. No more messages for that event will be sent until the application calls another Windows Sockets function that re-enables the particular message. For instance, if there is data to be read from a socket and the application has enabled notification of **FD_READ** events, Windows Sockets will send a single **FD_READ** event to the indicated window. When the application calls the **recv** or **recvfrom** function, **FD_READ** event generation is re-enabled. If more data is waiting on the socket's receive queue after **recv** or **recvfrom** has been called, another **FD_READ** event will be sent to the window. If no more data remains, no **FD_READ** event will be generated until more data arrives.

This behavior allows an application to be fully event driven. As long as data remains in the receive queue, for instance, **FD_READ** event messages will be generated. An application can read data in small chunks without worrying about emptying the queue all at once. If more data remains following a read, another **FD_READ** message will be generated and the application will read more data when it processes the message.

Table 5.12 shows the functions that re-enable generation of the specified events.

Invoking **WSAAsyncSelect** on a socket automatically makes the socket non-blocking, as if **ioctlsocket** had been invoked. As long as the event mask is non-zero, any attempt to put the socket into blocking mode using **ioctlsocket** will fail. To set a socket back to blocking mode, call **WSAAsyncSelect** with an event mask of zero before using **ioctlsocket**.

The **WSAAsyncSelect** function returns 0 if no errors occur. If an error occurs, it returns **SOCKET_ERROR**; the specific error can be retrieved by calling **WSAGetLastError**.

Table 5.12	Re-enabling functions for socket events
Event	**Functions that Re-enable Event Generation**
FD_ACCEPT	**accept**
FD_CLOSE	None—this can occur only once for a given socket
FD_CONNECT	None—this can occur only once for a given socket
FD_OOB	**recv**
FD_READ	**recv, recvfrom**
FD_WRITE	**send, sendto**

For more information about some of the finer points on using **WSAAsyncSelect**, consult the Windows Sockets specification that is included on the companion CD-ROM.

WSACancelAsyncRequest

The **WSACancelAsyncRequest** function cancels an outstanding asynchronous database lookup. The **WSACancelAsyncRequest** function is declared as:

```
int PASCAL FAR WSACancelAsyncRequest(HANDLE hAsyncTaskHandle);
```

The **hAsyncTaskHandle** parameter is the asynchronous task handle identifying the database lookup task. This task handle was returned to the application as the result of a successful call to a **WSAAsyncGetXByY** function.

WSACancelAsyncRequest returns 0 if no errors occur. It returns **SOCKET_ERROR** if an error occurs; the specific error code can be retrieved using **WSAGetLastError**.

WSACancelBlockingCall

The **WSACancelBlockingCall** function cancels a Windows Sockets function that is currently blocking. The **WSACancelBlockingCall** is declared as:

```
int PASCAL FAR WSACancelBlockingCall(void);
```

The **WSACancelBlockingCall** function takes no parameters. Because there can be only one blocking call in effect at a time, the blocking call to cancel is unambiguous.

The blocking function terminates as soon as possible. Note that because the blocking functionality is really being emulated by a message dispatch loop, the thread of control must pass back to the message loop before the call will exit. The cancelled blocking call returns the **WSAEINTR** error.

If **WSACancelBlockingCall** is successful, it returns 0. If an error occurs, **WSACancelBlockingCall** returns **SOCKET_ERROR**; the specific error code can be retrieved using **WSAGetLastError**.

WSACleanup

The **WSACleanup** function terminates the use of Windows Sockets. The **WSACleanup** function is declared as:

```
int PASCAL FAR WSACleanup(void);
```

Before using Windows Sockets services, an application must call **WSAStartup** to register itself with the Windows Sockets implementation. When the program finishes using Windows Sockets services, it must call **WSACleanup**. The **WSACleanup** function deregisters the application from the Windows Sockets implementation and frees any resources associated with the application.

If the application has stream sockets that are open at the time **WSACleanup** is called, those sockets are reset. Any sockets that were closed with **closesocket** prior to **WSACleanup** being called are closed normally, including sockets that still have data pending on the transmit queue. The data is sent as it would be if **WSACleanup** had not been called.

If **WSACleanup** is successful, it returns 0. If an error occurs, **WSACleanup** returns **SOCKET_ERROR**; the specific error code can be retrieved using **WSAGetLastError**.

WSAGetLastError

The **WSAGetLastError** function retrieves the specific error code associated with the last Windows Sockets function invoked. The **WSAGetLastError** function is declared as:

```
int PASCAL FAR WSAGetLastError(void);
```

WSAGetLastError returns the specific error code for the last Windows Sockets function invoked by the thread. Note that errors are *thread-specific* and not application-specific. The error returned by **WSAGetLastError** may be set by the application by calling **WSASetLastError**.

WSAIsBlocking

The **WSAIsBlocking** function allows an application to determine whether a Windows Sockets blocking operation is in progress. The **WSAIsBlocking** function is declared as:

```
BOOL PASCAL FAR WSAIsBlocking(void);
```

The **WSAIsBlocking** function returns TRUE if a blocking call is in progress and FALSE otherwise.

The **WSAIsBlocking** function typically is used to prevent a user from starting another network operation in programs that use blocking Windows Sockets functionality. Because messages still are dispatched to the application even when a blocking call is in progress, a user could potentially select a menu item or invoke an accelerator that would start a second network task. An application can use **WSAIsBlocking** to disable menu items that invoke network tasks when it receives a **WM_INITMENUPOPUP** message.

WSASetBlockingHook

The **WSASetBlockingHook** function sets an application-defined blocking hook function. The **WSASetBlockingHook** function is declared as:

```
FARPROC PASCAL FAR WSASetBlockingHook(FARPROC lpBlockFunc);
```

The **lpBlockFunc** parameter is a pointer to the new blocking hook function. The blocking hook function can be restored as the default blocking hook function using the **WSAUnhookBlockingHook** function.

When a Windows Sockets API function blocks, Windows Sockets enters a loop similar to the following code:

```
for(;;) {
    /* flush messages for good user response */
    while(BlockingHook())
      ;
    /* check for WSACancelBlockingCall() */
    if(operation_cancelled())
      break;
    /* check to see if operation completed */
    if(operation_complete())
      break;   /* normal completion */
}
```

The loop simply calls the blocking hook repeatedly while polling for the completion of the network operation. The default blocking hook has the following form:

```
BOOL DefaultBlockingHook(void) {
    MSG msg;
```

```
BOOL ret;
/* get the next message if any */
 ret = (BOOL)PeekMessage(&msg,NULL,0,0,PM_REMOVE);
/* if we got one, process it */
if (ret) {
    TranslateMessage(&msg);
    DispatchMessage(&msg);
}
/* TRUE if we got a message */
return ret;
}
```

A replacement blocking hook should follow the same form as the default blocking hook. Additional code can be added to that shown in the default blocking hook, but none should be taken away. In particular, the Windows message dispatch functionality must be preserved. If the functionality is not preserved, all Windows messages will stop flowing through the system (under Windows 3.1) and the user will not be able to interact with the system.

The **WSASetBlockingHook** function returns a pointer to the previous blocking hook function or **NULL** if an error occurs. The specific error code can be retrieved using **WSAGetLastError**.

An application should save the function pointer returned from **WSASetBlockingHook** and restore it using **WSASetBlockingHook** when it removes its own blocking hook. This process allows nested calls to **WSASetBlockingHook** to be made at various parts of a program with correct results. In particular, library functions that call **WSASetBlockingHook** should restore the previous blocking hook function to prevent an application's custom blocking hook from being removed. If the application knows that it will not call **WSASetBlockingHook** recursively, it can simply discard the returned value and call the **WSAUnhookBlockingHook** function to restore the default blocking hook.

WSASetLastError

The **WSASetLastError** function sets the error code that is returned by **WSAGetLastError**. The **WSASetLastError** function is declared as:

```
void PASCAL FAR WSASetLastError(int iError);
```

The **iError** parameter specifies the error code to be returned by subsequent calls to **WSAGetLastError**. Any subsequent call to a Windows Sockets function other than **WSAGetLastError** overwrites the error code.

WSAStartup

The **WSAStartup** function informs Windows Sockets that the application will use network services and must be the first Windows Sockets function called by an application. The **WSAStartup** function is declared as:

```
int PASCAL FAR WSAStartup(WORD wVersionRequired, LPWSADATA lpWSAData);
```

The **wVersionRequired** (also known as **wVersionRequested**) parameter indicates the highest version of Windows Sockets with which the application is known to work. The major revision number is in the *low-order* byte while the minor revision number is in the *high-order* byte. Note that this format often is perceived as "backwards." The **lpWSAData** is a pointer to a **WSADATA** structure, which returns information about the Windows Sockets implementation to the caller of **WSAStartup**. The **WSADATA** structure is defined as:

```
typedef struct WSAData {
  WORD          wVersion;
  WORD          wHighVersion;
  char          szDescription[WSADESCRIPTION_LEN+1];
  char          szSystemStatus[WSASYS_STATUS_LEN+1];
  unsigned short iMaxSockets;
  unsigned short iMaxUdpDg;
  char FAR *    lpVendorInfo;
} WSADATA;
```

The **wVersion** and **wHighVersion** members are described in Table 5.13.

The **szDescription** field is a null-terminated string provided for the Windows Sockets supplier to describe the particular implementation. Typically, this string includes a description of the implementation along with revision numbers and any other information that might be relevant.

The **szSystemStatus** is a null-terminated string used to return information about the particular configuration of the implementation. An application can present the information in **szDescription** and **szSystemStatus** to users to assist in diagnosis when problems occur.

The **iMaxSockets** field identifies the maximum number of sockets that an application potentially can use. Note that this field may represent the number of global sockets that the Windows Sockets implementation supports across all network applications. There is no guarantee that an application can allocate that many sockets, but the number can be used by applications to test absolute limits.

Table 5.13	WSAStartup version negotiation scenarios				
Versions Supported by the Application	Versions Supported by the Winsock Implementation	wVersion Required	wVersion	wHigh Version	Negotiation Result
1.1	1.1	1.1	1.1	1.1	Version 1.1 will be used
1.0 1.1	1.0	1.1	1.0	1.0	Version 1.0 will be used
1.0	1.0 1.1	1.0	1.0	1.1	Version 1.0 will be used
1.1	1.0 1.1	1.1	1.1	1.1	Version 1.1 will be used
1.1	1.0	1.1	1.0	1.0	Version supported by the implementation is unacceptable to the application, and the application refuses to run
1.0	1.1	1.0	—	—	WSAStartup returns WSAVERNOTSUPPORTED
1.0 1.1	1.0 1.1	1.1	1.1	1.1	Version 1.1 will be used
1.1 2.0	1.1	2.0	1.1	1.1	Version 1.1 will be used
2.0	1.1	2.0	1.1	1.1	Version supported by the implementation is unacceptable to the application, and the application refuses to run

For instance, if the implementation is configured to support fewer sockets than a single application needs to function, the application can inform the user and refuse to run. Sometimes, the Windows Sockets implementation can be reconfigured to support more sockets.

The **iMaxUdpDg** field specifies the size, in bytes, of the largest UDP datagram that can be sent or received by the implementation. If the implementation imposes no limits on datagram size, **iMaxUdpDg** will be 0. The minimum value of **iMaxUdpDg** for a compliant Windows Sockets implementation is 512.

The **lpVendorInfo** field is a pointer to vendor-specific information. Some Windows Sockets implementations support advanced features that are vendor-specific. This field allows the implementation to communicate other configuration parameters to the application. The structure of the data returned is implementation-specific and outside the scope of the Winsock specification.

When a Windows Sockets application starts up, the application and the Windows Sockets implementation negotiate to use a particular version of the Winsock API. The application indicates the highest version of the Winsock API that it can use in the **wVersionRequired** parameter. When the **WSAStartup** call is invoked, the Windows Sockets implementation checks the requested Winsock API version with the lowest Winsock API version it supports. If the requested version is greater than or equal to the lowest version the implementation supports, the **WSAStartup** call succeeds. The Windows Sockets implementation then returns the highest version of the Winsock API it supports in the **wHighVersion** member of the **WSADATA** structure. The implementation also stores the lower of either its highest version or the version requested in the **wVersion** member of the **WSADATA** structure; this is the version of the Winsock API that will be used if it's acceptable to the application. The application should consult the **wVersion** member to determine whether the version is acceptable to it. Table 5.13 shows some of the various possible negotiation scenarios and their outcomes.

An application can call **WSAStartup** more than once if it needs to retrieve the **WSADATA** structure more than once—for example, when an application uses a Winsock library that also needs to call **WSAStartup**. In all cases, **WSACleanup** needs to be called the same number of times as **WSAStartup**. That is, the calls must be balanced.

If no errors occur, **WSAStartup** returns 0. If an error occurs, **WSAStartup** returns the error code directly. There is no need to call **WSAGetLastError** to retrieve the error code. In fact, an application *should not* call **WSAGetLastError** because the implementation might not have initialized correctly and might be unable to store the error code (if it were unable to allocate any memory, for instance).

WSAUnhookBlockingHook

The **WSAUnhookBlockingHook** function restores the default blocking hook. The **WSAUnhookBlockingHook** function is declared as:

```
int PASCAL FAR WSAUnhookBlockingHook(void);
```

WSAUnhookBlockingHook always restores the default blocking hook. If an application wants to restore the previous blocking hook returned by the previous call to **WSASetBlockingHook**, it should call **WSASetBlockingHook** again with the previous function pointer as a parameter.

Winsock Errors

Windows Sockets defines error codes for many error conditions. In general, Windows Sockets functions return **SOCKET_ERROR** when an error occurs. The specific error code resulting from the most recent API function call is always available from **WSAGetLastError**. The error code returned by **WSAGetLastError** is specific to the thread that issued the Windows Sockets API call and is not shared globally. Error reporting works correctly in a multithreaded environment with no need for synchronization between threads for access to the **WSAGetLastError** function.

Table 5.14 lists, in numeric order, the various Windows Sockets functions. For more information about the errors that can be generated by a specific Windows Sockets API function, see the description of the function in the Windows Sockets API specification.

Table 5.14 Windows Sockets errors		
Windows Sockets Error Code	**Value**	**Description**
WSAEINTR	10004	Returned when a blocking call is cancelled with WSACancelBlockingCall
WSAEBADF	10009	As in standard C
WSAEACCES	10013	As in standard C
WSAEFAULT	10014	As in standard C
WSAEINVAL	10022	As in standard C
WSAEMFILE	10024	As in standard C
WSAEWOULDBLOCK	10035	Returned when the socket is in non-blocking mode and the requested operation would block
WSAEINPROGRESS	10036	Returned if an illegal Winsock API function is invoked while a blocking function is in progress; note that some Winsock functions are allowed such as WSACancelBlockingCall and WSAIsBlocking
WSAEALREADY	10037	Returned if an attempt is made to cancel an asynchronous operation that has already completed
WSAENOTSOCK	10038	Indicates that the specified socket descriptor is not valid for this application
WSAEDESTADDRREQ	10039	Indicates that a destination address was required but none was supplied to the function
WSAEMSGSIZE	10040	On reception of data, indicates that a datagram was too large to fit in the supplied buffer and was truncated; on transmission, indicates that the supplied datagram was larger than the maximum datagram size supported by the Windows Sockets implementation

Table 5.14   Windows Sockets errors (continued)

Windows Sockets Error Code	Value	Description
WSAEPROTOTYPE	10041	Indicates that the specified protocol does not match the other parameters in the call
WSAENOPROTOOPT	10042	Indicates that the protocol option is unknown or invalid
WSAEPROTONOSUPPORT	10043	Indicates that the specified protocol is not supported by the Windows Sockets implementation
WSAESOCKTNOSUPPORT	10044	Indicates that the specified socket type is not supported by the specified address family
WSAEOPNOTSUPP	10045	Indicates that the socket does not support the specified operation—for instance, the listen function being invoked on a datagram socket
WSAEPFNOSUPPORT	10046	As in BSD
WSAEAFNOSUPPORT	10047	Indicates that the specified address family is not supported by the Windows Sockets implementation or cannot be used with the indicated socket
WSAEADDRINUSE	10048	Indicates that the specified address is already in use
WSAEADDRNOTAVAIL	10049	Indicates that the specified address is not available from the local machine
WSAENETDOWN	10050	Indicates a problem with the network subsystem
WSAENETUNREACH	10051	Indicates that the network cannot be reached from this host at this time
WSAENETRESET	10052	Indicates that the connection was dropped and must be reset
WSAECONNABORTED	10053	Indicates that the connection was aborted because of a timeout or other error condition
WSAECONNRESET	10054	Indicates that the connection was reset by the remote host
WSAENOBUFS	10055	Indicates that the Windows Sockets implementation is out of buffer space or the space provided in an API call by the application was too small to hold the requested information
WSAEISCONN	10056	Indicates that the specified socket is already connected
WSAENOTCONN	10057	Indicates that the specified socket is not connected
WSAESHUTDOWN	10058	Indicates that the socket has had the requested functionality shut down
WSAETOOMANYREFS	10059	As in BSD
WSAETIMEDOUT	10060	Indicates that a connection attempt timed out before the connection could be established
WSAECONNREFUSED	10061	Indicates that a connection attempt was forcefully rejected
WSAELOOP	10062	As in BSD
WSAENAMETOOLONG	10063	As in BSD

Table 5.14 Windows Sockets errors (continued)

Windows Sockets Error Code	Value	Description
WSAEHOSTDOWN	10064	As in BSD
WSAEHOSTUNREACH	10065	As in BS
WSASYSNOTREADY	10091	Returned by WSAStartup to indicate that the network subsystem is not yet ready for communication
WSAVERNOTSUPPORTED	10092	Returned by WSAStartup to indicate that the Windows Sockets DLL does not support the requested Winsock protocol version
WSANOTINITIALISED	10093	Returned by all Winsock API functions prior to a successful WSAStartup being performed
WSAHOST_NOT_FOUND	11001	Indicates that the requested database information does not exist, as confirmed by an authoritative host
WSATRY_AGAIN	11002	Indicates that the requested information was not found but the answer was not authoritative
WSANO_RECOVERY	11003	Indicates that a non-recoverable error occurred
WSANO_DATA	11004	Indicates that the name supplied was valid but no information of the requested type is in the database

C++ Winsock Classes

The asynchronous extensions to Windows Sockets provide superior performance in the Windows environment. Use C++ to gain these performance benefits and reduce the associated complexity.

The previous two chapters introduced the concept of sockets and the Windows Sockets API that is used to program them. In this chapter, we'll examine the major models of Windows Sockets programming and learn about the asynchronous Windows Sockets API. We'll compare the asynchronous API to the synchronous API in the Windows environment and discover why we should use the asynchronous API. Finally, we'll learn to manage the added complexity of the asynchronous API using a set of reusable C++ classes.

Synchronous Winsock

As discussed in Chapter 4, the Windows Sockets synchronous API is modeled after the traditional Berkeley Sockets API. The compatibility between the two APIs is very helpful when an older body of Unix code needs to be ported to the Windows environment.

In general, the Windows Sockets synchronous API tends to favor procedural programming using blocking sockets. Programs tend to read from and write to sockets in a blocking manner, relying on the operating system to allow the system to progress when there is no data to read or the socket has accepted its capacity of data to send and is waiting to empty the queue. The synchronous API works wonderfully in a command-line oriented, pre-emptive multitasking environment like Unix. It's not as well suited to Windows.

To resolve the issues of blocking calls in the Windows event-driven, cooperative multitasking environment, the Winsock API fakes blocking calls using a blocking hook that contains an event dispatch loop. Unfortunately, the simulated blocking used by Windows Sockets has some limitations. In particular, only one blocking call is allowed to be active at a time. This limitation has some striking ramifications for the user interface design of the program.

Although a blocked program takes a temporary detour while waiting for a network event to occur, as far as Windows is concerned, it is not really blocked. Rather, it's sitting in a polling loop that also dispatches Windows messages, as shown here:

```
for(;;) {
    /* flush messages for good user response */
    while(BlockingHook())
        ;
    /* check for WSACancelBlockingCall() */
    if(operation_cancelled())
        break;
    /* check to see if operation completed */
    if(operation_complete())
        break;      /* normal completion */
}

BOOL DefaultBlockingHook(void) {
    MSG msg;
    BOOL ret;
    /* get the next message if any */
      ret = (BOOL)PeekMessage(&msg,NULL,0,0,PM_REMOVE);
    /* if we got one, process it */
    if (ret) {
            TranslateMessage(&msg);
            DispatchMessage(&msg);
    }
    /* TRUE if we got a message */
    return ret;
}
```

If a window message destined for the "blocked" program is put into the Windows message queue, it is dispatched to a window procedure in the program. The user interface belonging to the program is still active. A user can pick menu choices and type keystrokes that will be sent to the program. Problems can result if the user invokes a menu choice that will start another network activity. Because the program is already sitting in a blocking network function, no other network functions can be invoked, and an error results when the second network operation is attempted.

To prevent this occurrence, a Windows program using the synchronous blocking API must ensure that a second network operation cannot be started while the first operation sits in the blocking loop. The program either will have to disable all the menu items and keystrokes that could lead to the start of another network operation, a complex process if there are many routes, or disable the user interface entirely by capturing the mouse and keyboard and putting up the hour-glass cursor.

Of the choices, the first is preferable from the user's point of view. The user will be unable to start a second network operation, but at least the rest of the system is still usable. The user can switch to another running program and continue to work while the first program waits for the network operation to complete. This operation can be complex for the programmer to accomplish, however.

In the second scenario, the user is stuck staring at the hour-glass cursor waiting for the network operation to complete before more useful work can be accomplished. The Windows multitasking environment has effectively become a single-tasking environment, as far as networking is concerned.

In both cases, it's impossible for two networking operations to progress at the same time within the same application. The user would not be able to simultaneously send an email message and check the server to see if email has arrived.

The problem of the synchronous Windows Sockets API can be overcome by two methods; both methods use non-blocking sockets. In the first method, all sockets are made non-blocking, and the **select** function polls the status of the sockets of interest. Sockets are then read or written as data becomes available or is able to be queued for transmission. To avoid the problem of blocking calls reoccurring, however, the **select** function must be invoked with a **timeout** value of 0, leading to non-blocking operation. To keep polling, and at the same time allow window messages to flow through the system, code similar to a blocking hook would have to be used, as follows:

```
struct timeval timeout = {0, 0};
while (!select(..., &timeout)) {
    if (PeekMessage(...)) {
        TranslateMessage(...);
        DispatchMessage(...);
    }
}
```

Although this code works, it's still a poor solution. CPU cycles are burned while effectively doing nothing but repeatedly calling the **select** function. This technique is a poor use of resources and doesn't fit well with the Windows event-driven model.

A much better solution to the whole problem is to use non-blocking sockets with the Windows Sockets asynchronous API extensions.

Asynchronous Winsock: The Good, The Bad, and The Ugly

Using the Windows Sockets asynchronous API extensions is the best way to program sockets under Windows. They allow a program to support multiple concurrent network tasks without taking CPU time to perform polling. Using the asynchronous extensions, a user can both send email and check for the presence of incoming messages on a remote server, in the same application program, at the same time.

The asynchronous Winsock extensions operate by sending window messages to a window whenever the status of a socket changes or when an asynchronous database function completes its lookup. Socket state changes are indicated to an application using the **WSAAsyncSelect** function. Asynchronous database lookup is performed using the **WSAAsyncGetXByY** functions. Each of the standard database functions has a similarly named asynchronous counterpart.

WSAAsyncSelect

Figure 6.1 shows the sequence of events involved in using **WSAAsyncSelect** to determine the status of a socket.

The sequence of events is as follows:

1. First, the application creates the socket of interest. The socket is bound to a local address, then **WSAAsyncSelect** is invoked on the socket to specify asynchronous events in which the program is interested. In this example, the call to **WSAAsyncSelect** specifies that the program is interested in connection events. The call to **WSAAsyncSelect** specifies which window will receive notices of socket state changes and the window message to send to the window when the state changes occur. The **WSAAsyncSelect** function makes the socket non-blocking, just as if the **ioctlsocket** function were invoked on the socket with the **FIONBIO** command.

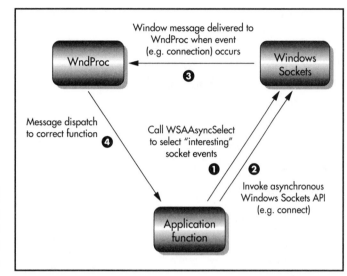

Figure 6.1

Sequence of events using WSAAsyncSelect to determine socket status.

2. An asynchronous socket function is invoked on the socket. Figure 6.1 shows the **connect** function being invoked. Since the socket is non-blocking, the **connect** function returns immediately, before the connection to the remote node has been established. The program can continue to do other tasks. No blocking hook is used, so the program may invoke other Winsock API functions at any time.

3. At some later time, Winsock completes the connection to the remote host. Winsock sends a message to the window specified in the original call to **WSAAsyncSelect** for the socket. Parameters of the message indicate the socket whose status is being reported, the status change, and a result code associated with the status change.

4. The window procedure processes the message and dispatches it to a routine within the program that handles it. If the connection is completed with no errors, the program then sends or receives data using the socket. If an error occurs, the program can inform the user with a dialog box or other means.

WSAAsyncGetXByY

Figure 6.2 shows the sequence of events for asynchronous database functions.

The sequence of events is as follows:

1. The application invokes an asynchronous database function (**WSAAsyncGetXByY**). The call to the asynchronous function specifies a win-

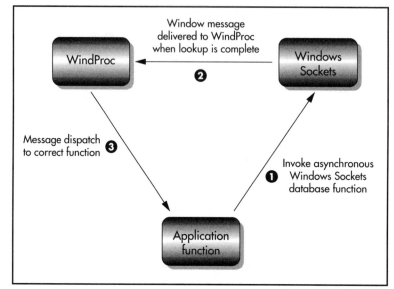

Figure 6.2

Sequence of events for asynchronous database functions.

dow to receive a window message when the database lookup is complete and an application-defined message to send to the window. The database lookup is started and the function returns. The function return value is an "asynchronous task handle," which identifies the asynchronous task when it later completes. The application continues to run while the database lookup progresses. Because the application does not use a blocking hook, there are no restrictions on invoking other Winsock functions. The application may continue to work on other network tasks while Winsock performs the database lookup.

2. When the lookup is complete, Winsock sends the window message specified in the asynchronous database call to the window also specified in the call. Parameters of the window message specify the asynchronous task handle, originally returned as the result of the asynchronous database call and a result code.

3. The window procedure dispatches the message to a function within the program that further processes it. If no errors occur, the program can make use of the database information.

Window Message Processing

The asynchronous Winsock extensions work quite well. They integrate the network programming API into the same event-driven structure as the rest of the Windows API.

In spite of the benefits, however, the asynchronous Winsock programming model has some problems. To process the window messages that occur when a socket's status changes or when a database lookup is complete, a programmer typically uses one of two techniques: Direct the window messages to the main application window or create separate windows to handle each socket or database lookup.

Centralizing the message processing by using the main application window is conceptually easy, but adds considerable complexity in practice. If more than one socket will be used in the application at once or more than one database lookup will be in progress, a list of socket descriptors and asynchronous task handles must be kept. The main window procedure will look up information associated with the socket descriptor or task handle in the list and dispatch the state change or completion message to an appropriate routine based on the information, as shown in Figure 6.3. This approach forces the network processing to be integrated into the core of the application, which makes it very difficult to create a library of routines to perform common network functions (for instance, implementing the mail protocols). Each time the routines are used, additional code must be added to the main window procedure of the application for them to operate correctly.

Figure 6.3

Centralized message processing.

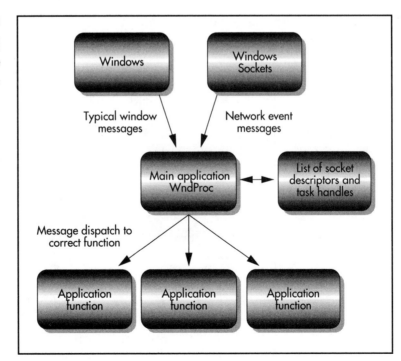

In the second message processing method, the program creates a hidden window to receive the window messages. The window uses a separate window procedure from the main application window procedure to keep the network window messages out of the main application message processing. This approach simplifies the main application and allows network code to be reused more easily. An unfortunate side effect is the use of precious space in Windows' USER heap for each window created. This scheme is shown in Figure 6.4.

Better Window Message Processing

A third method for Winsock event message processing typically works better than either of the two previously described. The application creates a single hidden window at startup. The window is a central resource to which all Winsock events are directed. The window procedure for the window only processes Winsock event messages. When a piece of code expects to receive a Winsock event message, it adds the socket descriptor or asynchronous task handle to a list that the window procedure for the hidden window can use to dispatch the window message to the proper function.

This technique keeps the window message processing out of the main application, which makes reusable network code easy to write and integrate into a set of

Figure 6.4

Using hidden windows with a specialized Winsock message processing window procedure.

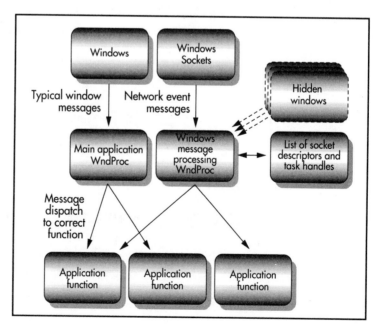

libraries or DLLs. This technique also reduces the number of windows that have to be created to handle Winsock messages to a single window, which consequently reduces the amount of memory devoted to keeping track of the window.

Programming Winsock with C++

Many Internet protocols, such as SMTP and NNTP, are easily implemented as state machines (as we'll see in the following chapters). Using object-oriented programming (OOP) and C++, these state machines can be implemented as objects. This protocol implementation method integrates well with the Winsock asynchronous programming model. Instead of dispatching Winsock asynchronous messages to a function within the program, the message is dispatched to an object that has registered for that message. The protocol object treats the message as an input to the state machine and drives the protocol forward.

Other C++ objects can also be designed to assist with Windows Sockets programming. As we'll see in the following section, using objects that represent sockets and Internet addresses can help us program more efficiently.

Object-based Message Dispatch

Using C++, we can easily develop a generic message dispatch system that implements the "better" message dispatch system described previously. The system is extensible to allow any object to receive Winsock messages. Figure 6.5 shows how the message dispatch system is implemented.

As Figure 6.5 shows, the system uses a single hidden window to be the destination of Windows Sockets messages. This approach keeps Windows Sockets messages out of the main application window procedure. The amount of memory required for the system is also reduced by using a single hidden window. The window procedure for the hidden window receives messages from Winsock and dispatches them to individual objects, using a callback mechanism. The objects wanting to receive Winsock messages register with a container object, **sg_clWparamList**, that stores pairs of socket descriptors or asynchronous task handles and the address of the object to receive a callback. The message dispatch system works as follows:

1. Whenever a task needs to be performed, an object implementing that task is created by the application or another object. Examples of task objects include socket objects or host database lookup objects.

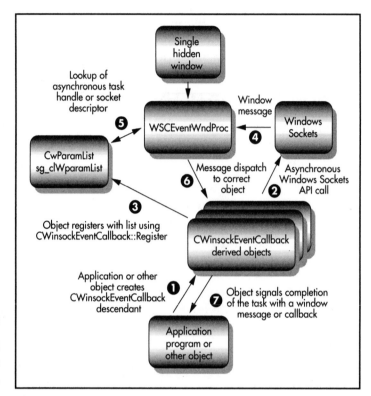

Figure 6.5

The Winsock classes
event dispatch
mechanism.

Each object that needs to receive Windows Sockets events is derived from the abstract class **CWinsockEventCallback**. The **CWinsockEventCallback** class provides two functions to register and deregister a derived object with the **sg_clWparamList** object, a function to determine the window handle of the hidden window, and a callback function that the hidden window procedure invokes when it dispatches a message to the object. The callback function is undefined in the **CWinsockEventCallback** class and declared to be **virtual**. Objects wanting to receive Windows Sockets events simply inherit the interface defined by the callback function, and provide the callback function to process the message once it's delivered by the dispatch system.

2. After the object is created, it calls a Winsock function to start an asynchronous operation. In the parameters of the call, the object specifies the window handle of the hidden window and a custom window message. If the call is a **WSAAsyncGetXByY** database lookup, the call returns an asynchronous task handle. If the call is **WSAAsyncSelect**, the object has already called Winsock to create a socket descriptor.

3. The object registers the socket descriptor or asynchronous task handle returned from the Winsock function with the **sg_clWparamList** object, providing a pointer to itself in the process. At this point, the asynchronous call is progressing and the setup is complete. The object now simply waits for the callback to be invoked.

4. When the asynchronous operation completes, Winsock sends the custom window message to the hidden window, as specified in the original parameters of the asynchronous Winsock function.

5. The window procedure for the hidden window, **WSCEventWndProc** ("WSC" stands for "Windows Sockets Classes"), receives the window message. It retrieves the address of the object, to which it will dispatch the message from the **sg_clWparamList** object using the socket descriptor or asynchronous task handle specified in the window message.

6. The window procedure invokes the callback function of the **CWinsockEventCallback**-derived object.

7. The callback function for the object processes the message. If the event was generated at the completion of an asynchronous database lookup, the object typically deregisters itself with the **sg_clWparamList** object. If the event pertained to a socket, the object might generate more Winsock asynchronous calls with resulting callbacks. At some point, the object will complete its work and deregister itself with the **sg_clWparamList** object. Finally, it signals that the overall operation is complete, using either a window message or callback function to the main program or the master object.

The **CWinsockEventCallback** class, the **CwParamList** class, and the **WSCEventWndProc** function are shown in Listings 6.1 and 6.2.

Starting Up and Shutting Down

A Windows Sockets program must explicitly call **WSAStartup** and **WSACleanup** to initialize and shut down Windows Sockets. Further, each time **WSAStartup** is called, the returned version numbers must be checked to ensure that the version of Windows Sockets implemented by the WINSOCK.DLL module is acceptable to the program. In most cases, this task is rote work for the program.

To automate these tasks, we'll use a class named **CWinsock**. The constructor for **CWinsock** calls **WSAStartup** automatically. The requested version of Winsock and the minimum acceptable version are specified as parameters to the constructor. The constructor automatically checks to ensure the WINSOCK.DLL module is acceptable. **CWinsock**'s destructor automatically calls **WSACleanup**.

Initializing Winsock is now simple: Define an object of type **CWinsock** as a program global, then check to see if it initialized correctly in **WinMain**, as shown here:

```
CWinsock g_wsWinsock(0x0101, 0x0101);

INT WINAPI WinMain(HINSTANCE hInstance, HINSTANCE hPrevInstance,
    LPSTR lpszCmdParam, INT nCmdShow)
{
    ...

    if (g_wsWinsock.LastError() != WSANOERROR) {
        ReportWSAError("Error: Can't startup Winsock.",
            g_wsWinsock.LastError(), NULL, hInstance);
        return FALSE;
    }

    ...
}
```

C++ ensures that the **CWinsock** destructor is called automatically when the program exits, even if an error occurs. This call eliminates complicated processing in the face of non-recoverable errors.

The **CWinsock** class is defined in Listings 6.1 and 6.2.

Internet Addresses

Internet addresses frequently are used in sockets programming. In fact, writing code to manipulate a **sockaddr** or **sockaddr_in** structure can quickly turn into a part-time programming job. Because the addresses and port number fields of a **sockaddr_in** structure are stored in network—rather than host—byte order within the structures, it's easy to create bugs. A lot of the drudgery associated with these address structures can be eliminated by creating a C++ class to hold Internet addresses.

The **CSockAddr** class, as defined in Listings 6.3 and 6.4, is exactly what we need. This program wraps a class around a **sockaddr_in** structure and provides access functions to manipulate the address and port number fields of the structure. The program always uses host byte order for these quantities; the conversions to network byte order and back again take place automatically.

Dealing With Databases

Almost every Winsock program accesses one or more of the network databases during its execution. Typically, the program looks up the IP address of a remote host, using the host name entered by a user. To avoid retyping all the code necessary to perform a database lookup, we can create an object to do it for us. The **CHost** and **CService** classes that are shown in Listings 6.5, 6.6, 6.7, and 6.8 perform host and service database lookups.

Although the different databases are accessed using several different functions of the form **WSAAsyncGetXByY**, most of the setup code is common among the databases. The **CAsyncDB** class (Listings 6.9 and 6.10) is an ancestor of the **CHost** and **CService** classes and provides much of this common code. The **CAsyncDB** class provides a pure virtual function named **StartWinsockLookup**, which is overridden in each of the descendants. The **StartWinsockLookup** function is called by the **CAsyncDB** class to invoke the appropriate Winsock database routine.

The **CAsyncDB** class is descended from **CWinsockEventCallback**. When the asynchronous lookup is complete, the message dispatch system shown back in Figure 6.5 sends the completion message to the correct **CAsyncDB**-derived object.

Figure 6.6 shows the inheritance diagram for these classes. A **CProtocol** class was not defined because typically it is not used. It would be very easy to create such a class using **CAsyncDB** as an ancestor, however.

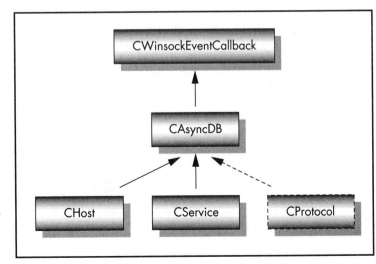

Figure 6.6

Database object inheritance diagram.

To access the information returned as the result of the database lookup, each individual class provides appropriate access functions. **CHost** provides access functions appropriate to accessing a **hostent** structure. **CService** provides access functions appropriate to accessing a **servent** structure.

We'll learn more about how these classes are used in later chapters.

Streaming Sockets

Sockets clearly are a center point of Windows Sockets programming. Without sockets, no information gets sent between nodes, which makes network programming considerably less interesting. Using C++, a socket class can be built to help with socket programming. The **CStreamSocket** class in Listings 6.11 and 6.12 implements just such a class.

The **CStreamSocket** class provides services to assist in the programming of stream sockets used exclusively for the Internet protocols described in this book. The **CStreamSocket** class cannot be used for datagram sockets. Ideally, in a generalized Winsock class library, a set of related classes would be provided, as shown in Figure 6.7. A general **CSocket** class would be an ancestor to more specialized **CStreamSocket** and **CDatagramSocket** classes. In our case, because the **CStreamSocket** class is all we need to implement the protocols described in this book, it's the only class provided.

The **CStreamSocket** class has a socket descriptor as a private variable and provides a set of functions that mimic the standard Windows Sockets socket functions to manipulate the socket. A **CStreamSocket** can connect to a remote node or can be used to accept connections. The **CStreamSocket** class is descended from **CWinsockEventCallback**. The class receives status change notifications for the socket and passes them on to other objects descended from the **CStreamCallback** class.

Figure 6.7

Ideal CSocket inheritance diagram.

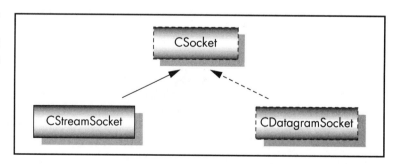

The abstract **CStreamCallback** class is used to receive callbacks from a **CStreamSocket** object. Typically, a master object creates a **CStreamSocket** class in order to implement a protocol. The master object would inherit the **CStreamCallback** interface and would receive notifications of socket state changes through the **StreamCallback** member function of the **CStreamCallback** interface.

Programming non-blocking stream sockets can be quite complex. The need to handle situations in which the **send** function is invoked to transmit data and returns **WSAEWOULDBLOCK** can complicate a program's logic. Ideally, no call to **send** should block or return **WSAEWOULDBLOCK**. The **send** function blocks or returns **WSAEWOULDBLOCK** because the outgoing data buffers internal to the Windows Sockets implementation fill while waiting for the remote host to acknowledge the receipt of transmitted data. At some point, the buffers are full and the Windows sockets implementation won't accept any more data.

The **CStreamSocket** class compensates for this behavior by checking the value returned by the **send** function for the **WSAEWOULDBLOCK** error. If this error occurs, the **CStreamSocket** class simply adds the data buffer passed to its **Send** function to a queue. As the remote host acknowledges transmitted data and the buffers in the Windows Sockets implementation empty, an **FD_WRITE** event is sent to the **CStreamSocket** class. The class then de-queues the first buffer on its local queue and sends whatever data it can. It continues sending data from the queued buffers until the queue is empty or the **send** function returns **WSAEWOULDBLOCK**. The **CStreamSocket** class invokes the **StreamCallback** function of the parent object for each queued buffer when it is finally written to the socket. This step allows the parent object to reuse buffers after the data in them is finally transmitted and the buffers are freed.

The **CStreamSocket** destructor automatically invokes the **closesocket** function to deallocate the resources associated with a socket object that has been destroyed. This ensures that a "socket descriptor leak," a close cousin of the familiar memory leak, will not occur easily because a program forgets to call **closesocket** when it is done with a socket.

We'll learn more about how to use a **CStreamSocket** object in later chapters.

Miscellaneous Functions

The CWINSOCK.H and CWINSOCK.CPP files, Listings 6.1 and 6.2, provide a few more functions that are helpful in Winsock programming. In particular, the

ReportWSAError and **WSCFatalError** functions can be used to help deal with errors that occur in Windows Sockets programming.

The **ReportWSAError** function displays an error message describing a Windows Sockets result code in a message box. The function takes an error message string and the Winsock error code as inputs. Using the error code, the function retrieves a string describing the Winsock error from the program's string resource table and integrates it with the string passed to it as a parameter. The supplied string allows the program to give the error message some context, and the Winsock error message description tells the user exactly what went wrong. Figure 6.8 shows an example of the resulting message box.

The **WSCFatalError** terminates the program as the result of a fatal error. The function simply displays a message box with a supplied error message, then terminates the program using the system **exit** function.

Summary

In this chapter, we've developed a system for dispatching asynchronous Winsock messages to objects that wish to receive them using C++. Client objects that wish to receive the messages are descended from the **CWinsockEventCallback** class. The dispatch system uses a single hidden window and a separate window procedure. This procedure keeps the memory requirements for the system very low and does not force the main application window procedure to process the messages.

The **CWinsock** class is used to start up and shut down Winsock. If given the appropriate version numbers, the class automatically checks to see that the WINSOCK.DLL version is usable by the application. Using the **CWinsock** class is as simple as creating a global object of the **CWinsock** class and checking to ensure that Winsock started correctly.

Database lookup is a common Winsock programming task. The **CHost** and **CService** classes provide this functionality. Both **CHost** and **CService** are de-

Figure 6.8

An example of the message box produced by ReportWSAError.

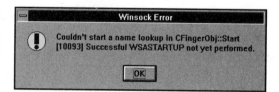

scended from the **CAsyncDB** class, which provides the common code for asynchronous database lookup of all types. Although a **CProtocol** class is not described here, it is a simple exercise to create one using **CAsyncDB** as an ancestor, if needed.

Finally, we examined a **CStreamSocket** class designed to provide enhanced socket programming features. **CStreamSocket** allows a program to easily use asynchronous Winsock services on stream socket connections. The **CStreamSocket** class notifies other objects of changes in the socket state, using callbacks to objects descended from **CStreamCallback**.

CStreamSocket provides buffering services for calls to **send**. If a call to **send** returns **WSAEWOULDBLOCK**, the **CStreamSocket** class buffers the remaining user data. The data is sent at a later time when Winsock indicates that it has free buffer space available. A callback is generated when all the data in a buffer has been sent, informing the application that the data may be reused.

In the next chapter, we'll examine an application that uses the classes described in this chapter—a Finger protocol client.

Listing 6.1 CWINSOCK.H

```
/*
    File: CWINSOCK.H
    Description:
        Header file for CWINSOCK.CPP.

        A few classes and miscellaneous functions for dealing with
        Winsock in a more friendly manner.  Note that classes
        encapsulating sockets and addresses can be found in separate
        files.
    Copyright 1995, David G. Roberts
*/

#ifndef _CWINSOCK_H
#define _CWINSOCK_H

#include <windows.h>
#include "winsock.h"

/* CONSTANTS */
#define WPARAM_TYPE_HANDLE      0
#define WPARAM_TYPE_SOCKET      1

// I can't believe that Winsock doesn't define this on its own.
#define WSANOERROR  0
```

```
// Private window messages.  Note that we don't have to keep these
// unique, even within the application, since they'll just be sent to
// our own window proc.
#define WM_WSAGETHOSTBYADDR      (WM_USER + 0)
#define WM_WSAGETHOSTBYNAME      (WM_USER + 1)
#define WM_WSAGETPROTOBYNAME     (WM_USER + 2)
#define WM_WSAGETPROTOBYNUMBER   (WM_USER + 3)
#define WM_WSAGETSERVBYNAME      (WM_USER + 4)
#define WM_WSAGETSERVBYPORT      (WM_USER + 5)
#define WM_WSAASYNCSELECT        (WM_USER + 6)


/* MACROS */
// A quick macro to denote an unused argument parameter.  This simply
// references the parameter in its own expression, which the optimizer
// will eliminate.
#define UNUSED_PARAMETER(x) x


/* MISC FUNCTIONS */
BOOL WSCCreateEventWindow(HINSTANCE hInstance,
     HINSTANCE hPrevInstance);
HWND WSCGetEventWindow(void);
void ReportWSAError(LPCSTR lpszMsg, int iError, HWND hwnd,
     HINSTANCE hInstance);
void WSCFatalError(LPCSTR lpszMsg);

/*
    Class: CWinsock
    Description:
        This class is used to initialize Winsock in an application
        and retrieve information about the particular Winsock
        implementation running under it.  A single instance of this
        class should be created as a global or as a local in WinMain.
        The constructor of this class calls WSAStartup and the
        destructor calls WSACleanup.  This ensures that the calls
        are balanced without the programmer having to remember to call
        WSACleanup at program exit.
*/
class CWinsock {
private:
    WSADATA m_wsaData;            // Holds results of WSAStartup call
    int     m_iLastError;         // Last error from Winsock call
    BOOL    m_bNeedCleanup;       // Indicates WSAStartup was successful
                                  //   and the destructor should call
                                  //   WSACleanup
public:
    CWinsock(WORD wVersionRequested, WORD wMinVersion);
    ~CWinsock();
    int LastError(void) { return m_iLastError; };
    LPWSADATA GetWSAData(void) { return (LPWSADATA)&m_wsaData; };
};

/*
    Class: CWinsockEventCallback
```

```
        Description:
            This class is used to receive a callback whenever a Winsock
            window message is received by the Winsock event window.
            Objects needing to get a callback should inherit this
            class and override the WinsockEventCallback member function.
*/
class CWinsockEventCallback {
protected:
        void Register(WPARAM wParam, int iType);
        void Deregister(WPARAM wParam, int iType);
        HWND GetEventWindow(void) { return WSCGetEventWindow(); };
public:
        // Override this with the desired functionality.
        virtual void WinsockEventCallback(HWND hwnd, UINT msg,
            WPARAM wParam, LPARAM lParam) = 0;
};


#endif // #ifndef _CWINSOCK_H
```

Listing 6.2   CWINSOCK.CPP

```
/*
        File: CWINSOCK.CPP
        Description:
            A few classes and miscellaneous functions for dealing with
            Winsock in a more friendly manner.  Note that classes
            encapsulating sockets and addresses can be found in separate
            files.
        Copyright 1995, David G. Roberts
*/


#include <stdlib.h>
#include "cwinsock.h"
#include "myassert.h"


/* MODULE PRIVATE TYPES */


/*
        Class: CwParamList
        Description:
            A small class used to keep a linked list of pointers to
            CWinsockEventCallback objects, keyed with a WPARAM for lookup.
            CwParamList objects are used to keep lists of outstanding
            Winsock asynchronous callbacks so the private Winsock window
            can dispatch them to the appropriate objects.  Since both
            sockets and Winsock asynchronous handles don't have to be
            unique between each other, a second type value is used to
            distinguish between the two for lookup purposes.

            Note: This class could easily be implemented with a number of
            off-the-shelf container class libraries, but it was
            implemented here for cross-compiler compatibility.
```

```
*/
class CwParamList {
private:
    struct SListNode {
        SListNode *                 lplnNext;
        SListNode *                 lplnPrev;
        WPARAM                      wParam;
        int                         iType;
          CWinsockEventCallback * lpecbCallback;
    };
    SListNode    m_lnHead;
    SListNode    m_lnTail;
     SListNode * FindNode(WPARAM wParam, int iType);
public:
    BOOL  Add(WPARAM wParam, int iType,
        CWinsockEventCallback * lpecbCallback);
    BOOL  Remove(WPARAM wParam, int iType);
    BOOL  Find(WPARAM wParam, int iType,
        CWinsockEventCallback * & lpecbCallback);
    CwParamList();
    ~CwParamList();
};


/* MODULE VARIABLES */
static BOOL       sg_bWinsockStarted = FALSE;
static HWND       sg_hwndWSCEventWindow = NULL;
static char       sg_szWSCWindowClass[] = "WSAEventWindow";
CwParamList       sg_clWparamList;


/* MODULE PRIVATE DECLARATIONS */
static LRESULT CALLBACK WSCEventWndProc(HWND hwnd, UINT msg,
    WPARAM wParam, LPARAM lParam);


/**********************************************************************
     PUBLIC CLASS MEMBER FUNCTIONS
**********************************************************************/

/*

     Function: CWinsock::CWinsock
     Description:
         Constructor for the CWinsock class.  Initializes Winsock by
         calling WSAStartup and checking to make sure the Winsock DLL
         version is compatible with the application.
     Inputs:
         wVersionRequested — The maximum Winsock version the app
             supports.
         wMinVersion — The minimum Winsock version the app supports.
     Outputs:
         No direct outputs.
         The result of this function can be retrieved by calling
         CWinsock::LastError.
*/
CWinsock::CWinsock(WORD wVersionRequested, WORD wMinVersion)
```

```
{
    // Make sure we haven't started Winsock already.
    ASSERT(sg_bWinsockStarted == FALSE);

    // Start up Winsock.
    m_iLastError = WSAStartup(wVersionRequested,
        (LPWSADATA)&m_wsaData);

    // If we got an error, get out of here and indicate that we don't
    // need any cleanup in the destructor.
    if (m_iLastError != WSANOERROR) {
        // Indicate that we don't need to be cleaned up
        m_bNeedCleanup = FALSE;
        return;
    }

    // Indicate that we're up and running.
    sg_bWinsockStarted  = TRUE;
    m_bNeedCleanup      = TRUE;

    // See if the DLL and the app each support a common version.
    // Check to make sure that the version the DLL returns in wVersion
    // is at least enough to satisfy the applications needs.
    if (HIBYTE(m_wsaData.wVersion) < HIBYTE(wMinVersion) ||
        (HIBYTE(m_wsaData.wVersion) == HIBYTE(wMinVersion) &&
        LOBYTE(m_wsaData.wVersion) < LOBYTE(wMinVersion)) ) {
        // The DLL version is incompatible, so fake a
        // WSAVERNOTSUPPORTED error.
        m_iLastError = WSAVERNOTSUPPORTED;
    }
}


/*
    Function: CWinsock::~CWinsock
    Description:
        Destructor for CWinsock class.  The function calls WSACleanup
        to terminate use of a Winsock DLL.  If WSACleanup returns an
        error condition, the function reports it to the user using
        MessageBox.  Note that the application can't report
        the error itself since it's occuring in the destructor and
        there is no way to pass it to the app.  Further, if the
        CWinsock class instance is a global variable, then the
        destructor will be called as the app exits, so there is no
        chance for the app to handle the error.
    Inputs:
        None.
    Outputs:
        None.
*/
CWinsock::~CWinsock()
{
    char szErrorMsg[80];
```

```
        // If WSAStartup wasn't successful (because the required DLL
        // version wasn't compatible), then don't call WSACleanup.
        if (!m_bNeedCleanup)
            return;
        // Clean up Winsock and report any error that might occur.
        if (WSACleanup() == SOCKET_ERROR) {
            m_iLastError = WSAGetLastError();
            wsprintf(szErrorMsg,
                "Winsock reported error [%d] when shutting down.",
                m_iLastError);
            MessageBox(NULL, szErrorMsg, "Winsock Error",
                MB_OK | MB_ICONEXCLAMATION);
        }

        // Indicate that we're shut down.
        sg_bWinsockStarted = FALSE;
}

/*

    Function: CWinsockEventCallback::Register
    Description:
        Registers a CWinsockEventCallback object with the
        WSCEventWndProc.  This allows the WndProc to callback the
        object when a window message is received.
    Inputs:
        wParam - wParam value to register a callback for.
        iType - Equals WPARAM_TYPE_HANDLE if wParam is a Winsock task
            handle, or WPARAM_TYPE_SOCKET if wParam is a socket
            number.
    Outputs:
        None.
*/
void CWinsockEventCallback::Register(WPARAM wParam, int iType)
{
    if (!sg_clWparamList.Add(wParam, iType, this)) {
        // Some sort of error happened.
        WSCFatalError("Can't register CWinsockEventCallback object.");
    }
}

/*

    Function: CWinsockEventCallback::Deregister
    Description:
        Deregisters a CWinsockEventCallback object that had previously
        been registered with CWinsockEventCallback::Register.
    Inputs:
        wParam - wParam value to register a callback for.
        iType - Equals WPARAM_TYPE_HANDLE if wParam is a Winsock task
            handle, or WPARAM_TYPE_SOCKET if wParam is a socket
            number.
    Outputs:
        None.
```

```
*/
void CWinsockEventCallback::Deregister(WPARAM wParam, int iType)
{
      if (!sg_clWparamList.Remove(wParam, iType)) {
          // Some sort of error happened.
          WSCFatalError(
                "Can't deregister CWinsockEventCallback object.");
      }
}


/**********************************************************************
      PRIVATE CLASS MEMBER FUNCTIONS
**********************************************************************/


/*
      Function: CwParamList::CwParamList
      Description:
          Constructor of the CwParamList class.   Initializes internal
          list structure.
      Inputs:
          None.
      Outputs:
          None.
*/
CwParamList::CwParamList()
{
      m_lnHead.lplnNext = &m_lnTail;
      m_lnHead.lplnPrev = NULL;
      m_lnTail.lplnNext = NULL;
      m_lnTail.lplnPrev = &m_lnHead;
}


/*
      Function: CwParamList::~CwParamList
      Description:
          Destructor for the CwParamList class.  Takes care of deleting
          any orphan nodes remaining on in the list.
*/
CwParamList::~CwParamList()
{
      SListNode * lplnNext;
      SListNode * lplnCurrent;

      // Delete all orphaned nodes in list.
      lplnNext = m_lnHead.lplnNext;
      while (lplnNext != &m_lnTail) {
          lplnCurrent = lplnNext;
          lplnNext    = lplnCurrent->lplnNext;
          delete lplnCurrent;
      };
}
```

```
/*
      Function: CwParamList::Add
      Description:
          Adds a node to a CwParamList.
      Inputs:
          wParam — Key for the list management routines.  Typically
              either a Winsock asyncronous task handle or a socket
              descriptor.
          iType — Equals WPARAM_TYPE_HANDLE if wParam is a Winsock task
              handle, or WPARAM_TYPE_SOCKET if wParam is a socket
              number.
          lpecbCallback — A pointer to a CWinsockEventCallback that is
              stored in the list node and accessed according to the key.
      Outputs:
          The function returns TRUE if the information can be added to
          the list.  If there is no memory to allocate a new list node
          or a node with the same wParam key is already in the list,
          the function returns FALSE.
*/
BOOL CwParamList::Add(WPARAM wParam, int iType,
    CWinsockEventCallback * lpecbCallback)
{
    // Check some stuff
    ASSERT(lpecbCallback != NULL);

    // See if a node with that wParam/iType key already exists.
    SListNode * lplnNewNode = FindNode(wParam, iType);
    // If so, we have an error condition.
    if (lplnNewNode != NULL)
        return FALSE;

    // Create a new node and link it to the front of the list.
    lplnNewNode = new SListNode;
    if (lplnNewNode == NULL)
        return FALSE;
    // Fill in info.
    lplnNewNode->wParam             = wParam;
    lplnNewNode->iType              = iType;
    lplnNewNode->lpecbCallback    = lpecbCallback;
    // Set links in new node.
    lplnNewNode->lplnNext           = m_lnHead.lplnNext;
    lplnNewNode->lplnPrev           = &m_lnHead;
    // Set previous pointer in following node.
    m_lnHead.lplnNext->lplnPrev  = lplnNewNode;
    // Set next pointer in head node.
    m_lnHead.lplnNext               = lplnNewNode;

    return TRUE;
}


/*
      Function: CwParamList::Remove
      Description:
```

```
            Removes a node from the CwParamList.
        Inputs:
            wParam - Key indicating which node to remove.
            iType - Equals WPARAM_TYPE_HANDLE if wParam is a Winsock task
                handle, or WPARAM_TYPE_SOCKET if wParam is a socket
                number.
        Outputs:
            The function returns TRUE if the node can be removed.
            The function returns FALSE if a node with the specified key
            cannot be located in the list.
*/
BOOL CwParamList::Remove(WPARAM wParam, int iType)
{
    // See if we can find the node.
    SListNode * lplnNode = FindNode(wParam, iType);
    if (lplnNode == NULL)
        return FALSE;
    // Set pointers to bypass the indicated node.
    lplnNode->lplnPrev->lplnNext    = lplnNode->lplnNext;
    lplnNode->lplnNext->lplnPrev    = lplnNode->lplnPrev;
    // Delete the node.
    delete lplnNode;
    return TRUE;
}


/*

    Function: CwParamList::Find
    Description:
        Find a node in the list and return its lpecbCallback info.
        This function is little more than a wrapper for
        CwParamList::FindNode but it keeps the internal structure of
        the list data hidden.
    Inputs:
        wParam - Key for finding the info.
        iType - Equals WPARAM_TYPE_HANDLE if wParam is a Winsock task
            handle, or WPARAM_TYPE_SOCKET if wParam is a socket
            number.
        lplpecbCallback - Reference to a pointer to a callback
            object.  The pointer will be filled in with the data from
            the found node.
    Outputs:
        The function returns TRUE if it is successful.
        The function returns FALSE if the wParam key isn't valid and a
        corresponding node can't be found.
*/
BOOL CwParamList::Find(WPARAM wParam, int iType,
    CWinsockEventCallback * & lpecbCallback)

{
    // Find the node.
    SListNode * lplnNode = FindNode(wParam, iType);
    if (lplnNode == NULL)
        return FALSE;
```

```
        // Copy the pointer to the callback object into the output
        // parameter.
        lpecbCallback = lplnNode->lpecbCallback;
        return TRUE;
}


/*

    Function: CwParamList::FindNode
    Description:
        Finds a list node in the linked list and returns a pointer
        to it.
    Input:
        wParam - Search key of the node to find.
        iType - Equals WPARAM_TYPE_HANDLE if wParam is a Winsock task
            handle, or WPARAM_TYPE_SOCKET if wParam is a socket
            number.
    Output:
        Returns a FAR pointer to a CwParamList::SListNode if
        successful.  Returns NULL if the given wParam key can't be
        located in the list.
*/
CwParamList::SListNode * CwParamList::FindNode(WPARAM wParam,
    int iType)
{
    // Start at the first node after the head.
    SListNode * lplnNode = m_lnHead.lplnNext;

    // Walk the list until we get to the tail.
    while (lplnNode != &m_lnTail) {
        // If we have a match, return a pointer to the node.
        if (lplnNode->wParam == wParam && lplnNode->iType == iType)
            return lplnNode;
        // Move on...
        lplnNode = lplnNode->lplnNext;
    }
    return NULL;
}


/************************************************************************
    MISC FUNCTIONS
************************************************************************/

/*

    Function: WSCCreateEventWindow
    Description:
        Creates a window to receive Winsock events.
    Inputs:
        hInstance - The instance handle of the application.
    Outputs:
        BOOL - Returns TRUE if the function was successful, and FALSE
            if an error occurred.
*/
```

```
BOOL WSCCreateEventWindow(HINSTANCE hInstance,
    HINSTANCE hPrevInstance)
{
    // Check arguments.
    ASSERT(hInstance != NULL);

    // We can't do this twice.
    if (sg_hwndWSCEventWindow != NULL)
        return FALSE;

    if (!hPrevInstance) {
        // Create the window class.
        WNDCLASS wc;
        wc.style            = 0;
        wc.lpfnWndProc      = WSCEventWndProc;
        wc.cbClsExtra       = 0;
        wc.cbWndExtra       = 0;
        wc.hInstance        = hInstance;
        wc.hIcon            = NULL;
        wc.hCursor          = NULL;
        wc.hbrBackground    = NULL;
        wc.lpszMenuName     = NULL;
        wc.lpszClassName    = sg_szWSCWindowClass;

        BOOL bResult = RegisterClass(&wc);
        if (!bResult)
            return FALSE;
    }

    // Create the window itself.  Note that the window is by default
    // invisible and we simply never show it with ShowWindow.
    sg_hwndWSCEventWindow = CreateWindow(
        sg_szWSCWindowClass,              // window class name
        "",                               // window title text
        0,                                // window style
        CW_USEDEFAULT, CW_USEDEFAULT,     // position = default
        CW_USEDEFAULT, CW_USEDEFAULT,     // size = default
        NULL,                             // no parent window
        NULL,                             // menu = window class default
        hInstance,                        // window owner
        NULL);                            // no additional creation data

    if (sg_hwndWSCEventWindow == NULL)
        return FALSE;
    else
        return TRUE;
}

/*

    Function: WSCGetEventWindow
    Description:
        Returns the handle of the window created by
```

```
          WSCCreateEventWindow to receive Winsock events.  This is
               typically passed to a WSAAsyncGetXByY or WSAAsyncSelect call.
*/
HWND  WSCGetEventWindow(void)
{
     return sg_hwndWSCEventWindow;
}


/*

     Function: ReportWSAError
     Description:
          Generates a message box in response to a Winsock error.  The
          message box contains a bit of text passed to the function as
          well as a textual description of the error corresponding to
          the iError argument.  HWnd is used by MessageBox and the
          parent window and hInstance is used by LoadString to get the
          Winsock error text string resource.
     Inputs:
          lpszMsg — A pointer to a text message to be printed before
               the error message.
          iError — The Winsock error number.
          hwnd — Window to use as the message box parent.
          hInstance — The application instance handle.  This is used to
               read the error message string from the application's
               string resource table using LoadString.  This cannot be
               NULL.
     Outputs:
          None.
*/
void ReportWSAError(LPCSTR lpszMsg, int iError, HWND hwnd,
     HINSTANCE hInstance)
{
     // Make sure arguments are cool.
     ASSERT(lpszMsg != NULL);
     ASSERT(hInstance != NULL);

     // Convert iError == 0 to WSABASEERR.
     if (iError == 0)
         iError = WSABASEERR;

     // Retrieve the error message text.  This may fail if Windows is
     // out of memory (which could also be the cause of the Winsock
     // error).
     char szErrorMsg[81];
     int cErrMsgLen = LoadString(hInstance, iError, szErrorMsg,
         sizeof(szErrorMsg)) - 1; // -1 for the '\0' terminator.
     // If we couldn't find the error message text, fill in something.
     if (cErrMsgLen == 0)
         wsprintf(szErrorMsg, "[%d] Unknown Error", iError);

     // Create the final error message string.
     int cMsgLen = lstrlen(lpszMsg);
```

```
    // Need 80 bytes for message, 80 bytes for error text, 2 bytes for
    // CRLF, 1 byte for period, 1 byte for '\0'.
    const int FINAL_MSG_SIZE = (80 + 80 + 2 + 1 + 1);
    char szFinalMsg[FINAL_MSG_SIZE];
    // Copy message to final string, truncating to make room for
    // all the other text, if necessary.
    if ((cMsgLen + cErrMsgLen + 4) > FINAL_MSG_SIZE) {
        lstrcpyn(szFinalMsg, lpszMsg, FINAL_MSG_SIZE - 4 -
            cErrMsgLen);
    }
    else {
        lstrcpy(szFinalMsg, lpszMsg);
    }
    lstrcat(szFinalMsg, "\r\n");
    lstrcat(szFinalMsg, szErrorMsg);
    lstrcat(szFinalMsg, ".");

    // Display it using MessageBox.
    MessageBox(hwnd, szFinalMsg, "Winsock Error",
        MB_OK | MB_ICONEXCLAMATION);
}

void WSCFatalError(LPCSTR lpszMsg)
{
    MessageBox(NULL, lpszMsg, "Winsock Classes Fatal Error",
        MB_OK | MB_ICONEXCLAMATION);
    exit(1);
}


/***********************************************************************
    MODULE PRIVATE FUNCTIONS
***********************************************************************/

/*
    Function: WSCEventWndProc
    Description:
        This function is used to receive all Winsock related event
        messages.  The function corresponds to a hidden, private
        window that CWinsock allocates.  When a message arrives,
        WSCEventWndProc finds a callback routine corresponding to the
        message and dispatches the event to that routine to be
        handled.
    Inputs:
        The standard set of WndProc messages: hwnd, msg, wParam,
        lParam.
    Outputs:
        Standard WndProc LRESULT.
*/
static LRESULT CALLBACK WSCEventWndProc(HWND hwnd, UINT msg,
    WPARAM wParam, LPARAM lParam)
{
    CWinsockEventCallback * lpecCallback;
```

```
switch (msg) {
    // Since all these messages all use task handles, we can unify
    // their processing.
    case WM_WSAGETHOSTBYADDR:
    case WM_WSAGETHOSTBYNAME:
    case WM_WSAGETPROTOBYNAME:
    case WM_WSAGETPROTOBYNUMBER:
    case WM_WSAGETSERVBYNAME:
    case WM_WSAGETSERVBYPORT:
        // Look up task handle.
        if (sg_clWparamList.Find(wParam, WPARAM_TYPE_HANDLE,
            lpecCallback)) {
            // Make sure we aren't off in the weeds.
            ASSERT(lpecCallback != NULL);
            // Dispatch control to appropriate callback function.
            lpecCallback->WinsockEventCallback(hwnd, msg,
                wParam, lParam);
            return 0;
        }
        else {
            // We didn't find an entry for the task handle.
            return 0;
        }
    case WM_WSAASYNCSELECT:
        // Look up socket.
        if (sg_clWparamList.Find(wParam, WPARAM_TYPE_SOCKET,
            lpecCallback)) {
            // Make sure we aren't off in the weeds.
            ASSERT(lpecCallback != NULL);
            // Dispatch control to appropriate callback function.
            lpecCallback->WinsockEventCallback(hwnd, msg,
                wParam, lParam);
            return 0;
        }
        else {
            // We didn't find an entry for the socket.
            return 0;
        }
    default:
        return DefWindowProc(hwnd, msg, wParam, lParam);
    }
}
```

Listing 6.3 CSOCKADR.H

```
/*
    File: CSOCKADR.H
    Description:
        An Internet family socket address class.
    Copyright 1995, David G. Roberts
*/
```

```
#ifndef _CSOCKADR_H
#define _CSOCKADR_H

#include <windows.h>
#include "winsock.h"

/*
     Class: CSockAddr
     Description:
          The CSockAddr class is an encapsulation of a Winsock
          sockaddr/sockaddr_in structure.  The class eliminates the
          common error of forgetting to specify address or port numbers
          in host byte order.  If used with other objects that generate
          addresses in given formats compatible with this object, an
          application need not know of Internet address formats and thus
          may not have to change when converted to support IPv6.

          Note that all address and port numbers given and returned
          as integers are in host byte order.  The functions convert
          them to network byte order as appropriate.
*/
class CSockAddr {
private:
     SOCKADDR_IN      m_sinAddr;  // The address itself.
public:
     // Constructors and destructors
     CSockAddr() { m_sinAddr.sin_family = AF_INET; }; // Default
     CSockAddr(const CSockAddr& csaSockAddr) // Copy constructor
          : m_sinAddr(csaSockAddr.m_sinAddr) {};
     CSockAddr(const SOCKADDR& saSockAddr)
          : m_sinAddr(*(SOCKADDR_IN FAR *)&saSockAddr) {};
     CSockAddr(const SOCKADDR_IN& sinSockAddr)
          : m_sinAddr(sinSockAddr) {};
     CSockAddr(const u_short ushPort, const u_long ulAddr)
          { Set(ushPort, ulAddr); };
     ~CSockAddr() {};      // Destructor
     // Overloaded operator= functions.
     const CSockAddr& operator=(const CSockAddr& csaSockAddr);
     const CSockAddr& operator=(const SOCKADDR& saSockAddr)
          { m_sinAddr = *(SOCKADDR_IN FAR *)&saSockAddr;
            return *this; };
     const CSockAddr& operator=(const SOCKADDR_IN& sinSockAddr)
          { m_sinAddr = sinSockAddr; return *this; };
     // Functions for manipulating portions of SOCKADDR_IN after
     // construction time.
     void Set(const u_short ushPort, const u_long ulAddr);
     u_short Port(void) const
          { return ntohs(m_sinAddr.sin_port); };
     void Port(const u_short ushPort)
          { m_sinAddr.sin_port = htons(ushPort); };
     u_long Addr(void) const
          { return ntohl(m_sinAddr.sin_addr.s_addr); };
```

```
    void Addr(const u_long ulAddr)
        { m_sinAddr.sin_addr.s_addr = htonl(ulAddr); };
    // Conversion operators so we can use CSockAddr with Winsock
    // functions.
/*
    operator  const SOCKADDR&() const
        { return *((SOCKADDR *) &m_sinAddr); };
    operator const SOCKADDR_IN&() const
        { return m_sinAddr; };
*/
    operator SOCKADDR()
        { return *((SOCKADDR *) &m_sinAddr); };
    operator SOCKADDR_IN()
        { return m_sinAddr; };
    operator LPSOCKADDR()
        { return (LPSOCKADDR) & m_sinAddr; };
    operator LPSOCKADDR_IN()
        { return (LPSOCKADDR_IN) & m_sinAddr; };
};


#endif // #ifndef _CSOCKADR_H
```

Listing 6.4 CSOCKADR.CPP

```
/*
    File: CSOCKADR.CPP
    Description:
        An Internet family socket address class.
    Copyright 1995, David G. Roberts
*/

#include "csockadr.h"

/*
    Function: CSockAddr::operator=
    Description:
        Handle assignment operator.
*/
const CSockAddr& CSockAddr::operator=(const CSockAddr& csaSockAddr)
{
    if (&csaSockAddr != this) {
        // Copy the structure.
        m_sinAddr = csaSockAddr.m_sinAddr;
    }
    return *this;
}

/*
    Function: CSockAddr::Set
    Description:
        Set the port and address info to the specified values.
        The port and address values are specified in host byte
```

```
                order in the parameter list and are converted by the
                function.
*/
void CSockAddr::Set(const u_short ushPort, const u_long ulAddr)
{
    m_sinAddr.sin_family          = AF_INET;
    m_sinAddr.sin_port            = htons(ushPort);
    m_sinAddr.sin_addr.s_addr     = htonl(ulAddr);
}
```

Listing 6.5   CASYNCDB.H

```
/*
        File: CASYNCDB.H
        Description:
            A virtual class to perform Winsock asynchronous database
            lookup.
        Copyright 1995, David G. Roberts
*/

#ifndef _CASYNCDB_H
#define _CASYNCDB_H

#include <windows.h>
#include "winsock.h"
#ifndef _CWINSOCK_H
#include "cwinsock.h"
#endif

/* CONSTANTS */
/* Error codes */
#define ASYNCDBERR_NOERROR              0
#define ASYNCDBERR_INPROGRESS           1
#define ASYNCDBERR_NOTINPROGRESS        2

/*
        Class: CAsyncDBCallback
        Description:
            A class describing a callback interface used by CAsyncDB to
            inform another object that an asynchronous lookup has
            completed. Classes using a CAsyncDB derived class for
            asynchronous lookup should inherit this callback class
            interface and override the virtual function appropriately.
*/
class CAsyncDBCallback {
public:
    // iToken will contain the token value passed to the lookup class
    //    when it is constructed.
    // iError will contain a Winsock error number.
    virtual void AsyncDBCallback(int iToken, int iError) = 0;
};
```

```
/*
    Class: CAsyncDB
    Description:
        CAsyncDB is used to look up service port numbers.
*/
class CAsyncDB : protected CWinsockEventCallback {
public:
    enum STATE { INVALID, INPROGRESS, VALID };
protected:
    char *              m_pBuffer;        // Buffer for lookup info.
    CAsyncDBCallback *  m_pCallback;      // Pointer to callback object.
    int                 m_iToken;         // Callback token.
    STATE               m_stState;        // Current lookup state.
    HANDLE              m_hWSATask;       // Winsock task handle.
    int                 m_iLastError;     // Last error for this object.

    // Make the event callback private so that only the event dispatch
    // window can "see" it.  It won't be visible to users of the
    // class.
    virtual void WinsockEventCallback(HWND hwnd, UINT msg,
        WPARAM wParam, LPARAM lParam);

    // This function should be customized in all classes that inherit
    // from this base class.  It's what kicks off the actual lookup
    // in Winsock and is specific to the information that is being
    // looked up.
    virtual HANDLE StartWinsockLookup(void) = 0;
private:
    // Hide this stuff so the compiler doesn't generate default
    // versions of them and nobody can use them by mistake.
    CAsyncDB(CAsyncDB&);        // Copy constructor
    operator=(CAsyncDB&);       // Assignment operator.
public:
    CAsyncDB(void)
            : m_pBuffer(new char[MAXGETHOSTSTRUCT]), m_pCallback(NULL),
        m_iToken(0), m_stState(INVALID) {};
    virtual ~CAsyncDB();        // Virtual destructor because it's a base
                                // class.
    int StartLookup(CAsyncDBCallback * pCallback, int iToken);
    int StopLookup(void);
    STATE State(void) { return m_stState; };
    int LastError(void) { return m_iLastError; };
};

#endif
```

Listing 6.6 CASYNCDB.CPP

```
/*
    File: CASYNCDB.CPP
    Description:
        A virtual class to perform Winsock asynchronous database
    lookup.
```

```
     Copyright 1995, David G. Roberts
*/

#include "casyncdb.h"
#include "myassert.h"

/*
     Function: CAsyncDB::~CAsyncDB
     Description:
          Destructor for CAsyncDB class.  Ensures that any pending
          lookup is cancelled before the object is destroyed.
*/
CAsyncDB::~CAsyncDB()
{
    // Make sure we stop anything that's currently in progress.
    StopLookup();
    delete[] m_pBuffer;
}


/*
     Function: CAsyncDB::StartLookup
     Description:
          Starts a lookup process using a CAsyncDB object.  The object
          must not have a lookup pending.  This means that object may
          have been created using the default constructor, a previous
          lookup is complete, or it was cancelled using StopLookup.
     Inputs:
          pCallback — pointer to the object to receive the callback.
          iToken — a user-specified value that is passed to the
             callback.
     Outputs:
          Returns an error code if a problem occured.  The error can be
          a Winsock error or a private ASYNCDBERR_* code.
          ASYNCDBERR_NOERROR will be returned if no error occurs.
*/
int CAsyncDB::StartLookup(CAsyncDBCallback * pCallback, int iToken)
{
    // If something is already going, don't interrupt it.  The caller
    // must invoke StopLookup first.
    if (m_stState == INPROGRESS)
        return m_iLastError = ASYNCDBERR_INPROGRESS;
    // Okay, now we're going.
    m_stState   = INPROGRESS;

    // Kick off the lookup.
    m_hWSATask = StartWinsockLookup();

    // Did something go wrong?
    if (m_hWSATask == NULL) {
        // Save error for future use.
        m_stState       = INVALID;
        return m_iLastError = WSAGetLastError();
    }
```

```
    // Set up the callback.
    m_pCallback = pCallback;
    m_iToken = iToken;
    Register((WPARAM)m_hWSATask, WPARAM_TYPE_HANDLE);

    return ASYNCDBERR_NOERROR;
}

/*

    Function: CAsyncDB::StopLookup
    Description:
        Stops an in progress lookup.
    Inputs: None.
    Outputs:
        Returns an error code if a problem occured.  The error can be
        a Winsock error or a private ASYNCDBERR_* code.
        ASYNCDBERR_NOERROR will be returned if no error occurs.
*/
int CAsyncDB::StopLookup(void)
{
    // See if we're really in progress.
    if (m_stState != INPROGRESS)
        return m_iLastError = ASYNCDBERR_NOTINPROGRESS;

    // Okay, now the address state is invalid.
    m_stState = INVALID;

    // Remove task handle from event callback list.
    Deregister((WPARAM)m_hWSATask, WPARAM_TYPE_HANDLE);
    m_pCallback = NULL;
    m_iToken = 0;

    // Cancel the lookup with Winsock.
    int iCancelResult = WSACancelAsyncRequest(m_hWSATask);
    if (iCancelResult == SOCKET_ERROR)
        m_iLastError = WSAGetLastError();
    // Map WSAEINVAL and WSAEALREADY to no error.  We'll assume that
    // the task handle really was valid but that Winsock has finished
    // the lookup.  Our application hasn't dispatched the Winsock
    // event message that is probably sitting in the message queue
    // right now, which is why we think the operation is still active
    // while Winsock doesn't.
    if (iCancelResult == SOCKET_ERROR && (m_iLastError == WSAEINVAL ||
        m_iLastError == WSAEALREADY)) {
        // Make function return 0, but leave m_iLastError set to real
        // error code, just in case somebody wants to check this.
        iCancelResult = 0;
    }

    // Return an error code.
    if (iCancelResult == 0)
        return ASYNCDBERR_NOERROR;
    else
```

```
                    return m_iLastError;
}

/*
        Function: CAsyncDB::WinsockEventCallback
        Description:
                Virtual function to handle the Winsock event message.
                Basically, this just deregisters the callback, gets the
                address from the SERVENT structure, stores it away so the
                app can retrieve it later, and finally calls the completion
                callback function.
        Inputs:
                Standard wndproc parameters.
        Outputs: None.
*/
void CAsyncDB::WinsockEventCallback(HWND hwnd, UINT msg,
        WPARAM wParam, LPARAM lParam)
{
        UNUSED_PARAMETER(hwnd);
        UNUSED_PARAMETER(msg);

        // Check our parameters.
        ASSERT((HANDLE) wParam == m_hWSATask);

        // Deregister the event callback.
        Deregister((WPARAM)m_hWSATask, WPARAM_TYPE_HANDLE);

        // Break out the result code.
        int iError = WSAGETASYNCERROR(lParam);

        if (iError == 0) {
            // No error, so now we're valid.
            m_stState   = VALID;
            m_iLastError = ASYNCDBERR_NOERROR;
        }
        else {
            // Some error occurred.
            m_stState = INVALID;
            m_iLastError = iError;
        }

        // Invoke the completion callback.
        ASSERT(m_pCallback != NULL);
        CAsyncDBCallback * pCallback = m_pCallback;
        m_pCallback = NULL;
        pCallback->AsyncDBCallback(m_iToken, iError);
}
```

Listing 6.7   CHOST.H

```
/*
        File: CHOST.H
        Description:
```

```
        A class to perform host name lookup.
        Copyright 1995, David G. Roberts
*/


#ifndef _CHOST_H
#define _CHOST_H

#include <windows.h>
#include "winsock.h"
#ifndef _CWINSOCK_H
#include "cwinsock.h"
#endif
#ifndef _CSOCKADR_H
#include "csockadr.h"
#endif
#ifndef _CASYNCDB_H
#include "casyncdb.h"
#endif


/*
    Class: CHost
    Description:
        CHost is used to look up host names and determine their
        addresses.
*/
class CHost : public CAsyncDB {
private:
    int       m_iAddrIndex;
    LPCSTR    m_lpszHostName;

    // Override the CAsyncDB member to start the async lookup specific
    // to CHost.
     virtual HANDLE StartWinsockLookup(void);

    // Hide this stuff so the compiler doesn't generate default
    // versions of them and nobody can use them by mistake.
    CHost(CHost&);        // Copy constructor
     operator=(CHost&);   // Assignment operator.
public:
    CHost(void)
        : CAsyncDB(), m_iAddrIndex(0) {};
    CHost(LPCSTR lpszHostName, CAsyncDBCallback * pCallback,
        int iToken) : CAsyncDB(), m_iAddrIndex(0)
        { StartLookup(lpszHostName, pCallback, iToken); };
    ~CHost() {};
    int StartLookup(LPCSTR lpszHostName, CAsyncDBCallback * pCallback,
        int iToken)
        { m_lpszHostName = lpszHostName;
         return CAsyncDB::StartLookup(pCallback, iToken); };
    CSockAddr FirstAddr(BOOL *);
    CSockAddr NextAddr(BOOL *);
};


#endif
```

Listing 6.8 CHOST.CPP

```
/*
    File: CHOST.CPP
    Description:
        A class to perform host name lookup.
    Copyright 1995, David G. Roberts
*/

#include "chost.h"
#include "myassert.h"

/*
    Function: StartWinsockLookup
    Description:
        Virtual function provided to CAsyncDB to kick off the right
        type of lookup.
*/
HANDLE CHost::StartWinsockLookup(void)
{
    return WSAAsyncGetHostByName(GetEventWindow(),
        WM_WSAGETHOSTBYNAME, m_lpszHostName, (char FAR *) m_pBuffer,
        MAXGETHOSTSTRUCT);
}

/*
    Function: CHost::FirstAddr
    Description:
        Retrieves the first host address following a lookup.
    Inputs:
        pbResult — pointer to a BOOL indicating whether the
        operation was successful (it won't be successful if the
        CHost state is invalid or if the looked up host doesn't have
        even one address for some reason).
    Outputs:
        Returns a CSockAddr.
*/
CSockAddr CHost::FirstAddr(BOOL * pbResult)
{
    ASSERT(pbResult != NULL);

    // If we're still looking something up, indicate failure.
    if (m_stState != VALID) {
        *pbResult = FALSE;
        return CSockAddr(0, 0);
    }
    m_iAddrIndex = 0;         // Move us to the first index.
    // Make sure this entry is valid.
    if (((HOSTENT *)m_pBuffer)->h_addr_list[m_iAddrIndex] == NULL) {
        *pbResult = FALSE;
        return CSockAddr(0, 0);
    }
    // Get it.
    CSockAddr saResult(0, ntohl(*(u_long FAR *)
```

```
                (((HOSTENT *)m_pBuffer)->h_addr_list[m_iAddrIndex])));
        m_iAddrIndex++;              // Move us to the next index.
        *pbResult = TRUE;
        return saResult;
}


/*

     Function: CHost::NextAddr
     Description:
          Retrieves the next host address following a lookup.
     Inputs:
          pbResult – pointer to a BOOL indicating whether the
          operation was successful (it won't be successful if the
          CHost state is invalid or if there are no more addresses
          for the host).
     Outputs:
          Returns a CSockAddr.
*/
CSockAddr CHost::NextAddr(BOOL * pbResult)
{
        ASSERT(pbResult != NULL);

        // If we're still looking something up, indicate failure.
        if (m_stState != VALID) {
            *pbResult = FALSE;
            return CSockAddr(0, 0);
        }
        // Make sure this entry is valid.
         if (((HOSTENT *)m_pBuffer)->h_addr_list[m_iAddrIndex] == NULL) {
            *pbResult = FALSE;
            return CSockAddr(0, 0);
        }
        // Get it.
         CSockAddr saResult(0, ntohl(*(u_long FAR *)
              (((HOSTENT *)m_pBuffer)->h_addr_list[m_iAddrIndex])));
        m_iAddrIndex++;              // Move us to the next index.
        *pbResult = TRUE;
        return saResult;
}
```

Listing 6.9   CSERVICE.H

```
/*
     File: CSERVICE.H
     Description:
          A class to perform service lookup.
     Copyright 1995, David G. Roberts
*/

#ifndef _CSERVICE_H
#define _CSERVICE_H

#include <windows.h>
#include <winsock.h>
```

```
#ifndef _CWINSOCK_H
#include "cwinsock.h"
#endif
#ifndef _CSOCKADR_H
#include "csockadr.h"
#endif
#ifndef _CASYNCDB_H
#include "casyncdb.h"
#endif


/*
    Class: CService
    Description:
        CService is used to look up host names and determine their
        addresses.
*/
class CService : public CAsyncDB {
private:
    LPCSTR    m_lpszServiceName;
    LPCSTR    m_lpszProtoName;

    // Override the CAsyncDB member to start the async lookup
    // specific to CService.
    virtual HANDLE StartWinsockLookup(void);

    // Hide this stuff so the compiler doesn't generate default
    // versions of them and nobody can use them by mistake.
    CService(CService&);      // Copy constructor
    operator=(CService&);     // Assignment operator.
public:
    CService(void) : CAsyncDB() {};
    CService(LPCSTR lpszServiceName, LPCSTR lpszProtoName,
        CAsyncDBCallback * pCallback, int iToken)
        : CAsyncDB()
          { StartLookup(lpszServiceName, lpszProtoName, pCallback,
          iToken); };
    virtual ~CService() {};
    int StartLookup(LPCSTR lpszServiceName, LPCSTR lpszProtoName,
        CAsyncDBCallback * pCallback, int iToken)
        { m_lpszServiceName = lpszServiceName;
        m_lpszProtoName = lpszProtoName;
         return CAsyncDB::StartLookup(pCallback, iToken); };
    u_short Port(void);
};

#endif
```

Listing 6.10 CSERVICE.CPP

```
/*
    File: CSERVICE.CPP
    Description:
        A class to perform serice lookup.
```

```
    Copyright 1995, David G. Roberts
*/


#include "cservice.h"
#include "myassert.h"


/*
    Function: CService::StartWinsockLookup
    Description:
        Handle the callback from CAsyncDB to start the asynchronous
        database function.
*/
HANDLE CService::StartWinsockLookup(void)
{
    // Simply kick of an asynchronous getservbyname operation.
    return WSAAsyncGetServByName(GetEventWindow(),
        WM_WSAGETHOSTBYNAME, m_lpszServiceName, m_lpszProtoName,
        (char FAR *) m_pBuffer, MAXGETHOSTSTRUCT);
}


/*
    Function: CService::Port
    Description:
        Get the port number of the service once it has been
        looked up.  Note that the function returns the port number
        in host byte order, suitable for passing to CSockAddr.
*/
u_short CService::Port(void)
{
    if (m_stState != VALID)
        return 0;
    return ntohs(((SERVENT *)m_pBuffer)->s_port);
}
```

Listing 6.11 CSOCKET.H

```
/*
    File: CSOCKET.H
    Description:
        Class to encapsulate a Windows socket.
    Copyright 1995, David G. Roberts
*/


#ifndef _CSOCKET_H
#define _CSOCKET_H


#include <windows.h>
#include "winsock.h"
#ifndef _CWINSOCK_H
#include "cwinsock.h"
#endif
#ifndef _CSOCKADR_H
#include "csockadr.h"
```

```
#endif

class CStreamCallback {
public:
    enum STREAMEVENT { SE_CONNECT, SE_ACCEPT, SE_DATAREADY,
        SE_DATASENT, SE_CLOSE };
    virtual void StreamCallback(int iToken, STREAMEVENT iEvent,
        int iError, char FAR * lpBuffer) = 0;
};

class CStreamSocket : private CWinsockEventCallback {
private:
    // BufferDescriptor used to chain buffered transmit data.
    struct BufferDescriptor {
        BufferDescriptor *   m_pbdNext;
        char FAR *           m_lpOriginalBuffer;
        char FAR *           m_lpCurrentBuffer;
        int                  m_iLength;

        BufferDescriptor(char FAR * lpOriginalBuffer,
            char FAR * lpCurrentBuffer, int iLength)
            : m_pbdNext(NULL), m_lpOriginalBuffer(lpOriginalBuffer),
            m_lpCurrentBuffer(lpCurrentBuffer), m_iLength(iLength) {};
    };

    // State that a socket goes through.
    enum SOCKETSTATE { IDLE, CONNECTING, CONNECTED, LISTENING };

    SOCKET               m_s;
    int                  m_iLastError;
    CStreamCallback *    m_pCallback;
    int                  m_iToken;
    SOCKETSTATE          m_iState;
    BufferDescriptor *   m_pbdHead;
    BufferDescriptor *   m_pbdTail;

    virtual void WinsockEventCallback(HWND, UINT, WPARAM, LPARAM);

    // Private constructor used during AcceptConnection.
    CStreamSocket(SOCKET, CStreamCallback *, int);

    // Private functions to manage the send queue.
    void AddTail(char FAR *, char FAR*, int);
    void DeleteHead(void);

    // Make these off limits so nobody uses them.
    CStreamSocket(CStreamSocket&);              // Copy constructor.
    CStreamSocket& operator=(CStreamSocket&); // Assignment operator.
public:
    // Constructor and destructor.
    CStreamSocket(void)
            : m_s(INVALID_SOCKET), m_iLastError(WSANOERROR),
            m_pCallback(NULL), m_iToken(0), m_iState(IDLE),
```

```
                m_pbdHead(NULL), m_pbdTail(NULL) {};
        virtual ~CStreamSocket();
        // CStreamSocket managment functions.
        BOOL DataQueued(void)
                { return (m_pbdHead != NULL) ? TRUE : FALSE; };
        int LastError() { return m_iLastError; };
        void SetCallback(CStreamCallback * pCallback, int iToken)
                { m_pCallback = pCallback; m_iToken = iToken; };
        // General socket functions.
        CStreamSocket * Accept(CStreamCallback * pCallback, int iToken,
                CSockAddr * pcsaAddr = NULL);
        int Bind(CSockAddr& saBindAddr);
        int Close(void);
        int Connect(CSockAddr& saForeignAddr);
        int GetPeerName(CSockAddr * psaPeerName);
        int GetSockName(CSockAddr * psaSockName);
        int GetSockOpt(int iLevel, int iOptName, char * pOptVal,
                int * pnLen);
        int IoctlSocket(long lCommand, u_long * pArg);
        int Listen(CSockAddr& saServiceAddr, int iQueueLen);
        int Open(void);
        int Receive(char FAR * lpBuffer, int * piBuffLength,
                int iFlags = 0);
        int Send(char FAR * lpBuffer, int iLength, int iFlags = 0);
        int SetSockOpt(int iLevel, int iOptName, char * pOptVal,
                int nLen);
};

#endif
```

Listing 6.12 CSOCKET.CPP

```
/*
        File: CSOCKET.CPP
        Description:
                Class to encapsulate a Windows socket.
        Copyright 1995, David G. Roberts
*/

#include "csocket.h"
#include "myassert.h"

/*
        Function: CStreamSocket::WinsockEventCallback
        Description:
                Receives Winsock events from the event dispatch
                mechansim.
        Inputs:
                Standard Windows message parameters.
        Output:
                None.
*/
void CStreamSocket::WinsockEventCallback(HWND hwnd, UINT msg,
```

```
        WPARAM wParam, LPARAM lParam)
{

    UNUSED_PARAMETER(hwnd);
    UNUSED_PARAMETER(msg);
    UNUSED_PARAMETER(wParam);

    // If we've removed the socket callback function for some reason,
    // then don't bother calling it.  Simply ignore the message.
    if (m_pCallback == NULL)
        return;
    // Crack apart the event code and error code.
    int iEvent = WSAGETSELECTEVENT(lParam);
    int iError = WSAGETSELECTERROR(lParam);
    switch (iEvent) {
        case FD_ACCEPT:
            ASSERT(m_iState == LISTENING);
            m_pCallback->StreamCallback(m_iToken,
                CStreamCallback::SE_ACCEPT, iError, NULL);
            break;
        case FD_CLOSE:
            m_pCallback->StreamCallback(m_iToken,
                CStreamCallback::SE_CLOSE, iError, NULL);
            break;
        case FD_CONNECT:
            ASSERT(m_iState == CONNECTING);
            if (iError == WSANOERROR) {
                // If no error, signal that we now want read, write,
                // and close events and move the CStreamSocket
                // state to CONNECTED.
                WSAAsyncSelect(m_s, WSCGetEventWindow(),
                    WM_WSAASYNCSELECT,
                    FD_READ | FD_WRITE | FD_CLOSE);
                m_iState = CONNECTED;
            }
            m_pCallback->StreamCallback(m_iToken,
                CStreamCallback::SE_CONNECT, iError, NULL);
            break;
        case FD_READ:
            // Invoke the callback and say that there's data to be
            // read. Following this, somebody should call the
            // Receive member function to actually get the data.
            m_pCallback->StreamCallback(m_iToken,
                CStreamCallback::SE_DATAREADY, iError, NULL);
            break;
        case FD_WRITE:
            // Winsock has some buffer space.  Do we have any data?
            while (m_pbdHead != NULL) {
                // Yes, so try to send it.
                int iSentLength;
                do {
                    iSentLength = send(m_s,
                        m_pbdHead->m_lpCurrentBuffer,
                        m_pbdHead->m_iLength, 0);
```

```
                    if (iSentLength != SOCKET_ERROR) {
                        m_pbdHead->m_lpCurrentBuffer += iSentLength;
                        m_pbdHead->m_iLength -= iSentLength;
                    }
                } while (iSentLength != SOCKET_ERROR &&
                    m_pbdHead->m_iLength > 0);
                if (m_pbdHead->m_iLength > 0) {
                    // There's still more data left.  Figure out why.
                    m_iLastError = WSAGetLastError();
                    if (m_iLastError != WSAEWOULDBLOCK) {
                        // Something bad happened.  Dequeue the
                        // buffer and invoke the callback with the
                        // bad news.
                        char FAR * lpOriginalBuffer =
                            m_pbdHead->m_lpOriginalBuffer;
                        DeleteHead();
                        m_pCallback->StreamCallback(m_iToken,
                            CStreamCallback::SE_DATASENT,
                            m_iLastError,
                            lpOriginalBuffer);

                    }
                    else {
                        // Else error == WSAEWOULDBLOCK, which means
                        // that Winsock is just out of space.  We'll
                        // just break out of the enclosing while loop
                        // and continue to send the buffer when
                        // Winsock sends us another FD_WRITE event.
                        break;
                    }
                }
                else {
                    // We completed sending that buffer.  Dequeue
                    // it and invoke the callback.
                    char FAR * lpOriginalBuffer =
                        m_pbdHead->m_lpOriginalBuffer;
                    DeleteHead();
                    m_iLastError = WSANOERROR;
                    m_pCallback->StreamCallback(m_iToken,
                        CStreamCallback::SE_DATASENT, m_iLastError,
                        lpOriginalBuffer);
                }
            } // while (m_pbdHead != NULL)
        break;
    default:
        // The event is unknown, so simply ignore it.
        break;
    }
}


/*

    Function:
        CStreamSocket::CStreamSocket(SOCKET, CStreamCallback *, int)
```

```
    Description:
        A private constructor used to create a newly connected
        CStreamSocket in Accept.
    Inputs:
        s - socket descriptor of new socket from Winsock.
        pCallback - the callback function for the new CStreamSocket.
        iToken - the token value of the new CStreamSocket.
    Outputs: None.
*/
CStreamSocket::CStreamSocket(SOCKET s, CStreamCallback * pCallback,
    int iToken)
    : m_s(s), m_iLastError(WSANOERROR), m_pCallback(pCallback),
    m_iToken(iToken), m_iState(CONNECTED)
{
    WSAAsyncSelect(m_s, WSCGetEventWindow(), WM_WSAASYNCSELECT,
        FD_READ | FD_WRITE | FD_CLOSE);
}


/*
    Function: CStreamSocket::~CStreamSocket
    Description:
        Destructor for CStreamSocket.
    Inputs: None.
    Outputs: None.
*/
CStreamSocket::~CStreamSocket()
{
    // Close out the socket.
    if (m_s != INVALID_SOCKET)
        Close();
}


/*
    Function: CStreamSocket::Accept
    Description:
        Accepts a connection from a foreign host.  The socket should
        have already been put in a listening state by calling Listen.
    Inputs:
        pCallback - the callback function to be associated with the
            newly created CStreamSocket.
        iToken - the token value to be passed with the callback for
            the newly created CStreamSocket.
        lpsaAddr - an optional parameter to hold the address of the
            foreign host.
        lpiAddrLen - on input, the length of the data structure
            pointedto by lpsaAddr.  On exit, the length of the data
            written to the structure.
    Output:
        A pointer to a newly created CStreamSocket.  The socket can be
        destroyed with 'delete' at a later time.  If an error occurs,
        NULL is returned and the error code may be retrieved using
        LastError.  If the code is WSAEWOULDBLOCK, then there is no
        connection waiting.
```

```
*/
CStreamSocket * CStreamSocket::Accept(CStreamCallback * pCallback,
    int iToken, CSockAddr * pcsaAddr)
{
    ASSERT(m_s != INVALID_SOCKET && m_iState == LISTENING);

    // Try to accept the incoming connection.
    SOCKADDR saAddr;
    int iAddrLen = sizeof(saAddr);
    SOCKET s = accept(m_s, &saAddr, &iAddrLen);
    if (s == INVALID_SOCKET) {
        m_iLastError = WSAGetLastError();
        return NULL;
    }
    if (pcsaAddr != NULL)
        *pcsaAddr = saAddr;
    // If successful, create a new CStreamSocket
    CStreamSocket * pssNew = new CStreamSocket(s, pCallback, iToken);
    if (pssNew == NULL)
        return NULL;
    return pssNew;
}


/*

    Function: CStreamSocket::Bind
    Description:
        Binds a socket to an address.  If the socket has not yet
        been opened, the socket is first opened.
    Input:
        saBindAddr - reference to the socket address to bind to.
    Output:
        WSANOERROR if no error occurred or another Winsock
        error code.
*/
int CStreamSocket::Bind(CSockAddr& saBindAddr)
{
    int iError;

    // If socket has not yet be opened, then open it.
    if (m_s == INVALID_SOCKET) {
        ASSERT(m_iState == IDLE);
        iError = Open();
        if (iError != WSANOERROR)
            return iError;
    }

    // Bind the socket to the specified address.
    iError = bind(m_s, (LPSOCKADDR) saBindAddr, sizeof(SOCKADDR));
    if (iError == SOCKET_ERROR) {
        m_iLastError = WSAGetLastError();
        return m_iLastError;
    }
    return m_iLastError = WSANOERROR;
```

```
}

/*

     Function: CStreamSocket::Close
     Description:
         Closes a socket.
     Inputs: None.
     Output:
         WSANOERROR if no error occurred or another Winsock
         error code.
*/
int CStreamSocket::Close(void)
{
    // It's okay to close an already closed socket.
    if (m_s == INVALID_SOCKET)
        return m_iLastError = WSANOERROR;
    // Make sure we don't get any more callbacks.
    Deregister((WPARAM) m_s, WPARAM_TYPE_SOCKET);
    // Delete all the queued buffer descriptors.  Note that no
    // callbacks are given.  Presumably, the receiver of the that
    // callbacks knows we're being closed and won't miss them.
    while (m_pbdHead != NULL)
        DeleteHead();
    // Close the socket.
    if (closesocket(m_s) == SOCKET_ERROR)
        m_iLastError = WSAGetLastError();
    else
        m_iLastError = WSANOERROR;
    // We're now idle.
    m_s = INVALID_SOCKET;
    m_iState = IDLE;
    return m_iLastError;
}


/*

     Function: CStreamSocket::Connect
     Description:
         Start the connection process.  When the connection
         is set up, the application will receive a callback.
     Input:
         saForeignAddr — the remote address to connect to.
     Output:
         WSANOERROR if no errors occurred or other Winsock
         error.
*/
int CStreamSocket::Connect(CSockAddr& saForeignAddr)
{
    int iError;

    // If socket has not yet be opened, then open it.
    if (m_s == INVALID_SOCKET) {
        ASSERT(m_iState == IDLE);
        iError = Open();
```

```
                if (iError != WSANOERROR)
                    return iError;
        }
        // Set us up to receive connect events.
        iError = WSAAsyncSelect(m_s, WSCGetEventWindow(),
            WM_WSAASYNCSELECT, FD_CONNECT);
        if (iError == SOCKET_ERROR)
            return m_iLastError = WSAGetLastError();
        // Try to connect us.
        iError = connect(m_s, (LPSOCKADDR) saForeignAddr,
            sizeof(SOCKADDR));
        if (iError == SOCKET_ERROR) {
            m_iLastError = WSAGetLastError();
            if (m_iLastError == WSAEWOULDBLOCK) {
                // We would have blocked, so the connection is in
                // progress. Set our state to connecting and wait for the
                // callback event.
                m_iState = CONNECTING;
            }
            return m_iLastError;
        }
        // Somehow we got lucky and the call didn't block.  So indicate
        // that we're connected.
        m_iState = CONNECTED;
        return m_iLastError = WSANOERROR;
}


/*

    Function: CStreamSocket::GetPeerName
    Description:
        Gets the address and port information of the remote host.
    Input:
        psaPeerName - pointer to a CSockAddr object which will hold
            the result.
    Output:
        The peer address is placed in the structure pointed to by
        psaPeerName.
        The function returns WSANOERROR if no errors occurred or
        another Winsock error code.
*/
int CStreamSocket::GetPeerName(CSockAddr * psaPeerName)
{
    // See if we have a valid socket.
    if (m_s == INVALID_SOCKET) {
        return m_iLastError = WSAENOTSOCK;
    }

    int nLen = sizeof(SOCKADDR);
    int iError = getpeername(m_s, (LPSOCKADDR)(*psaPeerName), &nLen);
    if (iError == SOCKET_ERROR) {
        m_iLastError = WSAGetLastError();
        return m_iLastError;
    }
```

```
        return m_iLastError - WSANOERROR;
}


/*

    Function: CStreamSocket::GetSockName
    Description:
        Gets the address and port that the socket is bound to.
        If the socket has not been opened, it is opened and bound
        to INADDR_ANY, port 0.
    Input:
        psaSockName - pointer to a CSockAddr object which will hold
            the result.
    Output:
        The local address is placed in the structure pointed to by
        psaSockName.
        The function returns WSANOERROR if no errors occurred or
        another Winsock error code.
*/
int CStreamSocket::GetSockName(CSockAddr * psaSockName)
{
    int iError;

    // If socket has not yet be opened, then open it and bind it.
    if (m_s == INVALID_SOCKET) {
        ASSERT(m_iState == IDLE);
        iError = Open();
        if (iError != WSANOERROR)
            return iError;
        CSockAddr saTemp(INADDR_ANY, 0);
        iError = Bind(saTemp);
        if (iError != WSANOERROR)
            return iError;
    }

    // Get it's name.
    int nLen = sizeof(SOCKADDR);
    iError = getpeername(m_s, (LPSOCKADDR)(*psaSockName), &nLen);
    if (iError == SOCKET_ERROR) {
        m_iLastError = WSAGetLastError();
        return m_iLastError;
    }
    return m_iLastError = WSANOERROR;
}


/*

    Function: CStreamSocket::GetSockOpt
    Description:
        Gets the value of a current socket option.
    Inputs:
        iLevel - the level of the socket option.
        iOptName - the name of the option.
        pOptVal - pointer to a buffer to receive the option value.
        pnLen - pointer to an integer holding the length of the
            buffer.
```

```
    Outputs:
        Sets *pnLen to the length of the data returned in the
        buffer.
        Directly returns a Winsock error value or WSANOERROR if
        no errors occurred.
*/
int CStreamSocket::GetSockOpt(int iLevel, int iOptName,
    char * pOptVal, int * pnLen)
{
    int iError;

    // If socket has not yet be opened, then open it.
    if (m_s == INVALID_SOCKET) {
        ASSERT(m_iState == IDLE);
        iError = Open();
        if (iError != WSANOERROR)
            return iError;
    }

    // Get the socket option information.
    iError = getsockopt(m_s, iLevel, iOptName, pOptVal, pnLen);
    if (iError == SOCKET_ERROR) {
        m_iLastError = WSAGetLastError();
        return m_iLastError;
    }

    return m_iLastError = WSANOERROR;
}


/*
    Function: CStreamSocket::IoctlSocket
    Description:
        Changes the current mode of a socket.
    Inputs:
        lCommand - the command to invoke on the socket.
        pArg - pointer to an argument for the command.
    Outputs:
        Returns a Winsock error code or WSANOERROR if no errors
        occurred.
*/
int CStreamSocket::IoctlSocket(long lCommand, u_long * pArg)
{
    int iError;

    // If socket has not yet be opened, then open it.
    if (m_s == INVALID_SOCKET) {
        ASSERT(m_iState == IDLE);
        iError = Open();
        if (iError != WSANOERROR)
            return iError;
    }

    // Get the socket option information.
```

```
        iError = ioctlsocket(m_s, lCommand, pArg);
        if (iError == SOCKET_ERROR) {
            m_iLastError = WSAGetLastError();
            return m_iLastError;
        }
        return m_iLastError = WSANOERROR;
    }


/*
        Function: CStreamSocket::Listen
        Description:
            Put the socket into listening mode.
        Inputs:
            saServiceAddr — the address to bind the socket to
                before listening.
            iQueueLen — the length of the queue passed to
                Winsock "listen".
        Output:
            WSANOERROR if no errors occurred.
            Other Winsock error as necessary.
*/
int CStreamSocket::Listen(CSockAddr& saServiceAddr,
    int iQueueLen)
{
    int iError;

    // If socket has not yet be opened, then open it.
    if (m_s == INVALID_SOCKET) {
        ASSERT(m_iState == IDLE);
        iError = Open();
        if (iError != WSANOERROR)
            return iError;
    }
    // Bind the socket to the specified port and interface address.
    iError = bind(m_s, (LPSOCKADDR) saServiceAddr, sizeof(SOCKADDR));
    if (iError == SOCKET_ERROR)
        return m_iLastError = WSAGetLastError();
    // Set us up to listen with the specified connection queue length.
    iError = listen(m_s, iQueueLen);
    if (iError == SOCKET_ERROR)
        return m_iLastError = WSAGetLastError();
    // Make Winsock generate accept notification messages.
    iError = WSAAsyncSelect(m_s, WSCGetEventWindow(),
        WM_WSAASYNCSELECT, FD_ACCEPT);
    m_iState = LISTENING;
    return m_iLastError = WSANOERROR;
}


/*
        Function: CStreamSocket::Open
        Description:
            Open a socket for communcation.
        Inputs: None.
```

```
        Output:
            WSANOERROR if no error occurred.
            Other Winsock error as returned from "socket" or
            "ioctlsocket".
*/
int CStreamSocket::Open(void)
{
    // Make sure we don't have something open.
    ASSERT(m_s == INVALID_SOCKET && m_iState == IDLE);
    // Create the socket.
    m_s = socket(AF_INET, SOCK_STREAM, 0);
    if (m_s == INVALID_SOCKET)
        return m_iLastError = WSAGetLastError();
    // Make the socket non-blocking.
    u_long ulFlag = 1;
    // Note, the compiler may give a warning about the FIONBIO
    // constant below.  Ignore the warning; everything is okay.
    int iError = ioctlsocket(m_s, FIONBIO, &ulFlag);
    if (iError == SOCKET_ERROR) {
        closesocket(m_s);
        m_s = INVALID_SOCKET;
        return m_iLastError = WSAGetLastError();
    }
    // Register the callbacks.
    Register((WPARAM) m_s, WPARAM_TYPE_SOCKET);
    return m_iLastError = WSANOERROR;
}


/*
    Function: CStreamSocket::Receive
    Description:
        Get received data from the socket.
    Inputs:
        lpBuffer — pointer to the buffer to receive the data.
        piBuffLength — a pointer to an integer that
            contains the length of the buffer.
        iFlags — flags passed to Winsock "recv" function.
    Outputs:
        piBuffLength — on exit, the integer
            is overwritten with the amount of data actually
            read from the socket.  If the connection is
            closed gracefully, the returned length will be
            zero.
        Directly returns the error code returned from "recv".
*/
int CStreamSocket::Receive(char FAR * lpBuffer, int * piBuffLength,
    int iFlags)
{
    int iReceivedLength = recv(m_s, lpBuffer, *piBuffLength, iFlags);
    if (iReceivedLength == SOCKET_ERROR) {
        *piBuffLength = 0;
        return m_iLastError = WSAGetLastError();
    }
```

```
        *piBuffLength = iReceivedLength;
        return m_iLastError = WSANOERROR;
}


/*

    Function: CStreamSocket::Send
    Description:
        Send data using the socket.  If the result of the
        transmission attempt is WSAEWOULDBLOCK, the buffer
        containing the data is queued until the socket will
        accept the data.
    Inputs:
        lpBuffer - pointer to the buffer to be sent.
        iLength - length of the buffer.
        iFlags - flags to be passed to Windows Sockets send
            function.
    Outputs:
        WSANOERROR - no errors occurred.
        WSAEWOULDBLOCK - some or all of the data could not be
            accepted at this time.  The buffer has been queued
            for later transmission and a callback will be
            generated when the data is sent.
        Other - other Winsock errors as returned by "send".
*/
int CStreamSocket::Send(char FAR * lpBuffer, int iLength, int iFlags)
{
    ASSERT(m_iState == CONNECTED);

    // See if there's stuff on the queue.
    if (m_pbdHead != NULL) {
        // Yup, so we're already waiting to send stuff.  Simply chain
        // this buffer to the end.
        AddTail(lpBuffer, lpBuffer, iLength);
        return m_iLastError = WSAEWOULDBLOCK;
    }
    // There's no data on the queue, so simply try to send the data.
    char FAR * lpOriginalBuffer = lpBuffer;
    int iSentLength;
    do {
        iSentLength = send(m_s, lpBuffer, iLength, iFlags);
        if (iSentLength != SOCKET_ERROR) {
            lpBuffer += iSentLength;
            iLength -= iSentLength;
        }
    } while (iSentLength != SOCKET_ERROR && iLength > 0);
    if (iLength > 0) {
        // We didn't send all the data.  Find out why.
        m_iLastError = WSAGetLastError();
        if (m_iLastError == WSAEWOULDBLOCK) {
            // Winsock ran out of buffer space, so buffer the
            // remaining data.
            AddTail(lpOriginalBuffer, lpBuffer, iLength);
            return WSAEWOULDBLOCK;
```

```
            }
            else {
                // Something bad happened.  Tell the caller.
                return m_iLastError;
            }
        }
    else {
        // All the data got sent, so return with no error.  Note that
        // we don't call the callback routine because we could get in
        // a recursive loop if the callback routine tries to send more
        // data.  Depending on how many times we looped, we might run
        // out of stack space.  The caller should use a return value
        // of WSANOERROR in lieu of a callback to indicate that the
        // buffer is free.
        return m_iLastError = WSANOERROR;
    }
}


/*

    Function: CStreamSocket::SetSockOpt
    Description:
        Set a current socket option.
    Inputs:
        iLevel - the level of the socket option.
        iOptName - the name of the socket option.
        pOptVal - pointer to a buffer containing the new value for
            the socket option.
        nLen - the length of the data in the buffer.
    Output:
        Returns a Winsock error code or WSANOERROR if no errors
        occurred.
*/
int CStreamSocket::SetSockOpt(int iLevel, int iOptName,
    char * pOptVal, int nLen)
{
    int iError;

    // If socket has not yet be opened, then open it.
    if (m_s == INVALID_SOCKET) {
        ASSERT(m_iState == IDLE);
        iError = Open();
        if (iError != WSANOERROR)
            return iError;
    }

    // Get the socket option information.
    iError = setsockopt(m_s, iLevel, iOptName, pOptVal, nLen);
    if (iError == SOCKET_ERROR) {
        m_iLastError = WSAGetLastError();
        return m_iLastError;
    }
    return m_iLastError = WSANOERROR;
}
```

```
/*
     Function: CStreamSocket::AddTail
     Description:
         Add a buffer to the end of the sending queue.
     Inputs:
         lpOriginalBuffer — pointer to the buffer as originally
             passed to Send.  We need this to identify the buffer
             to the application in the completion callback.
         lpCurrentBuffer — pointer to the first byte of data
             remaining in the buffer.
         iLength — the length of data remaining to be sent.
     Output:
         None.
*/
void CStreamSocket::AddTail(char FAR * lpOriginalBuffer,
     char FAR * lpCurrentBuffer, int iLength)
{
     BufferDescriptor * pbdNew = new BufferDescriptor(lpOriginalBuffer,
         lpCurrentBuffer, iLength);
     if (m_pbdHead == NULL) {
         // The list was empty.
         m_pbdHead = m_pbdTail = pbdNew;
     }
     else {
         // Chain the buffer to the end.
         m_pbdTail->m_pbdNext = pbdNew;
         m_pbdTail = pbdNew;
     }
}


/*
      Function: CStreamSocket::DeleteHead
     Description:
         Remove a buffer from the head of the sending queue.
     Inputs: None.
     Outputs: None.
*/
void CStreamSocket::DeleteHead(void)
{
     ASSERT(m_pbdHead != NULL);

     BufferDescriptor * pbdNextHead = m_pbdHead->m_pbdNext;
     delete m_pbdHead;
     m_pbdHead = pbdNextHead;
     if (m_pbdHead == NULL)  // If we just deleted the last in
         m_pbdTail = NULL;   //    the chain...
}
```

A First Winsock Programming Project

The Finger protocol allows you to retrieve information about a remote user. Learn how to program Windows Sockets using the C++ classes developed in the previous chapter as we implement a Finger protocol client.

My grandfather always used to say, "In order to learn how to ride, you've got to get up on the horse." Well, all right, my grandfather never said that, and he raised beef, not horses, but he was the sort of man who *would have* said that if he had been a horse man rather than a cow man. He did say, "Practice makes perfect," although I think somebody else probably took credit for that one. So what do horses, cows, and practice have to do with Winsock programming? Horses and cows don't have much at all to do with Winsock programming. Practice has a lot to do with it. It's about time we rolled up our sleeves and got into a real programming assignment.

In this chapter, we'll build a complete Winsock program: a client implementing the Finger protocol described in RFC 1288. We'll see our C++ classes from the previous chapter in action, and we'll implement a protocol using a state-machine model and the Winsock asynchronous extensions.

The Finger Protocol

Why use the Finger protocol as a first project? Well, the Finger protocol is a fairly simple, yet truly useful protocol. The Finger protocol allows you to retrieve information about a remote user on a remote host. The specific information returned about a user is up to the remote host but generally includes such things as the user's real name, his or her login name, and the last time the user logged into the remote host. Other information can include the remote user's telephone number or office number, which are useful in a campus environment when you want to contact a professor or professional colleague.

Some servers allow each user to specify a *plan file*, the text of which is returned in addition to the typical Finger information. The plan file was originally used to specify information about the user's current project, such as how far behind schedule it was. These days, plan files are used to include personal statements about the user. Modern plan files commonly include political ranting and the user's public encryption key for such programs as Pretty Good Privacy (PGP).

The Finger protocol works as follows:

- Using TCP, a Finger client program makes a connection with the Finger server on the remote host. The server is typically contacted at the well-known port number 79.
- The client sends the server a query consisting of a single line of text, typically the name of the remote user of interest.
- The server processes the query and then sends the client a response. When the response has been sent, the server closes the connection.
- The client receives the data, closes its end of the connection, then displays the response to the user.

The format of the data exchanged is fairly simple. All data is 8-bit ASCII. Lines are terminated with a carriage-return and a linefeed (ASCII 13 followed by ASCII 10, also written as CRLF), as they are in DOS.

Internet Text Data Conventions

The CRLF end-of-line convention is used in many Internet protocols. The use of ASCII characters and CRLF has been around since the early days of the Internet. These standards reflect an attempt to overcome the numerous textual conventions in use on different systems throughout the early Internet. Although host systems may use EBCDIC character sets or a carriage return (ASCII 13) by itself as a line termination character, they always exchange textual data over the network using ASCII and CRLF line terminators.

We'll see these same conventions reappear as we implement other protocols such as SMTP, POP, NNTP, and FTP in following chapters.

As I said, the Finger protocol is fairly simple, yet it contains all the elements of programs twice its size—connections must be opened and closed, data must be sent and received, and remote host names must be looked up in the host database. Because of its simplicity, implementing a Finger client makes a great first Windows Sockets programming task. Perhaps this fact explains the numerous Finger clients available on the Net.

The Finger Program

The Finger client application we'll implement is fairly simple: a Single Document Interface (SDI) Windows application with a couple of menus. The client area of the application window displays the text returned from the server. The client area is scrollable so that the user can read all of the text if it is long.

Figure 7.1 shows a screen shot of the program after some Finger information has been retrieved from the server.

The File menu of the program contains only two menu choices: Connect... and Exit. The Help menu contains only an About... menu item. The Connect menu choice brings up a dialog box that allows the user to make a connection to a remote Finger server. The Connect dialog box is shown in Figure 7.2.

Figure 7.1

The results of a Finger query.

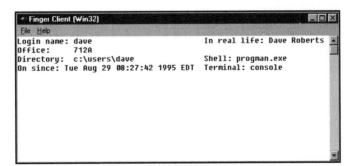

```
Finger Client (Win32)                                    _ □ ×
File  Help
Login name: dave                      In real life: Dave Roberts
Office:     712A
Directory:  c:\users\dave             Shell: progman.exe
On since: Tue Aug 29 08:27:42 1995 EDT  Terminal: console
```

Figure 7.2

The Finger
client Connect
dialog box.

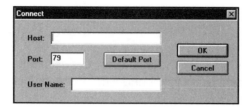

The Host edit control allows the user to type the name of the remote host to which to connect. The User Name edit control allows the user to specify the text that is passed to the remote server by the client. Typically, the text is the name of a remote user. The Port edit control allows the user to specify the port address on which the remote server is listening. The Default Port button sets the number in the Port edit box back to the standard Finger port number, 79.

When the user selects the OK button in the Connect dialog box, the application makes contact with the remote server, sends it the text in the User Name edit control, and waits for a reply. When the reply arrives, the application displays it in the client area of the application window.

Project Overview

The Finger client project consists of 11 main files along with associated include files. The set of main files is shown in Table 7.1.

Table 7.1 Main files in the Finger client project

File	Description	Reference
CASYNCDB.CPP	Asynchronous database lookup base class	Listing 6.6
CFINGOBJ.CPP	A class to implement the Finger protocol	Listing 7.5
CHOST.CPP	Host information lookup class	Listing 6.8
CSOCKADR.CPP	Internet address class	Listing 6.4
CSOCKET.CPP	Stream socket class	Listing 6.12
CTL3DV2.LIB	Import library for the 3D controls DLL	On CD-ROM in binary format
CWINSOCK.CPP	The CWinsock class and other infrastructure functions and classes	Listing 6.2
FINGER.CPP	The main application file for the Finger client application	Listing 7.1
FINGER.DEF	Linker definition file for the Finger client project	Listing 7.2
FINGER.RC	Resources for the Finger client application	Listing 7.3
WINSOCK.LIB	Import library for WINSOCK.DLL	On CD-ROM in binary format

The companion CD-ROM provides project files for Borland C++ (FINGER.IDE) and Microsoft Visual C++ (FINGER.MAK) environments. If you use the integrated development environments associated with each of these compilers, you can simply open the appropriate project file and compile. If you use the command-line version of either of these compilers or another compiler tool-set, you'll have to create the appropriate make file or project file for the environment.

Starting Up Winsock

Listing 7.1 shows the source code for the main Finger client application. The code that implements the user interface is standard Windows code. Windows Sockets is started using a global object of the **CWinsock** class:

```
CWinsock      g_wsWinsock(0x0101, 0x0101);
```

The parameters of the **CWinsock** constructor specify the minimum and maximum versions of the Winsock specification that the application can tolerate. **CWinsock** automatically calls **WSAStartup** in its constructor and compares the supplied version numbers to the version numbers in the **WSADATA** structure returned by **WSAStartup**. If the version numbers returned by **WSAStartup** are incompatible with the version numbers supplied by the application, the **CWinsock** constructor stores **WSAVERNOTSUPPORTED** as the startup error code. Note that **WSAVERNOTSUPPORTED** may be forced as the error type even when **WSAStartup** returns 0, if the Windows Sockets implementation cannot support the minimum version desired by the application.

Later, in the **WinMain** function, the application calls the **InitWinsock** function. The **InitWinsock** function checks the error code stored in the **g_wsWinsock** object to ensure that the Windows Sockets implementation started correctly. If Windows Sockets started correctly, the **InitWinsock** function calls **WSCCreateEventWindow** to create the hidden window, which will be used to receive and dispatch Windows Sockets asynchronous event messages. Next, **InitWinsock** looks up the service port number for the Finger service using a *blocking* call:

```
struct servent FAR * lpBuffer  = getservbyname("finger", "tcp");
```

To prevent the application from initializing and allowing the user to try to connect, the mouse is captured in the **WinMain** function around the call to

InitWinsock. This step prevents the user from choosing the Connect... menu item while the application is blocking in the **getservbyname** function in **InitWinsock.** Remember that although the **getservbyname** call blocks, window message dispatching is still occurring, even to our application. Capturing the mouse simply cuts off all meaningful events for a short time while the service lookup completes, as follows:

```
// Since initializing Winsock can take some time (because we
// get the default Finger port using blocking calls), put
// up an hourglass cursor so the user knows we're working on
// something and not just out to lunch.
 SetCapture(g_hFrame);
 SetCursor(LoadCursor(NULL, IDC_WAIT));

// Make sure Winsock initialized and get the event dispatch
// mechanism up and running.
 if (!InitWinsock(g_hFrame, hInstance, hPrevInstance)) {
    ReleaseCapture();
    return 0;
}

 ReleaseCapture();
```

When **InitWinsock** returns, Windows Sockets has been initialized and the default port for the Finger service has been obtained. The application then enters its normal message loop and dispatches messages appropriately.

Starting Finger

When the user selects the Connect menu item, the real work begins. Choosing Connect causes the **OnNetworkConnect** function to be called.

The **OnNetworkConnect** function first puts up the Connect dialog box. The Connect dialog box, shown in Figure 7.2, allows the user to enter the name of the remote server, the port on which to contact the server, and the Finger protocol user text string. When the user fills in the information correctly and selects the OK button, the dialog box returns, and the **OnNetworkConnect** function passes the host name, port number, and user text string to a newly created **CFingerObj** object. The creation of the **CFingerObj** starts the Finger protocol.

The **OnNetworkConnect** function disables the Connect menu item and prevents the user from selecting it until the previous Finger query ends. Although the **CFingerObj** uses the asynchronous Winsock API, which allows more than one network operation to be in progress at once, the application we've implemented is an SDI application. We disable the menu choice because of user interface limitations, not because of Winsock limitations. We could easily create a Multiple Document Interface (MDI) application that allows more than one Finger query to be in progress at once. Our **CFingerObj** class could be used for the MDI application, as well.

If the user selects the Cancel button in the connect dialog box, the **OnNetworkConnect** function simply returns without creating the Finger object or disabling the Connect menu item.

Implementing Finger: CFingerObj

Our implementation of the Finger protocol will be done in a separate C++ class named **CFingerObj**. This class encapsulates all knowledge of the Finger protocol, as well as the interactions needed with Windows Sockets and the Windows Sockets asynchronous message dispatch system described in Chapter 6. Figure 7.3 shows the usage model for the **CFingerObj** class, as implemented in Listings 7.4 and 7.5.

When the application wants to perform a Finger protocol query, it creates a **CFingerObj** object, and passes the remote server name, Finger port number, and user text as parameters to the **CFingerObj** constructor. Additional parameters to the constructor include a window that requires a message when the object finishes its work, the message to send, and the application instance handle. Some of the error reporting routines in the object use the instance handle to access the string table that contains the text of the Winsock error messages.

Figure 7.3

The CFingerObj class usage model.

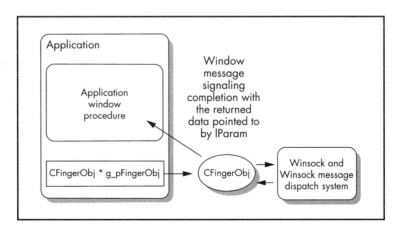

When the object completes the Finger protocol query, it sends a message to the window specified in the constructor. The **lParam** of the message points to a series of text lines returned from the remote server in response to the query. The application then deletes the object and displays the text returned from the server in the application window.

Note that the interaction between the **CFingerObj** class and the application is minimal. This design makes the **CFingerObj** very reusable. You can include it in various projects without a great deal of rework to the application. The application only needs to start Winsock, create the Finger object, and process the results returned from the server.

Implementing Finger as a State Machine

The actual Finger protocol is implemented by **CFingerObj** using a state machine, the Winsock classes described in Chapter 6, and the Winsock asynchronous extension API. Implementing the Finger protocol as a state machine makes the implementation fairly easy. Figure 7.4 shows the basic structure of the system.

Figure 7.4

CFingerObj state-machine implementation.

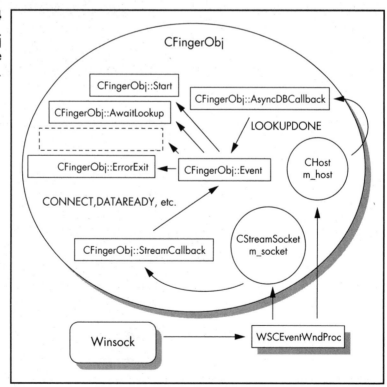

As Figure 7.4 shows, the **CFingerObj** class uses two other objects: **CHost** and **CStreamSocket**, to get much of its work done. The **CHost** object looks up the address of the remote server using the host name passed to the **CFingerObj** constructor. The **CStreamSocket** class sends the user text to the remote server and retrieves the response text.

We described both the **CHost** and **CStreamSocket** classes in Chapter 6. They interface with the message dispatch system also described in Chapter 6. The **CFingerObj** class inherits the **CAsyncDBCallback** and **CStreamCallback** abstract classes. The **CAsyncDBCallback** and **CStreamCallback** classes provide the **CFingerObj** class with two interfaces that the **CHost** and **CStreamSocket** classes invoke to communicate certain events. Examples of such events are that the host lookup is complete or that data has arrived at the socket to be read. The specific interface functions are **AsyncDBCallback** and **StreamCallback**.

The **CFingerObj** class provides implementations of the **AsyncDBCallback** and **StreamCallback** functions, which turn the callbacks from the **CHost** and **CStreamSocket** objects into state-machine events. Specifically, the **AsyncDBCallback** and **StreamCallback** functions invoke the **Event** function with an event code. The **Event** function then dispatches the event to an appropriate function that implements one state of the state machine. The **Event** function works as follows:

```
void CFingerObj::Event(EVENT ev)
{
    m_evEvent = ev;

    BOOL bContinue = FALSE;

    do {
        switch (m_stState) {
            case START:
                bContinue = Start(m_evEvent);
                break;
            case AWAITLOOKUP:
                bContinue = AwaitLookup(m_evEvent);
                break;
            case MAKECONNECTION:
                bContinue = MakeConnection(m_evEvent);
                break;
            case AWAITCONNECTION:
                bContinue = AwaitConnection(m_evEvent);
                break;
```

```
          case CONNECTED:
                  bContinue = Connected(m_evEvent);
                  break;
            case AWAITDATA:
                  bContinue = AwaitData(m_evEvent);
                  break;
            case CLOSED:
                  bContinue = Closed(m_evEvent);
                  break;
            case ERROREXIT:
                  bContinue = ErrorExit(m_evEvent);
                  break;
            case FINISH:
                  bContinue = FALSE;
                  break;
        }
     } while (bContinue);
}
```

Each state in the state machine, except the Finish state, has a corresponding state function. The **Event** function is simply a large switch statement that dispatches the event to the appropriate function. The state function returns a Boolean value that determines whether the state machine should continue to the next state after visiting the current state. The **m_stState** variable holds the current state of the machine. To move the machine to a following state, a state function changes the **m_stState** variable to the appropriate value. The **m_evEvent** variable holds the event that is examined by each state function.

State Machine Description

The state machine implemented in the **CFingerObj** class is fairly simple. It consists of nine states with six possible input events. Figure 7.5 shows the state machine and the possible transitions between the states. The possible input events are defined by this set of enumerated constants:

```
enum EVENT { NULLEVENT, LOOKUPDONE, CLOSE, CONNECT, DATAREADY,
        DATASENT };
```

These events are generated by the **AsyncDBCallback** and **StreamCallback** functions in response to callbacks from the **CHost** and **CStreamSocket** objects that the **CFingerObj** class uses. The **AsyncDBCallback** function generates the **LOOKUPDONE** event when a host lookup completes. The other events, except

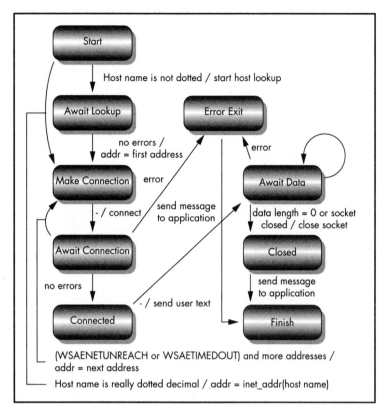

Figure 7.5

Finger client state machine.

for **NULLEVENT**, are generated by the **StreamCallback** function to indicate changes in the **CStreamSocket** object state. The **NULLEVENT** event is generated by other states in the machine when the **Event** function should continue to the following state. **NULLEVENT** indicates that the current event was consumed by the machine and that there is no event for the next state.

Some states respond to specific events and ignore any other events. Other states, notably Make Connection and Connected, simply fall through to the next state without needing another event.

Start

The Start state is entered when the **CFingerObj** constructor is called. The Start state examines the remote host name passed to the **CFingerObj** constructor to determine whether it is really a host name or an Internet address in dotted-decimal format. If the host name is really a host name, the Start state begins the host lookup processing using the **CHost** object and transitions the state machine to the Await Lookup state.

If the host name is really a dotted-decimal address, the machine sets the connection address to the dotted-decimal address and transitions the state machine to the Make Connection state.

Await Lookup

The Await Lookup state waits for the **LOOKUPDONE** event. When a **LOOKUPDONE** event arrives, indicating that the host lookup is complete, the Await Lookup state examines the error code returned as the result of the lookup. If no errors occurred, the Await Lookup state sets the connection address to the first host address for the remote host in the host data. It then transitions the machine to the Make Connection state.

If an error occurred as the result of the host lookup, the Await Lookup state transitions the machine to the Error Exit state.

Make Connection

The Make Connection state does not wait for any events. It simply starts the process of trying to connect the **CStreamSocket** object to the remote host, using the Internet address found in the host data or the result of converting a dotted-decimal address that was passed in the host name string. After starting the connection process on the socket, the Make Connection state transitions the machine to the Await Connection state.

Await Connection

The Await Connection state waits for the result of the socket connection attempt. When a **CONNECT** event arrives, the Await Connection state examines the error code produced as a result. If there are no errors, the machine transitions to the Connected state.

An error during a connection attempt triggers one of two outcomes. If the error is **WSAENETUNREACH** or **WSAETIMEDOUT**, the Await Connection state determines if the host has more than one Internet address. Some high-availability servers have more than one network interface (known as being "multi-homed"). The error may be with the particular network interface that the previous connection attempted to use. If more addresses exist for the host, the Await Connection state sets the connection address to the next address in the host data and transitions back to the Make Connection state. The behavior continues until the host addresses are exhausted or a connection is made.

If the connection result was an error and the error code was not **WSAENETUNREACH** or **WSAETIMEDOUT**, the machine transitions to the Error Exit state.

Connected

The Connected state responds unconditionally to all events, even **NULLEVENT**. It simply sends the user text string to the remote host using the connected socket. The machine then transitions to the Await Data state.

Await Data

The Await Data state captures the response text sent back to **CFingerObj** from the remote server. The Await Data state responds to the **DATAREADY** and **CLOSE** events. The **DATAREADY** event is sent when data arrives at the socket, or when data is read from the socket but more data still remains on the receive queue. As the data arrives, the Await Data state collects it and scans for a CRLF pair, which marks the end of a line of text. As lines of text are identified, they are stored in memory for later return to the main application. The machine remains in the Await Data state as long as the socket is not closed and no error occurs.

The Await Data state knows that the other end of the connection is closed when it responds to a **DATAREADY** event and finds that either no data can be read from the socket or the **CLOSE** event arrived. The local end of the connection is then closed and the machine transitions to the Closed state.

If an error occurs while the response text from the server is arriving, the state machine transitions to the Error Exit state.

Closed

The Closed state is entered when the Await Data state receives an indication that the socket was closed. At this point, all the response data from the remote Finger server is collected. The Closed state manipulates the data structures that were allocated to hold the data and sends a message back to the application indicating that the **CFingerObj** object has completed its work. In the **wParam** of the window message, the Close state indicates the number of lines of text returned from the remote server. The **lParam** points to an array of character pointers, which in turn point to the lines of text.

After the window message is sent, the state machine transitions to the Finish state.

Finish

The Finish state is the terminal state of the state machine. The state is not implemented with a separate function, but rather handled with code in the **Event** function. The Finish state simply swallows all events that are fed to it. This step precludes events arriving after an error condition. The Finish state has no transitions. The state machine cannot be restarted once it reaches the Finish state. To perform another Finger lookup, the application must create another **CFingerObj** object.

Error Exit

The Error Exit state can be entered from several states when an error occurs. The Error Exit state simply performs any necessary cleanup and sends a message to the application window indicating that no lines of text were received. Error messages are printed in the state when the error is recognized, before transitioning to the Error Exit state. After the internal data structures are cleaned up and the message is sent to the application, the machine transitions to the Finish state.

Summary

The event-driven nature of the asynchronous Winsock extension API works well with the implementation of protocols as high-level state machines. In this chapter, we explored the design of a Finger protocol client.

We implemented the Finger protocol in a self-contained object class, **CFingerObj**. The **CFingerObj** class used **CHost** and **CStreamSocket** objects, described in Chapter 6, to perform much of the work of host lookup and socket management. The **CHost** and **CStreamSocket** objects receive callback messages from the Winsock event dispatch system that we developed in Chapter 6.

The **CHost** and **CStreamSocket** objects then perform callbacks to **CFingerObj** using the interfaces it inherited from the **CAsyncDBCallback** and **CStreamCallback** classes. **CFingerObj** overrides the **AsyncDBCallback** and

StreamCallback functions. They take the incoming callbacks and turn them into events for the Finger protocol state machine. When the **CFingerObj** class completes its work, it sends a window message back to the application. The parameters of the window message identify the location and size of the response text returned from the remote Finger server.

The **CFingerObj** class encapsulates the Finger protocol implementation within a single reusable class. You can easily add the Finger protocol to almost any program with very little modification to the main program.

We will use the state machine implementation technique to implement other protocols in later chapters. We'll see how to use this technique to implement protocols for mail transmission and reception, and network news reading.

Listings

This section includes the following listings for the files that are necessary for our Finger client project:

Listing 7.1 shows the main application file, FINGER.CPP.
Listing 7.2 is the linker definition file, FINGER.DEF.
Listing 7.3 is the Finger client application resource file, FINGER.RC.
Listing 7.4 is the header file for the **CFingerObj** class, CFINGOBJ.H.
Listing 7.5 is the implementation file for the **CFingerObj** class, CFINGOBJ.CPP.

Listing 7.1 FINGER.CPP

```
/*
    File: FINGER.CPP
    Description:
        A simple client that implements the Finger protocol.
    Copyright 1995, David G. Roberts
*/

#include <windows.h>
#include <windowsx.h>
#include "ctl3d.h"
#include "winsock.h"
#include "cfingobj.h"
#include "finger.rh"
#include "myassert.h"

/*
    CONSTANTS
```

```
*/
#define DEFAULT_FINGER_PORT 79
#define WM_FINGERDONE      WM_USER

/*
    MACROS
*/
#define min(a, b) (((a) < (b)) ? (a) : (b))
#define max(a, b) (((a) > (b)) ? (a) : (b))
// Microsoft Visual C++ 1.5 WINDOWSX.H doesn't include this macro,
// so define it
#ifndef GET_WM_COMMAND_ID
#ifdef WIN32
#define GET_WM_COMMAND_ID(wp, lp)   LOWORD(wp)
#else
#define GET_WM_COMMAND_ID(wp, lp)   (wp)
#endif
#endif


/*
    TYPES
*/
typedef int INT;
typedef BOOL FAR * LPBOOL;

/*
    GLOBAL VARIABLES
*/
#ifdef WIN32
#define WINVERSION "32"
#else
#define WINVERSION "16"
#endif
char        g_szAppName[] = "FINGER";
char        g_szFullAppName[] = "Finger Client (Win" WINVERSION ")";
HWND        g_hFrame;
HINSTANCE   g_hInstance;
char *      g_pszHost;
u_short     g_ushPort;
u_short     g_ushDefaultPort;
char *      g_pszUser;
CWinsock    g_wsWinsock(0x0101, 0x0101);
char **     g_ppszFingerLines = NULL;
int         g_iNumLines = 0;
int         g_iLineHeight;
int         g_iClientHeight;
CFingerObj* g_pFingerObj = NULL;

/*
    FUNCTION PROTOTYPES
*/
void        CleanupInstance(HINSTANCE);
BOOL CALLBACK ConnectDlgProc(HWND, UINT, WPARAM, LPARAM);
LRESULT CALLBACK FrameWndProc(HWND, UINT, WPARAM, LPARAM);
```

```
BOOL        InitWinsock(HWND, HINSTANCE, HINSTANCE);
BOOL        InitApp(HINSTANCE);
BOOL        InitInstance(HINSTANCE);
void        InitError(void);
INT WINAPI  WinMain(HANDLE, HANDLE, LPSTR, INT);

/*
    MESSAGE HANDLER PROTOTYPES
*/
void    OnCommand(HWND, int, HWND, UINT);
void    OnFingerDone(HWND, WPARAM, LPARAM);
void    OnKey(HWND, UINT, BOOL, int, UINT);
void    OnPaint(HWND);
BOOL    OnSetCursor(HWND, HWND, UINT, UINT);
void    OnSize(HWND, UINT, int, int);
void    OnVScroll(HWND, HWND, UINT, int);

/*
    WM_COMMAND HANDLER PROTOTYPES
*/
void    OnFileExit(HWND);
void    OnHelpAbout(HWND);
void    OnNetworkConnect(HWND);


/***********************************************************************
    WINMAIN
***********************************************************************/


/*
    Function: WinMain
    Description:
        Good ol' WinMain.
*/
INT WINAPI WinMain(HINSTANCE hInstance, HINSTANCE hPrevInstance,
    LPSTR lpszCmdParam, INT nCmdShow)
{
    UNUSED_PARAMETER(lpszCmdParam);

    // Save our instance handle for later.
    g_hInstance = hInstance;

    // If no other instance is running, initialize the application
    // window classes.
    if (!hPrevInstance) {
        if (!InitApp(hInstance)) {
            InitError();
            return 0;
        }
    }

    // Initialize all instance-specific stuff.  In particular, create
    // the frame window.
```

```
    if (!InitInstance(hInstance)) {
        InitError();
        return 0;
    }

    // Since initializing Winsock can take some time (because we
    // get the default Finger port using blocking calls), put
    // up an hourglass cursor so the user knows we're working on
    // something and not just out to lunch.
    SetCapture(g_hFrame);
    SetCursor(LoadCursor(NULL, IDC_WAIT));

    // Make sure Winsock initialized and get the event dispatch
    // mechanism up and running.
    if (!InitWinsock(g_hFrame, hInstance, hPrevInstance)) {
        ReleaseCapture();
        return 0;
    }

    ReleaseCapture();

    // Show the frame window and cause it to be repainted.
    ShowWindow(g_hFrame, nCmdShow);
    UpdateWindow(g_hFrame);

    // Do the message loop.
    MSG msg;
    while (GetMessage((LPMSG)&msg, NULL, 0, 0)) {
        TranslateMessage(&msg);
        DispatchMessage(&msg);
    }

    // Clean up before we exit.
    CleanupInstance(hInstance);

    return msg.wParam;
}


/*
    Function: InitError
    Description:
        Handles putting up a message box for the application if it
        cannot be initialized.
*/
void InitError(void)
{
    char szMessage[80];

    wsprintf(szMessage, "ERROR: Cannot initialize %s.",
        (LPSTR)g_szFullAppName);
    // Use NULL for hwnd because application probably doesn't have
    // its window created yet.
```

```
        MessageBox(NULL, szMessage, g_szAppName, MB_ICONSTOP | MB_OK);
}


/*
    Function: InitApp
    Description:
        Registers the application's window classes and performs
        initialization that must be done for all application
        instances.  The function returns TRUE if successful and no
        errors occur, and FALSE otherwise.
*/
BOOL InitApp(HINSTANCE hInstance)
{
    WNDCLASS wc;
    BOOL bResult;

    wc.style           = CS_HREDRAW | CS_VREDRAW; // class style
    wc.lpfnWndProc     = FrameWndProc;            // window proc
    wc.cbClsExtra      = 0;                        // no extra
    wc.cbWndExtra      = 0;                        // no extra
    wc.hInstance       = hInstance;               // class owner
    wc.hIcon           = LoadIcon(hInstance, g_szAppName); // icon
    wc.hCursor         = LoadCursor(NULL, IDC_ARROW); // cursor
    wc.hbrBackground   = (HBRUSH) GetStockObject(WHITE_BRUSH); // bg
    wc.lpszMenuName    = g_szAppName; // menu resource name
    wc.lpszClassName   = g_szAppName; // window class name

    bResult = RegisterClass(&wc);

    return bResult;
}


/*
    Function: InitInstance
    Description:
        Performs instance specific initialization, like the creation
        of the frame window, etc.  The function returns TRUE if
        successful and no errors occur, and FALSE otherwise.
*/
BOOL InitInstance(HINSTANCE hInstance)
{
    g_hFrame = CreateWindow(
        g_szAppName,                       // window class name
        g_szFullAppName,                   // window title text
        WS_OVERLAPPEDWINDOW | WS_VSCROLL,  // window style
        CW_USEDEFAULT, CW_USEDEFAULT,      // position = default
        CW_USEDEFAULT, CW_USEDEFAULT,      // size = default
        NULL,                              // no parent window
        NULL,                              // menu = window class default
        hInstance,                         // window owner
        NULL);                             // no additional creation data
```

```
    if (!g_hFrame)
        return FALSE;

    // Initialize Microsoft 3D controls (CTL3D)
    Ctl3dRegister(hInstance);
    Ctl3dAutoSubclass(hInstance);

    return TRUE;
}


/*
    Function: InitWinsock
    Description:
        Make sure Winsock is up and running and that the Winsock event
        dispatch window is created.  Further, preform any actions that
        have to take place before the application window is created.
*/
BOOL InitWinsock(HWND hwnd, HINSTANCE hInstance,
    HINSTANCE hPrevInstance)
{
    // Make sure that we didn't have any problems
    // starting up Winsock.
    if (g_wsWinsock.LastError() != WSANOERROR) {
        ReportWSAError("Error: Can't startup Winsock.",
            g_wsWinsock.LastError(), NULL, hInstance);
        return FALSE;
    }

    // Create the Winsock message dispatch window.
    if (!WSCCreateEventWindow(hInstance, hPrevInstance)) {
        MessageBox(hwnd,
            "Error: Could not create the Winsock message window.",
            "Winsock Error", MB_OK | MB_ICONEXCLAMATION);
        return FALSE;
    }


    // Look up the default port for Finger service.  Note that we'll
    // use a blocking call here since we're only doing this at
    // startup and won't need to have two of these going at once.
    struct servent FAR * lpBuffer  = getservbyname("finger", "tcp");
    if (lpBuffer == NULL) {
        // Potential problem.
        int iError = WSAGetLastError();
        if (iError == WSANO_DATA) {
            // No big deal, we just couldn't find an entry for Finger
            // in the services database.  Use the normal default
            // finger port.
            g_ushDefaultPort = DEFAULT_FINGER_PORT;
        }
        else {
            // Whoa!  Real problem of some sort.  Signal it.
            ReportWSAError(
                "Error looking up Finger service port number",
```

```
                    iError, hwnd, hInstance);
                return FALSE;
            }
        }
        else {
            // No problem, so get the port number from the buffer
            // structure. Remember that the port is in network byte
            // order!!
            g_ushDefaultPort = ntohs(lpBuffer->s_port);
        }
        g_ushPort = g_ushDefaultPort;    // Current port is the default.

        return TRUE;
}


/*
    Function: CleanupInstance
    Description:
        Do any instance specific clean up before the application
        quits.
*/
void CleanupInstance(HINSTANCE hInstance)
{
    // Clean up Microsoft 3D controls (CTL3D)
    Ctl3dUnregister(hInstance);
}

/**********************************************************************
    WINDOW AND DIALOG PROCS
**********************************************************************/

/*
    Function: FrameWndProc
    Description:
        Window procedure for the application frame window.
*/
LRESULT CALLBACK FrameWndProc(HWND hwnd, UINT msg, WPARAM wParam,
    LPARAM lParam)
{
    HDC hdc;
    TEXTMETRIC tm;

    switch (msg) {
        case WM_CREATE:
            // Initialize the host and user strings.
            g_pszHost = new char[1];
            g_pszHost[0] = '\0';
            g_pszUser = new char[1];
            g_pszUser[0] = '\0';
            // Figure out the height of the text.
            hdc = GetDC(hwnd);
            SelectObject(hdc, GetStockObject(SYSTEM_FIXED_FONT));
```

```
                GetTextMetrics(hdc, &tm);
                g_iLineHeight = tm.tmHeight;
                ReleaseDC(hwnd, hdc);
                return 0;
        HANDLE_MSG(hwnd, WM_COMMAND, OnCommand);
        HANDLE_MSG(hwnd, WM_KEYDOWN, OnKey);
        HANDLE_MSG(hwnd, WM_PAINT, OnPaint);
        HANDLE_MSG(hwnd, WM_SETCURSOR, OnSetCursor);
        HANDLE_MSG(hwnd, WM_SIZE, OnSize);
        HANDLE_MSG(hwnd, WM_VSCROLL, OnVScroll);
        case WM_DESTROY:
            // Delete all the finger text.
            if (g_ppszFingerLines != NULL) {
                // Delete the text of each line.
                for (int i = 0; i < g_iNumLines; i++)
                    delete[] g_ppszFingerLines[i];
                // Delete the block of line pointers.
                delete[] g_ppszFingerLines;
            }
            PostQuitMessage(0);
            return 0;
        case WM_FINGERDONE:
            OnFingerDone(hwnd, wParam, lParam);
            return 0;
        default:
            return DefWindowProc(hwnd, msg, wParam, lParam);
    }
}


/*
    Function: ConnectDlgProc
    Description:
        Dialog proc for the connect dialog.
*/
BOOL CALLBACK ConnectDlgProc(HWND hwndDlg, UINT msg, WPARAM wParam,
    LPARAM lParam)
{
    int     id;
    BOOL    bTranslated;
    unsigned uPort;
    int     nLen;

    UNUSED_PARAMETER(lParam);

    switch (msg) {
        case WM_INITDIALOG:
            // Initialize dialog edit boxes with info from last time.
            SetDlgItemText(hwndDlg, IDD_HOST, g_pszHost);

            // Set the dialog box focus to the host name edit box and
            // select all the text in it so that the user can simply
            // type over the old name if so desired.
            SetFocus(GetDlgItem(hwndDlg, IDD_HOST));
            Edit_SetSel(GetDlgItem(hwndDlg, IDD_HOST), 0, -1);
```

```
                // Set port value text using SetDlgItemInt to do the
                // int->text conversion for us.
                SetDlgItemInt(hwndDlg, IDD_PORT, g_ushPort, FALSE);

                // Set the user name string.
                SetDlgItemText(hwndDlg, IDD_USER, g_pszUser);

                // Return FALSE because we set the focus to the host edit
                // box control.
                return FALSE;
        case WM_COMMAND:
                // Explode wParam and lParam into constituent parts.
                id = GET_WM_COMMAND_ID(wParam, lParam);
                switch (id) {
                    case IDOK:
                        // Retrieve the port number first.  Use a
                        // temporary first, just in case things don't go
                        // well.
                        uPort = GetDlgItemInt(hwndDlg, IDD_PORT,
                            (LPBOOL) &bTranslated, FALSE);
                        // If things didn't go well, set the focus to the
                        // port edit box, select all the text in it, and
                        // beep.
                        if (!bTranslated) {
                            SetFocus(GetDlgItem(hwndDlg, IDD_PORT));
                            Edit_SetSel(GetDlgItem(hwndDlg, IDD_PORT),
                                0, -1);
                            MessageBeep(MB_ICONHAND);
                            return TRUE;
                        }
                        // Get the text length from the host edit box.
                        nLen = Edit_GetTextLength(GetDlgItem(hwndDlg,
                            IDD_HOST));
                        // If the user has given us a blank string, set
                        // the focus back to the edit box and beep.
                        if (nLen == 0) {
                            SetFocus(GetDlgItem(hwndDlg, IDD_HOST));
                            Edit_SetSel(GetDlgItem(hwndDlg, IDD_HOST),
                                0, -1);
                            MessageBeep(MB_ICONHAND);
                            return TRUE;
                        }
                        // Retrieve the host and user text and update the
                        // g_ushPort variable with the temporary.
                        delete[] g_pszHost;
                        g_pszHost = new char[nLen + 1];
                        GetDlgItemText(hwndDlg, IDD_HOST, g_pszHost,
                            nLen + 1);
                        nLen = Edit_GetTextLength(GetDlgItem(hwndDlg,
                            IDD_USER));
                        delete[] g_pszUser;
                        g_pszUser = new char[nLen + 1];
```

```
                GetDlgItemText(hwndDlg, IDD_USER, g_pszUser,
                    nLen + 1);
                g_ushPort = (u_short)uPort;
                EndDialog(hwndDlg, TRUE);
                return TRUE;
            case IDCANCEL:
                EndDialog(hwndDlg, FALSE);
                return TRUE;
            case IDD_DEFAULTPORT:
                // Set the port edit text to the default.
                SetDlgItemInt(hwndDlg, IDD_PORT, g_ushDefaultPort,
                    FALSE);
                return TRUE;
        } // switch (id)
    } // switch (msg)
    return FALSE;
}


/**********************************************************************
    WINDOW MESSAGE HANDLERS
**********************************************************************/

/*
    Function: OnCommand
    Description:
        Handle WM_COMMAND messages.
*/
void OnCommand(HWND hwnd, int id, HWND hwndCtl, UINT codeNotify)
{
    // Dispatch command
    switch (id) {
        case IDM_FILEEXIT:
            OnFileExit(hwnd);
            break;
        case IDM_FILECONNECT:
            OnNetworkConnect(hwnd);
            break;
        case IDM_HELPABOUT:
            OnHelpAbout(hwnd);
            break;
        default:
        // ...Or let DefWindowProc handle it if it's not ours
        FORWARD_WM_COMMAND(hwnd, id, hwndCtl, codeNotify,
            DefWindowProc);
    }
}


/*
    Function: OnFingerDone
    Description:
        Handle a WM_FINGERDONE message sent by the Finger object
        when it's done with a lookup.  The wParam contains the number
```

```
                  of lines of data and the lParam contains a pointer to an
                  array of character pointers to the actual null-terminated
                  lines.
*/
void OnFingerDone(HWND hwnd, WPARAM wParam, LPARAM lParam)
{
      ASSERT(g_pFingerObj != NULL);

      // Delete the Finger object, set the cursor back to normal, and
      // enable the File|Connect menu choice once again.
      delete g_pFingerObj;
      g_pFingerObj = NULL;
      SetCursor(LoadCursor(NULL, IDC_ARROW));
      EnableMenuItem(GetMenu(hwnd), IDM_FILECONNECT, MF_ENABLED);
      // First delete the old data.
      if (g_ppszFingerLines != NULL) {
          // Delete the text of each line.
          for (int i = 0; i < g_iNumLines; i++)
              delete[] g_ppszFingerLines[i];
          // Delete the block of line pointers.
          delete[] g_ppszFingerLines;
      }
      // Make the new data active.
      g_ppszFingerLines = (char **) lParam;
      g_iNumLines = (int) wParam;
      // Update the vertical scroll bar.
      SetScrollRange(hwnd, SB_VERT, 0, g_iNumLines - 1, FALSE);
      SetScrollPos(hwnd, SB_VERT, 0, TRUE);
      // Force our window to update.
      InvalidateRect(hwnd, NULL, TRUE);
}


void OnKey(HWND hwnd, UINT vk, BOOL fDown, int cRepeat, UINT flags)
{
      UNUSED_PARAMETER(fDown);

      // Translate keystrokes to appropriate scroll messages.
      switch (vk) {
          case VK_HOME:
              SendMessage(hwnd, WM_VSCROLL, SB_TOP, 0L);
              break;
          case VK_END:
              SendMessage(hwnd, WM_VSCROLL, SB_BOTTOM, 0L);
              break;
          case VK_UP:
              SendMessage(hwnd, WM_VSCROLL, SB_LINEUP, 0L);
              break;
          case VK_DOWN:
              SendMessage(hwnd, WM_VSCROLL, SB_LINEDOWN, 0L);
              break;
          case VK_PRIOR:
              SendMessage(hwnd, WM_VSCROLL, SB_PAGEUP, 0L);
              break;
          case VK_NEXT:
```

```
                SendMessage(hwnd, WM_VSCROLL, SB_PAGEDOWN, OL);
                break;
            default:
                FORWARD_WM_KEYDOWN(hwnd, vk, cRepeat, flags,
                    DefWindowProc);
                break;
        }
}


/*
    Function: OnPaint
    Description:
        Handler for WM_PAINT messages.
*/
void OnPaint(HWND hwnd)
{
    PAINTSTRUCT ps;
    HDC hdc = BeginPaint(hwnd, &ps);
    if (g_iNumLines > 0) {
        SelectObject(hdc, GetStockObject(SYSTEM_FIXED_FONT));
        RECT rect;
        GetClientRect(hwnd, &rect);
        int iLineY = rect.top;
        int iLineIndex = GetScrollPos(hwnd, SB_VERT);
        // Print all the text lines in the window, starting with
        // the top.
        while (iLineY <= rect.bottom && iLineIndex < g_iNumLines) {
            TabbedTextOut(hdc, rect.left, iLineY,
                g_ppszFingerLines[iLineIndex],
                lstrlen(g_ppszFingerLines[iLineIndex]),
                0, NULL, rect.left);
            iLineY += g_iLineHeight;
            iLineIndex++;
        }
    }
    EndPaint(hwnd, &ps);
}


/*
    Function: OnSetCursor
    Description:
        Set the cursor to an hour glass when it's in the client area
        and a lookup is in progress.
*/
BOOL OnSetCursor(HWND hwnd, HWND hwndCursor, UINT codeHitTest,
    UINT msg)
{
    UNUSED_PARAMETER(hwnd);
    UNUSED_PARAMETER(hwndCursor);
    UNUSED_PARAMETER(msg);

    // If a lookup is in progress and the cursor is in the client area
    // or the vertical scroll bar, change it to an hourglass.
```

```
        if (g_pFingerObj != NULL && (codeHitTest == HTCLIENT ||
            codeHitTest == HTVSCROLL)) {
            SetCursor(LoadCursor(NULL, IDC_WAIT));
            return TRUE;
        }
        else // Else pass the WM_SETCURSOR message to DefWindowProc.
            return FORWARD_WM_SETCURSOR(hwnd, hwndCursor, codeHitTest,
                msg, DefWindowProc);
}


/*
    Function: OnSize
    Description:
        Handle a WM_SIZE message.  In particular, store the
        vertical height to be used for calculating the number of lines
        to scroll when a page scroll is requested.
*/
void OnSize(HWND hwnd, UINT state, int cx, int cy)
{
    UNUSED_PARAMETER(hwnd);
    UNUSED_PARAMETER(state);
    UNUSED_PARAMETER(cx);

    // Save the client height for paging the scroll area when
    // processing WM_VSCROLL.
    g_iClientHeight = cy;
}


/*
    Description: OnVScroll
    Description:
        Handle scrolling of the Finger text in the client window.
        Note that this uses a very, very, very simple algorithm that
        repaints the entire client window each time a scroll occurs.
        This is pretty ugly and could be made more pretty using a
        spiffy algorithm that used ScrollWindow and just repainted the
        exposed portion of the client window following the scroll.
*/
void OnVScroll(HWND hwnd, HWND hwndCtl, UINT code, int pos)
{
    UNUSED_PARAMETER(hwndCtl);

    // If we're in progress on a lookup, the scroll bar is locked out.
    if (g_pFingerObj != NULL)
        return;

    int iCurrentPos = GetScrollPos(hwnd, SB_VERT);

    switch (code) {
        case SB_TOP:
            iCurrentPos = 0;
            break;
```

```
            case SB_BOTTOM:
                iCurrentPos = g_iNumLines - 1;
                break;
            case SB_LINEUP:
                iCurrentPos-;
                break;
            case SB_LINEDOWN:
                iCurrentPos++;
                break;
            case SB_PAGEUP:
                iCurrentPos -= g_iClientHeight / g_iLineHeight;
                break;
            case SB_PAGEDOWN:
                iCurrentPos += g_iClientHeight / g_iLineHeight;
                break;
            case SB_THUMBPOSITION:
                iCurrentPos = pos;
                break;
        }
        iCurrentPos = max(0, min(iCurrentPos, g_iNumLines - 1));
        if (iCurrentPos != GetScrollPos(hwnd, SB_VERT)) {
            SetScrollPos(hwnd, SB_VERT, iCurrentPos, TRUE);
            InvalidateRect(hwnd, NULL, TRUE);
        }
}


/***********************************************************************
    WM_COMMAND HANDLERS
***********************************************************************/

/*
    Function: OnFileExit
    Description:
        Exits the application in response to a IDM_FILEEXIT message.
*/
void OnFileExit(HWND hwnd)
{
    SendMessage(hwnd, WM_CLOSE, 0, 0L);
}


/*
    Function: OnHelpAbout
    Description:
        Pops up the "About..." dialog box in response to IDM_HELPABOUT
        command messages.
*/
void OnHelpAbout(HWND hwnd)
{
    char szTitle[100];
    char szInfo[200];

    wsprintf(szTitle, "About %s", (LPSTR)g_szFullAppName);
    wsprintf(szInfo, "%s\r\nCopyright \251 1995\r\n"
```

```
            "David G. Roberts\r\n\r\nAn example program from the book\r\n"
            "'Developing for the Internet with Windows Sockets'",
            (LPSTR)g_szFullAppName);
    MessageBox(hwnd, szInfo, szTitle, MB_OK);
}


/*

    Function: OnNetworkConnect
    Description:
        Pops up a dialog box to get the user's input regarding the
        host and port to connect to.
*/
void OnNetworkConnect(HWND hwnd)
{
    FARPROC lpfnConnect = MakeProcInstance((FARPROC) ConnectDlgProc,
        g_hInstance);
    BOOL bResult = DialogBox(g_hInstance, "CONNECT", hwnd,
        (DLGPROC) lpfnConnect);
    FreeProcInstance(lpfnConnect);
    if (bResult == FALSE)
        return;
    // We're off and running.  Gray out the "Connect" menu item so
    // that the user can't select it again before we're done.
    EnableMenuItem(GetMenu(hwnd), IDM_FILECONNECT, MF_GRAYED);
    g_pFingerObj = new CFingerObj(g_pszHost, g_ushPort, g_pszUser,
        hwnd, WM_FINGERDONE, g_hInstance);
}
```

Listing 7.2 FINGER.DEF

```
NAME        FINGER
DESCRIPTION 'Finger Client, Copyright 1995, David G. Roberts'
EXETYPE     WINDOWS
STUB        'WINSTUB.EXE'
CODE        PRELOAD MOVABLE DISCARDABLE
DATA        PRELOAD MOVABLE
HEAPSIZE    32768
STACKSIZE   8192
```

Listing 7.3 FINGER.RC

```
/************************************************************************



FINGER.RC

produced by Borland Resource Workshop



************************************************************************/

#include "finger.rh"
#include "errno.rc"
CONNECT DIALOG 32, 22, 219, 84
```

```
STYLE DS_MODALFRAME | WS_POPUP | WS_VISIBLE | WS_CAPTION | WS_SYSMENU
CAPTION "Connect"
FONT 8, "MS Sans Serif"
{
 DEFPUSHBUTTON "OK", IDOK, 160, 24, 50, 14
 PUSHBUTTON "Cancel", IDCANCEL, 160, 42, 50, 14
 LTEXT "Host:", -1, 12, 15, 20, 8
 LTEXT "Port:", -1, 12, 36, 16, 8
 LTEXT "User Name:", -1, 12, 62, 44, 8
 EDITTEXT IDD_HOST, 36, 13, 108, 12
 EDITTEXT IDD_PORT, 36, 34, 32, 12
 EDITTEXT IDD_USER, 56, 60, 88, 12
 PUSHBUTTON "Default Port", IDD_DEFAULTPORT, 88, 33, 56, 15
}
FINGER MENU
{
 POPUP "&File"
 {
  MENUITEM "&Connect...", IDM_FILECONNECT
  MENUITEM "E&xit", IDM_FILEEXIT
 }

 POPUP "&Help"
 {
  MENUITEM "&About...", IDM_HELPABOUT
 }

}

FINGER ICON "finger.ico"
```

Listing 7.4 CFINGOBJ.H

```
/*
    File: CFINGOBJ.H
    Description:
        An class to implement the finger protocol.
    Copyright 1995, David G. Roberts
*/

#ifndef _CFINGOBJ_H
#define _CFINGOBJ_H


#include <windows.h>
#include "winsock.h"
#ifndef _CSOCKADR_H
#include "csockadr.h"
#endif
#ifndef _CHOST_H
#include "chost.h"
#endif
#ifndef _CSOCKET_H
#include "csocket.h"
#endif
```

```
/*
    Class: CFingerObj
    Description:
        Implements the finger protocol.  Sends a program-defined
        message to a window when the protocol is complete along with
        the lines of text returned from the remote host.
*/
class CFingerObj : private CAsyncDBCallback, private CStreamCallback {
    enum STATE { START, AWAITLOOKUP, MAKECONNECTION, AWAITCONNECTION,
        CONNECTED, AWAITDATA, CLOSED, ERROREXIT, FINISH };
    enum EVENT { NULLEVENT, LOOKUPDONE, CLOSE, CONNECT, DATAREADY,
        DATASENT };
    enum CONSTANTS { BUFFER_QUANTUM = 128 };

    struct LineNode {
        LineNode *  m_plnNext;
        char *      m_pszLine;

        LineNode() : m_plnNext(NULL), m_pszLine(NULL) {};
    };

    char *      m_pszHost;
    u_short     m_ushPort;
    char *      m_pszUser;
    HWND        m_hwnd;
    int         m_iMessage;
    HINSTANCE   m_hInstance;
    STATE       m_stState;
    EVENT       m_evEvent;
    int         m_iError;
    char FAR *  m_lpSentBuffer;
    CSockAddr   m_saAddr;
    BOOL        m_bDotted;
    CHost       m_host;
    CStreamSocket m_stream;
    LineNode    m_lnHead;
    LineNode *  m_plnTail;
    char *      m_pDataBuffer;
    unsigned    m_uDataSize;
    unsigned    m_uBufferSize;

    // Event dispatch function.
    void Event(EVENT ev);
    // Functions for each state.
    BOOL Start(EVENT ev);
    BOOL AwaitLookup(EVENT ev);
    BOOL MakeConnection(EVENT ev);
    BOOL AwaitConnection(EVENT ev);
    BOOL Connected(EVENT ev);
    BOOL AwaitData(EVENT ev);
    BOOL Closed(EVENT ev);
    BOOL ErrorExit(EVENT ev);
```

```
    // Helpful error reporting function.
    void ErrorWithHostName(LPCSTR lpszTitle, LPCSTR lpszErrorMsg);

    // Callbacks.
    virtual void AsyncDBCallback(int iToken, int iError);
    virtual void StreamCallback(int iToken, STREAMEVENT iEvent,
        int iError, char FAR * lpBuffer);
public:
    CFingerObj(LPCSTR lpszHost, u_short ushPort, LPCSTR lpszUser,
        HWND hwnd, int iMessage, HINSTANCE hInstance);
    ~CFingerObj();
};

#endif
```

Listing 7.5 CFINGOBJ.CPP

```
/*
    File: CFINGOBJ.CPP
    Description:
        An class to implement the finger protocol.
    Copyright 1995, David G. Roberts
*/


#include "cfingobj.h"
#include "myassert.h"


/*
    Function: CFingerObj::CFingerObj
    Description:
        Constructor for the CFingerObj class. Stores the constructor
        parameters in class member variables and kicks off the
        state machine at the Start state.
*/
CFingerObj::CFingerObj(LPCSTR lpszHost, u_short ushPort,
    LPCSTR lpszUser, HWND hwnd, int iMessage, HINSTANCE hInstance)
    : m_pszHost(new char[lstrlen(lpszHost) + 1]), m_ushPort(ushPort),
    m_pszUser(new char[lstrlen(lpszUser) + 1]), m_hwnd(hwnd),
    m_iMessage(iMessage), m_hInstance(hInstance),
    m_stState(START), m_evEvent(NULLEVENT), m_stream(),
    m_plnTail(&m_lnHead),
    m_pDataBuffer(new char[BUFFER_QUANTUM]), m_uDataSize(0),
    m_uBufferSize(BUFFER_QUANTUM)
{
    m_stream.SetCallback(this, 0);
    lstrcpy(m_pszHost, lpszHost);
    lstrcpy(m_pszUser, lpszUser);
    Event(NULLEVENT);
}


/*
    Function: CFingerObj::~CFingerObj
```

```
        Description:
            Destructor for the CFingerObj class.  Simply deletes the
            memory which was allocated in the constructor.
*/
CFingerObj::~CFingerObj()
{
    delete[] m_pszHost;
    delete[] m_pszUser;
    delete[] m_pDataBuffer;
}


/*
    Function: CFingerObj::AsyncDBCallback
    Description:
        The function which handles the completion callback from
        the CHost object.  The error code from the host lookup
        is saved and a LOOKUPDONE event generated to the state
        machine.
*/
void CFingerObj::AsyncDBCallback(int iToken, int iError)
{
    UNUSED_PARAMETER(iToken);    // Eliminate the compiler warning.

    m_iError = iError;
    Event(LOOKUPDONE);
}


/*
    Function: CFingerObj::StreamCallback
    Description:
        This function receives callback from the CStreamSocket
        object.  The function turns the various CStreamSocket events
        into events for the CFingerObj state machine.
*/
void CFingerObj::StreamCallback(int iToken, STREAMEVENT iEvent,
    int iError, char FAR *lpBuffer)
{
    UNUSED_PARAMETER(iToken);    // Eliminate the compiler warning.

    m_iError = iError;
    m_lpSentBuffer = lpBuffer;
    switch (iEvent) {
        case CStreamCallback::SE_ACCEPT:
            // Error!  We are connecting to someone else, not
            // accepting connections from others.
            WSCFatalError(
            "Received SE_ACCEPT event in CFingerObj::StreamCallback");
        case CStreamCallback::SE_CLOSE:
            Event(CLOSE);
            break;
        case CStreamCallback::SE_CONNECT:
            Event(CONNECT);
```

```
            break;
        case CStreamCallback::SE_DATAREADY:
            Event(DATAREADY);
            break;
        case CStreamCallback::SE_DATASENT:
            Event(DATASENT);
            break;
        default:
            break;
    }
}


/*
    Function: CFingerObj::Event
    Description:
        The main function for the state machine.  It dispatches
        the input event to the appropriate state function.  If
        the state function returns TRUE, the machine continues to
        dispatch the event to the next function.  Presumably, the
        previous state function has set m_evEvent to NULLEVENT
        in order to "swallow" the prior event.
*/
void CFingerObj::Event(EVENT ev)
{
    m_evEvent = ev;

    BOOL bContinue = FALSE;

    do {
        switch (m_stState) {
            case START:
                bContinue = Start(m_evEvent);
                break;
            case AWAITLOOKUP:
                bContinue = AwaitLookup(m_evEvent);
                break;
            case MAKECONNECTION:
                bContinue = MakeConnection(m_evEvent);
                break;
            case AWAITCONNECTION:
                bContinue = AwaitConnection(m_evEvent);
                break;
            case CONNECTED:
                bContinue = Connected(m_evEvent);
                break;
            case AWAITDATA:
                bContinue = AwaitData(m_evEvent);
                break;
            case CLOSED:
                bContinue = Closed(m_evEvent);
                break;
            case ERROREXIT:
```

```
                    bContinue = ErrorExit(m_evEvent);
                    break;
                case FINISH:
                    bContinue = FALSE;
                    break;
            }
    } while (bContinue);
}


/*
    Function: CFingerObj::Start
    Description:
        The first function of the state machine.  Starts a host
        lookup for the host name given to the CFingerObj constructor.
*/
BOOL CFingerObj::Start(EVENT ev)
{
    int iError;
    UNUSED_PARAMETER(ev);    // Eliminate the compiler warning.

    // Note: this little test won't work when IPv6 is deployed
    // and IP addresses move to 128 bits.  We're assuming IP addresses
    // are 32 bits wide and can fit in a u_long.
    u_long addr = inet_addr(m_pszHost);
    // Note: the INADDR_NONE constant on the following line may
    // generate a warning.  Ignore it.  It's fine.
    if (addr == INADDR_NONE) {
        // Addr must be a host name. Kick off a lookup.
        m_bDotted = FALSE;
        iError = m_host.StartLookup(m_pszHost, this, 0);
        if (iError != WSANOERROR) {
            ReportWSAError(
                "Couldn't start a name lookup in CFingerObj::Start",
                iError, m_hwnd, m_hInstance);
            m_stState = ERROREXIT;
            m_evEvent = NULLEVENT;
            return TRUE;
        }
        m_stState = AWAITLOOKUP;
        return FALSE;
    }
    else {
        // Addr was in dotted decimal notation.
        m_bDotted = TRUE;
        addr = ntohl(addr);
        m_saAddr.Addr(addr);
        m_stState = MAKECONNECTION;
        m_evEvent = NULLEVENT;
        return TRUE;
    }
}
```

```
BOOL CFingerObj::AwaitLookup(EVENT ev)
{
    // We're only expecting a LOOKUPDONE event.
    if (ev != LOOKUPDONE)
        return FALSE;
    if (m_iError != WSANOERROR) {
        // Something didn't go right.
        if (m_iError == WSAHOST_NOT_FOUND || m_iError == WSANO_DATA ||
            m_iError == WSATRY_AGAIN) {
            // Okay, we couldn't find the name string in the database.
            // Use a nice dialog box to inform the user.
            ErrorWithHostName("Host Not Found",
                "Couldn't find an address for host '%s'.");
        }
        else {
            // Some other sort of error occurred.  Alert the user with
            // the more ugly dialog box.
            const char szFormat[] =
                "Unexpected error while looking up address "
                "for host '%s'.";
            char * pszMsg = new char[sizeof(szFormat) +
                lstrlen(m_pszHost) + 1];
            wsprintf(pszMsg, szFormat, (LPSTR)m_pszHost);
            ReportWSAError(pszMsg, m_iError, m_hwnd, m_hInstance);
            delete[] pszMsg;
        }
        m_stState = ERROREXIT;
        m_evEvent = NULLEVENT;
        return TRUE;
    }
    // Set our address to the first address from the host lookup.
    BOOL bResult;
    m_saAddr = m_host.FirstAddr(&bResult);
    if (bResult != TRUE) {
        MessageBox(m_hwnd, "Error accessing address after lookup.",
            "Error", MB_OK | MB_ICONEXCLAMATION);
        m_stState = ERROREXIT;
        m_evEvent = NULLEVENT;
        return TRUE;
    }
    m_stState = MAKECONNECTION;
    m_evEvent = NULLEVENT;
    return TRUE;
}


BOOL CFingerObj::MakeConnection(EVENT ev)
{
    UNUSED_PARAMETER(ev);    // Eliminate the compiler warning.

    // Okay, we've got our address.  Fill in the port and try to make
    // a connection.
    m_saAddr.Port(m_ushPort);
```

```
        int iError = m_stream.Connect(m_saAddr);
        if (iError != WSANOERROR && iError != WSAEWOULDBLOCK) {
            // Something went wrong.  We don't expect anything right here,
            // so don't bother making things too pretty.
            const char szFormat[] =
                "Error while connecting to foreign host '%s'.";
            char * pszMsg = new char[sizeof(szFormat) +
                lstrlen(m_pszHost) + 1];
            wsprintf(pszMsg, szFormat, (LPSTR)m_pszHost);
            ReportWSAError(pszMsg, iError, m_hwnd, m_hInstance);
            delete[] pszMsg;
            m_stState = ERROREXIT;
            m_evEvent = NULLEVENT;
            return TRUE;
        }
        m_stState = AWAITCONNECTION;
        m_evEvent = NULLEVENT;
        return FALSE;
}


BOOL CFingerObj::AwaitConnection(EVENT ev)
{
    if (ev != CONNECT)
        return FALSE;
    // See if we connected or had an error.
    if (m_iError == 0) {
        // Everything was okay.  We're now connected.  Move on.
        m_stState = CONNECTED;
        m_evEvent = NULLEVENT;
        return TRUE;
    }
    // Okay, something went wrong.  See what it was.
    if (m_iError == WSAENETUNREACH || m_iError == WSAETIMEDOUT) {
        // Perhaps we can't reach the foreign host on the primary
        // address.  If the foreign host has multiple addresses, try
        // one of the others until we're out of addresses.
        BOOL bResult;
        m_saAddr = m_host.NextAddr(&bResult);
        if (!m_bDotted && bResult == TRUE) {
            // We didn't have a dotted address to begin with and
            // the host has more addresses left, so try again.
            m_stream.Close();
            m_stState = MAKECONNECTION;
            m_evEvent = NULLEVENT;
            return TRUE;
        }
        // Okay, there are no more addresses left to try.  Generate
        // a user friendly error.
        if (m_iError == WSAENETUNREACH) {
            ErrorWithHostName("Network Unreachable",
                "The network for host '%s' is unreachable.");
        }
```

```
        else if (m_iError == WSAETIMEDOUT) {
            ErrorWithHostName("Connection Timed Out",
                "Connection attempt timed out while trying "
                "to reach host '%s'.");
        }
        m_stState = ERROREXIT;
        m_evEvent = NULLEVENT;
        return TRUE;
    }
    // Okay, we got an error.  See if it's something we might expect
    // and try to make it sound a bit nicer.
    if (m_iError == WSAECONNREFUSED) {
        // We reached the other host but they refused us.
        ErrorWithHostName("Connection Refused",
            "Host '%s' refused the connection on the specified port. "
            "Either you used the wrong port number or the desired "
            "service is not running on the host.");
        m_stState = ERROREXIT;
        m_evEvent = NULLEVENT;
        return TRUE;
    }
    // It was something unexpected (like we're out of socket
    // descriptors).  Signal with an ugly error message.
    const char szFormat[] =
        "Error while connecting to host '%s'.";
    char * pszMsg = new char[sizeof(szFormat) +
        lstrlen(m_pszHost) + 1];
    wsprintf(pszMsg, szFormat, (LPSTR)m_pszHost);
    ReportWSAError(pszMsg, m_iError, m_hwnd, m_hInstance);
    delete[] pszMsg;
    m_stState = ERROREXIT;
    m_evEvent = NULLEVENT;
    return TRUE;
}


BOOL CFingerObj::Connected(EVENT ev)
{
    UNUSED_PARAMETER(ev);

    // Send the name of the user followed by a CRLF pair.
    int iError = m_stream.Send(m_pszUser, lstrlen(m_pszUser));
    if (iError != WSANOERROR && iError != WSAEWOULDBLOCK) {
        // We expect to either have the data sent with no errors or
        // to block waiting for Winsock (in reality, with this little
        // data it should never block).  If something else happened,
        // flag the error.
        ReportWSAError("Error trying to send data.", iError, m_hwnd,
            m_hInstance);
        m_stState = ERROREXIT;
        m_evEvent = NULLEVENT;
        return TRUE;
    }
```

```
        iError = m_stream.Send("\015\012", 2);  // CRLF = 15,12 (octal)
        if (iError != WSANOERROR && iError != WSAEWOULDBLOCK) {
            ReportWSAError("Error trying to send data.", iError, m_hwnd,
                m_hInstance);
            m_stState = ERROREXIT;
            m_evEvent = NULLEVENT;
            return TRUE;
        }
        m_stState = AWAITDATA;
        m_evEvent = NULLEVENT;
        return FALSE;
}

BOOL CFingerObj::AwaitData(EVENT ev)
{
    int iLength;
    int iError;
    char * pNewBuffer;
    unsigned i;
    unsigned j;
    BOOL bFound;
    LineNode * plnNewNode;

    switch (ev) {
        case DATAREADY:
            // Figure out how much space is left in the buffer.
            // Read that number of bytes, max.
            iLength = m_uBufferSize - m_uDataSize;
            iError = m_stream.Receive(m_pDataBuffer + m_uDataSize,
                &iLength, 0);
            if (iError == WSANOERROR && iLength > 0) {
                m_uDataSize += iLength;
                do {
                    // Scan for a CRLF.
                    bFound = FALSE;
                    for (i = 0; i < m_uDataSize; i++) {
                        if (m_pDataBuffer[i] == '\015' &&
                            (i + 1) < m_uDataSize &&
                            m_pDataBuffer[i + 1] == '\012') {
                                bFound = TRUE;
                                break;
                        }
                    }
                    if (bFound) {
                        // Allocate a new line node and add it to the
                        // end of the linked list.
                        plnNewNode = new LineNode;
                        m_plnTail->m_plnNext = plnNewNode;
                        m_plnTail = plnNewNode;
                        // Allocate space for the line data.  At this
                        // point, i equals the number of characters
                        // in the line minus the CRLF.  Allocate
```

```
                    // enough for the characters before the CRLF
                    // and the null terminator.
                    plnNewNode->m_pszLine = new char[i + 1];
                    // Copy the characters to the line buffer.
                    for (j = 0; j < i; j++) {
                        plnNewNode->m_pszLine[j] =
                            m_pDataBuffer[j];
                    }
                    plnNewNode->m_pszLine[i] = '\0';
                    // Copy the characters in the data buffer
                    // following the CRLF down to the start of
                    // the buffer.
                    i += 2; // Skip over the CRLF pair.
                    for (j = 0; j < (m_uDataSize - i); j++) {
                        m_pDataBuffer[j] = m_pDataBuffer[i + j];
                    }
                    m_uDataSize -= i;
                }
                else {
                    // See if our buffer is totally full.  If so,
                    // then enlarge it by another quantum.
                    if (m_uDataSize == m_uBufferSize) {
                        pNewBuffer = new char[m_uBufferSize +
                            BUFFER_QUANTUM];
                        for (i = 0; i < m_uBufferSize; i++) {
                            pNewBuffer[i] = m_pDataBuffer[i];
                        }
                        delete[] m_pDataBuffer;
                        m_pDataBuffer = pNewBuffer;
                        m_uBufferSize += BUFFER_QUANTUM;
                    }
                }
            } while (bFound && m_uDataSize > 0);
            return FALSE;
        }
        // Either an error or end-of-file.
        m_stream.Close();
        if (iError != WSANOERROR) {
            // An error.  Report it and error exit.
            ReportWSAError("Error receiving data.", iError,
                m_hwnd, m_hInstance);
            m_stState = ERROREXIT;
            m_evEvent = NULLEVENT;
            return TRUE;
        }
        // End-of-file.  The socket was closed gracefully.
        m_stState = CLOSED;
        m_evEvent = NULLEVENT;
        return TRUE;
    case CLOSE:
        m_stream.Close();
        m_stState = CLOSED;
        m_evEvent = NULLEVENT;
        return TRUE;
```

```
        default:
            return FALSE;
    }
}


BOOL CFingerObj::Closed(EVENT ev)
{
    UNUSED_PARAMETER(ev);

    // Count the number of lines in the text.
    int iNumLines = 0;
    LineNode * plnNode = m_lnHead.m_plnNext;
    while (plnNode != NULL) {
        iNumLines++;
        plnNode = plnNode->m_plnNext;
    }

    // Allocate a block of pointers to each of the lines and
    // convert the list of LineNodes to an array of line pointers.
    if (iNumLines > 0) {
        char **ppszLinePointers = new char*[iNumLines];
        plnNode = m_lnHead.m_plnNext;
        int i = 0;
        while (plnNode != NULL) {
            ppszLinePointers[i] = plnNode->m_pszLine;
            LineNode * plnNext = plnNode->m_plnNext;
            delete plnNode;
            plnNode = plnNext;
            i++;
        }
        ASSERT(i == iNumLines);
        PostMessage(m_hwnd, m_iMessage, (WPARAM) iNumLines,
            (LPARAM) ppszLinePointers);
    }
    else {
        PostMessage(m_hwnd, m_iMessage, 0, 0);
    }

    m_stState = FINISH;
    m_evEvent = NULLEVENT;
    return TRUE;
}


BOOL CFingerObj::ErrorExit(EVENT ev)
{
    UNUSED_PARAMETER(ev);   // Eliminate the compiler warning.

    // If we've got some lines allocated already, free them up.
    LineNode * plnNode = m_lnHead.m_plnNext;
    while (plnNode != NULL) {
        delete[] plnNode->m_pszLine;
        LineNode * plnNext = plnNode->m_plnNext;
```

```
        delete plnNode;
        plnNode = plnNext;
    }

    // Close up the socket and inform the window that we're done but
    // have no text for it.
    m_stream.Close();
    PostMessage(m_hwnd, m_iMessage, 0, 0);
    m_stState = FINISH;
    m_evEvent = NULLEVENT;
    return TRUE;
}

void CFingerObj::ErrorWithHostName(LPCSTR lpszTitle,
    LPCSTR lpszErrorMsg)
{
    char * pszFinalMsg = new char[lstrlen(lpszErrorMsg) +
        lstrlen(m_pszHost) + 1];
    wsprintf(pszFinalMsg, lpszErrorMsg, (LPSTR)m_pszHost);
    MessageBox(m_hwnd, pszFinalMsg, lpszTitle,
        MB_OK | MB_ICONEXCLAMATION);
    delete[] pszFinalMsg;
}
```

Internet Message Format: RFC 822

Electronic mail and network news are two of the most popular services on the Internet. In this chapter, we'll learn the structure of Internet text messages that carry email and news data.

I hated learning to type. Yep, it's probably hard to believe that a fellow who writes and programs as much as I do simply hated learning to type, but that was the case.

I had just finished my final exams in junior high school. I had all summer to sit and think about nothing except what I would do with my freedom. All summer to goof off and not even think about teachers, books, or classes. All summer to not think about math, not think about English, and not think about history. Summer is a glorious time for a teenage boy.

Not so from my mother's perspective. To my mother summer vacation meant the beginning of life as chauffeur. She had to cart me all over town because I didn't yet have my driver's license. It meant that she could listen to me complain forever about how bored I was because my friends were on vacation. It meant that she would go crazy watching me with nothing to do. Clearly, this wouldn't do.

Every year, my mom and I went through the same ritual: I'd bask in the glory of having too much free time and she'd try to figure out something that would fill all that time, get me out of the house, and keep me from staring blankly at the television all afternoon. This year it was typing lessons.

My mother had decided that it was time I learned how to type. I was going to enter high school the following year and would be facing term papers. I wanted to be a programmer when I grew up. I was using computers at school. Clearly this was something worthy that I could be learning over the summer, and it would keep me out of her hair for at least part of the time. So, off we went to the bookstore to get one of the "Teach Yourself Typing in 21 Days" books.

Well, that shattered my dreams of a summer filled with nothing but nothing.

```
aaaa ssss dddd ffff jjjj kkkk llll ;;;;
AaAa SsSs DdDd FfFf sad sad Sad SAD lad lad Lad LAD
```

So it went. Drill after drill after drill. Every morning I practiced my typing. We had this mechanical typewriter with a ribbon and keys that actually struck the paper. Yes, it was ancient technology—even for those days. The keys jammed a lot because my fingers weren't quite long enough at the time, but I just kept at it, whining all the while. Mom didn't buy it. "Keep at it," she said. "You'll get it eventually." Home keys, finger placement—I learned it all. Over and over and over. All summer long, one hour a day, every weekday (I got weekends off. Hey, mom wasn't a tyrant, just a taskmaster).

And you know what? By the end of the summer I was pretty good. Heck I was great! I moved past repeating letters fairly quickly and got down to real words. I stared at my fingers quite a bit, but I was finally getting the hang of it. Toward the end of the summer, I was nearing the final chapters of "Teach Yourself Typing in 21 Days" (yes, it took far longer than 21 days—who do they think they're kidding, anyway?). At the end of the book, there were sections on business letters and memos. I remember practicing [sic]:

```
To:      Steve Wozniak, Appple computer
Frpm:    David Roberts
Subject: Your offer

Dear Woz,
I regret to ifmorm you that I'll be unable to accept your offer to become Chief
Executive officer of Apple computer.  My mom has me practising my typing and I'll be
unable to spend the right amoutn of time on your pojects.  Yes, I kow that you'll pay
me a huge amount of $$$$$ and I'll be able to buy the coolest car when I'm 16, but that's
life.  Besides, it seems liek Steve Jobs would be really mad if we kicked him out.

Regretfully,
David G. Roberts, esq. and cool guy

PS: What were you guys thinkig with that Apple ][, anyway?  Who bought one of those?
```

Okay, so I had an active imagination. But this brings us to the topic of this chapter—the format of Internet text messages.

When the ARPANET was blazing a trail through cyberspace, email was one of the first services. Much of the early development of the protocols that ran on the ARPANET (and on the Internet today) was conducted by researchers using email. From the beginning, users needed standards for the format of email messages so that computer systems could interpret the messages properly and deliver them to the correct recipients. Later, network news became a popular service on the Internet. Following the example of the pre-existing format for email messages, the news service adopted a similar format.

The format of Internet mail and news messages is described in RFC 822. In this chapter, we'll review this important format to prepare us for later chapters on mail and news protocols. The material that is presented here is simply an overview. As always, consult the official RFC for definitive answers on fine questions.

Basic Message Structure

The basic Internet message structure is that of an informal office memo, similar to that letter I wrote to Woz. The message structure consists of a set of header lines that describe the sender and receiver of the message, the date, subject, and a few other things. Figure 8.1 shows an example of a message.

The headers are followed by a blank line (a single CRLF pair) and the body of the message, which is composed of lines of text. The blank line is logically part of the header block and not part of the message body; the header block is terminated with the first blank header line. The body of the message is optional and may be absent. An empty message simply consists of a series of headers followed by a

Figure 8.1

Sample email message.

```
From:       David Roberts <dave@droberts.com>
To:         jeffd@coriolis.com (Jeff Duntemann)
Subject:    That deadline
Date:       Sun, 9 Jul 95 14:10 PDT
Message-ID: <abcdefg-0123456@droberts.com>

Jeff,

I know I'm late with chapter 8.  It seems my grandmother died and
I won't be able to have it for you.  Yes, I know my grandmother died
when I was supposed to get you chapter 7 as well.  This was my other
grandmother.

- Dave Roberts
```

blank line. All characters are 7-bit ASCII characters, and lines are terminated with a CRLF pair.

Message Headers

Mail software uses the message headers to process the message as it flows through the network. The headers provide information about the sender, receiver, and subject to humans. The Internet mail system uses a store-and-forward model. A mail message can be processed by multiple intermediate Message Transport Agents (MTAs) on its way to the final receiver. The headers must be interpreted and manipulated by the intermediate MTAs. Similarly, the network news system is a relay network. Messages are replicated and copied from system to system until every system that desires a copy of the message has one.

The format of the headers must be well-defined to allow the message headers to be interpreted while messages pass from host to host. In this section, we'll examine the general format of header lines.

General Header Format

Each header is logically a single line of text composed of a header name followed by a colon (":") and a header body, collectively called a header field. For example:

```
Header-Name: This is a header
```

The header name is a single lexical token with no spaces in it. The header name must start at the first character on the header line. No white space characters can precede the header name.

The header name is case insensitive—"Header-Name" is equivalent to "hEaDeR-NaMe" which is equivalent to "HEADER-NAME." In general, any printable ASCII character (values 33 to 126, except for ":") can occur in a header name field.

The header body can be structured or unstructured, depending on the particular header name. For instance, the "Date" header body has a very specific format while the "Subject" header body is an unstructured line of text. Each header field is parsed by its own scanning function during processing.

The header ends at the first CRLF pair encountered after the header starts. The following section describes the exception to this rule.

Long Header Lines

In many cases, the header body may not be able to fit on a single line of text of reasonable length. Rather than force headers to be 500 characters in length, RFC 822 allows header lines to be "folded" onto multiple lines. Typically, lines longer than 72 characters are folded to remain readable on a standard 80-character-wide terminal.

A header line is folded by inserting a CRLF pair followed by one or more linear white space characters (spaces or tabs) and the remaining text. The header line can be folded more than once if the line is very long. Figure 8.2 shows a folded header line.

When the header line is processed, it is first "unfolded." The first line of the header is read and the character following the terminating CRLF pair is tested to see if it begins with a tab or a space. A tab or space at the beginning of the next header line indicates that it was folded, so the following line is read and concatenated with the previous line. This process continues until a line is read that does not begin with a linear white space character. The sequence of the CRLF pair followed by linear white space is replaced in the concatenated header text by a single space character before processing begins. After the header is "unfolded," it is processed normally.

Structured Header Bodies

The body text for headers with structured bodies generally conforms to the following rules:

- White space is ignored when parsing the header body.
- Comments can be embedded in the header body. Comments are enclosed in parentheses and must not appear in literal strings (those that appear between double quotation marks). The data in the comment is ignored by a program that parses the header body, but it might provide useful information to a human interpreter. Comments are retained with the message through all intermediate MTAs.
- Literal strings provide a method to include spaces and parentheses in a single lexical token. A literal string is delimited by double quotation marks.

Figure 8.2

A long header line that has been folded.

```
Subject: This is a really long subject line.
         Rather than have it wrap at inconvenient places on
         the receiver's terminal, we'll insert line breaks
         between words and use the header folding
         mechanism.
```

Additional rules are provided in RFC 822, but the previous rules handle the majority of common cases.

Common Headers

Many types of headers can occur in mail and news messages. Some of them are required, and others are optional.

From

The *From* header specifies who sent the message. The body of the From header contains a single email address—that of the originator of the message. The From header is required.

To

The *To* header specifies a list of primary recipients of the message. The body of the To header contains a list of email addresses separated by commas. Any number of recipients can be specified. The To header is not required, but if it is not included, either the Cc or Bcc header must appear.

Cc and Bcc

The *Cc* and *Bcc* headers specify a list of secondary recipients of the message. Neither the Cc nor Bcc header is required if the To header is specified. All messages must contain at least one of the To, Cc, or Bcc headers.

The Cc and Bcc headers are similar to the To header. The message is delivered to all the recipients. The Cc header is primarily for humans to distinguish those recipients who received a courtesy copy. The Bcc header operates identically to the Cc header but allows the mail system to remove the header from copies of the message sent to the To and Cc list. (Bcc originated from the term "Blind Carbon Copy," back from those ancient times again.)

Subject

The *Subject* header allows the message sender to describe the contents of the message. This header assists mail User Agents (UAs) to create summaries of all arrived messages and help the message reader quickly see the topic. A user can read the text presented on the Subject line to prioritize the new messages when choosing the messages to read. The body of the Subject header is unstructured and can contain any characters up to the terminating CRLF pair. The Subject header is not required.

Date

The *Date* header specifies the date that the message was created and given to the mail system. It is a structured header with the following format:

```
[ Day "," ] Day-of-Month Month Year Hour ":" Minute [ ":" Second ] Timezone
```

For instance,

```
Sun, 09 Jul 1995 15:01 PDT
Sun, 9 Jul 95 15:01:37 PDT
```

are both valid dates.

The Date header is included in the message to assist in diagnostic processing and to allow UAs to sort incoming messages according to the date sent. Generally, the Date header is created by the UA just before the message is handed to the mail system for delivery. The Date header is required.

Message-ID

The *Message-ID* header uniquely identifies a message to the global mail system. The Message-ID header has a structured body and uses the following format:

```
"<" Unique Text ">"
```

The unique text can be anything that is guaranteed to be unique. Generally, the unique text follows a format something like the following:

```
Unique "@" Hostname
```

The addition of the hostname helps qualify the rest of the unique text. The unique part of this format is typically a series of characters based on the current date and time ("19950101143015" for January 1, 1995, at 2:30:15, for instance). This text is concatenated with some other random text or a sequence number maintained by the mail system. This technique reduces the probability of a duplicate Message-ID.

A UA can use Message-IDs to uniquely identify its messages and to search for a specific message.

Reply-To

The *Reply-To* header specifies an alternate reply address for the message. Typically, when a user wants to reply to a given message, a UA takes the address that appears in the From header and uses it as the To header of the reply message. In some cases, the From header may not indicate the correct reply address. This situation can occur when a user generates the original message on a system other than the one they typically use to read their mail. In this case, the user will want to specify his or her home mail system in a Reply-To header, so that responses will be addressed to the correct location.

Sometimes, a user wants to identify a different user to which to respond. For instance, a secretary may generate a message announcing a meeting but may specify the address of the manager who called the meeting in the Reply-To field. Potential meeting attendees can indicate their attendance plans or ask questions about the meeting topic directly to the manager.

Fields Added by MTAs

Some headers are not generated by users or UAs, but by MTAs while the message passes through the mail system. In particular, a *Received* header is added to the header block by each intermediate MTA as it receives the message. When administrators are trying to diagnose a mail problem, the series of Received headers allows them to determine the path that the message took to reach its final destination. Each Received header includes the date and time that the message was received, which allows administrators to determine how long the message stayed on each intermediate system.

Extension Headers

RFC 822 provides for *Extension* headers. Extension headers contain extra information for which no header has been officially defined. The mail system ignores the Extension headers, and their bodies are considered to be composed of unstructured text. Extension headers are distinguished by their use of a leading "X-" as the first two characters of the header name. UAs often include an "X-Mailer" or "X-User-Agent" header to identify the name and revision of the UA that generated the message. This information can help diagnose bugs in the formats of generated messages.

Other Headers

Many other headers can be included in RFC 822 message. In general, these headers are used infrequently or are less important than the headers described previously. Consult RFC 822 for more information about other headers, their uses, and the structure of their bodies.

Address Format

The From and To headers are the two most important headers in a message. These headers identify the sender and the receivers of the message. Each header contains a list of email addresses, which are structured like this

```
Local-Part "@" Domain
```

where Domain is a series of sub-domains separated by periods. When included in the From, To, Cc, and Bcc headers, the addresses can be in one of the two following forms:

```
Address
Phrase "<" Address ">"
```

The second form allows the inclusion of human-readable text before the address (the "Phrase"), which is not interpreted by the mail system. Examples of the address formats are:

```
dave@droberts.com
Dave Roberts <dave@droberts.com>
```

Some UAs use the first address form but include human-readable text in a comment following the address, for example:

```
dave@droberts.com (Dave Roberts)
```

Note that this last format is equivalent to the first format as far as the processing agent (either a UA or intermediate agent) is concerned. It simply contains a comment string that is ignored.

What's Next?

Now that we understand the format of Internet messages, we'll take a look at how messages are transported through the mail system. In the next chapter, we'll start building our own mail user agent that will use the SMTP protocol to interface with the mail system.

Sending Mail: SMTP

Electronic mail is one of the most frequently used services on the Internet. Learn about the Simple Mail Transport Protocol in this chapter, as we begin to build a simple mail user agent.

Electronic mail is one of the oldest and most popular services on the modern Internet. Email was one of the original ARPANET services. Today, an email address appears on almost every business card in the world. In fact, many radio and TV shows have set up email accounts to receive viewer feedback.

In this chapter, we'll examine the Simple Mail Transport Protocol, which is used to transfer email messages throughout the Internet. Additionally, we'll begin to construct a simple email user agent application. We'll discuss how the SMTP protocol is added to the user agent to allow delivery of mail to a remote server. Later chapters will describe the protocols and programming necessary to allow the user agent to pick up delivered mail and send and receive binary and multimedia files and objects.

SMTP Model

The Internet mail system relies on the Simple Mail Transport Protocol (SMTP), described in RFC 821, to deliver email messages between Internet hosts. SMTP describes both a protocol for interaction between hosts and a conceptual model for mail delivery and routing. This section describes the conceptual model; in the next section, we'll examine the actual protocol that is used to exchange email.

RFC 821 describes a store-and-forward model for mail delivery. Mail user agents generate messages at the requests of users, format them according to RFC 822 specifications, and hand them to the SMTP mail system for delivery. In the course of delivery, a message may be handled by multiple Internet hosts on the way to its final destination.

The exact number of machines that handle a message on the way to the final destination depends on the mail configuration at both the sender's and receiver's site. SMTP does not *require* multiple nodes to handle a message; SMTP simply allows it. A message may be delivered directly between the sending and receiving nodes.

In general, direct delivery between two nodes is the most common case when both of the nodes belong to the same company, university, or other administrative group. When a message must be delivered between administrative groups, the delivery is typically performed via multiple nodes ("hopping").

Network managers often configure the mail system at their site to route the mail entering or leaving the administrative group through one or more master email servers. The master servers may be used to centralize email routing information, provide security, and collect usage statistics. The set of email servers is often hierarchical. A company typically has one or more servers that transfer mail with the outside world. The next level of hierarchy may include servers for each individual geographic location. The final level of hierarchy may service individual departments within the organization—the chemistry department at a university or the finance department within a corporation, for instance. Figure 9.1 shows a typical set of hierarchical servers.

Figure 9.1

A set of hierarchical email servers for a multinational company.

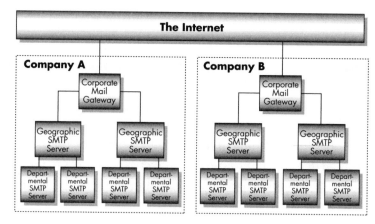

Messages that are sent between machines at the lowest level of the hierarchy are usually delivered with one hop. Messages that must be delivered between other machines traverse the hierarchy as necessary to reach their destination. An intercorporate message often requires three to five hops while it exits the sender's corporation and another three to five hops as it enters the receiver's corporation.

The exact method that email is routed is configuration-specific. Network managers may configure a server to use many methods to determine which system should receive the message next, including static configurations or internal databases. When mail is transferred between corporations or universities on the global Internet, information in the DNS is used to determine which central server, if any, should receive mail for an administrative group.

Email delivery is not strictly limited to the Internet. Many other systems that do not use SMTP can exchange email with the Internet mail system. Some of these systems are store-and-forward bulletin board systems (BBSs) that use dial-up rather than constant connectivity models. Other systems use the ISO X.400 email standard. Still other systems may use proprietary email protocols or protocols developed for mainframe operating systems. In each case, a gateway system is used to adapt to the different email protocols. The gateway connects to the different systems using the native protocols of both systems (UUCP and SMTP, for instance), and handles any reformatting of messages between the native formats for each system (between X.400 and RFC 822 formats, for instance). Figure 9.2 shows how email systems can be connected.

SMTP

SMTP is an application-level, client-server protocol used to exchange email messages between machines in the Internet mail system. The SMTP client is the message transfer agent (MTA) that has the message needing to be transferred. At the end of the exchange, the server accepts the message or an error occurs.

SMTP uses stream connections (TCP) to carry the data exchanged between the client and server. The client contacts the server on well-known port 21. SMTP uses an ASCII text-based, request-response protocol to transfer messages. The client sends a series of commands to the server, which returns a reply code in response to each command. The reply code indicates whether the command succeeded or failed, or whether more data should be sent. The interaction between the client and the server is lock-step. The client always waits for the server to respond before sending the next command.

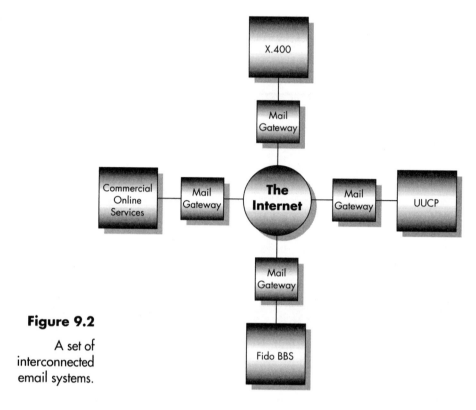

Figure 9.2

A set of interconnected email systems.

Commands and Reply Codes

Each SMTP command has a similar format—a short command name, possibly followed by some parameters. The command names are not case-sensitive, although the parameters might be (mailbox names, for instance). Here are some command examples:

```
HELO droberts.com
MAIL FROM:<dave@droberts.com>
RCPT TO:<jeffd@coriolis.com>
```

Server replies have a rigid syntax. Each server reply begins with a three-digit numeric code that indicates whether the command succeeded or failed. The first digit gives the overall result of the command (success or failure, possibly pending further command interaction). The second digit indicates a response category (syntax, information, connection, or the mail system). The third digit indicates a finer gradation of the code specified in the second digit. Following the numeric code may be a space and then some text that describes an error. The numeric code is intended to be interpreted by a program, while the error message is to be interpreted by a human. Here are some examples of reply messages:

```
250 OK
354 Start mail input; end with <CRLF>.<CRLF>
500 Syntax error, command unrecognized
```

Sometimes the human-readable text from the server will not fit on a single 80-character line. Rather than generate long lines, SMTP allows multi-line responses. All lines of the multi-line response except the last line put a hyphen character ("-") in place of a space as the character following the numeric reply code. The server indicates the last line of the response by using the standard format: a space after the numeric reply code. The numeric code in each line of the multi-line response must be the same. In general, a program is free to ignore all the lines of the multi-line response except the last one. Figure 9.3 shows an example multi-line response.

SMTP Protocol Sequence

The SMTP protocol sequence is very straightforward. For a simple mail exchange, only five commands (HELO, MAIL, RCPT, DATA, and QUIT) must be given.

1. When the client first contacts the server, the server sends a greeting message. The greeting indicates that the server is ready to accept commands. The client waits until the greeting message is received before sending any commands.

2. The client identifies itself to the server using the HELO command.

3. The client starts a mail transaction using the MAIL command. The MAIL command identifies the sender's mailbox.

4. When the MAIL command has been accepted, the recipients of the message are identified using RCPT commands. Each recipient in the To, Cc, and Bcc headers is listed using a RCPT command.

Figure 9.3

An example of a multi-line server reply.

```
500-This is a multiline response message.  The reply
500-code is '500' which indicates that I did not recognize
500-the command you gave me.  Had I recognized the command
500-I would not have returned this code.  In the future,
500-please by more careful and only give me commands that I
500-understand.
500 Syntax error, command unrecognized
```

5. When the client has identified all the recipients, it indicates that it is ready to transfer the message to the server by sending the DATA command. If the DATA command is accepted, the server returns a 354 reply code. This code is an intermediate reply code and indicates that the DATA command was successful and the server is ready for data transfer.

6. All lines sent by the client following the reception of the 354 reply code are actual message lines. The message text is formatted according to RFC 822, with each line ending with CRLF.

7. When all the lines of the message have been sent, the client indicates the end of the message by sending a line containing just a single period.

8. When the server receives the termination indicator, it sends a reply code indicating whether the message text was received correctly.

9. The client sends a QUIT command to terminate the session.

10. The server replies to the QUIT command with a reply code and closes the connection.

Steps 3 through 8 can be repeated as many times as necessary when more than one message needs to be sent to the same destination.

Figure 9.4 shows a sample SMTP protocol exchange. In the example, text sent by the client is indicated with "C:" and text returned by the server is indicated with "S:"

In step 7, the client indicates the end of the message by sending a line containing just a single period character followed by CRLF. To keep the server from confusing a single line with a period that might occur in the message text with the actual end of message indication, a *quoting rule* is invoked on all lines in the message text that begin with a period character. If the first character of a line is a period, the client inserts another period before the line is sent, effectively turning the first period into two periods. The end of message line is not quoted. When the server receives any line starting with a period, it checks to see if it contains only a single period. If so, it's the end of message indicator. If not, the client must have inserted the first period character. The server strips the first period from the line and treats the remainder of the line as message text.

```
S: 220 mythical.com   Sooper-Dooper SMTP Version 1
C: HELO droberts.com
S: 250 Nice to meet you droberts.com
C: MAIL FROM:<dave@droberts.com>
S: 250 OK
C: RCPT TO:<smith@mythical.com>
S: 250 OK
C: RCPT TO:<jones@mythical.com>
S: 250 OK
C: DATA
S: 354 Okay, give me that text. Terminate with <CRLF>.<CRLF>
C: To: smith@mythical.com, jones@mythical.com
C: From: dave@droberts.com
C: Date: 20 Jan 95 13:24 PST
C: Message-ID: <1234@droberts.com>
C:
C: This is the message body.
C: blah... blah...
C: ..This line starts with a period but it's quoted.
C: ..
C: The previous line contained a single period which didn't
C: end the message because it was quoted.
C: Here's the real last line of the message.
C: .
S: 250 OK
C: QUIT
S: 221 mythical.com   Seeya!   Closing connection.
```

Figure 9.4

A sample SMTP protocol session.

SMTP Object: CSMTP

Although the SMTP protocol is simple, we don't want to reprogram it every time we need to add mail-sending functionality to a program. In this section, we'll look at a C++ class that sends email messages using the SMTP client protocol—**CSMTP**. The **CSMTP** class provides a simple interface that allows email functionality to be added to an application with little additional programming.

Using the CSMTP Class

The interface to the **CSMTP** class is very simple. The header file containing the **CSMTP** class is shown in Listing 9.1. A program can send a message simply by creating a **CSMTP** object, then invoking the **SendMessage** member function of the object. The **SendMessage** member function is prototyped as follows:

```
BOOL CSMTP::SendMessage(LPCSTR lpszHost, u_short ushPort,
        istream * pisMsgStream, LPCSTR lpszFrom,
        CAddrList * palAddrList);
```

The **lpszHost** and **ushPort** parameters identify the remote SMTP server to which the message will first be transferred. This server might not be the final destination of the message; it might be an intermediate host that will forward the message toward the ultimate destination.

The **pisMsgStream** parameter is a pointer to a C++ input stream that contains the message. Typically, this input stream is connected to a file, but it may also be a string if the message is very short. The **CSMTP** object reads the message from this stream, line by line, to send it.

The **lpszFrom** parameter indicates the mailbox of the message sender. This string is sent to the SMTP server in the MAIL command.

The **palAddrList** parameter points to a list of destination address strings to which the message is addressed. A RCPT command is sent to the SMTP server for each address in the list.

The **CSMTP** class is an abstract base class; it provides the basic functionality of the SMTP protocol but not a specific callback mechanism to inform the program when the message has been sent. Instead, two classes are derived from the **CSMTP** class: **CSMTPWithWinMsg** and **CSMTPWithCallback**. When the **CSMTP** class completes its interaction with the server (either the message was sent successfully or an error occurred), it invokes the **DoCallback** pure-virtual function. This function is provided by each of the derived classes and provides the appropriate completion message: a window message for **CSMTPWithWinMsg** and a function callback for **CSMTPWithCallback**. In both cases, the callback uses a result code to indicate whether the message was sent successfully.

Functional Overview

The implementation of the **CSMTP** class is similar to the implementation of the **CFingObj** class in Chapter 7. The SMTP protocol is implemented as a state machine. Windows Sockets events are processed and translated into events that drive the SMTP protocol state machine forward. Listing 9.2 shows the implementation of the **CSMTP** class.

The **CSMTP** class has one major difference from the **CFingObj** class, however: the **CSMTP** object does not manage its TCP connection setup. The **CFingObj** class included functionality that attempted to connect with all of a remote host's Internet addresses in the event that certain error conditions were encountered for some addresses. This process allows a connection to be established with a remote host when one of its multiple network interfaces has a malfunction. This functionality is common to many different applications and has been put into a class of its own: a connection manager class named **CConnMgr**.

The **CConnMgr** class takes a host name, port, and socket, and establishes a connection using the socket to the remote host. It then generates a callback when the connection is established or if a connection cannot be established using any of the remote host's addresses. The code for **CConnMgr** can be found on the companion CD-ROM.

The basic state machine operation is similar to that used in the **CFingObj** class with some subtle differences. In the **CSMTP** class, the state variable is a pointer to a member function. Dispatch to a state is accomplished by calling the function through the dereferenced pointer. See the **Event** function in Listing 9.2. The state function returns TRUE if the state processed the event, and FALSE otherwise. After a given state processes the event, the current event is set to **EV_NULLEVENT** and the next state is invoked. If the state responds to null events, it returns **TRUE** and the state machine continues to the next state, again using the null event. If the next state does not respond to null events, it returns FALSE and the **Event** function exits.

The effect of this behavior is that most state functions are called twice: once with **EV_NULLEVENT** when the previous state transitions to the current state and once when the next event occurs. This approach assumes that the **State** function does not process null events. If the state does respond to null events, the machine will transition when the first null event is passed to the state.

The **CSMTP** class performs more processing on the text that is returned from the remote server than the **CFingObj** class performs. The **CFingObj** class simply collects the reply text for the application to display; the **CSMTP** class must interpret the text as an SMTP reply.

When the **StreamCallback** member function receives an indication that data has arrived from the remote server, it first checks to see if it received a full line of text. If so, it checks to see if the character following the three-digit reply code is the hyphen character ("-"). If so, the reply is part of a multi-line response and the line is simply discarded (the program waits for the last line of a multi-line response). If the character following the reply code is not a hyphen, the line is either a single line response or the last line of a multi-line response. In this case, the

StreamCallback function takes the first digit of the numeric response code and turns it into an event to the state machine: **EV_CODE_1**, **EV_CODE_2**, and so on. All the remaining digits and the text description are ignored.

SMTP State Machine

The state machine in the **CSMTP** class contains 13 states, as shown in Figure 9.5. Each state has a corresponding state function, which are described in the following pages. Note that the figure and descriptions do not show some of the more subtle transitions in the state machine, typically error conditions. For an exact description of the state machine, consult the code in Listing 9.2.

Start

The *Start* state is entered when the **CSMTP** object is directed to send a message using the **SendMessage** member function. The Start state simply directs the connection manager object to connect with the remote server and transitions the state machine to the Await Connection state.

Figure 9.5

The CSMTP state machine.

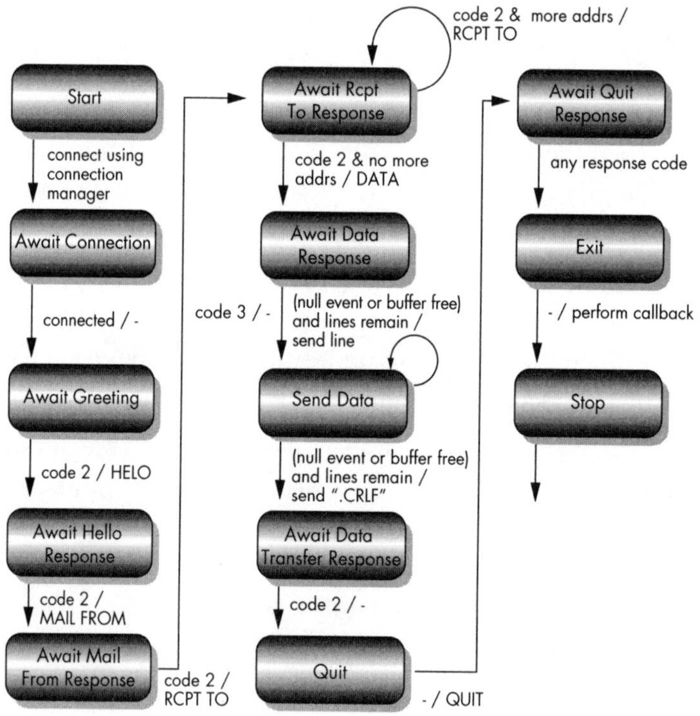

Await Connection

The *Await Connection* state waits for a connection to the remote server to be established by the connection manager. When the connection manager is finished, it returns a result to the **CSMTP::ConnMgrCallback** function, which is turned into an **EV_CONNECT** or **EV_ERROR** event to the **CSMTP** state machine. If the Await Connection state receives the **EV_CONNECT** event, the state machine transitions to the Await Greeting state. If it receives **EV_ERROR**, the state machine transitions to the Exit state.

Await Greeting

The *Await Greeting* state waits for the remote server to send the initial greeting after a connection is successfully established. The greeting message starts with an initial reply code of 220, so the Await Greeting state looks for an **EV_CODE_2** event. Once the **EV_CODE_2** event is received, the HELO command is sent to identify the local machine to the remote server. All other SMTP reply codes cause the state machine to enter the Exit state. After the HELO command is sent, the state machine transitions to the Await Hello Response state.

Await Hello Response

The *Await Hello Response* state waits for the response to the HELO command. If the server returns a reply code starting with 2, the MAIL command is sent to identify the sender of the current message. The state machine then transitions to the Await Mail From Response state. If a reply code beginning with anything other than 2 is returned in response to the HELO command, the state machine transitions to the Quit state.

Await Mail From Response

The *Await Mail From Response* state waits for the server's reply to the MAIL command. If the server returns a positive reply, the state machine sends the first of possibly multiple RCPT commands. The state machine then transitions to the Await Rcpt To Response state. If the server's reply to the MAIL command indicates a problem, the state machine transitions to the Quit state.

Await Rcpt To Response

The *Await Rcpt To Response* state waits for the server's response to the last RCPT command. If the server's reply is positive, the code checks to see if more destination addresses remain in the address list. If so, the code sends another RCPT command and the state machine remains in the Await Rcpt To Response state to wait for the server's reply. If no more addresses remain, the state machine sends the DATA command and transitions to the Await Data Response state. If the initial response to the previous RCPT command indicates that a problem occurred, the state machine transitions to the Quit state.

Await Data Response

The *Await Data Response* state waits for the server's reply to the DATA command. Normally, the server replies with a 354 reply code, which is a positive intermediate response indicating that the client should now send the mail message text. If the Await Data Response state receives an **EV_CODE_3** event, the state machine transitions to the Send Data state. If the server returns any other response, the state machine transitions to the Quit state.

Send Data

The *Send Data* state transmits the message text, and responds to the **EV_NULLEVENT** event. On each entry to the Send Data state that is caused by an **EV_NULLEVENT** or **EV_BUFFERFREE** event, the code reads another line of text from the input stream containing the message. The state does not expect any reply code from the server during the time it is sending the message. Any such reply code indicates that some error has occurred at the server, and the state machine transitions to the Quit state.

Before sending the line of text, the code performs some preprocessing. First, it clears the high bit of each character. RFC 821 specifies that SMTP message text may include only 7-bit ASCII characters with the high-order bit of each octet cleared. Although the composer of the message should have formatted the message using only 7-bit ASCII, clearing high-order bits ensures that only 7-bit ASCII is transferred.

Next, the code checks the first character of the message line to see if it is equal to a period. If so, the code first sends an additional period character to comply with SMTP's transparency rules.

Finally, the code sends the actual line to the socket and returns to the Event dispatcher. The state machine remains in the Send Data state.

When the input message stream is exhausted, the code sends a single period followed by CRLF, which signals the end of the message to the server. The state machine then transitions to the Await Data Transfer Response state.

Normally, while data is being sent, the state machine repeatedly dispatches control to the Send Data state with an **EV_NULLEVENT** event. A line of text is sent with each call of the **SendData** function. If the message is long, the TCP buffer in the Windows Sockets implementation may fill up and a call to the **send** function may return **WSAEWOULDBLOCK**. When this occurs, the code sets a flag, **m_bBufferQueued**, indicating the condition and simply returns. The next call to the **SendData** function with **EV_NULLEVENT** returns FALSE, which stops the event dispatch loop for the state machine. Later, when Winsock indicates that the socket is ready to accept more data, the flag is cleared (in **CSMTP::StreamCallback**) and an **EV_BUFFERFREE** event is sent to the state machine, which causes another line to be sent. The state machine then sends more lines of text until the buffer becomes full again or the end of the message text is reached.

Await Data Transfer Response

Once the end-of-message indicator is sent (the ".CRLF" sequence), the server sends back a reply code indicating whether the transfer was successful. The *Await Data Transfer Response* state waits for this indication. If the state receives an **EV_CODE_2** event, the transfer was successful and the state machine transitions to the Quit state with a successful result code (**RESULT_SUCCESS**). If any other code is received, the state machine transitions to the Quit state with a failure result code (**RESULT_FAILURE**).

Quit

The *Quit* state terminates the connection with the server by sending the QUIT command, which causes the state machine to transition to the Await Quit Response state.

Await Quit Response

The *Await Quit Response* state waits for the reply code from the server in response to the QUIT command. This process is a mere formality. The message has already been sent and accepted by the server. Virtually all event' input to this state cause the state machine to transition to the Exit state. The Await Quit Response does not discriminate among any result codes returned by the server.

Exit

The *Exit* state cleans up before the state machine enters the Stop state. The Exit state closes the socket being used to communicate with the remote server, deletes some memory allocated when the state machine was started, and performs a callback to let the main program know that it has completed its work. The state machine then transitions to the Stop state.

When the Exit state performs the callback, it calls the **CSMTP::DoCallback** virtual function. The **CSMTPWithWinMsg** and **CSMTPWithCallback** classes override this function to create the appropriate callback behavior for the derived classes.

Stop

The *Stop* state is the final state of the state machine. It simply ignores all events, acting as a sink for any spurious events that may occur after the state machine has encountered an error.

Mail Client

To demonstrate our **CSMTP**-derived classes, we'll develop a mail client application, appropriately named Mail Client. Mail Client is a simple MUA. This agent allows a user to compose messages, send them using SMTP, retrieve messages from a remote host using the POP3 protocol, encode and decode files using the UUENCODE algorithm, and attach files to email using the MIME mail extensions protocol. We'll use Mail Client as a demonstration program for the next few chapters as we implement POP3, UUENCODE, and MIME.

Mail Client is a very limited mail user agent. It cannot reply to messages, forward messages to other users, or file messages in multiple folders. You can easily add these features by building on the existing features.

Figure 9.6 shows a screen shot of the mail client program. Mail Client is an MDI application with separate windows to edit messages, view messages, and review a mailbox summary listing.

Configuration

Before using Mail Client, we must configure a few parameters. Figure 9.7 shows the configuration dialog box that is displayed when the user chooses Mail|Configure.

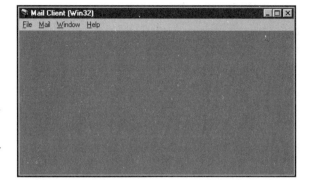

Figure 9.6

The Mail Client application.

Three sets of information must be configured: SMTP server information, user information, and POP server information.

We use the SMTP section of the configuration information dialog box to specify the name and port number of the remote SMTP server. Mail Client does not perform direct delivery of outgoing mail to the final destination. Instead, Mail Client sends each message to a local server, which then routes the message to the final destination or to the next intermediate transport agent. The name of the server machine must be entered into the SMTP Server text box. The port number on which to contact the server can be configured as well, although it's unusual not to use the default of 25.

We use the User Information section of the Configure dialog box to specify a return address and user name. Mail Client needs this information to compose a message that forms the From header field. This information ensures that messages have a proper return address independent of the actual machine that the user may be using to compose the mail.

We use the POP section of the configuration dialog to configure server information for the POP3 protocol. We'll discuss the POP3 protocol in the next chapter.

Figure 9.7

The Configure dialog box.

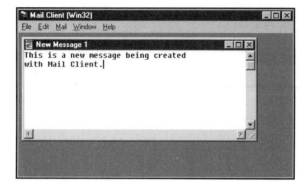

Figure 9.8

Creating a
new message.

Creating A Message

To create a message, the user selects File|New Message. This action creates an editor window in which the user can type the message text. Figure 9.8 shows a message being created.

The message must be addressed and sent after the message text is written. The user chooses Mail|Send to notify Mail Client that the message editing is complete and the message is ready to send. Mail Client then displays the Addressing Information dialog box, shown in Figure 9.9. The user enters the To address to which to send the message, and an optional Cc address. The user can also enter a subject line that describes the contents of the message. The Attachment text box shows that a binary attachment will be sent with the message along with the message text. We'll look at this functionality in a later chapter on the MIME protocol.

Once the message addressing information is complete, the user selects OK and the message is sent. Mail Client creates a valid RFC 822 message in a temporary file, creates a **CSMTPWithWinMsg** object, and tells the object to send the message in the temporary file. While the message is being sent, Mail Client iconizes the editor window. If the message is sent successfully, Mail Client destroys the editor window. If an error occurs during the interaction with the SMTP server, Mail Client displays a notification and redisplays the message in the editor window. The user can then try to correct the problem and resend the message (by changing the SMTP configuration parameters, for instance).

The Mail Client Project

Our Mail Client project contains many files, as shown in Table 9.1. In this section, we'll examine the implementation of two of the files, MAILCLI.CPP and

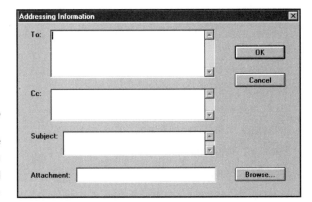

Figure 9.9

The
Information
Addressing
dialog box.

MAILEDIT.CPP. MAILCLI.CPP implements the main Mail Client MDI frame window. MAILEDIT.CPP implements the message editing window and handles message composition and the creation and destruction of the **CSMTP** object used to send the message.

Table 9.1	Mail Client project files	
File	**Description**	**Reference**
CASYNCDB.CPP	Asynchronous database lookup base class	Listing 6.6
CBASE64.CPP	BASE64 encoding for the MIME protocol	Chapter 12
CCONNMGR.CPP	Connection manager class	On CD-ROM in binary format
CFILEMAP.CPP	Poor-person's memory mapped file class	Chapter 12
CHOST.CPP	Host information lookup class	Listing 6.8
CLIST.CPP	Simple list class	On CD-ROM in binary format
CMIME.CPP	Class for parsing MIME-formatted messages	Chapter 12
CPOP3.CPP	Mail retrieval class using the POP3 protocol	Chapter 10
CSMTP.CPP	SMTP class	Listing 9.2
CSOCKADR.CPP	Internet address class	Listing 6.4
CSOCKET.CPP	Stream socket class	Listing 6.12
CSTRLIST.CPP	Simple list of strings descended from CList class	On CD-ROM in binary format
CTL3DV2.LIB	Import library for the 3D controls DLL	On CD-ROM in binary format
CUUENDEC.CPP	UUENCODE algorithm class	Chapter 11

Table 9.1	Mail Client project files (continued)	
File	**Description**	**Reference**
CWINSOCK.CPP	The CWinsock class and other infrastructure functions and classes	Listing 6.2
MAILBOX.CPP	File that implements the mailbox child window for Mail Client	Chapter 10
MAILCLI.CPP	Main file for the Mail Client project	Listing 9.7
MAILCLI.DEF	Linker definition file for the Mail Client project	Listing 9.6
MAILEDIT.CPP	Mail editor child window for the Mail Client project	Listing 9.8
MAILVIEW.CPP	File that implements the mail viewing child window for Mail Client	Chapter 10
PARSDATE.CPP	Functions for parsing an RFC 822 style date	Chapter 10
RFC822.CPP	Various functions for creating and parsing RFC 822 headers	Listing 9.10
UTILITY.CPP	A set of general-purpose utility functions	On CD-ROM in binary format
WINSOCK.LIB	Import library for WINSOCK.DLL	On CD-ROM in binary format

Main Program

The MAILCLI.CPP file, shown in Listing 9.7, is the main file for the Mail Client project. MAILCLI.CPP contains the **WinMain** function, the implementation of the MDI frame window, and the Configure dialog box.

The **WinMain** function is fairly conventional. It calls the **InitApp** function to register window classes for the frame window and various MDI child windows. Next, the **WinMain** function loads the menus used by each of the MDI child windows, and the accelerator key table. It then calls **InitInstance** to create the frame window.

Once the window and menu management code execute, **WinMain** calls **InitWinsock** to initialize the network-specific functionality. **InitWinsock** verifies that the global **CWinsock** object initialized correctly, ensuring that **WSAStartup** was called successfully. If so, **InitWinsock** creates the event dispatch window for the Winsock classes.

Once Winsock is initialized, the frame window is made visible and is updated. **WinMain** then enters a standard event dispatch loop.

The **FrameWndProc** function is the window procedure for the frame window class. The **FrameWndProc** function simply dispatches window messages to individual message-handling functions. Mail Client uses the "message-cracker" macros defined in the WINDOWSX.H header file to enhance portability between the Win16 (Windows 3.1) and Win32 (Windows NT and Windows 95) environments.

One of the first messages sent to the frame window is **WM_CREATE**. The **OnCreate** function in MAILCLI.CPP is called to handle this message. Note that **OnCreate** is declared to be a **static** function. Its definition is local to the MAILCLI.CPP file. As we'll see, the MAILEDIT.CPP file contains a window procedure for the editor MDI child window. MAILEDIT.CPP also defines a function named **OnCreate** to handle **WM_CREATE** messages sent to the editor child window. Don't confuse these two functions. Although they share the same name, each function is local to the file in which it is located, and is associated with the window procedure in the same file as itself.

The first responsibility of the **OnCreate** function in MAILCLI.CPP is to create the MDI client window. The MDI client window manages the MDI child windows.

Once the client window is created, **OnCreate** reads the Mail Client configuration information from an application-specific initialization file using the Windows **GetPrivateProfileXXX** functions. A set of global variables is initialized with the information. These variables will be accessed and set when the user invokes the Configure dialog box.

The Configure dialog box is displayed when the user chooses Configure from the Mail menu. Invoking a menu choice first causes the **OnCommand** function to be called from **FrameWndProc**. **OnCommand** then calls **OnMailConfigure** to handle this menu choice.

The **OnMailConfigure** function displays the Configure dialog box. The **ConfigureDlgProc** function is the dialog procedure for the Configure dialog box. When the user selects the OK button, **ConfigureDlgProc** grabs all the configuration information from the text boxes in the dialog box, performs some validity checking on them, and sets the configuration global variables to the retrieved values. The dialog box is then terminated. Once the dialog box is removed, **OnMailConfigure** writes the values in the configuration global variables to the Mail Client initialization file so the user won't have to re-enter them when the program is next run.

Most of the other code in MAILCLI.CPP is related to the creation or management of MDI child windows. When the user selects the File|New Message menu command, the **OnFileNewMessage** function is eventually called, which causes the creation of a new message editing window. When the user selects the File|Open Mailbox menu command, the **OnFileOpenMailbox** function is called, which causes the creation of the mailbox child window.

Mail Edit Window

An MDI child window that edits messages is created when the user chooses the File|New Message menu choice. The code implementing the editor child window is contained in the MAILEDIT.CPP file, shown in Listing 9.8.

The **EditorWndProc** function serves as the window procedure for the message editor window class. Just like **FrameWndProc**, **EditorWndProc** simply dispatches window messages to individual handler functions using the WINDOWSX.H message-cracker macros.

When an editor child window is created, **OnCreate** in MAILEDIT.CPP is called to handle the **WM_CREATE** window message. **OnCreate** first allocates an **EDITORDATA** structure that holds some variables local to each editor window. A pointer to the editor data is stored in the window data associated with the window. Next, **OnCreate** creates a multi-line edit control. The handle of the edit control is stored in the **EDITORDATA** structure associated with the editor MDI child window. The edit control fills the entire client area of the editor child window and is used to edit the message contents. Once the edit control is created, its font is set to the default system fixed-pitch font.

The user creates the message contents in the editor control, which provides full cut-and-paste capability. After the message is created, the user selects the Mail|Send menu command, which calls the **OnMailSend** function.

The **OnMailSend** function is the main function in the MAILEDIT.CPP file. It obtains the address information for the message from the user, composing an RFC 822 message by using the addressing information and contents of the message in the edit control. It then creates a **CSMTP** object to deliver the message.

The **OnMailSend** function's first task is to obtain the address information from the user. **OnMailSend** displays the Addressing Information dialog box. The **AddressDlgProc** function is the dialog procedure for the Addressing Information dialog box. When the dialog box is created, **OnMailSend** passes a pointer to an **ADDRESSDLGINFO** structure to the dialog box in the **lParam** of the **WM_INITDIALOG** message. The dialog procedure will use the **ADDRESSDLGINFO** structure to return the address and subject information to the **OnMailSend** function when the dialog box returns.

When the user selects "OK" in the Addressing Information dialog box, the **AddressDlgProc** function retrieves the values of the To and Cc edit controls, splits the strings into a list of separate addresses, and returns the address and subject information to the **OnMailSend** function.

When the dialog box terminates, **OnMailSend** performs some checks to ensure that the user entered a minimum amount of information into the dialog box. In particular, it determines that at least one destination address was specified in the To or Cc text boxes. **OnMailSend** also ensures that any attachment file actually exists. This process is covered more fully in a later chapter on the MIME protocol.

If everything checks, **OnMailSend** disables the Mail|Send menu choice (so that the user can't try to send the same message again while it is being sent), iconizes the editor window, and alters the window title to indicate that the message is in the process of being sent. **OnMailSend** then creates an RFC 822 message in a temporary file. The message headers are created based on the address and subject information provided in the Addressing Information dialog box. The message is also given a Message-ID header and Date header. Additional headers are included for the MIME protocol if the message has a file attachment or includes non-US-ASCII characters (such as ISO 8859-1 characters). Following the message headers, the message body is retrieved from the edit control window and written to the temporary file.

Once the temporary file is created, **OnMailSend** creates a **CSMTPWithWinMsg** object. **OnMailSend** indicates that the editor child window should be sent a **WM_CSMTPDONE** message when the **CSMTPWithWinMsg** object finishes sending of the message. The **WM_CSMTPDONE** message is a private window message defined in the MAILEDIT.CPP file. **OnMailSend** then invokes the **SendMessage** member function on the object. **OnMailSend** indicates that the temporary file containing the message should be sent to the remote server specified in the global configuration variables.

When the **CSMTPWithWinMsg** class completes its task, it sends the editor window a **WM_CSMTPDONE** window message. Receipt of this message causes the **OnCSMTPDone** function to be called. First, the **OnCSMTPDone** function deletes the **CSMTPWithWinMsg** object and deletes the temporary file in which the message was created. The list of destination addresses is also deleted, and the Mail|Send menu item is re-enabled. If the parameters associated with the **WM_CSMTPDONE** message indicate that the message was transmitted without an error occuring, the window simply closes itself. If the message transmission had any problems, the editor window is reactivated and an error dialog box notifies the user that something happened. The user can try to correct the problem and then resend the message.

Listings

This section includes the following listings for the files that are necessary for the first part of our Mail Client project. Other files are included in later chapters and on the companion CD-ROM.

Listing 9.1 is the header file for the **CSMTP** class, CSMTP.H.

Listing 9.2 is the implementation file for the **CSMTP** class, CSMTP.CPP.

Listing 9.3 is the header file containing the global variable declarations for the Mail Client project, MAILCLIG.H.

Listing 9.4 is the resource file for the Mail Client project, MAILCLI.RC.

Listing 9.5 is the resource header file for the Mail Client project, MAILCLI.RH.

Listing 9.6 is the linker definition file for the Mail Client project, MAILCLI.DEF.

Listing 9.7 is the main implementation file for the Mail Client project, MAILCLI.CPP. It contains the implementation of the MDI frame window and the Configure dialog box.

Listing 9.8 is the implementation file for the editor MDI child window, MAILEDIT.CPP. It contains all of the window procedure code to handle the window. It also contains the code to compose a message and interface with the **CSMTP** class.

Listing 9.9 is the header file for the RFC822.CPP file, RFC822.H.

Listing 9.10 shows RFC822.CPP. This file contains a number of functions related to RFC 822, including functions to create a unique message ID string as well as format the current date and time in RFC 822 format. Additional functions parse RFC 822 header bodies. These additional functions will be used in later chapters.

Listing 9.1 CSMTP.H

```
/*
    File: CSMTP.H
    Description:
        A class for sending email messages via SMTP (RFC 821).
    Copyright 1995, David G. Roberts
*/

#ifndef _CSMTP_H
#define _CSMTP_H

#ifndef _CSOCKET_H
#include "csocket.h"
#endif
#ifndef _CCONNMGR_H
#include "cconnmgr.h"
#endif
#ifndef _CADDRLST_H
#include "caddrlst.h"
#endif
#include <iostream.h>

/*
    Class: CSMTP
    Description:
        Implementes the SMTP protocol.
*/
class CSMTP : private CConnMgrCallback, private CStreamCallback {
public:
    enum RESULT { RESULT_ABORT, RESULT_SUCCESS, RESULT_FAILURE };
protected:
    RESULT          m_result;
private:
    enum CONSTANTS { MAX_REPLY_SIZE = 512, MAX_LINE_SIZE = 1001 };
    enum EVENT { EV_NULLEVENT, EV_CONNECT, EV_CLOSE, EV_CODE_1,
        EV_CODE_2, EV_CODE_3, EV_CODE_4, EV_CODE_5, EV_BUFFERFREE,
        EV_ERROR, EV_ABORT};
    typedef BOOL (CSMTP::*PSTATEFUNC)(EVENT ev);

    CConnMgr        m_connmgr;
    CStreamSocket   m_sock;
    char            m_szReplyBuffer[MAX_REPLY_SIZE];
    int             m_iReplyLen;
    char            m_szLineBuffer[MAX_LINE_SIZE];
```

```
    BOOL            m_bBufferQueued;
    PSTATEFUNC       m_pState;
    int             m_iError;
    char *          m_pszHost;
    u_short         m_ushPort;
    istream *        m_pisMsgStream;
    char *          m_pszFrom;
    CAddrList *      m_palAddrList;
    BOOL            m_bDoCallback;

    // State machine interface.
    void Event(EVENT ev);
    void NextState(PSTATEFUNC pState) { m_pState = pState; };

    // State functions.
    BOOL Start(EVENT ev);
    BOOL AwaitConnection(EVENT ev);
    BOOL AwaitGreeting(EVENT ev);
    BOOL AwaitHelloResponse(EVENT ev);
    BOOL AwaitMailFromResponse(EVENT ev);
    BOOL AwaitRcptToResponse(EVENT ev);
    BOOL AwaitDataResponse(EVENT ev);
    BOOL SendData(EVENT ev);
    BOOL AwaitDataTransferResponse(EVENT ev);
    BOOL Quit(EVENT ev);
    BOOL AwaitQuitResponse(EVENT ev);
    BOOL Exit(EVENT ev);
    BOOL Stop(EVENT ev);

    // Virtual function called when the CSMTP state machine has
    // finished.
    virtual void DoCallback(void) = 0;

    // Aux functions.
    BOOL ReadReplyData(void);
    BOOL LineComplete(void);
    void ShrinkReceiveBuffer(void);

    virtual void ConnMgrCallback(int iToken,
        CConnMgrCallback::RESULT result);
    virtual void StreamCallback(int iToken, STREAMEVENT iEvent,
        int iError, char FAR * lpBuffer);

    // Eliminate the use of the copy constructor and operator=.
    CSMTP(const CSMTP&);
    operator=(const CSMTP&);
public:
    CSMTP() { m_connmgr.SetCallback(this, 0); };
    virtual ~CSMTP() { Abort(FALSE); };

    BOOL SendMessage(LPCSTR lpszHost, u_short ushPort,
        istream * pisMsgStream, LPCSTR lpszFrom,
        CAddrList * palAddrList);
```

```
        void Abort(BOOL bDoCallback);
};

/*
    Class: CSMTPWithWinMsg
    Description:
        Descendant of the CSMTP class.  Sends a window message
        back to the application when the message has been sent.
*/
class CSMTPWithWinMsg : public CSMTP {
private:
    HWND m_hwnd;
    UINT m_msg;
    int  m_iToken;

    virtual void DoCallback(void);
public:
    CSMTPWithWinMsg(HWND hwnd, UINT msg, int iToken) :
        m_hwnd(hwnd), m_msg(msg), m_iToken(iToken) {};
    ~CSMTPWithWinMsg() {};
};

/*
    Class: CSMTPCallback
    Description:
        Used with CSMTPWithCallback.  An object wishing to receive
        a callback from a CSMTP object should inherit this class.
*/
class CSMTPCallback {
public:
    virtual void SMTPCallback(int iToken, CSMTP::RESULT result) = 0;
};

/*
    Class: CSMTPWithCallback
    Description:
        Descendant of the CSMTP class.  Provides a callback when
        the message has been sent.  An object wishing to receive
        the callback should inherit CSMTPCallback.
*/
class CSMTPWithCallback : public CSMTP {
private:
    CSMTPCallback * m_pCallback;
    int  m_iToken;

    virtual void DoCallback(void);
public:
    CSMTPWithCallback(CSMTPCallback * pCallback, int iToken) :
        m_pCallback(pCallback), m_iToken(iToken) {};
    ~CSMTPWithCallback() {};
};
#endif
```

Listing 9.2 CSMTP.CPP

```
/*
    File: CSMTP.CPP
    Description:
        A class for sending email messages via SMTP (RFC 821).
    Copyright 1995, David G. Roberts
*/

#include "csmtp.h"
#include "myassert.h"

const char CR = '\015';
const char LF = '\012';

// Used to include at the end of text.  The compiler will splice
// strings.
// Use like m_sock.Send("Foo" CRLF,...).
#define CRLF "\015\012"

/*
    Function: CSMTP::Event
    Description:
        The event dispatch loop for the state machine.
*/
void CSMTP::Event(EVENT ev)
{
    while ((this->*m_pState)(ev)) {
        ev = EV_NULLEVENT;
    };
}


/*
    Function: CSMTP::StreamCallback
    Description:
        Receives callbacks from the CStreamSocket object and
        conditions them into appropriate events for the SMTP
        state machine.  In particular, when a line of response
        text comes back from the server, this function reads it,
        and if a full line of text is present, interprets the
        text to generate an EV_CODE_X event.
*/
void CSMTP::StreamCallback(int iToken, STREAMEVENT iEvent, int iError,
    char FAR *lpBuffer)
{
    UNUSED_PARAMETER(iToken);    // Eliminate the compiler warning.

    m_iError = iError;
    switch (iEvent) {
        case CStreamCallback::SE_CLOSE:
            Event(EV_CLOSE);
            break;
```

```
    case CStreamCallback::SE_DATAREADY:
        // Read the data.
        if (ReadReplyData()) {
            // If no errors, see if we have a complete reply line.
            if (LineComplete()) {
                // Yes, it's a complete line.  See if the line is
                // a continuation reply (of the form "250-Foo").
                if (m_szReplyBuffer[3] != '-') {
                    // If not, save the first character (should
                    // be the leading digit of a numeric reply
                    // code.
                    char ch = m_szReplyBuffer[0];
                    // Eliminate the line from the receive buffer.
                    ShrinkReceiveBuffer();
                    // Turn the character code into a state
                    // machine event.
                    switch (ch) {
                        case '1': Event(EV_CODE_1); break;
                        case '2': Event(EV_CODE_2); break;
                        case '3': Event(EV_CODE_3); break;
                        case '4': Event(EV_CODE_4); break;
                        case '5': Event(EV_CODE_5); break;
                        default:
                            WSCFatalError(
                                "Invalid SMTP reply received "
                                "in CSMTP.");
                    }
                }
                else {
                    // Yes, it was a continuation line.  Just
                    // throw it in the bit bucket.
                    ShrinkReceiveBuffer();
                }
            }
        }
        else {
            // Something went wrong.
            WSCFatalError("Couldn't read from socket in CSMTP.");
        }
        break;
    case CStreamCallback::SE_DATASENT:
        if (lpBuffer == (char FAR *)m_szLineBuffer) {
            m_bBufferQueued = FALSE;
            Event(EV_BUFFERFREE);
        }
        break;
    default:
        // Error!  Something we weren't expecting.
        WSCFatalError(
            "Unexpected socket event in CSMTP::StreamCallback");
        break;
    }
}
```

```
/*
        Function: CSMTP::ReadReplyData
        Description:
            When data arrives at the socket to be read, this function
            is called to read it into a local buffer.  The function
            ensures that data already in the buffer is preserved and
            that we don't read more than we can handle.  The function
            normally returns TRUE.  If an error occurs during the read,
            it returns FALSE.
*/
BOOL CSMTP::ReadReplyData(void)
{
    // Figure out how much room is left in the buffer.
    int iBufferLen = MAX_REPLY_SIZE - m_iReplyLen;
    ASSERT(iBufferLen > 0);

    // Receive the data.
    int iResult = m_sock.Receive(&m_szReplyBuffer[m_iReplyLen],
        &iBufferLen);

    if (iResult == WSANOERROR || iResult == WSAEWOULDBLOCK) {
        // If no errors, update the length of the data in the buffer.
        m_iReplyLen += iBufferLen;
        return TRUE;
    }
    else {
        // Save the error and signal it.
        m_iError = iResult;
        return FALSE;
    }
}


/*
        Function: CSMTP::LineComplete
        Description:
            This function is called when data arrives on the socket
            and has been read into a local buffer.  The function returns
            true if a full line of text is present in the buffer
            (i.e., that a CRLF has been found).  It returns FALSE if
            it cannot find a CRLF in the current data.
*/
BOOL CSMTP::LineComplete(void)
{
    ASSERT(m_iReplyLen <= MAX_REPLY_SIZE);

    for (int i = 0; i < m_iReplyLen; i++) {
        if ((m_szReplyBuffer[i] == CR) && ((i + 1) < m_iReplyLen) &&
            (m_szReplyBuffer[i + 1] == LF)) {
            return TRUE;
        }
    }
    return FALSE;
}
```

```
/*
     Function: CSMTP::ShrinkReceiveBuffer
     Description:
          This function is called to remove a full line of response
          text from the buffer when it has been processed.  Any
          text that remains in the buffer following the processed
          line is moved to the front of the buffer.
*/
void CSMTP::ShrinkReceiveBuffer(void)
{
     ASSERT(m_iReplyLen <= MAX_REPLY_SIZE);

     // Find the CRLF at the end of the line.
     for (int i = 0; i < m_iReplyLen; i++) {
          if ((m_szReplyBuffer[i] == CR) && ((i + 1) < m_iReplyLen) &&
             (m_szReplyBuffer[i + 1] == LF)) {
               // Set i equal to the character following the CRLF.
               i += 2;
               // Copy the characters following the CRLF to the beginning
               // of the line.
               for (int j = 0; j < m_iReplyLen - i; j++) {
                    m_szReplyBuffer[j] = m_szReplyBuffer[i + j];
               }
               // Subtract number of characters removed from the current
               // number of characters in the buffer.
               m_iReplyLen -= i;
               // Break out of the for(i) loop.
               break;
          }
     }
}


/*
     Function: CSMTP::ConnMsgCallback
     Description:
          Receives callbacks from the connection manager object
          and turns them into events for the SMTP state machine.
*/
void CSMTP::ConnMgrCallback(int iToken,
     CConnMgrCallback::RESULT result)
{
     UNUSED_PARAMETER(iToken);

     ASSERT(result != CConnMgrCallback::INVALID_RESULT);

     // Turn connection callback result into events.
     switch (result) {
          case CConnMgrCallback::OK_CONNECTED:
             Event(EV_CONNECT);
             break;
          case CConnMgrCallback::ERR_NOTCONNECTED:
             m_iError = m_connmgr.LastError();
```

```
                Event(EV_ERROR);
                break;
        }
}


/*

    Function: CSMTP::Abort
    Description:
        Public function called when the program wants to abort
        the SMTP transfer.  The function generates an EV_ABORT
        event to the state machine.
*/
void CSMTP::Abort(BOOL bDoCallback)
{
    m_bDoCallback = bDoCallback;
    Event(EV_ABORT);
}


/*

    Function: CSMTP::SendMessage
    Description:
        The function that kicks off SMTP processing.  The parameters
        specify the host and port to connect to, a stream from
        which to draw the message, the from address, and a list
        of recipients.  The function stores away the necessary
        information and starts the SMTP state machine in the
        START state.
*/
BOOL CSMTP::SendMessage(LPCSTR lpszHost, u_short ushPort,
    istream * pisMsgStream, LPCSTR lpszFrom, CAddrList * palAddrList)
{
    ASSERT(lpszHost != NULL);
    ASSERT(lpszFrom != NULL);
    ASSERT(palAddrList != NULL);

    // Make sure we're currently stopped.
    // Store parameters away.
    m_pszHost = new char[lstrlen(lpszHost) + 1];
    lstrcpy(m_pszHost, lpszHost);
    m_ushPort = ushPort;
    m_pisMsgStream = pisMsgStream;
    m_pszFrom = new char[lstrlen(lpszFrom) + 1];
    lstrcpy(m_pszFrom, lpszFrom);
    m_palAddrList = palAddrList;

    // Initialize our state correctly.
    m_iReplyLen = 0;
    m_bBufferQueued = FALSE;
    m_bDoCallback = TRUE;

    // Start us off.
    NextState(&CSMTP::Start);
```

```
        Event(EV_NULLEVENT);

    return TRUE;
}


/*
      Function: CSMTP::Start
      Description:
            Start the state machine.  Fire off the connection manager
            to try to connect and then go to the AWAITCONNECTION state.
*/
BOOL CSMTP::Start(EVENT ev)
{
      UNUSED_PARAMETER(ev);

      // Make the connection to the remote host.  Let the connection
      // manager do all the work.
      m_connmgr.Connect(m_pszHost, m_ushPort, &m_sock, this, 0);
      NextState(&CSMTP::AwaitConnection);
      return TRUE;
}


/*
      Function:  CSMTP::AwaitConnection
      Description:
            Wait for the connection event from the connection
            manager or an error.  If the connection succeeded, wait
            for the greeting message from the server.
*/
BOOL CSMTP::AwaitConnection(EVENT ev)
{
      switch (ev) {
          case EV_ABORT:
              m_connmgr.Abort();
              m_result = RESULT_ABORT;
              NextState(&CSMTP::Exit);
              break;
          case EV_CONNECT:
              NextState(&CSMTP::AwaitGreeting);
              break;
          case EV_ERROR:
              m_result = RESULT_FAILURE;
              NextState(&CSMTP::Exit);
              break;
          default:
              return FALSE;
      }
      return TRUE;
}


/*
      Function:  CSMTP::AwaitGreeting
```

```
        Description:
                Waits for the remote SMTP server to send the initial
                greeting.
*/
BOOL CSMTP::AwaitGreeting(EVENT ev)
{
        int iResult;
        char szMyHostName[80];

        switch (ev) {
            case EV_ABORT:
                m_result = RESULT_ABORT;
                NextState(&CSMTP::Exit);
                break;
            case EV_CLOSE:
                // Hmmm... unexpected close of the socket from the other
                // end.
                m_result = RESULT_FAILURE;
                NextState(&CSMTP::Exit);
                break;
            case EV_CODE_2:
                // Okay, we got the greeting.  Send the HELO message in
                // response.
                if (gethostname(szMyHostName, sizeof(szMyHostName)) ==
                    SOCKET_ERROR) {
                    m_iError = WSAGetLastError();
                    m_result = RESULT_FAILURE;
                    NextState(&CSMTP::Exit);
                }
                else {
                    wsprintf(m_szLineBuffer, "HELO %s" CRLF,
                        (LPSTR)szMyHostName);
                    iResult = m_sock.Send(m_szLineBuffer,
                        lstrlen(m_szLineBuffer));
                    if (iResult == WSANOERROR ||
                        iResult == WSAEWOULDBLOCK) {
                        NextState(&CSMTP::AwaitHelloResponse);
                    }
                    else {
                        m_iError = iResult;
                        m_result = RESULT_FAILURE;
                        NextState(&CSMTP::Exit);
                    }
                }
                break;
            case EV_CODE_1:
            case EV_CODE_3:
            case EV_CODE_4:
            case EV_CODE_5:
                // All other codes are unexpected and generate a failure.
                m_result = RESULT_FAILURE;
                NextState(&CSMTP::Exit);
```

```
                break;
            default:
                return FALSE;
    }
    return TRUE;
}


/*

    Function: CSMTP::AwaitHelloResponse
    Description:
        Waits for the response to the HELO command.
*/
BOOL CSMTP::AwaitHelloResponse(EVENT ev)
{
    int iResult;

    switch (ev) {
        case EV_ABORT:
            m_result = RESULT_ABORT;
            NextState(&CSMTP::Exit);
            break;
        case EV_CLOSE:
            // Hmmm... unexpected close of the socket from the
            // other end.
            m_result = RESULT_FAILURE;
            NextState(&CSMTP::Exit);
            break;
        case EV_CODE_2:
            wsprintf(m_szLineBuffer, "MAIL FROM:<%s>" CRLF,
                (LPSTR)m_pszFrom);
            iResult = m_sock.Send(m_szLineBuffer,
                lstrlen(m_szLineBuffer));
            if (iResult == WSANOERROR || iResult == WSAEWOULDBLOCK) {
                NextState(&CSMTP::AwaitMailFromResponse);
            }
            else {
                m_iError = iResult;
                m_result = RESULT_FAILURE;
                NextState(&CSMTP::Exit);
            }
            break;
        case EV_CODE_1:
        case EV_CODE_3:
        case EV_CODE_4:
        case EV_CODE_5:
            // All other codes are unexpected and generate a failure.
            m_result = RESULT_FAILURE;
            NextState(&CSMTP::Quit);      // Now go send QUIT.
            break;
        default:
            return FALSE;
    }
```

```
    return TRUE;
}


/*

    Function: CSMTP::AwaitMailFromResponse
    Description:
        Awaits for the response from the MAIL FROM command.
*/
BOOL CSMTP::AwaitMailFromResponse(EVENT ev)
{
    int iResult;
    char * pszRecipient;

    switch (ev) {
        case EV_ABORT:
            m_result = RESULT_ABORT;
            NextState(&CSMTP::Exit);
            break;
        case EV_CLOSE:
            // Hmmm... unexpected close of the socket from the
            // other end.
            m_result = RESULT_FAILURE;
            NextState(&CSMTP::Exit);
            break;
        case EV_CODE_2:
            pszRecipient = m_palAddrList->First();
            ASSERT(pszRecipient != NULL);
            wsprintf(m_szLineBuffer, "RCPT TO:<%s>" CRLF,
                (LPSTR)pszRecipient);
            iResult = m_sock.Send(m_szLineBuffer,
                lstrlen(m_szLineBuffer));
            if (iResult == WSANOERROR || iResult == WSAEWOULDBLOCK) {
                NextState(&CSMTP::AwaitRcptToResponse);
            }
            else {
                m_iError = iResult;
                m_result = RESULT_FAILURE;
                NextState(&CSMTP::Exit);
            }
            break;
        case EV_CODE_1:
        case EV_CODE_3:
        case EV_CODE_4:
        case EV_CODE_5:
            // All other codes are unexpected and generate a failure.
            m_result = RESULT_FAILURE;
            NextState(&CSMTP::Quit);
            break;
        default:
            return FALSE;
    }
    return TRUE;
}
```

```
/*
    Function: CSMTP::AwaitRcptToResponse
    Description:
        Waits for the response from the RCPT command.
        If there are more recipients remaining, it sends another
        RCPT command and waits for the response again.
*/
BOOL CSMTP::AwaitRcptToResponse(EVENT ev)
{
    int iResult;
    char * pszRecipient;

    switch (ev) {
        case EV_ABORT:
            m_result = RESULT_ABORT;
            NextState(&CSMTP::Exit);
            break;
        case EV_CLOSE:
            // Hmmm... unexpected close of the socket from the
            // other end.
            m_result = RESULT_FAILURE;
            NextState(&CSMTP::Exit);
            break;
        case EV_CODE_2:
            pszRecipient = m_palAddrList->Next();
            if (pszRecipient == NULL) {
                lstrcpy(m_szLineBuffer, "DATA" CRLF);
                iResult = m_sock.Send(m_szLineBuffer,
                    lstrlen(m_szLineBuffer));
                if (iResult == WSANOERROR || iResult ==
                    WSAEWOULDBLOCK) {
                    NextState(&CSMTP::AwaitDataResponse);
                }
                else {
                    m_iError = iResult;
                    m_result = RESULT_FAILURE;
                    NextState(&CSMTP::Exit);
                }
            }
            else {
                wsprintf(m_szLineBuffer, "RCPT TO:<%s>" CRLF,
                    (LPSTR)pszRecipient);
                iResult = m_sock.Send(m_szLineBuffer,
                    lstrlen(m_szLineBuffer));
                if (iResult == WSANOERROR || iResult ==
                    WSAEWOULDBLOCK) {
                    NextState(&CSMTP::AwaitRcptToResponse);
                }
                else {
                    m_iError = iResult;
                    m_result = RESULT_FAILURE;
                    NextState(&CSMTP::Exit);
                }
            }
```

```
                break;
            case EV_CODE_1:
            case EV_CODE_3:
            case EV_CODE_4:
            case EV_CODE_5:
                // All other codes are unexpected and generate a failure.
                m_result = RESULT_FAILURE;
                NextState(&CSMTP::Quit);
                break;
            default:
                return FALSE;
    }
    return TRUE;
}


/*
    Function: CSMTP::AwaitDataResponse
    Description:
        Waits for the response from the DATA command.
*/
BOOL CSMTP::AwaitDataResponse(EVENT ev)
{
    switch (ev) {
        case EV_ABORT:
            m_result = RESULT_ABORT;
            NextState(&CSMTP::Exit);
            break;
        case EV_CLOSE:
            // Hmmm... unexpected close of the socket from the
            // other end.
            m_result = RESULT_FAILURE;
            NextState(&CSMTP::Exit);
            break;
        case EV_CODE_3:
            // Okay, here we go.
            NextState(&CSMTP::SendData);
            break;
        case EV_CODE_1:
        case EV_CODE_2:
        case EV_CODE_4:
        case EV_CODE_5:
            // All other codes are unexpected and generate a failure.
            m_result = RESULT_FAILURE;
            NextState(&CSMTP::Quit);
            break;
        default:
            return FALSE;
    }
    return TRUE;
}
```

```
/*
     Function: CSMTP::SendData
     Description:
         Sends the lines of text making up the message.  If the
         lines start with ".", the transparency rules are invoked
         to escape the leading "." character.  If the socket
         transmit buffer becomes full and a write command blocks,
         the function quits sending data until the buffer becomes
         free again.
*/
BOOL CSMTP::SendData(EVENT ev)
{
    int iResult;

    switch (ev) {
        case EV_ABORT:
            m_result = RESULT_ABORT;
            NextState(&CSMTP::Exit);
            break;
        case EV_CLOSE:
            // Hmmm... unexpected close of the socket from the
            // other end.
            m_result = RESULT_FAILURE;
            NextState(&CSMTP::Exit);
            break;
        case EV_CODE_1:
        case EV_CODE_2:
        case EV_CODE_3:
        case EV_CODE_4:
        case EV_CODE_5:
            // All other codes are unexpected and generate a failure.
            m_result = RESULT_FAILURE;
            NextState(&CSMTP::Quit);
            break;
        case EV_NULLEVENT:
            // This stops the machine from progressing when we fill up
            // the socket's buffer.  The machine will progress when
            // the socket sends a SE_DATASENT, which is converted to
            // EV_BUFFERFREE by the StreamCallback function.
            if (m_bBufferQueued) {
                return FALSE;
            }
            // Else fall through.
        case EV_BUFFERFREE:
            if (m_pisMsgStream->peek() == EOF) {
                // Send ".CRLF"
                lstrcpy(m_szLineBuffer, "." CRLF);
                iResult = m_sock.Send(m_szLineBuffer,
                    lstrlen(m_szLineBuffer));
                if (iResult == WSANOERROR || iResult ==
                    WSAEWOULDBLOCK) {
                        NextState(&CSMTP::AwaitDataTransferResponse);
```

```
            }
        else {
            m_iError = iResult;
            m_result = RESULT_FAILURE;
            NextState(&CSMTP::Exit);
        }
    }
    else {
        // Get a line of data from the stream.
        m_pisMsgStream->getline(m_szLineBuffer,
            MAX_LINE_SIZE);
        int iLineLength = lstrlen(m_szLineBuffer);
        if (iLineLength > (MAX_LINE_SIZE - 3)) {
            // Whoa!  The line we read was too long.
            m_result = RESULT_FAILURE;
            NextState(&CSMTP::Exit);
        }
        else {
            // Strip all the high bits to make sure we don't
            // violate SMTP's 7-bit US-ASCII coding
            // requirement.
            for (int i = 0; i < iLineLength; i++) {
                m_szLineBuffer[i] =
                    (char) (m_szLineBuffer[i] & 0x7F);
            }
            lstrcat(m_szLineBuffer, CRLF);  // Add CRLF.
            if (m_szLineBuffer[0] == '.') {
                // It's got a leading period, so add one, as
                // per SMTP transparency rules.
                // (RCF 821, 4.5.2).
                iResult = m_sock.Send(".", 1);
                if (iResult != WSANOERROR && iResult !=
                    WSAEWOULDBLOCK) {
                    m_iError = iResult;
                    m_result = RESULT_FAILURE;
                    NextState(&CSMTP::Exit);
                    return TRUE;
                }
            }
            // Send the line.
            iResult = m_sock.Send(m_szLineBuffer,
                lstrlen(m_szLineBuffer));
            if (iResult == WSANOERROR) {
                // If we didn't block, then keep going.
                return TRUE;
            }
            else if (iResult == WSAEWOULDBLOCK) {
                // We blocked, so signal that buffer is queued
                // and keep going.  Note that the EV_NULLEVENT
                // handling above will stop the machine.
                m_bBufferQueued = TRUE;
                return TRUE;
```

```
                        }
                      else {
                            m_iError = iResult;
                            m_result = RESULT_FAILURE;
                            NextState(&CSMTP::Exit);
                      }
                }
           }
        default:
            return FALSE;
    }
    return TRUE;
}


/*
    Function: CSMTP::AwaitDataTransferResponse
    Description:
        Waits for the response after the data has been sent.
*/
BOOL CSMTP::AwaitDataTransferResponse(EVENT ev)
{
    switch (ev) {
        case EV_ABORT:
            m_result = RESULT_ABORT;
            NextState(&CSMTP::Exit);
            break;
        case EV_CLOSE:
            // Hmmm... unexpected close of the socket from the
            // other end.
            m_result = RESULT_FAILURE;
            NextState(&CSMTP::Exit);
            break;
        case EV_CODE_2:
            // It worked!!
            m_result = RESULT_SUCCESS;
            NextState(&CSMTP::Quit);
            break;
        case EV_CODE_1:
        case EV_CODE_3:
        case EV_CODE_4:
        case EV_CODE_5:
            // All other codes are unexpected and generate a failure.
            m_result = RESULT_FAILURE;
            NextState(&CSMTP::Quit);
            break;
        default:
            return FALSE;
    }
    return TRUE;
}
```

```
/*
      Function: CSMTP::Quit
      Description:
          We're all done.  The data has been sent.  Send the QUIT
          command to close the connection.
*/
BOOL CSMTP::Quit(EVENT ev)
{
      UNUSED_PARAMETER(ev);

    int iResult;

    lstrcpy(m_szLineBuffer, "QUIT" CRLF);
    iResult = m_sock.Send(m_szLineBuffer, lstrlen(m_szLineBuffer));
    if (iResult == WSANOERROR || iResult == WSAEWOULDBLOCK) {
        NextState(&CSMTP::AwaitQuitResponse);
    }
    else {
        m_iError = iResult;
        m_result = RESULT_FAILURE;
        NextState(&CSMTP::Exit);
    }
    return TRUE;
}


/*
      Function: CSMTP::AwaitQuitResponse
      Description:
          Waits for the response to the QUIT command.
*/
BOOL CSMTP::AwaitQuitResponse(EVENT ev)
{
    switch (ev) {
        case EV_ABORT:
            m_result = RESULT_ABORT;
            NextState(&CSMTP::Exit);
          break;
        case EV_CLOSE:  // Just about anything is okay.  We
        case EV_CODE_1: // transferred the message, so just move on.
        case EV_CODE_2: // Note that success or failure is indicated
        case EV_CODE_3: // before this state is entered, so don't
        case EV_CODE_4: // mess with it here.
        case EV_CODE_5:
            NextState(&CSMTP::Exit);
          break;
        default:
            return FALSE;
    }
    return TRUE;
}

/*
    Function: CSMTP::Exit
```

```
        Description:
            Deletes all the allocated memory, performs the completion
            callback (which is either a window message or a function
            callback), and transitions to the Stop state.
*/
BOOL CSMTP::Exit(EVENT ev)
{
    UNUSED_PARAMETER(ev);     // Eliminate the compiler warning.

    // Close the socket.
    m_sock.Close();

    // Free up the stuff we allocated when we started.
    delete[] m_pszHost;
    delete[] m_pszFrom;

    // Now, invoke the callback with the connection attempt result.
    if (m_bDoCallback) {
        DoCallback();
    }

    NextState(&CSMTP::Stop);
    return TRUE;
}


/*
    Function: CSMTP::Stop
    Description:
        The final state of the state machine.  Ignores all events.
*/
BOOL CSMTP::Stop(EVENT ev)
{
    UNUSED_PARAMETER(ev);
    // Simply ignore all events.
    return FALSE;
}

/********************************************************************
    Callbacks for specialized CSMTP derivatives.
********************************************************************/
/*
    Function: CSMTPWithWinMsg::DoCallback
    Description:
        Turn the state machine completion into a window message.
*/
void CSMTPWithWinMsg::DoCallback(void)
{
    PostMessage(m_hwnd, m_msg, m_iToken, m_result);
}

/*
    Function: CSMTPWithCallback::DoCallback
```

```
    Description:
         Turn the state machine completion into a function callback.
*/
void CSMTPWithCallback::DoCallback(void)
{
    m_pCallback->SMTPCallback(m_iToken, m_result);
}
```

Listing 9.3   MAILCLIG.H

```
/*
    File: MAILCLIG.H
    Description:
         The global variable declarations for MAILCLI.
    Copyright 1995, David G. Roberts
*/


#ifdef DECLARE
#define INIT(x)
#define EXTERN extern
#else
#define INIT(x) x
#define EXTERN
#endif


/*
    CONSTANTS
*/
#define MAX_PATH_LENGTH      260
#define MAX_FILENAME_LENGTH  255


/*
    MACROS
*/
// Microsoft Visual C++ 1.5 WINDOWSX.H doesn't include these macros
// like Borland does.
#ifndef GET_WM_COMMAND_ID
#ifdef WIN32
#define GET_WM_COMMAND_ID(wp, lp)      LOWORD(wp)
#else
#define GET_WM_COMMAND_ID(wp, lp)     (wp)
#endif
#endif


#ifndef GET_WM_COMMAND_HWND
#ifdef WIN32
#define GET_WM_COMMAND_HWND(wp, lp)        (HWND)(lp)
#else
#define GET_WM_COMMAND_HWND(wp, lp)        (HWND)LOWORD(lp)
#endif
#endif
```

```
#ifndef GET_WM_COMMAND_CMD
#ifdef WIN32
#define GET_WM_COMMAND_CMD(wp, lp)          HIWORD(wp)
#else
#define GET_WM_COMMAND_CMD(wp, lp)          HIWORD(lp)
#endif
#endif


#ifndef GET_WM_COMMAND_MPS
#ifdef WIN32
#define GET_WM_COMMAND_MPS(id, hwnd, cmd)       \
        (WPARAM)MAKELONG(id, cmd), (LONG)(hwnd)
#else
#define GET_WM_COMMAND_MPS(id, hwnd, cmd)       \
        (WPARAM)(id), MAKELONG(hwnd, cmd)
#endif
#endif


#ifndef GET_WM_MDISETMENU_MPS
#ifdef WIN32
#define GET_WM_MDISETMENU_MPS(hmenuF, hmenuW) (WPARAM)hmenuF, (LONG)hmenuW
#else
#define GET_WM_MDISETMENU_MPS(hmenuF, hmenuW) 0, MAKELONG(hmenuF, hmenuW)
#endif
#endif


#ifndef GET_EM_SETSEL_MPS
#ifdef WIN32
#define GET_EM_SETSEL_MPS(iStart, iEnd) \
        (WPARAM)(iStart), (LONG)(iEnd)
#else
#define GET_EM_SETSEL_MPS(iStart, iEnd) \
        0, MAKELONG(iStart, iEnd)
#endif
#endif


/*
    GLOBAL VARIABLES
*/
#ifdef WIN32
#define WINVERSION "32"
#else
#define WINVERSION "16"
#endif
EXTERN HWND         g_hFrame;
EXTERN HWND         g_hClient;
EXTERN HINSTANCE    g_hInstance;
EXTERN char         g_szAppName[] INIT(= "MAILCLI");
EXTERN char         g_szFullAppName[]
                         INIT(= "Mail Client (Win" WINVERSION ")");
EXTERN char         g_szFrameClass[] INIT(= "MAILCLIFRAME");
```

```
EXTERN char          g_szMailboxClass[] INIT(= "MAILBOXCHILD");
EXTERN char           g_szViewerClass[] INIT(= "VIEWERCHILD");
EXTERN char           g_szEditorClass[] INIT(= "EDITORCHILD");
EXTERN HMENU         g_hFrameMenu;
EXTERN HMENU         g_hMailboxMenu;
EXTERN HMENU         g_hViewerMenu;
EXTERN HMENU         g_hEditorMenu;
EXTERN HMENU          g_hFrameWindowMenu;
EXTERN HMENU          g_hMailboxWindowMenu;
EXTERN HMENU          g_hViewerWindowMenu;
EXTERN HMENU          g_hEditorWindowMenu;
EXTERN HACCEL        g_hAccel;
EXTERN char *        g_pszSMTPServer;
EXTERN u_short       g_ushSMTPPort;
EXTERN u_short        g_ushSMTPDefaultPort;
EXTERN char *        g_pszPOPServer;
EXTERN u_short       g_ushPOPPort;
EXTERN u_short        g_ushPOPDefaultPort;
EXTERN char *        g_pszMailbox;
EXTERN char *        g_pszPassword;
EXTERN char *        g_pszUserName;
EXTERN char *        g_pszUserAddress;
EXTERN char          g_szIniFile[] INIT(= "mailcli.ini");
EXTERN char *        g_pszWorkingDirectory;
EXTERN CWinsock      g_wsWinsock INIT((0x0101, 0x0101));
EXTERN BOOL          g_bConfigured INIT(= FALSE);
EXTERN char          g_szMessageDir[MAX_PATH_LENGTH];
EXTERN char          g_szMailboxFile[MAX_PATH_LENGTH];

/*
    GLOBAL FUNCTIONS
*/
void ForwardDefFrameProc(HWND, UINT, WPARAM, LPARAM);
HWND GetMDIActiveChild(HWND);
BOOL VerifyDlgInt(HWND, int, BOOL);
BOOL VerifyDlgText(HWND, int);
void SetEditErrorFocus(HWND, int);
```

Listing 9.4 MAILCLI.RC

```
/***************************************************************************
MAILCLI.RC
***************************************************************************/

#include "mailcli.rh"
#include "errno.rc"
CONFIGURE DIALOG 13, 44, 284, 161
STYLE DS_MODALFRAME | WS_POPUP | WS_VISIBLE | WS_CAPTION | WS_SYSMENU
CAPTION "Configure"
FONT 8, "MS Sans Serif"
{
  DEFPUSHBUTTON "OK", IDOK, 75, 140, 50, 14
```

```
    PUSHBUTTON "Cancel", IDCANCEL, 159, 140, 50, 14
    EDITTEXT IDD_SMTPSERVER, 47, 25, 84, 15, ES_AUTOHSCROLL | WS_BORDER | WS_TABSTOP
    EDITTEXT IDD_SMTPPORT, 47, 45, 32, 15
    PUSHBUTTON "Default", IDD_DEFAULTSMTPPORT, 84, 45, 46, 15
    EDITTEXT IDD_NAME, 48, 84, 84, 15, ES_AUTOHSCROLL | WS_BORDER | WS_TABSTOP
    EDITTEXT IDD_ADDRESS, 48, 108, 84, 15, ES_AUTOHSCROLL | WS_BORDER | WS_TABSTOP
    EDITTEXT IDD_POPSERVER, 184, 25, 84, 15, ES_AUTOHSCROLL | WS_BORDER | WS_TABSTOP
    EDITTEXT IDD_POPPORT, 184, 46, 32, 15
    PUSHBUTTON "Default", IDD_DEFAULTPOPPORT, 221, 46, 46, 15
    EDITTEXT IDD_MAILBOX, 192, 84, 76, 15, ES_AUTOHSCROLL | WS_BORDER | WS_TABSTOP
    EDITTEXT IDD_PASSWORD, 192, 104, 76, 15, ES_AUTOHSCROLL | ES_PASSWORD | WS_BORDER |
WS_TABSTOP
  LTEXT "Name", -1, 16, 84, 24, 12
  LTEXT "Address", -1, 16, 108, 32, 12
  LTEXT "Server", -1, 15, 26, 28, 12
  LTEXT "Port", -1, 15, 46, 28, 12
  GROUPBOX "SMTP: Outbound Mail", -1, 7, 8, 132, 60, BS_GROUPBOX
  LTEXT "Server", -1, 152, 26, 28, 12
  LTEXT "Port", -1, 152, 46, 28, 12
  GROUPBOX "POP: Inbound Mail", -1, 144, 8, 132, 124, BS_GROUPBOX
  LTEXT "Mailbox", -1, 152, 85, 28, 12
  LTEXT "Password", -1, 152, 105, 36, 12
  GROUPBOX "User Information", -1, 7, 72, 132, 60, BS_GROUPBOX
}
FRAMEMENU MENU
{
  POPUP "&File"
  {
    MENUITEM "&New Message", IDM_FILENEWMESSAGE
    MENUITEM "&Open Mailbox", IDM_FILEOPENMAILBOX
    MENUITEM "&Close", IDM_FILECLOSE
    MENUITEM SEPARATOR
    MENUITEM "E&xit", IDM_FILEEXIT
  }

  POPUP "&Mail"
  {
    MENUITEM "&Configure...", IDM_MAILCONFIGURE
  }

  POPUP "&Window"
  {
    MENUITEM "&Cascade\tShift+F5", IDM_WINDOWCASCADE
    MENUITEM "&Tile\tShift+F4", IDM_WINDOWTILE
    MENUITEM "Arrange &Icons", IDM_WINDOWARRANGE
    MENUITEM "Close &All", IDM_WINDOWCLOSEALL
  }

  POPUP "&Help"
  {
    MENUITEM "&About...", IDM_HELPABOUT
  }
```

```
}
MAILCLI ACCELERATORS
{
  "^Z", IDM_EDITUNDO, ASCII
  VK_DELETE, IDM_MAILDELETEMESSAGE, VIRTKEY
  "^X", IDM_EDITCUT, ASCII
  "^C", IDM_EDITCOPY, ASCII
  "^V", IDM_EDITPASTE, ASCII
  VK_F5, IDM_WINDOWCASCADE, VIRTKEY, SHIFT
  VK_F4, IDM_WINDOWTILE, VIRTKEY, SHIFT
}


EDITORMENU MENU
{
  POPUP "&File"
  {
    MENUITEM "&New Message", IDM_FILENEWMESSAGE
    MENUITEM "&Open Mailbox", IDM_FILEOPENMAILBOX
    MENUITEM "&Close", IDM_FILECLOSE
    MENUITEM SEPARATOR
    MENUITEM "E&xit", IDM_FILEEXIT
  }

  POPUP "&Edit"
  {
    MENUITEM "&Cut\tCtrl+X", IDM_EDITCUT
    MENUITEM "&Copy\tCtrl+C", IDM_EDITCOPY
    MENUITEM "&Paste\tCtrl+V", IDM_EDITPASTE
  }

  POPUP "&Mail"
  {
    MENUITEM "&Send", IDM_MAILSEND
    MENUITEM "&UUENCODE...", IDM_MAILUUENCODE
    MENUITEM SEPARATOR
    MENUITEM "&Configure...", IDM_MAILCONFIGURE
  }

  POPUP "&Window"
  {
    MENUITEM "&Cascade\tShift+F5", IDM_WINDOWCASCADE
    MENUITEM "&Tile\tShift+F4", IDM_WINDOWTILE
    MENUITEM "Arrange &Icons", IDM_WINDOWARRANGE
    MENUITEM "Close &All", IDM_WINDOWCLOSEALL
  }

  POPUP "&Help"
  {
    MENUITEM "&About...", IDM_HELPABOUT
  }

}
```

```
MAILBOXICON ICON "mailbox.ico"

EDITORICON ICON "mailedit.ico"
VIEWERICON ICON "mailview.ico"
ADDRESSING DIALOG 6, 15, 276, 178
STYLE DS_MODALFRAME | WS_POPUP | WS_VISIBLE | WS_CAPTION | WS_SYSMENU
CAPTION "Addressing Information"
FONT 8, "MS Sans Serif"
{
  DEFPUSHBUTTON "OK", IDOK, 212, 24, 50, 14
  PUSHBUTTON "Cancel", IDCANCEL, 212, 52, 50, 14
  LTEXT "To:", -1, 12, 8, 60, 8
  LTEXT "Cc:", -1, 12, 68, 60, 8
  LTEXT "Subject:", -1, 12, 112, 60, 8
  EDITTEXT IDD_TO, 32, 8, 160, 48, ES_MULTILINE | ES_AUTOVSCROLL | WS_BORDER |
WS_VSCROLL | WS_TABSTOP
  EDITTEXT IDD_CC, 32, 68, 160, 32, ES_MULTILINE | ES_AUTOVSCROLL | WS_BORDER |
WS_VSCROLL | WS_TABSTOP
  EDITTEXT IDD_SUBJECT, 44, 112, 148, 24, ES_MULTILINE | ES_AUTOVSCROLL | WS_BORDER |
WS_VSCROLL | WS_TABSTOP
  LTEXT "Attachment:", -1, 12, 152, 44, 8
  EDITTEXT IDD_ATTACHMENT, 57, 149, 136, 15, ES_AUTOHSCROLL | WS_BORDER | WS_TABSTOP
  PUSHBUTTON "Browse...", IDD_BROWSE, 212, 149, 50, 14
}
MAILBOXMENU MENU
{
  POPUP "&File"
  {
    MENUITEM "&New Message", IDM_FILENEWMESSAGE
    MENUITEM "&Open Mailbox", IDM_FILEOPENMAILBOX
    MENUITEM "&Close", IDM_FILECLOSE
    MENUITEM SEPARATOR
    MENUITEM "E&xit", IDM_FILEEXIT
  }

  POPUP "&Mail"
  {
    MENUITEM "Retrieve", IDM_MAILRETRIEVE
    MENUITEM "&View Message", IDM_MAILVIEWMESSAGE
    MENUITEM "&Delete Message", IDM_MAILDELETEMESSAGE
    MENUITEM SEPARATOR
    MENUITEM "&Configure...", IDM_MAILCONFIGURE
  }

  POPUP "&Window"
  {
    MENUITEM "&Cascade\tShift+F5", IDM_WINDOWCASCADE
    MENUITEM "&Tile\tShift+F4", IDM_WINDOWTILE
    MENUITEM "Arrange &Icons", IDM_WINDOWARRANGE
    MENUITEM "Close &All", IDM_WINDOWCLOSEALL
  }
```

```
POPUP "&Help"
{
  MENUITEM "&About...", IDM_HELPABOUT
}

}

VIEWERMENU MENU
{
 POPUP "&File"
 {
   MENUITEM "&New Message", IDM_FILENEWMESSAGE
   MENUITEM "&Open Mailbox", IDM_FILEOPENMAILBOX
   MENUITEM "&Close", IDM_FILECLOSE
   MENUITEM SEPARATOR
   MENUITEM "E&xit", IDM_FILEEXIT
 }

 POPUP "&Edit"
 {
   MENUITEM "&Cut\tCtrl+X", IDM_EDITCUT, GRAYED
   MENUITEM "&Copy\tCtrl+C", IDM_EDITCOPY
   MENUITEM "&Paste\tCtrl+V", IDM_EDITPASTE, GRAYED
 }

 POPUP "&Mail"
 {
   MENUITEM "First Body Part", IDM_MAILFIRSTBODYPART
   MENUITEM "Next Body Part", IDM_MAILNEXTBODYPART
   MENUITEM SEPARATOR
   MENUITEM "&UUDECODE...", IDM_MAILUUDECODE
   MENUITEM SEPARATOR
   MENUITEM "&Configure...", IDM_MAILCONFIGURE
 }

 POPUP "&Window"
 {
   MENUITEM "&Cascade\tShift+F5", IDM_WINDOWCASCADE
   MENUITEM "&Tile\tShift+F4", IDM_WINDOWTILE
   MENUITEM "Arrange &Icons", IDM_WINDOWARRANGE
   MENUITEM "Close &All", IDM_WINDOWCLOSEALL
 }

 POPUP "&Help"
 {
   MENUITEM "&About...", IDM_HELPABOUT
 }

}


APPICON ICON "mailbox.ico"
```

Listing 9.5 MAILCLI.RH

```
/**************************************************************************
mailcli.rh
**************************************************************************/

#define   IDM_MAILNEXTBODYPART        103
#define   IDM_MAILFIRSTBODYPART       102
#define   IDM_MAILUUENCODE            33
#define   IDM_FIRSTCHILD              1000
#define   IDM_MAILUUDECODE            101
#define   IDM_MAILRETRIEVE            103
#define   IDM_MAILDELETEMESSAGE       102
#define   IDM_MAILVIEWMESSAGE         101
#define   IDD_CC                      102
#define   IDD_SUBJECT                 103
#define   IDD_ATTACHMENT              104
#define   IDD_BROWSE                  105
#define   IDD_TO                      101
#define   IDM_FILECLOSE               13
#define   IDM_FILEOPENMAILBOX         12
#define   IDM_FILENEWMESSAGE          10
#define   IDM_FILEEXIT                11

#define   IDM_EDITUNDO                20
#define   IDM_EDITCUT                 21
#define   IDM_EDITCOPY                22
#define   IDM_EDITPASTE               23

#define   IDM_MAILCONFIGURE           30
#define   IDM_MAILSEND                32

#define   IDM_WINDOWCASCADE           40
#define   IDM_WINDOWTILE              41
#define   IDM_WINDOWARRANGE           42
#define   IDM_WINDOWCLOSEALL          43

#define   IDM_HELPABOUT               50


#define   IDD_SMTPSERVER              100
#define   IDD_SMTPPORT                101
#define   IDD_DEFAULTSMTPPORT         102
#define   IDD_POPSERVER               103
#define   IDD_POPPORT                 104
#define   IDD_DEFAULTPOPPORT          105
#define   IDD_MAILBOX                 106
#define   IDD_PASSWORD                107
#define   IDD_ADDRESS                 109
#define   IDD_NAME                    108
```

Listing 9.6   MAILCLI.DEF

```
NAME        MAILCLI
DESCRIPTION 'Mail Client, Copyright 1995, David G. Roberts'
EXETYPE     WINDOWS
STUB        'WINSTUB.EXE'
CODE        PRELOAD MOVABLE DISCARDABLE
DATA        PRELOAD MOVABLE
HEAPSIZE    32768
STACKSIZE   8192
```

Listing 9.7   MAILCLI.CPP

```cpp
/*
    File: MAILCLI.CPP
    Description:
        A simple mail client.
    Copyright 1995, David G. Roberts
*/

#ifdef __BORLANDC__
#include <dir.h>
#else
#include <direct.h>
#define mkdir _mkdir
#define getcwd _getcwd
#endif
#include <stdlib.h>
#include <windows.h>
#include <windowsx.h>
#include "ctl3d.h"
#include "winsock.h"
#include "cwinsock.h"
#include "mailcli.rh"
#include "myassert.h"

/*
    CONSTANTS
*/
#define DEFAULT_SMTP_PORT    25

#define FRAME_WINDOW_MENU_POS    2
#define EDITOR_WINDOW_MENU_POS   3
#define MAILBOX_WINDOW_MENU_POS  2
#define VIEWER_WINDOW_MENU_POS   3

#define MAILBOX_NAME        "mailbox.txt"
#define MESSAGE_DIR         "messages"

/*
    TYPES
*/
typedef int INT;
```

```
typedef BOOL FAR * LPBOOL;

/*
    GLOBALS
*/
#include "mailclig.h"

/*
    FUNCTION PROTOTYPES
*/
void            CleanupInstance(HINSTANCE);
BOOL CALLBACK ConfigureDlgProc(HWND, UINT, WPARAM, LPARAM);
LRESULT CALLBACK FrameWndProc(HWND, UINT, WPARAM, LPARAM);
LRESULT CALLBACK EditorWndProc(HWND, UINT, WPARAM, LPARAM);
BOOL            InitWinsock(HINSTANCE, HINSTANCE);
BOOL            InitApp(HINSTANCE);
BOOL            InitInstance(HINSTANCE);
void            InitError(void);
LRESULT CALLBACK MailboxWndProc(HWND, UINT, WPARAM, LPARAM);
INT WINAPI   WinMain(HANDLE, HANDLE, LPSTR, INT);
LRESULT CALLBACK ViewerWndProc(HWND, UINT, WPARAM, LPARAM);

/*
    MESSAGE HANDLER PROTOTYPES
*/
static void OnClose(HWND hwnd);
static void OnCommand(HWND, int, HWND, UINT);
BOOL OnCreate(HWND, CREATESTRUCT FAR*);

/*
    WM_COMMAND HANDLER PROTOTYPES
*/
static void OnFileNewMessage(HWND);
static void OnFileClose(HWND);
static void OnFileExit(HWND);
static void OnFileOpenMailbox(HWND);
static void OnMailConfigure(HWND);
static void OnWindowCloseAll(HWND);
static BOOL CALLBACK CloseEnumProc(HWND, LPARAM);
static void OnHelpAbout(HWND);

/*********************************************************************
    WINMAIN
*********************************************************************/

/*
    Function: WinMain
    Description:
        Good ol' WinMain.
*/
INT WINAPI WinMain(HINSTANCE hInstance, HINSTANCE hPrevInstance,
    LPSTR lpszCmdParam, INT nCmdShow)
{
```

```
    UNUSED_PARAMETER(lpszCmdParam);

  // Save off our instance handle for later.
  g_hInstance = hInstance;

  // Use the current directory to fix some paths.
  _fullpath(g_szMessageDir, MESSAGE_DIR, sizeof(g_szMessageDir));
  _fullpath(g_szMailboxFile, MAILBOX_NAME, sizeof(g_szMailboxFile));

  // Make sure a message directory exits.
  // If not, create it.  An error will result if the
  // directory already exists.  Ignore it.
  mkdir(g_szMessageDir);

  // If no other instance is running, initialize the application
  // window classes.
  if (!hPrevInstance) {
      if (!InitApp(hInstance)) {
          InitError();
          return 0;
      }
  }


  // Load all our menus.
  g_hFrameMenu     = LoadMenu(hInstance, "FRAMEMENU");
  g_hMailboxMenu   = LoadMenu(hInstance, "MAILBOXMENU");
  g_hViewerMenu    = LoadMenu(hInstance, "VIEWERMENU");
  g_hEditorMenu    = LoadMenu(hInstance, "EDITORMENU");

  // Get the handle of the Window submenu for each MDI menu.
  g_hFrameWindowMenu = GetSubMenu(g_hFrameMenu,
      FRAME_WINDOW_MENU_POS);
  g_hEditorWindowMenu = GetSubMenu(g_hEditorMenu,
      EDITOR_WINDOW_MENU_POS);
  g_hMailboxWindowMenu = GetSubMenu(g_hMailboxMenu,
      MAILBOX_WINDOW_MENU_POS);
  g_hViewerWindowMenu = GetSubMenu(g_hViewerMenu,
      VIEWER_WINDOW_MENU_POS);

  // Load the accellerators.
  g_hAccel = LoadAccelerators(hInstance, g_szAppName);

  // Initialize all instance specific stuff.  In particular, create
  // the frame window.
  if (!InitInstance(hInstance)) {
      InitError();
      return 0;
  }

  // Since initializing Winsock can take some time (because we
  // get the default Finger port using blocking calls), put
  // up an hourglass cursor so the user knows we're working on
```

```
   // something and not just out to lunch.
    SetCapture(g_hFrame);
    SetCursor(LoadCursor(NULL, IDC_WAIT));

    // Make sure Winsock initialized and get the event dispatch
    // mechanism up and running.
    if (!InitWinsock(hInstance, hPrevInstance)) {
        ReleaseCapture();
        return 0;
    }

    ReleaseCapture();

    // Show the frame window and cause it to be repainted.
    ShowWindow(g_hFrame, nCmdShow);
    UpdateWindow(g_hFrame);

    // Do the message loop.
    MSG msg;
    while (GetMessage((LPMSG)&msg, NULL, 0, 0)) {
        if (!TranslateMDISysAccel(g_hClient, &msg) &&
            !TranslateAccelerator(g_hFrame, g_hAccel, &msg)) {
            TranslateMessage(&msg);
            DispatchMessage(&msg);
        }
    }

    DestroyMenu(g_hFrameMenu);
    DestroyMenu(g_hMailboxMenu);
    DestroyMenu(g_hViewerMenu);
    DestroyMenu(g_hEditorMenu);

    // Clean up before we exit.
    CleanupInstance(hInstance);

    return msg.wParam;
}

/*

    Function: InitError
    Description:
        Handles putting up a message box for the application if it
        cannot be initialized.
*/
void InitError(void)
{
    char szMessage[80];

    wsprintf(szMessage, "ERROR: Cannot initialize %s.",
        (LPSTR)g_szFullAppName);
    // Use NULL for hwnd because application probably doesn't have
    // its window created yet.
```

```
        MessageBox(NULL, szMessage, g_szAppName, MB_ICONSTOP | MB_OK);
}


/*

    Function: InitApp
    Description:
          Registers the application's window classes and performs
          initialization that must be done for all application
          instances.  The function returns TRUE if successful and no
          errors occur, and FALSE otherwise.
*/
BOOL InitApp(HINSTANCE hInstance)
{
    WNDCLASS wc;

    // Register the frame window class.

    wc.style              = CS_HREDRAW | CS_VREDRAW;
    wc.lpfnWndProc        = FrameWndProc;
    wc.cbClsExtra         = 0;
    wc.cbWndExtra         = 0;
    wc.hInstance          = hInstance;
    wc.hIcon              = LoadIcon(hInstance, "APPICON");
    wc.hCursor            = LoadCursor(NULL, IDC_ARROW);
    wc.hbrBackground      = (HBRUSH) (COLOR_APPWORKSPACE + 1);
    wc.lpszMenuName       = NULL;
    wc.lpszClassName      = g_szFrameClass;

    if (!RegisterClass(&wc))
        return FALSE;

    // Register the mailbox child window class.
    wc.style              = CS_HREDRAW | CS_VREDRAW;
    wc.lpfnWndProc        = MailboxWndProc;
    wc.cbClsExtra         = 0;
    wc.cbWndExtra         = sizeof(void FAR *);
    wc.hInstance          = hInstance;
    wc.hIcon              = LoadIcon(hInstance, "MAILBOXICON");
    wc.hCursor            = LoadCursor(NULL, IDC_ARROW);
    wc.hbrBackground      = (HBRUSH) (COLOR_WINDOW + 1);
    wc.lpszMenuName       = NULL;
    wc.lpszClassName      = g_szMailboxClass;

    if (!RegisterClass(&wc))
        return FALSE;

    // Register the message viewer child window class.
    wc.style              = CS_HREDRAW | CS_VREDRAW;
    wc.lpfnWndProc        = ViewerWndProc;
    wc.cbClsExtra         = 0;
    wc.cbWndExtra         = sizeof(void FAR *);
    wc.hInstance          = hInstance;
```

```
    wc.hIcon              = LoadIcon(hInstance, "VIEWERICON");
     wc.hCursor             = LoadCursor(NULL, IDC_ARROW);
     wc.hbrBackground       = (HBRUSH) (COLOR_WINDOW + 1);
     wc.lpszMenuName        = NULL;
     wc.lpszClassName       = g_szViewerClass;

    if (!RegisterClass(&wc))
        return FALSE;

    // Register the message editor child window class.
    wc.style              = CS_HREDRAW | CS_VREDRAW;
    wc.lpfnWndProc        = EditorWndProc;
    wc.cbClsExtra         = 0;
    wc.cbWndExtra         = sizeof(void FAR *);
    wc.hInstance          = hInstance;
    wc.hIcon               = LoadIcon(hInstance, "EDITORICON");
    wc.hCursor             = LoadCursor(NULL, IDC_ARROW);
    wc.hbrBackground       = (HBRUSH) (COLOR_WINDOW + 1);
    wc.lpszMenuName       = NULL;
    wc.lpszClassName      = g_szEditorClass;

    if (!RegisterClass(&wc))
        return FALSE;

    return TRUE;
}


/*
    Function: InitInstance
    Description:
        Performs instance specific initialization, like the
        creation of the frame window, etc.  The function returns
        TRUE if successful and no errors occur, and FALSE otherwise.
*/
BOOL InitInstance(HINSTANCE hInstance)
{
    g_hFrame = CreateWindow(
        g_szFrameClass,                // window class name
        g_szFullAppName,               // window title text
        WS_OVERLAPPEDWINDOW | WS_CLIPCHILDREN, // window style
        CW_USEDEFAULT, CW_USEDEFAULT,  // position = default
        CW_USEDEFAULT, CW_USEDEFAULT,  // size = default
        NULL,                          // no parent window
        g_hFrameMenu,                  // menu = window class default
        hInstance,                     // window owner
        NULL);                         // no additional creation data

    if (!g_hFrame)
        return FALSE;

    // Initialize Microsoft 3D controls (CTL3D)
    Ctl3dRegister(hInstance);
```

```
    Ctl3dAutoSubclass(hInstance);

    return TRUE;
}

/*
    Function: InitWinsock
    Description:
        Make sure Winsock is up and running and that the Winsock event
        dispatch window is created.  Further, perform any actions that
        have to take place before the application window is created.
*/
BOOL InitWinsock(HINSTANCE hInstance, HINSTANCE hPrevInstance)
{
    // Make sure that we didn't have any problems
    // starting up Winsock.
    if (g_wsWinsock.LastError() != WSANOERROR) {
        ReportWSAError("Error: Can't startup Winsock.",
            g_wsWinsock.LastError(), NULL, g_hInstance);
        return FALSE;
    }

    // Create the Winsock message dispatch window.
    if (!WSCCreateEventWindow(hInstance, hPrevInstance)) {
        MessageBox(g_hFrame,
            "Error: Could not create the Winsock message window.",
            "Winsock Error", MB_OK | MB_ICONEXCLAMATION);
        return FALSE;
    }

    return TRUE;
}

/*
    Function: CleanupInstance
    Description:
        Do any instance specific clean-up before the application
        quits.
*/
void CleanupInstance(HINSTANCE hInstance)
{
    // Clean up Microsoft 3D controls (CTL3D)
    Ctl3dUnregister(hInstance);
}

/***********************************************************************
    WINDOW AND DIALOG PROCS
***********************************************************************/

/*
    Function: FrameWndProc
    Description:
```

```
         Window procedure for the application frame window.
*/
LRESULT CALLBACK FrameWndProc(HWND hwnd, UINT msg, WPARAM wParam,
    LPARAM lParam)
{
    switch (msg) {
        HANDLE_MSG(hwnd, WM_CREATE, OnCreate);
        HANDLE_MSG(hwnd, WM_CLOSE, OnClose);
        HANDLE_MSG(hwnd, WM_COMMAND, OnCommand);
        case WM_DESTROY:
            // Delete all the config info.
            delete[] g_pszSMTPServer;
            delete[] g_pszPOPServer;
            delete[] g_pszMailbox;
            delete[] g_pszPassword;
            delete[] g_pszUserName;
            delete[] g_pszUserAddress;
            // Post the quit message.
            PostQuitMessage(0);
            return 0;
        default:
            return DefFrameProc(hwnd, g_hClient, msg, wParam, lParam);
    }
}


/*
    Function: ConfigureDlgProc
    Description:
        Dialog proc for the Configure dialog.
*/
BOOL CALLBACK ConfigureDlgProc(HWND hwnd, UINT msg, WPARAM wParam,
    LPARAM lParam)
{
    int     id;
    BOOL    bTranslated;
    int     nLen;

    UNUSED_PARAMETER(lParam);

    switch (msg) {
        case WM_INITDIALOG:
            // Initialize dialog edit boxes.
            SetDlgItemText(hwnd, IDD_SMTPSERVER, g_pszSMTPServer);
            SetDlgItemInt(hwnd, IDD_SMTPPORT, g_ushSMTPPort, FALSE);
            SetDlgItemText(hwnd, IDD_POPSERVER, g_pszPOPServer);
            SetDlgItemInt(hwnd, IDD_POPPORT, g_ushPOPPort, FALSE);
            SetDlgItemText(hwnd, IDD_MAILBOX, g_pszMailbox);
            SetDlgItemText(hwnd, IDD_PASSWORD, g_pszPassword);
            SetDlgItemText(hwnd, IDD_NAME, g_pszUserName);
            SetDlgItemText(hwnd, IDD_ADDRESS, g_pszUserAddress);
            return TRUE;
        case WM_COMMAND:
```

```
        // Explode wParam and lParam into constituent parts.
    id = GET_WM_COMMAND_ID(wParam, lParam);
  switch (id) {
      case IDOK:
              // Verify all the fields.
              if (!(VerifyDlgText(hwnd, IDD_SMTPSERVER) &&
                    VerifyDlgInt(hwnd, IDD_SMTPPORT, FALSE) &&
                    VerifyDlgText(hwnd, IDD_POPSERVER) &&
                    VerifyDlgInt(hwnd, IDD_POPPORT, FALSE) &&
                    VerifyDlgText(hwnd, IDD_MAILBOX) &&
                    VerifyDlgText(hwnd, IDD_PASSWORD) &&
                    VerifyDlgText(hwnd, IDD_NAME) &&
                    VerifyDlgText(hwnd, IDD_ADDRESS))) {
                  return TRUE;
      }
              // Now that we've verified everything, retrieve
          // it all "for real."
          // First the SMTP server...
          delete[] g_pszSMTPServer;
          nLen = Edit_GetTextLength(GetDlgItem(hwnd,
             IDD_SMTPSERVER));
          g_pszSMTPServer = new char[nLen + 1];
          GetDlgItemText(hwnd, IDD_SMTPSERVER,
             g_pszSMTPServer, nLen + 1);
          // ...Then the SMTP port...
          g_ushSMTPPort = (u_short) GetDlgItemInt(hwnd,
              IDD_SMTPPORT, (LPBOOL) &bTranslated, FALSE);
          // ...Then the POP server...
          delete[] g_pszPOPServer;
          nLen = Edit_GetTextLength(GetDlgItem(hwnd,
             IDD_POPSERVER));
          g_pszPOPServer = new char[nLen + 1];
          GetDlgItemText(hwnd, IDD_POPSERVER,
             g_pszPOPServer, nLen + 1);
          // ...Then the POP port...
          g_ushPOPPort = (u_short) GetDlgItemInt(hwnd,
              IDD_POPPORT, (LPBOOL) &bTranslated, FALSE);
          // ...Then the mailbox name...
          delete[] g_pszMailbox;
          nLen = Edit_GetTextLength(GetDlgItem(hwnd,
             IDD_MAILBOX));
          g_pszMailbox = new char[nLen + 1];
          GetDlgItemText(hwnd, IDD_MAILBOX, g_pszMailbox,
             nLen + 1);
          // ...Then the password string...
          delete[] g_pszPassword;
          nLen = Edit_GetTextLength(GetDlgItem(hwnd,
             IDD_PASSWORD));
          g_pszPassword = new char[nLen + 1];
          GetDlgItemText(hwnd, IDD_PASSWORD, g_pszPassword,
             nLen + 1);
          // ...Then the user name string...
```

```
                    delete[] g_pszUserName;
                        nLen = Edit_GetTextLength(GetDlgItem(hwnd,
                            IDD_NAME));
                        g_pszUserName = new char[nLen + 1];
                    GetDlgItemText(hwnd, IDD_NAME,
                            g_pszUserName, nLen + 1);
                    // ...Then the user address string.
                    delete[] g_pszUserAddress;
                        nLen = Edit_GetTextLength(GetDlgItem(hwnd,
                            IDD_ADDRESS));
                        g_pszUserAddress = new char[nLen + 1];
                        GetDlgItemText(hwnd, IDD_ADDRESS,
                            g_pszUserAddress, nLen + 1);
                    // Now we're done.
                        EndDialog(hwnd, TRUE);
                        return TRUE;
                    case IDCANCEL:
                        EndDialog(hwnd, FALSE);
                        return TRUE;
                    case IDD_DEFAULTSMTPPORT:
                        SetDlgItemInt(hwnd, IDD_SMTPPORT,
                            g_ushSMTPDefaultPort, FALSE);
                        return TRUE;
                    case IDD_DEFAULTPOPPORT:
                        SetDlgItemInt(hwnd, IDD_POPPORT,
                            g_ushPOPDefaultPort, FALSE);
                        return TRUE;
            } // switch (id)
    } // switch (msg)
    return FALSE;
}


/*********************************************************************
    WINDOW MESSAGE HANDLERS
*********************************************************************/

/*
    Function: OnClose
    Description:
        Handles a WM_CLOSE message to the frame window.
*/
void OnClose(HWND hwnd)
{
    // Send ourselves a Close All menu command message to close up
    // the children.
    SendMessage(hwnd, WM_COMMAND, IDM_WINDOWCLOSEALL, 0);
    if (GetWindow(g_hClient, GW_CHILD) == NULL) {
        // If the client window has no children, then all the children
        // are closed and we can continue.  Call the default window
        // proc to have it post a destroy message.
        FORWARD_WM_CLOSE(hwnd, ForwardDefFrameProc);
    }
```

```
    // One of the client's children didn't close, so simply return.
    // The user can't exit.
}


/*

    Function: OnCommand
    Description:
        Handle WM_COMMAND messages.
*/
void OnCommand(HWND hwnd, int id, HWND hwndCtl, UINT codeNotify)
{
    // Dispatch command...
    switch (id) {
        case IDM_FILENEWMESSAGE:
            OnFileNewMessage(hwnd);
            break;
        case IDM_FILECLOSE:
            OnFileClose(hwnd);
            break;
        case IDM_FILEEXIT:
            OnFileExit(hwnd);
            break;
        case IDM_FILEOPENMAILBOX:
            OnFileOpenMailbox(hwnd);
            break;
        case IDM_MAILCONFIGURE:
            OnMailConfigure(hwnd);
            break;
        case IDM_WINDOWCASCADE:
            SendMessage(g_hClient, WM_MDICASCADE, 0, 0);
            break;
        case IDM_WINDOWARRANGE:
            SendMessage(g_hClient, WM_MDIICONARRANGE, 0, 0);
            break;
        case IDM_WINDOWTILE:
            SendMessage(g_hClient, WM_MDITILE, 0, 0);
            break;
        case IDM_WINDOWCLOSEALL:
            OnWindowCloseAll(hwnd);
            break;
        case IDM_HELPABOUT:
            OnHelpAbout(hwnd);
            break;
        default:
            // ...Or send it to the active child window and see if it
            // processes it.
            HWND hwndChild = GetMDIActiveChild(g_hClient);
            if (IsWindow(hwndChild)) {
                FORWARD_WM_COMMAND(hwndChild, id, hwndCtl, codeNotify,
                    SendMessage);
            }
            break;
    }
```

```
        // Always forward it to DefFrameProc after we're done.
        FORWARD_WM_COMMAND(hwnd, id, hwndCtl, codeNotify,
            ForwardDefFrameProc);
}


/*
    Function: OnCreate
    Description:
        Handle creation of the main frame window.  Creates the MDI
        client window to manage MDI children and initializes the mail
        configuration information.
*/
BOOL OnCreate(HWND hwnd, CREATESTRUCT FAR* lpCreateStruct)
{
    UNUSED_PARAMETER(lpCreateStruct);

    CLIENTCREATESTRUCT ClientCreate;

    // Create the MDI client window.
    ClientCreate.hWindowMenu = g_hFrameWindowMenu;
    ClientCreate.idFirstChild = IDM_FIRSTCHILD;
    g_hClient = CreateWindow(
        "MDICLIENT",                // window class name
        NULL,                       // no title for the client window
        WS_CHILD | WS_CLIPCHILDREN | WS_VISIBLE, // window style
        0, 0,                       // position at 0,0
        0, 0,                       // no size
        hwnd,                       // parent is the frame window
        (HMENU) 1,                  // Not really a menu. A child
                                    // window number when doing MDI.
        g_hInstance,                // owning instance
        (LPSTR)&ClientCreate);      // additional creation data

    // Set up the default ports for SMTP and POP.
    g_ushSMTPDefaultPort = 25;
    g_ushPOPDefaultPort = 110;

    // Initialize the configuration information.
    const int STR_BASE = 10;
    const int STR_GROW_QUANTUM = 10;
    int iStrLen;
    int iReadLen;

    // Assume we're going to do everything right.
    g_bConfigured = TRUE;

    // Get the SMTP server name.
    iStrLen = STR_BASE;
    g_pszSMTPServer = new char[1];
    do {
        delete[] g_pszSMTPServer;
        iStrLen += STR_GROW_QUANTUM;
```

```
        g_pszSMTPServer = new char[iStrLen];
          iReadLen = GetPrivateProfileString("SMTP", "Server", "",
              g_pszSMTPServer, iStrLen, g_szIniFile);
    } while (iReadLen >= iStrLen - 1);
    if (lstrcmp(g_pszSMTPServer, "") == 0) {
        // If a null string got in the file or there was no entry,
        // then we still aren't configured.
        g_bConfigured = FALSE;
    }


    // Get the SMTP port number.
    g_ushSMTPPort = (u_short) GetPrivateProfileInt("SMTP", "Port", 0,
        g_szIniFile);
    if (g_ushSMTPPort == 0) {
        g_ushSMTPPort = g_ushSMTPDefaultPort;
        g_bConfigured = FALSE;
    }


    // Get the POP server name.
    iStrLen = STR_BASE;
    g_pszPOPServer = new char[1];
    do {
        delete[] g_pszPOPServer;
        iStrLen += STR_GROW_QUANTUM;
        g_pszPOPServer = new char[iStrLen];
          iReadLen = GetPrivateProfileString("POP", "Server", "",
              g_pszPOPServer, iStrLen, g_szIniFile);
    } while (iReadLen >= iStrLen - 1);
    if (lstrcmp(g_pszPOPServer, "") == 0) {
        // If a null string got in the file or there was no entry,
        // then we still aren't configured.
        g_bConfigured = FALSE;
    }


    // Get the POP port number.
    g_ushPOPPort = (u_short) GetPrivateProfileInt("POP", "Port", 0,
        g_szIniFile);
    if (g_ushPOPPort == 0) {
        g_ushPOPPort = g_ushPOPDefaultPort;
        g_bConfigured = FALSE;
    }


    // Get the POP mailbox name.
    iStrLen = STR_BASE;
    g_pszMailbox = new char[1];
    do {
        delete[] g_pszMailbox;
        iStrLen += STR_GROW_QUANTUM;
        g_pszMailbox = new char[iStrLen];
          iReadLen = GetPrivateProfileString("POP", "Mailbox", "",
              g_pszMailbox, iStrLen, g_szIniFile);
    } while (iReadLen >= iStrLen - 1);
```

```
if (lstrcmp(g_pszMailbox, "") == 0) {
    // If a null string got in the file or there was no entry,
    // then we still aren't configured.
    g_bConfigured = FALSE;
}

// Get the POP mailbox password.
iStrLen = STR_BASE;
g_pszPassword = new char[1];
do {
    delete[] g_pszPassword;
    iStrLen += STR_GROW_QUANTUM;
    g_pszPassword = new char[iStrLen];
    iReadLen = GetPrivateProfileString("POP", "Password", "",
        g_pszPassword, iStrLen, g_szIniFile);
} while (iReadLen >= iStrLen - 1);
if (lstrcmp(g_pszPassword, "") == 0) {
    // If a null string got in the file or there was no entry,
    // then we still aren't configured.
    g_bConfigured = FALSE;
}

// Get the user name.
iStrLen = STR_BASE;
g_pszUserName = new char[1];
do {
    delete[] g_pszUserName;
    iStrLen += STR_GROW_QUANTUM;
    g_pszUserName = new char[iStrLen];
    iReadLen = GetPrivateProfileString("UserInfo", "Name", "",
        g_pszUserName, iStrLen, g_szIniFile);
} while (iReadLen >= iStrLen - 1);
if (lstrcmp(g_pszUserName, "") == 0) {
    // If a null string got in the file or there was no entry,
    // then we still aren't configured.
    g_bConfigured = FALSE;
}

// Get the user address.
iStrLen = STR_BASE;
g_pszUserAddress = new char[1];
do {
    delete[] g_pszUserAddress;
    iStrLen += STR_GROW_QUANTUM;
    g_pszUserAddress = new char[iStrLen];
    iReadLen = GetPrivateProfileString("UserInfo", "Address", "",
        g_pszUserAddress, iStrLen, g_szIniFile);
} while (iReadLen >= iStrLen - 1);
if (lstrcmp(g_pszUserAddress, "") == 0) {
    // If a null string got in the file or there was no entry,
    // then we still aren't configured.
    g_bConfigured = FALSE;
}
```

```
        return TRUE;
}


/***********************************************************************
     WM_COMMAND HANDLERS
***********************************************************************/

/*
     Function: OnFileNewMessage
     Description:
          Create a new message editor window in which to compose
          a message.
*/
void OnFileNewMessage(HWND hwnd)
{
     MDICREATESTRUCT mdicreate;
     static int iNewIndex = 1;
     char szTitle[20];

     UNUSED_PARAMETER(hwnd);

     // Create the new window title.
     wsprintf(szTitle, "New Message %d", iNewIndex);
     iNewIndex++;

     mdicreate.szClass    = g_szEditorClass;
     mdicreate.szTitle    = szTitle;
     mdicreate.hOwner     = g_hInstance;
     mdicreate.x          = CW_USEDEFAULT;
     mdicreate.y          = CW_USEDEFAULT;
     mdicreate.cx         = CW_USEDEFAULT;
     mdicreate.cy         = CW_USEDEFAULT;
     mdicreate.style      = 0;
     mdicreate.lParam     = NULL;

     // Send a message to the client window to create the new child.
     SendMessage(g_hClient, WM_MDICREATE, 0,
          (LPARAM) (LPMDICREATESTRUCT) &mdicreate);
}

/*
     Function: OnFileClose
     Description:
          Close the currently active MDI child window.
*/
void OnFileClose(HWND hwnd)
{
     UNUSED_PARAMETER(hwnd);

     HWND hChild = GetMDIActiveChild(g_hClient);

     if (hChild == NULL)
          return;
```

```
        if (SendMessage(hChild, WM_QUERYENDSESSION, 0, 0)) {
               SendMessage(g_hClient, WM_MDIDESTROY, (WPARAM) hChild, 0);
        }
}


/*
     Function: OnFileExit
     Description:
          Exits the application in response to a IDM_FILEEXIT message.
*/
void OnFileExit(HWND hwnd)
{
     SendMessage(hwnd, WM_CLOSE, 0, 0L);
}


/*
     Function: OnFileOpenMailbox
     Description:
          Create a new mailbox window.
*/
void OnFileOpenMailbox(HWND hwnd)
{
     MDICREATESTRUCT mdicreate;

     UNUSED_PARAMETER(hwnd);

     mdicreate.szClass    = g_szMailboxClass;
     mdicreate.szTitle    = "Mailbox";
     mdicreate.hOwner     = g_hInstance;
     mdicreate.x          = CW_USEDEFAULT;
     mdicreate.y          = CW_USEDEFAULT;
     mdicreate.cx         = CW_USEDEFAULT;
     mdicreate.cy         = CW_USEDEFAULT;
     mdicreate.style      = 0;
     mdicreate.lParam     = NULL;

     // Send a message to the client window to create the new child.
     SendMessage(g_hClient, WM_MDICREATE, 0,
         (LPARAM) (LPMDICREATESTRUCT) &mdicreate);
}


/*
     Function: OnMailConfigure
     Description:
          Pops up a dialog box to configure all the server name and port
          information.
*/
void OnMailConfigure(HWND hwnd)
{
     // Put up the dialog box.
     FARPROC lpfnConfigure =
            MakeProcInstance((FARPROC) ConfigureDlgProc, g_hInstance);
```

```
    BOOL bResult = DialogBox(g_hInstance, "CONFIGURE", hwnd,
        (DLGPROC) lpfnConfigure);
     FreeProcInstance(lpfnConfigure);

    // We're only configured if we were configured before or we just
    // got configured.  If we weren't before and the user hit cancel,
    // we still aren't.
     g_bConfigured = g_bConfigured || bResult;

    // Write out the INI file.
    char szPort[20];
    if (bResult) { // Only do this if the user hit OK.
        WritePrivateProfileString("SMTP", "Server", g_pszSMTPServer,
            g_szIniFile);
        wsprintf(szPort, "%u", g_ushSMTPPort);
        WritePrivateProfileString("SMTP", "Port", szPort,
            g_szIniFile);
        WritePrivateProfileString("POP", "Server", g_pszPOPServer,
            g_szIniFile);
        wsprintf(szPort, "%u", g_ushPOPPort);
        WritePrivateProfileString("POP", "Port", szPort, g_szIniFile);
        WritePrivateProfileString("POP", "Mailbox", g_pszMailbox,
            g_szIniFile);
        WritePrivateProfileString("POP", "Password", g_pszPassword,
            g_szIniFile);
        WritePrivateProfileString("UserInfo", "Name",
            g_pszUserName, g_szIniFile);
        WritePrivateProfileString("UserInfo", "Address",
            g_pszUserAddress, g_szIniFile);
    }
}


/*
    Function: OnWindowCloseAll
    Description:
        Attempts to close all the child windows.
*/
void OnWindowCloseAll(HWND hwnd)
{
    UNUSED_PARAMETER(hwnd);

    // Simply enumerate all the child windows, calling CloseEnumProc
    // for each one.
    FARPROC lpfnCloseEnum = MakeProcInstance((FARPROC) CloseEnumProc,
        g_hInstance);
    EnumChildWindows(g_hClient, (WNDENUMPROC) lpfnCloseEnum, 0);
    FreeProcInstance(lpfnCloseEnum);
}


/*
    Function: CloseEnumProc
    Description:
```

```
            The enumeration function used in the OnWindowCloseAll
            function.
*/
BOOL CALLBACK CloseEnumProc(HWND hwnd, LPARAM lParam)
{
      UNUSED_PARAMETER(lParam);

      // EnumChildWindows picks up the title windows of iconized child
      // windows.  Skip over these icon titles by checking to see if
      // they are owned by anybody.  Icon titles are owned while child
      // windows aren't.
      if (GetWindow(hwnd, GW_OWNER) != NULL) {
         return TRUE;
      }
      // Restore the child window to normal size.
      SendMessage(GetParent(hwnd), WM_MDIRESTORE, (WPARAM) hwnd, 0);
      // Ask the child whether we can close it.
      if (!SendMessage(hwnd, WM_QUERYENDSESSION, 0, 0)) {
         // If not, move on.
         return TRUE;
      }
      // Close it!
      SendMessage(GetParent(hwnd), WM_MDIDESTROY, (WPARAM) hwnd, 0);
      // Go to the next child window.
      return TRUE;
}


/*
      Function: OnHelpAbout
      Description:
         Pops up the About dialog box in response to IDM_HELPABOUT
         command messages.
*/
void OnHelpAbout(HWND hwnd)
{
      char szTitle[100];
      char szInfo[200];

      wsprintf(szTitle, "About %s", (LPSTR)g_szFullAppName);
      wsprintf(szInfo, "%s\r\nCopyright \251 1995\r\n"
         "David G. Roberts\r\n\r\nAn example program from the book\r\n"
         "'Developing for the Internet with Windows Sockets'",
         (LPSTR)g_szFullAppName);
      MessageBox(hwnd, szInfo, szTitle, MB_OK);
}

/**************************************************************
      UTILITY FUNCTIONS
**************************************************************/


/*
      Function: ForwardDefFrameProc
```

```
        Description:
                A short routine that provides some syntactic sugar to allow
                the windowsx.h FORWARD_WM_COMMAND macro to work with
                DefFrameProc.  Normally, FORWARD_WM_COMMAND packages its
                parameters and tries to call a function with the normal number
                and types of WndProc parameters (HWND, UINT, WPARAM, LPARAM).
                DefFrameProc requires the client HWND to also be present.
                Use FOWARD_WM_COMMAND to call this procedure which then adds
                the client HWND and calls DefFrameProc.
*/
void ForwardDefFrameProc(HWND hwnd, UINT msg, WPARAM wParam,
    LPARAM lParam)
{
    DefFrameProc(hwnd, g_hClient, msg, wParam, lParam);
}


/*

    Function: GetMDIActiveChild
    Description:
        This is one function that differs between Win16 and Win32.
        GetMDIActiveChild isolates those differences in this function
        rather than writing Win16/Win32 specific code everywhere.
*/
HWND GetMDIActiveChild(HWND hwndClient)
{
#ifdef WIN32
    return (HWND) SendMessage(hwndClient, WM_MDIGETACTIVE, 0, 0);
#else
    return (HWND) LOWORD(SendMessage(hwndClient, WM_MDIGETACTIVE,
        0, 0));
#endif
}


/*

    Function: VerifyDlgInt
    Description:
        Verifies that an edit field in a dialog box contains a valid
        integer.  The function works by calling GetDlgItemInt on the
        edit control and checking the bTranslated argument.  The
        caller may specify a signed or unsigned translation with the
        bSigned function argument.  If the item doesn't translate,
        the function highlights the text in the edit box, beeps, and
        returns FALSE.
*/
BOOL VerifyDlgInt(HWND hwnd, int iDlgItem, BOOL bSigned)
{
    BOOL bTranslated;

    // Try to retrieve the number.
    GetDlgItemInt(hwnd, iDlgItem, (LPBOOL) &bTranslated,
        bSigned);
    // If things didn't go well, set the focus to the
```

```
        // edit box, select all the text in it, and beep.
        if (!bTranslated) {
            SetEditErrorFocus(hwnd, iDlgItem);
            return FALSE;
        }
        return TRUE;
}


/*

    Function: VerifyDlgText
    Description:
        Verfies that an edit text control in a dialog box contains
        some text (i.e., is not null).  If the length of the text in
        the control is zero, the function sets the focus to the edit
        text item, beeps, and returns FALSE.
*/
BOOL VerifyDlgText(HWND hwnd, int iDlgItem)
{
    // Get the text length from the edit box.
    int nLen = Edit_GetTextLength(GetDlgItem(hwnd, iDlgItem));
    // If the user has given us a blank string, set the
    // focus back to the edit box and beep.
    if (nLen == 0) {
        SetEditErrorFocus(hwnd, iDlgItem);
        return FALSE;
    }
    return TRUE;
}


/*

    Function: SetEditErrorFocus
    Description:
        Sets the focus to a given dialog control, selects all its
        text, and beeps.  The dialog window handle is specified by
        hwnd and the id of the dialog item by iDlgItem.
*/
void SetEditErrorFocus(HWND hwnd, int iDlgItem)
{
    SetFocus(GetDlgItem(hwnd, iDlgItem));
    Edit_SetSel(GetDlgItem(hwnd, iDlgItem), 0, -1);
    MessageBeep(MB_ICONSTOP);
}
```

Listing 9.8 MAILEDIT.CPP

```
/*
    File: MAILEDIT.CPP
    Description:
        Implements the editor window class for Mail Client.
    Copyright 1995, David G. Roberts
*/

#include <dos.h>
```

```
#include <fstream.h>
#include <stdlib.h>
#include <windows.h>
#include <windowsx.h>
#include "mailcli.rh"
#include "myassert.h"
#include "cwinsock.h"
#include "csmtp.h"
#include "caddrlst.h"
#include "rfc822.h"
#include "cuuendec.h"
#include "cbase64.h"

#define DECLARE
#include "mailclig.h"

/*
    CONSTANTS
*/
#define EDITCTLID         1
#define WM_CSMTPDONE      WM_USER
const char cszSendingText[] = ": Sending...";

/*
    TYPES
*/

/*
    Structure: EDITORDATA
    Description:
        A collection of private data allocated in WM_CREATE
        processing for the editor MDI child window.  A pointer to
        this structure is stored in the Windows data structures.
*/
struct EDITORDATA {
    HWND         hwndEdit;
    char *       pszTempFile;
    CAddrList * palAddrList;
    CSMTPWithWinMsg * pcsmtp;
    ifstream     ifsMsgStream;
    BOOL         bSending;

    EDITORDATA() : hwndEdit(NULL), pszTempFile(NULL),
        palAddrList(NULL), pcsmtp(NULL), bSending(FALSE) {};
    ~EDITORDATA();
};

EDITORDATA::~EDITORDATA()
{
    // Note: delete the CSMTP object before the address list and
    // before we close the stream.  The CSMTP object could be using
    // these things.
```

```
    if (bSending) {
        bSending = FALSE;
        delete pcsmtp;
        pcsmtp = NULL;
        ifsMsgStream.close();
        unlink(pszTempFile);
        delete[] pszTempFile;
        pszTempFile = NULL;
        delete palAddrList;
        palAddrList = NULL;
    }

}


// A macro to help us the get the pointer from the extra window
// storage area that compensates for the pointer size differences
// of different memory models.  Note that we have to the size test
// in real code rather than a preprocessor test because MSVC 1.5
// doesn't support the "sizeof" operator in preprocessor
// expressions.
#define GETEDITORDATA(hwnd) \
    ( (sizeof(EDITORDATA*) != 2) ? \
    (EDITORDATA *)GetWindowLong(hwnd, 0) : \
    (EDITORDATA *)GetWindowWord(hwnd, 0) )


/*
    Structure: ADDRESSDLGINFO
    Description:
        The set of data returned from the addressing info dialog.
        The structure simply collects this info together so that
        a simple pointer can be passed to the dialog.
*/
struct ADDRESSDLGINFO {
    CAddrList * pToAddrList;
    CAddrList * pCcAddrList;
    char *      pszSubject;
    char *      pszFullName;

    ADDRESSDLGINFO() : pToAddrList(NULL), pCcAddrList(NULL),
        pszSubject(NULL), pszFullName(NULL) {};
    // Make sure memory gets released.
    ~ADDRESSDLGINFO() {
        if (pToAddrList != NULL) delete pToAddrList;
        if (pCcAddrList != NULL) delete pCcAddrList;
        if (pszSubject != NULL) delete[] pszSubject;
        if (pszFullName != NULL) delete[] pszFullName;
    };
};


/*
    LOCAL FUNCTIONS
*/
```

```
static void OnCommand(HWND hwnd, int id, HWND hwndCtl,
    UINT codeNotify);
static BOOL OnCreate(HWND, CREATESTRUCT FAR*);
static void OnCSMTPDone(HWND, UINT, WPARAM, LPARAM);
static void OnDestroy(HWND);
static void OnMDIActivate(HWND, BOOL, HWND, HWND);
static BOOL OnQueryEndSession(HWND hwnd);
static void OnSize(HWND, UINT, int, int);

// MENU HANDLERS
static void OnMailSend(HWND);
static void OnMailUuencode(HWND hwnd);

// UTILITY FUNCTIONS
static BOOL AddressStringToList(char *, CAddrList *);
static void OutputAddrList(char *, CAddrList *, CAddrList *,
    ofstream&);
static void OutputMessageText(HWND, ofstream&);
static void ConvertToQP(char *, int, char *);
static void QuoteCharacter(unsigned char, char *);
static void CreateBoundary(char *, int);
static void OutputAttachment(char *, ofstream&);

/*************************************************************************
    WINDOW AND DIALOG BOX PROCEDURES
*************************************************************************/

/*
    Function: EditorWndProc
    Description:
        Window procedure for the editor MDI child window.
        Dispatches all the window messages to the correct handling
        routines.
*/
LRESULT CALLBACK EditorWndProc(HWND hwnd, UINT msg, WPARAM wParam,
    LPARAM lParam)
{
    switch (msg) {
        HANDLE_MSG(hwnd, WM_COMMAND, OnCommand);
        HANDLE_MSG(hwnd, WM_CREATE, OnCreate);
        HANDLE_MSG(hwnd, WM_DESTROY, OnDestroy);
        HANDLE_MSG(hwnd, WM_MDIACTIVATE, OnMDIActivate);
        HANDLE_MSG(hwnd, WM_QUERYENDSESSION, OnQueryEndSession);
        HANDLE_MSG(hwnd, WM_SIZE, OnSize);
        case WM_CSMTPDONE:
            OnCSMTPDone(hwnd, msg, wParam, lParam); return 0;
    }
    return DefMDIChildProc(hwnd, msg, wParam, lParam);
}

/*
    Function: AddressDlgProc
```

```
    Description:
          The dialog procedure for the Addressing Information dialog box.
          Most of the code is devoted to extracting all the info
          when the user hits the OK button.
*/
BOOL CALLBACK AddressDlgProc(HWND hwnd, UINT msg, WPARAM wParam,
    LPARAM lParam)
{
    int id;
    ADDRESSDLGINFO FAR * lpAddrInfo;
    int iTextLen;
    char * pszText;
    BOOL bParsedOK;
    OPENFILENAME ofn;
    static char *szFilter[] = { "All Files (*.*)", "*.*", "", "" };
     char szFullName[MAX_PATH_LENGTH];
     char szFileName[MAX_FILENAME_LENGTH];
    BOOL bResult;

    switch (msg) {
        case WM_COMMAND:
             id = GET_WM_COMMAND_ID(wParam, lParam);
            switch (id) {
                case IDOK:
                     // Retrieve the pointer we stuffed away when we
                     // were first created.
                     lpAddrInfo = (ADDRESSDLGINFO FAR *)
                         GetWindowLong(hwnd, DWL_USER);
                     // Get text length of To: box.
                      iTextLen = Edit_GetTextLength(GetDlgItem(hwnd,
                        IDD_TO));
                     // Allocate string.
                     pszText = new char[iTextLen + 1];
                     // Get text from To: box into string.
                      GetDlgItemText(hwnd, IDD_TO, pszText,
                        iTextLen + 1);
                     // Allocate a list of addresses.
                     lpAddrInfo->pToAddrList = new CAddrList;
                     // Parse the addresses.
                     bParsedOK = AddressStringToList(pszText,
                        lpAddrInfo->pToAddrList);
                    delete[] pszText;
                     // If things didn't go right, then delete the
                     // allocated memory and return.
                    if (!bParsedOK) {
                        delete lpAddrInfo->pToAddrList;
                        SetEditErrorFocus(hwnd, IDD_TO);
                        return TRUE;
                    }

                     // Now do the same for the Cc text.
                     // Get text length of Cc: box.
```

```
    iTextLen = Edit_GetTextLength(GetDlgItem(hwnd,
        IDD_CC));
  // Allocate string.
  pszText = new char[iTextLen + 1];
  // Get text from To: box into string.
  GetDlgItemText(hwnd, IDD_CC, pszText,
      iTextLen + 1);
  // Allocate a list of addresses.
  lpAddrInfo->pCcAddrList = new CAddrList;
  // Parse the addresses.
  bParsedOK = AddressStringToList(pszText,
      lpAddrInfo->pCcAddrList);
  delete[] pszText;
  // If things didn't go right, then delete the
  // allocated memory and return.
  if (!bParsedOK) {
      delete lpAddrInfo->pToAddrList;
      delete lpAddrInfo->pCcAddrList;
      SetEditErrorFocus(hwnd, IDD_CC);
      return TRUE;
  }
  // Now extract the subject text.
    iTextLen = Edit_GetTextLength(GetDlgItem(hwnd,
      IDD_SUBJECT));
  lpAddrInfo->pszSubject = new char[iTextLen + 1];
  GetDlgItemText(hwnd, IDD_SUBJECT,
      lpAddrInfo->pszSubject, iTextLen + 1);
  // Now extract the attachment filename text.
    iTextLen = Edit_GetTextLength(GetDlgItem(hwnd,
      IDD_ATTACHMENT));
  lpAddrInfo->pszFullName = new char[iTextLen + 1];
  GetDlgItemText(hwnd, IDD_ATTACHMENT,
      lpAddrInfo->pszFullName, iTextLen + 1);

  EndDialog(hwnd, TRUE);
  return TRUE;
case IDCANCEL:
  EndDialog(hwnd, FALSE);
  return TRUE;
case IDD_BROWSE:
  // Set up the OPENFILENAME structure in
  // preparation for browsing.

  ofn.lStructSize          = sizeof(OPENFILENAME);
  ofn.hwndOwner            = hwnd;
  ofn.hInstance            = NULL;
  ofn.lpstrFilter          = szFilter[0];
  ofn.lpstrCustomFilter    = NULL;
  ofn.nMaxCustFilter       = 0;
  ofn.nFilterIndex         = 1;
  ofn.lpstrFile            = szFullName;
  ofn.nMaxFile             = sizeof(szFullName);
```

```
                    lstrcpy(szFullName, "");
                        ofn.lpstrFileTitle        = szFileName;
                        ofn.nMaxFileTitle         = sizeof(szFileName);
                        lstrcpy(szFileName, "");
                        ofn.lpstrInitialDir       = NULL;
                        ofn.lpstrTitle            = "Attach File";
                        ofn.Flags                 = OFN_HIDEREADONLY;
                        ofn.nFileOffset           = 0;
                        ofn.nFileExtension        = 0;
                        ofn.lpstrDefExt           = NULL;
                        ofn.lCustData             = 0;
                        ofn.lpfnHook              = NULL;
                        ofn.lpTemplateName        = NULL;

                        bResult = GetOpenFileName(&ofn);

                        if (bResult) {
                                SetWindowText(GetDlgItem(hwnd, IDD_ATTACHMENT),
                                    szFullName);
                        }
                        break;
                } // End switch (id)
                break;
            case WM_INITDIALOG:
                // Stuff away the pointer to the user data.
                SetWindowLong(hwnd, DWL_USER, (LONG) lParam);
                // Set the focus to the To: edit control so the user can
                // immediately start typing.
                SetFocus(GetDlgItem(hwnd, IDD_TO));
                return 0;  // Return 0 because we set focus to IDD_TO.
        } // End switch (msg)
        return FALSE;
}


/************************************************************************
     MESSAGE HANDLING FUNCTIONS
 ************************************************************************/

/*
     Function: OnCommand
     Description:
         Handles WM_COMMAND messages for the MDI child window.
*/
void OnCommand(HWND hwnd, int id, HWND hwndCtl, UINT codeNotify)
{
     EDITORDATA * pdata = GETEDITORDATA(hwnd);

     if (hwndCtl == NULL) {
         // It's a window message.
         switch (id) {
             case IDM_EDITCUT:
                 SendMessage(pdata->hwndEdit, WM_CUT, 0, 0);
```

```
                            return;
                    case IDM_EDITCOPY:
                            SendMessage(pdata->hwndEdit, WM_COPY, 0, 0);
                        return;
                    case IDM_EDITPASTE:
                            SendMessage(pdata->hwndEdit, WM_PASTE, 0, 0);
                        return;
                    case IDM_MAILSEND:
                        OnMailSend(hwnd);
                        return;
                    case IDM_MAILUUENCODE:
                        OnMailUuencode(hwnd);
                        return;
            }
        }
        else {
            ASSERT(id == EDITCTLID);
            // It's from our control.
            if (codeNotify == EN_ERRSPACE) {
                MessageBox(hwnd, "Editor out of space.", "Error",
                    MB_OK | MB_ICONEXCLAMATION);
                return;
            }
        }
        // Make sure the default child proc sees things we don't
        // process ourselves!
        FORWARD_WM_COMMAND(hwnd, id, hwndCtl, codeNotify,
            DefMDIChildProc);
}


/*

    Function: OnCreate
    Description:
        Handles WM_CREATE messages.  The function creates the
        editor control child window and allocates a private data
        area associated with the MDI child window to hold a set
        of private variables.
*/
BOOL OnCreate(HWND hwnd, CREATESTRUCT FAR* lpCreateStruct)
{
    UNUSED_PARAMETER(lpCreateStruct);

    // Allocate some private window data for ourselves.
    EDITORDATA * pdata = new EDITORDATA;

    // Note that we must do the following test with real code
    // rather than in the preprocessor because MSVC 1.5
    // doesn't support the "sizeof" operator in preprocessor
    // expressions! Gak!  Note that one or the other of the
    // following SetWindowXXX statements may generate a
    // warning.  The warning may involve the fact that the condition
    // is always true, one of the lines will never be executed, or
```

```
    // that the pointer is being converted to shorter or longer type
    // than it should be.
    if (sizeof(EDITORDATA *) != 2)
        SetWindowLong(hwnd, 0, (LONG) pdata);
    else
        SetWindowWord(hwnd, 0, (WORD) pdata);

    // Create a multiline edit control to do our work for us.
    pdata->hwndEdit = CreateWindow(
        "EDIT",                         // class name
        NULL,                           // window name
        WS_CHILD | WS_VISIBLE |         // window styles
        WS_HSCROLL | WS_VSCROLL | ES_LEFT |
        ES_MULTILINE | ES_AUTOHSCROLL | ES_AUTOVSCROLL,
        0,0,0,0,                        // location and size
        hwnd,                           // parent
        (HMENU) EDITCTLID,              // child id, not really a menu
        g_hInstance,                    // program instance
        NULL);                          // creation data
    // Set the edit control's font to a fixed pitch.
    HFONT hfont = GetStockFont(SYSTEM_FIXED_FONT);
    SetWindowFont(pdata->hwndEdit, hfont, FALSE);
    return TRUE;
}


/*

    Function: OnCSMTPDone
    Description:
        Processes the private WM_CSMTPDONE window message that is
        sent by the CSMTP object when it completes its operation.
        This function takes care of deleting all the various data
        that was needed for CSMTP to operate.  If CSMTP was
        successful, this function deletes the editor child window
        (self destructs), otherwise, it informs the user that an
        error has occurred and allows the user to retry the operation
        after correcting the problem.
*/
void OnCSMTPDone(HWND hwnd, UINT msg, WPARAM wToken, LPARAM lResult)
{
    UNUSED_PARAMETER(msg);
    UNUSED_PARAMETER(wToken);

    EDITORDATA * pdata = GETEDITORDATA(hwnd);

    pdata->bSending = FALSE;
    delete pdata->pcsmtp;
    pdata->pcsmtp = NULL;
    pdata->ifsMsgStream.close();
    unlink(pdata->pszTempFile);
    delete[] pdata->pszTempFile;
    pdata->pszTempFile = NULL;
    delete pdata->palAddrList;
    pdata->palAddrList = NULL;
```

```
        EnableMenuItem(g_hEditorMenu, IDM_MAILSEND, MF_ENABLED);

        if (lResult == CSMTP::RESULT_SUCCESS ||
            lResult == CSMTP::RESULT_ABORT) {
            SendMessage(hwnd, WM_CLOSE, 0, 0);
        }
        else {
            int iOldLength = GetWindowTextLength(hwnd);
            char * pszNewTitle = new char[iOldLength + 1];
            GetWindowText(hwnd, pszNewTitle, iOldLength + 1);
            int iNewLength = iOldLength - lstrlen(cszSendingText);
            pszNewTitle[iNewLength] = '\0';
            SetWindowText(hwnd, pszNewTitle);
            delete[] pszNewTitle;

            pdata->bSending = FALSE;

            SendMessage(g_hClient, WM_MDIRESTORE, (WPARAM) hwnd, 0);
            SendMessage(g_hClient, WM_MDIACTIVATE, (WPARAM) hwnd, 0);
            MessageBox(hwnd,
                "Could not send message!  Check configuration and "
                "addressing information and try again.", "Error",
                MB_OK | MB_ICONEXCLAMATION);
        }
}


/*
    Function: OnDestroy
    Description:
        Handles WM_DESTROY processing.  Simply deletes the private
        data associated with the window before it is destroyed.
*/
void OnDestroy(HWND hwnd)
{
    // Deallocate our private window data before we go away.
    EDITORDATA * pdata = GETEDITORDATA(hwnd);
    delete pdata;
}


/*
    Function: OnMDIActivate
    Description:
        Handles WM_MDIACTIVATE messages.  The function takes care of
        putting the editor menu in place and enabling/disabling
        the "Send" menu choice based on whether a SMTP session is
        already in progress for this message.  If the window is
        being deactivated, the frame menu is put in place.
*/
void OnMDIActivate(HWND hwnd, BOOL fActive, HWND hwndActivate,
    HWND hwndDeactivate)
```

```
{
    UNUSED_PARAMETER(hwndActivate);
    UNUSED_PARAMETER(hwndDeactivate);

    if (fActive) {
        // Put our menu in place.
        SendMessage(g_hClient, WM_MDISETMENU,
            GET_WM_MDISETMENU_MPS(g_hEditorMenu,
                g_hEditorWindowMenu));
        EDITORDATA * pdata = GETEDITORDATA(hwnd);
        // Enable/disable the Mail|Send menu item.
        if (pdata->bSending) {
            EnableMenuItem(g_hEditorMenu, IDM_MAILSEND, MF_GRAYED);
        }
        else {
            EnableMenuItem(g_hEditorMenu, IDM_MAILSEND, MF_ENABLED);
        }
        // Make sure keystrokes go to the edit control.
        SetFocus(pdata->hwndEdit);
    }
    else {
        // We're being deactivated, so put the main menu in place.
        SendMessage(g_hClient, WM_MDISETMENU,
            GET_WM_MDISETMENU_MPS(g_hFrameMenu,
                g_hFrameWindowMenu));
    }
    DrawMenuBar(g_hFrame);
}


/*
    Function: OnQueryEndSession
    Description:
        Handles WM_QUERYENDSESSION window messages.  The function
        throws up a warning message box if the user tries to close
        the window while the message is being sent via SMTP.
*/
BOOL OnQueryEndSession(HWND hwnd)
{
    EDITORDATA * pdata = GETEDITORDATA(hwnd);
    if (pdata->bSending) {
        SendMessage(g_hClient, WM_MDIRESTORE, (WPARAM) hwnd, 0);
        int iResult = MessageBox(hwnd,
            "Message still being sent.  Close anyway?",
            "Close Anyway?", MB_YESNO | MB_ICONQUESTION);
        if (iResult == IDYES)
            return TRUE;
        else
            return FALSE;
    }
    else {
        return TRUE;
    }
}
```

```
/*
    Function: OnSize
    Description:
        Handle WM_SIZE window messages.  Makes sure that the edit
        control inside the window gets resized when the user
        resizes the child MDI window.
*/
void OnSize(HWND hwnd, UINT state, int cx, int cy)
{
    UNUSED_PARAMETER(state);

    EDITORDATA * pdata = GETEDITORDATA(hwnd);
    MoveWindow(pdata->hwndEdit, 0, 0, cx, cy, TRUE);
    // Must make sure we forward this to the default child proc
    // as well!
    FORWARD_WM_SIZE(hwnd, state, cx, cy, DefMDIChildProc);
}


/************************************************************************
    MENU HANDLERS
************************************************************************/

/*
    Function: OnMailSend
    Description:
        The function that kicks off the sending of a message.  The
        function first displays a dialog box that allows the user to
        edit the address list and subject of the message.  Next, the
        function creates the RFC822 compliant message in a temporary
        file, which is then handed to the SMTP object to deliver.
*/
void OnMailSend(HWND hwnd)
{
    ADDRESSDLGINFO adi;

    // Force the user to be configured before progressing.
    if (!g_bConfigured) {
        MessageBox(hwnd, "You must configure the mail parameters "
            "before sending mail.", "Can't Send Message",
            MB_OK | MB_ICONSTOP);
        return;
    }

    // Put up the Addressing Information dialog box.
    FARPROC lpfnAddressProc =
        MakeProcInstance((FARPROC) AddressDlgProc, g_hInstance);
    BOOL bResult = DialogBoxParam(g_hInstance, "ADDRESSING", hwnd,
        (DLGPROC) lpfnAddressProc,
        (LPARAM)(ADDRESSDLGINFO FAR *) &adi);
    FreeProcInstance(lpfnAddressProc);

    // Don't do anything if the user hits Cancel.
    if (bResult == FALSE)
        return;
```

```
    // Make sure it's addressed to somebody.
    if (adi.pToAddrList->First() == NULL &&
        adi.pCcAddrList->First() == NULL) {
        MessageBox(hwnd, "You must supply at least one destination "
            "address.", "Can't Send Message", MB_OK | MB_ICONSTOP);
        return;
    }

    // See if there is an attachment and if so, whether the file
    // exists or not.
    BOOL bAttachment;
    if (lstrcmp(adi.pszFullName, "") != 0) {
        bAttachment = TRUE;
        OFSTRUCT ofs;
        HFILE hfile = OpenFile(adi.pszFullName, &ofs, OF_EXIST);
        if (hfile == HFILE_ERROR) {
            MessageBox(hwnd, "Attachment file can't be opened.",
                "Can't Send Message", MB_OK | MB_ICONSTOP);
            return;
        }
    }
    else {
        bAttachment = FALSE;
    }

    // Capture the mouse, 'cause this could take more than an
    // instant.
    SetCapture(g_hFrame);
    HCURSOR hcursorSave = SetCursor(LoadCursor(NULL, IDC_WAIT));

    // Block sending.
    EDITORDATA * pdata = GETEDITORDATA(hwnd);
    pdata->bSending = TRUE;
    EnableMenuItem(g_hEditorMenu, IDM_MAILSEND, MF_GRAYED);

    // Fiddle with the window text and make the window iconic.
    int iOldLength = GetWindowTextLength(hwnd);
    int iNewLength = iOldLength + lstrlen(cszSendingText) + 1;
    char * pszNewTitle = new char[iNewLength];
    GetWindowText(hwnd, pszNewTitle, iOldLength + 1);
    lstrcat(pszNewTitle, cszSendingText);
    SetWindowText(hwnd, pszNewTitle);
    delete[] pszNewTitle;
    ShowWindow(hwnd, SW_MINIMIZE);
    SendMessage(g_hClient, WM_MDINEXT, (WPARAM)hwnd, 0);

    // Create the RFC822 message from the body text and the addressing
    // information the user has entered.

    // Get a temp filename from Windows.
    pdata->pszTempFile = new char[MAX_PATH_LENGTH];
    GetTempFileName(0, "MAIL", 0, pdata->pszTempFile);
```

```
// Open a standard C++ output stream.
  ofstream ofsMsgStream(pdata->pszTempFile);

// Compose the message.  Note that we use '\n' line terminators
// rather than the explicit "\r\n" that RFC 822 requires.  The
// standard end-of-line convention in DOS is actually "\r\n" but
// not in C/C++.  The standard C/C++ libraries handle converting
// our '\n' to "\r\n" as the file is written.  When it's read back
// in in the CSMTP object, the "\r\n" in the file is converted
// back to just '\n', which the CSMTP object then converts back
// to "\r\n" for SMTP purposes.  It's a torturous route, but it
// works.
  char szDate[MAX_DATE_LENGTH];
  GetCurrentRFC822Date(szDate);
ofsMsgStream << "Date: " << szDate << '\n';
ofsMsgStream << "From: " << g_pszUserName << " <" <<
      g_pszUserAddress << ">\n";

// Allocate the combined To: & CC: list that will be passed to the
// SMTP object for delivery.
  pdata->palAddrList = new CAddrList;

// Output the To: list.
  OutputAddrList("To: ", adi.pToAddrList, pdata->palAddrList,
      ofsMsgStream);

// Output the Cc: list.
  OutputAddrList("Cc: ", adi.pCcAddrList, pdata->palAddrList,
      ofsMsgStream);

// Write out the subject.
  if (lstrcmp(adi.pszSubject, "") != 0) {
      ofsMsgStream << "Subject: " << adi.pszSubject << '\n';
  }

// Create a message ID.
  char szMessageID[MAX_MESSAGE_ID_LENGTH];
  GetMessageID(szMessageID);
ofsMsgStream << "Message-ID: <" << szMessageID << ">\n";

// We're doing MIME.
  ofsMsgStream << "MIME-Version: 1.0\n";

// Some advertising... :-)
  ofsMsgStream << "X-Mail-Agent: Mail Client\n";
  ofsMsgStream << "X-Mail-Agent: From the book, \"Developing for "
      "the Internet with WinSock\"\n";
  ofsMsgStream << "X-Mail-Agent: By Dave Roberts\n";

  if (bAttachment == FALSE) {
      OutputMessageText(pdata->hwndEdit, ofsMsgStream);
  }
```

```
    else {
        // Create some boundary text.
        char szBoundary[30];
         CreateBoundary(szBoundary, sizeof(szBoundary));
        // Output the multipart/mixed content type with the
        // boundary.
         ofsMsgStream << "Content-Type: multipart/mixed;\n" <<
            "  boundary=\"" << szBoundary << "\"\n";
        ofsMsgStream << '\n';   // Blank line between header/body.
        // Output the boundary which starts a body part.
        ofsMsgStream << '\n' << "-" << szBoundary << '\n';
        // Output the text portion of the file.
         OutputMessageText(pdata->hwndEdit, ofsMsgStream);
        // Output the boundary which separates the text and the
        // attachment.
        ofsMsgStream << '\n' << "-" << szBoundary << '\n';
        // Output the attachment.
         OutputAttachment(adi.pszFullName, ofsMsgStream);
        // Output the boundary which terminates all body parts.
        ofsMsgStream << '\n' << "-" << szBoundary << "-\n";
    }

    ofsMsgStream.close();

    // Release the mouse.
    SetCursor(hcursorSave);
    ReleaseCapture();

    // Create the CSMTP object and let 'er rip!
    pdata->ifsMsgStream.open(pdata->pszTempFile);
    pdata->pcsmtp = new CSMTPWithWinMsg(hwnd, WM_CSMTPDONE, 0);
    pdata->pcsmtp->SendMessage(g_pszSMTPServer, g_ushSMTPPort,
        &(pdata->ifsMsgStream), g_pszUserAddress,
        pdata->palAddrList);
}


/*
    Function: OnMailUuencode
    Description:
        Handle the UUENCODE menu choice.  UUENCODE a file and
        insert it into the editing buffer.
*/
void OnMailUuencode(HWND hwnd)
{
    char szBuffer[82];
    CUUENC cuuenc(hwnd);

    // Capture the mouse, 'cause this could take more than an
    // instant.
    SetCapture(g_hFrame);
    HCURSOR hcursorSave = SetCursor(LoadCursor(NULL, IDC_WAIT));
```

```
    EDITORDATA * pdata = GETEDITORDATA(hwnd);

    // Turn off redraw so this goes a lot faster.
    SetWindowRedraw(pdata->hwndEdit, FALSE);

    // Move the caret to the start of the current line.
    // This ensures that all the uuencoded text is contained on
    // separate lines.  In particular, it ensures that the "begin"
    // text doesn't have text on the line in front of it, thus
    // screwing up decoding.
    int iLineStart = (int) SendMessage(pdata->hwndEdit, EM_LINEINDEX,
        (WPARAM)-1, 0); // -1 = this line.
    SendMessage(pdata->hwndEdit, EM_SETSEL,
        GET_EM_SETSEL_MPS(iLineStart, iLineStart));

    // Encode a file.
    int iResult = cuuenc.EncodeLine(szBuffer, sizeof(szBuffer));
    while (iResult == CUUENC::RESULT_OK) {
        lstrcat(szBuffer, "\r\n");
        SendMessage(pdata->hwndEdit, EM_REPLACESEL, 0,
            (LPARAM)(LPCSTR) szBuffer);
        iResult = cuuenc.EncodeLine(szBuffer, sizeof(szBuffer));
    }

    // Turn on redraw again.
    SetWindowRedraw(pdata->hwndEdit, TRUE);

    // Release the captured mouse.
    SetCursor(hcursorSave);
    ReleaseCapture();

    // Figure out what happened.
    if (iResult == CUUENC::RESULT_DONE) {
        // Handle the last line.
        lstrcat(szBuffer, "\r\n");
        SendMessage(pdata->hwndEdit, EM_REPLACESEL, 0,
            (LPARAM)(LPCSTR) szBuffer);
    }
    else if (iResult == CUUENC::RESULT_ERROR) {
        // Deal with any error that cropped up.
        MessageBox(hwnd, "An error occurred during encoding.",
            "Error", MB_OK | MB_ICONEXCLAMATION);
    }
}


/**********************************************************************
    UTILITY FUNCTIONS
**********************************************************************/

/*
    Function: AddressStringToList
    Description:
```

```
        Take a string containing a series of comma-separated
          email addresses, break them into individual strings,
          and add them to an address list.
*/
BOOL AddressStringToList(char * pszAddressString, CAddrList * pAddrList)
{
    char szAddress[80];
    int iAddrStringIndex = 0;

    // Do this until we hit the end of the input string.
    while (pszAddressString[iAddrStringIndex] != '\0') {
        int iAddressIndex = 0;
        char c = pszAddressString[iAddrStringIndex];
        // Copy characters from the input string to the address
        // string until we hit a null or a comma.
        while (c != '\0' && c != ',' &&
            iAddressIndex < sizeof(szAddress)) {
            // Copy all non-whitespace characters to the holding
            // string.
            if (c != ' ' && c != '\t') {
                szAddress[iAddressIndex] = c;
                iAddressIndex++;
            }
            iAddrStringIndex++;
            c = pszAddressString[iAddrStringIndex];
        }
        if (iAddressIndex == sizeof(szAddress)) {
            // If we ran out of room, error.
            return FALSE;
        }
        // Terminate the holding string.
        szAddress[iAddressIndex] = '\0';
        // Move past the comma of the input string.
        if (c != '\0') {
            iAddrStringIndex++;
        }
        // If we got a valid string, add it to the list.
        if (iAddressIndex > 0) {
            pAddrList->Add(szAddress);
        }
    }
    return TRUE;
}


/*
    Function: OutputAddrList
    Description:
        Output a list of addresses in an email address header
        to an output stream.
```

```
*/
void OutputAddrList(char * pszHeader, CAddrList * palHeaderList,
    CAddrList * palTotalList, ofstream &ofsMsgStream)
{
    // Create the To: list.
    if (palHeaderList->First() != NULL) {
        char szLine[73];  // 72 + null
        lstrcpy(szLine, pszHeader);
        lstrcat(szLine, palHeaderList->First());
        int iLineLen = lstrlen(szLine);
        palTotalList->Add(palHeaderList->First());
        char * pszNextAddr = palHeaderList->Next();
        if (pszNextAddr == NULL) {
            ofsMsgStream << szLine << '\n';
        }
        else {
            lstrcat(szLine, ",");
            iLineLen++;
            while (pszNextAddr != NULL) {
                while (pszNextAddr != NULL &&
                    /* space + comma */
                    ((iLineLen + lstrlen(pszNextAddr) + 2) <
                    sizeof(szLine))) {
                    // Add a space after the previous comma.
                    lstrcat(szLine, " ");
                    iLineLen++;
                    lstrcat(szLine, pszNextAddr);
                    iLineLen += lstrlen(pszNextAddr);
                    palTotalList->Add(pszNextAddr);
                    pszNextAddr = palHeaderList->Next();
                    if (pszNextAddr != NULL) {
                        // If there's another one, add a comma.
                        lstrcat(szLine, ",");
                        iLineLen++;
                    }
                }
                ofsMsgStream << szLine << '\n';
                lstrcpy(szLine, "   ");  // Add 3 spaces.
                iLineLen = lstrlen(szLine);
            } // end while
        } // end else
    } // end if
}


/*
    Function: OutputMessageText
    Description:
        Outputs a text mail body part to a stream.  Includes
        Content-Type and Content-Transfer-Encoding headers
        describing the text.  Handles ISO 8859-1 text by using
        quoted-printable encoding.
*/
```

```
void OutputMessageText(HWND hwndEdit, ofstream& ofsMsgStream)
{
    // Search the message text to see if any of the characters have
    // the high bit set.  If so, then the character set is ISO 8859-1.
    BOOL bISOCharset = FALSE;
    int iNumLines = (int)SendMessage(hwndEdit, EM_GETLINECOUNT, 0, 0);
    int i;
    for (i = 0; i < iNumLines; i++) {
        char szLineBuffer[500];
        // Get the line from the edit control.
        // First indicate the size of the buffer in the first couple
        // of bytes (pretty wierd way to do this, Microsoft...).
        // Leave 1 byte for the terminator which EM_GETLINE won't put
        // in.
        *(WORD *)szLineBuffer = sizeof(szLineBuffer) - 1;
        int iLength = (int) SendMessage(hwndEdit, EM_GETLINE, i,
            (LPARAM) (char FAR *) szLineBuffer);
        // EM_GETLINE doesn't terminate the string, so add a null.
        szLineBuffer[iLength] = '\0';
        for (int j = 0; szLineBuffer[j] != '\0'; j++) {
            if (0x80 & szLineBuffer[j]) {
                bISOCharset = TRUE;
                break;
            }
        }
        if (bISOCharset == TRUE)
            break;
    }

    ofsMsgStream << "Content-Type: text/plain; charset=";
    ofsMsgStream << (bISOCharset ? "iso-8859-1\n" : "us-ascii\n");
    ofsMsgStream << "Content-Transfer-Encoding: ";
    ofsMsgStream << (bISOCharset ? "quoted-printable\n" : "7bit\n");

    // Blank line separating headers and body.
    ofsMsgStream << '\n';

    // Output the lines of the message.
    iNumLines = (int) SendMessage(hwndEdit, EM_GETLINECOUNT, 0, 0);
    for (i = 0; i < iNumLines; i++) {
        char szLineBuffer[500];
        // Get the line from the edit control.
        // First indicate the size of the buffer in the first couple
        // of bytes (pretty wierd way to do this, Microsoft...).
        // Leave 1 byte for the terminator which EM_GETLINE won't put
        // in.
        *(WORD *)szLineBuffer = sizeof(szLineBuffer) - 1;
        int iLength = (int) SendMessage(hwndEdit, EM_GETLINE, i,
            (LPARAM) (char FAR *) szLineBuffer);
        // EM_GETLINE doesn't terminate the string, so add a null.
        szLineBuffer[iLength] = '\0';
        if (bISOCharset) {
```

```
                    // Check for characters with high-bit set and convert
                      // them to quoted printable.
                      char szSecondBuffer[500];
                        ConvertToQP(szSecondBuffer, sizeof(szSecondBuffer),
                          szLineBuffer);
                      ofsMsgStream << szSecondBuffer << '\n';
                }
            else {
                    // It's ASCII, so simply write it to the file.
                    ofsMsgStream << szLineBuffer << '\n';
                }
        }
    }
}


/*

    Function: ConvertToQP
    Description:
        Converts a line of 8-bit characters into quoted-printable
        encoding.
*/
void ConvertToQP(char * pszAfter, int nLen, char * pszBefore)
{
    int iAfter = 0;
    int iBefore = 0;
    int nLineLength = 0;
    // Note that we stop a bit before we overrun the after buffer
    // because we could have one character generate 3 quoted
    // characters, a soft line break could be inserted, and
    // we still need to insert a null terminator.
    while ((iAfter < nLen - 6) && pszBefore[iBefore] != '\0') {
        char c = pszBefore[iBefore];
        // Is it a whitespace character?
        if (IsLWSP(c)) {
            // Quoted printable encoding doesn't allow a space or tab
            // at the end of a line.  See if there are more
            // non-whitespace characters following.  If not, encode
            // this character as "=09" or "=20".
            int iTestIndex = iBefore + 1;
            BOOL bNonLWSPFollows = FALSE;
            while (pszBefore[iTestIndex] != '\0') {
                if (!IsLWSP(pszBefore[iTestIndex])) {
                    bNonLWSPFollows = TRUE;
                    break;
                }
                iTestIndex++;
            }
            if (bNonLWSPFollows) {
                // Non-whitespace follows, so we're okay.
                pszAfter[iAfter] = c;
                iAfter++;
                nLineLength++;
            }
```

```
            else {
                   // Just whitespace at the end of the line, so quote
                   // this one.
                    QuoteCharacter(c, &pszAfter[iAfter]);
                   iAfter += 3;
                   nLineLength += 3;
               }
       }
       // Is 33 <= c <= 60 or 62 <= c <= 126?
       else if ((33 <= c && c <= 60) || (62 <= c && c <= 126)) {
           // It's a normal character and doesn't have to be
           // quoted.
           pszAfter[iAfter] = c;
           iAfter++;
           nLineLength++;
       }
       else {
              QuoteCharacter(c, &pszAfter[iAfter]);
              iAfter += 3;
              nLineLength += 3;
       }

       // Check the line length
       if (nLineLength >= 75 && pszBefore[iBefore + 1] != '\0') {
           pszAfter[iAfter++] = '=';
           pszAfter[iAfter++] = '\n';
           nLineLength = 0;
       }
       iBefore++;
   }
   pszAfter[iAfter] = '\0';
}


/*
    Function: QuoteCharacter
    Description:
        Convert a single character into quoted-printable encoding.
*/
void QuoteCharacter(unsigned char c, char * pszBuffer)
{
    const char szHexDigit[] = "0123456789ABCDEF";
    pszBuffer[0] = '=';
    pszBuffer[1] = szHexDigit[(c >> 4) & 0xF];
    pszBuffer[2] = szHexDigit[c & 0xF];
}


/*
    Function: CreateBoundary
    Description:
        Creates a virtually unique message body separation boundary.
        Uses pseudo-random characters as filler to reduce the
        chance that a body part contains the boundary text somewhere.
```

```
*/
void CreateBoundary(char * szBuffer, int nLen)
{
    // From MIME RFC definition.
    const char szBCharsNoSpace[] =
          "0123456789abcdefghijklmnopqrstuvwxyz"
          "ABCDEFGHIJKLMNOPQRSTUVWXYZ'()+_,-./:=?";
    const char szStart[] = "=_ Boundary ";
    // Fill up as much of the buffer as we can with the starting
    // text.
    int i = 0;
    while (i < nLen - 1 && szStart[i] != '\0') {
        szBuffer[i] = szStart[i];
        i++;
    }
    // Then fill the rest of the buffer with random stuff to make
    // it virtually unique.
    while (i < nLen - 1) {
        szBuffer[i] = szBCharsNoSpace[rand() %
              sizeof(szBCharsNoSpace)];
        i++;
    }
    szBuffer[i] = '\0';
}


/*
    Function: OutputAttachment
    Description:
        Output the attachment body part to a stream.  The function
          outputs Content-Type and Content-Transfer-Encoding
        headers and converts the specified file to BASE64 encoding.
*/
void OutputAttachment(char * pszFileName, ofstream& ofsMsgStream)
{
    // Output the header info.
    ofsMsgStream << "Content-Type: application/octet-stream\n";
    ofsMsgStream << "Content-Transfer-Encoding: base64\n";
    ofsMsgStream << '\n';

    // Create an encoder object and have it open the attached file.
    CBase64Enc b64encoder;
    int iResult = b64encoder.OpenFile(pszFileName);
    if (iResult != CBase64Enc::RESULT_OK)
        return;
    // Encode all the data in the file and write it to the output
    // stream one line at a time.
    char szLine[80];
    iResult = b64encoder.EncodeLine(szLine, sizeof(szLine));
    while (iResult == CBase64Enc::RESULT_OK) {
        ofsMsgStream << szLine << '\n';
        iResult = b64encoder.EncodeLine(szLine, sizeof(szLine));
    }
}
```

Listing 9.9   RFC822.H

```
/*
     File: RFC822.H
     Description:
          A bunch of functions used for RFC 822 stuff.
     Copyright 1995, David G. Roberts
*/

#ifndef _RFC822_H
#define _RFC822_H

/*
     CONSTANTS
*/
#define MAX_DATE_LENGTH 40
#define MAX_MESSAGE_ID_LENGTH 80

/*
     RFC 822 Definitions
*/
#define IsCHAR(c)      (0 <= c && c <= 127)
#define IsALPHA(c)     ((65 <= c && c <= 90) || (97 <= c && c <= 122))
#define IsDIGIT(c)     (48 <= c && c <= 57)
#define IsCTL(c)       ((0 <= c && c <= 31) || (127 == c))
#define CR             ((char)13)
#define LF             ((char)10)
#define SPACE          ((char)32)
#define HTAB           ((char)9)
#define IsCR(c)        (c == CR)
#define IsLF(c)        (c == LF)
#define IsSPACE(c)     (c == SPACE)
#define IsLWSP(c)      (c == SPACE || c == HTAB)
extern const char szSpecials[];
extern const char szTSpecials[];
#define IsSPECIAL(c)       IsInSet(c, szSpecials)
#define IsTSPECIAL(c)      IsInSet(c, szTSpecials)

/*
     TOKEN VALUES
*/
#define TOKEN_ERROR       -1
#define TOKEN_ATOM         1
#define TOKEN_MIMETOKEN    2
#define TOKEN_QSTRING      3
#define TOKEN_DOMLIT       4
#define TOKEN_COMMENT      5
#define TOKEN_SPECIAL      6
#define TOKEN_TSPECIAL     7
#define TOKEN_CTL          8
#define TOKEN_END          9
```

```
/*
        FUNCTION DECLARATIONS
*/
void GetCurrentRFC822Date(char * pszBuffer);
void GetMessageID(char * pszBuffer);

/*
        PARSING FUNCTIONS
*/
BOOL IsInSet(const int c, const char * szSet);
char * SkipLWSP(char * pszBuffer);
char * GetToken(BOOL bMIME, char * pszHeader, char * pszBuffer,
    int nLen, int * piType);

#endif
```

Listing 9.10   RFC822.CPP

```
/*
        File: RFC822.CPP
        Description:
            A bunch of functions used for RFC 822 stuff.
        Copyright 1995, David G. Roberts
*/


#include <time.h>
#include <windows.h>
#include "winsock.h"
#include "rfc822.h"
#include "myassert.h"


/*

        Function: GetCurrentRFC822Date
        Description:
            Gets the current date in RFC 822 format. The input buffer
            must be large enough to hold the resulting date (size it at
            least as large as MAX_DATE_LENGTH, defined in RFC822.H).
*/
void GetCurrentRFC822Date(char * pszBuffer)
{
    struct tm * ptm;
    time_t curtime;
    const char * szDays[] = { "Sun", "Mon", "Tue", "Wed",
        "Thu", "Fri", "Sat" };
    const char * szMonths[] = { "Jan", "Feb", "Mar", "Apr", "May",
        "Jun", "Jul", "Aug", "Sep", "Oct", "Nov", "Dec" };

    // Set the _tzname, _daylight, and _timezone variables.
    tzset();
    // Get the current time.
    time(&curtime);
    ptm = localtime(&curtime);
```

```
    // Fill out the buffer.
    wsprintf(pszBuffer, "%s, %02d %s %02d %02d:%02d:%02d %s",
        (LPSTR)szDays[ptm->tm_wday],
        ptm->tm_mday,
        (LPSTR)szMonths[ptm->tm_mon],
        ptm->tm_year,
        ptm->tm_hour,
        ptm->tm_min,
        ptm->tm_sec,
        (LPSTR)_tzname[_daylight]);
}


/*

    Function: GetMessageID
    Description:
        Creates a text string message ID, virtually guaranteed to be
        unique on this host.  The message ID string consists of a
        string of digits, representing the current date and time, a
        message counter value, an "at-sign" (@), and the host name.
        The current date and time and the counter value make the
        string unique.  There is a remote possibility that if you
        had another program running on the same machine at the same
        time that it could send a message with the same message ID,
        but this possibility is very remote.
*/
void GetMessageID(char * pszBuffer)
{
    struct tm * ptm;
    time_t curtime;
    static unsigned long counter = 0;
    char szHostName[100];

    // Get the current time.
    time(&curtime);
    ptm = localtime(&curtime);
    gethostname(szHostName, sizeof(szHostName));
    wsprintf(pszBuffer, "%02d%02d%02d%02d%02d%02d.%lu@%s",
        ptm->tm_mon + 1, ptm->tm_mday, ptm->tm_year, ptm->tm_hour,
        ptm->tm_min, ptm->tm_sec, counter, (LPSTR)szHostName);
    counter++;
}

/*****************************************************************
    Parsing Functions
*****************************************************************/

// Standard RFC 822 specials.
const char szSpecials[] = "()<>@,;:\\\".[]";
// MIME (RFC 1521) tspecials
const char szTSpecials[] = "()<>@,;:\\\"/[]?=";

/*

    Function: IsInSet
```

```
      Description:
            Returns TRUE if the specified character is a part of the
            given character set.
*/
BOOL IsInSet(const int c, const char * szSet)
{
    int i;

    for (i = 0; szSet[i] != '\0'; i++)
        if (szSet[i] == c) return TRUE;
    return FALSE;
}


/*
      Function: SkipLWSP
      Description:
            Returns the first character of the specified string
            that is not a linear whitespace character.
*/
char * SkipLWSP(char * pszBuffer)
{
    while (IsLWSP(*pszBuffer))
        pszBuffer++;
    return pszBuffer;
}


/*
      Function: LexAtom
      Description:
            Gets an atom from the specified header.  Returns the
            first character that could not be consumed. The buffer length
            is specified in nLen and must be long enough to hold the
            entire token.
*/
char * LexAtom(char * pszHeader, char * pszBuffer, int nLen)
{
    int iHeader = 0;
    int iBuffer = 0;
    char c = pszHeader[iHeader++];
    while (!IsSPECIAL(c) && !IsSPACE(c) && !IsCTL(c) &&
        iBuffer < (nLen - 1)) {
        pszBuffer[iBuffer++] = c;
        c = pszHeader[iHeader++];
    }
    pszBuffer[iBuffer] = '\0';
    return pszHeader + iHeader - 1;
}


/*
      Function: LexQText
```

```
    Description:
        Gets quoted text from the specified header.  Returns the
        first character that could not be consumed. The buffer length
        is specified in nLen and must be long enough to hold the
        entire token.
*/
char * LexQText(char * pszHeader, char * pszBuffer, int nLen)
{
    int iHeader = 0;
    int iBuffer = 0;
    char c = pszHeader[iHeader++];
    while (c != '"' && iBuffer < (nLen - 1)) {
        // Skip over quoted pairs.
        if (c == '\\') {
            pszBuffer[iBuffer++] = pszHeader[iHeader++];
        }
        else {
            pszBuffer[iBuffer++] = c;
        }
        c = pszHeader[iHeader++];
    }
    pszBuffer[iBuffer] = '\0';
    return pszHeader + iHeader - 1;
}


/*
    Function: LexDText
    Description:
        Gets a domain literal from the specified header. Returns the
        first character that could not be consumed. The buffer length
        is specified in nLen and must be long enough to hold the
        entire token.
*/
char * LexDText(char * pszHeader, char * pszBuffer, int nLen)
{
    int iHeader = 0;
    int iBuffer = 0;
    char c = pszHeader[iHeader++];
    while (c != '[' && c != ']' && iBuffer < (nLen - 1)) {
        // Skip over quoted pairs.
        if (c == '\\') {
            pszBuffer[iBuffer++] = pszHeader[iHeader++];
        }
        else {
            pszBuffer[iBuffer++] = c;
        }
        c = pszHeader[iHeader++];
    }
    pszBuffer[iBuffer] = '\0';
    return pszHeader + iHeader - 1;
}
```

```
/*
    Function: LexCText
    Description:
        Gets comment text from the specified header.  Returns the
        first character that could not be consumed. The buffer length
        is specified in nLen and must be long enough to hold the
        entire token.
*/
char * LexCText(char * pszHeader, char * pszBuffer, int nLen)
{
    int iHeader = 0;
    int iBuffer = 0;
    int iNestLevel = 0;
    char c = pszHeader[iHeader++];
    while ((c != ')' || iNestLevel != 0) && iBuffer < (nLen - 1)) {
        // Skip over quoted pairs.
        if (c == '\\') {
            pszBuffer[iBuffer++] = pszHeader[iHeader++];
        }
        else {
            pszBuffer[iBuffer++] = c;
            if (c == '(')
                iNestLevel++;
            if (c == ')')
                iNestLevel-;
        }
        c = pszHeader[iHeader++];
    }
    pszBuffer[iBuffer] = '\0';
    return pszHeader + iHeader - 1;
}


/*
    Function: LexMIMEToken
    Description:
        Gets MIME token from the specified header.  A MIME token
        is defined in RFC 1521 and is slightly different than an
        RFC 822 atom.  The function returns the first character in
        the stream that could not be consumed.
*/
char * LexMIMEToken(char * pszHeader, char * pszBuffer, int nLen)
{
    int iHeader = 0;
    int iBuffer = 0;
    char c = pszHeader[iHeader++];
    while (!IsTSPECIAL(c) && !IsSPACE(c) && !IsCTL(c) &&
            iBuffer < (nLen - 1)) {
        pszBuffer[iBuffer++] = c;
        c = pszHeader[iHeader++];
    }
    pszBuffer[iBuffer] = '\0';
    return pszHeader + iHeader - 1;
}
```

```
/*
    Function: GetToken
    Description:
        Gets an RFC 822 token of some sort from the buffer.  The
        buffer is filled with the token and the integer specified
        by piType is set to the token type.  The next character
        following the token is returned.  If an error occurs,
        *piType is set to TOKEN_ERROR and the function return value
        indicates where the error occurred.  If bMIME is true, the
        function looks for MIME tokens rather than RFC 822 atoms.
        Note that the enclosing characters of quoted text,
        domain literals, and comments ( "\"[]()" ) is stripped
        from the token before it is returned.

        Note that pszBuffer must be non-NULL and nLen must 2 or more
        (2 for special or CTL and terminating null).
*/
char * GetToken(BOOL bMIME, char * pszHeader, char * pszBuffer,
    int nLen, int * piType)
{
    ASSERT(pszBuffer != NULL);
    ASSERT(nLen >= 2);

    // Skip over any leading white space characters.
    pszHeader = SkipLWSP(pszHeader);
    if (*pszHeader == '\0') {
        // We're at the end of the string.
        *pszBuffer = '\0';
        *piType = TOKEN_END;
        return pszHeader;
    }
    else if (*pszHeader == '"') {
        // Parse some quoted text.
        pszHeader = LexQText(pszHeader + 1, pszBuffer, nLen);
        // See if we stopped because of terminating quote.
        if (*pszHeader == '"') {
            // Yes, so everything was okay.
            *piType = TOKEN_QSTRING;
            return pszHeader + 1;
        }
        else {
            // Nope.  Signal error.
            *piType = TOKEN_ERROR;
            return pszHeader;
        }
    }
    else if (*pszHeader == '[') {
        // Parse a domain literal.
        pszHeader = LexDText(pszHeader + 1, pszBuffer, nLen);
        // See if we stopped because of terminating ']'.
        if (*pszHeader == ']') {
            // Yes, so everything was okay.
```

```
                    *piType = TOKEN_DOMLIT;
                    return pszHeader + 1;
            }
            else {
                    // Nope.  Signal error.
                    *piType = TOKEN_ERROR;
                    return pszHeader;
            }
    }
    else if (*pszHeader == '(') {
        // Parse a comment.
        pszHeader = LexCText(pszHeader + 1, pszBuffer, nLen);
        // See if we stopped because of terminating ')'.
        if (*pszHeader == ')') {
                // Yes, so everything was okay.
                *piType = TOKEN_DOMLIT;
                return pszHeader + 1;
        }
        else {
                // Nope.  Signal error.
                *piType = TOKEN_ERROR;
                return pszHeader;
        }
    }
    else if (IsCTL(*pszHeader)) {
        *piType = TOKEN_CTL;
        pszBuffer[0] = *pszHeader;
        pszBuffer[1] = '\0';
        return pszHeader + 1;
    }
    else if (bMIME) {
        // Parse MIME tokens and tspecials.
        if (IsTSPECIAL(*pszHeader)) {
            *piType = TOKEN_TSPECIAL;
            pszBuffer[0] = *pszHeader;
            pszBuffer[1] = '\0';
            return pszHeader + 1;
        }
        else {
             pszHeader = LexMIMEToken(pszHeader, pszBuffer, nLen);
            *piType = TOKEN_MIMETOKEN;
            return pszHeader;
        }
    }
    else {
        // Parse RFC 822 atoms and specials.
        if (IsSPECIAL(*pszHeader)) {
            *piType = TOKEN_SPECIAL;
            pszBuffer[0] = *pszHeader;
            pszBuffer[1] = '\0';
            return pszHeader + 1;
        }
```

```
        else {
             pszHeader = LexAtom(pszHeader, pszBuffer, nLen);
             *piType = TOKEN_ATOM;
             return pszHeader;
        }
    }
}
```

Retrieving Mail: POP

CHAPTER 10

Receiving mail is just as important as sending it. In this chapter, find out how to retrieve mail using the Post Office Protocol.

I loved getting letters in the mail when I was a kid. It didn't happen often but when it did, I was always very excited. I marveled at the amount of mail my parents received, most of which they simply glanced at and threw away. To increase the amount of mail that I got, I learned to write to friends and relatives. My friends and relatives would answer my letters and then I got mail; I hadn't learned about junk mail and bills yet.

Now that we have the ability to send electronic mail using Mail Client's SMTP capability, we'll need to add mail reception capability to receive the replies our messages will generate. In this chapter, we'll examine the Post Office Protocol, Version 3 (POP3), which is used by end nodes to collect the mail that was sent to them. Then we'll develop a C++ class that implements the POP3 protocol. Finally, we'll see what changes are necessary for Mail Client to receive and display messages.

Post Office Protocol

RFC 1460 describes the Post Office Protocol, Version 3. POP3 (sometimes just abbreviated as POP), which is a simple protocol used by end nodes to retrieve mail from mail servers. This section describes the POP3 usage model and the basics of the protocol itself.

The POP Model

You might be wondering why POP exists at all. Isn't SMTP responsible for delivering mail between nodes? Why do we need another protocol to handle any aspect of mail delivery? The answers are: yes, SMTP is responsible for mail delivery, but unfortunately, SMTP doesn't work well for nodes that are switched off or are connected to the network only periodically.

Figure 10.1 shows two nodes that are exchanging mail with one another along with a couple of intermediate SMTP nodes. In this case, the ultimate receiver of the message is on the machine named "receiver.mythical.com".

SMTP works well as long as receiver.mythical.com remains switched on and connected to the network. If receiver.mythical.com is switched off or becomes disconnected from the network, as shown in Figure 10.2, server.mythical.com is unable to create an SMTP session with receiver.mythical.com and transfer the messages across the last hop. Server.mythical.com will try to make a connection for a couple of days before it finally gives up. Server.mythical.com then generates an error message and sends it back to the sender of the message. The error message indicates that some problem occurred and contact could not be made with receiver.mythical.com.

For server machines, being switched off or being disconnected from the network is typically the result of some sort of problem. Either the machine crashed or the network interface was damaged or disconnected. For many personal computers, however, being switched off or becoming disconnected is a regular part of a daily cycle. Office PCs are often switched off at night and over the weekend. Laptop PCs are often disconnected from the network as users leave the office to travel with them. SMTP does not handle these types of situations well, so another protocol must be developed.

Figure 10.1

SMTP allows end-to-end delivery of messages.

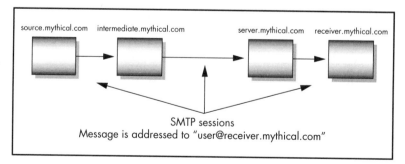

Figure 10.2

SMTP requires that all nodes in the path remain on and connected; otherwise, an error is generated.

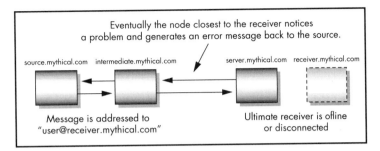

POP allows a server machine to act as a "post office" for other nodes that are frequently switched off or disconnected from the network. Using our sample configuration, users get email addresses of the form "user@server.mythical.com" in place of "user@receiver.mythical.com". As shown in Figure 10.3, SMTP delivers messages between the sender and the server machine. Because the server machine remains online and connected to the network, SMTP is able to deliver messages to it. Any error that may occur is caused by a true network error.

When the destination PC comes online, it establishes a POP session with the server and retrieves the mail stored on the server for an individual user. Because the PC (not the server) initiates the connection, the PC can control the timing of message transfers. If a PC is switched off over the weekend, all messages that arrive during that time simply are stored on the server until the PC is switched on Monday morning and is ready to collect them. In network lingo, SMTP is a "push" protocol and POP is a "pull" protocol.

When an end node wishes to send mail, it still uses SMTP, rather than POP. SMTP is used because the node can control when it tries to send outbound messages while it is connected. SMTP and POP do not require the same intermediate servers; they can be configured asymmetrically, as shown in Figure 10.4.

Figure 10.3

POP3 allows a server machine to provide a user mailbox, from which the POP client retrieves messages.

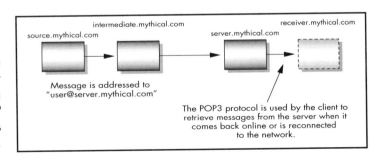

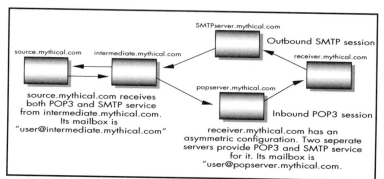

Figure 10.4

SMTP and POP
can use an
asymmetric
configuration.

Commands and Responses

POP uses a simple command and response protocol similar to that used in SMTP. All commands and responses are transferred as lines of ASCII text terminated by CRLF. Commands are simple keywords possibly followed by an argument. Examples of commands are shown in Figure 10.5.

Responses consist of a success indicator followed by more text, as shown in Figure 10.6. The format of the text depends on the command that generated it. Sometimes, as in the case of the STAT command, the reply text contains useful information that must be parsed by the program. For other commands, the text is intended to be interpreted by a human, not by a program. Only two success indicators are used: "+OK" and "-ERR". POP does not use numeric response codes like SMTP does.

Figure 10.5

Example of
POP3
commands.

```
USER dave
PASS foobar
STAT
LIST 3
QUIT
```

Figure 10.6

Example of
POP3 responses.

```
+OK 2 messages
+OK message deleted
-ERR no such message
-ERR could not access mailbox
-ERR no such user
```

Sample POP3 Session

In this section, we'll examine the command sequence used to retrieve a series of messages from a POP3 server. Not all POP3 commands are described here; a POP3 client may use different sequences of commands, depending on its needs. The command sequence described here is simply an example of what is typically used.

A simple POP session uses only six commands and follows this sequence:

1. First, the client initiates a connection with a host. The client connects to POP3's well-known port 110 using TCP.

2. The server, upon receiving a connection, sends back a greeting response to the client. The greeting is a single line of the form "+OK ...". A greeting example might be: "+OK server.mythical.com POP3 ready".

3. When the client receives the greeting, it must indicate the mailbox name that it will be manipulating with the USER command. The USER command takes a single argument: the name of the user. The server responds to a valid user name with a positive reply.

4. To prevent unauthorized users from gaining access to another person's mailbox, the client must follow the USER command with a PASS command. The PASS command takes a single argument: the password for the mailbox name indicated in the previous USER command. If the password is correct for the indicated user name, the server responds with a positive reply.

5. Now that the client has indicated a user mailbox name and has authenticated itself with the server, it can manipulate the user mailbox. First, the client issues a STAT command, which retrieves statistics about the user mailbox. The STAT command takes no arguments. The server replies to the STAT command with a reply in the following format: "+OK nn mm", where "nn" indicates the number of messages in the mailbox and "mm" indicates the total size of those messages. For example, the server might reply with "+OK 2 538", which means that two messages with a total size of 538 bytes are in the mailbox.

6. When the mailbox statistics have been retrieved, the client can start to retrieve all the messages in the mailbox. For each message indicated in the STAT response, the client performs the following two actions:

- First, the client issues the RETR command to retrieve a message. The RETR command takes one argument: the message number to retrieve. The messages are numbered 1 through nn (returned in the STAT response). If the RETR argument indicates a valid message number, the server returns a positive response ("+OK...CRLF") followed by the message text itself. As with SMTP, each line of the message is sent as ASCII text and is terminated with a CRLF character sequence. The end of the message is indicated with the ".CRLF" sequence. Lines beginning with a period are preceded with an additional period that is stripped out by the client. The end-of-message indication (".CRLF") indicates the end of the RETR command response to the client.

- After the client receives the message, it deletes it from the mailbox on the server using the DELE command. The DELE command takes a single argument: the message number to delete. If the argument indicates a valid message number, the message is marked for deletion and the server responds with a positive indication.

- When all the messages in the mailbox have been retrieved and deleted, the client sends a QUIT command to terminate the session. The QUIT command takes no arguments. The server responds to the QUIT command with a positive reply and then closes the TCP connection.

Figure 10.7 shows a sample POP3 session.

Figure 10.7

A sample POP3 session.

```
S: +OK server.droberts.com POP3 ready
C: USER dave
S: +OK User is dave
C: PASS clambake
S: +OK dave's maildrop has 2 messages
C: STAT
S: +OK 2 538
C: RETR 1
S: +OK 252 bytes
S: <server sends message #1>
S: .
C: DELE 1
S: +OK message 1 deleted
C: RETR 2
S: +OK 286 bytes
S: <server sends message #2>
S: .
C: DELE 2
S: +OK message 2 deleted
C: QUIT
S: +OK goodbye...
```

The CPOP3 Class

Just as we encapsulated SMTP functionality in the **CSMTP** class, we will encapsulate the functionality of the POP3 protocol in its own class. By encapsulating the POP3 functionality, we'll create a standalone POP3 protocol module that can be reused in many different programs. In this section, we take a look at the high-level design of our class, named **CPOP3**.

Using the CPOP3 Class

Our **CPOP3** class is very easy to use. As with our **CSMTP** class, a program simply creates an object of the class and invokes a member function to start the POP3 retrieval process. The **CPOP3** class connects with the server, retrieves all the messages in the specified mailbox, stores each message in a separate file, disconnects from the server, and informs the program that it has finished its work. The specification of the **CPOP3** class is shown in the CPOP3.H file, Listing 10.1.

The member used to start the retrieval process is prototyped like this:

```
BOOL CPOP3::RetrieveMessages(LPCSTR lpszHost, u_short ushPort,
    LPCSTR lpszUser, LPCSTR lpszPassword, LPCSTR lpszPathName,
    CStringList * pslFileList);
```

The **lpszHost** and **ushPort** arguments identify the host name and port number of the remote server.

The **lpszUser** and **lpszPassword** arguments point to the user mailbox name and associated password. These strings are passed to the server in the USER and PASS commands during the POP3 session.

The **lpszPathName** argument points to directory name where the retrieved message files should be located.

The **pslFileList** argument points to a **CStringList** object. As messages are retrieved from the server, unique file names are generated for each associated message file. The file names are stored in the **CStringList** object pointed to by **pslFileList**. When the **CPOP3** object completes the retrieval process, the program uses the file names stored in the **CStringList** object to access the messages.

The **CPOP3** class is an abstract base class. It has a pure virtual function named **DoCallback**, which is used to generate a callback to the program that created the object. The **CPOP3** class has two descendants, **CPOP3WithWinMsg** and **CPOP3WithCallback**. Each of these classes provides a **DoCallback** function that is invoked when **CPOP3** finishes the retrieval process. The **DoCallback** function implemented by the **CPOP3WithWinMsg** class generates a window message while the **CPOP3WithCallback** class generates a function callback.

Functional Overview

Like the **CSMTP** and **CFingObj** classes, **CPOP3** is implemented as a state machine. Listing 10.2 shows the implementation of the **CPOP3** class. The state machine mechanism is similar to that used in the **CSMTP** class. Like the **CSMTP** class, the **CPOP3** class uses a connection manager object (**CConnMgr**) to establish a connection with the remote server.

The state machine mechanisms used by the **CPOP3** class are similar to those used by the **CSMTP** class, with a few exceptions. The SMTP protocol is a push protocol. Most of the data transfer in an SMTP exchange is from the client to the server. In the **CSMTP** class, reply codes from the server are converted into state machine events that drive the state machine forward. The exact text returned in the reply is not significant to the state machine, so it is discarded when the event is generated (review the **CSMTP::StreamCallback** function in Listing 9.2).

In the POP protocol, most of the data exchanged between the client and server is directed towards the client. Lines of data received by the client may be either reply codes or lines of message text. Instead of converting POP reply codes ("+OK..." or "-ERR...") to state machine events, the **CPOP3** class simply sends an **EV_DATAREADY** event to the state machine for every line of text received from the server (see **CPOP3::StreamCallback**, Listing 10.2). The state machine interprets the line of text as a reply code or a line of message data, depending on its current state.

CPOP3 State Machine

The state machine implemented in the **CPOP3** class contains 14 states. A graphical representation of the state machine is shown in Figure 10.8. The code that implements the state machine is shown in Listing 10.2.

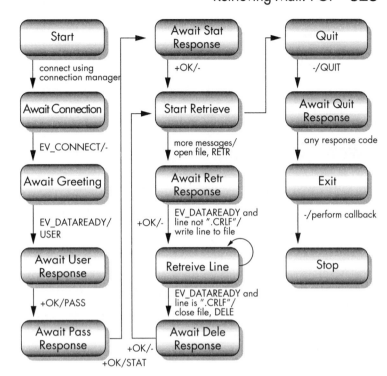

Figure 10.8

The CPOP3 state machine.

Start

The *Start* state activates when the **CPOP3::RetrieveMessages** function is invoked. The start state begins the connection process with the remote host. A **CConnMgr** object is used to manage the connection process. Once the **CConnMgr** object begins the connection process, the **CPOP3** state machine transitions to the Await Connection state.

Await Connection

The *Await Connection* state waits for the callback event after the **CConnMgr** object completes its work. If a TCP connection was successfully established between the local host and remote server, an **EV_CONNECT** event is sent to the state machine from the connection manager callback function, **CPOP3::ConnMgrCallback**. This event causes the **CPOP3** state machine to transition to the Await Greeting state. If a connection cannot be established, the **CPOP3::ConnMgrCallback** function sends an **EV_ERROR** event, which causes the **CPOP3** state machine to transition to the Exit state.

Await Greeting

The *Await Greeting* state waits for the remote server to send the initial positive reply greeting. The Await Greeting state waits to receive an **EV_DATAREADY** event. When the event arrives, the code sends a POP3 USER command to indicate the mailbox of interest and then transitions the state machine to the Await User Response state.

Await User Response

The *Await User Response* state waits to receive the server reply to the previous USER command. When the state receives an **EV_DATAREADY** event, it checks the text string for a leading "+OK" using the **CPOP3::PositiveResponse** function. This function returns TRUE if the string in the reply line buffer (**m_szReplyLineBuffer**) begins with "+OK". If the server response is positive, the code sends a PASS command and then transitions the state machine to the Await Pass Response state. If the server reply to the USER command is anything other than "+OK", the state machine transitions to the Quit state.

Await Pass Response

The *Await Pass Response* state waits for the server reply to the PASS command. If the server reply is positive, the client is authenticated with the server and can manipulate the indicated mailbox contents. The code issues a STAT command to the server to determine the number of messages in the user mailbox. The state machine then transitions to the Await Stat Response state.

Await Stat Response

The *Await Stat Response* state waits for the server reply to the STAT command. When the state receives an **EV_DATAREADY** event, it checks to see if the response was positive. If so, the code extracts the number of messages in the mailbox from the response line text using the **sscanf** standard C library function. The number of messages is stored in the **m_iTotalMessages** member variable. The state machine then transitions to the Start Retrieve state.

Start Retrieve

The *Start Retrieve* state is the first state of a loop that retrieves each message in the mailbox and deletes it. The Start Retrieve state responds to the **EV_NULLEVENT** event. The code associated with the state executes as soon as the state is entered.

The **CPOP3** state machine keeps a count of the number of messages that are retrieved during the session. This count is initialized when the POP3 session is started. The current count is compared with the total number of messages in the mailbox, as indicated in the STAT command reply. If all of the messages in the mailbox have been retrieved, the state machine transitions to the Quit state.

If more messages remain in the mailbox, the code begins the message retrieval process. First, the code opens a new file to hold the retrieved message. The file name is composed of a random string of characters, virtually guaranteed to be unique, and is located in the directory specified by the **lpszPathName** argument to the **CPOP3::RetrieveMessages** function.

When the file is open, the Start Retrieve code sends a POP3 RETR command to the server, specifying the current message number as the RETR command. The state machine then transitions to the Await Retr Response state.

Await Retr Response

The *Await Retr Response* state waits for the server's reply to the RETR command. If the response is positive, the server sends the message text following the reply line. The state machine transitions to the Retrieve Line state to receive the lines of message text. If the server reply to the RETR command is negative, the state machine aborts the retrieval process by transitioning to the Quit state. Any unretrieved messages are left on the server.

Retrieve Line

The *Retrieve Line* state receives each line of the message text and stores it in the message file. Each time an **EV_DATAREADY** event is received by this state, the reply line text is checked to see if it contains the end-of-message indicator (".CRLF") using the **MessageTerminator** function. If it does not contain the end-of-message indicator, the line of text is written to the file and the state machine remains in the Retrieve Line state. If the line begins with a period, all characters following the first period are written to the file. This behavior implements the transparency rules that allow a line containing a single period to be included as real message text.

If **MessageTerminator** returns TRUE for the given line of text, the file is closed and a DELE command is sent to the server to delete the message from the mailbox. The state machine then transitions to the Await Dele Response state.

Await Dele Response

The *Await Dele Response* state waits for the server's reply to the DELE command. If the response is positive, the state machine transitions to the Start Retrieve state to begin the retrieval of any remaining messages.

Quit

The *Quit* state terminates the POP3 session by sending a QUIT command to the server. The Quit state is normally entered from the Start Retrieve state when all the messages in the mailbox have been retrieved. It can also be entered if a negative reply code is received from the server to any command during the session. After sending the QUIT command, the state machine transitions to the Await Quit Response state.

Await Quit Response

The *Await Quit Response* state simply waits for the server's reply to the QUIT command. When an **EV_DATAREADY** event is received, the state machine transitions to the Exit state. The Await Quit Response state does not bother checking the reply line for a positive or negative response because the response must be positive according to the POP3 protocol.

Exit

The *Exit* state closes the connection to the server, deletes some of the string memory allocated in the **CPOP3::RetrieveMessages** function, and invokes the **DoCallback** virtual member function. The class-specific behavior defined for **DoCallback** generates either a window message or a function callback to inform the program that the POP3 session has concluded. When the program receives the callback, it uses the file names contained in the **CStringList** object, which is pointed to in the call to **CPOP3::RetrieveMessages** function, to manipulate the individual message files. After performing the callback, the state machine transitions to the Stop state.

Stop

The *Stop* state is a black hole for state machine events. The Stop state simply ignores all events, serving as a sink for any spurious events that may occur following some sort of error.

Additions to Mail Client

Our Mail Client project includes two modules that contain the code for retrieving messages, generating a summary mailbox listing, and viewing an entire message. MAILBOX.CPP is shown in Listing 10.3 and MAILVIEW.CPP is shown in Listing 10.4. Let's look at the functionality of these modules.

MAILBOX.CPP

The MAILBOX.CPP file implements the mailbox summary listing window. The mailbox window contains a scrollable list box of message summaries, as shown in Figure 10.9. The user can select messages to view according to the date the message was sent, the originator of the message, and subject of the message. Double clicking on a message summary or selecting the Mail|View Message menu the vertical bar choice creates a message viewing window. While the mailbox window is active, the user can select Mail|Retrieve from the menu bar to retrieve messages from a remote mailbox using the POP3 protocol. After the messages are retrieved, their summaries are added to the summary listing in the mailbox window.

The **MailboxWndProc** function is the window procedure for the mailbox window. The message-cracking macros contained in WINDOWSX.H separate the

Figure 10.9

The mailbox summary listing window.

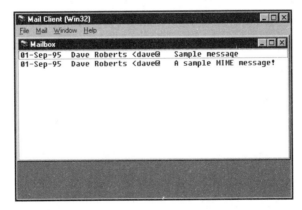

wParam and **lParam** variables into parameters suitable for each message type, then dispatch each message type to a separate handling function. Each message handling function is a static function. This approach keeps the function names local to the MAILBOX.CPP file and prevents name clashes with similarly named functions in other modules.

The **OnCreate** function is called when the window procedure receives a **WM_CREATE** message. The **OnCreate** function creates a structure containing private data (the **MAILBOXDATA** structure) and stores a pointer to it in the window. The function then creates a list box control within the MDI child window. The list box control contains the message summaries.

Once the list box is created, the code disables the File|Open Mailbox menu item on each of the possible menus in the program. This step prevents the user from trying to open another mailbox window (only one mailbox window can be open at a time).

Next, the code calls the **ReadMailbox** function, which reads previously stored message summaries from the disk. Saving the previous set of message summaries on disk prevents the program from having to parse through the actual messages each time the mailbox window is created.

The **ReadMailbox** function stores the message summaries in a **CSummaryList** data structure. The **CSummaryList** class is derived from the **CList** class and is used to store a list of **SUMMARYINFO** structures. The **SUMMARYINFO** structure stores the file name of the corresponding message, the From and Subject fields from the message, and the time the message was sent. A pointer to the **CSummaryList** object is contained in the **MAILBOXDATA** structure associated with the mailbox window.

Once the **ReadMailbox** function reads the stored message summaries from disk, the **OnCreate** function calls the **CreateMailboxItems** function. The **CreateMailboxItems** function takes the summary list pointed to from the **MAILBOXDATA** structure associated with the window and generates a list box item for each summary.

Once the list box is filled with the message summaries, the user can select a message to view by double clicking on one of the items or by selecting the item and choosing Mail|View Message. Each of these actions invokes the **OnMailView** function.

The **OnMailView** function finds the SUMMARYINFO item in the **CSummaryList** data structure associated with the currently selected list box entry. The **OnMailView** code then creates a viewer window and passes a pointer to the message file name in the **lParam** of the **WM_CREATE** message sent to the viewer window. The viewer code uses the file name to open the message file and display the message in the viewer window.

Choosing the Mail|Retrieve menu item invokes the **OnMailRetrieve** function. The **OnMailRetrieve** function creates a **CPOP3WithWinMsg** object to retrieve messages from the remote POP3 server. The **OnMailRetrieve** function indicates to the **CPOP3WithWinMsg** object that a **WM_CPOP3DONE** message should be sent to the mailbox window when the **CPOP3** object completes the retrieval process. The **WM_CPOP3DONE** message is simply defined as **WM_USER**.

Next, **OnMailRetrieve** creates a string list object that the **CPOP3** object will use to store the names of the message files into which each retrieved message is stored.

Finally, **OnMailRetrieve** invokes the **RetrieveMessages** member function of the **CPOP3** object to start the retrieval process. A flag is set in the **MAILBOXDATA** structure associated with the mailbox window to indicate that a retrieval is in process. If the user attempts to close the mailbox window while the flag is set, the program displays a warning. The code then disables the Mail|Retrieve menu item to prevent the user from starting another retrieval process until the first one has completed.

> *Note: Why do we allow the user to start only one retrieval process at a time, when the asynchronous Winsock extensions allow us to have multiple network operations in progress at the same time? The reason for limiting the number of retrieval processes is that both retrieval processes would be manipulating the same mailbox on the remote server at the same time. The POP3 protocol indicates that only one client should have control of the remote user mailbox at a time, so a second retrieval process would fail when the POP3 client tried to authenticate with the server.*
>
> *Our program does allow multiple network processes to occur at the same time, however. Although only a single POP3 session is allowed at once, the program can be sending mail using an SMTP session (or even sending multiple messages with multiple SMTP sessions) while a POP3 session is in progress. The ability to run multiple processes is the advantage that the asynchronous Winsock extensions bring.*

When the **CPOP3WithWinMsg** object completes the POP3 retrieval process, it sends the mailbox window a **WM_CPOP3DONE** message. The **MailboxWndProc** function dispatches the message to the **OnCPOP3Done** function.

The **OnCPOP3Done** function first reenables the Mail|Retrieve menu item. The code then deletes the **CPOP3WithWinMsg** object.

If the **WM_CPOP3DONE** message indicates that an error occurred during the POP3 session, the **OnCPOP3Done** function displays an error message for the user. Otherwise, the function iterates through the list of file names and creates a **SUMMARYINFO** node in the **CSummaryList** data structure for each new message.

Once the **CSummaryList** data structure is updated with the new messages, the function writes the summaries to disk using the **WriteMailbox** function and updates the list box using the **CreateMailboxItems** function.

Finally, the function displays a message box that tells the user how many new messages were retrieved from the remote server.

MAILVIEW.CPP

The MAILVIEW.CPP file (Listing 10.4) contains the implementation of the viewer window. The viewer window displays the contents of a message selected in the mailbox window, as shown in Figure 10.10. Multiple viewer windows may be active at one time, each displaying a separate message.

Much of the code in MAILVIEW.CPP provides viewing capabilities for MIME messages. This code will be explained in Chapter 12. MAILVIEW.CPP also includes code to assist with the decoding of UUENCODED messages. This code will be described in Chapter 11. This section includes only a brief description of the MAILVIEW.CPP file.

The window procedure for the viewer window is the **ViewerWndProc** function. As with other window procedures in the Mail Client program, the message-cracker macros contained in WINDOWSX.H are used to dispatch messages to handling functions.

The **OnCreate** function is invoked when the window is first created. Each viewer window contains a read-only edit control that displays the text of the message.

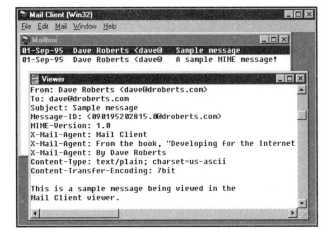

Figure 10.10

The viewer window.

The **OnCreate** function creates the edit control and stores the window handle for the control in a **VIEWERDATA** structure associated with the viewer window.

After the edit control is created, the **OnCreate** function uses the file name passed to the viewer window from the mailbox window to create a complete path name to the message. The path name is used to open and parse the message. Assuming the message is a simple message and not a multipart MIME message (see Chapter 12), the parsing is insignificant. If the message is a multipart MIME message, each constituent part is identified.

Once the message is parsed, the first part is displayed using the **ViewMessagePart** function. If the message is a simple message, it contains only one part and the whole message is displayed.

The **ViewMessagePart** function displays the text of the message in the read-only edit control. Although the exact operation of **ViewMessagePart** is dependent on MIME, the functionality used to display plain text messages is fairly simple. The message is read one line at a time and the text is inserted into the edit control using an **EM_REPLACESEL** message, which is sent to the control. When all the lines of the message are inserted into the control, the file containing the message is closed. The user can scroll through the message using the scroll bars provided by the edit control.

That's it for now. We'll learn more about the MIME and viewing multipart messages in Chapter 12.

Listings

This section includes the following listings for the files that provide mail retrieving and viewing capability to the Mail Client project:

Listing 10.1 is the header file for the CPOP3.CPP file, CPOP3.H.

Listing 10.2 is the implementation file for the **CPOP3** class, CPOP3.CPP.

Listing 10.3 is the module that implements the mailbox window, MAILBOX.CPP.

Listing 10.4 is the module that implements the message viewer window, MAILVIEW.CPP.

Listing 10.1 CPOP3.H

```
/*
    File: CPOP3.H
    Description:
        A class for retrieving email messages via POP3 (RFC 1460).
    Copyright 1995, David G. Roberts
*/

#ifndef _CPOP3_H
#define _CPOP3_H

#ifndef _CSOCKET_H
#include "csocket.h"
#endif
#ifndef _CCONNMGR_H
#include "cconnmgr.h"
#endif
#ifndef _CSTRLIST_H
#include "cstrlist.h"
#endif
#include <fstream.h>

class CPOP3 : private CConnMgrCallback, private CStreamCallback {
public:
    enum RESULT { RESULT_ABORT, RESULT_SUCCESS, RESULT_FAILURE,
        RESULT_NOMAIL };
protected:
    RESULT          m_result;
private:
    enum CONSTANTS { MAX_REPLY_SIZE = 1001, MAX_LINE_SIZE = 200 };
    enum EVENT { EV_NULLEVENT, EV_CONNECT, EV_CLOSE, EV_DATAREADY,
        EV_ERROR, EV_ABORT};
    typedef BOOL (CPOP3::*PSTATEFUNC)(EVENT ev);

    CConnMgr        m_connmgr;
    CStreamSocket   m_sock;
```

```
char            m_szReceiveBuffer[MAX_REPLY_SIZE];
int             m_iReceiveBufferLen;
char            m_szReplyLineBuffer[MAX_REPLY_SIZE];
char            m_szLineBuffer[MAX_LINE_SIZE];
PSTATEFUNC      m_pState;
int             m_iError;
char *          m_pszHost;
u_short         m_ushPort;
char *          m_pszUser;
char *          m_pszPassword;
char *          m_pszPathName;
CStringList *   m_pslFileList;
char            m_szFileName[255];
int             m_iTotalMessages;
int             m_iRetrieved;
BOOL            m_bDoCallback;
ofstream        m_ofsFile;

// State machine interface.
void Event(EVENT ev);
void NextState(PSTATEFUNC pState) { m_pState = pState; };

// State functions.
BOOL Start(EVENT ev);
BOOL AwaitConnection(EVENT ev);
BOOL AwaitGreeting(EVENT ev);
BOOL AwaitUserResponse(EVENT ev);
BOOL AwaitPassResponse(EVENT ev);
BOOL AwaitStatResponse(EVENT ev);
BOOL StartRetrieve(EVENT ev);
BOOL AwaitRetrResponse(EVENT ev);
BOOL RetrieveLine(EVENT ev);
BOOL AwaitDeleResponse(EVENT ev);
BOOL Quit(EVENT ev);
BOOL AwaitQuitResponse(EVENT ev);
BOOL Exit(EVENT ev);
BOOL Stop(EVENT ev);

// Virtual function called when the CPOP3 state machine has
// finished.
virtual void DoCallback(void) = 0;

// Aux functions.
BOOL ReadReplyData(void);
BOOL LineComplete(void);
void CopyLine(void);
void ShrinkReceiveBuffer(void);
BOOL PositiveResponse(void);
BOOL MessageTerminator(void);
void NewFileName(char * pszPathName, char * pszFileName,
    char * pszFullName);

virtual void ConnMgrCallback(int iToken,
    CConnMgrCallback::RESULT result);
```

```
    virtual void StreamCallback(int iToken, STREAMEVENT iEvent,
        int iError, char FAR * lpBuffer);

    // Eliminate the use of the copy constructor and operator=.
    CPOP3(const CPOP3&);
    operator=(const CPOP3&);
public:
    CPOP3() { m_connmgr.SetCallback(this, 0); };
    virtual ~CPOP3() { Abort(FALSE); };

    BOOL RetrieveMessages(LPCSTR lpszHost, u_short ushPort,
        LPCSTR lpszUser, LPCSTR lpszPassword, LPCSTR lpszPathName,
        CStringList * pslFileList);
    void Abort(BOOL bDoCallback);
};

class CPOP3WithWinMsg : public CPOP3 {
private:
    HWND m_hwnd;
    UINT m_msg;
    int  m_iToken;

    virtual void DoCallback(void);
public:
    CPOP3WithWinMsg(HWND hwnd, UINT msg, int iToken) :
        m_hwnd(hwnd), m_msg(msg), m_iToken(iToken) {};
    ~CPOP3WithWinMsg() {};
};

class CPOP3Callback {
public:
    virtual void SMTPCallback(int iToken, CPOP3::RESULT result) = 0;
};

class CPOP3WithCallback : public CPOP3 {
private:
    CPOP3Callback * m_pCallback;
    int  m_iToken;

    virtual void DoCallback(void);
public:
    CPOP3WithCallback(CPOP3Callback * pCallback, int iToken) :
        m_pCallback(pCallback), m_iToken(iToken) {};
    ~CPOP3WithCallback() {};
};
#endif
```

Listing 10.2 CPOP3.CPP

```
/*
    File: CPOP3.CPP
    Description:
```

```
        A class for retrieving email messages via POP3 (RFC 1460).
    Copyright 1995, David G. Roberts
*/

#include <ctype.h>   // need toupper()
#include <stdlib.h>  // need srand()/rand()
#include <time.h>    // need time()
#include "cpop3.h"
#include "myassert.h"

const char CR = '\015';
const char LF = '\012';

// Used to include at the end of text.  The compiler will splice
// strings.
// Use like m_sock.Send("Foo" CRLF,...).  Note that we have to use a
// macro rather than a string constant because we need the
// preprocessor to perform a textual substitution so the string
// splicing will work.
#define CRLF "\015\012"

/*
    Function: CPOP3::Event
    Description:
        The state machine event dispatch loop.
*/
void CPOP3::Event(EVENT ev)
{
    while ((this->*m_pState)(ev)) {
        ev = EV_NULLEVENT;
    };
}


/*
    Function: CPOP3::StreamCallback
    Description:
        Invoked when events occur on the socket.
*/
void CPOP3::StreamCallback(int iToken, STREAMEVENT iEvent, int iError,
    char FAR *lpBuffer)
{
    UNUSED_PARAMETER(iToken);    // Eliminate the compiler warning.
    UNUSED_PARAMETER(lpBuffer);

    m_iError = iError;
    switch (iEvent) {
        case CStreamCallback::SE_CLOSE:
            Event(EV_CLOSE);
            break;
        case CStreamCallback::SE_DATAREADY:
            // Read the data.
            if (ReadReplyData()) {
```

```
                    while (LineComplete()) {
                            CopyLine();
                            ShrinkReceiveBuffer();
                            Event(EV_DATAREADY);
                        }
                }
                else {
                    // Something went wrong.
                    WSCFatalError("Couldn't read from socket in CPOP3.");
                }
                break;
            case CStreamCallback::SE_DATASENT:
                // All commands to the server are one line.
                // Even if something blocks, we'll wait for a response
                // before sending another one, which means that the buffer
                // will be free again before we use it.
                break;
            default:
                // Error!  Something we weren't expecting.
                WSCFatalError(
                        "Unexpected socket event in CPOP3::StreamCallback");
                break;
        }
    }
}


/*

    Function: CPOP3::ReadReplyData
    Description:
        Calculates the amount of data the receiver buffer can
        receive at this time and reads it from the socket.
*/
BOOL CPOP3::ReadReplyData(void)
{
    // Figure out how much room is left in the buffer.
    int iBufferLen = MAX_REPLY_SIZE - m_iReceiveBufferLen;
    ASSERT(iBufferLen > 0);

    // Receive the data.
    int iResult = m_sock.Receive(
            &m_szReceiveBuffer[m_iReceiveBufferLen], &iBufferLen);

    if (iResult == WSANOERROR || iResult == WSAEWOULDBLOCK) {
        // If no errors, update the length of the data in the buffer.
        m_iReceiveBufferLen += iBufferLen;
        return TRUE;
    }
    else {
        // Save the error and signal it.
        m_iError = iResult;
        return FALSE;
    }
}
```

```
/*
     Function: CPOP3::LineComplete
     Description:
          Determines if the buffer contains a line of text terminated
          with CRLF.
*/
BOOL CPOP3::LineComplete(void)
{
     ASSERT(m_iReceiveBufferLen <= MAX_REPLY_SIZE);

     for (int i = 0; i < m_iReceiveBufferLen; i++) {
         if ((m_szReceiveBuffer[i] == CR) &&
             ((i + 1) < m_iReceiveBufferLen) &&
             (m_szReceiveBuffer[i + 1] == LF)) {
             return TRUE;
         }
     }
     return FALSE;
}


/*
     Function: CPOP3::CopyLine
     Description:
          Copies a line from the receive buffer to the reply line
          buffer.
*/
void CPOP3::CopyLine(void)
{
     ASSERT(m_iReceiveBufferLen <= MAX_REPLY_SIZE);

     for (int i = 0; i < m_iReceiveBufferLen; i++) {
         if ((m_szReceiveBuffer[i] == CR) &&
             ((i + 1) < m_iReceiveBufferLen) &&
             (m_szReceiveBuffer[i + 1] == LF)) {
             m_szReplyLineBuffer[i] = '\0';
             break;
         }
         else {
             m_szReplyLineBuffer[i] = m_szReceiveBuffer[i];
         }
     }
}


/*
     Function: CPOP3::ShrinkReceiveBuffer
     Description:
          Deletes the first line of CRLF terminated text from the
          receiver buffer (presumably after it has been moved to the
          reply line buffer).
*/
void CPOP3::ShrinkReceiveBuffer(void)
{
     ASSERT(m_iReceiveBufferLen <= MAX_REPLY_SIZE);
```

```
        // Find the CRLF at the end of the line.
      for (int i = 0; i < m_iReceiveBufferLen; i++) {
          if ((m_szReceiveBuffer[i] == CR) &&
              ((i + 1) < m_iReceiveBufferLen) &&
              (m_szReceiveBuffer[i + 1] == LF)) {
              // Set i equal to the character following the CRLF.
              i += 2;
              // Copy the characters following the CRLF to the beginning
              // of the line.
              for (int j = 0; j < m_iReceiveBufferLen - i; j++) {
                  m_szReceiveBuffer[j] = m_szReceiveBuffer[i + j];
              }
              // Subtract number of characters removed from the current
              // number of characters in the buffer.
              m_iReceiveBufferLen -= i;
              // Break out of the for(i) loop.
              break;
          }
      }
}


/*
    Function: CPOP3::PositiveResponse
    Description:
        Returns TRUE if the reply line buffer beings with "+OK"
        and FALSE otherwise.
*/
BOOL CPOP3::PositiveResponse(void)
{
    // See if we have a "+OK..." response
    if (m_szReplyLineBuffer[0] == '+' &&
        toupper(m_szReplyLineBuffer[1]) == 'O' &&
        toupper(m_szReplyLineBuffer[2]) == 'K')
        return TRUE;
    else
        return FALSE;
}


/*
    Function: CPOP3::MessageTerminator
    Description:
        Returns TRUE if the line simply contains a single period
        character, indicating the end of the message text.
*/
BOOL CPOP3::MessageTerminator(void)
{
    if (m_szReplyLineBuffer[0] == '.' &&
        m_szReplyLineBuffer[1] == '\0')
        return TRUE;
    else
        return FALSE;
}
```

```
/*
     Function: CPOP3::NewFileName
     Description:
         Creates a random, unique file name to store a received
         message in.
*/
void CPOP3::NewFileName(char * pszPathName, char * pszFileName,
    char * pszFullName)
{
    char szTrialName[13];   // All file names will be 8.3 format.
    HFILE hfile;

    do {
        // Choose eight random letters.
        for (int i = 0; i < 8; i++) {
            int r = rand() % 26;
            szTrialName[i] = (char)( 'a' + r );
        }
        // Tack on a ".txt" extension.
        szTrialName[8] = '\0';
        lstrcat(szTrialName, ".txt");
        // Make the file name = the trial name.
        lstrcpy(pszFileName, szTrialName);
        // Build the full name from the path name and the trial name.
        lstrcpy(pszFullName, pszPathName);
        lstrcat(pszFullName, "\\");
        lstrcat(pszFullName, szTrialName);
        // See if the file already exists.
        OFSTRUCT ofstructTemp;
        hfile = OpenFile(pszFullName, &ofstructTemp, OF_EXIST);
        // If not, choose another name.
    } while (hfile != HFILE_ERROR);
}


/*
     Function: CPOP3::ConnMgrCallback
     Description:
         The callback function for the connection manager object.
         The function conditions the connection manager results and
         creates events for the CPOP3 state machine.
*/
void CPOP3::ConnMgrCallback(int iToken,
    CConnMgrCallback::RESULT result)
{
    UNUSED_PARAMETER(iToken);

    ASSERT(result != CConnMgrCallback::INVALID_RESULT);

    // Turn connection callback result into events.
    switch (result) {
        case CConnMgrCallback::OK_CONNECTED:
            Event(EV_CONNECT);
```

```
                break;
            case CConnMgrCallback::ERR_NOTCONNECTED:
                m_iError = m_connmgr.LastError();
                Event(EV_ERROR);
                break;
    }
}

/*

    Function: CPOP3::Abort
    Description:
        Called when the program wants to abort the current POP3
        session.  Injects an EV_ABORT event into the state machine.
        The bDoCallback argument determines whether the program
        wants a callback to be generated.  This might be useful if
        some code requires the CPOP3 callback in order to clean up
        allocated memory or other things.
*/
void CPOP3::Abort(BOOL bDoCallback)
{
    m_bDoCallback = bDoCallback;
    Event(EV_ABORT);
}


/*

    Function: CPOP3::RetrieveMessages
    Description:
        This starts the whole thing off.
*/
BOOL CPOP3::RetrieveMessages(LPCSTR lpszHost, u_short ushPort,
    LPCSTR lpszUser, LPCSTR lpszPassword, LPCSTR lpszPathName,
    CStringList * pslFileList)
{
    ASSERT(lpszHost != NULL);
    ASSERT(pslFileList != NULL);

    // Make sure we're currently stopped.
    // Store parameters away.
    m_pszHost = new char[lstrlen(lpszHost) + 1];
    lstrcpy(m_pszHost, lpszHost);
    m_ushPort = ushPort;
    m_pszUser = new char[lstrlen(lpszUser) + 1];
    lstrcpy(m_pszUser, lpszUser);
    m_pszPassword = new char[lstrlen(lpszPassword) + 1];
    lstrcpy(m_pszPassword, lpszPassword);
    m_pszPathName = new char[lstrlen(lpszPathName) + 1];
    lstrcpy(m_pszPathName, lpszPathName);
    m_pslFileList = pslFileList;

    // Initialize our state correctly.
    m_iReceiveBufferLen = 0;
    m_bDoCallback = TRUE;
```

```
        // Seed the random number generator so we can generate
        // unique file names to store messages in.
        time_t curtime = time(NULL);
        srand((unsigned)curtime);

        // Start us off.
        NextState(&CPOP3::Start);
        Event(EV_NULLEVENT);

        return TRUE;
}


/*
        Function: CPOP3::Start
        Description:
            The first state in the state machine.
*/
BOOL CPOP3::Start(EVENT ev)
{
        UNUSED_PARAMETER(ev);

        // Make the connection to the remote host.  Let the connection
        // manager do all the work.
        m_connmgr.Connect(m_pszHost, m_ushPort, &m_sock, this, 0);
        NextState(&CPOP3::AwaitConnection);
        return TRUE;
}


/*
        Function: CPOP3::AwaitConnection
        Description:
            Awaits the results of the connection manager's connection
        attempt.
*/
BOOL CPOP3::AwaitConnection(EVENT ev)
{
        switch (ev) {
            case EV_ABORT:
                m_connmgr.Abort();
                m_result = RESULT_ABORT;
                NextState(&CPOP3::Exit);
                break;
            case EV_CONNECT:
                NextState(&CPOP3::AwaitGreeting);
                break;
            case EV_ERROR:
                m_result = RESULT_FAILURE;
                NextState(&CPOP3::Exit);
                break;
            default:
                return FALSE;
        }
        return TRUE;
}
```

```
/*
       Function: CPOP3::AwaitGreeting
       Description:
           Waits for the line of greeting text from the remote
           POP3 server.
*/
BOOL CPOP3::AwaitGreeting(EVENT ev)
{
     int iResult;

     switch (ev) {
         case EV_ABORT:
             m_result = RESULT_ABORT;
             NextState(&CPOP3::Exit);
           break;
         case EV_CLOSE:
             // Hmmm... unexpected close of the socket from the
             // other end.
             m_result = RESULT_FAILURE;
             NextState(&CPOP3::Exit);
           break;
         case EV_DATAREADY:
             // Okay, we're connected and we have the greeting.
             // Ignore the greeting message (should be "+OK..."
             // but who knows).
             wsprintf(m_szLineBuffer, "USER %s" CRLF,
                 (LPSTR)m_pszUser);
             iResult = m_sock.Send(m_szLineBuffer,
                 lstrlen(m_szLineBuffer));
             if (iResult == WSANOERROR ||
                 iResult == WSAEWOULDBLOCK) {
                 NextState(&CPOP3::AwaitUserResponse);
             }
             else {
                 m_iError = iResult;
                 m_result = RESULT_FAILURE;
                 NextState(&CPOP3::Exit);
             }
           break;
         default:
             return FALSE;
     }
     return TRUE;
}


/*
       Function: CPOP3::AwaitUserResponse
       Description:
           Waits for the server's reply to the USER command.
*/
BOOL CPOP3::AwaitUserResponse(EVENT ev)
{
     int iResult;
```

```
    switch (ev) {
        case EV_ABORT:
            m_result = RESULT_ABORT;
            NextState(&CPOP3::Exit);
            break;
        case EV_CLOSE:
            // Hmmm... unexpected close of the socket from the
            // other end.
            m_result = RESULT_FAILURE;
            NextState(&CPOP3::Exit);
            break;
        case EV_DATAREADY:
            if (PositiveResponse()) {
                // We got an "+OK..." response.  Send the password.
                wsprintf(m_szLineBuffer, "PASS %s" CRLF,
                    (LPSTR)m_pszPassword);
                iResult = m_sock.Send(m_szLineBuffer,
                    lstrlen(m_szLineBuffer));
                if (iResult == WSANOERROR ||
                    iResult == WSAEWOULDBLOCK) {
                    NextState(&CPOP3::AwaitPassResponse);
                }
                else {
                    m_iError = iResult;
                    m_result = RESULT_FAILURE;
                    NextState(&CPOP3::Exit);
                }
            }
            else {
                // All other responses generate a failure.
                m_result = RESULT_FAILURE;
                NextState(&CPOP3::Quit);     // Now go send QUIT.
            }
            break;
        default:
            return FALSE;
    }
    return TRUE;
}


/*
    Function: CPOP3::AwaitPassResponse
    Description:
        Waits for the server's reply to the PASS command.
*/
BOOL CPOP3::AwaitPassResponse(EVENT ev)
{
    int iResult;

    switch (ev) {
        case EV_ABORT:
            m_result = RESULT_ABORT;
```

```
                    NextState(&CPOP3::Exit);
                     break;
                case EV_CLOSE:
                     // Hmmm... unexpected close of the socket from the
                     // other end.
                     m_result = RESULT_FAILURE;
                     NextState(&CPOP3::Exit);
                     break;
                case EV_DATAREADY:
                     if (PositiveResponse()) {
                         // We got an "+OK..." response.
                         // Ask for the mailbox statistics.
                         lstrcpy(m_szLineBuffer, "STAT" CRLF);
                         iResult = m_sock.Send(m_szLineBuffer,
                             lstrlen(m_szLineBuffer));
                         if (iResult == WSANOERROR ||
                             iResult == WSAEWOULDBLOCK) {
                             NextState(&CPOP3::AwaitStatResponse);
                         }
                         else {
                             m_iError = iResult;
                             m_result = RESULT_FAILURE;
                             NextState(&CPOP3::Exit);
                         }
                     }
                     else {
                         // All other responses generate a failure.
                         m_result = RESULT_FAILURE;
                         NextState(&CPOP3::Quit);     // Now go send QUIT.
                     }
                     break;
            default:
                 return FALSE;
        }
     return TRUE;
}


/*
     Function: CPOP3::AwaitStatResponse
     Description:
         Waits for the server's reply to the STAT command.  When the
         reply comes, the function extracts the message count from
         the line of reply text.
*/
BOOL CPOP3::AwaitStatResponse(EVENT ev)
{
     switch (ev) {
         case EV_ABORT:
             m_result = RESULT_ABORT;
             NextState(&CPOP3::Exit);
             break;
         case EV_CLOSE:
```

```
                // Hmmm... unexpected close of the socket from the
                // other end.
                m_result = RESULT_FAILURE;
                NextState(&CPOP3::Exit);
            break;
        case EV_DATAREADY:
            if (PositiveResponse()) {
                // We got an "+OK..." response.
                // Parse the response for the message count.
                if (sscanf(m_szReplyLineBuffer, "+OK %d",
                    &m_iTotalMessages) != 1) {
                    // If the response didn't contain a count of
                    // messages following the +OK, something's wrong.
                    m_result = RESULT_FAILURE;
                    NextState(&CPOP3::Exit);
                }
                else {
                    // Set the current message count to zero.
                    m_iRetrieved = 0;
                    NextState(&CPOP3::StartRetrieve);
                }
            }
            else {
                // All other responses generate a failure.
                m_result = RESULT_FAILURE;
                NextState(&CPOP3::Quit);        // Now go send QUIT.
            }
            break;
        default:
            return FALSE;
    }
    return TRUE;
}


/*
    Function: CPOP3::StartRetrieve
    Description:
        Starts the retrieval process by creating and opening a file
        to hold the message and sending the RETR command to the
        server.
*/
BOOL CPOP3::StartRetrieve(EVENT ev)
{
    UNUSED_PARAMETER(ev);

    // Have we retrieved all the messages.
    if (m_iRetrieved >= m_iTotalMessages) {
        // Yes, so just quit gracefully with a success indication.
        // Note that this will happen even if there are no messages.
        // The caller should be prepared to find no message file names
        // in the file name list.
        m_result = RESULT_SUCCESS;
```

```
            NextState(&CPOP3::Quit);
             return TRUE;
        }

        // Find a unique file name, open a stream for it.
        char szFullName[260];
        NewFileName(m_pszPathName, m_szFileName, szFullName);
        m_ofsFile.open(szFullName);

        // Send a RETR command to get the current message.
        wsprintf(m_szLineBuffer, "RETR %d" CRLF, m_iRetrieved + 1);
        int iResult = m_sock.Send(m_szLineBuffer,
            lstrlen(m_szLineBuffer));
        if (iResult == WSANOERROR || iResult == WSAEWOULDBLOCK) {
            NextState(&CPOP3::AwaitRetrResponse);
        }
        else {
            m_iError = iResult;
            m_result = RESULT_FAILURE;
            NextState(&CPOP3::Exit);
        }
        return TRUE;
}


/*
    Function: CPOP3::AwaitRetrResponse
    Description:
        Waits for the server's reply to the RETR command.
*/
BOOL CPOP3::AwaitRetrResponse(EVENT ev)
{
    switch (ev) {
        case EV_ABORT:
            m_result = RESULT_ABORT;
            NextState(&CPOP3::Exit);
            break;
        case EV_CLOSE:
            // Hmmm... unexpected close of the socket from the
            // other end.
            m_result = RESULT_FAILURE;
            NextState(&CPOP3::Exit);
            break;
        case EV_DATAREADY:
            if (PositiveResponse()) {
                NextState(&CPOP3::RetrieveLine);
            }
            else {
                // All other responses generate a failure.
                m_result = RESULT_FAILURE;
                NextState(&CPOP3::Quit);    // Now go send QUIT.
            }
            break;
```

```
            default:
                return FALSE;
        }
    return TRUE;
}


/*

    Function: CPOP3::RetrieveLine
    Description:
        This state machine state retrieves each line of message
        text and writes it to the message file until the end of
        message indication is found (".CRLF").  It then sends
        the DELE command to delete the message.
*/
BOOL CPOP3::RetrieveLine(EVENT ev)
{
    int iResult;

    switch (ev) {
        case EV_ABORT:
            m_result = RESULT_ABORT;
            NextState(&CPOP3::Exit);
            break;
        case EV_CLOSE:
            // Hmmm... unexpected close of the socket from the
            // other end.
            m_result = RESULT_FAILURE;
            NextState(&CPOP3::Exit);
            break;
        case EV_DATAREADY:
            if (MessageTerminator()) {
                // The message is done.  Close up the file
                m_ofsFile.close();
                // Tell the server to delete the message from the
                // mailbox when the session concludes.
                wsprintf(m_szLineBuffer, "DELE %d" CRLF,
                    m_iRetrieved + 1);
                iResult = m_sock.Send(m_szLineBuffer,
                    lstrlen(m_szLineBuffer));
                if (iResult == WSANOERROR ||
                    iResult == WSAEWOULDBLOCK) {
                    NextState(&CPOP3::AwaitDeleResponse);
                }
                else {
                    m_iError = iResult;
                    m_result = RESULT_FAILURE;
                    NextState(&CPOP3::Exit);
                }
            }
            else {
                // Write the line to the file, followed by a local
                // line terminator.
                if (m_szReplyLineBuffer[0] == '.') {
```

```
                            // If the line starts with a period then it was
                                // stuffed there, so skip over it when writing
                            // to the file.
                                m_ofsFile << &(m_szReplyLineBuffer[1]) << '\n';
                        }
                        else {
                                m_ofsFile << m_szReplyLineBuffer << '\n';
                        }
                            // No need to set the state.  Stay in RetrieveLine
                            // until we get the message terminator.
                    }
                    break;
            default:
                    return FALSE;
        }
        return TRUE;
}


/*
      Function: CPOP3::AwaitDeleResponse
      Description:
            Waits for the server's reply to the DELE command.
*/
BOOL CPOP3::AwaitDeleResponse(EVENT ev)
{
    switch (ev) {
        case EV_ABORT:
                m_result = RESULT_ABORT;
                NextState(&CPOP3::Exit);
                break;
        case EV_CLOSE:
                // Hmmm... unexpected close of the socket from the
                // other end.
                m_result = RESULT_FAILURE;
                NextState(&CPOP3::Exit);
                break;
        case EV_DATAREADY:
                if (PositiveResponse()) {
                    m_iRetrieved++;
                    m_pslFileList->Add(m_szFileName);
                    NextState(&CPOP3::StartRetrieve);
                }
                else {
                    // All other responses generate a failure.
                    m_result = RESULT_FAILURE;
                    NextState(&CPOP3::Quit);     // Now go send QUIT.
                }
                break;
        default:
                return FALSE;
    }
    return TRUE;
}
```

```
/*
    Function: CPOP3::Quit
    Description:
        Sends the QUIT command to the server to end the POP3 session.
*/
BOOL CPOP3::Quit(EVENT ev)
{
    UNUSED_PARAMETER(ev);

    int iResult;

    lstrcpy(m_szLineBuffer, "QUIT" CRLF);
    iResult = m_sock.Send(m_szLineBuffer, lstrlen(m_szLineBuffer));
    if (iResult == WSANOERROR || iResult == WSAEWOULDBLOCK) {
        NextState(&CPOP3::AwaitQuitResponse);
    }
    else {
        m_iError = iResult;
        m_result = RESULT_FAILURE;
        NextState(&CPOP3::Exit);
    }
    return TRUE;
}


/*
    Function: CPOP3::AwaitQuitResponse
    Description:
        Waits for the server's reply to the QUIT command.  Note that
        the state accepts any reply.  Theoretically the protocol
        only allows the server to reply with +OK, but it doesn't
        really matter at this point.
*/
BOOL CPOP3::AwaitQuitResponse(EVENT ev)
{
    switch (ev) {
        case EV_ABORT:
            m_result = RESULT_ABORT;
            NextState(&CPOP3::Exit);
            break;
        case EV_CLOSE:          // Just about anything is okay.
        case EV_DATAREADY:
            NextState(&CPOP3::Exit);
            break;
        default:
            return FALSE;
    }
    return TRUE;
}

/*
    Function: CPOP3::Exit
    Description:
```

```
            The Exit state closes the socket, deallocates memory
            allocated when the state machine started, and calls
            DoCallback to perform the appropriate callback behavior.
*/
BOOL CPOP3::Exit(EVENT ev)
{
    UNUSED_PARAMETER(ev);    // Eliminate the compiler warning.

    // Close the socket.
    m_sock.Close();

    // Free up the stuff we allocated when we started.
    delete[] m_pszHost;
    delete[] m_pszUser;
    delete[] m_pszPassword;
    delete[] m_pszPathName;

    // Now, invoke the callback with the connection attempt result.
    if (m_bDoCallback) {
        DoCallback();
    }

    NextState(&CPOP3::Stop);
    return TRUE;
}


/*

    Function: CPOP3::Stop
    Description:
            The Stop state simply devours any and all events sent to it
            without doing anything with them.  This causes any spurious
            events that may still be generated after the state machine
            completes to be ignored.
*/
BOOL CPOP3::Stop(EVENT ev)
{
    UNUSED_PARAMETER(ev);
    // Simply ignore all events.
    return FALSE;
}


/***********************************************************************
    Callbacks for specialized CPOP3 derivatives.
***********************************************************************/

void CPOP3WithWinMsg::DoCallback(void)
{
    PostMessage(m_hwnd, m_msg, m_iToken, m_result);
}


void CPOP3WithCallback::DoCallback(void)
{
    m_pCallback->SMTPCallback(m_iToken, m_result);
}
```

Listing 10.3 MAILBOX.CPP

```
/*
    File: MAILBOX.CPP
    Description:
        Implements the mailbox window for Mail Client.
    Copyright 1995, David G. Roberts
*/

#include <ctype.h>
#include <dos.h>
#include <io.h>
#include <stdlib.h>
#include <time.h>
#include <fstream.h>
#include <windows.h>
#include <windowsx.h>
#include "mailcli.rh"
#include "myassert.h"
#include "cwinsock.h"
#include "clist.h"
#include "cstrlist.h"
#include "cpop3.h"
#include "rfc822.h"
#include "parsdate.h"
#include "utility.h"

#define DECLARE
#include "mailclig.h"

/*
    CONSTANTS
*/
#define LBCTLID        1
#define WM_CPOP3DONE      WM_USER

/*
    MACROS
*/
#define min(a, b) (((a) < (b)) ? (a) : (b))
#define max(a, b) (((a) > (b)) ? (a) : (b))

/*
    TYPES
*/

// A little collection structure to hold summary data about
// a particular message.  Note that the collection deletes all the
// string members upon destruction.  Make copies beforehand!
struct SUMMARYINFO {
    char *  pszFileName;
    char *  pszFrom;
```

```
    char *  pszSubject;
     time_t  time;

      SUMMARYINFO() : pszFileName(NULL), pszFrom(NULL),
          pszSubject(NULL), time(0) {};
      SUMMARYINFO(char * pszfn, char * pszfr, char * pszsub, time_t d) :
           pszFileName(pszfn), pszFrom(pszfr), pszSubject(pszsub),
          time(d) {};
      ~SUMMARYINFO() {
           if (pszFileName != NULL) delete[] pszFileName;
           if (pszFrom != NULL) delete[] pszFrom;
           if (pszSubject != NULL) delete[] pszSubject;
     };
};

// A list class to manage SUMMARYINFO data.  Derived from CList.
class CSummaryList : public CList {
protected:
     virtual int Compare(void * pvThing1, void * pvThing2);
     virtual void DeleteData(void * pvThing);
public:
     CSummaryList() { };
     ~CSummaryList();
     void Add(SUMMARYINFO * psi) { CList::Add((void *) psi); };
     void Insert(SUMMARYINFO * psi) { CList::Insert((void *) psi); };
     SUMMARYINFO * First(void)
          { return (SUMMARYINFO *) CList::First(); };
     SUMMARYINFO * Next(void)
          { return (SUMMARYINFO *) CList::Next(); };
};

CSummaryList::~CSummaryList()
{
     // Delete all the data in the list.
     SUMMARYINFO * psi = First();
     while (psi != NULL) {
         delete psi;
         psi = Next();
     }
}

int CSummaryList::Compare(void * pvThing1, void *pvThing2)
{
     SUMMARYINFO * psi1 = (SUMMARYINFO *) pvThing1;
     SUMMARYINFO * psi2 = (SUMMARYINFO *) pvThing2;

     if (psi1->time < psi2->time)
         return -1;
     else if (psi1->time == psi2->time)
         return 0;
     else
         return 1;
}
```

```
void CSummaryList::DeleteData(void * pvThing)
{
    delete (SUMMARYINFO *) pvThing;
}

// A little collection structure to hold some data that is associated
// with the mailbox window.
struct MAILBOXDATA {
    HWND                 hwndLB;
    BOOL                 bRetrieving;
    CSummaryList *       pslSummaryList;
    CPOP3WithWinMsg *    pcpop3;
    CStringList *        pslFileList;

    MAILBOXDATA() : hwndLB(NULL), bRetrieving(FALSE),
        pslSummaryList(new CSummaryList), pcpop3(NULL),
        pslFileList(NULL) {};
    ~MAILBOXDATA();
};

MAILBOXDATA::~MAILBOXDATA()
{
    if (bRetrieving) {
        bRetrieving = FALSE;
        pcpop3->Abort(FALSE);
        delete pcpop3;
        delete pslFileList;
    }
    delete pslSummaryList;
}

/*
    LOCAL FUNCTIONS
*/
static void OnCommand(HWND hwnd, int id, HWND hwndCtl,
    UINT codeNotify);
static void OnCPOP3Done(HWND, UINT, WPARAM, LPARAM);
static BOOL OnCreate(HWND, CREATESTRUCT FAR*);
static void OnDestroy(HWND);
static void OnMDIActivate(HWND, BOOL, HWND, HWND);
static BOOL OnQueryEndSession(HWND hwnd);
static void OnSize(HWND, UINT, int, int);

// MENU HANDLERS
static void OnMailDelete(HWND);
static void OnMailRetrieve(HWND);
static void OnMailView(HWND);

// UTILITY FUNCTIONS
void ReadMailbox(HWND);
void WriteMailbox(HWND);
void CreateMailboxItems(HWND);
```

```
SUMMARYINFO * GetSummaryInfo(char *);
char * GetHeaderData(char *, char *);

/************************************************************************
      WINDOW AND DIALOG BOX PROCEDURES
*************************************************************************/

/*
      Function: MailboxWndProc
      Description:
           Window procedure for the mailbox window class.
*/
LRESULT CALLBACK MailboxWndProc(HWND hwnd, UINT msg, WPARAM wParam,
      LPARAM lParam)
{
      switch (msg) {
            HANDLE_MSG(hwnd, WM_COMMAND, OnCommand);
            HANDLE_MSG(hwnd, WM_CREATE, OnCreate);
            HANDLE_MSG(hwnd, WM_DESTROY, OnDestroy);
            HANDLE_MSG(hwnd, WM_MDIACTIVATE, OnMDIActivate);
            HANDLE_MSG(hwnd, WM_QUERYENDSESSION, OnQueryEndSession);
            HANDLE_MSG(hwnd, WM_SIZE, OnSize);
          case WM_CPOP3DONE:
                OnCPOP3Done(hwnd, msg, wParam, lParam);
                return 0;
      }
      return DefMDIChildProc(hwnd, msg, wParam, lParam);
}


/************************************************************************
      MESSAGE HANDLING FUNCTIONS
*************************************************************************/

void OnCommand(HWND hwnd, int id, HWND hwndCtl, UINT codeNotify)
{
      if (hwndCtl == NULL) {
          // It's a window message.
          switch (id) {
              case IDM_MAILRETRIEVE:
                  OnMailRetrieve(hwnd);
                  return;
              case IDM_MAILVIEWMESSAGE:
                  OnMailView(hwnd);
                  return;
              case IDM_MAILDELETEMESSAGE:
                  OnMailDelete(hwnd);
                  return;
          }
      }
      else {
          ASSERT(id == LBCTLID);
          // It's from our control.
```

```
        if (codeNotify == LBN_DBLCLK) {
            OnMailView(hwnd);
            return;
        }
    }
    // Make sure the default child proc sees things we don't
    // process ourselves!
    FORWARD_WM_COMMAND(hwnd, id, hwndCtl, codeNotify,
        DefMDIChildProc);
}


void OnCPOP3Done(HWND hwnd, UINT msg, WPARAM wToken, LPARAM lResult)
{
    UNUSED_PARAMETER(msg);
    UNUSED_PARAMETER(wToken);

    MAILBOXDATA FAR * lpdata =
        (MAILBOXDATA FAR *)GetWindowLong(hwnd, 0);

    // We're done retrieving.  Re-enable the menu item and delete
    // the POP3 object.
    lpdata->bRetrieving = FALSE;
    EnableMenuItem(g_hMailboxMenu, IDM_MAILRETRIEVE, MF_ENABLED);
    delete lpdata->pcpop3;
    lpdata->pcpop3 = NULL;
    // If something went wrong, tell the user.
    if (lResult != CPOP3::RESULT_SUCCESS) {
        MessageBox(hwnd, "Error retrieving POP mail.", "POP Error",
            MB_OK | MB_ICONEXCLAMATION);
        delete lpdata->pslFileList;
        lpdata->pslFileList = NULL;
        return;
    }
    char * pszFileName = lpdata->pslFileList->First();
    // See if we retrieved any messages.
    if (pszFileName == NULL) {
        MessageBox(hwnd, "No messages retrieved.", "POP Result",
            MB_OK | MB_ICONEXCLAMATION);
        delete lpdata->pslFileList;
        lpdata->pslFileList = NULL;
        return;
    }
    int iMsgCount = 0;
    while (pszFileName != NULL) {
        iMsgCount++;
        // Create some summary data from the file.
        SUMMARYINFO * psiInfo = GetSummaryInfo(pszFileName);
        // Insert it into the summary list (which will order it
        // by the time field).
        lpdata->pslSummaryList->Insert(psiInfo);
        // Get the next file name.
        pszFileName = lpdata->pslFileList->Next();
    }
```

```
        // Update the mailbox on disk.
        WriteMailbox(hwnd);
        // Update the list box.
        CreateMailboxItems(hwnd);
        // Tell the user what we retrieved.
        char szMessage[80];
        if (iMsgCount == 1)
            lstrcpy(szMessage, "1 message retrieved.");
        else
            wsprintf(szMessage, "%d messages retrieved.", iMsgCount);
        MessageBox(hwnd, szMessage, "POP Result",
            MB_OK | MB_ICONEXCLAMATION);
        delete lpdata->pslFileList;
        lpdata->pslFileList = NULL;
}


BOOL OnCreate(HWND hwnd, CREATESTRUCT FAR* lpCreateStruct)
{
        UNUSED_PARAMETER(lpCreateStruct);

        // Allocate some private window data for ourselves.
        MAILBOXDATA FAR * lpdata = new MAILBOXDATA;
        SetWindowLong(hwnd, 0, (LONG) lpdata);
        // Create a list box control to do our work for us.
        lpdata->hwndLB = CreateWindow(
            "LISTBOX",                      // class name
            NULL,                           // window name
            WS_CHILD | WS_VISIBLE |         // window styles
            LBS_NOTIFY | WS_VSCROLL,
            0,0,0,0,                        // location and size
            hwnd,                           // parent
            (HMENU) LBCTLID,                // child id, not really a menu
            g_hInstance,                    // program instance
            NULL);                          // creation data
        // Set the list box control's font to a fixed pitch.
        HFONT hfont = GetStockFont(SYSTEM_FIXED_FONT);
        SetWindowFont(lpdata->hwndLB, hfont, FALSE);

        // Disable the menu item that allows creation of this window
        // type.  This means there can only be one mailbox window at
        // a time.
        EnableMenuItem(g_hFrameMenu, IDM_FILEOPENMAILBOX, MF_GRAYED);
        EnableMenuItem(g_hMailboxMenu, IDM_FILEOPENMAILBOX, MF_GRAYED);
        EnableMenuItem(g_hViewerMenu, IDM_FILEOPENMAILBOX, MF_GRAYED);
        EnableMenuItem(g_hEditorMenu, IDM_FILEOPENMAILBOX, MF_GRAYED);

        // Read the mailbox off disk and set it up.
        ReadMailbox(hwnd);
        CreateMailboxItems(hwnd);

        return TRUE;
}
```

```
void OnDestroy(HWND hwnd)
{
    // Deallocate our private window data before we go away.
    MAILBOXDATA FAR * lpdata =
        (MAILBOXDATA FAR *) GetWindowLong(hwnd, 0);
    delete lpdata;

    // Re-enable File|Open Mailbox
    EnableMenuItem(g_hFrameMenu, IDM_FILEOPENMAILBOX, MF_ENABLED);
    EnableMenuItem(g_hMailboxMenu, IDM_FILEOPENMAILBOX, MF_ENABLED);
    EnableMenuItem(g_hViewerMenu, IDM_FILEOPENMAILBOX, MF_ENABLED);
    EnableMenuItem(g_hEditorMenu, IDM_FILEOPENMAILBOX, MF_ENABLED);
}

void OnMDIActivate(HWND hwnd, BOOL fActive, HWND hwndActivate,
    HWND hwndDeactivate)
{
    UNUSED_PARAMETER(hwndActivate);
    UNUSED_PARAMETER(hwndDeactivate);

    if (fActive) {
        // Put our menu in place.
        SendMessage(g_hClient, WM_MDISETMENU,
            GET_WM_MDISETMENU_MPS(g_hMailboxMenu,
                g_hMailboxWindowMenu));
        MAILBOXDATA FAR * lpdata =
            (MAILBOXDATA FAR*) GetWindowLong(hwnd, 0);
        // Enable/disable the Mail|Send menu item.
        if (lpdata->bRetrieving) {
            EnableMenuItem(g_hMailboxMenu, IDM_MAILRETRIEVE,
                MF_GRAYED);
        }
        else {
            EnableMenuItem(g_hMailboxMenu, IDM_MAILRETRIEVE,
                MF_ENABLED);
        }
        // Make sure keystrokes go to the list box control.
        SetFocus(lpdata->hwndLB);
    }
    else {
        // We're being deactivated, so put the main menu in place.
        SendMessage(g_hClient, WM_MDISETMENU,
            GET_WM_MDISETMENU_MPS(g_hFrameMenu, g_hFrameWindowMenu));
    }
    DrawMenuBar(g_hFrame);
}

BOOL OnQueryEndSession(HWND hwnd)
{
    MAILBOXDATA FAR * lpdata =
        (MAILBOXDATA FAR *) GetWindowLong(hwnd, 0);
    if (lpdata->bRetrieving) {
```

```
            SendMessage(g_hClient, WM_MDIRESTORE, (WPARAM) hwnd, 0);
            int iResult = MessageBox(hwnd,
                "Retrieving mail.  Close anyway?",
                "Close Anyway?", MB_YESNO | MB_ICONQUESTION);
            if (iResult == IDYES)
                return TRUE;
            else
                return FALSE;
        }
        else {
            return TRUE;
        }
}

void OnSize(HWND hwnd, UINT state, int cx, int cy)
{
        UNUSED_PARAMETER(state);

        MAILBOXDATA FAR * lpdata =
            (MAILBOXDATA FAR *) GetWindowLong(hwnd, 0);
        MoveWindow(lpdata->hwndLB, 0, 0, cx, cy, TRUE);
        // Must make sure we forward this to the default child proc
        // as well!
        FORWARD_WM_SIZE(hwnd, state, cx, cy, DefMDIChildProc);
}

/***********************************************************************
    MENU HANDLERS
***********************************************************************/

void OnMailRetrieve(HWND hwnd)
{
        MAILBOXDATA FAR * lpdata =
            (MAILBOXDATA FAR *) GetWindowLong(hwnd, 0);

        lpdata->pcpop3 = new CPOP3WithWinMsg(hwnd, WM_CPOP3DONE, 0);
        lpdata->pslFileList = new CStringList;
        lpdata->pcpop3->RetrieveMessages(g_pszPOPServer, g_ushPOPPort,
            g_pszMailbox, g_pszPassword, g_szMessageDir,
            lpdata->pslFileList);
        lpdata->bRetrieving = TRUE;
        EnableMenuItem(g_hMailboxMenu, IDM_MAILRETRIEVE, MF_GRAYED);
}

void OnMailView(HWND hwnd)
{
        MAILBOXDATA FAR * lpdata =
            (MAILBOXDATA FAR *) GetWindowLong(hwnd, 0);
        // Get the current selection index from the list box.
        int iCurSel = ListBox_GetCurSel(lpdata->hwndLB);
        if (iCurSel < 0) {
            MessageBox(hwnd, "You must make a selection first.",
```

```
                "Whoops!", MB_OK | MB_ICONHAND);
            return;
    }
    // Find the right summary info entry in the list that
    // corresponds to the selection index.
     SUMMARYINFO * psi = lpdata->pslSummaryList->First();
    for (int i = 0; i < iCurSel; i++, psi = lpdata->pslSummaryList->Next())
        ; // Null loop body.
    ASSERT(psi != NULL);
    // Create the viewer window and give it the message filename.
     MDICREATESTRUCT mdicreate;
     mdicreate.szClass    = g_szViewerClass;
     mdicreate.szTitle    = "Viewer";
     mdicreate.hOwner     = g_hInstance;
     mdicreate.x          = CW_USEDEFAULT;
     mdicreate.y          = CW_USEDEFAULT;
     mdicreate.cx         = CW_USEDEFAULT;
     mdicreate.cy         = CW_USEDEFAULT;
     mdicreate.style      = 0;
     mdicreate.lParam     =
            (LPARAM)(LPSTR)DuplicateString(psi->pszFileName);

    // Send a message to the client window to create the new child.
     SendMessage(g_hClient, WM_MDICREATE, 0,
         (LPARAM) (LPMDICREATESTRUCT) &mdicreate);

    return;
}

void OnMailDelete(HWND hwnd)
{
    MAILBOXDATA FAR * lpdata =
        (MAILBOXDATA FAR *) GetWindowLong(hwnd, 0);
    // Get the current selection index from the list box.
     int iCurSel = ListBox_GetCurSel(lpdata->hwndLB);
    if (iCurSel < 0) {
        MessageBox(hwnd, "You must make a selection first.",
            "Whoops!", MB_OK | MB_ICONHAND);
        return;
    }
    // Find the right summary info entry in the list that
    // corresponds to the selection index.
     SUMMARYINFO * psi = lpdata->pslSummaryList->First();
    for (int i = 0; i < iCurSel; i++, psi =
        lpdata->pslSummaryList->Next())
        ; // Null loop body.
    ASSERT(psi != NULL);
    // Delete the disk message file.
     char szFullName[MAX_PATH_LENGTH];
     lstrcpy(szFullName, g_szMessageDir);
     lstrcat(szFullName, "\\");
     lstrcat(szFullName, psi->pszFileName);
```

```
    unlink(szFullName);
     // Delete the node.
     lpdata->pslSummaryList->Delete(psi);
     // Update the mailbox on disk.
     WriteMailbox(hwnd);
     // Update the list box.
     CreateMailboxItems(hwnd);
}


/**********************************************************************
     UTILITY FUNCTIONS
**********************************************************************/

void ReadMailbox(HWND hwnd)
{
    MAILBOXDATA FAR * lpdata =
         (MAILBOXDATA FAR *) GetWindowLong(hwnd, 0);
     ifstream ifsFile(g_szMailboxFile);
    const int LINESIZE = 256;
    char szLine[LINESIZE];

    while (ifsFile.peek() != EOF) {
         SUMMARYINFO * psi = new SUMMARYINFO;
          ifsFile.getline(szLine, LINESIZE);
          psi->pszFileName = DuplicateString(szLine);
          ifsFile.getline(szLine, LINESIZE);
          psi->pszFrom = DuplicateString(szLine);
          ifsFile.getline(szLine, LINESIZE);
          psi->pszSubject = DuplicateString(szLine);
          ifsFile.getline(szLine, LINESIZE);
          psi->time = (time_t) atol(szLine);
           lpdata->pslSummaryList->Insert(psi);
    }
     ifsFile.close();
}


void WriteMailbox(HWND hwnd)
{
    MAILBOXDATA FAR * lpdata =
         (MAILBOXDATA FAR *) GetWindowLong(hwnd, 0);
     ofstream ofsFile(g_szMailboxFile);

     SUMMARYINFO * psi = lpdata->pslSummaryList->First();
    while (psi != NULL) {
         ofsFile << psi->pszFileName << '\n';
         ofsFile << psi->pszFrom << '\n';
         ofsFile << psi->pszSubject << '\n';
         ofsFile << (long) psi->time << '\n';
          psi = lpdata->pslSummaryList->Next();
    }
     ofsFile.close();
}
```

```
void CreateMailboxItems(HWND hwnd)
{
    const char *Months[] = { "Jan", "Feb", "Mar", "Apr", "May", "Jun",
        "Jul", "Aug", "Sep", "Oct", "Nov", "Dec" };
    const int MAXFROM = 20;
    const int MAXSUBJECT = 50;

    // Clear out the list box.
    MAILBOXDATA FAR * lpdata =
        (MAILBOXDATA FAR *) GetWindowLong(hwnd, 0);
    HWND hwndLB = lpdata->hwndLB;
    SetWindowRedraw(hwndLB, FALSE);
    SendMessage(hwndLB, LB_RESETCONTENT, 0, 0);

    // Create a summary line for each item in the summary info list.
    SUMMARYINFO * psi = lpdata->pslSummaryList->First();
    while (psi != NULL) {
        // Format the summary line string using the information
        // in the summary record.
        char szSummaryLine[100];
        char szTruncFrom[MAXFROM + 1];
        char szTruncSubject[MAXSUBJECT + 1];
        struct tm * ptm = localtime(&(psi->time));
        lstrcpyn(szTruncFrom, psi->pszFrom, MAXFROM);
        lstrcpyn(szTruncSubject, psi->pszSubject, MAXSUBJECT);
        wsprintf(szSummaryLine, "%02d-%s-%02d   %-20s   %-50s",
            ptm->tm_mday, (LPSTR)Months[ptm->tm_mon], ptm->tm_year,
            (LPSTR)szTruncFrom, (LPSTR)szTruncSubject);
        ListBox_AddString(hwndLB, szSummaryLine);
        psi = lpdata->pslSummaryList->Next();
    }
    SetWindowRedraw(hwndLB, TRUE);
}

SUMMARYINFO * GetSummaryInfo(char * pszFileName)
{
    SUMMARYINFO * psiResult = new SUMMARYINFO;

    // Save the file name.
    psiResult->pszFileName = DuplicateString(pszFileName);

    // Get the From: header.
    char * pszHeaderData = GetHeaderData("From:", pszFileName);
    if (pszHeaderData == NULL) {
        // If we couldn't find the header, create a zero-length
        // null-terminated string.
        pszHeaderData = new char[1];
        *pszHeaderData = '\0';
    }
    psiResult->pszFrom = pszHeaderData;

    // Get the subject header.
```

```
   pszHeaderData = GetHeaderData("Subject:", pszFileName);
    if (pszHeaderData == NULL) {
        // If we couldn't find the header, create a zero-length
        // null terminated string.
        pszHeaderData = new char[1];
        *pszHeaderData = '\0';
    }
    psiResult->pszSubject = pszHeaderData;

    // Get the date header.
    pszHeaderData = GetHeaderData("Date:", pszFileName);
    if (pszHeaderData == NULL) {
        // If there was no date, pick a default time.
        psiResult->time = 0;
    }
    else {
        // Else parse the date to return a time_t value.
        psiResult->time = ParseDateString(pszHeaderData);
        delete[] pszHeaderData;
    }

    // Return the SUMMARYINFO structure to the caller.
    return psiResult;
}

char * GetHeaderData(char * pszHeader, char * pszFileName)
{
    int i;
    char szFullName[MAX_PATH_LENGTH];
    lstrcpy(szFullName, g_szMessageDir);
    lstrcat(szFullName, "\\");
    lstrcat(szFullName, pszFileName);

    ifstream ifsMessage(szFullName);
    char szLineBuffer[1001];

    while (ifsMessage.peek() != EOF) {
        // Slurp up a line of data from the file.
        ifsMessage.getline(szLineBuffer, sizeof(szLineBuffer));
        // See if the line was simply a CRLF.
        if (lstrlen(szLineBuffer) == 0) {
            // If so, we reached the end of the headers before
            // finding the one we were looking for.  Exit the
            // while loop and return NULL.
            return NULL;
        }
        // See if this is the header we want.
        BOOL bMatch = TRUE;
        for (i = 0; i < lstrlen(pszHeader); i++) {
            if (tolower(pszHeader[i]) != tolower(szLineBuffer[i])) {
                // Nope, something didn't match.
                bMatch = FALSE;
```

```
                    break;
                }
            }
        // If we matched, break out.
        if (bMatch)
            break;
    }
    // At this point, i==lstrlen(pszHeader).
    // Advance i past any whitespace that might have followed
    // the colon after the header name.
    while (IsLWSP(szLineBuffer[i]))
        i++;
    // Now, shrink the line down, eliminating the header name,
    // colon, and any following white space but retaining all
    // the info we really care about.
    char * pszResult = new char[lstrlen(szLineBuffer) - i + 1];
    int j = 0;
    while (szLineBuffer[i] != '\0') {
        pszResult[j++] = szLineBuffer[i++];
    }
    pszResult[j] = '\0';
    // Now, check to see if the following line is folded.  If
    // so, we should append it on to the current data.
    while (ifsMessage.peek() != EOF) {
        // We still have more file, so read in another line.
        ifsMessage.getline(szLineBuffer, sizeof(szLineBuffer));
        // See if it starts with linear white space.  If not,
        // then the line is not folded further and we're done.
        if (!IsLWSP(szLineBuffer[0]))
            break;
        // Okay, the line is folded.
        // See how long the combined line will be when we've
        // appended this line to the previous ones.
        int iLength = lstrlen(pszResult) + lstrlen(szLineBuffer);
        char * pszTemp = new char[iLength + 1];
        lstrcpy(pszTemp, pszResult);
        lstrcat(pszTemp, szLineBuffer);
        delete[] pszResult;
        pszResult = pszTemp;
    }

    return pszResult;
}
```

Listing 10.4 MAILVIEW.CPP

```
/*
    File: MAILVIEW.CPP
    Description:
        Implements the viewer window class for Mail Client.
    Copyright 1995, David G. Roberts
*/
```

```
#include <string.h>
#include <dos.h>
#include <fstream.h>
#include <windows.h>
#include <windowsx.h>
#include "mailcli.rh"
#include "myassert.h"
#include "cwinsock.h"
#include "csmtp.h"
#include "caddrlst.h"
#include "rfc822.h"
#include "cuuendec.h"
#include "cmime.h"
#include "cbase64.h"

#define DECLARE
#include "mailclig.h"

/*
    CONSTANTS
*/
#define EDITCTLID        1

/*
    MACROS
*/
#define min(a, b) (((a) < (b)) ? (a) : (b))
#define max(a, b) (((a) > (b)) ? (a) : (b))

/*
    TYPES
*/

// VIEWERDATA holds some data associated with the viewer window.
struct VIEWERDATA {
    HWND       hwndEdit;
    CMIMEMsg * pMessage;

    VIEWERDATA::VIEWERDATA() { pMessage = NULL; };
    VIEWERDATA::~VIEWERDATA() { delete pMessage; };
};

/*
    LOCAL FUNCTIONS
*/
static void OnCommand(HWND hwnd, int id, HWND hwndCtl,
    UINT codeNotify);
static BOOL OnCreate(HWND, CREATESTRUCT FAR*);
static void OnDestroy(HWND);
static void OnMDIActivate(HWND, BOOL, HWND, HWND);
static void OnSize(HWND, UINT, int, int);
```

```c
/*
    MENU HANDLERS
*/
static void OnMailUudecode(HWND);

/*
    UTILITY FUNCTIONS
*/
void ViewMessagePart(HWND);
void ConvertQPToText(char *, char *, int);
int ConvertHexDigit(char);

/************************************************************************
    WINDOW AND DIALOG BOX PROCEDURES
************************************************************************/

/*
    Function: ViewerWndProc
    Description:
        Window proc for the viewer window.
*/
LRESULT CALLBACK ViewerWndProc(HWND hwnd, UINT msg, WPARAM wParam,
    LPARAM lParam)
{
    switch (msg) {
        HANDLE_MSG(hwnd, WM_COMMAND, OnCommand);
        HANDLE_MSG(hwnd, WM_CREATE, OnCreate);
        HANDLE_MSG(hwnd, WM_DESTROY, OnDestroy);
        HANDLE_MSG(hwnd, WM_MDIACTIVATE, OnMDIActivate);
        HANDLE_MSG(hwnd, WM_SIZE, OnSize);
    }
    return DefMDIChildProc(hwnd, msg, wParam, lParam);
}

/************************************************************************
    MESSAGE HANDLING FUNCTIONS
************************************************************************/

/*
    Function: OnCommand
    Description:
        Handles WM_COMMAND messages.
*/
void OnCommand(HWND hwnd, int id, HWND hwndCtl, UINT codeNotify)
{
    VIEWERDATA FAR *lpdata = (VIEWERDATA FAR *)GetWindowLong(hwnd, 0);

    if (hwndCtl == NULL) {
        // It's a window message.
        switch (id) {
            case IDM_EDITCOPY:
                SendMessage(lpdata->hwndEdit, WM_COPY, 0, 0);
```

```
                    return;
               case IDM_MAILFIRSTBODYPART:
                    lpdata->pMessage->FirstPart();
                   ViewMessagePart(hwnd);
                   return;
               case IDM_MAILNEXTBODYPART:
                   if (lpdata->pMessage->NextPart() == NULL) {
                       MessageBox(hwnd, "There are no more parts.",
                           "Notice", MB_OK | MB_ICONSTOP);
                   }
                   else
                        ViewMessagePart(hwnd);
                   return;
               case IDM_MAILUUDECODE:
                   OnMailUudecode(hwnd);
                   return;
           }
       }
       else {
            ASSERT(id == EDITCTLID);
            // It's from our control.
            if (codeNotify == EN_ERRSPACE) {
               MessageBox(hwnd, "Viewer out of space.", "Error",
                   MB_OK | MB_ICONEXCLAMATION);
               return;
           }
       }
       // Make sure the default child proc sees things we don't
       // process ourselves!
        FORWARD_WM_COMMAND(hwnd, id, hwndCtl, codeNotify,
           DefMDIChildProc);
}


/*
    Function: OnCreate
    Description:
        Creates the editor window in which the messages are
        displayed, parses the message, and displays the first
        body part.
*/
BOOL OnCreate(HWND hwnd, CREATESTRUCT FAR* lpCreateStruct)
{
    // Allocate some private window data for ourselves.
    VIEWERDATA FAR * lpdata = new VIEWERDATA;
    SetWindowLong(hwnd, 0, (LONG) lpdata);

    // Create a multiline edit control to do our work for us.
    lpdata->hwndEdit = CreateWindow(
        "EDIT",                         // class name
        NULL,                           // window name
        WS_CHILD | WS_VISIBLE |         // window styles
        WS_HSCROLL | WS_VSCROLL | ES_LEFT |
```

```
            ES_MULTILINE | ES_AUTOHSCROLL | ES_AUTOVSCROLL | ES_READONLY,
        0,0,0,0,                        // location and size
        hwnd,                           // parent
         (HMENU) EDITCTLID,             // child id, not really a menu
        g_hInstance,                    // program instance
        NULL);                          // creation data

    // Set the edit control's font to a fixed pitch.
    HFONT hfont = GetStockFont(SYSTEM_FIXED_FONT);
    SetWindowFont(lpdata->hwndEdit, hfont, FALSE);

    // Create the full file name from the message directory name
    // and the individual file name.
    char FAR * lpszFileName = (LPSTR)(((MDICREATESTRUCT FAR *)
            (lpCreateStruct->lpCreateParams))->lParam);
    char szFullName[MAX_PATH_LENGTH];
    lstrcpy(szFullName, g_szMessageDir);
    lstrcat(szFullName, "\\");
    lstrcat(szFullName, lpszFileName);
    delete[] lpszFileName;

    // Create the MIME message object.
    lpdata->pMessage = new CMIMEMsg;
    if (lpdata->pMessage->Parse(szFullName) != TRUE) {
        // Handle possible parsing error.
        MessageBox(hwnd, "Error parsing message.", "Error",
            MB_OK | MB_ICONEXCLAMATION);
        return FALSE;
    }

    // Move the first part of the message and view it.
    lpdata->pMessage->FirstPart();
    ViewMessagePart(hwnd);

    return TRUE;
}


/*
    Function: OnDestroy
    Description:
        Handles a WM_DESTROY message.
*/
void OnDestroy(HWND hwnd)
{
    // Deallocate our private window data before we go away.
    VIEWERDATA FAR *lpdata = (VIEWERDATA FAR *)GetWindowLong(hwnd, 0);
    delete lpdata;
}
/*
    Function: OnMDIActivate
    Description:
        Takes care of putting the viewer menu into the menu
        bar when the viewer window becomes active.
*/
```

```
void OnMDIActivate(HWND hwnd, BOOL fActive, HWND hwndActivate,
    HWND hwndDeactivate)
{
    UNUSED_PARAMETER(hwndActivate);
    UNUSED_PARAMETER(hwndDeactivate);

    if (fActive) {
        // Put our menu in place.
        SendMessage(g_hClient, WM_MDISETMENU,
            GET_WM_MDISETMENU_MPS(g_hViewerMenu,
                g_hViewerWindowMenu));
        VIEWERDATA FAR *lpdata =
            (VIEWERDATA FAR*)GetWindowLong(hwnd, 0);
        // Make sure keystrokes go to the edit control.
        SetFocus(lpdata->hwndEdit);
    }
    else {
        // We're being deactivated, so put the main menu in place.
        SendMessage(g_hClient, WM_MDISETMENU,
            GET_WM_MDISETMENU_MPS(g_hFrameMenu,
                g_hFrameWindowMenu));
    }
    DrawMenuBar(g_hFrame);
}

/*
    Function: OnSize
    Description:
        Notifies the editor child window whenever the viewer window
        gets resized.
*/
void OnSize(HWND hwnd, UINT state, int cx, int cy)
{
    UNUSED_PARAMETER(state);

    VIEWERDATA FAR *lpdata = (VIEWERDATA FAR *)GetWindowLong(hwnd, 0);
    MoveWindow(lpdata->hwndEdit, 0, 0, cx, cy, TRUE);
    // Must make sure we forward this to the default child proc
    // as well!
    FORWARD_WM_SIZE(hwnd, state, cx, cy, DefMDIChildProc);
}

/***********************************************************************
    MENU HANDLERS
***********************************************************************/

/*
    Function: OnMailUudecode
    Description:
        Handles a UUDECODE command from the menu bar.
*/
void OnMailUudecode(HWND hwnd)
```

```
{
    int iResult;

    // Capture the mouse, 'cause this could take more than an
    // instant.
    SetCapture(g_hFrame);
    HCURSOR hcursorSave = SetCursor(LoadCursor(NULL, IDC_WAIT));

    CUUDEC uudec(hwnd);
    VIEWERDATA FAR *lpdata = (VIEWERDATA FAR *)GetWindowLong(hwnd, 0);

    // Figure out how many lines there are in this viewer.
    int iCount = (int) SendMessage(lpdata->hwndEdit, EM_GETLINECOUNT,
        0, 0);
    for (int i = 0; i < iCount; i++) {
        char szLineBuffer[1000];
        // Get the line from the edit control.
        // First indicate the size of the buffer in the first couple
        // of bytes (pretty weird way to do this, Microsoft...).
        // Leave 1 byte for the terminator, which EM_GETLINE won't put
        // in.
        *(WORD *)szLineBuffer = sizeof(szLineBuffer) - 1;
        int iLength = (int) SendMessage(lpdata->hwndEdit, EM_GETLINE,
            i, (LPARAM) (char FAR *) szLineBuffer);
        // EM_GETLINE doesn't terminate the string, so add a null.
        szLineBuffer[iLength] = '\0';
        iResult = uudec.DecodeLine(szLineBuffer);
        if (iResult != CUUDEC::RESULT_OK)
            break;
    }

    // Release the mouse.
    SetCursor(hcursorSave);
    ReleaseCapture();

    // If something went wrong, signal it.
    if (iResult == CUUDEC::RESULT_ERROR) {
        MessageBox(hwnd, "An error occurred during decoding.",
            "Error", MB_OK | MB_ICONEXCLAMATION);
    }
}

/***********************************************************************
    UTILITY FUNCTIONS
***********************************************************************/

/*
    Function: ViewMessagePart
    Description:
        Given the current message body part, the function displays
        it in the viewer window if it's a text message.  If it's
        a different message type, the function offers to save it
        in a file.
```

```c
*/
void ViewMessagePart(HWND hwnd)
{
    int iResult;
    BOOL bResult;
    int iLength;
    char szRawBuffer[1000];
    char szDecodedBuffer[1000];
    CBase64Dec * pBase64Dec = new CBase64Dec;
    static char *szFilter[] = { "All Files (*.*)", "*.*", "", "" };
    char szFullName[MAX_PATH_LENGTH];
    char szFileName[MAX_FILENAME_LENGTH];

    VIEWERDATA FAR *lpdata = (VIEWERDATA FAR *)GetWindowLong(hwnd, 0);

    CMIMEBodyPart * pCurrentPart = lpdata->pMessage->CurrentPart();

    // Delete all the data in the viewer currently.
    SendMessage(lpdata->hwndEdit, EM_SETSEL,
        GET_EM_SETSEL_MPS(0, -1));
    SendMessage(lpdata->hwndEdit, EM_REPLACESEL, 0, (LPARAM) "");

    // Open up the body part so we can read it.
    if (pCurrentPart->Open() != TRUE) {
        MessageBox(hwnd, "Could not open body part.", "Error",
            MB_OK | MB_ICONEXCLAMATION);
        return;
    }

    // Figure out what the current body part type is.
    // Whatever it is, it shouldn't be a multipart node.  The
    // FirstPart and NextPart functions of CMIMEMsg should skip
    // over these and only give us the constituent parts of a
    // multipart.
    ASSERT(lstrcmpi(pCurrentPart->Type(), "multipart") != 0);

    if (lstrcmpi(pCurrentPart->Type(), "text") == 0) {
        // Figure out what character set it is using.
        CMIMEParamTuple * pTuple = pCurrentPart->FirstParam();
        while (pTuple != NULL &&
            lstrcmpi(pTuple->Param(), "charset") != 0) {
            pTuple = pCurrentPart->NextParam();
        }
        // See if we can handle it.
        if (pTuple != NULL &&
            lstrcmpi(pTuple->Value(), "us-ascii") != 0 &&
            lstrcmpi(pTuple->Value(), "iso-8859-1") != 0) {
            MessageBox(hwnd, "This message body part uses an "
                "unknown or unsupported character set.  It may not "
                "display correctly.", "Warning",
                MB_OK | MB_ICONEXCLAMATION);
        }
```

```
        // If it's not text/plain, throw up a disclaimer.
        if (lstrcmpi(pCurrentPart->SubType(), "plain") != 0) {
            MessageBox(hwnd, "This message part contains an unknown "
                "subtype of type text.  It may not display "
                "correctly.",
                "Warning", MB_OK | MB_ICONASTERISK);
    }


        // Put the text into the viewer.
        BOOL bFoundSeparator = FALSE;
        int iResult = pCurrentPart->FirstLine(szRawBuffer,
            sizeof(szRawBuffer));
        while (iResult >= 0) {
            // Decode buffer.
            if (bFoundSeparator) {
                if (lstrcmpi(pCurrentPart->Encoding(), "base64")
                    == 0) {
                    iLength = pBase64Dec->DecodeLine(szRawBuffer,
                        lstrlen(szRawBuffer),
                        (uchar *)szDecodedBuffer,
                        sizeof(szDecodedBuffer));
                    szDecodedBuffer[iLength] = '\0';
            }
                else if (lstrcmpi(pCurrentPart->Encoding(),
                    "quoted-printable") == 0) {
                    ConvertQPToText(szRawBuffer, szDecodedBuffer,
                        sizeof(szDecodedBuffer));
                }
                else {
                    lstrcpy(szDecodedBuffer, szRawBuffer);
                }
            }
            else {
                if (lstrcmp(szRawBuffer, "\r\n") == 0)
                    bFoundSeparator = TRUE;
                lstrcpy(szDecodedBuffer, szRawBuffer);
            }
            // Stuff the decoded text into the edit control
            SendMessage(lpdata->hwndEdit, EM_REPLACESEL, 0,
                (LPARAM) szDecodedBuffer);
            // Get the next line of raw text.
            iResult = pCurrentPart->NextLine(szRawBuffer,
                sizeof(szRawBuffer));
        }
    }
    else {
        // Treat everything else like application/octet-stream.

        // Put something in the edit box.
        SendMessage(lpdata->hwndEdit, EM_REPLACESEL, 0,
            (LPARAM) "*** NON-TEXT DATA ***\r\n");
```

```
       // Query the user if we should save it.
       iResult = MessageBox(hwnd,
           "This body part contains non-text data.  "
           "Would you like to save it to a file?", "Save?",
           MB_YESNO | MB_ICONQUESTION);
   if (iResult == IDNO)
       goto exit;

       // Open up a common file dialog box.
       szFullName[0] = szFileName[0] = '\0';
   OPENFILENAME ofn;
       memset(&ofn, 0, sizeof(OPENFILENAME));

       ofn.lStructSize        = sizeof(OPENFILENAME);
   ofn.hwndOwner          = hwnd;
   ofn.lpstrFilter        = szFilter[0];
   ofn.lpstrFile          = szFullName;
   ofn.nMaxFile           = sizeof(szFullName);
       ofn.lpstrFileTitle   = szFileName;
       ofn.nMaxFileTitle    = sizeof(szFileName);
       ofn.lpstrTitle       = "Save Non-Text Attachment";
   ofn.Flags               = OFN_HIDEREADONLY |
                               OFN_NOREADONLYRETURN |
                               OFN_OVERWRITEPROMPT;

       bResult = GetSaveFileName(&ofn);

   if (bResult == 0)
       goto exit;

   // Open up the file.
   OFSTRUCT ofs;
       HFILE hfile = OpenFile(szFullName, &ofs,
           OF_WRITE | OF_CREATE);
       if (hfile == HFILE_ERROR) {
           MessageBox(hwnd, "Could not open the output file.",
               "Error", MB_OK | MB_ICONEXCLAMATION);
           goto exit;
   }

       // Get each line, decode it, and write it to the file.
       BOOL bFoundSeparator = FALSE;
       int iResult = pCurrentPart->FirstLine(szRawBuffer,
           sizeof(szRawBuffer));
   while (iResult >= 0) {
           // Decode buffer.
           if (bFoundSeparator) {
               if (lstrcmpi(pCurrentPart->Encoding(), "base64")
                   == 0) {
                   iLength = pBase64Dec->DecodeLine(szRawBuffer,
                       lstrlen(szRawBuffer),
                       (uchar *)szDecodedBuffer,
```

```
                                   sizeof(szDecodedBuffer));
                  }
                    else if (lstrcmpi(pCurrentPart->Encoding(),
                       "quoted-printable") == 0) {
                        ConvertQPToText(szRawBuffer, szDecodedBuffer,
                           sizeof(szDecodedBuffer));
                        iLength = lstrlen(szDecodedBuffer);
                  }
                  else {
                        lstrcpy(szDecodedBuffer, szRawBuffer);
                  }
                   // Write it out.
                     _lwrite(hfile, (LPCSTR) szDecodedBuffer, iLength);
             }
             else {
                  if (lstrcmp(szRawBuffer, "\r\n") == 0)
                     bFoundSeparator = TRUE;
             }
              // Get the next line of raw text.
               iResult = pCurrentPart->NextLine(szRawBuffer,
                  sizeof(szRawBuffer));
        }
         _lclose(hfile);

    }

exit:
    // Close up the body part now that it's in the viewer.
     pCurrentPart->Close();

    // Put the caret at the beginning of the control and scroll it
    // into view.
     SendMessage(lpdata->hwndEdit, EM_SETSEL,
         GET_EM_SETSEL_MPS(0, 0));
#ifdef WIN32
     SendMessage(lpdata->hwndEdit, EM_SCROLLCARET, 0, 0);
#endif

    delete pBase64Dec;
}


/*
    Function: ConvertQPToText
    Description:
         Decodes quoted-printable encoded data.
*/
void ConvertQPToText(char * pszInput, char * pszOutput, int nLen)
{
    int iInputIndex = 0;
    int iOutputIndex = 0;

    while (iOutputIndex < (nLen - 1) &&
```

```
            pszInput[iInputIndex] != '\0') {
            char c = pszInput[iInputIndex++];
            if (c != '=') {
                pszOutput[iOutputIndex++] = c;
                continue;
            }
            // We found a '=' character.  See if we have a soft
            // line break or a hex-encoded character.
            c = pszInput[iInputIndex++];
            if (c == CR) {
                // Soft break.
                break;
            }
            else {
                pszOutput[iOutputIndex++] =
                    (char) (16 * ConvertHexDigit(c) +
                     ConvertHexDigit(pszInput[iInputIndex++]));
            }
        }
    }
    pszOutput[iOutputIndex] = '\0';
}


/*

    Function: ConvertHexDigit
    Description:
        Given an ASCII character, the function returns its
        hex value, if it has one, or -1 if the character is not
        a hex digit.
*/
int ConvertHexDigit(char c)
{
    if ('0' <= c && c <= '9')
        return c - '0';
    if ('A' <= c && c <= 'F')
        return c - 'A' + 10;
    if ('a' <= c && c <= 'f')
        return c - 'a' + 10;
    return -1;
}
```

Encoding Binary Data: UUENCODE

CHAPTER **11**

Sometimes we need to send binary data files through the Internet mail system. How can we send binary data when SMTP only supports the transfer of ASCII messages? Read on to learn about the UUENCODE format.

Although many people have total access to the Internet, others are not so fortunate. Some users only have network connectivity within their own organization and not with the global Internet. Sometimes this limitation reflects a lack of network infrastructure. Other times the restriction is an intentional restriction designed to increase network security. The theory is that by preventing access, you also prevent intrusion.

Even when such connectivity limitations exist, however, most users have email connectivity. Email is quickly becoming the universal network application. Although the SMTP protocol requires direct connectivity between hops, organizations can put an email gateway at the border of their network. The email gateway does not function as an IP router. It simply forwards SMTP messages between the organization and the outside world, not allowing IP packets to flow between the internal network and the global Internet. This environment keeps people from using the FTP protocol to transfer files to and from the outside world, for instance (because that would require direct IP connectivity), but allows them to exchange email.

What happens when the latest shareware game is uploaded to a network site, however? Or when the latest Windows utility becomes available? How can these users with crippled connectivity receive files that other users simply FTP? Since these users can still send and receive email, wouldn't it be nice if a friend on the outside could simply mail the files to them?

Of course, that's exactly what happens. Unfortunately, the Internet email system was designed when life was simple. It only supports the transfer of ASCII text messages. Although it's trivial to email a text file to a friend, the Internet email system won't allow you to email a file containing arbitrary binary data without performing some additional work. If you try to send binary data through the Internet email system, your message may be rejected by an intermediate node or corrupted on its way to the destination.

To send a file containing binary data through the Internet email system, the binary data must be encoded in a format that contains only 7-bit ASCII data. The encoded data may look like a random series of characters, but that isn't a problem. None of the intermediate message transfer agents along the path to the destination interprets the contents of message bodies. If the message contains nothing but ASCII text, no matter how unintelligible it looks, it will get through the network. One of the first and most popular encoding formats that has this property is the UUENCODE format.

In this chapter, we'll look at the UUENCODE format and some C++ classes that implement an encoder and decoder for the format. Finally, we'll see how we can use these classes to implement encoding and decoding functionality for the UUENCODE format in the Mail Client application.

The UUENCODE Format

The UUENCODE format is a simple 7-bit ASCII format that encodes a binary file along with control information to assist in decoding the file. The format comprises a series of short lines of text, suitable for transport through the Internet mail system. The rough format of a UUENCODED file is:

```
begin <permissions> <file name>
<lines of encoded data>
<zero line>
end
```

The first line of the format starts with "begin," followed by a number that encodes the file's security permissions and the file name. The three pieces of information are separated by spaces. The "begin" line is followed by short lines of UUENCODED file text. Each line of text begins with a code that determines how many bytes of encoded data the line contains. A line with a length value of zero marks the end of the encoded data. The last line of the format is "end." A sample UUENCODED file is shown in Figure 11.1.

Let's dissect the UUENCODE format line by line.

The numeric permissions indication is a three-digit number in *octal* format. It encodes the file's security permissions. Inclusion of the security permissions in the UUENCODE format allows them to be transported along with the encoded data. The decoded file can have the same permissions as the original file when it is recovered. The format of the permissions is the same as the typical permission bits used in the Unix file system.

Each digit of the octal number represents three permission bits: a read bit, write bit, and execute bit. If the bit is set, a user can read, write, or execute the given file.

The three octal digits encode permissions for the owner of the file, a group of users associated with the file, and for other users not directly associated with the file. Remember that Unix is a multi-user system. The permission bits reflect the desire for each user to control other users' access to his or her files.

The permissions indication has no direct equivalent in the DOS file system. The closest thing DOS has to a permission bit is the read-only bit. Generally, DOS systems can ignore the file permissions when decoding files and can set the permissions to "600" when encoding files. Setting the permissions to 600 allows a decoder on a Unix system to read and write the file but denies access to all other users on the system. This conservative policy errs on the side of being too protective rather than too open. If Unix users want to give other users access to the file, they can change the file permissions after decoding the file.

Figure 11.1

A UUENCODED file containing the sequence of bytes from 00h to FFh.

```
begin  600  TST0-255.BIN
M"$"'P0%!@<("0H+#!T'.#.!/#?&'=.Q'1$A.4%187&!!D:&QP='A\@(2(C)"4F)R@I*BLL
M+2X0.,#$R#.,SOU-C<X.3H[/#T'/T!T!!0!D-$149'2$E*2TQ-3]045)35%565UA9
M6EM<75Y?8&%B8V1E9F=H:6IK;&UN;U!Q<G-T=79W>'EZ>WQ]?G^&'@8*#B(F*BXR-CH^
M0$)$1DA*3$Y04E15E=96EQ>8&)D9F=I;&VO<G5W>7M]?X&#A8>)BXV/D9.5EYF;G9^@HJ2F
MJ*JLKK"RM+:XNKR^P,+$QL;(RLS.T-+4UMC:W-[@XN3F"6-K;W>'C9>9G:'E]?G^_P\?+S]/7V]_C\
?^?K[_/W^_R'_O\'"P\7&Q\C)RL/'S]/S\'_O\'CY^vC;_/W^_/4
`
end
```

Note: The NTFS file system used in Windows NT has much more sophisticated security features than DOS. The permission bits used in the UUENCODE format have direct equivalents in the NTFS file system. A program written to make use of NTFS features could set and interpret the UUENCODE mode bits compatibly.

A file name follows the permissions information on the "begin" line. The file name format is that used by the operating system on which the file was encoded. A DOS UUDECODE program should not expect a file name in "8.3" format. File names in other operating systems are typically less restrictive than in DOS, both in the length of the name and the allowable character set. A DOS UUDECODE program should either allow the user to change the file name to a legal DOS file name or use an algorithm to generate a valid DOS file name from the file name given on the "begin" line.

Lines of encoded text follow the "begin" line. Each line of encoded text begins with a count of the number of bytes encoded on the line, followed by the encoded bytes. The length information is also encoded so that it represents a valid ASCII character.

The encoding technique that is used in the UUENCODE format encodes 6 bits of binary data at a time. The 6-bit value is added to the ASCII value for the space character (32 decimal, 20 hex). The result is a printable ASCII character that represents the 6-bit value. Printable characters are used because some mail systems don't handle control characters well. For instance:

```
0  + SPACE = 32 = SPACE
1  + SPACE = 33 = !
2  + SPACE = 34 = "
3  + SPACE = 35 = #
4  + SPACE = 36 = $
5  + SPACE = 37 = %
...
63 + SPACE = 95 = _
```

Bytes are encoded in groups of three, or 24 bits at a time. The 24 bits are encoded as four characters, six bits per character. Figure 11.2 shows an example of the encoding process.

Except for the last line, each line of encoded data should contain a multiple of three data bytes, or four encoded characters. The first character in the line represents the number of bytes (not characters) encoded in the line, encoded using the same

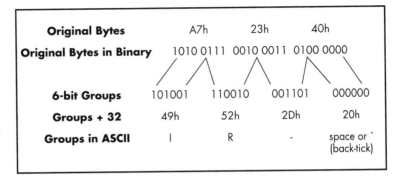

Figure 11.2

Encoding three bytes using the UUENCODE algorithm.

6-bit encoding scheme as the data. For example, if a line contains three data bytes, the first character on the line will be "#" followed by four characters representing the three encoded bytes. Common convention dictates that all lines except the last line contain 45 bytes of data, which results in an encoded length of "M".

If the length of the data file is not evenly divisible by three, the last encoding group will not contain three data bytes. In this case, the last 3-byte encoding group is padded on the right with zeros to make a full 3-byte group. The encoding then takes place as usual, and all four resulting characters are included on the encoded line. The length character included with the line contains the number of original data bytes encoded in the line, so the decoder knows that the last group of four characters does not represent three data bytes.

> Note: Lines other than the last line are allowed to use data lengths that are not a multiple of three. This flexibility results in inefficiency, however, because a full group of four characters must still be included on the line.

A line that contains zero data bytes marks the end of the encoded data. This line is encoded with a length byte of zero (the space character) followed by no other characters other than the end of line character or sequence.

Finally, the end of the format is signaled with a line containing only "end". This line is superfluous because the end of the encoded data already was signaled by the line containing a zero length. The end of format line still must be included, however.

For an example of the UUENCODE format, refer back to Figure 11.1, which shows the result of encoding the byte sequence: 00h, 01h, 02h, 03h, 04h, ... FEh, FFh.

Buggy Mail Transfer Agents

Although the UUENCODE format as described works well under most circumstances, some mail transfer agents (MTAs) can still corrupt the UUENCODED data. The problem occurs because some non-compliant MTAs strip trailing space characters from lines in the message text. Technically, this procedure violates the SMTP specification. MTAs are not supposed to alter the message body in any way, including the addition or removal of characters. Still, these MTAs do exist.

Presumably, such MTAs are trying to save communication bandwidth or message storage space by removing characters that aren't typically visible on a normal text message. Usually, you wouldn't miss a series of space characters that were removed from the end of a text line, but UUENCODED files need these characters. If a UUENCODED file contains space characters at the end of a line of encoded data, they may be stripped off, resulting in problems during decoding. The decoder will find that the line of encoded data is shorter than the byte count indicates it should be. Whatever gain in bandwidth or storage efficiency is achieved is outweighed by the havoc that this practice causes.

To get around the decoding problem, many UUENCODERs map the space character in the encoded text to the "back-tick" character ("`", ASCII value 96 decimal, 60 hex). The standard decoding process for each character is to take the ASCII value, subtract 32, then take the lower 6 bits of the result as the data. The "back-tick" character decodes as zero when this algorithm is used.

A UUENCODE Encoder/Decoder

Implementing a UUENCODE encoder and decoder is relatively simple. Listings 11.1 and 11.2 are the header file and implementation file for a pair of encoder and decoder classes, which we'll use for our Mail Client application.

To encode a file, the program creates an object of the **UUENC** class. The program then calls the **EncodeLine** member function with a pointer to a buffer to hold a line of encoded data and the length of the line.

The first call to **EncodeLine** causes the **UUENC** object to display a standard file dialog box that allows the user to open a file to encode. **EncodeLine** then returns the "begin" line in the buffer. Subsequent calls to **EncodeLine** return a line of encoded data from the file, eventually followed by the "end" line.

The value returned directly by **EncodeLine** signals whether the encoding process completed. When **EncodeLine** returns **RESULT_OK**, the buffer contains a valid line of the UUENCODE format, and the program should store the line of text appropriately. When the encoding process is complete, **EncodeLine** returns **RESULT_DONE**. The program then can destroy the **UUENC** object.

Decoding is similar. An object of the **UUDEC** class is created and each line of UUENCODE data is fed to the **DecodeLine** member function. The **DecodeLine** member function ignores all lines of text until a line containing "begin" is reached. The name of the encoded file is then parsed from the "begin" line, and a standard file dialog box is opened to allow the user to specify the file name and directory location for the decoding process. Note that this method allows the decoder to be fed the lines of header text from a message without first searching for the start of the UUENCODED data.

The program keeps feeding lines of text to the **DecodeLine** function as long as it returns **RESULT_OK**. When the decoder reaches the "end" line, **DecodeLine** returns **RESULT_DONE** and the program stops feeding it lines of text.

Using **UUENCODE** with Mail Client

The Mail Client program uses the **UUENC** and **UUDEC** classes to provide encoding and decoding capability for the UUENCODE format.

The MAILEDIT.CPP file (Listing 9.8) handles the encoding of files. When the user chooses the Mail|UUENCODE menu command while editing a new message, the **OnMailUuencode** function is invoked. **OnMailUuencode** creates a UUENC object and then repeatedly calls the **EncodeLine** member function. While **EncodeLine** returns **RESULT_OK**, **OnMailUuencode** inserts the encoded text into the edit control containing the message. When **EncodeLine** returns something other than **RESULT_OK**, **OnMailUuencode** stops inserting the lines of encoded text. If the result is **RESULT_DONE**, the **OnMailUuencode** function simply returns. If the result is **RESULT_ERROR**, an error message is displayed for the user.

The MAILVIEW.CPP file (Listing 10.4) handles the decoding of files. When the user chooses Mail|UUDECODE while viewing a message, the **OnMailUudecode** function is invoked. **OnMailUudecode** creates an object of the **UUDEC** class and begins feeding lines of message text to it. The decoder ignores all lines before the "begin" line, so the program makes no attempt to skip over any header lines that may be in the viewer. Lines of text are sent to the decoder as long as it returns **RESULT_OK**. When the decoder returns a result code other than **RESULT_OK**, the decoding process stops. If the decoder returns **RESULT_DONE**, the **OnMailUudecode** function simply exits. If the decoder returns **RESULT_ERROR**, an error message is displayed for the user.

As you can see, adding UUENCODE encoding and decoding functionality to a program is very simple.

Listings

This section includes the following file listings:

Listing 11.1 is the header file for the UUENC and UUDEC classes, UUENDEC.H.

Listing 11.2 is the implementation file for the UUENC and UUDEC classes, UUENDEC.CPP.

Listing 11.1 CUUENDEC.H

```
/*
    File: UUENDEC.H
    Description:
        UUENCODE/UUDECODE classes.
    Copyright 1995, David G. Roberts
*/

#ifndef _UUENDEC_H
#define _UUENDEC_H

#include <windows.h>
#include <commdlg.h>

class CUUDEC {
private:
    enum STATE { AWAIT_BEGIN, DECODING, AWAIT_END, DONE };
    STATE           m_state;
    HFILE           m_hfile;
    int             m_iMode;
    char            m_szFullName[260];
    char            m_szFileName[255];
    unsigned char   m_uchDecode[64];
    OPENFILENAME    m_ofn;
```

```
    // State functions.
     int AwaitBegin(char *);
     int Decode(char *);
     int AwaitEnd(char *);
public:
    CUUDEC(HWND hwnd);
    virtual ~CUUDEC();

    enum { RESULT_OK, RESULT_ERROR, RESULT_DONE, RESULT_CANCEL };
    int DecodeLine(char * pszLine);
    void Reset(void);
};

class CUUENC {
private:
    enum STATE { BEGIN, ENCODING, END, DONE };
    enum { MAXBYTESPERLINE = 45 };
    STATE            m_state;
    HFILE            m_hfile;
    char             m_szFullName[260];
    char             m_szFileName[255];
    unsigned char    m_uchBuffer[MAXBYTESPERLINE];
    OPENFILENAME     m_ofn;

    // State functions.
    int Begin(char *, int);
    int Encode(char *, int);
    int End(char *, int);
public:
    CUUENC(HWND hwnd);
    virtual ~CUUENC();

    enum { RESULT_OK, RESULT_ERROR, RESULT_DONE, RESULT_CANCEL,
        RESULT_SMALLBUFFER };
    int EncodeLine(char * pszLine, int nLength);
    void Reset(void);
};
#endif
```

Listing 11.2   CUUENDEC.CPP

```
/*
    File: UUENDEC.CPP
    Description:
        UUENCODE/UUDECODE classes.
    Copyright 1995, David G. Roberts
*/

#include <stdio.h>   // Needed for sscanf().
#include "cuuendec.h"
#include "myassert.h"
```

```
typedef unsigned char uchar;
#define SPACE               ((uchar)32)
// Remember, 077 = octal 77 = 0x3F = binary 00111111.
#define DECODE_CHAR(c)   ((((uchar)c) - SPACE) & 077)
#define ENCODE_BYTE(b)   (((uchar)(b) & 077) == 0 ? '`' : \
      (((uchar)(b) & 077) + SPACE))


/**********************************************************************
      UUDECODE
**********************************************************************/

/*
      Function: CUUDEC::CUUDEC
      Description:
          Constructor for CUUDEC class.  Puts the state machine into
          the AWAIT_BEGIN state and initializes the OPENFILENAME
          structure used for the save file common dialog box.
*/
CUUDEC::CUUDEC(HWND hwnd) : m_state(AWAIT_BEGIN), m_hfile(NULL)
{
      static char *szFilter[] = { "All Files (*.*)", "*.*", "", "" };

      m_ofn.lStructSize          = sizeof(OPENFILENAME);
      m_ofn.hwndOwner           = hwnd;
      m_ofn.hInstance           = NULL;       // Not using templates
                                              // so NULL is OK.
      m_ofn.lpstrFilter          = szFilter[0];
      m_ofn.lpstrCustomFilter  = NULL;
      m_ofn.nMaxCustFilter      = 0;
      m_ofn.nFilterIndex        = 1;
      m_ofn.lpstrFile           = m_szFullName;
      m_ofn.nMaxFile            = sizeof(m_szFullName);
      m_ofn.lpstrFileTitle      = m_szFileName;
      m_ofn.nMaxFileTitle       = sizeof(m_szFileName);
      m_ofn.lpstrInitialDir     = NULL;
      m_ofn.lpstrTitle          = "UUDECODE To";
      m_ofn.Flags               = OFN_HIDEREADONLY |
                                   OFN_NOREADONLYRETURN |
                                   OFN_OVERWRITEPROMPT;
      m_ofn.nFileOffset         = 0;          // Set by dialog.
      m_ofn.nFileExtension      = 0;          // Set by dialog.
      m_ofn.lpstrDefExt         = NULL;       // User chooses total name.
      m_ofn.lCustData           = 0;          // Not using hook.
      m_ofn.lpfnHook            = NULL;
      m_ofn.lpTemplateName      = NULL;       // Not using custom template.
}

/*
      Function: CUUDEC::~CUUDEC
      Description:
          Destructor for CUUDEC class.  Simply make sure the file we
          were working on is closed if this gets called while we're
```

```
                in the middle of something.
*/
CUUDEC::~CUUDEC()
{
    if (m_hfile != NULL) {
        _lclose(m_hfile);
    }
}


/*
     Function: CUUDEC::DecodeLine
     Description:
          Dispatch function for the state machine.  The user of the
          object calls DecodeLine with every line of interest in the
          file, buffer, or other data source.  This is repeated until
          DecodeLine returns a result value other than RESULT_OK.
          RESULT_DONE signals that the end of a uuencoded file has
          been reached and everything was successful.   RESULT_ERROR
          results if a problem cropped up during decoding.
          RESULT_CANCEL is returned if the user hits the cancel button
          in the save file common dialog box.
*/
int CUUDEC::DecodeLine(char * pszLine)
{
     ASSERT(pszLine != NULL);

     switch (m_state) {
          case AWAIT_BEGIN:
               return AwaitBegin(pszLine);
          case DECODING:
               return Decode(pszLine);
          case AWAIT_END:
               return AwaitEnd(pszLine);
          case DONE:
               return RESULT_DONE;
     }
      return RESULT_ERROR;
}


/*
     Function: CUUDEC::AwaitBegin
     Description:
          Waits for a line starting with the characters "begin"
          and containing a file mode and file name.  When this is
          found, it asks the user to confirm the file name and select
          a destination directory for the decode.  The file is then
          opened and the state changed to DECODING.
*/
int CUUDEC::AwaitBegin(char * pszLine)
{
     // Look for a line starting with "begin"
     const char szBegin[] = "begin ";
```

```
    for (int i = 0; i < lstrlen(szBegin); i++) {
        if (pszLine[i] != szBegin[i])
            return RESULT_OK;
    }
    // Found it.  Get the mode and file name.
    int iScanned = sscanf(pszLine, "begin %o %s", &m_iMode,
        m_szFullName);
    if (iScanned != 2)
        return RESULT_OK;
    // Display a save file dialog box to allow the user to confirm
    // the destination file name and specify the destination
    // directory.
    BOOL bResult = GetSaveFileName(&m_ofn);
    // If the user hits cancel, abort the whole thing.
    if (!bResult) {
        m_state = DONE;
        return RESULT_CANCEL;
    }
    // Open the file.  Handle any errors.
    m_hfile = _lcreat(m_szFullName, 0);
    if (m_hfile == HFILE_ERROR) {
        m_state = DONE;
        return RESULT_ERROR;
    }
    m_state = DECODING;
    return RESULT_OK;
}


/*

    Function: CUUDEC::Decode
    Description:
        Decode a line of uuencoded bytes and write them to the
        destination file.  Move to AWAIT_END if the end of the text
        is found.
*/
int CUUDEC::Decode(char * pszLine)
{
    // The first character of the line holds the number of bytes
    // that are encoded on this line.
    int nBytes = DECODE_CHAR(pszLine[0]);
    // If there are no bytes on this line, we're at the end.
    if (nBytes == 0) {
        // Close up the file and handle any error.
        if (_lclose(m_hfile) == HFILE_ERROR) {
            m_hfile = NULL;
            m_state = DONE;
            return RESULT_ERROR;
        }
        else {
            m_hfile = NULL;
            m_state = AWAIT_END;
            return RESULT_OK;
```

```
        }
    }

    // Decode the line of text.
    int iByteIndex = 0;
    int iCharIndex = 1;
    while (iByteIndex < nBytes) {
        // Note that nBytes may not be a multiple of 3, but the
        // number of characters on the line should be a multiple of 4.
        // If the number of encoded bytes is not a multiple of 3 then
        // extra pad characters should have been added to the text
        // by the encoder to make the character count a multiple of 4.
        if (pszLine[iCharIndex] == '\0' ||
            pszLine[iCharIndex + 1] == '\0' ||
            pszLine[iCharIndex + 2] == '\0' ||
            pszLine[iCharIndex + 3] == '\0') {
            // Something went wrong.  Close up the file.
            _lclose(m_hfile);
            m_hfile = NULL;
            m_state = DONE;
            return RESULT_ERROR;
        }
        // Decode the line in 3-byte (=4-character) jumps.
        m_uchDecode[iByteIndex]    =
            (uchar)((DECODE_CHAR(pszLine[iCharIndex]) << 2) |
            (DECODE_CHAR(pszLine[iCharIndex + 1]) >> 4));
        m_uchDecode[iByteIndex + 1] =
            (uchar)((DECODE_CHAR(pszLine[iCharIndex + 1]) << 4) |
            (DECODE_CHAR(pszLine[iCharIndex + 2]) >> 2));
        m_uchDecode[iByteIndex + 2] =
            (uchar)((DECODE_CHAR(pszLine[iCharIndex + 2]) << 6) |
            DECODE_CHAR(pszLine[iCharIndex + 3]));
        iByteIndex += 3;
        iCharIndex += 4;
    }
    // When all the bytes have been decoded, write them out to the
    // file.  Handle any write error.
    if (_lwrite(m_hfile, (LPCSTR)m_uchDecode, nBytes) !=
        (UINT)nBytes) {
        // Close up the file.
        _lclose(m_hfile);
        m_hfile = NULL;
        m_state = DONE;
        return RESULT_ERROR;
    }

    // We're ready for another line.
    return RESULT_OK;
}

/*

    Function: CUUDEC::AwaitEnd
```

```
        Description:
                According to the uuencode format, there should be a
                line with just "end" on it following the text.
*/
int CUUDEC::AwaitEnd(char * pszLine)
{
    // See if the line is "end"
    if (lstrcmp(pszLine, "end") == 0) {
        // Yep.  Whew!  Now we're really done.
        m_state = DONE;
        return RESULT_DONE;
    }
    else {
        // Nope.  Signal an error.  The data didn't follow the
        // standard uuencode format.  The decoded file on disk
        // may or may not be corrupted.  We have no way to tell.
        m_state = DONE;
        return RESULT_ERROR;
    }
}


/*
    Function: CUUDEC::Reset
    Description:
        Resets the decoder state machine.
*/
void CUUDEC::Reset(void)
{
    if (m_hfile != NULL) {
        _lclose(m_hfile);
    }
    m_state = AWAIT_BEGIN;
}


/***********************************************************************
    UUENCODE
***********************************************************************/

/*
    Function: CUUENC::CUUENC
    Description:
        Constructor for CUUENC class.  Puts the state machine into
        the BEGIN state and initializes the OPENFILENAME
        structure used for the save file common dialog box.
*/
CUUENC::CUUENC(HWND hwnd) : m_state(BEGIN), m_hfile(NULL)
{
    static char *szFilter[] = { "All Files (*.*)", "*.*", "", "" };

    m_ofn.lStructSize           = sizeof(OPENFILENAME);
    m_ofn.hwndOwner             = hwnd;
    m_ofn.hInstance             = NULL;      // Not using templates
```

```
                                       // so NULL is OK.
     m_ofn.lpstrFilter       = szFilter[0];
     m_ofn.lpstrCustomFilter = NULL;
     m_ofn.nMaxCustFilter    = 0;
     m_ofn.nFilterIndex      = 1;
     m_ofn.lpstrFile         = m_szFullName;
     m_ofn.nMaxFile          = sizeof(m_szFullName);
     m_ofn.lpstrFileTitle    = m_szFileName;
     m_ofn.nMaxFileTitle     = sizeof(m_szFileName);
     m_ofn.lpstrInitialDir   = NULL;
     m_ofn.lpstrTitle        = "UUDECODE To";
     m_ofn.Flags             = OFN_HIDEREADONLY;
     m_ofn.nFileOffset       = 0;          // Set by dialog box.
     m_ofn.nFileExtension    = 0;          // Set by dialog box.
     m_ofn.lpstrDefExt       = NULL;       // User chooses total name.
     m_ofn.lCustData         = 0;          // Not using hook.
     m_ofn.lpfnHook          = NULL;
     m_ofn.lpTemplateName    = NULL;       // Not using custom template.
}


/*

     Function: CUUENC::~CUUENC
     Description:
          Destructor for CUUENC class.  Simply make sure the file we
          were working on is closed if this gets called while we're
          in the middle of something.
*/
CUUENC::~CUUENC()
{
    if (m_hfile != NULL) {
        _lclose(m_hfile);
    }
}
/*

     Function: CUUENC::EncodeLine
     Description:
          Dispatch function for the state machine.  A user of this
          object calls EncodeLine repeatedly with a data buffer.
          EncodeLine dispatches the call to the right routine based
          on the state machine.  On each call, the state machine returns
          some data to the caller in the provided buffer and a result
          code.  If the code is RESULT_OK, the caller should store
          the returned data somewhere (usually a file or buffer) and
          call EncodeLine again.  Eventually, the end of the input file
          will be reached and EncodeLine will return RESULT_DONE.
          The user can then destroy the object or call CUUENC::Reset
          to reinitialize it.  If an error occurs during processing,
          RESULT_ERROR is returned.  If the user cancels out of the
          file selection dialog box, RESULT_CANCEL is returned.  If the
          supplied buffer is too small to hold the data that needs to
          be returned, RESULT_SMALLBUFFER is returned.  To avoid this,
          it's best to supply 80 characters minimum.
```

```
*/
int CUUENC::EncodeLine(char * pszLine, int nLength)
{
    ASSERT(pszLine != NULL);
    ASSERT(nLength > 0);

    switch (m_state) {
        case BEGIN:
            return Begin(pszLine, nLength);
        case ENCODING:
            return Encode(pszLine, nLength);
        case END:
            return End(pszLine, nLength);
        case DONE:
            return RESULT_DONE;
    }
    return RESULT_ERROR;
}


/*
    Function: CUUENC::Begin
    Description:
        Get the file to encode from the user using a standard file
        dialog, open it, and return the "begin..." line.  Returns
        RESULT_CANCEL if the user cancels out of the file dialog.
*/
int CUUENC::Begin(char *pszLine, int nLength)
{
    // Display an open file dialog box to allow the user to confirm
    // the destination file name and specify the destination
    // directory.
    lstrcpy(m_szFullName, "");
    BOOL bResult = GetOpenFileName(&m_ofn);
    // If the user hit cancel, abort the whole thing.
    if (!bResult) {
        m_state = DONE;
        return RESULT_CANCEL;
    }
    const char szBeginText[] = "begin 600 ";
    if (lstrlen(szBeginText) + lstrlen(m_szFileName) + 1 <=
        nLength) {
        // Open the file.  Handle any errors.
        m_hfile = _lopen(m_szFullName, OF_READ);
        if (m_hfile == HFILE_ERROR) {
            m_state = DONE;
            return RESULT_ERROR;
        }
        // Create the "begin..." line.
        lstrcpy(pszLine, szBeginText);
        lstrcat(pszLine, m_szFileName);
        // Now we're encoding.
        m_state = ENCODING;
```

```
            return RESULT_OK;
    }
    else {
        // The buffer was too small.
        m_state = DONE;
         return RESULT_SMALLBUFFER;
    }
}


/*

    Function: CUUENC::Encode
    Description:
        Reads a text line's-worth of bytes (typically 45) into a
        buffer, encodes them, and returns them to the user.
*/
int CUUENC::Encode(char * pszLine, int nLength)
{
    // Zero out the buffer.
    for (int i = 0; i < sizeof(m_uchBuffer); i++)
        m_uchBuffer[i] = 0;
    // Read a line's-worth of bytes from the file into the buffer.
    int nBytes = _lread(m_hfile, m_uchBuffer,
         sizeof(m_uchBuffer));
    // Handle the potential error.
    if (nBytes == HFILE_ERROR) {
        _lclose(m_hfile);
        m_hfile = NULL;
        m_state = DONE;
         return RESULT_ERROR;
    }
    // Make sure the text line buffer supplied by the user will
    // be large enough to hold all the coded text.  If not, inform
    // the user.
    // Line length is length byte + coded characters + string
    // terminator.
    int iLineLength = 1 +
        (((nBytes / 3) + (nBytes % 3) ? 1 : 0) * 4) + 1;
    if (iLineLength > nLength) {
        if (_lclose(m_hfile) == HFILE_ERROR) {
            m_hfile = NULL;
            m_state = DONE;
             return RESULT_ERROR;
        }
        else {
            m_hfile = NULL;
            m_state = DONE;
             return RESULT_SMALLBUFFER;
        }
    }
    // Encode the number of bytes in this line and store as first
    // character in the line.
     pszLine[0] = (char) ENCODE_BYTE(nBytes);
```

```
    // Encode all the bytes in this line.
    int iByteIndex = 0;
    int iCharIndex = 1;
    while (iByteIndex < nBytes) {
        pszLine[iCharIndex] =
            (char)(ENCODE_BYTE(m_uchBuffer[iByteIndex] >> 2));
        pszLine[iCharIndex + 1] =
            (char)(ENCODE_BYTE((m_uchBuffer[iByteIndex] << 4) |
                (m_uchBuffer[iByteIndex + 1] >> 4)));
        pszLine[iCharIndex + 2] =
            (char)(ENCODE_BYTE((m_uchBuffer[iByteIndex + 1] << 2) |
                (m_uchBuffer[iByteIndex + 2] >> 6)));
        pszLine[iCharIndex + 3] =
            (char)(ENCODE_BYTE(m_uchBuffer[iByteIndex + 2]));
        iByteIndex += 3;
        iCharIndex += 4;
    }
    // Add the line terminator.
    pszLine[iCharIndex] = '\0';
    // See if we hit the end of the file.
    if (nBytes == 0) {
        // Yup, so close it up, handling any error as appropriate.
        if (_lclose(m_hfile) == HFILE_ERROR) {
            m_hfile = NULL;
            m_state = DONE;
            return RESULT_ERROR;
        }
        else {
            m_hfile = NULL;
            m_state = END;
            return RESULT_OK;
        }
    }
    else {
        return RESULT_OK;
    }
}


/*
    Function: CUUENC::End
    Description:
        Returns the "end" line to the caller.
*/
int CUUENC::End(char * pszLine, int nLength)
{
    const char szEndText[] = "end";
    if (lstrlen(szEndText) + 1 <= nLength) {
        lstrcpy(pszLine, szEndText);
        m_state = DONE;
        return RESULT_DONE;
    }
    else {
```

```
            m_state = DONE;
                return RESULT_SMALLBUFFER;
        }
}


/*
        Function: CUUENC::Reset
        Description:
            Resets the encoder state machine.
*/
void CUUENC::Reset(void)
{
    if (m_hfile != NULL) {
        _lclose(m_hfile);
    }
    m_state = BEGIN;
}
```

Mail Extensions: MIME

MIME is new! MIME is hot! MIME allows stodgy old SMTP to carry binary and multimedia data. Read this chapter to find out how MIME works and how we can add MIME support to the Mail Client program.

The RFC 822 message format and the SMTP protocol defined by RFC 821 were released in 1982. It's now 1995, and the world of technology has advanced a great deal during the intervening 13 years.

In 1982, computer interfaces were more primitive than they are now. Although computer graphics existed, graphical user interfaces (GUIs) were not in common use. The Macintosh, which popularized GUIs as we know them today, came out in 1984—remember those "big brother" commercials? Computer multimedia consisting of video, graphics, and sound was the realm of science fiction. Because RFC 822 and SMTP were written in what seems like the dark ages of computer history, they support only the transport of 7-bit US-ASCII messages.

Of course, we're further along the technology advancement curve now, but most of the electronic mail communication that traverses the Internet today still contains ASCII text messages. A UUENCODED file or two may sneak in there somewhere, but for the most part we haven't advanced very far.

During those 13 intervening years, other email systems and protocols were developed. Proprietary LAN email products from manufacturers like Lotus and Microsoft and newer global standards like ISO X.400 appeared. Of course, these systems reaped the benefit of 20/20 hindsight. These newer systems and protocols all include support for binary and multimedia files.

Developing MIME

Not to be outdone by other system developers, the engineers at the Internet Engineering Task Force (IETF) started working on the problem of supporting binary and multimedia file transfers. The IETF is the body that develops and standardizes the Internet protocols. Most RFCs are the result of IETF working groups.

The task facing the IETF engineers was to design a protocol that allowed advanced email services including binary file attachments and multimedia support. The protocol had to remain compatible with the millions of Internet hosts already connected and using RFC 822 and SMTP. Creating a new from-the-ground-up standard would be an easier engineering task, but that approach would entail a massive upgrade, which is difficult to deploy. For example, if you or your mail recipient failed to acquire the new system, you'd have a problem sending email to each other.

The problem is even more difficult because SMTP mail is carried by many intermediate servers, not just the end points. Although you and your friend could buy new email packages to send multimedia email between your sites, your messages could be carried by intermediate systems that still expect RFC 822-compliant messages and connect using SMTP. A totally new standard might require these intermediate systems to upgrade as well.

MIME Services

In spite of these difficulties, the IETF engineers accomplished their task. The result is the Multipurpose Internet Mail Extensions (MIME) format, documented in RFCs 1521 and 1522. MIME is a new message format that is compatible with the older RFC 822 message format.

A MIME message includes additional information that helps MIME-compliant software to interpret the message contents. Older intermediate mail systems don't have to understand the new format, however. To them, a MIME message simply looks like an RFC 822 message, and they simply pass the message on to the destination. MIME allows the installed base of RFC 822 and SMTP software to be preserved whenever possible. Only the software at the end points of the communication (the software that generates and interprets the MIME format) must be upgraded to support MIME.

The MIME format enables the following new or improved mail services:

- *Transmission of binary files:* A message can contain binary data, which is encoded using a method similar to the UUENCODE format.
- *Multipart messages:* A MIME message can contain multiple parts rather than a single message body as RFC 822 specifies.
- *Message typing:* Message parts contain type information that allows the message receiver to display it properly. Common types include plain message text, binary file data, graphics image data, and video data. Each part of a multipart message has its own type information. You can compose one message containing text, video, and a binary file attachment. New types will be added to the standard as needed in the future.
- *New character sets:* RFC 822 allows only US-ASCII characters in message bodies. MIME messages specify the character set used to compose text message bodies. Message receivers can display the message using the appropriate character set. This feature allows foreign language communication, enabling the Internet to take its place as the universal global data network.
- *And much more:* The MIME format supports future growth. Different services are already starting to appear, based on the MIME framework. These services include message encryption and authentication and electronic commerce. Using the flexible typing feature of MIME message body parts, just about anything can be represented as a MIME type.

Basic Message Structure

The MIME message structure is documented in RFC 1521. The following sections of this chapter include a summarized description of the MIME format. For a detailed description of the format, consult RFC 1521.

The MIME format is based on the RFC 822 message format. It contains a message header followed by a message body. The MIME message format simply adds a few additional header fields to an RFC 822 message to identify the message as a MIME message. These header fields allow the receiver to parse the structure of the message body.

MIME header names follow the RFC 822 rules. They are case-insensitive and must be followed by a colon, then the header contents. MIME headers generally contain structured rather than freeform contents. RFC 1521 defines the parsing rules for each header.

MIME-Version Header Field

The MIME-Version header field identifies a message to receivers as a MIME message and specifies the version of the MIME standard to which the message complies. The current MIME version is 1.0. The MIME-Version header field is formatted as follows:

```
MIME-Version: 1.0
```

A message that does not contain the MIME-Version header field may be interpreted as a simple RFC 822 message by a MIME-capable receiver.

Content-Type Header Field

Each MIME message body has an associated type that tells the MIME receiver how to display or manipulate the body. The Content-Type header field identifies the message body type and provides other information that may be associated with that type. Here are some sample Content-Type headers:

```
Content-Type: text/plain; charset=us-ascii
Content-Type: image/jpeg
Content-Type: video/mpeg
Content-Type: multipart/mixed
Content-Type: application/octet-stream
```

A MIME type is composed of two type names separated by a forward slash character (/). The first name is the type name, and the second is the subtype name. Type names describe the general format of the data while subtypes give additional format information. The type name is enough to allow a receiver to assess its ability to "display" (is audio really "displayed"?) the data. For instance, when a MIME user agent written for a character-mode terminal encounters an image type, it knows that it won't be able to display it, whatever the format specified by the subtype.

Following the type and subtype is a series of optional parameters. Each parameter has a parameter name followed by an equal sign (=), followed by the parameter value. Parameters are separated from each other and the type and subtype by semicolons.

Parameters specify additional information that may be necessary for the receiver to display the type. In this first example above, the text/plain type uses a "charset" parameter to specify the character set of the text data.

A few types are used frequently. The text/plain type is the most-used type. It describes plain, unformatted text. The application/octet-stream type describes a stream of binary data and is often used as the type for general-purpose file attachments. The image/jpeg and video/mpeg types describe a particular image or video format. Other image and video subtypes exist as well.

Sometimes the composing user agent has a choice between two different types. For instance, if a JPEG image is attached to a message, a user agent could describe the data using the application/octet-stream or image/jpeg type. A simple user agent may just describe all attachments using the application/octet-stream type, preferring to let the receiving user handle it. A sophisticated user agent may notice that the attached file is an image, so it will use the image/jpeg type.

The Content-Type header field is optional. If it is not present, the body type defaults to text/plain using the US-ASCII character set.

Content-Transfer-Encoding Header Field

The Content-Transfer-Encoding header identifies an encoding for the data in the body. Because MIME messages usually contain binary data of some sort (a file, graphic image, stream of audio, and so on), the message body often must be encoded to comply with the RFC 822 format requirements.

The Content-Transfer-Encoding header field simply specifies an encoding format. The format name is case-insensitive. Here are some examples of the Content-Transfer-Encoding header field:

```
Content-Transfer-Encoding:  7-bit
Content-Transfer-Encoding:  quoted-printable
Content-Transfer-Encoding:  BASE64
```

MIME allows several different encoding formats. The sender can choose the encoding format, depending on the format of the data being sent. Of the five standard MIME encoding formats, three are used most often: 7-bit, quoted-printable, and base64. The following sections describe these formats.

Two other formats, 8-bit and binary, describe binary data that is not encoded. These encodings may be used for messages when SMTP is not the message transport protocol (remember that SMTP only allows 7-bit ASCII characters in message headers and bodies). Because the other encodings expand the message size, the 8-bit and binary encodings are more efficient if the sender knows that the message will not have to cross any SMTP mail transport links. Most often, special purpose systems use these formats.

The Content-Transfer-Encoding header field is optional. If it is not present, the encoding of the body defaults to 7-bit.

7-Bit

The 7-bit format identifies data that was not encoded. It is compatible with both RFC 822's and SMTP's requirements for short lines of ASCII text. The 7-bit format is commonly used for text messages.

Quoted-Printable

The quoted-printable encoding technique represents each byte of data by an equal sign (=) followed by two hexadecimal digits representing the byte value. Bytes with values in the range of printable ASCII characters (33 through 60 and 62 through 127, inclusive) can be represented by their ASCII equivalents. RFC 1521 also defines some other rules dealing with line breaks and the encoding of white space characters that occur at the end of a line. Consult RFC 1521 for the detailed encoding rules.

The quoted-printable encoding format typically is used to encode text messages that use 8-bit characters in addition to US-ASCII characters. Characters in the ASCII character set range are represented by themselves (they are not encoded); all other characters are encoded as an equal sign followed by two hexadecimal digits. Because many of the characters in a text message will be ASCII characters which will remain unencoded, a message encoded in this manner is often readable by a human when displayed by a non-MIME mail user agent. The user will see a few encoded characters, but most of the message will be readable.

A common example of this situation is when a message is composed in a foreign character set (ISO 8859-1, for instance, which is very similar to the Windows ANSI character set) and sent to a user who reads mail on a dialup terminal connection. Although the terminal won't be capable of displaying the newer ISO 8859-1 characters, the rest of the text will be readable.

The quoted-printable encoding format is not well-suited to encoding arbitrary binary data. Because three characters represent each encoded byte (the equal sign and two hexadecimal digits), this method greatly expands the size of the encoded data. This method is acceptable for textual data that contains a few accented characters or non-standard punctuation. It is not a good choice for a large binary file where every other byte needs to be encoded.

Base64

The Base64 encoding technique is used to encode data that people do not need to read. This encoding format is similar to the UUENCODE format discussed in the last chapter, but it cures some of the UUENCODE format's problems. Let's review the major problems.

The technique used by the UUENCODE format is generally sound. The UUENCODE format is simple and only results in roughly a 33 percent increase in size over the raw data. The UUENCODE format has a fatal flaw, however: It relies on the ASCII character set. Encoding is performed by taking data in 6-bit groups and adding the value of the 6 bits to the value of the ASCII space character (32 decimal).

Although the ASCII character set is the most common character encoding system in the world, not all computers use it. Before ASCII was developed, many computer systems used their own proprietary character sets. For instance, many IBM mainframes use the EBCDIC character set. In addition, not all character sets contain the same characters. Although most character sets include uppercase and lowercase roman letters, many character sets also include other punctuation marks or symbols.

For typical text email, the difference between character sets is usually not a problem. A version of SMTP running on an IBM mainframe using EBCDIC will translate between ASCII and EBCDIC for ingoing and outgoing messages, for instance. In cases where the translation software finds a character that cannot be represented equivalently during the translation, a multiple character sequence may be inserted or the character simply may be dropped. In most cases, this translation won't cause much of a problem. A human reading the message will often be able to understand it even when a translation glitch has occurred. For binary data encoded in the message, however, even the smallest alteration of the message text causes data corruption.

The UUENCODE format includes many characters from the ASCII character set that cannot be equivalently represented in other character sets. The Base64 encoding format attempts to retain the simplicity of the UUENCODE format but uses a set of characters that are equivalently represented in most character sets.

As I mentioned earlier, the Base64 encoding format is similar to the UUENCODE format. Groups of three bytes are split into four 6-bit encoding units just as in the UUENCODE algorithm. These 6-bit units are then encoded using the mapping shown in Table 12.1. All of the characters used to represent encoded data are roman letters, numbers, or the slash or equal character. These characters are included in every character set, so a message that undergoes translation from ASCII to EBCDIC or other character set won't be corrupted.

For instance, if the character "A" appears in the encoded message, it will be appear as an ASCII "A" on one side of the translation border. On the other side, it will appear as an EBCDIC "A." Although the character set value used to represent the "A" will change, a decoder on either side of the border knows that the "A" represents 6-bits of binary data with a value of 0. Of course, a decoder on the EBCDIC side of the border will have to recognize that it is interpreting a message body using the EBCDIC character set rather than the ASCII character set; but the data contained in the message will cross the border with no problems.

Table 12.1 The Base64 mapping

Value	Encoding	Value	Encoding	Value	Encoding	Value	Encoding
0	A	17	R	34	i	51	z
1	B	18	S	35	j	52	0
2	C	19	T	36	k	53	1
3	D	20	U	37	l	54	2
4	E	21	V	38	m	55	3
5	F	22	W	39	n	56	4
6	G	23	X	40	o	57	5
7	H	24	Y	41	p	58	6
8	I	25	Z	42	q	59	7
9	J	26	a	43	r	60	8
10	K	27	b	44	s	61	9
11	L	28	c	45	t	62	0
12	M	29	d	46	u	63	/
13	N	30	e	47	v		
14	O	31	f	48	w	Padding	=
15	P	32	g	49	x		
16	Q	33	h	50	y		

Unlike the UUENCODE format, the Base64 format has no concept of lines of characters. Although line breaks can (and should) be inserted to keep line lengths under 80 characters (for transmission using SMTP), all white space and line breaks are ignored during decoding. The Base64 format does begin each line with a character representing the length of the data encoded on a given line. The data is simply streamed out of the encoder, with line breaks inserted where necessary.

The end of Base64 encoded data is marked by the end of the message text or an equal character (=). This character pads the end of the text when the original data length is not a multiple of three. Three possible situations arise when the end of the data is reached:

- The original data length is a multiple of three. The result of the encoding is four valid characters. No padding is needed and the end of the data is signaled by the end of the message body.
- The last encoding group contains one valid data byte. Two zero-bytes are added to the encoding group. The result of the encoding is two characters that contain valid data. The other two characters are represented by the equal character to signal to the decoder that they do not contain any valid data.
- The last encoding group contains two valid data bytes. One zero-byte is added to the encoding group. The result of the encoding is three characters that contain valid data. The final, fourth character is represented by the equal characters to signal to the decoder that it does not contain any valid data.

Because the equal character represents padding, a decoder can stop processing input when it reaches the equal character.

Sample Message

Figure 12.1 shows a sample message. This message contains a text/plain body using the ISO 8859-1 character set, encoded with the quoted-printable encoding format. Note that the message is very readable even though it is encoded using the quoted-printable encoding format. A user reading this message would have only a small amount of trouble deciphering it (assuming the user knew a bit of Swedish).

Multipart Message Structure

Although MIME supports the use of exotic character sets and the encoding of binary files, MIME's greatest capability is its support for multipart messages.

Figure 12.1

A text/plain message with the ISO 8859-1 character set, encoded using the quoted-printable encoding format.

```
Date: Sun, 20 Aug 95 18:49:12 pdt
From: Dave Roberts <dave@droberts.com>
To: dave@droberts.com
Subject: Quoted Printable Example
Message-ID: <082095184912.0@droberts.com>
MIME-Version: 1.0
X-Mail-Agent: Mail Client
X-Mail-Agent: From the book, "Developing for
the Internet with Winsock" WinsockX-Mail-Agent:
By Dave Roberts
Content-Type: text/plain; charset=iso-8859-1
Content-Transfer-Encoding: quoted-printable

This is an example of quoted-printable
encoding.  The following word, "f=F6nster", is
Swedish for "window".  The character after the
"f" is an o with two small dots over it,
character
246 decimal in ISO 8859-1.
```

Multipart messages can include binary attachments along with text messages, image data that can serve to diagram what is explained in the text, or five video clips. Each part of a message may be related to the other parts or may have no connection whatsoever. Although most messages contain at least one text part explaining to the destination user what the other parts are, this is not a requirement. Figure 12.2 shows an example of a multipart MIME message.

Body Parts

Each section of a multipart body is called a *body part*. A body part is a similar to a MIME formatted message. A body part has its own header and body, separated by a blank line. The header of a body part contains standard MIME header fields that describe the type and encoding format of the body part. In Figure 12.2, the first body part is a text/plain body part encoded using the standard 7-bit format. The second body part is a file attachment given the application/octet-stream type and encoded using the Base64 encoding format. A receiving mail user agent uses the body part headers to display each body part.

A body part does not have to include MIME type and encoding headers. In this case, the body part starts with the blank line that separates the missing headers from the body of the body part (that sounds a little redundant). The MIME type defaults to text/plain using the US-ASCII character set and the encoding defaults to 7-bit.

Figure 12.2

An sample
multipart
message
containing a
text/plain
body part and
an
application/
octet-stream
body part.

```
Date: Sun, 20 Aug 95 19:15:53 pdt
From: Dave Roberts <dave@droberts.com>
To: dave@droberts.com
Subject: Multipart Example
Message-ID: <082095191553.0@droberts.com>
MIME-Version: 1.0
X-Mail-Agent: Mail Client
X-Mail-Agent: From the book, "Developing for the Internet with Winsock"
X-Mail-Agent: By Dave Roberts
Content-Type: multipart/mixed;
        boundary="=_ Boundary KTwEv,JE?148K4Gac"


-=_ Boundary KTwEv,JE?148K4Gac
Content-Type: text/plain; charset=us-ascii
Content-Transfer-Encoding: 7bit

This is a sample multipart message.  The first part contains a
text body part and the second contains a binary file attachment.


-=_ Boundary KTwEv,JE?148K4Gac
Content-Type: application/octet-stream
Content-Transfer-Encoding: base64
```

```
W211bnVdDQptZW51aXR1bT13aW5jZCwgV21uZG93cB3L0NEDQptZW51aXR1bT1kb3Nj
ZCwgRE9TIHcvQOQgDQptZW51aXR1bT13aW5kb3dzLCBXaW5kb3dzDQptZW51aXR1bT1k
b3MsIERPUwOKbWVudWRlZmF1bHQ9d21uY2QsMjANCgOKW2NvbW1vbl0NCkRPUz1ISUdI
LFVNQgOKREVWSUNFPUM6XHdpbmRvd3NcSElNRU0uU11TIC9ZX20bWVttOm9mwZgOKREVW
SUNFPUM6XHdpbmRvd3NcRU1NMzg2LkVYRSBSQUONCkJVRkZFU1M9NDAsMAOKZm1sZXM9
NTANCkxBU1REUk1WRT1aDQpGQOJTPTE2LDANC1NIRUxMPUM6XERPU1xDT01NQU5ELKNP
TSBD01xET1NcIC91OjEwMjQgL3ANCnJlbSBBERVZJQOU9QzpcRU1ERTIzMDBcRU1ERTIz
MDAuU11TDQpERVZJQOVISUdIPUM6XERPU1xBT1NJL1NZUwOKREVWSUNFSE1HSD1D01xE
T1NcUOVUVkVSLkVYRQOKU1RBQOtTPTksMjU2DQpbZG9zXQOKW3dpbmRv3NdDQpbZG9z
Y2RdDQpSRUOgKiogRnVOdXJlIIERvbWFpbiBQb3d1clNDUOkhIHYOLjAgU3VwcG9ydCAq
KgOKREVWSUNFSE1HSD1D01xQV1JTQ1NJIVxEQOFNOTUwLkVYRSAvQOEwEwMCA1IAOKREVW
SUNFSE1HSD1D01xQV1JTQ1NJIVxBU1BJRkNBBTS5TWVMgLOQgLO8gDQpERVZJQOVISUdI
PUM6XFBXU1NDU0khXEZEQOQuU11TIC9EOk1TQOQwMDAxDQpSRUOgKioqKiBFbmQg
UG93ZXJTQ1NJISB2NC4wIFN1cHBvcnQgKioqKgOKW3dpbmNkXQOKUkVNICoqIEZ1
dHVyZSBEb21haW4gUG93ZXJTQ1NJISB2NC4wIFN1cHBvcnQgKioNCkRFVk1DRUhJR0g9
QzpcUFdSU0NTSFcRENBTTk1MC5FWEUgL0NBMDAgNSANCkRFVK1DRUhJR0g9QzpcUFdS
U0NTSFcQVNQSUZDQU0uU11TIC9EIC9PIA0KREVWSUNFSE1HSD1D01xQV1JTQ1NJIVxG
RENE1NZUyAvRDpNU0ONEMDAwMQOKUkVNICoqKioqIKioqIogRW5kIFBvd2VyU0NTSEgdjQu
MCBTdXBwb3J0ICoqKioqKioNC1tjb21tb25dDQpkZXZpZ2U9Yzpcd21uZG93c1xpZZNNo
bHAuc31zDQo=
```

```
-=_ Boundary KTwEv,JE?148K4Gac-
```

MIME body parts are not full RFC 822 messages in themselves. Body part headers do not include the standard RFC 822 header fields (From, To, Date, and so on) and may be omitted altogether if the body part is compatible with the MIME header defaults.

Multipart Structure

As shown in Figure 12.2, multipart messages use the primary type "multipart." The multipart type signals the receiver that the message contains multiple sections. The multipart primary type has several different subtypes, each of which tells the receiving user agent the relationship between each of the multiple body parts.

For instance, the "alternative" subtype tells the receiving user agent that every body part contains a different version of the same information; each version is formatted differently. The receiving user agent can then choose the version of the message to display. For instance, a text message may be sent both with and without auxiliary formatting information (bold and italic characters, for instance). If the message is displayed on a character-mode terminal, the version without formatting information would be used. If the message is displayed on a PC using a graphical user interface, the version with formatting information would be used.

Another example might be a message that included video data and text data communicating the same information. If the message is displayed on a multimedia workstation, the video data would be played for the user. If the message is displayed on a character-mode terminal, just the text data would be displayed.

The "parallel" subtype tells the receiving user agent that the body parts should be displayed at the same time, if possible. For instance, a message might contain both a graphic image and an audio clip which explains the contents of the image. Using the "parallel" subtype, the user could view the image while listening to the audio. In some cases, parallel display of multiple body parts is not possible and the parts would simply be displayed sequentially.

In Figure 12.2, the "mixed" subtype tells the receiver that the body parts have no relationship to each other and can be presented in any way. In most cases, this subtype causes the receiver to display the body parts sequentially.

All messages of the multipart type follow the same structure, even if the subtypes are different. This format allows a receiver to parse a multipart message even when the subtype is unknown.

Boundaries

The multipart type uses a "boundary" parameter to specify a character sequence that separates each body part. In Figure 12.2 this sequence is:

```
=_ Boundary KTwEv.JE?148K4Gac
```

The character sequence can be from 1 to 70 characters long, chosen from a set of letters, numbers, and some punctuation marks, as defined in RFC 1521. The boundary characters can be a readable string (like "boundary") or a set of random characters (like the end of the boundary example above). Often, the composing mail user agent will generate at least a portion of the boundary randomly to reduce the chance that a line of data within a body part actually has the same data pattern. Alternatively, the message sender can scan the body part data to ensure that no conflicts occur between the boundary and a real line of data.

In the body of the message itself, a line that contains the boundary characters preceded by two minus characters (--) marks the beginning of a body part. A line that contains the boundary characters surrounded by two sets of two minus characters marks the end of all body parts in the multipart body.

For example:

```
—Boundary
Content-Type: text/plain

This is a text body part.

—Boundary
Content-Type: text/plain

This is a second text body part.

—Boundary—
```

The CRLF pairs both before and after the line that contains the boundary characters are considered part of the boundary itself. This convention allows the situation where the preceding body part does not end with a CRLF pair. If the body part does end with its own CRLF (as most text body parts do), two CRLF pairs will be inserted. One CRLF pair is part of the body part, and one is part of the boundary.

For example, the line of text just before the boundary in this example does not end with CRLF. The CRLF after the period belongs to the boundary.

```
This line doesn't end in CRLF.
—Boundary
```

In this example, the line of text does end with CRLF. The blank line preceeding the boundary belongs to the boundary, while the CRLF after the period belongs to the text.

```
This line ends with CRLF.

—Boundary
```

Recursive Encoding

A body part may itself have a multipart type, which allows the recursive encoding of multipart messages. The recursion depth has no limit. The only requirement is that each multipart boundary must be different so that the decoder can determine the recursive structure correctly. Figure 12.3 shows a message that contains a multipart/mixed body part as a section of another multipart/mixed message.

Adding MIME Support to Mail Client

Our Mail Client application contains simple MIME support. Mail Client implements these MIME features:

- Support for the ISO 8859-1 character set using the Windows ANSI character set. ISO 8859-1 characters are encoded using the quoted-printable encoding format.
- Attachment of binary files to messages using multipart messages. Files are automatically encoded using the Base64 encoding format.
- Parsing of all received messages.
- Decoding and display of all text messages, if possible. The user is warned before the display of all unknown text subtypes and character sets.
- Treatment of all unknown types as file attachments. The user is given the opportunity to save the decoded body part to a file for later viewing using a different application.

Although Mail Client only supports a handful of services, it's a start. For instance, you could easily add a JPEG image decoder to the program so that body parts of the image/jpeg type could be viewed from within the program itself. Alternatively, you could write a user configurable mapping between MIME types and "helper" applications. When the user tries to view a body part of an unknown type, the mapping table is consulted, the body part is saved to a file, and the helper application associated with the type is launched by Mail Client to view the saved body part.

Figure 12.3

Multipart body
parts may be
recursively
encoded.

```
Date: Sun, 20 Aug 95 19:16:00 pdt
From: Dave Roberts <dave@droberts.com>
To: dave@droberts.com
Subject: Multipart Example
Message-ID: <082095191600.4@droberts.com>
MIME-Version: 1.0
X-Mail-Agent: Mail Client
X-Mail-Agent: From the book, "Developing for the Internet with Winsock"
X-Mail-Agent: By Dave Roberts
Content-Type: multipart/mixed;
       boundary="=_ Boundary kow29Sia40SwsAG"


--=_ Boundary kow29Sia40SwsAG
Content-Type: text/plain; charset=us-ascii
Content-Transfer-Encoding: 7bit

This is a sample recursive multipart message.

--=_ Boundary kow29Sia40SwsAG
Content-Type: multipart/mixed;
       boundary="=_ Boundary Ai80,i934JEk20kls?"


--=_ Boundary Ai80,i934JEk20kls?
Content-Type: text/plain

This is a text/plain body part inside a multipart inside
a multipart.  The character set defaults to US-ASCII.
The encoding defaults to 7-bit.

--=_ Boundary Ai80,i934JEk20kls?

This is a second text/plain body part inside a multipart
inside a multipart.  It has no headers.
The type defaults to text/plain.
The character set defaults to US-ASCII.
The encoding defaults to 7-bit.
It does not end with a CRLF (remember that the
CRLF separating this line from the boundary
is part of the boundary itself).
--=_ Boundary Ai80,i934JEk20kls?-

--=_ Boundary kow29Sia40SwsAG-
```

Our Strategy

MIME support within the Mail Client application starts with the MAILEDIT.CPP and MAILVIEW.CPP files. Code within the MAILEDIT.CPP file (Listing 9.8) handles the generation and encoding of MIME messages. Code within the MAILVIEW.CPP file (Listing 10.4) handles the decoding and viewing of MIME messages. A handful of support files provide MIME parsing and Base64 encoding and decoding functionality.

The following sections describe the message composition and parsing functionality. Note that some of the files mentioned in these sections were presented in earlier chapters.

Composing MIME Messages

The **OnMailSend** function within the MAILEDIT.CPP file (Listing 9.8) collects the addressing, subject, and file attachment information from the user. It then generates a MIME-compliant message and creates a **CSMTP** object to send the message on its way.

Mail Client is capable of generating two types of messages:

* *Simple messages with a single-part message body of type text/plain.* The US-ASCII and ISO 8859-1 character sets are supported for the creation of the message. If a message uses ISO 8859-1 characters, they are encoded using the quoted-printable encoding format. Figure 12.1 shows an example of such a message.
* *Multipart messages containing text parts and file attachments.* The main message is given the multipart/mixed type. The text body part is given a text/plain type. As with the simple message type, the text may use either US-ASCII or ISO 8859-1 characters. If ISO 8859-1 characters are used, they are encoded using the quoted-printable format. The file attachment body part is given the application/octet-stream type. The file is encoded using the Base64 encoding format; the file is unconditionally Base64 encoded, even if it is a text file. Figure 12.2 shows an example of a message containing a file attachment.

The composition process is straightforward. Code within **OnMailSend** first generates a standard RFC 822 message header block. The header block contains Date, From, To, Cc, Subject, and Message-ID header fields.

Next, the code adds a MIME-Version header. **OnMailSend** generates MIME-compliant messages even when the message contains a single body of US-ASCII text. After the MIME-Version header, **OnMailSend** generates some X-Mail-Agent lines that identify the user agent (Mail Client) used to compose the message.

Once **OnMailSend** generates the header lines common to all messages, the code branches depending on whether or not a file was attached to the message by the user. If the message does not include an attached file, **OnMailSend** calls **OutputMessageText** to write the text portion of the message to the output file. **OutputMessageText** writes a Content-Type header and Content-Transfer-Encoding header to the output file, followed by a blank line and then the message text. If the message does not include an attached file, the Content-Type and Content-Transfer-Encoding headers become part of the main message header block. We'll come back to the **OutputMessageText** function in a moment.

If the message includes an attached file, **OnMailSend** outputs a multipart/mixed Content-Type header with a boundary character sequence. The boundary sequence is generated using the **CreateBoundary** function. The multipart/mixed Content-Type header field becomes part of the main message header block. **OnMailSend** then outputs a couple of blank lines and the message boundary character sequence.

After the boundary sequence is output, **OnMailSend** calls **OutputMessageText** to write the text portion of the message as the first body part of the multipart message. In this case, the text/plain Content-Type and Content-Transfer-Encoding headers that are output by **OutputMessageText** become the headers for the first body part.

When the text portion of the multipart message is output, **OnMailSend** writes a second boundary character sequence to end the first body part and begin the second. **OnMailSend** then calls **OutputAttachment** to write the file attachment body part.

The **OutputAttachment** function is similar to the **OutputMessageText** function. It writes an application/octet-stream Content-Type header field, followed by a Content-Transfer-Encoding header field. The Content-Transfer-Encoding header field indicates that the second body part is encoded using the Base64 encoding format. Once the second body part headers have been written, a blank line is output, followed by the Base64-encoded file attachment.

After the file attachment body part is written, **OnMailSend** writes the final boundary marker that indicates the end of all the body parts for the message. The output file is closed, and a **CSMTP** object is created to send the message.

OutputMessageText Function

The **OutputMessageText** function writes the text portion of an outgoing message. Before generating the headers and writing the message text to the output file, **OutputMessageText** determines whether the message contains any ISO 8859-1 characters.

Each line of the message text is retrieved from the window edit control. The **OutputMessageText** function looks at each character in the line to determine if it has its high-bit set. If so, the character is not US-ASCII; it is assumed to be ISO 8859-1. **OutputMessageText** sets the **bISOCharset** flag and starts to generate the message.

Once the character set is determined, **OutputMessageText** writes the headers to the file. The Content-Type header specifies the text/plain subtype using either the US-ASCII or ISO 8859-1 character sets, depending on the state of the **bISOCharset** flag. The Content-Transfer-Encoding header specifies 7-bit encoding if the **bISOCharset** flag is **FALSE** (US-ASCII needs no encoding) or quoted-printable encoding if the flag is **TRUE** (the ISO characters need to be encoded).

Next, **OutputMessageText** writes a blank line to separate the headers from the text body. The blank line is followed by each line from the edit control. If the **bISOCharset** flag is **TRUE**, each line of text is encoded using the quoted-printable encoding rules before it is written. If the **bISOCharset** flag is **FALSE**, the lines are written without any further processing.

Viewing MIME Messages

The MAILVIEW.CPP file (Listing 10.4) displays MIME messages when the user asks to view them. When the user selects a message to view in the mailbox window, the Mail Client program creates a message viewer window. It then passes a pointer to the message file name in the **lParam** parameter of the **WM_CREATE** message sent to the new window. The viewer window procedure, **ViewerWndProc**, sends the **WM_CREATE** message to the **OnCreate** function in the MAILVIEW.CPP file.

The **OnCreate** function allocates a structure to hold variables local to the viewer window. It stores a pointer to this structure in the Windows data structure associated with the window. Next, **OnCreate** creates a read-only edit control in the client portion of the viewer window. The edit control is used to view the text portions of messages.

After the edit control is created, **OnCreate** constructs the full path name of the message text file. **OnCreate** then creates a **CMIMEMsg** object and passes the message path name to the **Parse** member function. The **CMIMEMsg** class parses the MIME message and allows the rest of the viewer code to determine the types and encoding of the various body parts contained in the message.

After the message is parsed, **OnCreate** calls the **FirstPart** member function of the **CMIMEMsg** object. This function sets an internal pointer to the first body part of a multipart message or the only body part of a simple message. Finally, **OnCreate** calls the **ViewMessagePart** function to display the first body part.

Once the viewer window displays the first body part, the user may select the Mail/Next Body Part or Mail/First Body Part menu choice to move through each body part contained in the message. These menu choices cause the **OnCommand** function to execute the **FirstPart** and **NextPart** member functions of the **CMIMEMsg** class to step through the message body parts. (The **OnCommand** function handles all **WM_COMMAND** messages for the viewer window.) After each call to **FirstPart** and **NextPart**, **OnCommand** invokes the **ViewMessagePart** function to display the body part.

CMIMEMsg Class

An object of the **CMIMEMsg** class is used to parse each message that the viewer window displays. The **CMIMEMsg** class is defined in the CMIME.H and CMIME.CPP files, as shown in Listings 12.1 and 12.2. The **CMIMEMsg** class provides an interface to a tree-like data structure constructed out of **CMIMEBodyPart** objects. A **CMIMEBodyPart** object is used to represent each body part in the message. The tree-like data structure mimics the recursive structure of the MIME message itself.

Figure 12.4 shows the data structure as it would be allocated for a simple text-only message. The **CMIMEMsg** object points to the first body part in the message. In this example, the message has only one body part. The **CMIMEBodyPart** object stores the type and encoding attributes associated with the body part, as parsed from the MIME headers contained in the message. Figure 12.4 shows the data structure that would be constructed for the message shown in Figure 12.1.

Of course, more complex structures are possible if the MIME message contains multiple body parts. Figure 12.5 shows the structure that would be created for the message shown in Figure 12.2.

In Figure 12.5, the first **CMIMEBodyPart** object represents the top-level multi-part body part. The **m_pFirstChild** member of the multipart object points to another **CMIMEBodyPart** object that represents the first body part of the multi-part message. The first body part is a text/plain body part using the US-ASCII character set, encoded in standard 7-bit format.

The **m_pSibling** member of the text/plain body part points to the second body part. The second body part is an application/octet-stream body part encoded using the Base64 encoding format.

The data structure shown in Figure 12.6 would be generated to represent the message shown in Figure 12.3. This tree-like structure can be extended to handle any level of multipart recursion.

The message is parsed recursively. First, the **CMIMEMsg** object creates a **CMIMEBodyPart** object, passing the file name and starting and ending character index of the body part within the file to the **CMIMEBodyPart** constructor. The starting and ending character positions define the body part within the larger overall message. For the **CMIMEBodyPart** object created by the **CMIMEMsg**

Figure 12.4

The data structure constructed to represent a single body-part message.

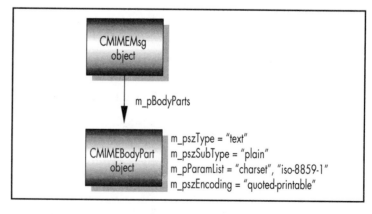

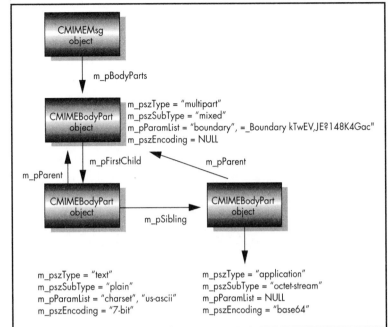

Figure 12.5

The data structure constructed to represent a multipart message with two body parts.

object, the starting character is 0 and the ending character is -1. The **CMIMEBodyPart** object replaces the -1 ending position with the length of the file when it begins parsing.

Next, the **CMIMEMsg** object invokes the **CMIMEBodyPart::Parse** function on the **CMIMEBodyPart** object. This function parses the body part as defined by the starting and ending character indexes.

The **Parse** function parses the body part headers using the **ParseHeaders** member function. This function finds the MIME headers (Content-Type and Content-Transfer-Encoding) and stores the body part type, subtype, parameters, and encoding in **CMIMEBodyPart** member variables.

If the body part type is "multipart," the **Parse** function calls the **ParseMultipart** function. The **ParseMultipart** function uses the boundary character string stored in the current body part parameter list to locate each recursive body part within the current body part. As the recursive (or child) body parts are found, new **CMIMEBodyPart** objects are created to represent each one. The starting and ending character positions of the child body part within the message file are passed to the **CMIMEBodyPart** constructor. The first child body part is linked to the

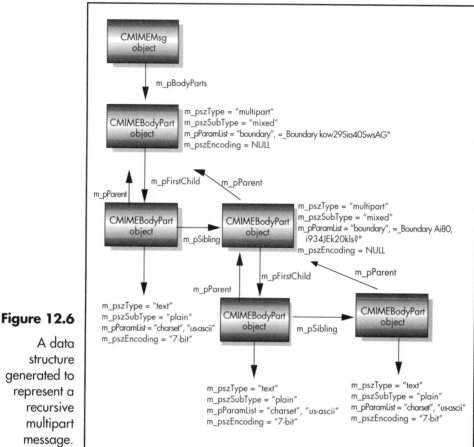

Figure 12.6

A data
structure
generated to
represent a
recursive
multipart
message.

parent body part using the **m_pFirstChild** pointer. Subsequent body parts are
linked to each other using the **m_pSibling** pointer in each child.

After the child body parts are found, the **Parse** member function is invoked on
each child **CMIMEBodyPart** object. This function starts the recursive parsing
process that generates the tree-like data structure shown in the previous figures.

ViewMessagePart Function

After the message is parsed, the viewer window code invokes the **ViewMessagePart**
function. The **ViewMessagePart** function displays the current body part in the
viewer window. The current body part changes as the user selects the Mail/Next
Body Part or Mail/First Body Part menu choice.

The **ViewMessagePart** function first gets a pointer to the current message body part from the **CMIMEMsg** object. Next, **ViewMessagePart** deletes all of the data in the viewer edit window. This data was the previous body part's data, so it must be disposed of before the current body part is displayed.

Once the edit window data is destroyed, the **ViewMessagePart** function determines the current body part's MIME type. The body part type should never be "multipart." The **CMIMEMsg::FirstPart** and **CMIMEMsg::NextPart** functions automatically skip over "multipart" nodes in the **CMIMEBodyPart** tree, moving on to their children instead. The current node must always be a "displayable" body part. The remainder of the display process depends on the body part type.

If the body part is a text body part, **ViewMessagePart** attempts to display it in the viewer edit control. First, **ViewMessagePart** checks the body part subtype and character set. If the subtype is not "plain" or the character set is not "us-ascii" or "iso-8859-1," **ViewMessagePart** warns the user that Mail Client does not include specific code to handle the body part. It informs the user that Mail Client will attempt to display the body part but because the subtype or character set is unfamiliar, the body part may not display correctly. This behavior demonstrates the usefulness of the MIME type/subtype system. Even if the viewer code does not recognize the specific body part subtype, it knows the body part contains textual information and tries to do the right thing.

After **ViewMessagePart** checks the subtype and character set and displays any necessary warning messages, it puts the message text into the viewer edit control. One by one, **ViewMessagePart** retrieves lines of text from the body part, decodes them, and puts the decoded text into the edit control. The decoding process handles all of the encoding formats (Base64, quoted-printable, 8-bit, 7-bit, and binary).

If the body part is not a text body part, **ViewMessagePart** treats it as an application/octet-stream body part. **ViewMessagePart** inserts the text "*** NON-TEXT DATA ***" in the viewer edit control and asks the user if the body part data should be saved to a file. If so, **ViewMessagePart** allows the user to enter a file name using the common file save dialog. If not, **ViewMessagePart** skips the file save operation and exits.

If the user enters a file name in which to save the data, **ViewMessagePart** opens the file. **ViewMessagePart** then retrieves the body text line by line, decodes it, and writes the decoded data to the file. All MIME encoding formats are supported.

When the decoding process is finished, the output file is closed and the **ViewMessagePart** function returns.

Base64 Encoding and Decoding

Short routines in the MAILEDIT.CPP and MAILVIEW.CPP files handle encoding and decoding of the quoted-printable encoding format. This encoding format is fairly simple; we will not discuss it further.

Base64 encoding and decoding is handled by the **CBase64Enc** and **CBase64Dec** classes. These classes are similar to the **CUUENC** and **CUUDEC** classes used to handle the UUENCODE format. Listings 12.3 and 12.4 show the CBASE64.H and CBASE64.CPP files that implement these classes.

The **CBase64Enc** class is simple to operate. A program simply creates a **CBase64Enc** object, invokes the **OpenFile** member function to open the file to encode, and repeatedly calls the **EncodeLine** member function to retrieve lines of encoded text. The **OpenFile** member function takes a pointer to a file path name as an argument. While the **CUUENC** class automatically displays a common file open dialog box to allow the user to select the file to encode, the **CBase64Enc** requires this step to be done outside of the encoder object itself. As with the **CUUENC** class, the **CBase64Enc** class returns **RESULT_DONE** from the **EncodeLine** member function when the object has processed all the data in the source file.

The **CBase64Dec** class has an interface similar to the **CBase64Enc** class. To decode Base64-encoded data, a program creates a **CBase64Dec** object, calls the **OpenFile** member function to specify the output file, and feeds the lines of Base64-encoded data to the **DecodeLine** member function. The **OpenFile** function takes the path of the output file as a parameter. The Base64 encoding format does not include the file name of the encoded data; indeed, the data may not have come from a file originally. Like the UUENCODE format, the program must supply a file name. The **DecodeLine** function is called repeatedly until the all of the text lines have been fed to the function. The **DecodeLine** function returns the number of bytes written to the file from the data contained in the line of encoded text.

Mail Client must know when to stop feeding lines of text to the decoder. Because the original data length may be a multiple of three, the data does not necessarily end with the Base64 pad character (the equal sign, =). The decoder has no way to tell if it has reached the end of the data. The program simply stops feeding the decoder data when it reaches the end of the data in a particular body part.

Listings

This section includes the following listings for the files that provide MIME functionality for the Mail Client program:

Listing 12.1 is the header file for the set of MIME parsing classes, CMIME.H.

Listing 12.2 is the implementation file for the set of MIME parsing classes, CMIME.CPP.

Listing 12.3 is the header file for the Base64 encoder and decoder classes, CBASE64.H.

Listing 12.4 is the implementation file for the Base64 encoder and decoder classes, CBASE64.CPP.

Listing 12.5 is the header file for a file mapping class, CFILEMAP.H. This class is used by the MIME parsing objects implemented in the CMIME.H and CMIME.CPP files. It allows random access to a file using an array-like notation. This functionality is implemented using C++ operator overloading.

Listing 12.6 is the implementation file for the file mapping class, CFILEMAP.CPP.

Listing 12.1 CMIME.H

```
/*
    File: CMIME.H
    Description:
        A bunch of functions for parsing and manipulating MIME
        messages and body parts.
    Copyright 1995, David G. Roberts
*/

#ifndef _CMIME_H
#define _CMIME_H

#include <windows.h>
#include "clist.h"
#include "cfilemap.h"

/*
    Class: CMIMEParamTuple
    Description:
        A simple class to store a 2-tuple of MIME parameter name and
        value strings.
```

```
*/
class CMIMEParamTuple {
private:
    char *  m_pszParam;
    char *  m_pszValue;
public:
    CMIMEParamTuple() : m_pszParam(NULL), m_pszValue(NULL) {};
    CMIMEParamTuple(const char * pszParam, const char * pszValue)
        { Param(pszParam); Value(pszValue); };
    CMIMEParamTuple(const CMIMEParamTuple&);
    ~CMIMEParamTuple();
    void Param(const char * pszParam);
    char * Param(void) { return m_pszParam; };
    void Value(const char * pszValue);
    char * Value(void) { return m_pszValue; };
    CMIMEParamTuple& operator=(const CMIMEParamTuple&);
};


/*
    Class: CMIMEParamList
    Description:
        A simple list of parameter tuples.  Uses CList as a base
        class and fills in the functionality appropriate for a list
        of CMIMEParamTuples.
*/
class CMIMEParamList : public CList {
private:
    virtual int Compare(void * pvThing1, void * pvThing2);
    virtual void DeleteData(void * pvThing);
public:
    // Constructor and destructor.
    CMIMEParamList() {};
    virtual ~CMIMEParamList();

    // Manipulation functions.
    void Add(CMIMEParamTuple * pTuple);
    void Insert(CMIMEParamTuple * pTuple);
    CMIMEParamTuple * First(void)
        { return (CMIMEParamTuple *) CList::First(); };
    CMIMEParamTuple * Next(void)
        { return (CMIMEParamTuple *) CList::Next(); };
};


/*
    Class: CMIMEBodyPart
    Description:
        Parses and stores data about individual MIME body parts.
        Handles multipart messages using a recursive parsing
        strategy.  When the parse is complete, a tree of
        CMIMEBodyPart nodes will have been constructed which
        represents all the body parts in the message.
*/
```

```
class CMIMEBodyPart {
private:
    char *              m_pszFilename;
    CFileMap            m_filemap;
    char *              m_pszType;
    char *              m_pszSubType;
    CMIMEParamList *    m_pParamList;
    char *              m_pszEncoding;
    long                m_lStart; // First char in the part
    long                m_lEnd; // Last char in the part + 1
    long                m_lCurrent;
    // Relationships to other body parts in the message.
    // Note that we don't use a CList-derived list of children
    // because we need to move more easily through the heirarchy
    // as we display the various body parts.
    CMIMEBodyPart *     m_pParent;
    CMIMEBodyPart *     m_pFirstChild;
    CMIMEBodyPart *     m_pSibling;

    // Private functions
    BOOL ParseHeaders(void);
    BOOL ParseMultipart(void);
    char * GetNextHeader(void);
    long FindCRLF(void);
    long StringSearch(char * pszString);
    BOOL HeaderCompare(char * pszHeader, char * pszHeaderName);
    BOOL ParseMIMEVersion(char * pszHeader);
    BOOL ParseContentType(char * pszHeader);
    BOOL ParseContentTransferEncoding(char * pszHeader);

public:
    CMIMEBodyPart(CMIMEBodyPart * pParent, char * pszFilename,
        long lStart, long lEnd);
    ~CMIMEBodyPart();

    BOOL Open(void);
    void Close(void);
    BOOL Parse(void);

    char * Type(void) { return m_pszType; };
    char * SubType(void) { return m_pszSubType; };
    char * Encoding(void) { return m_pszEncoding; };
    CMIMEParamTuple * FirstParam(void)
        { return m_pParamList->First(); };
    CMIMEParamTuple * NextParam(void)
        { return m_pParamList->Next(); };

    int FirstLine(char * pszLine, int nLen);
    int NextLine(char * pszLine, int nLen);

    CMIMEBodyPart * Parent(void) { return m_pParent; };
    CMIMEBodyPart * FirstChild(void) { return m_pFirstChild; };
```

```
    CMIMEBodyPart * Sibling(void) { return m_pSibling; };
};

/*
    Function: CMIMEMsg
    Description:
        An object which holds the top of the CMIMEBodyPart tree
        and allows a user to navigate the tree.  MIME viewers should
        create one of these objects and access individual body
        parts in the tree using the navigation functions.
*/
class CMIMEMsg {
private:
    CMIMEBodyPart * m_pBodyParts;
    CMIMEBodyPart * m_pCurrentPart;
public:
    CMIMEMsg() : m_pBodyParts(NULL), m_pCurrentPart(NULL) {};
    ~CMIMEMsg() { delete m_pBodyParts; };

    BOOL Parse(char *);

    CMIMEBodyPart * FirstPart(void);
    CMIMEBodyPart * NextPart(void);
    CMIMEBodyPart * CurrentPart(void) { return m_pCurrentPart; };
};

#endif
```

Listing 12.2   CMIME.CPP

```
/*
    File: CMIME.CPP
    Description:
        A bunch of functions for parsing and manipulating MIME
        messages and body parts.
    Copyright 1995, David G. Roberts
*/

#include <ctype.h>        // For tolower
#include "cmime.h"
#include "rfc822.h"
#include "utility.h"
#include "myassert.h"

#define UNUSED_PARAMETER(x) x

/************************************************************************.
    Class: CMIMEParamTuple
*************************************************************************/

/*
    Function: CMIMEParamTuple::CMIMEParamTuple
```

```
     Description:
          Copy constructor.  Make sure that we do more than a simple
          member-wise copy.  We need to actually duplicate the
          strings in the tuple.
*/
CMIMEParamTuple::CMIMEParamTuple(const  CMIMEParamTuple&  tuple)  :
     m_pszParam(NULL),  m_pszValue(NULL)
{
     Param(tuple.m_pszParam);
     Value(tuple.m_pszValue);
}


/*

     Function:  CMIMEParamTuple::~CMIMEParamTuple
     Description:
          Delete the param and value strings before the CMIMEParamTuple
          object is destroyed itself.
*/
CMIMEParamTuple::~CMIMEParamTuple()
{
     delete[] m_pszParam;
     delete[] m_pszValue;
}


/*

     Function:  CMIMEParamTuple::Param
     Description:
          Makes a local copy of the parameter string and stores it
          in the CMIMEParamTuple.
*/
void  CMIMEParamTuple::Param(const  char  *  pszParam)
{
     delete[] m_pszParam;
     if (pszParam != NULL) {
          m_pszParam = new char[lstrlen(pszParam) + 1];
          lstrcpy(m_pszParam, pszParam);
     }
     else
          m_pszParam = NULL;
}


/*

     Function:  CMIMEParamTuple::Value
     Description:
          Makes a local copy of the value string and stores it
          in the CMIMEParamTuple.
*/
void  CMIMEParamTuple::Value(const  char  *  pszValue)
{
     delete[] m_pszValue;
     if (pszValue != NULL) {
          m_pszValue = new char[lstrlen(pszValue) + 1];
          lstrcpy(m_pszValue, pszValue);
```

```
    }
    else
        m_pszValue = NULL;
}


/*
    Function:  CMIMEParamTuple::operator=
    Description:
        The overloaded assignment operator for the CMIMEParamTuple
        class.
*/
CMIMEParamTuple& CMIMEParamTuple::operator=
    (const CMIMEParamTuple& tuple)
{
    if (this != &tuple) {
        delete[] m_pszParam;
        delete[] m_pszValue;
        Param(tuple.m_pszParam);
        Value(tuple.m_pszValue);
    }
    return *this;
}


/************************************************************************
    Class: CMIMEParamList
************************************************************************/

/*
    Function:  CMIMEParamList::~CMIMEParamList
    Description:
        Deletes the pararm tuples before the list is destroyed.
*/
CMIMEParamList::~CMIMEParamList()
{
    CMIMEParamTuple * pTuple = First();
    while (pTuple != NULL) {
        delete pTuple;
        pTuple = Next();
    }
}


/*
    Function: CMIMEParamList::Compare
    Description:
        Simply returns 0.  A CMIMEParamList is unordered.  Returning
        0 causes an Insert operation to stop at the first element,
        which results in the element being stored at the beginning
        of the list.
*/
int CMIMEParamList::Compare(void * pvThing1, void * pvThing2)
{
    UNUSED_PARAMETER(pvThing1);
    UNUSED_PARAMETER(pvThing2);
```

```
    return 0;
}

/*
    Function: CMIMEParamList::DeleteData
    Description:
        Deletes an element of the list, in this case, a
        CMIMEParamTuple object.
*/
void CMIMEParamList::DeleteData(void * pvThing)
{
    delete ((CMIMEParamTuple *) pvThing);
}

/*
    Function: CMIMEParamList::Add
    Description:
        Add a tuple to the end of the list.  A copy of the tuple
        is made before it is added.
*/
void CMIMEParamList::Add(CMIMEParamTuple * pTuple)
{
    CMIMEParamTuple * pNewTuple = new CMIMEParamTuple(*pTuple);
    CList::Add(pNewTuple);
}

/*
    Function: CMIMEParamList::Insert
    Description:
        Insert a tuple into the list.  Because a CMIMEParamList is
        unordered, the tuple is inserted at the front of the list.
        A copy of the tuple is made before it is added.
*/
void CMIMEParamList::Insert(CMIMEParamTuple * pTuple)
{
    CMIMEParamTuple * pNewTuple = new CMIMEParamTuple(*pTuple);
    CList::Insert(pNewTuple);
}

/**********************************************************************
    Class: CMIMEBodyPart
**********************************************************************/

/*
    Function: CMIMEBodyPart::CMIMEBodyPart
    Description:
        Constructor for CMIMEBodyPart.  Just a huge initialization
        list for this one.
*/
CMIMEBodyPart::CMIMEBodyPart(CMIMEBodyPart * pParent,
    char * pszFilename, long lStart, long lEnd) :
    m_pszFilename(DuplicateString(pszFilename)),
```

```
    m_pszType(NULL), m_pszSubType(NULL),
     m_pParamList(new CMIMEParamList), m_pszEncoding(NULL),
     m_lStart(lStart), m_lEnd(lEnd),
     m_pParent(pParent), m_pFirstChild(NULL), m_pSibling(NULL)
{
}

/*
     Function: CMIMEBodyPart::~CMIMEBodyPart
     Description:
          Delete all the memory we allocated during this process.
*/
CMIMEBodyPart::~CMIMEBodyPart()
{
    Close();

    delete[]     m_pszFilename;
    delete[]     m_pszType;
    delete[]     m_pszSubType;
    delete       m_pParamList;
    delete[]     m_pszEncoding;

    // Delete all the children.
     CMIMEBodyPart * pChild, *pNextChild;
     pChild = m_pFirstChild;
     while (pChild != NULL) {
         pNextChild = pChild->m_pSibling;
         delete pChild;
         pChild = pNextChild;
    }
}

/*
     Function: CMIMEBodyPart::Open
     Description:
          Open the body part for parsing and reading.
*/
BOOL CMIMEBodyPart::Open(void)
{
    // Simply open the filemap object.
     return (m_filemap.Open(m_pszFilename) == CMM_NO_ERROR) ?
        TRUE : FALSE;
}

/*
     Function: CMIMEBodyPart::Close
     Description:
          Close the body part.  No more parsing or reading should
          be performed after this point.
*/
void CMIMEBodyPart::Close(void)
{
```

```
        // Simply close the filemap object.
        m_filemap.Close();
}


/*

      Function: CMIMEBodyPart::Parse
      Description:
            Parse the open body part.  The function first parses the
            headers.  If the headers indicate that the body part is
            multipart, then find the delimiters between the subparts and
            parse the subparts recursively.
*/
int CMIMEBodyPart::Parse(void)
{
    if (!m_filemap.IsOpen()) {
        return FALSE;
    }

    // Correct the values of start and end if they're set to
    // the defaults.
    if (m_lStart < 0)
        m_lStart = 0;
    if (m_lEnd < 0) {
        // Set lEnd to number of bytes in the file.
        m_lEnd = m_filemap.FileLength();
    }

    // Get all the headers of interest.
    ParseHeaders();

    // If this is a multipart message, parse it recursively.
    if (lstrcmpi(m_pszType, "multipart") == 0)
        if (ParseMultipart() != TRUE)
            return FALSE;

    return TRUE;
}


/*

      Function: CMIMEBodyPart::ParseMultipart
      Description:
            Use the specified boundary to locate the various body
            parts of the multipart message.  Create a CMIMEBodyPart
            for each body part and recursively call CMIMEBodyPart::Parse
            to parse the parts.  Returns TRUE if no errors occurred,
            or FALSE otherwise.
*/
BOOL CMIMEBodyPart::ParseMultipart(void)
{
    // Find the "boundary" parameter tuple.
    CMIMEParamTuple * pTuple = m_pParamList->First();
    while (pTuple != NULL) {
        if (lstrcmpi(pTuple->Param(), "boundary") == 0)
```

```
            break;
        pTuple = m_pParamList->Next();
    }
    if (pTuple == NULL)
        return FALSE;

    // Create the real boundary string.
    int nBoundaryLen = lstrlen(pTuple->Value());
    char * pszBoundary = new char[nBoundaryLen + 4 + 1];
    lstrcpy(pszBoundary, "\r\n—");
    lstrcat(pszBoundary, pTuple->Value());

    // Search for boundaries.
    long lBoundaryStart = StringSearch(pszBoundary);
    BOOL bFoundStartBoundary = FALSE;
    long lBodyPartStart, lBodyPartEnd;
    while (lBoundaryStart != -1) {
        // Okay, we found a boundary.  Is it a terminating boundary.
        BOOL bEndingBoundary = FALSE;
        if (m_filemap[m_lCurrent] == '-' &&
            m_filemap[m_lCurrent + 1] == '-') {
            bEndingBoundary = TRUE;
        }
        // Find the end of the line.
        long lBoundaryEnd = FindCRLF();
        if (lBoundaryEnd < 0) {
            delete[] pszBoundary;
            return FALSE;
        }
        lBoundaryEnd += 2;  // Jump over CRLF.
        if (lBoundaryEnd >= m_lEnd) {
            delete[] pszBoundary;
            return FALSE;
        }

        if (!bFoundStartBoundary) {
          // We haven't seen a starting boundary before.
            // See if we got an end before we got a start.
            if (bEndingBoundary) {
                delete[] pszBoundary;
                return FALSE;
            }
            lBodyPartStart = lBoundaryEnd;
            bFoundStartBoundary = TRUE;
        }
        else {
            // If we've already found a boundary before, then
            // this was a separating boundary or the terminating
            // boundary.
            lBodyPartEnd = lBoundaryStart;
            // Create a child body part and add it to the heirarchy.
            CMIMEBodyPart * pBodyPart = new CMIMEBodyPart(this,
```

```
                    m_pszFilename, lBodyPartStart, lBodyPartEnd);
              if (m_pFirstChild == NULL) {
                  m_pFirstChild = pBodyPart;
          }
          else {
                  // Add it to the end of the sibling chain.
                  CMIMEBodyPart * pChild = m_pFirstChild;
                  while (pChild->m_pSibling != NULL)
                      pChild = pChild->m_pSibling;
                  pChild->m_pSibling = pBodyPart;
          }

                  // The next body part starts right after this boundary.
                  lBodyPartStart = lBoundaryEnd;

            // If this was the terminating boundary, then we're
            // done.
              if (bEndingBoundary)
                  break;
         }

         // Find the next boundary.
           lBoundaryStart = StringSearch(pszBoundary);
     }

     delete[] pszBoundary;
     if (lBoundaryStart == -1)
         return FALSE;

    // Now we've found all the parts.  Traverse the child list
    // and have each child body part parse itself.
     CMIMEBodyPart * pChild = m_pFirstChild;
     while (pChild != NULL) {
         if (!(pChild->Open())) return FALSE;
         if (!(pChild->Parse())) return FALSE;
         pChild->Close();
         pChild = pChild->m_pSibling;
     }

     return TRUE;
}

/*
     Function: CMIMEBodyPart::ParseHeaders
     Description:
         Parse the body part headers to determine the content type
         and encoding of the message.
*/
BOOL CMIMEBodyPart::ParseHeaders(void)
{
     char * pszHeader;
     BOOL bResult;
```

```
   BOOL bFoundContentType = FALSE;
    BOOL bFoundEncoding = FALSE;

   // Start looking for headers at the start of the current
   // body part range.
   m_lCurrent = m_lStart;

   while ((pszHeader = GetNextHeader()) != NULL) {
      if (lstrcmp(pszHeader, "") == 0) {
            delete[] pszHeader;
            break;
      }
      else if (HeaderCompare(pszHeader, "MIME-Version")) {
            bResult = ParseMIMEVersion(pszHeader);
            if (bResult != TRUE) {
                delete[] pszHeader;
                return FALSE;
            }
      }
      else if (HeaderCompare(pszHeader, "Content-Type")) {
            bResult = ParseContentType(pszHeader);
            if (bResult != TRUE) {
                delete[] pszHeader;
                return FALSE;
            }
            bFoundContentType = TRUE;
      }
      else if
         (HeaderCompare(pszHeader, "Content-Transfer-Encoding")) {
            bResult = ParseContentTransferEncoding(pszHeader);
            if (bResult != TRUE) {
                delete[] pszHeader;
                return FALSE;
            }
            bFoundEncoding = TRUE;
      }
       delete[] pszHeader;
   }

   // Fill in the defaults if the appropriate headers were missing.
   if (!bFoundContentType) {
     m_pszType = DuplicateString("text");
     m_pszSubType = DuplicateString("plain");
   }
   if (!bFoundEncoding) {
     m_pszEncoding = DuplicateString("7bit");
   }

   return TRUE;
}

/*
    Function: CMIMEBodyPart::GetNextHeader
```

```
        Description:
            Find the next header in the file starting at m_lCurrent.
            Returns a newly created string with the header in it.
            The caller is responsible for deleteing the string when
            it is finished with the header.  The returned header has
            been unfolded and any trailing whitespace has been removed.
            All internal CRLFs have been converted to a single space.
            The final CRLF has been removed.
*/
char * CMIMEBodyPart::GetNextHeader(void)
{
    long lEndPos;
    long lStartPos = m_lCurrent;

    // Find the first CRLF pair that doesn't have linear whitespace
    // following it.
    do {
        lEndPos = FindCRLF();
        // Move the current position up.
        if (lEndPos >= 0) {
            m_lCurrent = lEndPos + 2;
        }
    } while (lEndPos >= 0 && IsLWSP(m_filemap[lEndPos + 2]));

    // If we couldn't find CRLF or an error occurred.
    if (lEndPos < 0)
        return NULL;

    // Push lEndPos to indicate the character following the CRLF.
    lEndPos += 2;

    // Calculate the header length.
    int nLen = (int)(lEndPos - lStartPos);
    ASSERT(nLen > 0);

    // Allocate a character string for it.
    char * pszHeader = new char[nLen + 1];
    // Copy the header to the buffer.  Replace CRLF pairs with a
    // single space character.
    BOOL bFoundCR = FALSE;
    int iCopyIndex = 0;
    for (int i = 0; i < nLen; i++) {
        char c = (char) m_filemap[lStartPos + i];
        // If we've just seen a CR, see if the next character is
        // an LF.
        if (bFoundCR) {
            if (c == LF) {
                // If so, simply add a space to the output string.
                pszHeader[iCopyIndex++] = ' ';
                bFoundCR = FALSE;
            }
            else {
```

```
                    // Else the previous CR was isolated by itself and
                    //   should be in the output string.
                    pszHeader[iCopyIndex++] = CR;
                    // Is the current character a CR
                    if (c == CR) {
                        // If so, make sure we check the next character
                        // for an LF.
                        bFoundCR = TRUE;
                    }
                    else {
                        // Nope.  Just copy it to the output.
                        pszHeader[iCopyIndex++] = c;
                        bFoundCR = FALSE;
                    }
                }
            }
        }
        else {
            // Is the character a CR.
            if (c == CR) {
                // Yes, so check the next character for LF.
                bFoundCR = TRUE;
            }
            else {
                // Nope. Copy it to the output.
                pszHeader[iCopyIndex++] = c;
                bFoundCR = FALSE;
            }
        }
    }

    // Remove any trailing whitespace and terminate the string.
    iCopyIndex-;
    while (IsLWSP(pszHeader[iCopyIndex]))
        iCopyIndex-;
    iCopyIndex++;
    pszHeader[iCopyIndex] = '\0';

    return pszHeader;
}


/*

    Function: CMIMEBodyPart::FindCRLF
    Description:
        Finds the next CRLF pair in the file after the position
        specified by m_lCurrent.  Returns the index in the file
        of the CR character.  Returns -1 if no CRLF pair can be found.

        The function uses a hard-coded Boyer-Moore string search
        algorithm.  It looks for LF every two characters.  When it
        finds one, it checks if the preceeding character was CR.
        If so, it's found one.  If not, it increments two locations
        and checks again.  If the current character was a CR rather
```

```
            than LF, it increments only one character in order to check
            the next character for LF.
*/
long CMIMEBodyPart::FindCRLF(void)
{
     long lSearch = m_lCurrent + 1;

     while (1) {
          int c = m_filemap[lSearch];
          if (c < 0)  // Error or EOF
              return -1;
          else if (c == LF) {
               if (m_filemap[lSearch - 1] == CR)
                   return lSearch - 1;  // Found it.
              else
                   lSearch += 2;
          }
          else if (c == CR)
              lSearch++; // Boyer-Moore step.
          else
              lSearch += 2;
     }
}


/*
     Function: CMIMEBodyPart::StringSearch
     Description:
          Searches for a string in the message text starting at
          m_lCurrent and ending at m_lEnd.  Returns the position of
          the first character in the string and advances m_lCurrent
          to the character following the string.  The function returns
          -1 if the string cannot be found before m_lEnd is reached.

          The function uses a Boyer-Moore string search algorithm in
          order to reduce the number of calls to CFileMap::Get
          and move through the string quickly.  Note, this is a
          pretty confusing search algorithm if you aren't used to it.
          Look it up in a textbook if you want more background
          (Sedgewick, "Algorithms in C," or Abrash, "Zen of Code
          Optimization," for instance).
*/
long CMIMEBodyPart::StringSearch(char * pszString)
{
     int iAdvanceTable[256];
     int i;

     ASSERT(pszString != NULL);
     int nLen = lstrlen(pszString);

     // If we've been asked to match a zero-length string, match it
     // immediately.
     if (nLen == 0)
         return m_lCurrent;
```

```
        // Fill in the the advance table with the default length.
        for (i = 0; i < 256; i++)
            iAdvanceTable[i] = nLen;
        // Fill in the corresponding positions in the advance table
        // with the positions of the characters in the search string.
        for (i = 0; i < nLen - 1; i++)
            iAdvanceTable[pszString[i]] = nLen - i - 1;

    int iAdvance;
    long lSearchPos = m_lCurrent + nLen - 1;
    while (lSearchPos < m_lEnd) {
        // Search from end of string back to front
        for (i = 0; i < nLen; i++) {
            int c = m_filemap[lSearchPos - i];
            if (c < 0) return -1;
            if (c != pszString[nLen - 1 - i]) {
                // We found a mismatch.  See how far we can
                // advance based on the mismatched character.
                iAdvance = iAdvanceTable[c] - i;
                // We always move forward, never back.
                if (iAdvance <= 0)
                    iAdvance = 1;
                break;
            }
        }
        if (i == nLen) {
            // We found it.
            m_lCurrent = lSearchPos + 1;
            return lSearchPos - (nLen - 1);
        }
        else {
            // Didn't find it, so advance the tail a bit more.
            lSearchPos += iAdvance;
        }
    }

    // Didn't find it before we ran out of room.
    return -1;
}

/*
    Function: CMIMEBodyPart::HeaderCompare
    Description:
        Compare a header with a header name.  If the header name
        equals the part of the header preceeding the first colon
        (and after whitespace has been stripped), then return TRUE,
        else return FALSE.  The comparison is case-insensitive.
*/
BOOL CMIMEBodyPart::HeaderCompare(char * pszHeader,
    char *pszHeaderName)
{
    // Find the first colon in the header.
```

```
    int i = 0;
    while (pszHeader[i] != ':')
        i++;
    // Now back up to skip any whitespace between the header
    // name and the colon.
    i-; // Skip back past colon.
    while (IsLWSP(pszHeader[i]))
        i-;
    i++; // i = length of header name.

    // Compare the lengths.
    if (i != lstrlen(pszHeaderName))
        return FALSE;

    // Compare the characters.
    for (int j = 0; j < i; j++)
        if (tolower(pszHeader[j]) != tolower(pszHeaderName[j]))
            return FALSE;

    return TRUE;
}


/*
    Function: CMIMEBodyPart::ParseMIMEVersion
    Description:
        Parse the MIME version header.  The function looks for
        version 1.0.  If version 1.0 is found and the header is
        syntactically correct, the function returns TRUE else it
        returns FALSE.
*/
BOOL CMIMEBodyPart::ParseMIMEVersion(char * pszHeader)
{
    ASSERT(pszHeader != NULL);

    // Allocate a token buffer.  The maximum token length could
    // be the size of the header minus the header name.  Allocate
    // one the size of the whole header, which is sure to be enough.
    int nTokenLen = lstrlen(pszHeader);
    char * pszToken = new char[nTokenLen];
    int iToken;

    // Move up to the colon separating the header name from
    // the header body.
    while (*pszHeader != ':' && *pszHeader != '\0')
        pszHeader++;
    if (*pszHeader == '\0') goto error;
    // Move past the colon.
    pszHeader++;

    // Look for the '1'.
    do {
        pszHeader = GetToken(FALSE, pszHeader, pszToken, nTokenLen,
```

```
            &iToken);
    } while (iToken == TOKEN_COMMENT);
    if (iToken != TOKEN_ATOM || lstrcmp(pszToken, "1") != 0)
        goto error;

    // Look for the '.'.
    do {
            pszHeader = GetToken(FALSE, pszHeader, pszToken, nTokenLen,
                &iToken);
    } while (iToken == TOKEN_COMMENT);
    if (iToken != TOKEN_SPECIAL || lstrcmp(pszToken, ".") != 0)
        goto error;

    // Look for the '0'.
    do {
            pszHeader = GetToken(FALSE, pszHeader, pszToken, nTokenLen,
                &iToken);
    } while (iToken == TOKEN_COMMENT);
    if (iToken != TOKEN_ATOM || lstrcmp(pszToken, "0") != 0)
        goto error;

    delete[] pszToken;
    return TRUE;

error:
    delete[] pszToken;
    return FALSE;
}


/*

    Function: CMIMEBodyPart::ParseContentType
    Description:
        Parses a Content-Type header.  The header name must have
        been checked previously.  The type and subtype fields are
        parsed from the header and stored in the node.  If
        parameters are present, they are parsed and stored in the
        parameter list.  If everything goes alright, the function
        returns TRUE.  If an error occurs, it returns FALSE.
*/
BOOL CMIMEBodyPart::ParseContentType(char * pszHeader)
{
    ASSERT(pszHeader != NULL);

    // Allocate a token buffer.  The maximum token length could
    // be the size of the header minus the header name.  Allocate
    // one the size of the whole header, which is sure to be enough.
    int nTokenLen = lstrlen(pszHeader);
    char * pszToken = new char[nTokenLen];
    int iToken;
    CMIMEParamTuple tuple;

    // Move up to the colon separating the header name from
    // the header body.
```

```
while (*pszHeader != ':' && *pszHeader != '\0')
    pszHeader++;
if (*pszHeader == '\0') goto error;
// Move past the colon.
pszHeader++;

// Get the type.
do {
        pszHeader = GetToken(TRUE, pszHeader, pszToken, nTokenLen,
          &iToken);
} while (iToken == TOKEN_COMMENT);
if (iToken != TOKEN_MIMETOKEN)
    goto error;
m_pszType = DuplicateString(pszToken);

// Get the "/" separator between the type and subtype.
do {
        pszHeader = GetToken(TRUE, pszHeader, pszToken, nTokenLen,
          &iToken);
} while (iToken == TOKEN_COMMENT);
if (iToken != TOKEN_TSPECIAL || *pszToken != '/')
    goto error;

// Get the subtype.
do {
        pszHeader = GetToken(TRUE, pszHeader, pszToken, nTokenLen,
          &iToken);
} while (iToken == TOKEN_COMMENT);
if (iToken != TOKEN_MIMETOKEN)
    goto error;
m_pszSubType = DuplicateString(pszToken);

// See if we have any parameters.
do {
        pszHeader = GetToken(TRUE, pszHeader, pszToken, nTokenLen,
          &iToken);
} while (iToken == TOKEN_COMMENT);
while (iToken == TOKEN_TSPECIAL && *pszToken == ';') {
    // Yes, we have a parameter.
    // Parse a token for the parameter name.
    do {
            pszHeader = GetToken(TRUE, pszHeader, pszToken, nTokenLen,
              &iToken);
    } while (iToken == TOKEN_COMMENT);
    if (iToken != TOKEN_MIMETOKEN)
        goto error;
    tuple.Param(pszToken);
    // Get the equals sign.
    do {
            pszHeader = GetToken(TRUE, pszHeader, pszToken, nTokenLen,
              &iToken);
    } while (iToken == TOKEN_COMMENT);
```

```
        if (iToken != TOKEN_TSPECIAL || *pszToken != '=')
            goto error;
        // Get the parameter value.
        do {
            pszHeader = GetToken(TRUE, pszHeader, pszToken, nTokenLen,
              &iToken);
        } while (iToken == TOKEN_COMMENT);
        if (iToken != TOKEN_MIMETOKEN && iToken != TOKEN_QSTRING)
            goto error;
        tuple.Value(pszToken);
        // Add the tuple to the list of parameters.
        m_pParamList->Add(&tuple);
        // See if have another following ';'.
        do {
            pszHeader = GetToken(TRUE, pszHeader, pszToken, nTokenLen,
              &iToken);
        } while (iToken == TOKEN_COMMENT);
    }

    // Okay, we should be at the end.
    delete[] pszToken;
    if (iToken != TOKEN_END)
        return FALSE;
    else
        return TRUE;

error:
    delete[] pszToken;
    return FALSE;
}


/*
    Function: CMIMEBodyPart::ParseContentTransferEncoding
    Description:
        Parse a Content-Transfer-Encoding header.  Sets the
        m_pszEncoding member to a string describing the encoding.
*/
int CMIMEBodyPart::ParseContentTransferEncoding(char * pszHeader)
{
    ASSERT(pszHeader != NULL);

    // Allocate a token buffer.  The maximum token length could
    // be the size of the header minus the header name.  Allocate
    // one the size of the whole header, which is sure to be enough.
    int nTokenLen = lstrlen(pszHeader);
    char * pszToken = new char[nTokenLen];
    int iToken;

    // Move up to the colon separating the header name from
    // the header body.
    while (*pszHeader != ':' && *pszHeader != '\0')
        pszHeader++;
```

```
    if (*pszHeader == '\0') goto error;
    // Move past the colon.
    pszHeader++;

    // Get the encoding.
    do {
         pszHeader = GetToken(TRUE, pszHeader, pszToken, nTokenLen,
             &iToken);
    } while (iToken == TOKEN_COMMENT);
    if (iToken != TOKEN_MIMETOKEN)
        goto error;
    m_pszEncoding = DuplicateString(pszToken);

    // Check if we're at the end.
    do {
         pszHeader = GetToken(TRUE, pszHeader, pszToken, nTokenLen,
             &iToken);
    } while (iToken == TOKEN_COMMENT);
    if (iToken != TOKEN_END)
        goto error;
    delete[] pszToken;
    return TRUE;

error:
    delete[] pszToken;
    return FALSE;
}


/*
    Function: CMIMEBodyPart::FirstLine
    Description:
        Returns the first line of text in the body part.  The CRLF
        is left in the text.  Simply resets the current pointer
        to the first byte of the body part and then calls NextLine.
*/
int CMIMEBodyPart::FirstLine(char * pszLine, int nLen)
{
    m_lCurrent = m_lStart;
    return NextLine(pszLine, nLen);
}


/*
    Function: CMIMEBodyPart::NextLine
    Description:
        Returns the next line of text in the body part.  The CRLF
        is left in the text.  Returns the number of characters
        transferred to the buffer, or -1 if there are no more lines
        of text.
*/
int CMIMEBodyPart::NextLine(char * pszLine, int nLen)
{
    if (m_lCurrent >= m_lEnd)
        return -1;
```

```
    BOOL bWasCR = FALSE;
    int iLineIndex = 0;
    while (m_lCurrent < m_lEnd && iLineIndex < (nLen - 1)) {
        int c = m_filemap[m_lCurrent++];
        if (c < 0) {
            return -1;
        }
        pszLine[iLineIndex++] = (char) c;
        if (c == LF && bWasCR)
            break;
        if (c == CR)
            bWasCR = TRUE;
        else
            bWasCR = FALSE;
    }
    pszLine[iLineIndex] = '\0';
    return iLineIndex;
}


/**********************************************************************
    Class: CMIMEMsg
**********************************************************************/

/*
    Function: CMIMEMsg::Parse
    Description:
        Parse the given filename.  Returns TRUE if the parse was
        successful or FALSE if an error occurred.
*/
BOOL CMIMEMsg::Parse(char * pszFilename)
{
    ASSERT(pszFilename != NULL);

    if (m_pBodyParts != NULL) return FALSE;

    m_pBodyParts = new CMIMEBodyPart(NULL, pszFilename, 0, -1);
    if (!(m_pBodyParts->Open())) return FALSE;
    if (!(m_pBodyParts->Parse())) return FALSE;
    m_pBodyParts->Close();

    return TRUE;
}


/*
    Function: CMIMEMsg::FirstPart
    Description:
        Moves to the first "viewable" body part in the tree,
        skipping over multipart nodes in favor of their
        children, as necessary.
*/
CMIMEBodyPart * CMIMEMsg::FirstPart(void)
{
```

```
    m_pCurrentPart = m_pBodyParts;
      while (m_pCurrentPart->FirstChild() != NULL)
          m_pCurrentPart = m_pCurrentPart->FirstChild();
      return m_pCurrentPart;
}


/*

     Function: CMIMEMsg::NextPart
     Description:
         Move to the next node in the MIME body part tree.  Returns
         the address of the next CMIMEBodyPart object in the tree
         or NULL if there are no more nodes in the tree.
*/
CMIMEBodyPart * CMIMEMsg::NextPart(void)
{
    // See if we can move sideways in the tree.
    CMIMEBodyPart * pTemp = m_pCurrentPart;
    while (pTemp != NULL && pTemp->Sibling() == NULL) {
        // If not, then move up until we can move sideways.
        pTemp = pTemp->Parent();
    }
    // See if we've gone through all the nodes.
     if (pTemp == NULL)
         return NULL;
     else
         pTemp = pTemp->Sibling();
     // If the node we found is a multipart node, move down as
     // far as possible.
     while (pTemp->FirstChild() != NULL)
         pTemp = pTemp->FirstChild();

    // Okay, we're there.
     return m_pCurrentPart = pTemp;
}
```

Listing 12.3   CBASE64.H

```
/*
     File: CBASE64.H
     Description:
         Implements a MIME BASE64 encoder/decoder.
     Copyright 1995, David G. Roberts
*/

#ifndef _CBASE64_H
#define _CBASE64_H

#include <windows.h>

typedef unsigned char uchar;

class CBase64Enc {
private:
```

```
    HFILE    m_hfile;
    uchar    m_uchBuffer[51];      // Must be multiple of 3.
public:
      enum { RESULT_OK, RESULT_ERROR, RESULT_DONE, RESULT_SMALLBUFFER };

      CBase64Enc() : m_hfile(NULL) {};
      virtual ~CBase64Enc()
          { if (m_hfile != NULL) _lclose(m_hfile); };

      int OpenFile(char * pszFileName);
      int EncodeLine(char * pszLine, int nLen);
};

class CBase64Dec {
private:
    HFILE    m_hfile;
    uchar    m_uchStoredChars[4];
    int      m_iChars;
public:
    enum { RESULT_OK = 0, RESULT_ERROR = -1 };

      CBase64Dec() : m_hfile(NULL), m_iChars(0) {};
      virtual ~CBase64Dec()
          { if (m_hfile != NULL) _lclose(m_hfile); };

      int OpenFile(char * pszFileName);
      int DecodeLine(char * pszLine, int nLineLen);
      int DecodeLine(char * pszLine, int nLineLen,
          uchar * uchBuffer, int nBufferLen);
};


#endif
```

Listing 12.4   CBASE64.CPP

```
/*
    File: CBASE64.CPP
    Description:
          Implements a MIME BASE64 encoder/decoder.
    Copyright 1995, David G. Roberts
*/

#include "cbase64.h"
#include "myassert.h"

int DecodeValue(const int c);

const char szBASE64CODE[] =
  "ABCDEFGHIJKLMNOPQRSTUVWXYZabcdefghijklmnopqrstuvwxyz0123456789+/";
#define ENCODE_BYTE(b) szBASE64CODE[((uchar)b) & 077];
```

```
// Calculate decoded character value.  Note that only legal
// characters should be given as input.
int DecodeValue(const int c)
{
    // Note that this works only on ASCII machines.
    if ('A' <= c && c <= 'Z')
        return c - 'A';
    if ('a' <= c && c <= 'z')
        return c - 'a' + 26;
    if ('0' <= c && c <= '9')
        return c - '0' + 52;
    if (c == '+')
        return 62;
    if (c == '/')
        return 63;
    if (c == '=')
        return -1;
    return -2;
}


/**********************************************************************
    Class: CBase64Enc
**********************************************************************/

/*
    Function: CBase64Enc::OpenFile
    Description:
        Opens the source file from which the data will be drawn.
*/
int CBase64Enc::OpenFile(char * pszFileName)
{
    // Open the file.  Handle any errors.
    m_hfile = _lopen(pszFileName, OF_READ);
    if (m_hfile == HFILE_ERROR) {
        m_hfile = NULL;
        return RESULT_ERROR;
    }
    else
        return RESULT_OK;
}


/*
    Function: CBase64Enc::EncodeLine
    Description:
        Reads a line's-worth of data from the file, encodes it,
        and returns it to the caller.
*/
int CBase64Enc::EncodeLine(char * pszLine, int nLen)
{
    // Our buffer size must be a multiple of 3.
    ASSERT(sizeof(m_uchBuffer) % 3 == 0);
```

```
    // Make sure the line buffer passed to us will be able to hold
    // all the encoded data.  If not, error.
    if (nLen < ((sizeof(m_uchBuffer) / 3) * 4 + 1))
        return RESULT_SMALLBUFFER;

    // Zero out the byte buffer so that when we reach the final
    // line and it's not full that it'll be padded with zero.
    for (int i = 0; i < sizeof(m_uchBuffer); i++)
        m_uchBuffer[i] = 0;

    // Read a line's-worth of bytes from the file.
    int nBytes = _lread(m_hfile, m_uchBuffer, sizeof(m_uchBuffer));
    int iByteIndex = 0;
    int iCharIndex = 0;
    while (nBytes > 0 && iByteIndex < nBytes) {
        pszLine[iCharIndex] =
            ENCODE_BYTE(m_uchBuffer[iByteIndex] >> 2);
        pszLine[iCharIndex + 1] =
            ENCODE_BYTE((m_uchBuffer[iByteIndex] << 4) |
                (m_uchBuffer[iByteIndex + 1] >> 4));
        if (iByteIndex + 1 < nBytes) {
            pszLine[iCharIndex + 2] =
                ENCODE_BYTE((m_uchBuffer[iByteIndex + 1] << 2) |
                    (m_uchBuffer[iByteIndex + 2] >> 6));
        }
        else {
            pszLine[iCharIndex + 2] = '=';
        }
        if (iByteIndex + 2 < nBytes) {
            pszLine[iCharIndex + 3] =
                ENCODE_BYTE(m_uchBuffer[iByteIndex + 2]);
        }
        else {
            pszLine[iCharIndex + 3] = '=';
        }
        iByteIndex += 3;
        iCharIndex += 4;
    }

    // Add the line terminator.
    pszLine[iCharIndex] = '\0';
    // See if we hit the end of the file.
    if (nBytes == 0) {
        // Yup, so close it up, handling any error as appropriate.
        if (_lclose(m_hfile) == HFILE_ERROR) {
            m_hfile = NULL;
            return RESULT_ERROR;
        }
        else {
            m_hfile = NULL;
            return RESULT_DONE;
        }
```

```
    }
    else {
        return RESULT_OK;
    }
}


/***********************************************************************
    Class: CBase64Dec
***********************************************************************/

/*
    Function: CBase64Dec::OpenFile
    Description:
        Open a file that we can write the characters to.
*/
int CBase64Dec::OpenFile(char * pszFileName)
{
    // Open the file.  Handle any errors.
    m_hfile = _lopen(pszFileName, OF_WRITE);
    if (m_hfile == HFILE_ERROR) {
        m_hfile = NULL;
        return RESULT_ERROR;
    }
    else
        return RESULT_OK;
}


/*
    Function: CBase64Dec::DecodeLine
    Description:
        Decode a line of data and write the bytes to the open file.
*/
int CBase64Dec::DecodeLine(char * pszLine, int nLineLen)
{
    uchar * uchBuffer = new uchar[nLineLen];
    int nDecodedLen = DecodeLine(pszLine, nLineLen,
        uchBuffer, nLineLen);
    if (nDecodedLen >= 0) {
        if (_lwrite(m_hfile, (LPCSTR)uchBuffer, nDecodedLen) ==
            (UINT)HFILE_ERROR)
            nDecodedLen = RESULT_ERROR;
    }
    delete[] uchBuffer;
    return nDecodedLen;
}


/*
    Function: CBase64Dec::DecodeLine
    Description:
        Simply decode a line of bytes.  Note that a file doesn't
            have to be opened to use this member function. Returns
            the count of the decoded bytes or -1 on error.
```

```
*/
int CBase64Dec::DecodeLine(char * pszLine, int nLineLen,
       uchar * uchBuffer, int nBufferLen)
{
    int iLineIndex = 0;
    int iBufferIndex = 0;

    while (iLineIndex < nLineLen) {
        // Group together four characters for decode.
        while (iLineIndex < nLineLen && m_iChars < 4) {
            int c = pszLine[iLineIndex++];
            // Ignore characters that aren't BASE64 characters
            // (e.g., spaces, CRLF, etc.).
            if (DecodeValue(c) != -2)
                m_uchStoredChars[m_iChars++] = (uchar) c;
        }

        if (m_iChars == 4) {
            // We've got four characters, so decode them.
            m_iChars = 0;

            // Decode first byte.
            if (iBufferIndex == nBufferLen) return RESULT_ERROR;
            uchBuffer[iBufferIndex++] = (uchar)
                (((uchar)DecodeValue(m_uchStoredChars[0]) << 2) |
                 ((uchar)DecodeValue(m_uchStoredChars[1]) >> 4));

            // Decode second byte.
            if (iBufferIndex == nBufferLen) return RESULT_ERROR;
            if (m_uchStoredChars[2] == '=') return iBufferIndex;
            uchBuffer[iBufferIndex++] = (uchar)
                (((uchar)DecodeValue(m_uchStoredChars[1]) << 4) |
                 ((uchar)DecodeValue(m_uchStoredChars[2]) >> 2));

            // Decode third byte.
            if (iBufferIndex == nBufferLen) return RESULT_ERROR;
            if (m_uchStoredChars[3] == '=') return iBufferIndex;
            uchBuffer[iBufferIndex++] = (uchar)
                (((uchar)DecodeValue(m_uchStoredChars[2]) << 6) |
                 ((uchar)DecodeValue(m_uchStoredChars[3])));
        }
    }

    // Return the count of decoded bytes.
    return iBufferIndex;
}
```

Listing 12.5   CFILEMAP.H

```
/*
    File: CFILEMAP.H
    Description:
        An object used to open and pseudo-memory-map a file.  The
        memory-mapping is simulated using C++ operator overloading.
```

```
    Copyright 1995, David G. Roberts
*/

#ifndef _CFILEMAP_H
#define _CFILEMAP_H

#include <windows.h>
#include <stdio.h>   // Just need EOF.
#include "myassert.h"

/** CONSTANTS **/
#define DEFAULT_BUFFER_SIZE        1024
// Errors
#define CMM_NO_ERROR               0
// Note that EOF is not really an error but is returned as one
// by Get.  It should be equal to -1, but you never know.  If it's
// not -1, then it might clash with some of the other errors.
#if (EOF != -1)
#error The end of file constant value is not -1.
#endif
#define CMM_NO_MEMORY              -2
#define CMM_OPEN_ERROR             -3
#define CMM_WRITE_ERROR            -4
#define CMM_READ_ERROR             -5
#define CMM_CLOSE_ERROR            -6
#define CMM_SEEK_ERROR             -7


/*
    Class: CFileMap
    Description:
        Implements a file mapping object.
*/
class CFileMap {
private:
    // Variables
    char *      m_pData;         // Pointer to file data
    unsigned    m_nBufferSize;   // Total size of buffer
    long        m_lBaseIndex;    // File index of first byte in buffer
    unsigned    m_uLen;          // Length of data within the buffer
    HFILE       m_hFile;         // Handle of open file
    int         m_iError;        // Most recent error code
    BOOL        m_bIsOpen;       // The file is open.

    // Private functions
    int FillBuffer(const long lBaseIndex);

public:
    // Constructor uses default buffer size if not provided.
    CFileMap(const unsigned nSize = DEFAULT_BUFFER_SIZE);
    ~CFileMap();

    int Open(LPCSTR Filename);
    int Close(void);
```

```
    BOOL IsOpen(void) { return m_bIsOpen; };
    long FileLength(void);
    int LastError(void) { return m_iError; };

    // Access Functions
    int Get(const long lIndex);
    int operator[](const long lIndex) { return Get(lIndex); };
    int ReadAndGet(const long lIndex);
};

inline int CFileMap::Get(const long lIndex)
{
    ASSERT(m_bIsOpen);

    // See if our buffer has the right data in it.
    if (m_lBaseIndex <= lIndex &&
        lIndex < (m_lBaseIndex + (long) m_nBufferSize)) {
        // Compute the offset of the byte in the buffer.
        unsigned uOffset = (unsigned) (lIndex - m_lBaseIndex);
        // Make sure we have that many bytes in the buffer.
        if (uOffset < m_uLen)
            return m_pData[uOffset];
        else
            return EOF;
    }
    else
        return ReadAndGet(lIndex);
}

#endif
```

Listing 12.6   CFILEMAP.CPP

```
/*
    File: CFILEMAP.CPP
    Description:
        An object used to open and pseudo-memory-map a file.  The
        memory-mapping is simulated using C++ operator overloading.
    Copyright 1995, David G. Roberts
*/

#include "cfilemap.h"

/*
    Function: CFileMap::CFileMap
    Description:
        Constructor for CFileMap class.  The function allocates a
        buffer cSize in length.
*/
CFileMap::CFileMap(const unsigned nSize) :
    m_pData(NULL), m_nBufferSize(nSize),
    m_hFile(NULL), m_iError(CMM_NO_ERROR), m_bIsOpen(FALSE)
```

```
{
}

/*
     Function: CFileMap::~CFileMap
     Description:
         Simply make sure the file is closed before we're destroyed.
*/
CFileMap::~CFileMap()
{
    // Make sure file is closed.
    Close();
}


/*
     Function: CFileMap::Open
     Description:
          Open the file, allocate the buffer, and read the first bytes
          of the file into it.
*/
int CFileMap::Open(LPCSTR lpszFilename)
{
    // Open file using Windows' _lopen.
     m_hFile = _lopen(lpszFilename, OF_READ | OF_SHARE_DENY_WRITE);
     if (m_hFile == HFILE_ERROR) {
         m_hFile = NULL;
          return m_iError = CMM_OPEN_ERROR;
     }

     // Allocate the buffer.
     m_pData = new char[m_nBufferSize];

     // Read as much of file into buffer as possible, starting from
     // beginning of file.
     FillBuffer(0L);

     m_bIsOpen = TRUE;

      return m_iError = CMM_NO_ERROR;
}

/*
     Function: CFileMap::Close
     Description:
          Delete the data buffer and close the file.
*/
int CFileMap::Close(void)
{
    // Get rid of the buffer.
    delete[] m_pData;
    m_pData = NULL;
```

```
        // Close the file.
        if (m_hFile == NULL)
            return m_iError = CMM_NO_ERROR;
        if (_lclose(m_hFile) == HFILE_ERROR)
            m_iError = CMM_CLOSE_ERROR;
        else
            m_iError = CMM_NO_ERROR;
        m_hFile = NULL;

        m_bIsOpen = FALSE;

        return m_iError;
    }

    /*
        Function: CFileMap::FileLength
        Description:
            Return the length of the file.
    */
    long CFileMap::FileLength(void)
    {
        LONG lSeekPos = _llseek(m_hFile, 0, 2); // Seek to end of file
        if (lSeekPos == HFILE_ERROR) {
            return m_iError = CMM_SEEK_ERROR;
        }
        else {
            m_iError = CMM_NO_ERROR;
            return lSeekPos;
        }
    }

    /*
        Function: CFileMap::FillBuffer
        Description:
            Fill the buffer with file data starting at lBaseIndex
            within the file.
    */
    int CFileMap::FillBuffer(const long lBaseIndex)
    {
        // Seek to correct position in file.
        LONG lSeekPos = _llseek(m_hFile, lBaseIndex, 0);
        if (lSeekPos == HFILE_ERROR || lSeekPos != lBaseIndex)
            return m_iError = CMM_SEEK_ERROR;

        // Read data in.
        UINT uResult = _lread(m_hFile, m_pData, m_nBufferSize);
        if (uResult == (UINT)HFILE_ERROR) {
            return m_iError = CMM_READ_ERROR;
        }
        if (uResult != m_nBufferSize) {
            // Zero fill remainder of buffer.
            for (unsigned i = uResult; i < m_nBufferSize; i++)
```

```
            m_pData[i] = 0;
    }

    // Update buffer variables.
    m_lBaseIndex    = lBaseIndex;
    m_uLen          = uResult;

    return m_iError = CMM_NO_ERROR;
}

/*

    Function: CFileMap::ReadAndGet
    Description:
        All access to the file data is through the Get member
        function.  The Get function is inlined for speed.  If the
        data is in the buffer, then the inlined code should execute
        quickly.  If the Get function determines that the desired
        data is not in the buffer, then it calls ReadAndGet to read
        the data into the buffer and return the appropriate data.
        Since reading the file is a slow operation, this code is
        put into its own function to save space in the inlined
        Get function.
*/
int CFileMap::ReadAndGet(const long lIndex)
{
    // We didn't have the right data, so get the right data
    long lBaseIndex = (lIndex / m_nBufferSize) * m_nBufferSize;
    int iResult = FillBuffer(lBaseIndex);
    if (iResult != CMM_NO_ERROR) {
        return m_iError = iResult;
    }

    // Try again...
    unsigned uOffset = (unsigned) (lIndex - m_lBaseIndex);
    if (uOffset < m_uLen)
        return m_pData[uOffset];
    else
        return EOF;
}

.
```

Network News Transport Protocol: NNTP

Extra! Extra! Read all about it! Network news is a distributed, public bulletin board system with a world-wide reach. In this chapter, find out how to make a network news client application.

Do you own an airplane and need a recommendation for replacement parts? Do you want to debate public policy? Are you looking for experts on compiler construction and object-oriented programming? You can find the answers you seek by reading network news.

In this chapter, we'll examine the network news system. First, we'll talk about the network news model. We'll examine the format of news articles and the protocols used to by client applications to retrieve articles from a news server. Finally, we'll build our own news client application and C++ object that implements the client/server news protocol.

Network News

Network news is a distributed, public bulletin board system. News messages, called *articles*, are arranged into a series of hierarchical subject groupings. The system includes groups about computers, groups about politics, groups about planes, groups about TV shows, and groups about almost everything else under the sun. The names of groups contain a series of subject categories separated by periods; for instance:

```
comp.protocols.tcp-ip
comp.lang.c
rec.games.chess
rec.games.programming
rec.food.chocolate
sci.archaeology
sci.bio.microbiology
```

The groups in the *comp* hierarchy deal with computers: computer architecture, networking protocols, programming languages, and operating systems, for instance. The groups in the *rec* hierarchy deal with recreational topics: computer and board games, pets, food, music, and TV shows. The groups in the *sci* hierarchy deal with scientific topics: archaeology, anthropology, mathematics, physics, and psychology.

Don't read anything in the *sci* hierarchy right before bedtime; you may be jolted awake by the sound of your head slamming forward on your keyboard.

Each level of hierarchy represents further specialization of the topic. Consider *rec.games.chess*, for example. Games are a form of recreation, and chess is a game. Other games are in the *rec.games* portion of the hierarchy, each in its own group.

How Information Flows

The network news system allows users to read articles and post responses or new articles in the subject category. A client/server methodology handles the interaction between users and the news system. Servers store the articles, and users read and post articles using client software.

Each server links to a set of other servers in the news system. Each server contacts its neighbors frequently to exchange new articles. When servers make contact, they exchange only articles that the other server does not have, which propagates copies of new articles throughout the news system.

A server need not accept articles from a specific newsgroup. Some system administrators configure their servers to reject certain newsgroups to eliminate some types of content. For example, a corporate server might not carry any of the groups in the *rec* hierarchy because they are not business-related. Refusing to accept articles from specified servers also reduces the amount of storage space needed to store articles.

The time between a new article being posted and its spread to the farthest reaches of the news network depends on the frequency of updates between servers. When server updates are frequent, copies of the article spread more quickly. If a server only makes contact with its neighbors once a day, its news will always be at least a day old. Many servers make contact several times a day. In most parts of the Internet, an article spreads world-wide within one day.

Articles from different sites may reach a particular server before those from other sites, because of the distributed manner in which information spreads. Sometimes, when someone posts an article, a user on a different site responds to the original posting, but the second article reaches a given server before the original article. The original article arrives eventually, but a user who happens to read the newsgroup may stumble on a reply to a question that, from that user's perspective, hasn't even been asked yet.

The set of servers exchanging network news articles comprise a network in itself. This virtual network is called USENET. Sites that exchange news articles do not need to connect directly use the TCP/IP protocol suite. Many sites connect to each other using the UUCP dial-up protocols. A USENET host *may not* be connected directly to the Internet itself.

How Articles Are Formatted

News articles use a format based on RFC 822 and described in RFC 1036. Like mail messages, news articles are ASCII text-based. They have a header block and body, separated by a blank line. News articles use a few extra headers to identify the topic group to which the article belongs. The additional headers are more useful to servers when they exchange articles than to clients when users read articles. If you want detailed information about the specific header differences, consult RFC 1036, which is provided on the companion CD-ROM.

NNTP

Network news clients interact with network news servers using the Network News Transport Protocol (NNTP), which is described in RFC 977. This section focuses on the interaction between clients and servers.

Servers also use NNTP to exchange articles. The interaction between servers is similar to that between a client and a server, but differences do exist. If you want more information about the services used by servers, consult RFC 977.

NNTP is a simple, text-based protocol similar to SMTP and POP3. All lines of text use the US-ASCII character set and CRLF new line sequence convention.

An NNTP session begins with a client contacting the server on well-known port 119 using TCP. When the connection is established, the server sends a greeting and then waits for the client to send commands. The server responds to each command with a reply, possibly followed by the text of all or a portion of a news article.

Commands

NNTP commands are contained on a single line of text, terminated with CRLF. A command consists of a command word followed by a parameter, if required. The parameter is separated from the command word with space characters. Commands and parameters are not normally case sensitive (the exception is message ID parameters). All command lines must be less than or equal to 512 characters long. This length includes the terminating CRLF sequence, which counts as two characters. Here are some sample NNTP command lines:

```
GROUP  rec.arts.startrek.misc
stat  10110
List
artiCLE  <2934@mythical.com>
```

Responses

After the client sends the server a command, the server responds. The server response consists of a single-line numeric response, possibly followed by additional text. The numeric response format is similar to that used with SMTP. The numeric response begins with a 3-digit numeric code. The three digits provide different levels of detail to the client.

The first digit indicates whether the command succeeded or failed. The first digit can be one of the following codes:

- Code "1" indicates an informational message.
- Code "2" indicates success.
- Code "3" is used for commands that require further interaction. It indicates success of the current part but not necessarily of the whole sequence.
- Code "4" indicates that the command was valid and understood, but the operation couldn't be performed for some reason.
- Code "5" indicates that the server did not understand the command.

The second digit indicates the response category: "0" for responses related to the connection, "1" for responses related to the selection of a newsgroup, and so on. Most clients simply interpret the first digit to determine whether the command succeeded or failed.

Other information may follow the 3-digit numeric response code on the same line. For instance, if a NEXT command generates no error, the server adds the index number and message ID of the next article to the line that follows the successful response code.

The server typically includes human-readable text after all numeric response codes and additional information. This text explains the meaning of the response to any human who might try to debug the exchange of commands and responses. The text is optional and is not standardized.

Many NNTP commands send additional data after the initial response line. For instance, if the client used the ARTICLE command to request the text of a particular article and no errors occurred, the server responds with a line that contains the 220 numeric response code, article index number, and article message ID string. The 220 response code indicates that the ARTICLE command was successful and that the text of the article will follow. The server then sends the text of the article line by line, terminating the article text with a line that contains a single period character. As with SMTP and POP3, NNTP inserts a period before every line of article text that begins with a period. The receiver strips out leading periods on received lines. This transparency behavior keeps valid article lines that contain only a single period from being confused with the end-of-data indication.

Article Indexes and Message IDs

An NNTP server uses article index numbers to identify individual articles during an NNTP session. A new article arriving at a server receives the next free index number within its associated newsgroup. Using the article index number, a client can retrieve the text of the article from the server.

Article index numbers are assigned locally. Because articles arrive at servers at different times, article number 5 in the *comp.lang.c* newsgroup on one server probably will not be article number 5 on a different server. Since articles are just used for communication with a given server, however, this does not present a problem.

NNTP commands also provide message ID strings along with article indexes. The message ID strings are parsed from the Message-ID header field of the articles themselves. Like article index numbers, message ID strings can be used to identify articles to the server. The server must search through a set of articles in a newsgroup to find the article with the right message ID string. This method can be slower than using index numbers.

Servers do not have infinite storage capacity. At some point, servers must discard old articles to reclaim space for newer articles. Discarded articles are called *expired*. Most NNTP server software allows the server system administrator to select the length of time that articles should be saved before they expire. The system administrator sets the length of time based on the amount of storage space available and how many articles arrive every day.

When articles expire, the remaining articles retain their index numbers. This procedure allows a client to store the index numbers of articles that the user read during previous sessions. Article index numbers remain persistent across NNTP sessions with the same server. When the user reads network news again, the user will not see the previously read articles.

Sample NNTP Session

A simple NNTP client uses only a few NNTP commands. This section describes the commonly used procedures necessary to select a newsgroup, generate an article summary list, and download article text for display. The sample session transcripts presented in this section use "S:" to indicate text sent by the server and "C:" to indicate text sent by the client.

Connecting

A TCP connection must be established before communication can occur between an NNTP client and server. The client initiates the connection to TCP port 119 on the server. After accepting the connection, the server sends a greeting response. The greeting response carries the 200 or 201 numeric response code to indicate whether the server allows clients to post articles. (200 if so, 201 if not.)

That's all there is to connecting. Unlike SMTP or POP3, the client does not have to identify itself or provide any authentication information.

Retrieving a List of Active Newsgroups

Users frequently want to see a list of available newsgroups. The LIST command provides a list of newsgroup names and other information associated with each newsgroup that the client can present to the user. Here is a typical list:

```
C: [connects to TCP port 119 on server]
S: 200 nntp.mythical.com ready - posting OK
C: LIST
S: 215 list of newsgroups follows
S: comp.protocols.tcp-ip 543 839 y
S: comp.lang.c 4030 5038 y
S: rec.games.chess 968 1016 y
S: rec.games.programming 4890 5390 y
S: rec.food.chocolate 234 984 y
S: sci.archaeology 982 1030 y
S: sci.bio.microbiology 39 50 n
S: .
```

The server replies to the LIST command with the 215 response code, which indicates that a list of newsgroups follows. Each line contains one newsgroup listing. In addition to the newsgroup name, each line contains two numbers and a "y" or "n."

The two numbers are the high and low index numbers of the current articles in the group. These numbers inform the user how many articles exist on the server for that newsgroup.

The "y" or "n" flag indicates whether the newsgroup allows posting. Some newsgroups are *moderated*. In this case, ordinary users cannot post to the newsgroup. Instead, all articles must be mailed to the group moderator, who reviews the material and posts it if it is appropriate. Moderated newsgroups are frequently used for special interest topics with limited readership. They help ensure that the articles in the group stay on topic and that responses to previous articles don't degenerate into needless arguments ("flame wars").

Selecting a Newsgroup

Before the NNTP client can retrieve information about any article, it must specify the name of a newsgroup to the NNTP server. The newsgroup name is specified using the GROUP command:

```
C: [connects to TCP port 119 on server]
S: 200 nntp.mythical.com ready — posting OK
C: GROUP comp.lang.c
S: 211 1009 4030 5038 comp.lang.c selected
```

The server responds to the GROUP command with a one-line response. The numeric response code indicates whether the command was successful. The 211 code in this example indicates success. The server returns code 411 when the GROUP command indicates that a newsgroup is not available on this server or does not exist.

The numbers following the numeric response code indicate the approximate number of articles in the newsgroup (1009, in this example) and the indexes of the first and last articles in the newsgroup. The first and last article indexes are the same numbers that the LIST command returns for the group.

The article count may not be exactly correct. Articles between the first and last articles in the group may have expired and may no longer be present on the server. The server virtually calculates the article count by simply subtracting the first article index number from the last article index number. If all the articles between the first and last index number are present, this method is accurate. If some articles have expired, the count will be higher than it should be. Some servers return an accurate count, no matter how many articles have expired. In this case, the count may not equal the last index minus the first index.

Once the client successfully executes the GROUP command, it can manipulate articles within the group.

Retrieving Article Headers

Many popular newsgroups carry a high traffic load. In one day, a server may receive a few hundred articles associated with a popular newsgroup. If a user doesn't read a high-traffic group for a few days, more than 1000 articles could be waiting when the group is next read.

Of course, nobody has time to read that many articles. Users who read these popular newsgroups typically are interested in only a few of the articles. It makes no sense to request the text of each article from the server. Instead, a summary listing of each of the articles allows the user to retrieve the ones of interest.

An article summary listing is similar to the email mailbox we implemented in the Mail Client program. A summary listing is generated from the article header fields and typically includes the date, originator of the article, and subject. To generate a summary listing, the NNTP client needs access to the headers for each of the articles. How can we get the headers without getting the articles, however? If we have to retrieve the articles anyway, we haven't saved the user any time by generating a summary listing.

Fortunately, NNTP allows the client to request just the headers of a specified article using the HEAD command. The server sends the header text but skips the body of the article, as shown here:

```
C: [connects to TCP port 119 on server]
S: 200 nntp.mythical.com ready — posting OK
C: GROUP comp.lang.c
S: 211 1009 4030 5038 comp.lang.c selected
C: HEAD 4030
S: 221 4030 <349845@mythical.com> Header follows
S: [...Header lines...]
S: .
```

The parameter to the HEAD command is an article index number or article message ID string. In this example, we've used the article index number.

The server responds to the HEAD command with a 221 response code if the article is available. It responds with a 423 response code if the specified article does not exist. Following the response code in the response line, the server includes the article index number (again) and the article message ID.

The server follows the response line with lines of header text, terminated by a single period on a line by itself.

Retrieving Multiple Headers Quickly

After selecting a newsgroup, an NNTP client application often needs to retrieve all of the headers in that newsgroup. NNTP provides the NEXT command to make this task painless.

During an NNTP session, the server keeps an internal *current article pointer.* This pointer specifies the current article. When a GROUP command occurs, the current article pointer is set to the first article in the group. The client can use the HEAD command without an argument to retrieve the header associated with the current article. NNTP provides two commands, NEXT and LAST, to move the current article pointer.

A client can retrieve headers quickly using the HEAD and NEXT commands; for instance:

```
C: [connects to TCP port 119 on server]
S: 200 nntp.mythical.com ready — posting OK
C: GROUP comp.lang.c
S: 211 10 4030 4040 comp.lang.c selected
C: HEAD
S: 221 4030 <349845@mythical.com> Header follows
S: [...Header lines for the first article...]
S: .
C: NEXT
S: 223 4031 <23498@blah.foo.edu> Article selected
C: HEAD
S: 221 4031 <23498@blah.foo.edu> Header follows
S: [...Header lines for the second article...]
S: .
C: NEXT
S: 223 4040 <982345@zip.bar.gov> Article selected
C: HEAD
S: 221 4040 <982345@zip.bar.gov> Header follows
S: [...Header lines for the third article...]
S: .
C: NEXT
S: 421 No next article
```

In this example, the client retrieves three articles from the server. The HEAD command retrieves the first article and then a sequence of NEXT and HEAD commands retrieves the other articles. The retrieval process stops when the client receives a 421 code from the server in response to a NEXT command.

Our mythical server first indicated that ten articles existed in the group (the number following the numeric response code in the GROUP response line). Only three articles were actually unexpired in the article range reported by the server, however. Remember that the number of articles returned by the server is approximate.

Notice that the NEXT command automatically skips over expired articles. Because of this behavior, the NEXT command helps improve client performance.

An alternative strategy for quick retrieval is to use the first and last article indexes returned in the GROUP command response to set up a loop. The client then issues multiple HEAD commands, using the loop index as the article number parameter in the HEAD command. In this case, however, the client would get an error message for each of the expired articles in the range. These messages slow performance.

Retrieving Articles

Once the client retrieves a list of headers and displays a summary list, the user can request that a specific article be displayed. To retrieve the article, the client uses the ARTICLE command. The ARTICLE command takes a single optional parameter: the index number or message ID of the article to retrieve. If no parameter is given, the ARTICLE command retrieves the article specified by the current article pointer.

The following example shows the client retrieving headers and then requesting the full text of the article that the user requested.

```
C: [connects to TCP port 119 on server]
S: 200 nntp.mythical.com ready — posting OK
C: GROUP comp.lang.c
S: 211 10 4030 4040 comp.lang.c selected
C: HEAD
S: 221 4030 <349845@mythical.com> Header follows
S: [...Header lines for the first article...]
S: .
C: NEXT
S: 223 4031 <23498@blah.foo.edu> Article selected
C: HEAD
S: 221 4031 <23498@blah.foo.edu> Header follows
S: [...Header lines for the second article...]
S: .
C: NEXT
S: 223 4040 <982345@zip.bar.gov> Article selected
C: HEAD
```

```
S: 221 4040 <982345@zip.bar.gov> Header follows
S: [...Header lines for the third article...]
S: .
C: NEXT
S: 421 No next article
C: ARTICLE 4031
S: 220 4031 <23498@blah.foo.edu> Article text follows
S: [...Full article text (headers and body)...]
S: .
```

Most interactive NNTP clients use the ARTICLE command with an index number or message ID parameter to retrieve a specific article. However, you could easily write a batch NNTP client that retrieved all of the articles in a set of newsgroups late at night. This NNTP client could use the NEXT and ARTICLE commands to retrieve every article in a group the same way that an interactive client might retrieve article headers.

Posting

After reading articles, users often want to express their opinions about what they just read. Sometimes users just want to post a message that doesn't respond to any specific issue; for instance, they may have a general question. NNTP allows a client to post a message into the news system using the POST command.

The POST command takes no arguments; it does not have to be issued after the GROUP command. The NNTP server deduces which newsgroup the article belongs to using the newsgroups header in the article itself. An article may specify multiple newsgroup names, separated by a comma. Consult RFC 1036 for more information about the newsgroups header and the format of network news articles.

If posting is allowed, the server replies to the POST command with a 340 numeric response code, indicating that it is waiting for the client to send the article text. The client then sends each line of the article text. The client indicates the end of the text by a line that contains a single period. As with text sent from the server to the client, the client inserts a period before the first character of lines that begin with a period character. The server removes the leading period character when it receives the line.

If no errors occur, the server returns numeric code 240 when the article termination sequence is received. If an error occurs for some reason (lack of disk space perhaps), the server returns code 441.

The following example shows how a message can be posted:

```
C: [connects to TCP port 119 on server]
S: 200 nntp.mythical.com ready - posting OK
C: POST
S: 340 Okay, send that text!!!
C: [...Client sends lines of article text...]
C: .
S: 240 Posting was successful
```

Ending an NNTP Session

The client terminates an NNTP session by sending the QUIT command. The QUIT command takes no parameters. The server responds to the QUIT command by sending the 205 reply code (unconditionally) and closes the TCP connection.

The following example shows a client posting a message and then quitting:

```
C: [connects to TCP port 119 on server]
S: 200 nntp.mythical.com ready - posting OK
C: POST
S: 340 Okay, send that text!!!
C: [...Client sends lines of article text...]
C: .
S: 240 Posting was successful
C: QUIT
S: 205 See-Ya! Closing connection...
S: [...server closes TCP connection...]
```

An NNTP Class: CNNTP

In this section, we'll examine the implementation of a C++ object that implements the NNTP protocol. Like the objects we implemented in previous chapters, this one is designed to be reusable. Although it supports only a small fraction of the total NNTP functionality, the object can be extended easily. The name of our NNTP class is **CNNTP**.

The **CNNTP** class is a bit more complicated than the **CSMTP** and **CPOP3** classes we've already implemented. Because the retrieval of headers and articles can take a long time, we will implement the **CNNTP** object so that it involves the application with the retrieval process. This method allows the application to update status messages as the NNTP session progresses.

The application interfaces to the **CNNTP** class through the following public member functions:

```
void Connect(HWND hwnd, UINT msg, char * pszHost,
     u_short ushPort);
void Group(HWND hwnd, UINT msg, char * pszGroup);
void Header(HWND hwnd, UINT msg);
void NextHeader(HWND hwnd, UINT msg);
void Article(HWND hwnd, UINT msg, long lArticle);
void Quit(HWND hwnd, UINT msg);
```

The programming model is fairly simple. Each function performs a specific task in the NNTP session. Each function takes a window handle and window message as its first two parameters. When the function has performed the associated task, the **CNNTP** object sends the specified window message to the specified window. Some of the functions accept additional parameters that are necessary for them to perform their task.

The **wParam** returned to the application in the window message indicates whether the function completed its task successfully. Normally, **wParam** is set to **CNNTP::RESULT_SUCCESS** or **CNNTP::RESULT_FAILURE**. Some functions return additional data in the message **lParam**.

The **Connect** member function connects a **CNNTP** object with the NNTP server. The **pszHost** parameter identifies the name of the host. The **ushPort** parameter specifies the TCP port (usually 119).

The **Group** member function sends the NNTP server the GROUP command. The newsgroup name is specified using the **pszGroup** parameter. If the **Group** function sends the application a **RESULT_SUCCESS** indication, the window message **lParam** is set to the number of messages in the group, as returned in the GROUP command response.

The **Header** function sends the server a HEAD command with no argument, which retrieves the header associated with the current article pointer. The **CNNTP** object stores the header text in a disk file. If the window message sent to the application after the operation completes indicates **RESULT_SUCCESS**, the **lParam** points to a **CNNTP::ARTICLEANDFILENAME** structure. The first member of the structure is a long integer that indicates the article index number of the returned header. The second member of the structure is a pointer to a string that indicates the name of the file in which the header text was stored. Both the **ARTICLEANDFILENAME** structure and string are allocated on the heap using the C++ **new** operator. The application must **delete** them after it finishes using them.

The **NextHeader** function causes the **CNNTP** object to retrieve the next header in sequence. The **CNNTP** object issues a NEXT command to the server. If the NEXT command succeeds, the **CNNTP** object automatically issues a HEAD command. As with the **Header** function, the header text is returned in a disk file and the **lParam** of the window message points to an **ARTICLEANDFILENAME** structure. If the NEXT command does not succeed or an error occurs, the window message result is **RESULT_FAILURE**. The application should assume that the NEXT command failed and no more headers can be retrieved.

After using the **Group** function, the application can use the **Header** function to retrieve the first header in a group. Additional headers after the first header can be retrieved using the **NextHeader** function.

The **Article** function allows the application to retrieve the text of a specific article. The **lArticle** parameter allows the application to specify the article number. If the **Article** function completion message indicates **RESULT_SUCCESS**, the **lParam** of the window message points to an **ARTICLEANDFILENAME** structure. The first member of the structure is the article index number. The article itself is returned to the application in a disk file. The second member of the **ARTICLEANDFILENAME** structure is a pointer to the disk filename. As with the **Header** and **NextHeader** functions, the application must delete the **ARTICLEANDFILENAME** structure and filename string.

The **Quit** function simply quits the current NNTP session. It causes the **CNNTP** object to send the **QUIT** function to the server. Unless something unexpected happens, the window message sent by the **Quit** function always indicates **RESULT_SUCCESS**.

The **CNNTP** class can process only one task at a time. After calling an interface function, the application should wait for the resulting window message before calling another interface function to perform a second task. If a second function is invoked before the first task completes, the **CNNTP** object will become confused.

Of course, the **CNNTP** class uses the Winsock asynchronous extensions, so multiple **CNNTP** objects can operate in the same program at the same time. Headers for multiple newsgroups or multiple articles can be retrieved at the same time using separate **CNNTP** objects.

CNNTP State Machine

The **CNNTP** class uses a state machine to implement the NNTP protocol. Figure 13.1 shows the **CNNTP** class state machine.

The state machine mechanics are essentially the same as the state machine in the **CPOP3** class. Unlike the **CPOP3** class, however, the **CNNTP** state machine decodes the numeric response codes returned from the server after an NNTP command and generates **EV_CODE1**, **EV_CODE2**, ... and **EV_CODE5** events to the state machine. The **CPOP3** class generated only simple **EV_DATAREADY** events for all responses.

Remember that the **CPOP3** state machine used **EV_DATAREADY** events because the **CPOP3::StreamCallback** function could not tell the difference between a response line and a line of message text. The **CNNTP** object uses a flag named **m_bDataMode** to determine whether lines of text returned from the server should be interpreted as lines of article text or numeric response lines.

Figure 13.1

The CNNTP class state machine.

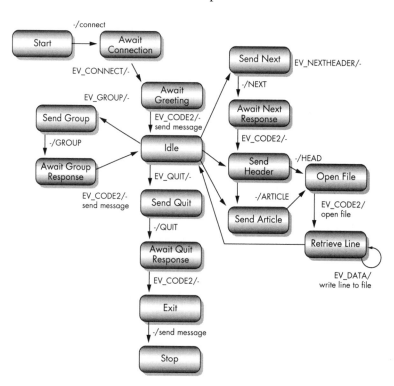

If the **m_bDataMode** flag is TRUE, the **CNNTP::StreamCallback** function interprets the line of received text as a line of article text. If the line contains just a single period, the **StreamCallback** function sends an **EV_ENDDATA** event to the state machine. If the line of text contains something other than a single period, the **StreamCallback** function sends the state machine an **EV_DATA** event.

If the **m_bDataMode** flag is FALSE, the **CNNTP::StreamCallback** function interprets the line of message text as a numeric response code. The CNNTP stream callback function injects **EV_CODE1** ... **EV_CODE5** events into the state machine depending on the first character of the response code.

In either case, the **CNNTP::StreamCallback** function makes the line of text associated with the state machine event available in the **m_szReplyLineBuffer** string. If the line is a server response, the state machine can use the line to retrieve the additional information that follows the numeric response code in some server responses. If the line is article text, the state machine writes the line to a file.

The **CNNTP** state machine uses 16 states. The following sections describe these states.

Note: The CNNTP class does not implement the ability to retrieve a list of available newsgroup names or post articles to the server. You could, however, add these features to the News Client program very easily.

Start

The state machine enters the *Start* state when the **Connect** member function is called. The Start state uses a **CConnMgr** object to create a socket connection to the NNTP server specified in the **Connect** function arguments. The state machine then transitions to the Await Connection state.

Await Connection

The *Await Connection* state waits for the results of the connection manager object's connection attempt. If the connection manager was successful, the state machine transitions to the Await Greeting state. The state machine transitions to the Exit state if the connection manager could not connect to the server.

Await Greeting

The *Await Greeting* state waits for the server to send the initial greeting message after the connection is established. Assuming the server sends an acceptable response, the state machine sends a window message with the **RESULT_SUCCESS** status code to the window specified in the call to the **Connect** function and transitions to the Idle state. If the server sends an unacceptable response (anything other than **EV_CODE2**), the state machine sends a **RESULT_FAILURE** message to the window and transitions to the Exit state.

Idle

As shown in Figure 13.1, the *Idle* state is entered when the state machine is not doing anything. The Idle state waits for the program to invoke another **CNNTP** command function. The command functions generate **EV_GROUP**, **EV_NEXTHEADER, EV_HEADER, EV_ARTICLE,** and **EV_QUIT** events to the state machine. The state machine transitions to the appropriate state for the command event received.

Send Group

The *Send Group* state is entered from the Idle state as the result of an **EV_GROUP** event. The Send Group state sends the server a GROUP command and then transitions to the Await Group Response state to wait for the server's reply.

Await Group Response

The *Await Group Response* state waits for the server's reply to the GROUP command sent by the Send Group state.

If the state machine receives an **EV_CODE2** event, a window message indicating **RESULT_SUCCESS** is sent to the application. The **lParam** of the window message is set to the number of messages in the group, as returned in the response line (the number after the numeric response code).

If the state machine receives an **EV_CODE4** event, a window message indicating **RESULT_FAILURE** is sent to the application.

In either case, the state machine transitions back to the Idle state.

Send Next

The *Send Next* state is entered from the Idle state when the state machine receives a **EV_NEXTHEADER** event. The Send Next state simply sends the server a NEXT command and transitions to the Await Next Response state.

Await Next Response

The *Await Next Response* state waits for the server's response to the NEXT command sent in the Send Next state. If the Await Next Response state receives **EV_CODE2**, it transitions to the Send Header state.

If it receives **EV_CODE4**, it sends a window message indicating **RESULT_FAILURE** to the application and transitions back to the Idle state. The server sends a 421 code when no article follows the current article in the current newsgroup.

Send Header

The *Send Header* state is entered from either the Idle state on receipt of an **EV_HEADER** event or the Await Next Response state after the NEXT command is sent to the server. The Send Header state simply sends the HEAD command to the server. No arguments are sent with the HEAD command, so the current article header is retrieved from the server. After sending the HEAD command, the state machine transitions to the Open File state.

Open File

The *Open File* state is entered from either the Send Header or Send Article state. The Open File state waits for the response code from the HEAD or ARTICLE command sent in the Send Header or Send Article state. If the state receives an **EV_CODE2** event indicating that the HEAD or ARTICLE command succeeded, the state generates a temporary filename to contain the data. It opens the file, sets the **m_bDataMode** flag to **TRUE**, and transitions the state machine to the Retrieve Line state.

If the Open File state receives an **EV_CODE4** event, it sends the application a **RESULT_FAILURE** indication and returns the state machine to the Idle state.

Retrieve Line

The *Retrieve Line* state captures lines of header and article text and writes them to the file opened in the Open File state. While the **m_bDataMode** flag is set to **TRUE**, the **StreamCallback** function continues to send either **EV_DATA** or **EV_ENDDATA** events to the state machine for each line that the server returns.

When the Retrieve Line state receives an **EV_DATA** event, it checks the first character of the line to see if it is a period. If not, the code writes the line of text to the file. If the first character is a period, all the characters following the first character are written to the file. This behavior implements the transparency rules for lines beginning with a period. After the line is written to the file, the state machine remains in the Retrieve Line state.

The **StreamCallback** function sends an **EV_ENDDATA** message to the state machine when it receives a line that contains only a single period. The Retrieve Line state sets the **m_bDataMode** flag back to FALSE, closes the header or article text file, and sends the application a window message. The **lParam** of the window message points to a newly allocated **ARTICLEANDFILENAME** structure, as described in a previous section.

After sending the window message, the state machine transitions back to the Idle state.

Send Article

The *Send Article* state is entered from the Idle state when the state machine receives an **EV_ARTICLE** event, as the result of the application calling the **Article** member function. The Send Article state simply sends an ARTICLE command to the server and transitions to the Open File state. The ARTICLE command includes the article index number passed to the **Article** function by the application.

Quit

The *Quit* state is entered from the Idle state when the state machine receives an **EV_QUIT** event. The Quit state sends the server a QUIT command and transitions to the Await Quit Response state.

Await Quit Response

The *Await Quit Response* state waits for the server to respond to the QUIT command sent in the Quit state. Almost any response is acceptable, although the server should send only a 205 reply code. The state machine simply transitions to the Exit state.

Exit

The *Exit* state is entered primarily from the Await Quit Response state. The Exit state closes the socket used for the NNTP connection and deletes any memory allocated by the **CNNTP** object while it was operating. The Exit state sends a window message to the application. Typically, this window message serves as the window message from the Quit command and indicates **RESULT_SUCCESS**.

Sometimes, the Exit state is entered from other states when a fatal error occurs. In this case, the message sent from the Exit state indicates **RESULT_FAILURE** or **RESULT_FATALERROR** to the application.

After sending the application a window message, the state machine transitions to the Stop state.

Stop

The *Stop* state is simply a black hole for state machine events. This state swallows all events and no action is taken. This process ensures that any spurious events that may be generated during an unusual error condition don't cause a problem before the **CNNTP** object is destroyed.

News Client Project

To demonstrate our new **CNNTP** class, we'll build a small network news client named News Client. (I'm very creative with names, don't you think?) News Client is not a full-featured news client, but it does allow a user to perform the most common operations: browsing articles in a group and reading them. Figure 13.2 illustrates the News Client application.

The News Client project is composed of 17 main files and a set of associated include files. Table 13.1 lists the project files along with a short description. Note that the Mail Client program also uses many of these files.

Figure 13.2

The News Client application.

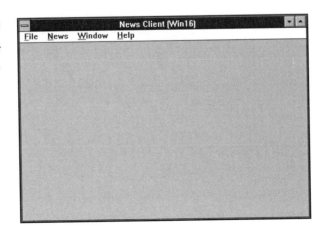

Table 13.1 News Client Project Files		
File	**Description**	**Reference**
CASYNCDB.CPP	Asynchronous database lookup base class	Listing 6.6
CCONNMGR.CPP	Connection manager class	On companion CD-ROM in binary form
CHOST.CPP	Host information lookup class	Listing 6.8
CLIST.CPP	Simple list class	On companion CD-ROM in binary form
CNNTP.CPP	NNTP protocol class	Listing 13.2
CSOCKADR.CPP	Internet address class	Listing 6.4
CSOCKET.CPP	Stream socket class	Listing 6.12
CTL3DV2.LIB	Import library for the 3D controls DLL	On companion CD-ROM in binary form
CWINSOCK.CPP	The CWinsock class and other infrastructure functions and classes	Listing 6.2
NEWSART.CPP	The application module that implements article retrieval and viewing capability	Listing 13.5
NEWSCLI.CPP	The main application module (where WinMain resides)	Listing 13.3
NEWSCLI.DEF	The linker definition file for the News Client project	Listing 13.6
NEWSCLI.RC	The source file for the project resources	Listing 13.7
NEWSGRP.CPP	The application module that retrieves article headers and displays a newsgroup article summary list	Listing 13.4
PARSDATE.CPP	Functions for parsing an RFC 822 style date	On companion CD-ROM in binary form
UTILITY.CPP	A set of general-purpose utility functions	On companion CD-ROM in binary form
WINSOCK.LIB	Import library for WINSOCK.DLL	On companion CD-ROM in binary form

The News Client program is structured much like the Mail Client program that we developed in previous chapters. I shamelessly swiped much of the code in NEWSCLI.CPP, NEWSGRP.CPP, and NEWSART.CPP from the Mail Client project to serve as a starting point for the News Client project. The following sections describe only the major differences—those related to the interaction of the program with the **CNNTP** class.

Configuration

The user must configure the program to connect with a server before using News Client. The user chooses the News|Configure menu choice to configure News Client.

Choosing News|Configure causes the program to execute the **OnNewsConfigure** function in NEWSCLI.CPP (Listing 13.3). This function displays the Configure dialog box, shown in Figure 13.3.

When the user enters the name of the server and port number, the **OnNewsConfigure** function writes the configuration to an initialization file stored in the WINDOWS directory. Each time the program restarts, it reads this file to restore the configuration parameters.

Selecting a Group

The user initiates a connection with the news server by choosing the File|Open Group menu choice. This action causes the **OnFileOpenGroup** function in the NEWSCLI.CPP module to be called.

The **OnFileOpenGroup** function displays the Open Group dialog box shown in Figure 13.4. The dialog box allows the user to enter the name of the group to open. News Client does not provide a list of available newsgroup names. The user must already know the name of a valid group.

After the user enters the newsgroup name, **OnFileOpenGroup** creates an MDI child window of the group window class. The title of the window becomes the name of the group entered by the user in the Open Group dialog box. When the group window is created, it retrieves the name of the group to open from its window title. This technique allows the title of the window to be set using the same information that must be passed to the window upon creation. Using this technique, the **OnFileOpenGroup** function can simply set the **lParam** of the **MDICREATESTRUCT** structure to **NULL** when the group window is created.

Figure 13.3

The News Client Configure dialog box.

Figure 13.4

Entering the name of a newsgroup.

Retrieving Headers

The group window class is implemented in the NEWSGRP.CPP application module, shown in Listing 13.4. The group window downloads all of the headers in the specified group and displays a summary listing to the user, as shown in Figure 13.5. The user can then select an article and request to view it.

The summary listing is created using a list box control. The list box control is created in the **OnCreate** function when it is called to handle the **WM_CREATE** window message that was sent to the window. After the list box is created, the **OnCreate** function retrieves the group name from the title of the window. The group name is stored in a set of private variables associated with the group window.

Next, the **OnCreate** function calls the **SetStatus** function to add a "connecting..." message after the group name in the window title. The **SetStatus** function (Listing 13.4) simply concatenates the group name with the specified status message and sets the window title to the resulting string.

After the status message is set, **OnCreate** creates a **CNNTP** object and invokes the **Connect** member function to connect to the server. The **OnCreate** function indicates that the **CNNTP** object should send a **WM_NNTPCONNECTED** message to the group window when it connects. The server name and port number configured by the user are included as parameters to the **Connect** function call.

After calling the **CNNTP::Connect** function, **OnCreate** sets the **bRetrieving** flag in the private window data to TRUE. If the user tries to close the group window

Figure 13.5

The group article summary window.

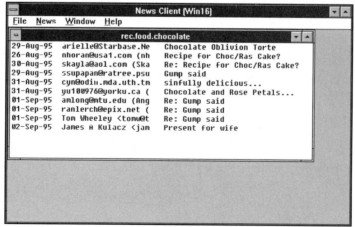

while the **bRetrieving** flag is set, News Client displays a message indicating that the program is connected to the server. The user can then cancel the operation if desired.

Finally, the **OnCreate** function returns.

The **WM_NNTPCONNECTED** message is a private window message. The NEWSGRP.CPP file defines several private messages for the **CNNTP** object to send back to the window. Each window message is defined relative to **WM_USER**, as shown here:

```
#define  WM_NNTPCONNECTED      WM_USER
#define  WM_NNTPGROUPDONE      (WM_USER + 1)
#define  WM_NNTPHEADERDONE     (WM_USER + 2)
#define  WM_NNTPQUITDONE       (WM_USER + 3)
```

When the **CNNTP** object connects to the server, it sends the window a **WM_NNTPCONNECTED** message. This message is handled by the **OnNNTPConnect** function.

The **OnNNTPConnect** function does minimal processing. It simply checks to see if the connection attempt was successful. If not, it displays an error message for the user and then closes the group window. If the operation was successful, it sets the retrieval status in the window title bar to "retrieving article count...." **OnNNTPConnect** then invokes the **CNNTP::Group** function. **OnNNTPConnect** passes the name of the group to the Group function and asks the **CNNTP** object to send a **WM_NNTPGROUPDONE** message to the window when the operation completes.

When the **CNNTP** object receives a response to the GROUP command sent to the server, it sends a **WM_NNTPGROUPDONE** message to the group window. The **WM_NNTPGROUPDONE** message is handled by the **OnNNTPGroupDone** function.

The **OnNNTPGroupDone** function first checks to see if the GROUP command sent to the server was successful. If not, the user probably entered an invalid group name. The **OnNNTPGroupDone** function informs the user of any error and closes the group window.

If the **CNNTP** object returned **RESULT_SUCCESS** from the **Group** function, the **OnNNTPGroupDone** function prepares to download all the headers in the group.

First, the **OnNNTPGroupDone** function stores the number of articles in the group in a private window variable. This information is returned in the **lParam** of the **WM_NNTPGROUPDONE** message and is used to update a progress status message as each header is retrieved.

Next, the **OnNNTPGroupDone** message updates the status message by calling the **SetRetrievalStatus** function. The **SetRetrievalStatus** function simply creates a progress message that indicates the completion percentage of the retrieval process. The **SetRetrievalStatus** function formats the progress message using the number of articles in the group (the number just stored) and then calls **SetStatus** to change the title bar of the window. Figure 13.6 shows the status message displayed as headers are downloaded.

Finally, the **OnNNTPGroupDone** function invokes the **CNNTP::Header** function to retrieve the first header in the group. The function call indicates that a **WM_NNTPHEADERDONE** message should be sent to the window when the header is retrieved.

WM_NNTPHEADERDONE messages are handled by the **OnNNTPHeaderDone** function. The **OnNNTPHeaderDone** function first checks to see if a header was retrieved successfully. If so, the function updates the count of the headers retrieved and sets the status message appropriately. Next, the function invokes the **CNNTP::NextHeader** function to start the retrieval of the next header. The **OnNNTPHeaderDone** function tells the **CNNTP** object to send a **WM_NNTPHEADERDONE** message to the window when the opera-

Figure 13.6

News Client updates a status message while it downloads headers.

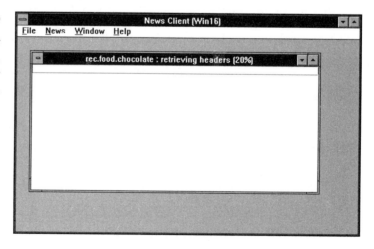

tion completes. When the next header is retrieved, the **OnNNTPHeaderDone** function is invoked again.

After the **OnNNTPHeaderDone** function starts the **CNNTP** object retrieving the next header, the function processes the current header. The **GetSummaryInfo** function is called to parse the appropriate information from the message header and create a **SUMMARYINFO** record for the article. The **GetSummaryInfo** function is virtually unchanged from the function of the same name in the Mail Client program.

You may wonder why the **OnNNTPHeaderDone** function invokes the **CNNTP::NextHeader** function *before* processing the current header. This sequence helps improve performance. The NNTP server can start finding and sending the appropriate article headers while the **OnNNTPHeaderDone** function processes the previous headers. This approach overlaps some of the processing and speeds up the overall retrieval process.

When the **WM_NNTPHEADERDONE** message indicates **RESULT_FAILURE**, no more articles are in the group. The **OnNNTPHeaderDone** function sets the status message to "closing connection" and invokes the **CNNTP::Quit** function to disconnect from the NNTP server. The **OnNNTPHeaderDone** function asks the **CNNTP** object to send the window a **WM_NNTPQUITDONE** message when the operation completes.

The **OnNNTPQuitDone** function is called to handle **WM_NNTPQUITDONE** messages. The **OnNNTPQuitDone** function reports any errors indicated by the **WM_NNTPQUITDONE** message. If no error occurred, **OnNNTPQuitDone** sets the connection status to an empty string, effectively setting the window title back to just the name of the newsgroup.

Finally, **OnNNTPQuitDone** calls **CreateArticleList** to put the list of **SUMMARYINFO** records created from the article headers into the group window's list box. The list displays the list of article summaries, allowing the user to select one.

Retrieving Articles

The article retrieval process starts when the user selects an article to view in the newsgroup article summary window. The user can select the article summary and the News/View Article menu choice or double click on the article summary. Either behavior invokes the **OnNewsViewArticle** function in NEWSGRP.CPP.

The **OnNewsViewArticle** function finds the **SUMMARYINFO** entry corresponding to the highlighted summary entry in the summary list box control. The **OnNewsViewArticle** function creates a **GROUPANDARTICLE** structure to hold the name of the group and the NNTP index number of the selected article. The function then creates an article viewer MDI child window. A pointer to the **GROUPANDARTICLE** structure is passed in the **lParam** member of the **MDICREATESTRUCT** used to create the window.

The article viewer window drives the article retrieval process. The article viewer window is implemented in the NEWSART.CPP module (Listing 13.5).

The article retrieval process starts when the article viewer window is created and receives a **WM_CREATE** window message. This **WM_CREATE** window message is handled by the **OnCreate** function in NEWSART.CPP.

The **OnCreate** function creates a read-only edit control in which to display the retrieved article text. Next, the **OnCreate** function retrieves the pointer to the **GROUPANDARTICLE** structure created in the **OnNewsViewArticle** function in NEWSGRP.CPP. The **OnCreate** function stores the data contained in the **GROUPANDARTICLE** structure in private window variables and deletes the structure itself.

The **OnCreate** function then creates a **CNNTP** object and invokes the **CNNTP::Connect** member function to connect to the NNTP server. The function then calls the **SetStatus** function in the NEWSART.CPP module, which sets a status message in the window title bar similar to that used in the NEWSGRP.CPP module.

As with the NEWSGRP.CPP module, the NEWSART.CPP module defines a set of private window messages used to communicate with the **CNNTP** object. These messages are private to the article viewer window. Although they have the same names as the similar messages used in the NEWSGRP.CPP module, they don't all have the same values.

After the **CNNTP** object connects with the server, the article viewer window selects the newsgroup specified in the **GROUPANDARTICLE** structure passed to it in the **WM_CREATE** message. The connection and group selection process is virtually identical to that used in the NEWSGRP.CPP module. The **WM_NNTPCONNECTED** message is handled by the **OnNNTPConnect** function, which calls the **CNNTP::Group** function. The resulting **WM_NNTPGROUPDONE** message is handled by the **OnNNTPGroupDone** function. Any errors that occur along the way are signaled to the user and the window is closed.

The **OnNNTPGroupDone** function starts the process of actually retrieving the article. The function calls the **SetStatus** function to display a "retrieving article" message in the window title bar and then calls the **CNNTP::Article** function. The call to the **CNNTP::Article** function includes the NNTP article index number passed to the window in the **GROUPANDARTICLE** structure when it was created.

The **CNNTP** object sends the window a **WM_NNTPARTICLEDONE** message when it retrieves the article. The **OnNNTPArticleDone** function handles this window message. As with message headers, the **CNNTP** object returns article text in a disk file. The **OnNNTPArticleDone** function calls the **PutFileIntoEditCtl** function to read the file containing the article and put the text into the read-only edit control. Figure 13.7 shows an article in the viewer after it was retrieved.

After deleting the structures and memory used to hold the name of the disk file and the disk file itself, the **OnNNTPArticleDone** function calls the **CNNTP::Quit** function to close the connection from the server.

The final **WM_NNTPQUITDONE** message is handled by the **OnNNTPQuitDone** function, which operates identically to the function of the same name in the NEWSGRP.CPP module.

That's it! We've just built a simple network news client application.

Figure 13.7

An article in the viewer window after retrieval.

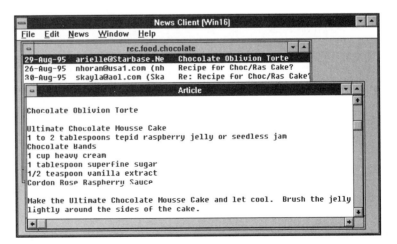

Listings

This section contains the listings of files used in the News Client project. The listings are:

Listing 13.1 is the header file for the **CNNTP** class, CNNTP.H.

Listing 13.2 is the implementation file for the **CNNTP** class, CNNTP.CPP.

Listing 13.3 is the main file for the News Client application, NEWSCLI.CPP.

Listing 13.4 is the code that implements the newsgroup article summary window for the News Client application, NEWSGRP.CPP.

Listing 13.5 is the code that implements the article viewer window for the News Client application, NEWSART.CPP.

Listing 13.6 is the linker definition file for the News Client application, NEWSCLI.DEF.

Listing 13.7 is the resource compiler source code for the News Client resources, NEWSCLI.RC.

Listing 13.8 is the header file containing identifier definitions of resource objects, NEWSCLI.RH.

Listing 13.1 CNNTP.H

```
/*
    File: CNNTP.H
    Description:
        A class for interacting with an NNTP server.
    Copyright 1995, David G. Roberts
*/

#ifndef _CNNTP_H
#define _CNNTP_H

#ifndef _CSOCKET_H
#include "csocket.h"
#endif
#ifndef _CCONNMGR_H
#include "cconnmgr.h"
#endif
#ifndef _CSTRLIST_H
#include "cstrlist.h"
#endif
#include <fstream.h>
```

```
class CNNTP : private CConnMgrCallback, private CStreamCallback {
public:
    enum RESULT { RESULT_ABORT, RESULT_SUCCESS, RESULT_FAILURE,
        RESULT_FATALERROR };
    struct ARTICLEANDFILENAME {
        long      lArticleNum;
        char *    pszFilename;
    };
private:
    enum CONSTANTS { MAX_REPLY_SIZE = 1001, MAX_LINE_SIZE = 200 };
    enum EVENT { EV_NULLEVENT, EV_CONNECT, EV_CLOSE, EV_DATA,
        EV_ENDDATA, EV_CODE1, EV_CODE2, EV_CODE3, EV_CODE4,
        EV_CODE5, EV_ERROR, EV_ABORT, EV_GROUP, EV_NEXTHEADER,
        EV_HEADER, EV_ARTICLE, EV_QUIT};
    typedef BOOL (CNNTP::*PSTATEFUNC)(EVENT ev);

    RESULT           m_result;
    CConnMgr         m_connmgr;
    CStreamSocket    m_sock;
    char             m_szReceiveBuffer[MAX_REPLY_SIZE];
    int              m_iReceiveBufferLen;
    char             m_szReplyLineBuffer[MAX_REPLY_SIZE];
    char             m_szLineBuffer[MAX_LINE_SIZE];
    PSTATEFUNC       m_pState;
    int              m_iError;
    char *           m_pszHost;
    u_short          m_ushPort;
    char             m_szFileName[255];
    BOOL             m_bDoCallback;
    ofstream         m_ofsFile;
    HWND             m_hwnd;
    UINT             m_msg;
    BOOL             m_bDataMode;
    char *           m_pszGroup;
    long             m_lArticle;

    // State machine interface.
    void Event(EVENT ev);
    void NextState(PSTATEFUNC pState) { m_pState = pState; };

    // State functions.
    BOOL Start(EVENT ev);
    BOOL AwaitConnection(EVENT ev);
    BOOL AwaitGreeting(EVENT ev);
    BOOL Idle(EVENT ev);
    BOOL SendGroup(EVENT ev);
    BOOL AwaitGroupResponse(EVENT ev);
    BOOL SendNext(EVENT ev);
    BOOL AwaitNextResponse(EVENT ev);
    BOOL SendHeader(EVENT ev);
    BOOL OpenFile(EVENT ev);
```

```
    BOOL RetrieveLine(EVENT ev);
    BOOL SendArticle(EVENT ev);
    BOOL Quit(EVENT ev);
    BOOL AwaitQuitResponse(EVENT ev);
    BOOL Exit(EVENT ev);
    BOOL Stop(EVENT ev);

    // Aux functions.
    BOOL ReadReplyData(void);
    BOOL LineComplete(void);
    void CopyLine(void);
    void ShrinkReceiveBuffer(void);
    BOOL MessageTerminator(void);

    virtual void ConnMgrCallback(int iToken,
        CConnMgrCallback::RESULT result);
    virtual void StreamCallback(int iToken, STREAMEVENT iEvent,
        int iError, char FAR * lpBuffer);

    // Eliminate the use of the copy constructor and operator=.
    CNNTP(const CNNTP&);
    operator=(const CNNTP&);
public:
    CNNTP() : m_pszHost(NULL), m_pszGroup(NULL)
        { m_connmgr.SetCallback(this, 0); };
    virtual ~CNNTP() { Abort(NULL, 0, FALSE); };

    void Connect(HWND hwnd, UINT msg, char * pszHost,
        u_short ushPort);
    void Group(HWND hwnd, UINT msg, char * pszGroup);
    void NextHeader(HWND hwnd, UINT msg);
    void Header(HWND hwnd, UINT msg);
    void Article(HWND hwnd, UINT msg, long lArticle);
    void Quit(HWND hwnd, UINT msg);

    void Abort(HWND hwnd, UINT msg, BOOL bDoCallback);

    int LastError(void) { return m_iError; };
};

#endif
```

Listing 13.2 CNNTP.CPP

```
/*
    File: CNNTP.CPP
    Description:
        A class for interacting with an NNTP server.
    Copyright 1995, David G. Roberts
*/

#include <ctype.h>  // need toupper()
#include <stdlib.h> // need srand()/rand()
```

```
#include <time.h>      // need time()
#include "cnntp.h"
#include "utility.h"
#include "myassert.h"


const char CR = '\015';
const char LF = '\012';


// Used to include at the end of text.  The compiler will
// splice strings.
// Use like m_sock.Send("Foo" CRLF,...).   Note that we have to use a
// macro rather than a string constant because we need the
// preprocessor to perform a textual substitution so the string
// splicing will work.
#define CRLF "\015\012"


void CNNTP::Event(EVENT ev)
{
    while ((this->*m_pState)(ev)) {
        ev = EV_NULLEVENT;
    };
}


void CNNTP::StreamCallback(int iToken, STREAMEVENT iEvent, int iError,
    char FAR *lpBuffer)
{
    UNUSED_PARAMETER(iToken);     // Eliminate the compiler warning.
    UNUSED_PARAMETER(lpBuffer);

    m_iError = iError;
    switch (iEvent) {
        case CStreamCallback::SE_CLOSE:
            Event(EV_CLOSE);
            break;
        case CStreamCallback::SE_DATAREADY:
            // Read the data.
            if (ReadReplyData()) {
                while (LineComplete()) {
                    CopyLine();
                    ShrinkReceiveBuffer();
                    if (m_bDataMode) {
                        if (MessageTerminator())
                            Event(EV_ENDDATA);
                        else
                            Event(EV_DATA);
                    }
                    else {
                        switch (m_szReplyLineBuffer[0]) {
                            case '1': Event(EV_CODE1); break;
                            case '2': Event(EV_CODE2); break;
                            case '3': Event(EV_CODE3); break;
                            case '4': Event(EV_CODE4); break;
```

```
                            case '5': Event(EV_CODE5); break;
                            default:
                                    // Something went wrong.
                                    Event(EV_ERROR); break;
                        }
                    }
                }
            }
            else {
                // Something went wrong.
                 WSCFatalError("Couldn't read from socket in CNNTP.");
            }
            break;
        case CStreamCallback::SE_DATASENT:
            // All commands to the server are one line.
            // Even if something blocks, we'll wait for a response
            // before sending another one, which means that the buffer
            // will be free again before we use it.
            break;
        default:
            // Error!  Something we weren't expecting.
            WSCFatalError(
                "Unexpected socket event in CNNTP::StreamCallback");
            break;
    }
}


BOOL CNNTP::ReadReplyData(void)
{
    // Figure out how much room is left in the buffer.
    int iBufferLen = MAX_REPLY_SIZE - m_iReceiveBufferLen;
    ASSERT(iBufferLen > 0);

    // Receive the data.
    int iResult = m_sock.Receive(
        &m_szReceiveBuffer[m_iReceiveBufferLen], &iBufferLen);

    if (iResult == WSANOERROR || iResult == WSAEWOULDBLOCK) {
        // If no errors, update the length of the data in the buffer.
        m_iReceiveBufferLen += iBufferLen;
        return TRUE;
    }
    else {
        // Save the error and signal it.
        m_iError = iResult;
        return FALSE;
    }
}


BOOL CNNTP::LineComplete(void)
{
    ASSERT(m_iReceiveBufferLen <= MAX_REPLY_SIZE);
```

```
    for (int i = 0; i < m_iReceiveBufferLen; i++) {
        if ((m_szReceiveBuffer[i] == CR) &&
            ((i + 1) < m_iReceiveBufferLen) &&
            (m_szReceiveBuffer[i + 1] == LF)) {
            return TRUE;
        }
    }
    return FALSE;
}

void CNNTP::CopyLine(void)
{
    ASSERT(m_iReceiveBufferLen <= MAX_REPLY_SIZE);

    for (int i = 0; i < m_iReceiveBufferLen; i++) {
        if ((m_szReceiveBuffer[i] == CR) &&
            ((i + 1) < m_iReceiveBufferLen) &&
            (m_szReceiveBuffer[i + 1] == LF)) {
            m_szReplyLineBuffer[i] = '\0';
            break;
        }
        else {
            m_szReplyLineBuffer[i] = m_szReceiveBuffer[i];
        }
    }
}

void CNNTP::ShrinkReceiveBuffer(void)
{
    ASSERT(m_iReceiveBufferLen <= MAX_REPLY_SIZE);

    // Find the CRLF at the end of the line.
    for (int i = 0; i < m_iReceiveBufferLen; i++) {
        if ((m_szReceiveBuffer[i] == CR) &&
            ((i + 1) < m_iReceiveBufferLen) &&
            (m_szReceiveBuffer[i + 1] == LF)) {
            // Set i equal to the character following the CRLF.
            i += 2;
            // Copy the characters following the CRLF to the beginning
            // of the line.
            for (int j = 0; j < m_iReceiveBufferLen - i; j++) {
                m_szReceiveBuffer[j] = m_szReceiveBuffer[i + j];
            }
            // Subtract number of characters removed from the current
            // number of characters in the buffer.
            m_iReceiveBufferLen -= i;
            // Break out of the for(i) loop.
            break;
        }
    }
}
```

```
BOOL  CNNTP::MessageTerminator(void)
{
     if (m_szReplyLineBuffer[0] == '.' &&
         m_szReplyLineBuffer[1] == '\0')
         return TRUE;
    else
         return FALSE;
}


void  CNNTP::ConnMgrCallback(int  iToken,
     CConnMgrCallback::RESULT  result)
{
     UNUSED_PARAMETER(iToken);

     ASSERT(result != CConnMgrCallback::INVALID_RESULT);

     // Turn connection callback result into events.
     switch (result) {
         case CConnMgrCallback::OK_CONNECTED:
             Event(EV_CONNECT);
            break;
         case CConnMgrCallback::ERR_NOTCONNECTED:
             m_iError = m_connmgr.LastError();
             Event(EV_ERROR);
            break;
    }
}


void  CNNTP::Abort(HWND  hwnd,  UINT  msg,  BOOL  bDoCallback)
{
    m_hwnd = hwnd;
    m_msg = msg;
     m_bDoCallback = bDoCallback;
     Event(EV_ABORT);
}


void  CNNTP::Connect(HWND  hwnd,  UINT  msg,
     char * lpszHost, u_short ushPort)
{
     ASSERT(lpszHost != NULL);

     // Store parameters away.
     m_hwnd = hwnd;
     m_msg = msg;
     m_pszHost = new char[lstrlen(lpszHost) + 1];
     lstrcpy(m_pszHost, lpszHost);
     m_ushPort = ushPort;

     // Initialize our state correctly.
     m_bDataMode = FALSE;
     m_iReceiveBufferLen = 0;
     m_bDoCallback = TRUE;
```

```
        // Start us off.
         NextState(&CNNTP::Start);
         Event(EV_NULLEVENT);
}

void CNNTP::Group(HWND hwnd, UINT msg, char * pszGroup)
{
        m_hwnd = hwnd;
        m_msg = msg;
         m_pszGroup = DuplicateString(pszGroup);
        m_bDoCallback = TRUE;
         Event(EV_GROUP);
}

void CNNTP::NextHeader(HWND hwnd, UINT msg)
{
        m_hwnd = hwnd;
        m_msg = msg;
         m_bDoCallback = TRUE;
          Event(EV_NEXTHEADER);
}

void CNNTP::Header(HWND hwnd, UINT msg)
{
        m_hwnd = hwnd;
        m_msg = msg;
         m_bDoCallback = TRUE;
          Event(EV_HEADER);
}

void CNNTP::Article(HWND hwnd, UINT msg, long lArticle)
{
        m_hwnd = hwnd;
        m_msg = msg;
         m_lArticle = lArticle;
         m_bDoCallback = TRUE;
          Event(EV_ARTICLE);
}

void CNNTP::Quit(HWND hwnd, UINT msg)
{
        m_hwnd = hwnd;
        m_msg = msg;
         m_bDoCallback = TRUE;
          Event(EV_QUIT);
}

BOOL CNNTP::Start(EVENT ev)
{
         UNUSED_PARAMETER(ev);

        // Make the connection to the remote host.  Let the connection
        // manager do all the work.
```

```
        m_connmgr.Connect(m_pszHost, m_ushPort, &m_sock, this, 0);
         NextState(&CNNTP::AwaitConnection);
        return TRUE;
}

BOOL  CNNTP::AwaitConnection(EVENT  ev)
{
        switch (ev) {
            case EV_ABORT:
                m_connmgr.Abort();
                m_result = RESULT_ABORT;
                NextState(&CNNTP::Exit);
               break;
            case EV_CONNECT:
                 NextState(&CNNTP::AwaitGreeting);
               break;
            case EV_ERROR:
                m_result = RESULT_FAILURE;
                NextState(&CNNTP::Exit);
               break;
            default:
                 return FALSE;
        }
        return TRUE;
}

BOOL  CNNTP::AwaitGreeting(EVENT  ev)
{
        switch (ev) {
            case EV_ABORT:
                m_result = RESULT_ABORT;
                NextState(&CNNTP::Exit);
               break;
            case EV_CLOSE:
                // Hmmm... unexpected close of the socket from the
                //other end.
                m_result = RESULT_FAILURE;
                NextState(&CNNTP::Exit);
               break;
            case EV_CODE2:
                // Okay, we're connected and we have the greeting.
                 PostMessage(m_hwnd, m_msg, RESULT_SUCCESS, 0);
                NextState(&CNNTP::Idle);
               break;
            case EV_ERROR:
            case EV_CODE1:
            case EV_CODE3:
            case EV_CODE4:
            case EV_CODE5:
                m_result = RESULT_FAILURE;
                NextState(&CNNTP::Exit);
               break;
```

```
            default:
                return FALSE;
    }
    return TRUE;
}

BOOL CNNTP::Idle(EVENT ev)
{
    switch (ev) {
        case EV_ABORT:
            m_result = RESULT_ABORT;
            NextState(&CNNTP::Exit);
            break;
        case EV_CLOSE:
            // Hmmm... unexpected close of the socket from the
            // other end.
            m_result = RESULT_FAILURE;
            NextState(&CNNTP::Exit);
            break;
        case EV_GROUP:
            NextState(&CNNTP::SendGroup);
            break;
        case EV_NEXTHEADER:
            NextState(&CNNTP::SendNext);
            break;
        case EV_HEADER:
            NextState(&CNNTP::SendHeader);
            break;
        case EV_ARTICLE:
            NextState(&CNNTP::SendArticle);
            break;
        case EV_QUIT:
            NextState(&CNNTP::Quit);
            break;
        default:
            return FALSE;
    }
    return TRUE;
}

BOOL CNNTP::SendGroup(EVENT ev)
{
    int iResult;

    switch (ev) {
        case EV_ABORT:
            m_result = RESULT_ABORT;
            NextState(&CNNTP::Exit);
            break;
        case EV_CLOSE:
            // Hmmm... unexpected close of the socket from the other
            // end.
```

```
                    m_result = RESULT_FAILURE;
                     NextState(&CNNTP::Exit);
                   break;
             case EV_NULLEVENT:
                // Send the GROUP command.
                   lstrcpy(m_szLineBuffer, "GROUP ");
                   lstrcat(m_szLineBuffer, m_pszGroup);
                   lstrcat(m_szLineBuffer, CRLF);
                  delete[] m_pszGroup;
                 m_pszGroup = NULL;
                  iResult = m_sock.Send(m_szLineBuffer,
                      lstrlen(m_szLineBuffer));
                  if (iResult == WSANOERROR || iResult == WSAEWOULDBLOCK) {
                      NextState(&CNNTP::AwaitGroupResponse);
                  }
                  else {
                      m_iError = iResult;
                      m_result = RESULT_FATALERROR;
                      NextState(&CNNTP::Exit);
                  }
                  break;
             default:
                  return FALSE;
        }
     return TRUE;
}

BOOL CNNTP::AwaitGroupResponse(EVENT ev)
{
     long lTotal;

     switch (ev) {
         case EV_ABORT:
              m_result = RESULT_ABORT;
               NextState(&CNNTP::Exit);
             break;
         case EV_CLOSE:
            // Hmmm... unexpected close of the socket from the
            // other end.
              m_result = RESULT_FAILURE;
               NextState(&CNNTP::Exit);
             break;
         case EV_CODE2:
            // Parse the return string.
               sscanf(m_szReplyLineBuffer, "%*ld %ld", &lTotal);
               PostMessage(m_hwnd, m_msg, RESULT_SUCCESS,
                   (LPARAM) lTotal);
              NextState(&CNNTP::Idle);
             break;
         case EV_CODE4:
              PostMessage(m_hwnd, m_msg, RESULT_FAILURE, 0);
              NextState(&CNNTP::Idle);
```

```
                break;
            case EV_ERROR:
            case EV_CODE1:
            case EV_CODE3:
            case EV_CODE5:
                // All other responses generate an error.
                m_result = RESULT_FATALERROR;
                NextState(&CNNTP::Quit);     // Try to quit.
            default:
                return FALSE;
        }
        return TRUE;
}

BOOL CNNTP::SendNext(EVENT ev)
{
        int iResult;

        switch (ev) {
            case EV_ABORT:
                m_result = RESULT_ABORT;
                NextState(&CNNTP::Exit);
              break;
            case EV_CLOSE:
              // Hmmm... unexpected close of the socket from the
              // other end.
                m_result = RESULT_FAILURE;
                NextState(&CNNTP::Exit);
              break;
            case EV_NULLEVENT:
              // Send the GROUP command.
                lstrcpy(m_szLineBuffer, "NEXT" CRLF);
                iResult = m_sock.Send(m_szLineBuffer,
                    lstrlen(m_szLineBuffer));
                if (iResult == WSANOERROR || iResult == WSAEWOULDBLOCK) {
                    NextState(&CNNTP::AwaitNextResponse);
                }
                else {
                    m_iError = iResult;
                    m_result = RESULT_FATALERROR;
                    NextState(&CNNTP::Exit);
                }
                break;
            default:
                return FALSE;
        }
        return TRUE;
}

BOOL CNNTP::AwaitNextResponse(EVENT ev)
{
        switch (ev) {
```

```
            case EV_ABORT:
                m_result = RESULT_ABORT;
                NextState(&CNNTP::Exit);
               break;
         case EV_CLOSE:
            // Hmmm... unexpected close of the socket from the
            // other end.
                m_result = RESULT_FAILURE;
                NextState(&CNNTP::Exit);
               break;
         case EV_CODE2:
                // Okay, the NEXT command succeeded.  Got get the
                // header itself.
                NextState(&CNNTP::SendHeader);
               break;
         case EV_CODE4:
                PostMessage(m_hwnd, m_msg, RESULT_FAILURE, 0);
                NextState(&CNNTP::Idle);
               break;
         case EV_ERROR:
         case EV_CODE1:
         case EV_CODE3:
         case EV_CODE5:
                // All other responses generate an error.
                m_result = RESULT_FATALERROR;
                NextState(&CNNTP::Quit);      // Try to quit.
         default:
                return FALSE;
    }
    return TRUE;
}


BOOL  CNNTP::SendHeader(EVENT ev)
{
    int iResult;

    switch (ev) {
        case EV_ABORT:
                m_result = RESULT_ABORT;
                NextState(&CNNTP::Exit);
               break;
        case EV_CLOSE:
                // Hmmm... unexpected close of the socket from the
                // other end.
                m_result = RESULT_FAILURE;
                NextState(&CNNTP::Exit);
               break;
          case EV_NULLEVENT:
            // Send the header command.
                lstrcpy(m_szLineBuffer, "HEAD" CRLF);
                iResult = m_sock.Send(m_szLineBuffer,
                    lstrlen(m_szLineBuffer));
```

```
            if (iResult == WSANOERROR || iResult == WSAEWOULDBLOCK) {
                NextState(&CNNTP::OpenFile);
            }
            else {
                m_iError = iResult;
                m_result = RESULT_FATALERROR;
                NextState(&CNNTP::Exit);
            }
            break;
        default:
            return FALSE;
    }
    return TRUE;
}


BOOL CNNTP::SendArticle(EVENT ev)
{
    int iResult;

    switch (ev) {
        case EV_ABORT:
            m_result = RESULT_ABORT;
            NextState(&CNNTP::Exit);
            break;
        case EV_CLOSE:
            // Hmmm... unexpected close of the socket from the
            // other end.
            m_result = RESULT_FAILURE;
            NextState(&CNNTP::Exit);
            break;
        case EV_NULLEVENT:
            // Send the header command.
            wsprintf(m_szLineBuffer, "ARTICLE %ld" CRLF, m_lArticle);
            iResult = m_sock.Send(m_szLineBuffer,
                lstrlen(m_szLineBuffer));
            if (iResult == WSANOERROR || iResult == WSAEWOULDBLOCK) {
                NextState(&CNNTP::OpenFile);
            }
            else {
                m_iError = iResult;
                m_result = RESULT_FATALERROR;
                NextState(&CNNTP::Exit);
            }
            break;
        default:
            return FALSE;
    }
    return TRUE;
}


BOOL CNNTP::OpenFile(EVENT ev)
{
```

```
    switch (ev) {
        case EV_ABORT:
            m_result = RESULT_ABORT;
            NextState(&CNNTP::Exit);
          break;
        case EV_CLOSE:
          // Hmmm... unexpected close of the socket from the
          // other end.
            m_result = RESULT_FAILURE;
            NextState(&CNNTP::Exit);
          break;
        case EV_CODE2:
            // Okay, get ready to receive the data.  Open a temp
            // file to contain it.
             sscanf(m_szReplyLineBuffer, "%*ld %ld", &m_lArticle);
             GetTempFileName(0, "NWZ", 0, m_szFileName);
             m_ofsFile.open(m_szFileName);
            m_bDataMode = TRUE;
             NextState(&CNNTP::RetrieveLine);
          break;
        case EV_CODE4:
             PostMessage(m_hwnd, m_msg, RESULT_FAILURE, 0);
             NextState(&CNNTP::Idle);
          break;
        case EV_ERROR:
        case EV_CODE1:
        case EV_CODE3:
        case EV_CODE5:
            // All other responses generate an error.
            m_result = RESULT_FATALERROR;
            NextState(&CNNTP::Quit);    // Try to quit.
        default:
            return FALSE;
    }
    return TRUE;
}

BOOL CNNTP::RetrieveLine(EVENT ev)
{
    ARTICLEANDFILENAME * pArtAndFile;

    switch (ev) {
        case EV_ABORT:
            m_bDataMode = FALSE;
            m_result = RESULT_ABORT;
            NextState(&CNNTP::Exit);
          break;
        case EV_CLOSE:
          // Hmmm... unexpected close of the socket from the
          // other end.
            m_bDataMode = FALSE;
            m_result = RESULT_FAILURE;
```

```
                NextState(&CNNTP::Exit);
                  break;
            case EV_ENDDATA:
                m_bDataMode = FALSE;
                // The data is done.  Close up the file
                m_ofsFile.close();
                // Post a message to the window.
                pArtAndFile = new ARTICLEANDFILENAME;
                pArtAndFile->lArticleNum = m_lArticle;
                  pArtAndFile->pszFilename = DuplicateString(m_szFileName);
                 PostMessage(m_hwnd, m_msg, RESULT_SUCCESS,
                      (LPARAM)pArtAndFile);
                 NextState(&CNNTP::Idle);
                break;
            case EV_DATA:
                // Write the line to the file, followed by a local
                // line terminator.
                 if (m_szReplyLineBuffer[0] == '.') {
                     // If the line starts with a period then it was
                     // stuffed there, so skip over it when writing
                     // to the file.
                      m_ofsFile << &(m_szReplyLineBuffer[1]) << '\n';
                }
                else {
                      m_ofsFile << m_szReplyLineBuffer << '\n';
                }
                break;
            default:
                 return FALSE;
        }
    }
    return TRUE;
}


BOOL CNNTP::Quit(EVENT ev)
{
    UNUSED_PARAMETER(ev);

    int iResult;

    // Send QUIT.
    lstrcpy(m_szLineBuffer, "QUIT" CRLF);
    iResult = m_sock.Send(m_szLineBuffer, lstrlen(m_szLineBuffer));
    if (iResult == WSANOERROR || iResult == WSAEWOULDBLOCK) {
        NextState(&CNNTP::AwaitQuitResponse);
    }
    else {
        m_iError = iResult;
        m_result = RESULT_FAILURE;
        NextState(&CNNTP::Exit);
    }
    return TRUE;
}
```

```
BOOL  CNNTP::AwaitQuitResponse(EVENT  ev)
{
    switch (ev) {
        case EV_ABORT:
            m_result = RESULT_ABORT;
            NextState(&CNNTP::Exit);
          break;
        case EV_CLOSE:        // Just about anything is okay.
        case EV_ERROR:
        case EV_CODE1:
        case EV_CODE2:
        case EV_CODE3:
        case EV_CODE4:
        case EV_CODE5:
            m_result = RESULT_SUCCESS;
            NextState(&CNNTP::Exit);
          break;
        default:
            return FALSE;
    }
    return TRUE;
}


BOOL  CNNTP::Exit(EVENT  ev)
{
    UNUSED_PARAMETER(ev);     // Eliminate the compiler warning.

    // Close the socket.
    m_sock.Close();

    // Delete some allocated memory.
    delete[] m_pszHost;
    delete[] m_pszGroup;

    // Send a callback.
    if (m_bDoCallback) {
        PostMessage(m_hwnd, m_msg, m_result, 0);
    }

    NextState(&CNNTP::Stop);
    return TRUE;
}


BOOL  CNNTP::Stop(EVENT  ev)
{
    UNUSED_PARAMETER(ev);
    // Simply ignore all events.
    return FALSE;
}
```

Listing 13.3 NEWSCLI.CPP

```
/*
     File: NEWSCLI.CPP
     Description:
          A simple news client.
     Copyright 1995, David G. Roberts
*/

#include <stdlib.h>
#include <windows.h>
#include <windowsx.h>
#include "ctl3d.h"
#include "cwinsock.h"
#include "newscli.rh"
#include "myassert.h"

/*
     CONSTANTS
*/
#define DEFAULT_NNTP_PORT     119

#define FRAME_WINDOW_MENU_POS     2
#define GROUP_WINDOW_MENU_POS     2
#define ARTICLE_WINDOW_MENU_POS 3

/*
     TYPES
*/
typedef int INT;
typedef BOOL FAR * LPBOOL;

/*
     GLOBALS
*/
#include "newsclig.h"

/*
     FUNCTION PROTOTYPES
*/
void          CleanupInstance(HINSTANCE);
BOOL CALLBACK ConfigureDlgProc(HWND, UINT, WPARAM, LPARAM);
BOOL CALLBACK GroupDlgProc(HWND, UINT, WPARAM, LPARAM);
LRESULT CALLBACK FrameWndProc(HWND, UINT, WPARAM, LPARAM);
BOOL          InitWinsock(HINSTANCE, HINSTANCE);
BOOL          InitApp(HINSTANCE);
BOOL          InitInstance(HINSTANCE);
void          InitError(void);
LRESULT CALLBACK GroupWndProc(HWND, UINT, WPARAM, LPARAM);
INT WINAPI    WinMain(HINSTANCE, HINSTANCE, LPSTR, INT);
LRESULT CALLBACK ArticleWndProc(HWND, UINT, WPARAM, LPARAM);
```

```
/*
     MESSAGE HANDLER PROTOTYPES
*/
static void OnClose(HWND hwnd);
static void OnCommand(HWND, int, HWND, UINT);
BOOL OnCreate(HWND, CREATESTRUCT FAR*);

/*
     WM_COMMAND HANDLER PROTOTYPES
*/
static void OnFileClose(HWND);
static void OnFileExit(HWND);
static void OnFileOpenGroup(HWND);
static void OnNewsConfigure(HWND);
static void OnWindowCloseAll(HWND);
static BOOL CALLBACK CloseEnumProc(HWND, LPARAM);
static void OnHelpAbout(HWND);

/***********************************************************************
     WINMAIN
***********************************************************************/

/*
     Function: WinMain
     Description:
         Good ol' WinMain.
*/
INT WINAPI WinMain(HINSTANCE hInstance, HINSTANCE hPrevInstance,
     LPSTR lpszCmdParam, INT nCmdShow)
{
     UNUSED_PARAMETER(lpszCmdParam);

     // Save off our instance handle for later.
     g_hInstance = hInstance;

     // If no other instance is running, initialize the application
     // window classes.
     if (!hPrevInstance) {
         if (!InitApp(hInstance)) {
             InitError();
             return 0;
         }
     }

     // Load all our menus.
     g_hFrameMenu    = LoadMenu(hInstance, "FRAMEMENU");
     g_hGroupMenu    = LoadMenu(hInstance, "GROUPMENU");
     g_hArticleMenu  = LoadMenu(hInstance, "ARTICLEMENU");

     // Get the handle of the Window submenu for each MDI menu.
     g_hFrameWindowMenu = GetSubMenu(g_hFrameMenu,
         FRAME_WINDOW_MENU_POS);
```

```
g_hGroupWindowMenu = GetSubMenu(g_hGroupMenu,
     GROUP_WINDOW_MENU_POS);
  g_hArticleWindowMenu = GetSubMenu(g_hArticleMenu,
     ARTICLE_WINDOW_MENU_POS);

 // Load the accelerators.
 g_hAccel = LoadAccelerators(hInstance, g_szAppName);

 // Initialize all instance specific stuff.  In particular, create
 // the frame window.
 if (!InitInstance(hInstance)) {
     InitError();
     return 0;
 }

 // Since initializing Winsock can take some time (because we
 // get the default Finger port using blocking calls), put
 // up an hourglass cursor so the user knows we're working on
 // something and not just out to lunch.
 SetCapture(g_hFrame);
 SetCursor(LoadCursor(NULL, IDC_WAIT));

 // Make sure Winsock initialized and get the event dispatch
 // mechanism up and running.
 if (!InitWinsock(hInstance, hPrevInstance)) {
     ReleaseCapture();
     return 0;
 }

 ReleaseCapture();

 // Show the frame window and cause it to be repainted.
 ShowWindow(g_hFrame, nCmdShow);
 UpdateWindow(g_hFrame);

 // Do the message loop.
 MSG msg;
 while (GetMessage((LPMSG)&msg, NULL, 0, 0)) {
     if (!TranslateMDISysAccel(g_hClient, &msg) &&
         !TranslateAccelerator(g_hFrame, g_hAccel, &msg)) {
         TranslateMessage(&msg);
         DispatchMessage(&msg);
     }
 }

 DestroyMenu(g_hFrameMenu);
 DestroyMenu(g_hGroupMenu);
 DestroyMenu(g_hArticleMenu);

 // Clean up before we exit.
 CleanupInstance(hInstance);
```

```
        return msg.wParam;
}

/*

    Function: InitError
    Description:
        Handles putting up a message box for the application if it
        cannot be initialized.
*/
void InitError(void)
{
    char szMessage[80];

    wsprintf(szMessage, "ERROR: Cannot initialize %s.",
        (LPSTR)g_szFullAppName);
    // Use NULL for hwnd because the application probably has not
    // created its window yet.
    MessageBox(NULL, szMessage, g_szAppName, MB_ICONSTOP | MB_OK);
}


/*

    Function: InitApp
    Description:
        Registers the application's window classes and performs
        initialization that must be done for all application
        instances.  The function returns TRUE if successful and no
        errors occur, and FALSE otherwise.
*/
BOOL InitApp(HINSTANCE hInstance)
{
    WNDCLASS wc;

    // Register the frame window class.

    wc.style              = CS_HREDRAW | CS_VREDRAW;
    wc.lpfnWndProc        = FrameWndProc;
    wc.cbClsExtra         = 0;
    wc.cbWndExtra         = 0;
    wc.hInstance          = hInstance;
    wc.hIcon              = LoadIcon(hInstance, "APPICON");
    wc.hCursor            = LoadCursor(NULL, IDC_ARROW);
    wc.hbrBackground      = (HBRUSH) (COLOR_APPWORKSPACE + 1);
    wc.lpszMenuName       = NULL;
    wc.lpszClassName      = g_szFrameClass;

    if (!RegisterClass(&wc))
        return FALSE;

    // Register the group child window class.
    wc.style              = CS_HREDRAW | CS_VREDRAW;
    wc.lpfnWndProc        = GroupWndProc;
    wc.cbClsExtra         = 0;
```

```
    wc.cbWndExtra          = sizeof(void FAR *);
    wc.hInstance           = hInstance;
    wc.hIcon               = LoadIcon(hInstance, "GROUPICON");
    wc.hCursor             = LoadCursor(NULL, IDC_ARROW);
    wc.hbrBackground       = (HBRUSH) (COLOR_WINDOW + 1);
    wc.lpszMenuName        = NULL;
    wc.lpszClassName       = g_szGroupClass;

    if (!RegisterClass(&wc))
        return FALSE;

    // Register the article viewer child window class.
    wc.style               = CS_HREDRAW | CS_VREDRAW;
    wc.lpfnWndProc         = ArticleWndProc;
    wc.cbClsExtra          = 0;
    wc.cbWndExtra          = sizeof(void FAR *);
    wc.hInstance           = hInstance;
    wc.hIcon               = LoadIcon(hInstance, "ARTICLEICON");
    wc.hCursor             = LoadCursor(NULL, IDC_ARROW);
    wc.hbrBackground       = (HBRUSH) (COLOR_WINDOW + 1);
    wc.lpszMenuName        = NULL;
    wc.lpszClassName       = g_szArticleClass;

    if (!RegisterClass(&wc))
        return FALSE;

    return TRUE;
}

/*
    Function: InitInstance
    Description:
        Performs instance specific initialization, like the
        creation of the frame window, etc.  The function returns
        TRUE if successful and no errors occur, and FALSE otherwise.
*/
BOOL InitInstance(HINSTANCE hInstance)
{
    g_hFrame = CreateWindow(
        g_szFrameClass,                     // window class name
        g_szFullAppName,                    // window title text
        WS_OVERLAPPEDWINDOW | WS_CLIPCHILDREN, // window style
        CW_USEDEFAULT, CW_USEDEFAULT,       // position = default
        CW_USEDEFAULT, CW_USEDEFAULT,       // size = default
        NULL,                               // no parent window
        g_hFrameMenu,                       // menu = window class default
        hInstance,                          // window owner
        NULL);                              // no additional creation data

    if (!g_hFrame)
        return FALSE;
```

```
    // Initialize Microsoft 3D controls (CTL3D)
     Ctl3dRegister(hInstance);
     Ctl3dAutoSubclass(hInstance);

    return TRUE;
}


/*

    Function: InitWinsock
    Description:
        Makes sure Winsock is up and running and that the Winsock event
        dispatch window is created.  Further, performs any actions that
        have to take place before the application window is created.
*/
BOOL InitWinsock(HINSTANCE hInstance, HINSTANCE hPrevInstance)
{
    // Make sure that we didn't have any problems
    // starting up Winsock.
    if (g_wsWinsock.LastError() != WSANOERROR) {
        ReportWSAError("Error: Can't startup Winsock.",
            g_wsWinsock.LastError(), NULL, g_hInstance);
        return FALSE;
    }

    // Create the Winsock message dispatch window.
    if (!WSCCreateEventWindow(hInstance, hPrevInstance)) {
        MessageBox(g_hFrame,
            "Error: Could not create the Winsock message window.",
            "Winsock Error", MB_OK | MB_ICONEXCLAMATION);
        return FALSE;
    }

    return TRUE;
}


/*

    Function: CleanupInstance
    Description:
        Does any instance specific clean-up before the application
        quits.
*/
void CleanupInstance(HINSTANCE hInstance)
{
    // Clean up Microsoft 3D controls (CTL3D)
    Ctl3dUnregister(hInstance);
}


/**********************************************************************
    WINDOW AND DIALOG PROCS
**********************************************************************/

/*

    Function: FrameWndProc
```

```
    Description:
        Window procedure for the application frame window.
*/
LRESULT CALLBACK FrameWndProc(HWND hwnd, UINT msg, WPARAM wParam,
    LPARAM lParam)
{
    switch (msg) {
        HANDLE_MSG(hwnd, WM_CREATE, OnCreate);
        HANDLE_MSG(hwnd, WM_CLOSE, OnClose);
        HANDLE_MSG(hwnd, WM_COMMAND, OnCommand);
        case WM_DESTROY:
            // Delete the config info.
            delete[] g_pszNNTPServer;
            // Post the quit message.
            PostQuitMessage(0);
            return 0;
        default:
            return DefFrameProc(hwnd, g_hClient, msg, wParam, lParam);
    }
}


/*
    Function: ConfigureDlgProc
    Description:
        Dialog proc for the configuration dialog.
*/
BOOL CALLBACK ConfigureDlgProc(HWND hwnd, UINT msg, WPARAM wParam,
    LPARAM lParam)
{
    int     id;
    BOOL    bTranslated;
    int     nLen;

    UNUSED_PARAMETER(lParam);

    switch (msg) {
        case WM_INITDIALOG:
            // Initialize dialog box edit controls.
            SetDlgItemText(hwnd, IDD_NNTPSERVER, g_pszNNTPServer);
            SetDlgItemInt(hwnd, IDD_NNTPPORT, g_ushNNTPPort, FALSE);
            return TRUE;
        case WM_COMMAND:
            // Explode wParam and lParam into constituent parts.
            id = GET_WM_COMMAND_ID(wParam, lParam);
            switch (id) {
                case IDOK:
                    // Verify all the fields.
                    if (!(VerifyDlgText(hwnd, IDD_NNTPSERVER) &&
                        VerifyDlgInt(hwnd, IDD_NNTPPORT, FALSE))) {
                            return TRUE;
                    }
                    // Now that we've verified everything, retrieve
                    // it all "for real."
```

```
                            // First the NNTP server....
                                delete[] g_pszNNTPServer;
                                 nLen = Edit_GetTextLength(GetDlgItem(hwnd,
                                    IDD_NNTPSERVER));
                                g_pszNNTPServer = new char[nLen + 1];
                                GetDlgItemText(hwnd, IDD_NNTPSERVER,
                                    g_pszNNTPServer, nLen + 1);
                            // ...Then the NNTP port.
                                 g_ushNNTPPort = (u_short) GetDlgItemInt(hwnd,
                                     IDD_NNTPPORT, (LPBOOL) &bTranslated, FALSE);
                            // Now we're done.
                                EndDialog(hwnd, TRUE);
                                return TRUE;
                        case IDCANCEL:
                                EndDialog(hwnd, FALSE);
                                return TRUE;
                        case IDD_DEFAULT:
                                SetDlgItemInt(hwnd, IDD_NNTPPORT,
                                        g_ushNNTPDefaultPort, FALSE);
                                return TRUE;
                    } // switch (id)
            } // switch (msg)
        return FALSE;
}


/*

    Function: GroupDlgProc
    Description:
        Dialog proc for the Open Group dialog box.
*/
BOOL CALLBACK GroupDlgProc(HWND hwnd, UINT msg, WPARAM wParam,
    LPARAM lParam)
{
    int     id;
    int     nLen;

    UNUSED_PARAMETER(lParam);

    switch (msg) {
        case WM_INITDIALOG:
            // Set the keyboard focus to the group edit control.
             SetFocus(GetDlgItem(hwnd, IDD_GROUP));
            return FALSE;
        case WM_COMMAND:
            // Explode wParam and lParam into constituent parts.
            id = GET_WM_COMMAND_ID(wParam, lParam);
            switch (id) {
                case IDOK:
                    // Verify the group field.
                     if (!(VerifyDlgText(hwnd, IDD_GROUP))) {
                            return TRUE;
                    }

                     nLen = Edit_GetTextLength(GetDlgItem(hwnd,
```

```
                      IDD_GROUP));
                    g_pszGroup = new char[nLen + 1];
                    GetDlgItemText(hwnd, IDD_GROUP,
                        g_pszGroup, nLen + 1);
                    // Now we're done.
                    EndDialog(hwnd, TRUE);
                    return TRUE;
                case IDCANCEL:
                    EndDialog(hwnd, FALSE);
                    return TRUE;
            } // switch (id)
    } // switch (msg)
    return FALSE;
}


/**********************************************************************
    WINDOW MESSAGE HANDLERS
**********************************************************************/


/*
    Function: OnClose
    Description:
        Handles a WM_CLOSE message to the frame window.
*/
void OnClose(HWND hwnd)
{
    // Send ourselves a Close All menu command message to close up
    // the children.
    SendMessage(hwnd, WM_COMMAND, IDM_WINDOWCLOSEALL, 0);
    if (GetWindow(g_hClient, GW_CHILD) == NULL) {
        // If the client window has no children, then all the children
        // are closed and we can continue.  Call the default window
        // proc to have it post a destroy message.
        FORWARD_WM_CLOSE(hwnd, ForwardDefFrameProc);
    }
    // One of the client's children didn't close, so simply return.
    // The user can't exit.
}


/*
    Function: OnCommand
    Description:
        Handle WM_COMMAND messages.
*/
void OnCommand(HWND hwnd, int id, HWND hwndCtl, UINT codeNotify)
{
    // Dispatch command.
    switch (id) {
        case IDM_FILECLOSE:
            OnFileClose(hwnd);
            break;
        case IDM_FILEEXIT:
```

```
                OnFileExit(hwnd);
                break;
            case IDM_FILEOPENGROUP:
                OnFileOpenGroup(hwnd);
                break;
            case IDM_NEWSCONFIGURE:
                OnNewsConfigure(hwnd);
                break;
            case IDM_WINDOWCASCADE:
                SendMessage(g_hClient, WM_MDICASCADE, 0, 0);
                break;
            case IDM_WINDOWARRANGE:
                SendMessage(g_hClient, WM_MDIICONARRANGE, 0, 0);
                break;
            case IDM_WINDOWTILE:
                SendMessage(g_hClient, WM_MDITILE, 0, 0);
                break;
            case IDM_WINDOWCLOSEALL:
                OnWindowCloseAll(hwnd);
                break;
            case IDM_HELPABOUT:
                OnHelpAbout(hwnd);
                break;
            default:
                // ...Or send it to the active child window and see if it
                // processes it.
                HWND hwndChild = GetMDIActiveChild(g_hClient);
                if (IsWindow(hwndChild)) {
                    FORWARD_WM_COMMAND(hwndChild, id, hwndCtl, codeNotify,
                        SendMessage);
                }
                break;
    }
    // Always forward it to DefFrameProc after we're done.
    FORWARD_WM_COMMAND(hwnd, id, hwndCtl, codeNotify,
        ForwardDefFrameProc);
}


/*
    Function: OnCreate
    Description:
        Handles creation of the main frame window.  Creates the MDI
        client window to manage MDI children and initializes the news
        configuration information.
*/
BOOL OnCreate(HWND hwnd, CREATESTRUCT FAR* lpCreateStruct)
{
    UNUSED_PARAMETER(lpCreateStruct);

    CLIENTCREATESTRUCT ClientCreate;

    // Create the MDI client window.
```

```
ClientCreate.hWindowMenu = g_hFrameWindowMenu;
  ClientCreate.idFirstChild = IDM_FIRSTCHILD;
  g_hClient = CreateWindow(
      "MDICLIENT",                                      // window class name
      NULL,                                             // no title for the client window
      WS_CHILD | WS_CLIPCHILDREN | WS_VISIBLE,          // window style
      0, 0,                                             // position at 0,0
      0, 0,                                             // no size
      hwnd,                                             // parent is the frame window
      (HMENU) 1,                                        // Not really a menu; a child
                                                        // window number when doing MDI
      g_hInstance,                                      // owning instance
      (LPSTR)&ClientCreate);                            // additional creation data

  // Set up the default port.
  g_ushNNTPDefaultPort = DEFAULT_NNTP_PORT;

  // Initialize the configuration information.
  const int STR_BASE = 10;
  const int STR_GROW_QUANTUM = 10;
  int iStrLen;
  int iReadLen;

  // Assume we're going to do everything right.
  g_bConfigured = TRUE;

  // Get the NNTP server name.
  iStrLen = STR_BASE;
  g_pszNNTPServer = new char[1];
  do {
      delete[] g_pszNNTPServer;
      iStrLen += STR_GROW_QUANTUM;
      g_pszNNTPServer = new char[iStrLen];
      iReadLen = GetPrivateProfileString("NNTP", "Server", "",
          g_pszNNTPServer, iStrLen, g_szIniFile);
  } while (iReadLen >= iStrLen - 1);
  if (lstrcmp(g_pszNNTPServer, "") == 0) {
      // If a null string got in the file or there was no entry,
      // then we still aren't configured.
      g_bConfigured = FALSE;
  }

  // Get the NNTP port number.
  g_ushNNTPPort = (u_short) GetPrivateProfileInt("NNTP", "Port", 0,
      g_szIniFile);
  if (g_ushNNTPPort == 0) {
      g_ushNNTPPort = g_ushNNTPDefaultPort;
      g_bConfigured = FALSE;
  }


  return TRUE;
}
```

```
/**********************************************************************
      WM_COMMAND HANDLERS
**********************************************************************/

/*
     Function: OnFileClose
     Description:
          Closes the currently active MDI child window.
*/
void OnFileClose(HWND hwnd)
{
     UNUSED_PARAMETER(hwnd);

     HWND hChild = GetMDIActiveChild(g_hClient);

   if (hChild == NULL)
      return;

    if (SendMessage(hChild, WM_QUERYENDSESSION, 0, 0)) {
         SendMessage(g_hClient, WM_MDIDESTROY, (WPARAM) hChild, 0);
    }
}


/*
     Function: OnFileExit
     Description:
          Exits the application in response to an IDM_FILEEXIT message.
*/
void OnFileExit(HWND hwnd)
{
     SendMessage(hwnd, WM_CLOSE, 0, 0L);
}


/*
     Function: OnFileOpenGroup
     Description:
          Creates a new group window.
*/
void OnFileOpenGroup(HWND hwnd)
{
    // Open a dialog box to get the group name.
    FARPROC lpfnGroup =
          MakeProcInstance((FARPROC) GroupDlgProc, g_hInstance);
    BOOL bResult = DialogBox(g_hInstance, "GROUP", hwnd,
        (DLGPROC) lpfnGroup);
    FreeProcInstance(lpfnGroup);

    // Abort if the user hit Cancel.
    if (bResult == FALSE)
       return;

    // Create the child window.
    MDICREATESTRUCT mdicreate;
```

```
        mdicreate.szClass    = g_szGroupClass;
        mdicreate.szTitle    = g_pszGroup;
        mdicreate.hOwner     = g_hInstance;
        mdicreate.x          = CW_USEDEFAULT;
        mdicreate.y          = CW_USEDEFAULT;
        mdicreate.cx         = CW_USEDEFAULT;
        mdicreate.cy         = CW_USEDEFAULT;
        mdicreate.style      = 0;
        mdicreate.lParam     = NULL;

        // Send a message to the client window to create the new child.
        SendMessage(g_hClient, WM_MDICREATE, 0,
            (LPARAM) (LPMDICREATESTRUCT) &mdicreate);

        delete[] g_pszGroup;
}


/*
        Function: OnNewsConfigure
        Description:
            Pops up a dialog box to configure all the server name and port
            information.
*/
void OnNewsConfigure(HWND hwnd)
{
        // Put up the dialog box.
        FARPROC lpfnConfigure =
            MakeProcInstance((FARPROC) ConfigureDlgProc, g_hInstance);
        BOOL bResult = DialogBox(g_hInstance, "CONFIGURE", hwnd,
            (DLGPROC) lpfnConfigure);
        FreeProcInstance(lpfnConfigure);

        // We're only configured if we were configured before or we just
        // got configured.  If we weren't before and the user hit cancel,
        // we still aren't.
        g_bConfigured = g_bConfigured || bResult;

        // Write out the INI file.
        char szPort[20];
        if (bResult) { // Only do this if the user hits OK.
            WritePrivateProfileString("NNTP", "Server", g_pszNNTPServer,
                g_szIniFile);
            wsprintf(szPort, "%u", g_ushNNTPPort);
            WritePrivateProfileString("NNTP", "Port", szPort,
                g_szIniFile);
        }
}


/*
        Function: OnWindowCloseAll
        Description:
            Attempts to close all the child windows.
```

```
*/
void OnWindowCloseAll(HWND hwnd)
{
     UNUSED_PARAMETER(hwnd);

     // Simply enumerate all the child windows, calling CloseEnumProc
     // for each one.
     FARPROC lpfnCloseEnum = MakeProcInstance((FARPROC) CloseEnumProc,
         g_hInstance);
     EnumChildWindows(g_hClient, (WNDENUMPROC) lpfnCloseEnum, 0);
     FreeProcInstance(lpfnCloseEnum);
}


/*
     Function: CloseEnumProc
     Description:
         The enumeration function used in the OnWindowCloseAll
         function.
*/
BOOL CALLBACK CloseEnumProc(HWND hwnd, LPARAM lParam)
{
     UNUSED_PARAMETER(lParam);

     // EnumChildWindows picks up the title windows of iconized child
     // windows.  Skip over these icon titles by checking to see if
     // they are owned by anybody.  Icon titles are owned while child
     // windows aren't.
     if (GetWindow(hwnd, GW_OWNER) != NULL) {
         return TRUE;
     }
     // Restore the child window to normal size.
     SendMessage(GetParent(hwnd), WM_MDIRESTORE, (WPARAM) hwnd, 0);
     // Ask the child whether we can close it.
     if (!SendMessage(hwnd, WM_QUERYENDSESSION, 0, 0)) {
         // If not, move on.
         return TRUE;
     }
     // Close it!
     SendMessage(GetParent(hwnd), WM_MDIDESTROY, (WPARAM) hwnd, 0);
     // Go to the next child window.
     return TRUE;
}


/*
     Function: OnHelpAbout
     Description:
         Pops up the "About..." dialog box in response to IDM_HELPABOUT
         command messages.
*/
void OnHelpAbout(HWND hwnd)
{
     char szTitle[100];
     char szInfo[200];
```

```
        wsprintf(szTitle, "About %s", (LPSTR)g_szFullAppName);
        wsprintf(szInfo, "%s\r\nCopyright \251 1995\r\n"
            "David G. Roberts\r\n\r\nAn example program from the book\r\n"
            "'Developing for the Internet with Windows Sockets'",
            (LPSTR)g_szFullAppName);
        MessageBox(hwnd, szInfo, szTitle, MB_OK);
}


/*********************************************************************
    UTILITY FUNCTIONS
*********************************************************************/


/*
    Function: ForwardDefFrameProc
    Description:
        A short routine that provides some syntactic sugar to allow
        the windowsx.h FORWARD_WM_COMMAND macro to work with
        DefFrameProc.  Normally, FORWARD_WM_COMMAND packages its
        parameters and tries to call a function with the normal number
        and types of WndProc parameters (HWND, UINT, WPARAM, LPARAM).
        DefFrameProc requires the client HWND to also be present.
        Use FOWARD_WM_COMMAND to call this procedure, which then adds
        the client HWND and calls DefFrameProc.
*/
void ForwardDefFrameProc(HWND hwnd, UINT msg, WPARAM wParam,
    LPARAM lParam)
{
    DefFrameProc(hwnd, g_hClient, msg, wParam, lParam);
}


/*
    Function: GetMDIActiveChild
    Description:
        This is one function that differs between Win16 and Win32.
        GetMDIActiveChild isolates those differences in this function
        rather than writing Win16/Win32 specific code everywhere.
*/
HWND GetMDIActiveChild(HWND hwndClient)
{
#ifdef WIN32
    return (HWND) SendMessage(hwndClient, WM_MDIGETACTIVE, 0, 0);
#else
    return (HWND) LOWORD(SendMessage(hwndClient, WM_MDIGETACTIVE,
        0, 0));
#endif
}

/*
    Function: VerifyDlgInt
    Description:
        Verifies that an edit control in a dialog box contains a valid
            integer.  The function works by calling GetDlgItemInt on the
```

```
            edit control and checking the bTranslated argument.  The
              caller may specify a signed or unsigned translation with the
              bSigned function argument.  If the item doesn't translate,
            the function highlights the text in the edit control, beeps, and
              returns FALSE.
*/
BOOL VerifyDlgInt(HWND hwnd, int iDlgItem, BOOL bSigned)
{
    BOOL bTranslated;

    // Try to retrieve the number.
     GetDlgItemInt(hwnd, iDlgItem, (LPBOOL) &bTranslated,
       bSigned);
    // If things didn't go well, set the focus to the
   // edit control, select all the text in it, and beep.
    if (!bTranslated) {
        SetEditErrorFocus(hwnd, iDlgItem);
        return FALSE;
    }
    return TRUE;
}


/*

    Function: VerifyDlgText
    Description:
        Verfies that an edit control in a dialog box contains
          some text (is not null).  If the length of the text in
          the control is zero, the function sets the focus to the edit
          text item, beeps, and returns FALSE.
*/
BOOL VerifyDlgText(HWND hwnd, int iDlgItem)
{
   // Get the text length from the edit control.
    int nLen = Edit_GetTextLength(GetDlgItem(hwnd, iDlgItem));
    // If the user has given us a blank string, set the
   // focus back to the edit control and beep.
    if (nLen == 0) {
        SetEditErrorFocus(hwnd, iDlgItem);
        return FALSE;
    }
    return TRUE;
}


/*

    Function: SetEditErrorFocus
    Description:
        Sets the focus to a given dialog control, selects all its
        text, and beeps.  The dialog window handle is specified by
        hwnd and the id of the dialog item by iDlgItem.
*/
void SetEditErrorFocus(HWND hwnd, int iDlgItem)
{
```

```
        SetFocus(GetDlgItem(hwnd, iDlgItem));
          Edit_SetSel(GetDlgItem(hwnd, iDlgItem), 0, -1);
          MessageBeep(MB_ICONSTOP);
}
```

Listing 13.4   NEWSGRP.CPP

```
/*
      File: NEWSGRP.CPP
      Description:
          Implements the group article selector for News Client.
      Copyright 1995, David G. Roberts
*/

#include <ctype.h>
#include <dos.h>
#include <io.h>
#include <stdlib.h>
#include <time.h>
#include <fstream.h>
#include <windows.h>
#include <windowsx.h>
#include "newscli.rh"
#include "myassert.h"
#include "cwinsock.h"
#include "clist.h"
#include "cnntp.h"
#include "cstrlist.h"
#include "rfc822.h"
#include "parsdate.h"
#include "utility.h"

#define DECLARE
#include "newsclig.h"

/*
    CONSTANTS
*/
#define LBCTLID          1
#define WM_NNTPCONNECTED        WM_USER
#define WM_NNTPGROUPDONE        (WM_USER + 1)
#define WM_NNTPHEADERDONE       (WM_USER + 2)
#define WM_NNTPQUITDONE         (WM_USER + 3)

/*
    TYPES
*/

// A little collection structure to hold summary data about
// a particular article.  Note that the collection deletes all the
// string members upon destruction.  Make copies beforehand!
```

```
struct SUMMARYINFO {
    char *  pszFrom;
    char *  pszSubject;
    time_t  time;
    long    lArticleNum;

     SUMMARYINFO() : pszFrom(NULL), pszSubject(NULL), time(0),
        lArticleNum(0) {};
    SUMMARYINFO(char * pszfr, char * pszsub, time_t d, int i) :
        pszFrom(pszfr), pszSubject(pszsub),
        time(d), lArticleNum(i) {};
    ~SUMMARYINFO() {
        delete[] pszFrom;
        delete[] pszSubject;
    };
};


// A list class to manage SUMMARYINFO data.  Derived from CList.
class CSummaryList : public CList {
protected:
    virtual int Compare(void * pvThing1, void * pvThing2);
    virtual void DeleteData(void * pvThing);
public:
    CSummaryList() { };
    ~CSummaryList();
    void Add(SUMMARYINFO * psi) { CList::Add((void *) psi); };
    void Insert(SUMMARYINFO * psi) { CList::Insert((void *) psi); };
    SUMMARYINFO * First(void)
        { return (SUMMARYINFO *) CList::First(); };
    SUMMARYINFO * Next(void)
        { return (SUMMARYINFO *) CList::Next(); };
};


CSummaryList::~CSummaryList()
{
    // Delete all the data in the list.
    SUMMARYINFO * psi = First();
    while (psi != NULL) {
        delete psi;
        psi = Next();
    }
}


int CSummaryList::Compare(void * pvThing1, void *pvThing2)
{
    SUMMARYINFO * psi1 = (SUMMARYINFO *) pvThing1;
    SUMMARYINFO * psi2 = (SUMMARYINFO *) pvThing2;

    if (psi1->lArticleNum < psi2->lArticleNum)
        return -1;
    else if (psi1->lArticleNum == psi2->lArticleNum)
        return 0;
```

```
    else
        return 1;
}

void CSummaryList::DeleteData(void * pvThing)
{
    delete (SUMMARYINFO *) pvThing;
}


// A little collection structure to hold some data that is associated
// with the group window.
struct GROUPDATA {
    HWND                hwndLB;
    BOOL                bRetrieving;
    CSummaryList *      pslSummaryList;
    char *              pszGroupName;
    CNNTP *             nntpobj;
    long                lTotal;
    long                lCurrent;

    GROUPDATA() : hwndLB(NULL), bRetrieving(FALSE),
        pslSummaryList(new CSummaryList), nntpobj(NULL) {};
    ~GROUPDATA();
};

GROUPDATA::~GROUPDATA()
{
    if (bRetrieving) {
        bRetrieving = FALSE;
        nntpobj->Abort(FALSE, NULL, 0);
        delete nntpobj;
    }
    delete pslSummaryList;
    delete[] pszGroupName;
}


/*
    LOCAL FUNCTIONS
*/
static void OnClose(HWND);
static void OnCommand(HWND, int, HWND, UINT);
static BOOL OnCreate(HWND, CREATESTRUCT FAR*);
static void OnDestroy(HWND);
static void OnMDIActivate(HWND, BOOL, HWND, HWND);
static void OnNNTPConnect(HWND, UINT, WPARAM, LPARAM);
static void OnNNTPGroupDone(HWND, UINT, WPARAM, LPARAM);
static void OnNNTPHeaderDone(HWND, UINT, WPARAM, LPARAM);
static void OnNNTPQuitDone(HWND, UINT, WPARAM, LPARAM);
static BOOL OnQueryEndSession(HWND hwnd);
static void OnSize(HWND, UINT, int, int);

// MENU HANDLERS
static void OnNewsViewArticle(HWND);
```

```
// UTILITY FUNCTIONS
void SetRetrievalStatus(HWND);
void SetStatus(HWND, char *);
void CreateArticleList(HWND);
SUMMARYINFO * GetSummaryInfo(char *, long);
char * GetHeaderData(char *, char *);


/***********************************************************************
     WINDOW AND DIALOG BOX PROCEDURES
***********************************************************************/


/*
     Function: GroupWndProc
     Description:
          The window procedure for the group window class.  The
          function simply dispatches window messages to smaller
          "handler" functions.
*/
LRESULT CALLBACK GroupWndProc(HWND hwnd, UINT msg, WPARAM wParam,
     LPARAM lParam)
{
     switch (msg) {
          HANDLE_MSG(hwnd, WM_CLOSE, OnClose);
          HANDLE_MSG(hwnd, WM_COMMAND, OnCommand);
          HANDLE_MSG(hwnd, WM_CREATE, OnCreate);
          HANDLE_MSG(hwnd, WM_DESTROY, OnDestroy);
          HANDLE_MSG(hwnd, WM_MDIACTIVATE, OnMDIActivate);
          HANDLE_MSG(hwnd, WM_QUERYENDSESSION, OnQueryEndSession);
          HANDLE_MSG(hwnd, WM_SIZE, OnSize);
          case WM_NNTPCONNECTED:
               OnNNTPConnect(hwnd, msg, wParam, lParam);
             break;
          case WM_NNTPGROUPDONE:
               OnNNTPGroupDone(hwnd, msg, wParam, lParam);
             break;
          case WM_NNTPHEADERDONE:
               OnNNTPHeaderDone(hwnd, msg, wParam, lParam);
             break;
          case WM_NNTPQUITDONE:
               OnNNTPQuitDone(hwnd, msg, wParam, lParam);
             break;
     }
      return DefMDIChildProc(hwnd, msg, wParam, lParam);
}


/***********************************************************************
     MESSAGE HANDLING FUNCTIONS
***********************************************************************/


/*
     Function: OnClose
     Description:
```

```
            Handles WM_CLOSE messages.  Simply determines if this is
            a good time to destroy the window, and if so, does the deed.
*/
void OnClose(HWND  hwnd)
{
     if (SendMessage(hwnd, WM_QUERYENDSESSION, 0, 0)) {
         SendMessage(g_hClient, WM_MDIDESTROY, (WPARAM) hwnd, 0);
     }
}


/*
     Function: OnCommand
     Description:
         Handles WM_COMMAND messages.
*/
void OnCommand(HWND  hwnd, int  id, HWND  hwndCtl, UINT  codeNotify)
{
     if (hwndCtl == NULL) {
         // It's a window message.
         switch (id) {
             case IDM_NEWSVIEWARTICLE:
                 OnNewsViewArticle(hwnd);
                 return;
         }
     }
     else {
         ASSERT(id == LBCTLID);
         // It's from our control.
         if (codeNotify == LBN_DBLCLK) {
             OnNewsViewArticle(hwnd);
             return;
         }
     }
     // Make sure the default child proc sees things we don't
     // process ourselves!
     FORWARD_WM_COMMAND(hwnd, id, hwndCtl, codeNotify,
         DefMDIChildProc);
}


/*
     Function: OnCreate
     Description:
         Handles WM_CREATE messages.  The function allocates
         private memory, creates a list box control to hold the
         summary listing, and then starts the header retrieval
         process.
*/
BOOL OnCreate(HWND  hwnd, CREATESTRUCT FAR*  lpCreateStruct)
{
     UNUSED_PARAMETER(lpCreateStruct);
```

```
    // Allocate some private window data for ourselves.
    GROUPDATA FAR * lpdata = new GROUPDATA;
    SetWindowLong(hwnd, 0, (LONG) lpdata);

    // Create a list box control to do our work for us.
    lpdata->hwndLB = CreateWindow(
        "LISTBOX",                  // class name
        NULL,                       // window name
        WS_CHILD | WS_VISIBLE |     // window styles
        LBS_NOTIFY | WS_VSCROLL,
        0,0,0,0,                    // location and size
        hwnd,                       // parent
        (HMENU) LBCTLID,            // child id, not really a menu
        g_hInstance,                // program instance
        NULL);                      // creation data

    // Set the edit control's font to a fixed pitch.
    HFONT hfont = GetStockFont(SYSTEM_FIXED_FONT);
    SetWindowFont(lpdata->hwndLB, hfont, FALSE);

    // Get the name of the group from the window title.
    int nLen = GetWindowTextLength(hwnd);
    lpdata->pszGroupName = new char[nLen + 1];
    GetWindowText(hwnd, lpdata->pszGroupName, nLen + 1);

    // Set the title to the group name + "connecting..."
    SetStatus(hwnd, " : connecting...");

    // Create a CNNTP object and have it connect.
    lpdata->nntpobj = new CNNTP;
    lpdata->nntpobj->Connect(hwnd, WM_NNTPCONNECTED, g_pszNNTPServer,
        g_ushNNTPPort);

    lpdata->bRetrieving = TRUE;

    return TRUE;
}


/*

    Function: OnDestroy
    Description:
        Handles WM_DESTROY messages.  The function simply deletes
        the window's private data structure.
*/
void OnDestroy(HWND hwnd)
{
    // Deallocate our private window data before we go away.
    GROUPDATA FAR * lpdata =
        (GROUPDATA FAR *) GetWindowLong(hwnd, 0);
    delete lpdata;
}
```

```
/*
     Function: OnMDIActivate
     Description:
          This function takes care of putting the appropriate menu
          into the menu bar when the window becomes active or inactive.
*/
void OnMDIActivate(HWND hwnd, BOOL fActive, HWND hwndActivate,
     HWND hwndDeactivate)
{
     UNUSED_PARAMETER(hwndActivate);
     UNUSED_PARAMETER(hwndDeactivate);

     if (fActive) {
         // Put our menu in place.
          SendMessage(g_hClient, WM_MDISETMENU,
              GET_WM_MDISETMENU_MPS(g_hGroupMenu,
                 g_hGroupWindowMenu));
          GROUPDATA FAR * lpdata =
              (GROUPDATA FAR*) GetWindowLong(hwnd, 0);
          // Make sure keystrokes go to the edit control.
          SetFocus(lpdata->hwndLB);
     }
     else {
          // We're being deactivated, so put the main menu in place.
          SendMessage(g_hClient, WM_MDISETMENU,
              GET_WM_MDISETMENU_MPS(g_hFrameMenu, g_hFrameWindowMenu));
     }
     DrawMenuBar(g_hFrame);
}


/*

     Function: OnNNTPConnect
     Description:
          This function handles WM_NNTPCONNECTED messages.
          If no errors occurred while connecting, the function
        selects the appropriate newsgroup.
*/
void OnNNTPConnect(HWND hwnd, UINT msg, WPARAM wParam, LPARAM lParam)
{
     UNUSED_PARAMETER(msg);
     UNUSED_PARAMETER(lParam);

     GROUPDATA FAR * lpdata =
          (GROUPDATA FAR *) GetWindowLong(hwnd, 0);

     if (wParam != CNNTP::RESULT_SUCCESS) {
          MessageBox(hwnd, "Could not connect to server!", "Error",
              MB_OK | MB_ICONEXCLAMATION);
          lpdata->bRetrieving = FALSE;
          delete lpdata->nntpobj;
          PostMessage(hwnd, WM_CLOSE, 0, 0);
         return;
     }
```

```
        // Set the title to the group name + "retrieving article count..."
        SetStatus(hwnd, " : retrieving article count...");

        lpdata->nntpobj->Group(hwnd, WM_NNTPGROUPDONE,
            lpdata->pszGroupName);
}

/*
    Function: OnNNTPGroupDone
    Description:
        This function handles WM_NNTPGROUPDONE messages sent to the
        window.  If no error occurred while trying to select the
        right group, this function starts retrieving the first
        header.
*/
void OnNNTPGroupDone(HWND hwnd, UINT msg, WPARAM wParam,
    LPARAM lParam)
{
    UNUSED_PARAMETER(msg);

    GROUPDATA FAR * lpdata =
        (GROUPDATA FAR *) GetWindowLong(hwnd, 0);

    if (wParam != CNNTP::RESULT_SUCCESS) {
        MessageBox(hwnd, "Invalid group name!", "Error",
            MB_OK | MB_ICONEXCLAMATION);
        lpdata->bRetrieving = FALSE;
        delete lpdata->nntpobj;
        PostMessage(hwnd, WM_CLOSE, 0, 0);
        return;
    }

    // Get the first and last article data.
    lpdata->lTotal = (long) lParam;
    lpdata->lCurrent = 0;

    // Get the first header.
    SetRetrievalStatus(hwnd);
    lpdata->nntpobj->Header(hwnd, WM_NNTPHEADERDONE);
}

/*
    Function: OnNNTPHeaderDone
    Description:
        This function is invoked when each header is retrieved.
        If no errors occurred, it parses the header and starts
        the retrieval process for the next.
*/
void OnNNTPHeaderDone(HWND hwnd, UINT msg, WPARAM wParam,
    LPARAM lParam)
{
    UNUSED_PARAMETER(msg);
```

```
        CNNTP::ARTICLEANDFILENAME * pArtAndFile;
        SUMMARYINFO * psi;
        GROUPDATA FAR * lpdata =
            (GROUPDATA FAR *) GetWindowLong(hwnd, 0);

        // Check return value from CNNTP object.
        switch (wParam) {
            case CNNTP::RESULT_SUCCESS:
                // Go to the next header before parsing the current
                // header to speed things up.
                lpdata->lCurrent++;
                SetRetrievalStatus(hwnd);
                  lpdata->nntpobj->NextHeader(hwnd, WM_NNTPHEADERDONE);

                // Parse the article header.
                pArtAndFile = (CNNTP::ARTICLEANDFILENAME *) lParam;
                psi = GetSummaryInfo(pArtAndFile->pszFilename,
                    pArtAndFile->lArticleNum);
                lpdata->pslSummaryList->Add(psi);

                // Delete the file and the memory allocated for the
                // ARTICLEANDFILENAME structure.
                unlink(pArtAndFile->pszFilename);
                delete[] pArtAndFile->pszFilename;
                delete pArtAndFile;

                break;
            case CNNTP::RESULT_FAILURE:
                // There are no more messages.
                SetStatus(hwnd, " : closing connection...");
                lpdata->nntpobj->Quit(hwnd, WM_NNTPQUITDONE);
                break;
            default:
                MessageBox(hwnd, "An error occurred while retrieving "
                    "article headers.", "Error!",
                    MB_OK | MB_ICONEXCLAMATION);
                lpdata->bRetrieving = FALSE;
                delete lpdata->nntpobj;
                PostMessage(hwnd, WM_CLOSE, 0, 0);
                break;
        }
        return;
}

/*
    Function: OnNNTPQuitDone
    Description:
        This function is invoked when the connection to the NNTP
        server has been closed.  It destroys the CNNTP object and
        reports any errors that might have occurred.
*/
void OnNNTPQuitDone(HWND hwnd, UINT msg, WPARAM wParam,
```

```
        LPARAM lParam)
{
    UNUSED_PARAMETER(msg);
    UNUSED_PARAMETER(lParam);

    GROUPDATA FAR * lpdata =
        (GROUPDATA FAR *) GetWindowLong(hwnd, 0);

    delete lpdata->nntpobj;
    lpdata->nntpobj = NULL;
    lpdata->bRetrieving = FALSE;

    if (wParam != CNNTP::RESULT_SUCCESS) {
        MessageBox(hwnd, "An error occurred while closing the "
            "connection.", "Error!",
            MB_OK | MB_ICONEXCLAMATION);
        lpdata->bRetrieving = FALSE;
        delete lpdata->nntpobj;
        PostMessage(hwnd, WM_CLOSE, 0, 0);
    }

    SetStatus(hwnd, "");

    CreateArticleList(hwnd);
}


/*
    Function: OnQueryEndSession
    Description:
        Handles WM_QUERYENDSESSION messages. Returns TRUE if the
        window should be closed, FALSE otherwise.
*/
BOOL OnQueryEndSession(HWND hwnd)
{
    GROUPDATA FAR * lpdata =
        (GROUPDATA FAR *) GetWindowLong(hwnd, 0);
    if (lpdata->bRetrieving) {
        SendMessage(g_hClient, WM_MDIRESTORE, (WPARAM) hwnd, 0);
        int iResult = MessageBox(hwnd,
            "Retrieving article headers.  Close anyway?",
            "Close Anyway?", MB_YESNO | MB_ICONQUESTION);
        if (iResult == IDYES)
            return TRUE;
        else
            return FALSE;
    }
    else {
        return TRUE;
    }
}


/*
    Function: OnSize
```

```
      Description:
         Notifies the list box child window whenever the viewer window
         gets resized.
*/
void OnSize(HWND hwnd, UINT state, int cx, int cy)
{
    UNUSED_PARAMETER(state);

    GROUPDATA FAR * lpdata =
         (GROUPDATA FAR *) GetWindowLong(hwnd, 0);
    MoveWindow(lpdata->hwndLB, 0, 0, cx, cy, TRUE);
    // Must make sure we forward this to the default child proc
    // as well!
    FORWARD_WM_SIZE(hwnd, state, cx, cy, DefMDIChildProc);
}


/***********************************************************************
    MENU HANDLERS
***********************************************************************/

/*
    Function: OnNewsViewArticle
    Description:
       This function is invoked when the user chooses News|View
       Article or double clicks on an article summary line in
         the group window.  The function creates a viewer MDI
         child window to retrieve and display the article.
*/
void OnNewsViewArticle(HWND hwnd)
{
    GROUPDATA FAR * lpdata =
         (GROUPDATA FAR *) GetWindowLong(hwnd, 0);
    // Get the current selection index from the list box.
    int iCurSel = ListBox_GetCurSel(lpdata->hwndLB);
    if (iCurSel < 0) {
        MessageBox(hwnd, "You must make a selection first.",
             "Whoops!", MB_OK | MB_ICONHAND);
        return;
    }
    // Find the right summary info entry in the list that
    // corresponds to the selection index.
    SUMMARYINFO * psi = lpdata->pslSummaryList->First();
    for (int i = 0; i < iCurSel; i++,
         psi = lpdata->pslSummaryList->Next())
         ; // Null loop body.

    // Create a little data structure to hold both the group
    // name and the article number.
    ASSERT(psi != NULL);
    GROUPANDARTICLE * pGroupAndArticle = new GROUPANDARTICLE;
    pGroupAndArticle->pszGroupName =
         DuplicateString(lpdata->pszGroupName);
    pGroupAndArticle->lArticleNum = psi->lArticleNum;
```

```
    // Create the viewer window.
     MDICREATESTRUCT mdicreate;
     mdicreate.szClass    = g_szArticleClass;
     mdicreate.szTitle    = "Article";
     mdicreate.hOwner     = g_hInstance;
     mdicreate.x          = CW_USEDEFAULT;
     mdicreate.y          = CW_USEDEFAULT;
     mdicreate.cx         = CW_USEDEFAULT;
     mdicreate.cy         = CW_USEDEFAULT;
     mdicreate.style      = 0;
     mdicreate.lParam     = (LPARAM)pGroupAndArticle;

     // Send a message to the client window to create the new child.
     SendMessage(g_hClient, WM_MDICREATE, 0,
         (LPARAM) (LPMDICREATESTRUCT) &mdicreate);

     return;
}


/*************************************************************************
     UTILITY FUNCTIONS
*************************************************************************/

/*
     Function: SetRetrievalStatus
     Description:
         This function sets the window title to show what percentage
         of the group's headers have been retrieved.
*/
void SetRetrievalStatus(HWND hwnd)
{
     GROUPDATA FAR * lpdata =
         (GROUPDATA FAR *) GetWindowLong(hwnd, 0);

     // Set the window title to indicate that we're retrieving
     // article headers.
     int iPercent = (int)((lpdata->lCurrent * 100) / lpdata->lTotal);
     const char pszStatusStr[] = " : retrieving headers (%d%%)";
     int nLen = lstrlen(pszStatusStr);
     char * pszTemp = new char[nLen + 10]; // 10 for percent and '\0'
     wsprintf(pszTemp, pszStatusStr, iPercent);
     SetStatus(hwnd, pszTemp);
     delete[] pszTemp;
}


/*
     Function: SetStatus
     Description:
         Changes the window title to include a status message.
         This is used to report the current connection status.
*/
void SetStatus(HWND hwnd, char * pszStatus)
```

```
{
    GROUPDATA FAR * lpdata =
        (GROUPDATA FAR *) GetWindowLong(hwnd, 0);
    int nLen = lstrlen(lpdata->pszGroupName) +
        lstrlen(pszStatus);
    char * pszTemp = new char[nLen + 1];
    lstrcpy(pszTemp, lpdata->pszGroupName);
    lstrcat(pszTemp, pszStatus);
    SetWindowText(hwnd, pszTemp);
    delete[] pszTemp;
}


/*
    Function: CreateArticleList
    Description:
        This function creates a series of summary lines from the
        list of summary nodes.  Each summary line is then put into
        the list box control.
*/
void CreateArticleList(HWND hwnd)
{
    const char *Months[] = { "Jan", "Feb", "Mar", "Apr", "May", "Jun",
        "Jul", "Aug", "Sep", "Oct", "Nov", "Dec" };
    const int MAXFROM = 20;
    const int MAXSUBJECT = 50;

    // Clear out the list box.
    GROUPDATA FAR * lpdata =
        (GROUPDATA FAR *) GetWindowLong(hwnd, 0);
    HWND hwndLB = lpdata->hwndLB;
    SetWindowRedraw(hwndLB, FALSE);
    SendMessage(hwndLB, LB_RESETCONTENT, 0, 0);

    // Create a summary line for each item in the summary info list.
    SUMMARYINFO * psi = lpdata->pslSummaryList->First();
    while (psi != NULL) {
        // Format the summary line string using the information
        // in the summary record.
        char szSummaryLine[100];
        char szTruncFrom[MAXFROM + 1];
        char szTruncSubject[MAXSUBJECT + 1];
        struct tm * ptm = localtime(&(psi->time));
        lstrcpyn(szTruncFrom, psi->pszFrom, MAXFROM);
        lstrcpyn(szTruncSubject, psi->pszSubject, MAXSUBJECT);
        wsprintf(szSummaryLine, "%02d-%s-%02d  %-20s  %-50s",
            ptm->tm_mday, (LPSTR)Months[ptm->tm_mon], ptm->tm_year,
            (LPSTR)szTruncFrom, (LPSTR)szTruncSubject);
        ListBox_AddString(hwndLB, szSummaryLine);
        psi = lpdata->pslSummaryList->Next();
    }
    SetWindowRedraw(hwndLB, TRUE);
}
```

```
/*
     Function: GetSummaryInfo
     Description:
          This function creates a summary info node from the header
          information in a disk file.
*/
SUMMARYINFO * GetSummaryInfo(char * pszFileName, long lArticleNum)
{
     SUMMARYINFO * psiResult = new SUMMARYINFO;

     // Set the article number.
     psiResult->lArticleNum = lArticleNum;

     // Get the From: header.
     char * pszHeaderData = GetHeaderData("From:", pszFileName);
     if (pszHeaderData == NULL) {
        // If we couldn't find the header, create a zero-length,
        // null-terminated string.
          pszHeaderData = new char[1];
          *pszHeaderData = '\0';
     }
     psiResult->pszFrom = pszHeaderData;

     // Get the subject header.
     pszHeaderData = GetHeaderData("Subject:", pszFileName);
     if (pszHeaderData == NULL) {
        // If we couldn't find the header, create a zero-length,
        // null-terminated string.
          pszHeaderData = new char[1];
          *pszHeaderData = '\0';
     }
     psiResult->pszSubject = pszHeaderData;

     // Get the date header.
     pszHeaderData = GetHeaderData("Date:", pszFileName);
     if (pszHeaderData == NULL) {
          // If there was no date, pick a default time.
          psiResult->time = 0;
     }
     else {
          // Else parse the date to return a time_t value.
          psiResult->time = ParseDateString(pszHeaderData);
          delete[] pszHeaderData;
     }

     // Return the SUMMARYINFO structure to the caller.
     return psiResult;
}


/*
     Function: GetHeaderData
     Description:
```

```
            This function reads a header field from a file containing
            a message.
*/
char * GetHeaderData(char * pszHeader, char * pszFileName)
{
    int i;
    ifstream ifsMessage(pszFileName);
    char szLineBuffer[1001];

    while (ifsMessage.peek() != EOF) {
        // Slurp up a line of data from the file.
          ifsMessage.getline(szLineBuffer, sizeof(szLineBuffer));
        // See if the line was simply a CRLF.
        if (lstrlen(szLineBuffer) == 0) {
            // If so, we reached the end of the headers before
            // finding the one we were looking for.  Exit the
            // while loop and return NULL.
            return NULL;
        }
        // See if this is the header we want.
        BOOL bMatch = TRUE;
        for (i = 0; i < lstrlen(pszHeader); i++) {
            if (tolower(pszHeader[i]) != tolower(szLineBuffer[i])) {
                // Nope, something didn't match.
                bMatch = FALSE;
                break;
            }
        }
        // If we matched, break out.
        if (bMatch)
            break;
    }
    // At this point, i==lstrlen(pszHeader).
    // Advance i past any whitespace that might have followed
    // the colon after the header name.
    while (IsLWSP(szLineBuffer[i]))
        i++;
    // Now, shrink the line down, eliminating the header name,
    // colon, and any following white space but retaining all
    // the info we really care about.
    char * pszResult = new char[lstrlen(szLineBuffer) - i + 1];
    int j = 0;
    while (szLineBuffer[i] != '\0') {
        pszResult[j++] = szLineBuffer[i++];
    }
    pszResult[j] = '\0';
    // Now, check to see if the following line is folded.  If
    // so, we should append it on to the current data.
    while (ifsMessage.peek() != EOF) {
        // We still have more file, so read in another line.
          ifsMessage.getline(szLineBuffer, sizeof(szLineBuffer));
        // See if it starts with linear white space.  If not,
```

```
            // then the line is not folded further and we're done.
              if (!IsLWSP(szLineBuffer[0]))
                 break;
              // Okay, the line is folded.
              // See how long the combined line will be when we've
              // appended this line to the previous ones.
               int iLength = lstrlen(pszResult) + lstrlen(szLineBuffer);
              char * pszTemp = new char[iLength + 1];
               lstrcpy(pszTemp, pszResult);
               lstrcat(pszTemp, szLineBuffer);
              delete[] pszResult;
              pszResult = pszTemp;
       }


       return pszResult;
}
```

Listing 13.5 NEWSART.CPP

```
/*
      File: NEWSART.CPP
      Description:
           Implements the article viewer window class for News Client.
      Copyright 1995, David G. Roberts
*/


#include <string.h>
#include <dos.h>
#include <fstream.h>
#include <windows.h>
#include <windowsx.h>
#include "newscli.rh"
#include "myassert.h"
#include "cnntp.h"

#define DECLARE
#include "newsclig.h"


/*
    CONSTANTS
*/
#define EDITCTLID          1
#define WM_NNTPCONNECTED       WM_USER
#define WM_NNTPGROUPDONE       (WM_USER + 1)
#define WM_NNTPARTICLEDONE     (WM_USER + 2)
#define WM_NNTPQUITDONE        (WM_USER + 3)


/*
    TYPES
*/


// ARTICLEDATA holds some data associated with the viewer window.
struct ARTICLEDATA {
```

```
    HWND          hwndEdit;
    char *        pszGroup;
    long          lArticleNum;
    CNNTP *       nntpobj;
    BOOL          bRetrieving;

    ARTICLEDATA::ARTICLEDATA()
        { pszGroup = NULL; nntpobj = NULL; bRetrieving = FALSE; };
    ARTICLEDATA::~ARTICLEDATA()
        { delete[] pszGroup; delete nntpobj; };
};

/*
    LOCAL FUNCTIONS
*/
static void OnClose(HWND);
static void OnCommand(HWND, int, HWND, UINT);
static BOOL OnCreate(HWND, CREATESTRUCT FAR*);
static void OnDestroy(HWND);
static void OnMDIActivate(HWND, BOOL, HWND, HWND);
static void OnNNTPConnect(HWND, UINT, WPARAM, LPARAM);
static void OnNNTPGroupDone(HWND, UINT, WPARAM, LPARAM);
static void OnNNTPArticleDone(HWND, UINT, WPARAM, LPARAM);
static void OnNNTPQuitDone(HWND, UINT, WPARAM, LPARAM);
static BOOL OnQueryEndSession(HWND hwnd);
static void OnSize(HWND, UINT, int, int);

/*
    UTILITY FUNCTIONS
*/
static void SetStatus(HWND, char *);
static BOOL PutFileIntoEditCtl(char *, HWND);

/************************************************************************
    WINDOW AND DIALOG BOX PROCEDURES
************************************************************************/

/*
    Function: ArticleWndProc
    Description:
        Window proc for the viewer window.
*/
LRESULT CALLBACK ArticleWndProc(HWND hwnd, UINT msg, WPARAM wParam,
    LPARAM lParam)
{
    switch (msg) {
        HANDLE_MSG(hwnd, WM_CLOSE, OnClose);
        HANDLE_MSG(hwnd, WM_COMMAND, OnCommand);
        HANDLE_MSG(hwnd, WM_CREATE, OnCreate);
        HANDLE_MSG(hwnd, WM_DESTROY, OnDestroy);
        HANDLE_MSG(hwnd, WM_MDIACTIVATE, OnMDIActivate);
        HANDLE_MSG(hwnd, WM_QUERYENDSESSION, OnQueryEndSession);
```

```
            HANDLE_MSG(hwnd, WM_SIZE, OnSize);
              case WM_NNTPCONNECTED:
                  OnNNTPConnect(hwnd, msg, wParam, lParam);
                break;
              case WM_NNTPGROUPDONE:
                  OnNNTPGroupDone(hwnd, msg, wParam, lParam);
                break;
              case WM_NNTPARTICLEDONE:
                  OnNNTPArticleDone(hwnd, msg, wParam, lParam);
                break;
              case WM_NNTPQUITDONE:
                  OnNNTPQuitDone(hwnd, msg, wParam, lParam);
                break;
        }
        return DefMDIChildProc(hwnd, msg, wParam, lParam);
}


/*********************************************************************
    MESSAGE HANDLING FUNCTIONS
*********************************************************************/

/*
    Function: OnClose
    Description:
        Determines if the window can be closed, and if so, destroys it.
*/
void OnClose(HWND hwnd)
{
    if (SendMessage(hwnd, WM_QUERYENDSESSION, 0, 0)) {
        SendMessage(g_hClient, WM_MDIDESTROY, (WPARAM) hwnd, 0);
    }
}


/*
    Function: OnCommand
    Description:
        Handles WM_COMMAND messages.
*/
void OnCommand(HWND hwnd, int id, HWND hwndCtl, UINT codeNotify)
{
    ARTICLEDATA FAR *lpdata =
        (ARTICLEDATA FAR *)GetWindowLong(hwnd, 0);

    if (hwndCtl == NULL) {
        // It's a window message.
        switch (id) {
            case IDM_EDITCOPY:
                SendMessage(lpdata->hwndEdit, WM_COPY, 0, 0);
                return;
        }
    }
    else {
```

```
        ASSERT(id == EDITCTLID);
          // It's from our control.
          if (codeNotify == EN_ERRSPACE) {
              MessageBox(hwnd, "Editor out of space.", "Error",
                  MB_OK | MB_ICONEXCLAMATION);
              return;
          }
    }
    // Make sure the default child proc sees things we don't
    // process ourselves!
    FORWARD_WM_COMMAND(hwnd, id, hwndCtl, codeNotify,
        DefMDIChildProc);
}


/*
    Function: OnCreate
    Description:
        Creates the editor window in which the messages are
        displayed, parses the message, and displays the first
        body part.
*/
BOOL OnCreate(HWND hwnd, CREATESTRUCT FAR* lpCreateStruct)
{
    // Allocate some private window data for ourselves.
    ARTICLEDATA FAR * lpdata = new ARTICLEDATA;
    SetWindowLong(hwnd, 0, (LONG) lpdata);

    // Create a multiline edit control to do our work for us.
    lpdata->hwndEdit = CreateWindow(
        "EDIT",                         // class name
        NULL,                           // window name
        WS_CHILD | WS_VISIBLE |         // window styles
        WS_HSCROLL | WS_VSCROLL | ES_LEFT |
        ES_MULTILINE | ES_AUTOHSCROLL | ES_AUTOVSCROLL | ES_READONLY,
        0,0,0,0,                        // location and size
        hwnd,                           // parent
        (HMENU) EDITCTLID,              // child id, not really a menu
        g_hInstance,                    // program instance
        NULL);                          // creation data

    // Set the edit control's font to a fixed pitch.
    HFONT hfont = GetStockFont(SYSTEM_FIXED_FONT);
    SetWindowFont(lpdata->hwndEdit, hfont, FALSE);

    // Get the group name and article number from the creation
    // parameters lParam.
    GROUPANDARTICLE * pGroupAndArt = (GROUPANDARTICLE *)
        (((MDICREATESTRUCT FAR *)
          (lpCreateStruct->lpCreateParams))->lParam);
    lpdata->pszGroup = pGroupAndArt->pszGroupName;
    lpdata->lArticleNum = pGroupAndArt->lArticleNum;
    delete pGroupAndArt;
```

```
    // Create the CNNTP object and start the article retrieval
    // process.
    lpdata->nntpobj = new CNNTP;
    lpdata->nntpobj->Connect(hwnd, WM_NNTPCONNECTED, g_pszNNTPServer,
        g_ushNNTPPort);
    SetStatus(hwnd, " : connecting...");

    lpdata->bRetrieving = TRUE;

    return TRUE;
}


/*
    Function: OnDestroy
    Description:
        Handles a WM_DESTROY message.
*/
void OnDestroy(HWND hwnd)
{
    // Deallocate our private window data before we go away.
    ARTICLEDATA FAR *lpdata =
        (ARTICLEDATA FAR *)GetWindowLong(hwnd, 0);
    delete lpdata;
}


/*
    Function: OnMDIActivate
    Description:
        Takes care of putting the viewer menu into the menu
        bar when the viewer window becomes active.
*/
void OnMDIActivate(HWND hwnd, BOOL fActive, HWND hwndActivate,
    HWND hwndDeactivate)
{
    UNUSED_PARAMETER(hwndActivate);
    UNUSED_PARAMETER(hwndDeactivate);

    if (fActive) {
        // Put our menu in place.
        SendMessage(g_hClient, WM_MDISETMENU,
            GET_WM_MDISETMENU_MPS(g_hArticleMenu,
                g_hArticleWindowMenu));
        ARTICLEDATA FAR *lpdata =
            (ARTICLEDATA FAR*)GetWindowLong(hwnd, 0);
        // Make sure keystrokes go to the edit control.
        SetFocus(lpdata->hwndEdit);
    }
    else {
        // We're being deactivated, so put the main menu in place.
        SendMessage(g_hClient, WM_MDISETMENU,
            GET_WM_MDISETMENU_MPS(g_hFrameMenu,
                g_hFrameWindowMenu));
```

```
    }
    DrawMenuBar(g_hFrame);
}

/*
    Function: OnNNTPConnect
    Description:
        This function is invoked when the WM_NNTPCONNECTED
        message is received.  It checks for errors and then
        selects the NNTP group.
*/
void OnNNTPConnect(HWND hwnd, UINT msg, WPARAM wParam, LPARAM lParam)
{
    UNUSED_PARAMETER(msg);
    UNUSED_PARAMETER(lParam);

    ARTICLEDATA FAR * lpdata =
        (ARTICLEDATA FAR *) GetWindowLong(hwnd, 0);

    if (wParam != CNNTP::RESULT_SUCCESS) {
        MessageBox(hwnd, "Could not connect to server!", "Error",
            MB_OK | MB_ICONEXCLAMATION);
        lpdata->bRetrieving = FALSE;
        delete lpdata->nntpobj;
        PostMessage(hwnd, WM_CLOSE, 0, 0);
        return;
    }

    // Set the title to the group name + "retrieving article count..."
    SetStatus(hwnd, " : selecting group...");

    lpdata->nntpobj->Group(hwnd, WM_NNTPGROUPDONE,
        lpdata->pszGroup);
}

/*
    Function: OnNNTPGroupDone
    Description:
        Invoked when the window receives a WM_NNTPGROUPDONE message.
        The function checks for errors and then starts the
        article download process.
*/
void OnNNTPGroupDone(HWND hwnd, UINT msg, WPARAM wParam,
    LPARAM lParam)
{
    UNUSED_PARAMETER(msg);
    UNUSED_PARAMETER(lParam);

    ARTICLEDATA FAR * lpdata =
        (ARTICLEDATA FAR *) GetWindowLong(hwnd, 0);

    if (wParam != CNNTP::RESULT_SUCCESS) {
```

```
        MessageBox(hwnd, "Invalid group name!", "Error",
            MB_OK | MB_ICONEXCLAMATION);
        lpdata->bRetrieving = FALSE;
        delete lpdata->nntpobj;
        PostMessage(hwnd, WM_CLOSE, 0, 0);
        return;
    }

    // Get the article.
    SetStatus(hwnd, " : retrieving article...");
    lpdata->nntpobj->Article(hwnd, WM_NNTPARTICLEDONE,
        lpdata->lArticleNum);
}

/*

    Function: OnNNTPArticleDone
    Description:
        Invoked when the window receives a WM_NNTPARTICLEDONE
        message.  It deals with any errors, puts the message text
        into the edit control window, and then closes the NNTP
        connection.
*/
void OnNNTPArticleDone(HWND hwnd, UINT msg, WPARAM wParam,
    LPARAM lParam)
{
    UNUSED_PARAMETER(msg);

    CNNTP::ARTICLEANDFILENAME * pArtAndFile;

    ARTICLEDATA FAR * lpdata =
        (ARTICLEDATA FAR *) GetWindowLong(hwnd, 0);

    // Check return value from CNNTP object.
    switch (wParam) {
        case CNNTP::RESULT_SUCCESS:
            // Parse the article header.
            pArtAndFile = (CNNTP::ARTICLEANDFILENAME *) lParam;

            // Put the file into the viewer.
            PutFileIntoEditCtl(pArtAndFile->pszFilename,
                lpdata->hwndEdit);

            // Delete the file and the memory allocated for the
            // ARTICLEANDFILENAME structure.
            unlink(pArtAndFile->pszFilename);
            delete[] pArtAndFile->pszFilename;
            delete pArtAndFile;

            // Quit.
            SetStatus(hwnd, " : closing connection...");
            lpdata->nntpobj->Quit(hwnd, WM_NNTPQUITDONE);
            break;
```

```
            case CNNTP::RESULT_FAILURE:
                // Something happened.  Bogus article number, perhaps?
                MessageBox(hwnd, "An error occurred while retrieving "
                    "the article.", "Error!",
                    MB_OK | MB_ICONEXCLAMATION);
               // Leave.
                SetStatus(hwnd, " : closing connection...");
                 lpdata->nntpobj->Quit(hwnd, WM_NNTPQUITDONE);
                break;
            default:
                MessageBox(hwnd, "An error occurred while retrieving "
                    "article headers.", "Error!",
                    MB_OK | MB_ICONEXCLAMATION);
                lpdata->bRetrieving = FALSE;
                delete lpdata->nntpobj;
                PostMessage(hwnd, WM_CLOSE, 0, 0);
                break;
    }
    return;
}


/*
    Function: OnNNTPQuitDone
    Description:
        Invoked when the window receives a WM_NNTPQUITDONE message.
        The function destroys the CNNTP object and reports
        any error that may have resulted.
*/
void OnNNTPQuitDone(HWND hwnd, UINT msg, WPARAM wParam,
    LPARAM lParam)
{
    UNUSED_PARAMETER(msg);
    UNUSED_PARAMETER(lParam);

    ARTICLEDATA FAR * lpdata =
        (ARTICLEDATA FAR *) GetWindowLong(hwnd, 0);

    delete lpdata->nntpobj;
    lpdata->nntpobj = NULL;
    lpdata->bRetrieving = FALSE;

    if (wParam != CNNTP::RESULT_SUCCESS) {
        MessageBox(hwnd, "An error occurred while closing the "
            "connection.", "Error!",
            MB_OK | MB_ICONEXCLAMATION);
        lpdata->bRetrieving = FALSE;
        delete lpdata->nntpobj;
        PostMessage(hwnd, WM_CLOSE, 0, 0);
    }

    SetStatus(hwnd, "");
}
```

```
/*
      Function: OnQueryEndSession
      Description:
          Handles WM_QUERYENDSESSION messages. Returns TRUE if the
          window should be closed, FALSE otherwise.
*/
BOOL OnQueryEndSession(HWND hwnd)
{
    ARTICLEDATA FAR * lpdata =
        (ARTICLEDATA FAR *) GetWindowLong(hwnd, 0);
    if (lpdata->bRetrieving) {
        SendMessage(g_hClient, WM_MDIRESTORE, (WPARAM) hwnd, 0);
        int iResult = MessageBox(hwnd,
            "Retrieving article.  Close anyway?",
            "Close Anyway?", MB_YESNO | MB_ICONQUESTION);
        if (iResult == IDYES)
            return TRUE;
        else
            return FALSE;
    }
    else {
        return TRUE;
    }
}


/*
      Function: OnSize
      Description:
          Notifies the editor child window whenever the viewer window
          gets resized.
*/
void OnSize(HWND hwnd, UINT state, int cx, int cy)
{
        UNUSED_PARAMETER(state);

        ARTICLEDATA FAR *lpdata =
            (ARTICLEDATA FAR *)GetWindowLong(hwnd, 0);
        MoveWindow(lpdata->hwndEdit, 0, 0, cx, cy, TRUE);
        // Must make sure we forward this to the default child proc
      // as well!
        FORWARD_WM_SIZE(hwnd, state, cx, cy, DefMDIChildProc);
}


/**********************************************************************
      UTILITY FUNCTIONS
**********************************************************************/

/*
      Function: SetStatus
      Description:
          Changes the window title to include a status message.
          This is used to report the current connection status.
```

```
*/
void SetStatus(HWND hwnd, char * pszStatus)
{
    const char szArticle[] = "Article";
    int nLen = lstrlen(szArticle) + lstrlen(pszStatus);
    char * pszTemp = new char[nLen + 1];
    lstrcpy(pszTemp, szArticle);
    lstrcat(pszTemp, pszStatus);
    SetWindowText(hwnd, pszTemp);
    delete[] pszTemp;
}


/*
    Function: PutFileIntoEditCtl
    Description:
        Reads a file and stuffs the text into the specified
      edit control.  Short, simple, and to the point.
*/
BOOL PutFileIntoEditCtl(char * pszFilename, HWND hwndEdit)
{
    // Open file.
    HFILE hFile = _lopen(pszFilename, OF_READ);
    if (hFile == HFILE_ERROR)
        return FALSE;

    // Determine file length by seeking to end of file.
    long lLength = _llseek(hFile, 0, 2);
    // Move back to beginning.
    _llseek(hFile, 0, 0);

#ifndef WIN32
    // Win16 _lread can only handle 0xFFFE bytes at a time.
    // If we're compiling for Win16, clamp lLength to 0xFFFE.
    if (lLength > 0xFFFE)
        lLength = 0xFFFE;
#endif

    // Allocate the buffer.
    char * pBuffer = new char[lLength + 1];
    if (pBuffer == NULL) {
        _lclose(hFile);
        return FALSE;
    }

    // Read the file into the buffer.
    if ((HFILE)_lread(hFile, pBuffer, (UINT) lLength) == HFILE_ERROR) {
        _lclose(hFile);
        return FALSE;
    }
    _lclose(hFile);

    // Terminate the buffer.
```

```
    pBuffer[lLength] = '\0';

    // Stuff the text into the viewer edit control.
    SetWindowText(hwndEdit, pBuffer);
    delete[] pBuffer;

    return TRUE;
}
```

Listing 13.6 NEWSCLI.DEF

```
NAME          NEWSCLI
DESCRIPTION   'News Client, Copyright 1995, David G. Roberts'
EXETYPE       WINDOWS
STUB          'WINSTUB.EXE'
CODE          PRELOAD MOVABLE DISCARDABLE
DATA          PRELOAD MOVABLE
HEAPSIZE      32768
STACKSIZE     8192
```

Listing 13.7 NEWSCLI.RC

```
/*****************************************************************************
NEWSCLI.RC
*****************************************************************************/

#include "newscli.rh"
#include "errno.rc"
FRAMEMENU MENU
{
 POPUP "&File"
 {
   MENUITEM "&Open Group", IDM_FILEOPENGROUP
   MENUITEM "&Close", IDM_FILECLOSE
   MENUITEM SEPARATOR
   MENUITEM "E&xit", IDM_FILEEXIT
 }

 POPUP "&News"
 {
   MENUITEM "&Configure...", IDM_NEWSCONFIGURE
 }

 POPUP "&Window"
 {
   MENUITEM "&Cascade\tShift+F5", IDM_WINDOWCASCADE
   MENUITEM "&Tile\tShift+F4", IDM_WINDOWTILE
   MENUITEM "Arrange &Icons", IDM_WINDOWARRANGE
   MENUITEM "Close &All", IDM_WINDOWCLOSEALL
 }
```

```
  POPUP "&Help"
  {
    MENUITEM "&About...", IDM_HELPABOUT
  }

}
NEWSCLI ACCELERATORS
{
  "^Z", IDM_EDITUNDO, ASCII
  "^X", IDM_EDITCUT, ASCII
  "^C", IDM_EDITCOPY, ASCII
  "^V", IDM_EDITPASTE, ASCII
  VK_F5, IDM_WINDOWCASCADE, VIRTKEY, SHIFT
  VK_F4, IDM_WINDOWTILE, VIRTKEY, SHIFT
}


GROUPMENU MENU
{
  POPUP "&File"
  {
    MENUITEM "&Open Group", IDM_FILEOPENGROUP
    MENUITEM "&Close", IDM_FILECLOSE
    MENUITEM SEPARATOR
    MENUITEM "E&xit", IDM_FILEEXIT
  }

  POPUP "&News"
  {
    MENUITEM "&View Article", IDM_NEWSVIEWARTICLE
    MENUITEM SEPARATOR
    MENUITEM "&Configure...", IDM_NEWSCONFIGURE
  }

  POPUP "&Window"
  {
    MENUITEM "&Cascade\tShift+F5", IDM_WINDOWCASCADE
    MENUITEM "&Tile\tShift+F4", IDM_WINDOWTILE
    MENUITEM "Arrange &Icons", IDM_WINDOWARRANGE
    MENUITEM "Close &All", IDM_WINDOWCLOSEALL
  }

  POPUP "&Help"
  {
    MENUITEM "&About...", IDM_HELPABOUT
  }

}

ARTICLEMENU MENU
{
```

```
POPUP "&File"
{
  MENUITEM "&Open Group", IDM_FILEOPENGROUP
  MENUITEM "&Close", IDM_FILECLOSE
  MENUITEM SEPARATOR
  MENUITEM "E&xit", IDM_FILEEXIT
}

POPUP "&Edit"
{
  MENUITEM "&Copy\tCtrl+C", IDM_EDITCOPY
}

POPUP "&News"
{
  MENUITEM "&Configure...", IDM_NEWSCONFIGURE
}

POPUP "&Window"
{
  MENUITEM "&Cascade\tShift+F5", IDM_WINDOWCASCADE
  MENUITEM "&Tile\tShift+F4", IDM_WINDOWTILE
  MENUITEM "Arrange &Icons", IDM_WINDOWARRANGE
  MENUITEM "Close &All", IDM_WINDOWCLOSEALL
}

POPUP "&Help"
{
  MENUITEM "&About...", IDM_HELPABOUT
}

}


CONFIGURE DIALOG 6, 15, 207, 49
STYLE DS_MODALFRAME | WS_POPUP | WS_VISIBLE | WS_CAPTION | WS_SYSMENU
CAPTION "Configure"
FONT 8, "MS Sans Serif"
{
  DEFPUSHBUTTON "OK", IDOK, 148, 6, 50, 14
  PUSHBUTTON "Cancel", IDCANCEL, 148, 24, 50, 14
  LTEXT "NNTP Server", -1, 12, 10, 48, 8
  LTEXT "NNTP Port", -1, 12, 31, 48, 8
  EDITTEXT IDD_NNTPSERVER, 59, 8, 72, 12
  EDITTEXT IDD_NNTPPORT, 59, 29, 28, 12
  PUSHBUTTON "Default", IDD_DEFAULT, 92, 28, 40, 14
}


GROUP DIALOG 6, 15, 207, 46
STYLE DS_MODALFRAME | WS_POPUP | WS_VISIBLE | WS_CAPTION | WS_SYSMENU
CAPTION "Open Group"
```

```
FONT 8, "MS Sans Serif"
{
  DEFPUSHBUTTON "OK", IDOK, 148, 6, 50, 14
  PUSHBUTTON "Cancel", IDCANCEL, 148, 24, 50, 14
  LTEXT "Group:", -1, 8, 8, 24, 8
  EDITTEXT IDD_GROUP, 8, 20, 128, 12
}


APPICON ICON "newscli.ico"


GROUPICON ICON "newsgrp.ico"


ARTICLEICON ICON "newsart.ico"
```

Listing 13.8   NEWSCLI.RH

```
/*************************************************************************
newscli.rh
*************************************************************************/

#define IDM_NEWSVIEWARTICLE 101
#define IDM_FIRSTCHILD   1000
#define IDM_NEWSCONFIGURE    30
#define IDM_FILEOPENGROUP    12
#define IDD_GROUP     101
#define IDD_DEFAULT  103
#define IDD_NNTPPORT     102
#define IDD_NNTPSERVER   101
#define IDM_FILECLOSE    13
#define IDM_FILEEXIT         11

#define IDM_EDITUNDO         20
#define IDM_EDITCUT          21
#define IDM_EDITCOPY         22
#define IDM_EDITPASTE        23


#define IDM_WINDOWCASCADE    40
#define IDM_WINDOWTILE       41
#define IDM_WINDOWARRANGE    42
#define IDM_WINDOWCLOSEALL   43

#define IDM_HELPABOUT        50
```

File Transfer Protocol: FTP

CHAPTER 14

The File Transfer Protocol is one of the oldest protocols in use on the Internet. Learn the ins and outs of this Internet mainstay in this chapter.

The File Transfer Protocol (FTP) is one of the oldest and most important protocols in use on the Internet today. FTP allows users to transfer files between network hosts. People have set up many FTP archive sites on the Internet. These sites allow users to retrieve games, utilities, source code, application programs, shareware distributions, and much, much more. All the RFCs that describe Internet protocols are available online in FTP archives.

In this chapter, we'll take a look at the problems FTP attempts to solve, the client-server model on which FTP is based, the various FTP commands and responses, and the data types that FTP transfers. Finally, we'll finish the chapter with a look at the public domain WS_FTP application written by John Junod.

The FTP Challenge

FTP has been around since the earliest days of the ARPANET. Remember that the original goals of the ARPANET included the sharing of information and resources between computer researchers. FTP was a fundamental component of the ARPANET architecture that allowed this sharing to occur.

Here's how it worked: Using FTP, researchers could transfer the results of experiments to colleagues across the network. Researchers could also use remote computers. The programs and data for an experiment were created on a local computer, then moved across the network using FTP. The programs were compiled on the remote computer and then run on the data set. The Telnet protocol controlled the remote computer. When the program completed, the results could be moved back to a local computer using FTP.

The original ARPANET goals are reflected in the following introduction to RFC 959, which describes the File Transfer Protocol:

> *The objectives of FTP are:*
>
> *1) to promote sharing of files (computer programs and/or data)*
>
> *2) to encourage indirect or implicit (via programs) use of remote computers*
>
> *3) to shield a user from variations in file storage systems among hosts, and*
>
> *4) to transfer data reliably and efficiently.*
>
> *FTP, though usable directly by a user at a terminal, is designed mainly for use by programs.*
>
> *The attempt in this specification is to satisfy the diverse needs of users of maxi-hosts, mini-hosts, personal workstations, and TACs, with a simple, and easily implemented protocol design.*

As the introduction describes, FTP is meant to be a simple, easy-to-implement protocol that satisfies a diverse set of needs. At the time FTP was created, the needs of such a protocol were indeed diverse. All sorts of computers existed, using all kinds of operating systems, file structures, and character sets. The fact that FTP was able to bridge the gap among these divergent systems is a testament to the skill of its designers.

Many of FTP's features are not in heavy use now. For instance, most of today's computers use the ASCII character set. Although FTP also supports the EBCDIC character set, a modern FTP client can easily omit this feature and still be very useable on the network.

This chapter concentrates on the parts of FTP that are most useful, and does not describe all of the FTP protocol. If you find yourself wondering, "Why did they do it that way?" however, you should consult RFC 959. Chances are the designers had very good reasons for creating FTP that way.

FTP Model

This section examines the client-server model used by FTP. Figure 14.1 shows a diagram of the model.

The FTP client communicates with the FTP server using two TCP connections: a control connection and a data connection. Using the control connection, the FTP client sends commands to the server and receives replies. Actual file data is transferred using the data connection.

Internally, the FTP client is composed of three logical modules: the user interface, protocol interpreter (PI), and data transfer process (DTP). The server has two modules: a protocol interpreter and a data transfer process.

Figure 14.1

The FTP client/ server model.

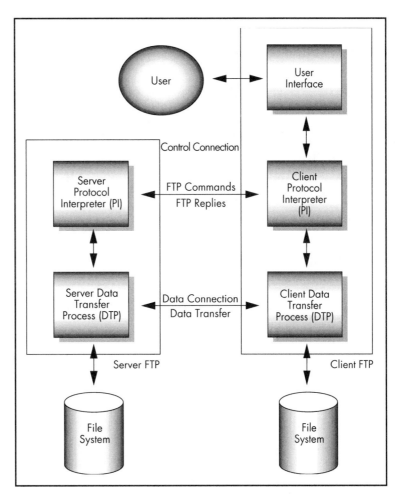

The user interface module creates the interface with which the user interacts. In a graphical environment like Microsoft Windows, the user interface module creates windows, menus, and buttons. An FTP client that was written to run in a terminal environment might provide a command line interface. Because a server does not interact directly with users, it does not need a user interface module. Some servers might implement a minimal user interface module that simply allows a system administrator to start, stop, or configure the FTP server process.

The PI module in the client and server interprets the FTP protocol and controls the DTP. The client PI generates FTP commands in response to user interface events and sends them to the server. It interprets the reply codes the server sends in response to the commands. The server PI interprets the commands sent from the client and generates responses to them. The FTP commands and responses are carried in the control connection.

The DTP module in the client and server transfers file data. Both client and server DTPs interact with the local file systems on their machines. The DTP converts between the native data formats on the local file system and the standard FTP data formats that are carried on the data connection.

The DTP modules also interact with the PI modules on the client and server. The PI module tells the DTP module when a data transfer is going to begin, the direction of the transfer, and the format of the data to be exchanged. The DTP module informs the PI module when the data transfer is complete or an error has occurred.

RFC 959 describes other models for the entities in an FTP system, as well. These models allow a single client to control data transfer between two remote hosts (rather than between a remote host and the local host). These models are used very rarely. In most cases, an FTP client transfers files only between itself and a remote server. Consult RFC 959 for more information about these FTP models.

The Control Connection

The control connection is the main connection in the FTP protocol. The client sets up the control connection when it first contacts the FTP server. Contact is made on well-known TCP port number 21. The control connection remains in place for the duration of the FTP session, in contrast to the data connection, which is set up as needed to transfer files.

The control connection carries text-based information and is similar to the SMTP, POP3, and NNTP connections. Commands and replies are sent as lines of 7-bit ASCII text, terminated with CRLF. Technically, the FTP control channel uses the Telnet protocol. The Telnet protocol allows the end-of-line sequence (among other parameters) to be negotiated between the client and server. In practice, the server never initiates a negotiation, so the client can simply use CRLF as the line termination sequence.

Commands

FTP commands are sent as a single line of text, terminated with CRLF. Each command name is a short string of alphabetic characters. Some commands are followed by a parameter. The parameter is separated from the command by space characters. Here are some sample FTP commands:

```
USER dave
CWD /pub/downloads
TYPE I
STOR foobar.zip
```

We'll take a look at the set of commonly used FTP commands in a later section.

Responses

FTP responses consist of a 3-digit numeric code followed by text. The numeric code is intended for the client PI, and the text is intended for a human who might be monitoring the control connection. The exact format of the reply is one line of text terminated with CRLF. The numeric code appears as the first three characters on the line. The numeric code is separated from the text by one or more space characters. The remaining text is not structured and varies from server to server. The text is not required and may be omitted. When text is omitted, the response line consists of the 3-digit code followed by CRLF.

The numeric code structure ensures that the first digit of the code gives the most detail. The first digit of the response code may be one of the following values:

1   Positive preliminary reply. The requested action is being initiated but has not completed. The client PI should expect another response line that indicates the final success or failure of the command. The client should not send another command to the server before receiving the final response to the current command.

2   Positive completion reply. The command completed successfully.

3   Positive intermediate reply. The command was accepted, and the server is now waiting for further information before the command can be completed.

4   Transient negative completion reply. The command could not be completed because of some error condition, but the situation is temporary. The client can retry the command at a later time to see if the error condition has resolved itself.

5   Permanent negative completion reply. The command could not be completed because of a permanent error condition. The error condition is not expected to resolve itself, and the client is not encouraged to retry the command.

The second digit of the response code indicates the category of the response:

0   Syntax — this reply code indicates a problem with the command syntax. The command may have been misspelled or is not implemented on this server.

1   Information — this is a reply for information or help.

2   Connection — this reply refers to the state of the control or data connection.

3   Authentication and Accounting — this reply refers to the login process.

4   Reserved — this code is reserved for future use.

5   File system — this reply refers to the state of the file system.

The third digit of the response code communicates a finer gradation of the previous response categories. The third digit can be used to distinguish between responses having the same first two digits.

Here are some sample FTP responses:

```
200 Command okay.
500 Syntax error, command unrecognized.
331 User name okay, need password.
250 Requested file action okay, completed.
```

Multiline Responses

Sometimes, the server needs to return more than a single line of text in an FTP response. Some FTP servers communicate policy statements when a user first signs on, for instance. FTP allows responses to span multiple response lines to accommodate these special cases.

A multiline FTP response is similar to a single-line response with one small difference. In a multiline response, the 3-digit numeric code is followed immediately by a hyphen character (-) rather than a space or CRLF.

The last line of a multiline response looks like a standard single-line response. The numeric response code is identical to that returned in the first line of the multiline response. The last line of a multiline response contains the numeric response code followed by a space or CRLF.

Multiple lines of text can occur between the first and last lines of the response. The intermediate lines of text can have any format except something that might be interpreted as the final response line. Most servers prefix each of the intermediate lines with the same numeric response code followed by a hyphen character, but this format is not required.

For example, most servers simply do this:

```
123-First line of response text.
123-Second line of response text.
123-Third line of response text.
123 Last line of response text.
```

This format is equally valid, however, and a well-written client should be prepared to encounter it:

```
123-First line of response text.
Second line of response text.
345 Third line of response text begins with numbers but not
the same code as the first. (This is the fourth line now.)
123 Last line of response text.
```

Data Transfer

The data connection transfers data between the sending and receiving hosts. Before data is transferred, the hosts must agree on the format of the data and the method of transmission that will be used. These options are described by the data type, data structure, and transfer mode.

Data Types

It may seem a simple task to transfer files between systems. Simply open a TCP connection and stuff the bytes through! What more could there be? This model works well when systems use the same operating system or at least the same set of standards that govern file types, character sets, and so on.

Remember, though, that FTP was purposely designed to work in a heterogeneous environment where such compatibility could not be taken for granted. As a result, FTP uses the concept of *data type* to help computers convert between equivalent representations of data on different systems. FTP supports four data types: ASCII, Image, EBCDIC, and Local. The following sections describe the ASCII, Image, and EBCDIC data types. The Local data type is not used very often; see RFC 959 for more information about the Local data type.

Every time a data file is transferred between systems, the client and server PIs inform the DTPs of the current data type. The data transfer is conducted using the necessary translations for the current data type.

The client changes the current data type using the TYPE command. We'll see how this change is accomplished in a later section.

In this section, we examine the types of data defined by FTP and how they are handled by the communicating systems.

ASCII

The *ASCII* data type transfers text files between systems. The sending host converts the text file from the native text format on the sending system to FTP's ASCII format. The receiving host converts the ASCII data to the native format on the receiving system. The ASCII format serves as a neutral format for the data transfer.

In practice, most modern computer systems already use ASCII characters in text files. The only part that causes problems is the representation of the end-of-line character or character sequence. Some systems use a single LF or single CR. Others, like DOS/Windows, use a combination CRLF pair. FTP's ASCII format defines the CRLF pair as the standard end-of-line character sequence for data transmitted between systems.

DOS/Windows applications already use this format. No conversion is needed between the data stored on disk and the data exchanged with the remote system. A DOS/Windows program simply reads data from disk and sends it to a socket.

The ASCII data type is the default data type selected when an FTP session begins. Support for the ASCII data type is mandatory.

Image

The *Image* data type transfers binary data between systems. This type identifies the data as a sequence of contiguous bits packed into 8-bit bytes. The data should be stored as a sequence of bits by each system involved in the transfer.

The FTP standard uses the "contiguous bits" phrase to handle cases where different computers have a different word size. For instance, many older computer systems used 36-bit words as their fundamental addressable unit. Most modern computer systems use 8-bit bytes. In this case, the Image data type simply tells the hosts to perform no translations on the data.

The Image type is one of the most-used data transfer types on the modern Internet. The Image type is used to transfer compressed archive files such as DOS Zip or Unix Tar files. These files are not text files and cannot be transferred using the ASCII data type.

Unfortunately, the Image type is not the FTP default data type. Many new users of FTP clients forget to set the date type to Image before transferring archived files. The ASCII type may introduce transformations on the raw data to conform to the FTP ASCII rules (such as converting between the local end-of-line standard and the FTP CRLF standard). The transformation can corrupt the binary data. More than one inexperienced user has downloaded a file only to find that it is corrupted.

Support for the Image data type is optional. In practice, however, the transfer of binary files between systems is so common that all FTP clients and servers must support this data type.

EBCDIC

The *EBCDIC* data type transfers EBCDIC text files between systems supporting the EBCDIC character set. If both systems use EBCDIC as the native character set, this data type loses no information during the transfer.

In Chapter 12 we discussed the subtle problems that may crop up when trying to convert between ASCII and EBCDIC character sets. We learned that files encoded using the Base64 encoding format use a limited set of characters that are present in both character sets. They can be converted between the two character sets without data loss. We noted that the UUENCODE format does not share this property because it uses characters from the ASCII character set that are not present in EBCDIC.

If two computer systems both support the EBCDIC character set, using the FTP ASCII data type to transfer a file between them could result in data loss. The sending system must convert EBCDIC characters to equivalent ASCII characters. This transformation introduces some alteration of the original data if the original file contains characters that cannot be represented equivalently in ASCII. The receiving system must convert the ASCII data back into EBCDIC. This transformation may also introduce some alterations to the data. The EBCDIC data type allows EBCDIC systems to transfer text files with no data alteration.

Support for the EBCDIC data type is optional. Because ASCII systems dominate the world, only applications written for EBCDIC systems need to support the EBCDIC data type.

Data Structures

In addition to data types, FTP also specifies a set of data structures. File systems used by different operating systems use different structures to store data. In some systems a file is simply a sequence of bytes; DOS and Unix use this structure. IBM mainframes often use a record-oriented structure. The FTP structure associated with a data transfer allows the receiver to interpret the source file system's structure and recover as much of it as possible.

FTP defines three data structures: *File, Record,* and *Page.* Of the three types, the File structure is used most often and is the default. The other structures are seldom used and are never used by systems running DOS/Windows. Many FTP servers don't even implement support for the Record and Page structures. Consult RFC 959 for more information about the other data structures.

The File structure assumes no internal structure for the data. The data is simply interpreted as a sequence of bytes. After the data is transformed according to the current data type (ASCII or Image, typically), no other transformations are needed to communicate the File structure.

The File structure is the default structure. This default is convenient for DOS/ Windows and Unix machines. The FTP client running on these operating systems does not have to execute an FTP command to change the current structure mode.

Although the FTP specification provides the STRU command to allow the client to specify the data structure, many servers using file systems supporting unstructured files don't implement anything other than the File structure.

Transfer Mode

After the format and structure of the data are agreed upon, the client and server must choose a data transfer mode. FTP defines three transfer modes: *Stream*, *Block*, and *Compressed*. The transfer modes indicate whether any framing information should be included in the data stream.

The Stream transfer mode simply transfers the file as a sequence of bytes. It relies on TCP's error control mechanisms to ensure that the data is received in sequence. The Block transfer mode transfers the data as a sequence of data blocks, each preceded by a header. The header indicates the length of the block and whether the block is the last block in the file. The Compressed transfer mode transfers compressed data. This mode uses a simple run-length compression algorithm.

The Stream transfer mode is the default transfer mode. Unfortunately, it is also the least reliable of the three modes. Because the Stream transfer mode includes no sequencing information in the data stream, the receiver cannot simply examine the data stream to tell when the end-of-file point is reached.

In Stream mode, closing the data connection signals the end-of-file. In some cases, this method causes problems. If the sender crashes or encounters some sort of fatal error, the connection might be closed before all of the data is transferred. In this case, the receiver mistakenly thinks that the end of the data has arrived. It closes the destination file and does not know that it received only a portion of the data.

The Block and Compressed transfer modes include enough sequencing information in the stream for the receiver to determine when the end-of-file is reached. The Block and Compressed transfer modes do not require the data connection to be closed after a file is transferred. Using the Block transfer mode, an interrupted file transfer can even be restarted at the point it failed.

Unfortunately, many FTP servers don't implement the Block or Compressed transfer modes. Because most servers do not implement them, many FTP clients do not use them, either. A user often has little choice but to accept the unreliability of the Stream transfer mode.

Managing the Data Connection

The data connection is managed by the DTPs in both the client and server. Unlike the control connection, the data connection is not necessarily stable throughout the FTP session. A data connection is opened when a file is transferred and closed afterwards.

> *Note: The data connection is closed to mark the end-of-file when the Stream transfer mode is in effect. The other transfer modes include auxiliary information that allows the receiver to determine the end-of-file. If these other transfer modes are in use, the data connection does not need to be closed after each file is transferred. In practice, however, most systems use the Stream transfer mode, so the data connection is closed after each file is transferred.*

Both client and server have a default data transfer port. The client's default port is the same port used for the control connection. The server's default port is the port number used for the control connection plus 1 (port 22 if the server is using well-known port 21 for the control connection).

Using the same port number for the client's control connection and the data transfer connection may seem a bit strange. Remember, however, that TCP identifies connections using the addresses and port numbers of both endpoints. As long as the server uses a different port number for its control and data connection, TCP views the connections as separate. Also remember that ports and sockets are not the same thing. Although the control and data connections may use the same port number, each connection is accessed using a separate socket descriptor.

When a data transfer starts, the client listens on its data transfer port. The server initiates the connection and the client accepts the connection request when it arrives. When the connection is established, data transfer can begin. If the stream transfer mode is in effect, the connection is closed when all data has been transferred. The closing of the connection indicates the end-of-file to the receiver.

Typically, the server always initiates the connection, whether it is the sender or receiver of the data that is being transferred. The PASV command alters this behavior. The PASV command indicates that the server should be the "passive" party in the connection and should wait for the client to contact it.

Both the client's and server's data transfer ports can be changed from the default using the PORT and PASV commands. The PORT command specifies the data port with which the server should connect. The PASV command instructs the server that the client will contact it. The server's response to the PASV command indicates a new port number that should be used to make contact.

This feature is used frequently. TCP does not allow a connection to be established between the same hosts using the same port numbers immediately after a similar connection has been closed. TCP disallows this connection because it uses the host addresses and port numbers to identify data belonging to a connection. Imagine that during the previous connection a packet containing data was lost. At some point, TCP would notice that the data did not arrive and would retransmit it. After all the data is sent, the connection would be closed.

Now imagine that the lost data packet was not lost at all, but simply very, very delayed. If a new connection using the same port numbers is opened immediately after the first connection closes, the delayed packet could arrive after the new connection is opened. And because the addresses and port numbers on both ends of the connection match, TCP might think that this newly arriving data packet belongs to the new connection, not the old connection. Instead of discarding the packet, TCP might insert it into the new data stream. This scenario is clearly a problem, so TCP enforces a delay period before a connection that uses the same address and port endpoints can be reopened.

TCP's behavior interacts with the Stream transfer mode to force FTP to move the data connection port of one of the end-points with each data transfer. The Stream transfer mode forces the data connection to be closed after every file is transferred. If more than one file must be transferred, the same ports cannot be used for the connection because of TCP's waiting period. To avoid this situation, most FTP clients never use the default data port. Instead, they issue a new PORT command before each new transfer to move the data connection to a new client port.

An alternative strategy is to issue PASV commands, forcing the client to take the responsibility of making contact with the server on the data connection.

A Sample FTP Session

Previous sections described the formats of commands, replies, data types, data structures, transfer modes, and management of the data connection. In this section, we'll look at a sample FTP session. We'll explain the commands issued by the client and the responses returned from the server.

In this analysis, the text example associated with the control channel is prefaced by "C:" and "S:" to indicate whether the client or server sends the text. Data communicated on the data channel is prefaced by "D:". Informative or descriptive text is surrounded by square brackets ([ ]).

An FTP session starts when the client PI contacts the server PI on the control connection's well-known port. When the control connection is opened, the server responds with a positive greeting response.

```
C: [contacts server on well-known port 21]
S: 220 Service ready.
```

Before the client can request file transfers, it must authenticate itself with the server. The first step in the authentication process is to send a user name to the server with the USER command.

```
C: USER dave
S: 331 Password required for dave.
```

If the user name is valid, the server responds with code 331 or code 230. Code 331 indicates the user name is valid but a password is needed to complete the authentication sequence. Code 230 indicates the user name is valid and no further information is needed. An invalid user name returns a response code starting with 4 or 5. In this case, the server responded with code 331, so we need to send a password.

The password is sent using the PASS command.

```
C: PASS cool!
S: 230 User dave logged in.
```

If the password is correct, the server returns a 230 response code. If the password is incorrect, the server returns a code starting with 4 or 5. After the PASS command is accepted, the client is authenticated and can issue further commands.

The first command the client might want to issue is the Change Working Directory command (CWD). The CWD command specifies a new working directory on the server. All commands executed to send and receive files take path names relative to the current working directory as arguments.

```
C: CWD /pub/downloads
S: 250 CWD command successful.
```

Once the client sets a new working directory, it can retrieve a list of filenames in the directory. The filenames can be formatted or unformatted. The LIST command returns a formatted directory list. The NLST command returns a simple list of filenames. If the names are formatted, the server returns a directory listing in its "native" format. The client must interpret the listing. If the listing is unformatted, the server returns a simple list of filenames, one per line.

Subdirectory names are typically returned as part of a directory listing. If the client requests an unformatted listing, the listing may not distinguish between files and subdirectories. Intelligent client programs typically request formatted directory listings, then try to parse them using knowledge of the host system's type returned in the System Type (SYST) command. The directory entries are then separated from the filename entries and presented to the user. The WS_FTP application presented later in this chapter performs this type of intelligent parsing.

The directory listing is sent over the data connection. Before issuing the LIST or NLST command, the client should issue a PORT command to tell the server on which port to contact it.

The PORT command takes six numbers as parameters, separated from each other with commas and from the PORT command with a space. The numbers encode the client's IP address and data port number. Each byte of the address and port number is represented as a decimal integer and written in network byte order. The following PORT command instructs the server to contact the client at IP address 15.0.0.1 and port 5135.

```
C: PORT 15,0,0,1,20,15
S: 200 PORT command successful.
```

Once the PORT command completes successfully, the directory listing can be retrieved. In this example, we'll use the NLST command to receive a simple unformatted list of files. The data transfer occurs in ASCII format.

```
C: NLST
S: 150 Opening ASCII mode data connection for file list.
D: readme.txt
D: foo.zip
D: bar.doc
S: 226 Transfer complete.
```

After retrieving a directory listing, the user might want to retrieve a file. In our example, the user wants to get the *readme.txt* file. Before performing the actual transfer, the client must again inform the host of the port on which to open the data connection.

```
C: PORT 15,0,0,1,20,16
S: 200 PORT command successful.
```

To retrieve the file, the client sends the RETR command. The RETR command takes the name of the file to retrieve as its argument.

The file is transferred across the data connection using the current data type, data structure, and transfer mode. We haven't changed any of these settings, so the file is transferred using the ASCII data type, File structure, and Stream transfer mode. Because *readme.txt* appears to be a text file, these settings are valid.

```
C: RETR readme.txt
S: 150 Opening ASCII mode data connection for readme.txt (5739 bytes).
D: [... The file transfers...]
S: 226 Transfer complete.
```

Initially, the server returns code 150, indicating that the filename is valid and the server is ready to open the data connection with the client. When the data connection is opened, the data is transferred. After the file is transferred, the data connection is closed to indicate end-of-file to the client. The server returns code 226 on the control channel to indicate the transfer is complete.

At this point, the client might want to upload a file. This transfer might be done in a different directory to keep uploaded files separate from other files on the site. First, the client changes to a different directory:

```
C: CWD /pub/uploads
S: 250 CWD command successful.
```

In our example, the client wants to upload a file containing binary data. Before the transfer begins, the client switches to the Image data type. This change keeps the server from trying to interpret the binary data as a text file and possibly corrupting it. The client changes the data type using the TYPE command. The TYPE command takes a single letter as its argument. "I" specifies the Image data type, "A" specifies ASCII, and "E" specifies EBCDIC.

```
C: TYPE I
S: 200 Type set to I.
```

Once the type is set correctly, the client again changes the port number for the data connection:

```
C: PORT 15,0,0,1,20,17
S: 200 PORT command successful.
```

The file transfer begins when the client executes the STOR command. The STOR command's argument is the filename that the server should use to name the resulting file. The filename does not need to match the name used on the client.

```
C: STOR binfile.zip
S: 150 Opening BINARY mode data connection for binfile.zip.
D: [... The file transfers...]
S: 226 Transfer complete.
```

As with the RETR command, the server first returns an intermediate reply code to indicate that it is ready to open the data connection with the client. The server returns the 226 code when the transfer concludes.

At this point, the user may have completed all the work he or she intends to do. The client can terminate the FTP session using the QUIT command.

```
C: QUIT
S: 221 Goodbye.
S: [server closes connection...]
```

Upon receiving the QUIT command, the server simply sends a 221 reply code and closes the control connection. The FTP session is now complete.

Many other commands are useful to an FTP client. Some commands create and remove subdirectories; other commands rename or delete files on the server. RFC 959 describes these commands in more detail.

Sample FTP Client: WS_FTP

I've used a great little FTP client application for quite a while: WS_FTP. This program, shown in Figure 14.2, was written by John Junod and is one of the better FTP clients available. John has released both executable versions of WS_FTP and the source code into the public domain. Rather than reinvent the wheel and try to duplicate John's great work, we'll examine WS_FTP's source as the sample application for this chapter.

WS_FTP is a good example for this chapter because it differs from the other sample programs. John implemented WS_FTP using the synchronous Windows Sockets API. Although we've used the asynchronous Windows Sockets API for the previous sample programs, the synchronous API is also effective, as long as you can live with its limitations. WS_FTP demonstrates what can be accomplished using the synchronous API.

> *Note: Many versions of WS_FTP are available on the Internet. The version described here is 93.12.05, which is slightly older than the most recent binary version. Since version 93.12.05 was written, John signed a deal with a software company to use WS_FTP in a commercial product. The arrangement allows John to release new versions of WS_FTP but prohibits him from making the source code available. Fortunately, version 93.12.05 includes the basic functionality of the newer versions.*

Project Overview

WS_FTP was written in C using a pre-Visual C++ Microsoft compiler. A makefile is provided that works with Visual C++ 1.5.

Figure 14.2

The main WS_FTP user interface.

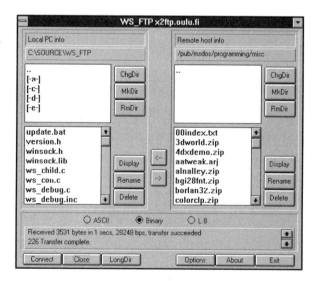

Note: Borland users will have to construct their own project files and may have to perform a small porting job. I haven't tried to do this myself and can't say what changes are needed. John says WS_FTP was originally written using Borland C but he switched to Microsft C. He says that the code should compile under Borland with few changes. I just used Microsoft C and didn't test the theory myself

WS_FTP includes a number of source modules. Table 14.1 summarizes the modules.

Table 14.1	WS_FTP Modules	
File	**Description**	**Reference**
VERSION.H	A header file that contains a definition for the VERSION symbol.	Listing 14.1
WS_CHILD.C	A set of functions to create and redraw the child controls and windows in the main window.	On CD-ROM
WS_CON.C	The set of functions that manage the control connection. This set includes sending commands to the server and receiving responses.	Listing 14.2
WS_DEBUG.C	A set of functions to create and manage a debug window.	On CD-ROM
WS_DEBUG.INC	A file that is included in WS_DEBUG.C.	On CD-ROM
WS_ERROR.C	Two functions to format and display Windows Sockets error messages	On CD-ROM
WS_FTP.DEF	The linker definition file for the WS_FTP project.	On CD-ROM
WS_FTP.DLG	A source file for the resource compiler that defines the various dialog boxes used in WS_FTP. This file is included in WS_FTP.RC when it is compiled.	On CD-ROM
WS_FTP.H	The main header file for WS_FTP. The file contains the control IDs for the various buttons, menus, and so on that WS_FTP uses along with function prototypes for all the modules.	Listing 14.3
WS_FTP.RC	The main resource compiler source file for the WS_FTP project.	On CD-ROM
WS_GLOB.C	Source file for all the global variables used in WS_FTP.	On CD-ROM
WS_GLOB.H	A header file that contains external declarations for all the global variables defined in WS_GLOB.C.	Listing 14.4
WS_HOST.C	The file that includes functions to handle processing of the Host dialog box and to parse the formatted directory listings of several system types.	On CD-ROM
WS_IP.C	This file contains a number of functions to simplify programming with the synchronous Windows Sockets API. The functions collect common sequences of socket calls into single functions. This code is based on code published by W. Richard Stevens in *UNIX Network Programming*.	On CD-ROM
WS_MAIN.C	The file that includes WinMain, the window procedure for the frame window, and a few dialog boxes.	On CD-ROM
WS_PAINT.C	The file that contains some of the routines to paint portions of the main window.	On CD-ROM

Most of WS_FTP's Windows Sockets code is located WS_CON.C and WS_IP.C. WS_CON.C contains the code that implements the FTP protocol. WS_IP.C contains functions that perform common sequences of socket commands (creating and connecting a socket, for instance).

Exploring WS_CON.C

WS_CON.C contains all the juicy FTP code. Let's focus our attention there. In this section we'll take a high-level look at the code in WS_CON.C.

WS_FTP uses a small series of functions to execute FTP commands. The FTP authentication sequence, for example, is handled in the **DoConnect** function. The **DoConnect** function takes one argument: the name of the FTP server to which the connection should be made. The **DoConnect** function creates the socket for the control connection and connects it using the **connectTCP** function. Once the socket is connected, **DoConnect** reads the FTP server's greeting response. If the greeting is positive, **DoConnect** sends USER and PASS commands to authenticate the user with the server. If everything goes as planned, **DoConnect** exits with the control connection set up and the client authenticated with the server. Figure 14.3 shows the dialog box that activates **DoConnect**.

Other commands also have their own functions. For instance, the CWD command is executed using the **DoCWD** function. **DoCWD** immediately passes control to the **command** function to send a CWD command and return the server's response.

Simple commands that require only a single response from the server and do not involve a data transfer are handled using the **command** function. The **command** function takes the control socket, formatting string, and variable argument list as parameters. The **command** function formats a command string using **sprintf**, the formatting string, and the set of variable arguments.

After the command string is formatted, the **command** function passes control to the **getreply** function. The **getreply** function sends the command string to the

Figure 14.3

The WS_FTP
HOST dialog
box.

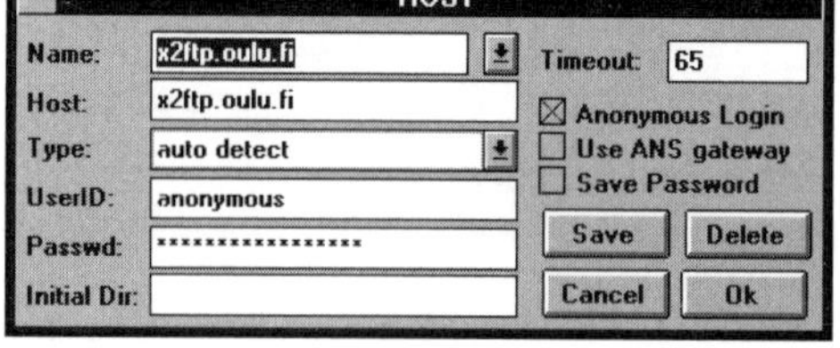

server using the **SendPacket** function. The server's reply is read using the **ReadDisplayLine** function. The **ReadDisplayLine** function automatically handles the return of multiline responses and returns the first digit of the numeric response code as an integer.

Commands that involve the retrieval of a file are handled by the **RetrieveFile** function.

The **RetrieveFile** function takes the socket descriptor of the control connection, a string indicating the FTP command to be performed, a string indicating the file name in which to store the returned data, and a character indicating the data type for the transfer. The **RetrieveFile** function first sends a correct TYPE command before the file is received.

After the TYPE command is sent, the **RetrieveFile** function creates a listening socket for the data connection and sends a PORT command to the server to identify its port number. These actions are performed in the **GetFTPListenSocket** function.

Once the PORT command is sent, **RetrieveFile** calls the **command** function to send the main command and return the server's preliminary response. If the preliminary response is positive, **RetrieveFile** calls the Winsock function **accept** to accept the incoming data connection from the server.

Once the data connection is established, **RetrieveFile** calls the **ReadMass** function to read all the server's data into a file. When **ReadMass** returns, **RetrieveFile** calls **DoClose** to close the data connection, updates some status, and exits.

The **SendFile** function handles file transfers to the server. It operates virtually identically to **RetrieveFile**. The exception is that **SendFile** calls **SendMass** rather than **ReadMass** to send the file to the server once the data connection is established.

That's most of it! WS_FTP calls each of the primitive functions to perform processing in response to buttons the user presses on the main frame window. The rest of the code simply handles the display and update of the user interface.

Listings

This section contains the header files and the WS_CON.C file. See Table 14.1 for a complete list of all WS_FTP files.

Listing 14.1 VERSION.H

```
/*************************************************************************
    Windows Sockets Client Application Support Module

    Written by:
        John A. Junod               Internet: <junodj@gordon-emh2.army.mil>
        267 Hillwood Street                    <zj8549@trotter.usma.edu>
        Martinez, GA 30907          CompuServe: 72321,366

    This program executable and all source code is released into the public
    domain.  It would be nice (but is not required) to give me a little
    credit.for any use of this code.

    THE INFORMATION AND CODE PROVIDED IS PROVIDED AS IS WITHOUT WARRANTY
    OF ANY KIND, EITHER EXPRESS OR IMPLIED, INCLUDING BUT NOT LIMITED TO
    THE IMPLIED WARRANTIES OF MERCHANTABILITY AND FITNESS FOR A PARTICULAR
    PURPOSE. IN NO EVENT SHALL JOHN A. JUNOD BE LIABLE FOR ANY DAMAGES
    WHATSOEVER INCLUDING DIRECT, INDIRECT, INCIDENTAL, CONSEQUENTIAL, LOSS
    OF BUSINESS PROFITS OR SPECIAL DAMAGES, EVEN IF JOHN A. JUNOD HAS BEEN
    ADVISED OF THE POSSIBILITY OF SUCH DAMAGES.


*************************************************************************/

#define VERSION "93.12.05"
```

Listing 14.2 WS_CON.C

```
/*************************************************************************
    Windows Sockets Client Application Support Module

    Written by:
        John A. Junod               Internet: <junodj@gordon-emh2.army.mil>
        267 Hillwood Street                    <zj8549@trotter.usma.edu>
        Martinez, GA 30907          Compuserve: 72321,366

    This program executable and all source code is released into the public
    domain.  It would be nice (but is not required) to give me a little
    credit for any use of this code.

    THE INFORMATION AND CODE PROVIDED IS PROVIDED AS IS WITHOUT WARRANTY
    OF ANY KIND, EITHER EXPRESS OR IMPLIED, INCLUDING BUT NOT LIMITED TO
    THE IMPLIED WARRANTIES OF MERCHANTABILITY AND FITNESS FOR A PARTICULAR
    PURPOSE. IN NO EVENT SHALL JOHN A. JUNOD BE LIABLE FOR ANY DAMAGES
    WHATSOEVER INCLUDING DIRECT, INDIRECT, INCIDENTAL, CONSEQUENTIAL, LOSS
    OF BUSINESS PROFITS OR SPECIAL DAMAGES, EVEN IF JOHN A. JUNOD HAS BEEN
    ADVISED OF THE POSSIBILITY OF SUCH DAMAGES.

*************************************************************************/

#include "ws_glob.h"
#include "ws_ftp.h"
#include <stdio.h>
```

```
#include <stdarg.h>
#include <ctype.h>
#include <io.h>
#include <fcntl.h>
#include <sys\stat.h>
#include <time.h>
#include <stdlib.h>   // atoi()

//extern int errno;
extern int nHostType;
extern BOOL bAborted;     // timer routine may set this

/*
// send a message on the control socket, read and display the resulting
// message and return the result value
*/
int getreply(SOCKET ctrl_skt,LPSTR cmdstring)
{
   int iRetCode=0;

   iCode=0;
   if(strncmp(cmdstring,"PASS ",5)==0)
     DoAddLine("PASS xxxxxx");
   else
     DoAddLine(cmdstring);
   if(ctrl_skt==INVALID_SOCKET) {
     DoAddLine("Not connected");
   } else {
     if(SendPacket(ctrl_skt,cmdstring)!=-1)
        iRetCode=ReadDisplayLine(ctrl_skt);
   }
   return(iRetCode);  // 0 - 5
}

int command(SOCKET ctrl_skt, char *fmt,...)
{
    va_list args;
    char szBuf[90];
    int  iRetCode;

    va_start(args,fmt);
    vsprintf(szBuf,fmt,args);
    va_end(args);
    return(getreply(ctrl_skt,szBuf));
}

int qcommand(SOCKET ctrl_skt, char *fmt,...)
{
    va_list args;
    char szBuf[90];
    int  iRetCode;
```

```
    va_start(args,fmt);
     vsprintf(szBuf,fmt,args);
     va_end(args);
     command(ctrl_skt,szBuf);
     return iCode ;
}

// return a string pointer to ON or OFF based on the flag
char *onoff(BOOL flag)
{
    if(flag) return("ON"); else return("OFF");
}

// process CWD
int DoCWD(SOCKET ctrl_skt,LPSTR path)
{
    if(command(ctrl_skt,"CWD %s",path)==FTP_ERROR && iCode==500) {
        command(ctrl_skt,"XCWD %s",path);
    }
    return(iCode/100);
}

// process PWD
int DoPWD(SOCKET ctrl_skt)
{
    if(command(ctrl_skt,"PWD")==FTP_ERROR && iCode==500) {
        command(ctrl_skt,"XPWD");
    }
    return(iCode/100);
}

// process MKD
int DoMKD(SOCKET ctrl_skt,LPSTR pathname)
{
    if(command(ctrl_skt,"MKD %s",pathname)==FTP_ERROR && iCode==500) {
        command(ctrl_skt,"XMKD %s",pathname);
    }
    return(iCode/100);
}

// process RMD
int DoRMD(SOCKET ctrl_skt,LPSTR pathname)
{
    if(command(ctrl_skt,"RMD %s",pathname)==FTP_ERROR && iCode==500)
        command(ctrl_skt,"XRMD %s",pathname);
    return(iCode/100);
}

// process DELE
int DoDELE(SOCKET ctrl_skt,LPSTR pathname)
{
    command(ctrl_skt,"DELE %s",pathname);
```

```
    return(iCode/100);
}

// process user command
int DoQUOTE(SOCKET ctrl_skt,LPSTR string)
{
    if(strncmp(string,"LIST",4)==0 ||
        strncmp(string,"NLST",4)==0)
        DoDirList(ctrl_skt,string);
    else
        command(ctrl_skt,string);
    return(iCode/100);
}

// process chmod
int DoCHMOD(SOCKET ctrl_skt,LPSTR modes,LPSTR filename)
{
    return(command(ctrl_skt,"SITE CHMOD %s %s",modes,filename));
}

extern BOOL bHELP;

// initial connection
SOCKET DoConnect(LPSTR ftp_host)
{
    int iLength,iRetCode;
    int iFlag=1;
    char host[80] ;
    SOCKET ctrl_skt;

    if(bConnected) {
        DoAddLine("Already connected!");
        return(INVALID_SOCKET);
    }
    // let other routines know that we are busy
    bCmdInProgress++;

    bHELP=FALSE;

    if(use_gateway)
        strcpy(host, szGateHost) ;
    else
        strcpy(host, ftp_host) ;

    // create a connected socket
    if((ctrl_skt=connectTCP(host,"ftp"))==INVALID_SOCKET) {
        //DoAddLine("connection failed");
        DoPrintf("Connection to %s failed",host) ;
        bCmdInProgress-;
        return(INVALID_SOCKET);
    }
    // get information about local end of the connection
```

```
iLength = sizeof (saCtrlAddr);
 if (getsockname(ctrl_skt,(struct sockaddr *)&saCtrlAddr, &iLength)
    ==SOCKET_ERROR)
{
   ReportWSError("getsockname",WSAGetLastError());
  bCmdInProgress-;
  DoClose(ctrl_skt);
   return(INVALID_SOCKET);
}
// show remote end address
DoPrintf("[%u] from %s port %u",ctrl_skt,
          inet_ntoa(saCtrlAddr.sin_addr),
          ntohs(saCtrlAddr.sin_port));
// get initial message from remote end
while((iRetCode=ReadDisplayLine(ctrl_skt))==FTP_PRELIM && !bAborted)   // 93.12.04
   if(nHostType==HOST_TYPE_AUTO) {
      if(strstr(szMsgBuf,"(EXOS")!=NULL)
        nHostType=HOST_TYPE_U5000;
  }
// if it succeeded
if(iRetCode==FTP_COMPLETE) {
   if(nHostType==HOST_TYPE_AUTO) {
      if(strstr(szMsgBuf,"(EXOS")!=NULL)
        nHostType=HOST_TYPE_U5000;
  }
   if (setsockopt(ctrl_skt, SOL_SOCKET, SO_OOBINLINE,
       (LPSTR)&iFlag, sizeof(iFlag))==SOCKET_ERROR)
  {
      ReportWSError("setsockopt",WSAGetLastError());
  }
  // have to reset this so "command" will work
  bCmdInProgress-;

  if(use_gateway)
    { // send our userid
      if((iRetCode=command(ctrl_skt,"USER %s",szGateUserID))==FTP_CONTINUE)
    { // if the remote system requires a password, send it.
        iRetCode=command(ctrl_skt,"PASS %s",szGatePassWord);
  }
    if(iRetCode!=FTP_COMPLETE)
    { // if we failed to successfully log on
      DoAddLine("Gateway logon failure, so quitting");
      DoClose((SOCKET)ctrl_skt);
      return(INVALID_SOCKET);
  }

    if((iRetCode=qcommand(ctrl_skt,"site %s",ftp_host))==FTP_ERROR)
  {
      DoAddLine("Connect to final destination failed, so quitting");
      DoClose((SOCKET)ctrl_skt);
     bConnected=0;
      return(INVALID_SOCKET);
```

```
      }
       bConnected=1;
     } // end of gateway connect

     // send our userid to the ftp_host
      if((iRetCode=command(ctrl_skt,"USER %s",szUserID))==FTP_CONTINUE) // || 1)
     {
        while(szPassWord[0]==0) {
           StdInputPassword(szPassWord,"Need a password:");
        }
       // if the remote system requires a password, send it
          if((iRetCode=command(ctrl_skt,"PASS %s",szPassWord))==FTP_CONTINUE)
         {
          // if the remote system requires an account, send it
            StdInput(NULL,"Need an account:");
             iRetCode=command(ctrl_skt,"ACCT %s",szDlgEdit);
         }
     }
      // if we are successfully logged on,.....
      if(iRetCode!=FTP_COMPLETE) // || 0)
     {
        DoAddLine("logon failure, so quitting");
        DoClose((SOCKET)ctrl_skt);
       bConnected=0;
        return(INVALID_SOCKET);
     }
      bConnected=1;
   } else {
      DoPrintf("unk open msg \"%s\" %u",szMsgBuf,iCode);
      // allow other processes to work
      bCmdInProgress--;
      DoClose((SOCKET)ctrl_skt);
      return(INVALID_SOCKET);
   }
   wsprintf(szString,"WS_FTP %s",szRemoteHost);
   SetWindowText(hWndMain,szString);
   return (ctrl_skt);
}

int DoDirList(SOCKET ctrl_skt,LPSTR szCMD)
{
   int nRC,nBell;
   nBell=bBell; bBell=0;
   nRC=RetrieveFile(ctrl_skt,szCMD,szTmpFile,TYPE_A);
   bBell=nBell;
   return(nRC);
}

int SendFile(SOCKET ctrl_skt,LPSTR szCMD,LPSTR localfile,char stype)
{
   int iRetCode;
   int iLength;
```

```
    iCode=0;
  // if we don't have a valid control socket, can't do anything
  if(ctrl_skt==INVALID_SOCKET) {
    DoAddLine("no ctrl_skt, ignored");
    return(0);
  }
  // if we are doing something, don't try to do this
  if(bCmdInProgress) {
    DoAddLine("command in process, ignored");
    return(0);
  }
  // if the requested type is not the same as the default type
  if(cType!=stype) {
    if(stype==TYPE_L)
      command(ctrl_skt,"TYPE L 8");
   else
      command(ctrl_skt,"TYPE %c",stype);
    cType=stype;
  }
  // create a listener socket, if it is successful
  if((listen_socket=GetFTPListenSocket(ctrl_skt))!=INVALID_SOCKET) {
    // send command to see the result of this all
    iRetCode=command((SOCKET)ctrl_skt,szCMD);
    // read the control channel (should return 1xx if it worked)
    if(iRetCode==FTP_PRELIM) {
      // wait for connection back to us on the listen socket
       SetTimer(hWndMain,10,uiTimeOut*1000,NULL);
      // get our data connection
       iLength=sizeof(saSockAddr1);
       data_socket=accept(listen_socket,(struct sockaddr far *)&saSockAddr1,
                          (int far *)&iLength);
      // turn off the timeout timer
       KillTimer(hWndMain,10);
      // if it failed, we have to quit this
       if(data_socket==INVALID_SOCKET) {
          ReportWSError("accept",WSAGetLastError());
          listen_socket=DoClose(listen_socket);
         iRetCode=0;
      } else {
         // we don't need the listener socket anymore
          listen_socket=DoClose(listen_socket);
         // inform user of the connection
          DoPrintf("[%u] accept from %s port %u", data_socket,
              inet_ntoa(saSockAddr1.sin_addr),ntohs(saSockAddr1.sin_port));
         // copy the file
          iRetCode=SendMass(data_socket,localfile,stype==TYPE_I);
         // close the socket
          data_socket=DoClose(data_socket);
          // read the close control message (should return 2xx)
           iRetCode=ReadDisplayLine(ctrl_skt);
      }
    } else {
        listen_socket=DoClose(listen_socket);
```

```
        iRetCode=0;
          if(bBell) MessageBeep(MB_ICONEXCLAMATION);
      }
  } else {
      listen_socket=DoClose(listen_socket);
     iRetCode=0;
       if(bBell) MessageBeep(MB_ICONEXCLAMATION);
  }
   return(iRetCode);
}

int RetrieveFile(SOCKET ctrl_skt,LPSTR szCMD,LPSTR localfile,char rtype)
{
   int iRetCode;
   int iLength;

   iCode=0;
   // if we don't have a valid control socket, can't do anything
   if(ctrl_skt==INVALID_SOCKET) {
      DoAddLine("no ctrl_skt, ignored");
     return(0);
   }
   // if we are doing something, don't try to do this
   if(bCmdInProgress) {
      DoAddLine("command in process, ignored");
     return(0);
   }
   // if the requested type is not the same as the default type
   if(cType!=rtype) {
     if(rtype==TYPE_L)
        command(ctrl_skt,"TYPE L 8");
     else
         command(ctrl_skt,"TYPE %c",rtype);
     cType=rtype;
   }
   // create a listener socket, if it is successful
   if((listen_socket=GetFTPListenSocket(ctrl_skt))!=INVALID_SOCKET) {
     // send command to see the result of this all
      iRetCode=command((SOCKET)ctrl_skt,szCMD);
     // read the control channel (should return 1xx if it worked)
     if(iRetCode==FTP_PRELIM) {
       // wait for connection back to us on the listen socket
        SetTimer(hWndMain,10,uiTimeOut*1000,NULL);
       // get our data connection
        iLength=sizeof(saSockAddr1);
        data_socket=accept(listen_socket,(struct sockaddr far *)&saSockAddr1,
                      (int far *)&iLength);
       // turn off the timeout timer
        KillTimer(hWndMain,10);
       // if it failed, we have to quit this
        if(data_socket==INVALID_SOCKET) {
           ReportWSError("accept",WSAGetLastError());
           listen_socket=DoClose(listen_socket);
          iRetCode=0;
```

```
          } else {
              // we don't need the listener socket anymore
                listen_socket=DoClose(listen_socket);
              // inform user of the connection
                DoPrintf("[%u] accept from %s port %u", data_socket,
                    inet_ntoa(saSockAddr1.sin_addr),ntohs(saSockAddr1.sin_port));
              // copy the file
                iRetCode=ReadMass(data_socket,localfile,rtype==TYPE_I);
              // shut the data socket down
                if(shutdown(data_socket,2)!=0)
                    ReportWSError("shutdown",WSAGetLastError());
              // close the data socket
                data_socket=DoClose(data_socket);
              // read the close control message (should return 2xx)
                iRetCode=ReadDisplayLine(ctrl_skt);
          }
      } else {
          listen_socket=DoClose(listen_socket);
          iRetCode=0;
          if(bBell) MessageBeep(MB_ICONEXCLAMATION);
      }

  } else {
      listen_socket=DoClose(listen_socket);
      iRetCode=0;
      if(bBell) MessageBeep(MB_ICONEXCLAMATION);
  }
  return(iRetCode);
}


// user close routine
SOCKET DoClose(SOCKET sockfd)
{
   LINGER linger;

   if(sockfd!=INVALID_SOCKET) {
     if(WSAIsBlocking()) {
        DoPrintf("[%u] Cancelled blocking call",sockfd);
        WSACancelBlockingCall();
        bAborted=TRUE;
     }
/*
     if(shutdown(sockfd,2)==SOCKET_ERROR)
        ReportWSError("shutdown",WSAGetLastError());
*/
/*   93.12.04 - so Lanera Winsock Works
     linger.l_onoff  = TRUE;
     linger.l_linger = 0;
      setsockopt(sockfd,SOL_SOCKET,SO_LINGER,
                 (LPSTR)&linger,sizeof(linger) );
*/
     if(closesocket(sockfd)==SOCKET_ERROR)
```

```
        ReportWSError("closesocket",WSAGetLastError());
      else {
          DoPrintf("[%u] Socket closed.",sockfd);
          sockfd=INVALID_SOCKET;
      }
  }

  if(sockfd!=INVALID_SOCKET)
      DoPrintf("[%u] Failed to close socket.",sockfd);

  return(sockfd);
}

int SendPacket(SOCKET sockfd,LPSTR msg)
{
  int i;

  if(sockfd==INVALID_SOCKET) return(-1);
  if(bCmdInProgress) {
      DoAddLine("command in progress, ignored");
      return (-1);
  }
  bCmdInProgress++;
  i=strlen(msg);
  strcpy(szSendPkt,msg);
  // append a CRLF to the end of outgoing messages
  szSendPkt[i++]='\r';
  szSendPkt[i++]='\n';
  szSendPkt[i]=0;
  i=sendstr(sockfd,szSendPkt,i);
  bCmdInProgress—;
  return (i);
}

int iMultiLine=0;
// read a reply (may be multiline) and display in debug window
int ReadDisplayLine(SOCKET sockfd)
{
  int iRetCode;
  int iContinue;
  char *s;
  char c;

  // can't do anything if we don't have a socket
  if(sockfd==INVALID_SOCKET) return(0);
  // let other routine know that we are doing something right now.
  bCmdInProgress++;
  // count the lines in the response
  iMultiLine++;
  // initialize some variables
  iContinue=0;
  // go read the line
  iRetCode=ReadLine(sockfd);
```

```
   // if it wasn't a valid value or the 4th char was a hyphen
   if(iRetCode<100 || iRetCode>599 || szMsgBuf[3]=='-')
     // then it is a continuation line
     iContinue=1;
   // send the line we read to our user/debug window
   DoAddLine((LPSTR)&szMsgBuf[0]);
   //   DoPrintf("iRetCode=%u, iContinue=%u",iRetCode,iContinue);
   // if the timer killed it
   if(bAborted) { iCode=iRetCode=421; iContinue=0; }
   // we only want to set the real return code in certain situations
   if((iMultiLine==1 || iCode==0) && iRetCode>99 && iRetCode<600)
     iCode=iRetCode;
   // handle continuation lines
   if(iContinue==1 || (iCode>0 && iMultiLine>1 && iRetCode!=iCode))
     ReadDisplayLine(sockfd);
   // count back down our multiline reponses
   iMultiLine--;
   // allow other processes to run
   bCmdInProgress--;
   // return only the first char of return code
   if(iCode>99 && iCode<600)
     return (iCode/100);
   else return 0;
}


// read a reply line back in from the sockfd and return the
// value at the beginning of the first line
int ReadLine(SOCKET sockfd)
{
   LPSTR szBuf;
   int nIndex;
   int iNumBytes,iN1,iN2,iN3;
   int iBytesRead;
   int iRetCode;
   int i;
   char *s;
   char c;

   // can't do anything if we don't have a socket
   if(sockfd==INVALID_SOCKET) return(0);
   // let other routines know that we are doing something right now
   bCmdInProgress++;
   // make sure we don't mistakenly think we timed out
   KillTimer(hWndMain,10); bAborted=FALSE;
   // zero our receive buffer
   memset(szMsgBuf,0,4096);
   // initialize some variables
   szBuf=szMsgBuf; iBytesRead=0; iRetCode=0;
   // set our timeout
   SetTimer(hWndMain,10,uiTimeOut*1000,NULL);
   // this routine is a little better as it read 80 characters at a time
   // (if it works:-)  Here we PEEK at what is available, find the LF etc...
```

```
while(iBytesRead<4000 && (iNumBytes=recv(sockfd,(LPSTR)szBuf,82,MSG_PEEK))>0)
{
    // Trumpet WinSock Alpha 15 always returns the len (82) from a recv
    // with MSG_PEEK.  I suppose this is an error??? The spec doesn't say
    // that MSG_PEEK returns something different than normal.
    KillTimer(hWndMain,10);
    iN1=iNumBytes;
  // must terminate the string so strchr doesn't go wild
    szBuf[iNumBytes]=0;
  // find a LF in the input if it exists
  //
    for(nIndex=0;nIndex<iNumBytes;nIndex++)
      if(szBuf[nIndex]==0 || szBuf[nIndex]==0x0a) {
        iNumBytes=nIndex+1;
        break;
      }
    // have to treat the UNISYS 5000 (EXOS driver) special.  It sends a
    // line with a CR at end and no LF and then follows it up with a
    // separate packet that has a CR/LF.  Usually this second packet is
    // not there when we peek but is when we read (answers my question
    // about the second receive containing new data!!... jaj 931024)
    if(iNumBytes>80 && nHostType==HOST_TYPE_U5000)
      for(nIndex=0;nIndex<iNumBytes;nIndex++)
        if(szBuf[nIndex]==0x0d) {
          iNumBytes=nIndex+2;
          break;
        }
    iN2=iNumBytes;
  // otherwise read up to the full length of what the first recv saw
    // Wonder what happens here if the second receive actually returns more
    // characters than the first receive and there was a LF in the extra data?
    iNumBytes=recv(sockfd,(LPSTR)szBuf,iNumBytes,0);
    // again, terminate the string
    szBuf[iNumBytes]=0;
    DoPrintf("[%u] readline %u - %u - %u %s",sockfd,iN1,iN2,iNumBytes,szBuf);
    // bump the receive buffer pointer
    szBuf+=iNumBytes;
    // count the bytes that we have read so far
    iBytesRead+=iNumBytes;
  // if the last character read was a LF, then stop
    if(*(szBuf-1)==0x0a)
      break;              // '\n') break;
    // otherwise reset the timer and go read more characters
    SetTimer(hWndMain,10,uiTimeOut*1000,NULL);
}
// if we are here, we have a line or an error or there was nothing to read
KillTimer(hWndMain,10);
// in any case terminate what we have
*szBuf=0;
// find the retcode at the beginning of the line
c=szMsgBuf[3]; szMsgBuf[3]=0; iRetCode=atoi(szMsgBuf); szMsgBuf[3]=c;
// if the timer killed it
```

```
      if(bAborted) iRetCode=421;
    // strip trailing blanks, CRs and LFs
     while(((i=strlen(szMsgBuf))>2 &&
            (szMsgBuf[i-1]==0x0a || szMsgBuf[i-1]==0x0d || szMsgBuf[i-1]==' '))
       szMsgBuf[i-1]=0;
    // unmark our progress
    bCmdInProgress--;

    return(iRetCode);
}


// based on WINTEL (ftp.c) and BSD (ftp.c)
SOCKET GetFTPListenSocket(SOCKET ctrl_skt)
{
     SOCKET listen_skt;
     int iLength;
     int iRetCode;
     char *a,*p;
     int iFlag=1;

    // create a data socket
      if((listen_skt=socket(AF_INET,SOCK_STREAM,IPPROTO_TCP))==INVALID_SOCKET)
     {
          ReportWSError("socket create",WSAGetLastError());
         return (INVALID_SOCKET);
     }
    // let system pick an unused port; we tell remote end with PORT cmd
      DoPrintf("[%u] going to listen %s port %u",listen_skt,
         inet_ntoa(saCtrlAddr.sin_addr),ntohs(saCtrlAddr.sin_port));

    if(bSendPort) {
        saCtrlAddr.sin_port=htons(0);
        saCtrlAddr.sin_family=AF_INET;
        saCtrlAddr.sin_addr.s_addr=0;
    } else
       // otherwise we attempt to reuse our ctrl_skt
        if(setsockopt(listen_skt,SOL_SOCKET,SO_REUSEADDR,
           (char *)&iFlag,sizeof(iFlag))==SOCKET_ERROR)
      {
          ReportWSError("setsockopt",WSAGetLastError());
         closesocket(listen_skt);
         return(INVALID_SOCKET);
      }
    // bind name to socket
     if( bind((SOCKET)listen_skt,(LPSOCKADDR)&saCtrlAddr,
              (int)sizeof(struct sockaddr))==SOCKET_ERROR)
     {
          ReportWSError("bind",WSAGetLastError());
         closesocket(listen_skt);
         return (INVALID_SOCKET);
     }
     // get the port name that we got for later transmission in PORT cmd
```

```
      iLength=sizeof(saCtrlAddr);
        if(getsockname(listen_skt,(struct  sockaddr  *)&saCtrlAddr,&iLength)<0)
      {
          ReportWSError("getsockname",WSAGetLastError());
          closesocket(listen_skt);
          return(INVALID_SOCKET);
      }
       // invoke listener
        if(listen(listen_skt,1)!=0)
      {
          ReportWSError("listen",WSAGetLastError());
          closesocket(listen_skt);
          return(INVALID_SOCKET);
      }

// inform remote end about our port that we created
      if(bSendPort)
     {
         struct sockaddr_in saTmpAddr;
        int iLength;

         iLength = sizeof (saTmpAddr);
          if (getsockname(ctrl_skt,(LPSOCKADDR)&saTmpAddr, &iLength)
          ==SOCKET_ERROR)
      {
            ReportWSError("getsockname",WSAGetLastError());
        }

        a = (char *)&saTmpAddr.sin_addr;
        p = (char *)&saCtrlAddr.sin_port;
#define   UC(b)    (((int)b)&0xff)
          if((iRetCode=command(ctrl_skt,"PORT %d,%d,%d,%d,%d,%d",
             UC(a[0]), UC(a[1]), UC(a[2]), UC(a[3]),
             UC(p[0]), UC(p[1])))!=FTP_COMPLETE) {
           DoPrintf("[%u] remote end didn't understand our port command.",listen_skt);
           return(listen_skt);
      }
    }
      DoPrintf("[%u] listener %s port %u",listen_skt,
          inet_ntoa(saCtrlAddr.sin_addr),ntohs(saCtrlAddr.sin_port));
      return(listen_skt);
}

// send a file through the data socket
int SendMass(SOCKET sockfd,LPSTR filename,BOOL binaryflag)
{
   int iNumBytes;
   int  iRetCode;
   int  iFileHandle;
   long lBytesWritten;
   time_t ttStart,ttStop,ttDiff;
```

```
   iRetCode=0;
   // if we don't have a socket, return an error
   if(sockfd==INVALID_SOCKET || !(bConnected)) return 0;
   // turn on a flag so other routines know we have a command in progress
   bCmdInProgress++;
   // initialize some vars
   lBytesWritten=0l; iRetCode=0;
   // at the moment we are ignoring the fact that the local destination file
   // may not open correctly
   if((iFileHandle=_lopen(filename,READ))== -1) {
      DoPrintf("failed to open file %s (%u)",filename,errno);
      if(bBell) MessageBeep(MB_ICONEXCLAMATION);
   } else {
     // get the start time
     ttStart=time(NULL);
     // loop to send output to remote end
     while((iNumBytes=_lread(iFileHandle,szMsgBuf,512))>0)
     {
        // this forces binary mode at the moment
         iRetCode=sendstr(sockfd,szMsgBuf,iNumBytes);
        // count the characters that we received
        lBytesWritten+=iNumBytes;

         wsprintf(szString,"%lu",lBytesWritten);
         SendMessage(hTxtLBytes,WM_SETTEXT,0,(LPARAM)szString);
     }
     // get the finish time
     ttStop=time(NULL);
     // if the output file is open, close it
     _lclose(iFileHandle);
     // show the user how we did
     SendMessage(hTxtLBytes,WM_SETTEXT,0,(LPARAM)NULL);
     ttDiff=ttStop-ttStart;
     if(ttDiff==0l) ttDiff=1l;
     DoPrintf("Transmitted %ld bytes in %ld secs, %ld bps, transfer %s",
        lBytesWritten,(long)ttDiff,
        lBytesWritten*8l/(long)(ttDiff),
        (iFileHandle==-1)?"failed":"succeeded");
     iRetCode=TRUE;
     if(bBell) MessageBeep(MB_OK);
   }
   // turn off our command in progress flag
   bCmdInProgress-;

   return (iRetCode);
}

// read information from the data socket into a file
int ReadMass(SOCKET sockfd,LPSTR filename,BOOL binaryflag)
{
   int   iNumBytes;
   int   iRetCode;
```

```
 int  iFileHandle;
 long lBytesRead;
 time_t ttStart,ttStop,ttDiff;

 // if we don't have a socket, return an error
 if(sockfd==INVALID_SOCKET || !(bConnected)) return 0;
 // turn on a flag so other routines know we have a command in progress
 bCmdInProgress++;
 // make sure we don't mistakenly think we timed out
 KillTimer(hWndMain,10); bAborted=FALSE;
 // initialize some vars
 lBytesRead=0l; iRetCode=0;
 // at the moment we are ignoring the fact that the local destination file
 // may not open correctly
 if((iFileHandle=_lcreat(filename,0))== -1)
    DoPrintf("failed to open file %s (%u)",filename,errno);
 // get the start time
 ttStart=time(NULL);
 // loop to receive input from remote end
 while(!bAborted && (iNumBytes=recv(sockfd,(LPSTR)szMsgBuf,4000,0))>0)
 {
    // write what we received if the file is open
    if(iFileHandle!= -1)
       _lwrite(iFileHandle,szMsgBuf,iNumBytes);
    // count the characters that we received
    lBytesRead+=iNumBytes;
    // update screen
    wsprintf(szString,"%lu",lBytesRead);
    SendMessage(hTxtRBytes,WM_SETTEXT,0,(LPARAM)szString);
 }
 // get the finish time
 ttStop=time(NULL);
 // if the output file is open, close it
 if(iFileHandle != -1)  _lclose(iFileHandle);
 // if we had a recv error, let us know about it
 if(iNumBytes==SOCKET_ERROR)
 {
    ReportWSError("recv",WSAGetLastError());
    if(lBytesRead==0l)
  {
      if(bBell) MessageBeep(MB_ICONEXCLAMATION);
     bCmdInProgress-;
     return(FALSE);
  }
 }
 SendMessage(hTxtRBytes,WM_SETTEXT,0,(LPARAM)NULL);

 ttDiff=ttStop-ttStart;
 if(ttDiff==0l) ttDiff=1l;
 // show the user how we did
 DoPrintf("Received %ld bytes in %ld secs, %ld bps, transfer %s",
    lBytesRead,(long)ttDiff,
```

```
    lBytesRead*81/(long)ttDiff,
     (iFileHandle==-1 || bAborted)?"failed":"succeeded");

  if(bBell) MessageBeep(MB_OK);
  // turn off our command in progress flag
  bCmdInProgress-;

  return (TRUE);
}
```

Listing 14.3   WS_FTP.H

```
/****************************************************************************
   Windows Sockets FTP Client Application Support Module

   Written by:
       John A. Junod              Internet: <junodj@gordon-emh2.army.mil>
       267 Hillwood Street                  <zj8549@trotter.usma.edu>
       Martinez, GA 30907         Compuserve: 72321,366

   This program executable and all source code is released into the public
   domain.  It would be nice (but is not required) to give me a little
   credit for any use of this code.

   THE INFORMATION AND CODE PROVIDED IS PROVIDED AS IS WITHOUT WARRANTY
   OF ANY KIND, EITHER EXPRESS OR IMPLIED, INCLUDING BUT NOT LIMITED TO
   THE IMPLIED WARRANTIES OF MERCHANTABILITY AND FITNESS FOR A PARTICULAR
   PURPOSE. IN NO EVENT SHALL JOHN A. JUNOD BE LIABLE FOR ANY DAMAGES
   WHATSOEVER INCLUDING DIRECT, INDIRECT, INCIDENTAL, CONSEQUENTIAL, LOSS
   OF BUSINESS PROFITS OR SPECIAL DAMAGES, EVEN IF JOHN A. JUNOD HAS BEEN
   ADVISED OF THE POSSIBILITY OF SUCH DAMAGES.

   ****************************************************************************/
/*
   MODULE: WS_FTP.H    (main program header file)
*/

#include <windows.h>

// **** Dialog box names
// #define DLG_ABOUT                510
// #define DLG_HOST                 520
// #define DLG_INPUT                530
// #define DLG_STATUS               540

// **** debug window menu definitions
// may be used by other functions!

// under COMMAND popup menu
#define CMD_CONNECT                1010
#define CMD_CLOSE                  1020
```

```
#define CMD_CWD                          1040
#define CMD_DELE                         1050
#define CMD_HELP                         1060
#define CMD_LIST                         1070
#define CMD_MKD                          1080
#define CMD_NLST                         1090
#define CMD_PWD                          1100
#define CMD_QUOTE                        1110
#define CMD_RETR                         1120
#define CMD_RMD                          1130
#define CMD_STATUS                       1140
#define CMD_STOR                         1150

#define CMD_TYPE_I                       1170
#define CMD_TYPE_A                       1180

#define CMD_SHFLAGS                      1200

// under OPTIONS popup menu
#define OPT_SETVIEWER                    1410

#define IDM_ABOUT                        1500
#define IDM_EXIT                         1600

// **** main window child window identifiers
// TXT = static text windows
// LST = list boxes
// BTN = push buttons
// RB  = radio buttons

// local side child windows
#define TXT_LDIRECTORY                   2110
#define LST_LDIRS                        2120
#define LST_LFILES                       2130
#define BTN_LCHANGE                      2140
#define BTN_LMKDIR                       2150
#define BTN_LRMDIR                       2160
#define BTN_LDISPLAY                     2170
#define BTN_LRENAME                      2180
#define BTN_LDELETE                      2190

// remote side child windows
#define TXT_HOSTNAME                     2200
#define TXT_RDIRECTORY                   2210
#define LST_RDIRS                        2220
#define LST_RFILES                       2230
#define BTN_RCHANGE                      2240
#define BTN_RMKDIR                       2250
#define BTN_RRMDIR                       2260
#define BTN_RDISPLAY                     2270
#define BTN_RRENAME                      2280
#define BTN_RDELETE                      2290
```

```
// transfer buttons
#define BTN_LOCAL_TO_REMOTE        2310
#define BTN_REMOTE_TO_LOCAL        2320


// configuration buttons
#define RB_ASCII                   2410
#define RB_BINARY                  2411
#define RB_L8                      2412


// information text windows
#define TXT_STATUS                 2510
#define TXT_RBYTES                 2520
#define TXT_LBYTES                 2530


// control buttons
#define BTN_CONNECT                2610
#define BTN_CLOSE                  2620
#define BTN_LONG                   2630
#define BTN_OPTION                 2635
#define BTN_ABOUT                  2640
#define BTN_EXIT                   2650


// input dialog controls
#define DLG_PROMPT                 3010
#define DLG_EDIT                   3020


// **** connect dialog box controls
#define DLG_EDT_HOST               4010
#define DLG_EDT_USERID             4020
#define DLG_EDT_PASSWD             4030
#define DLG_HOST_TIMEOUT           4040


// **** status dlg identifiers
#define CKB_BELL                   5010
#define CKB_CRSTRIP                5020
#define CKB_GLOBBING               5030
#define CKB_HASH                   5040
#define CKB_PROMPT                 5050
#define CKB_INTERACTIVE            5060
#define CKB_MCASE                  5070
#define CKB_PORT_CMDS              5080
#define CKB_RECV_UNIQUE            5090
#define CKB_STOR_UNIQUE            5100
#define CKB_VERBOSE                5110
#define CKB_AUTOSTART              5120
#define BTN_OPTIONS                5130
#define DLG_MAILADDR               5250


#define RB_SHOWCHECKS 8100

// **** misc definitions
#define TYPE_I 'I'
```

```
#define TYPE_A 'A'
#define TYPE_E 'E'
#define TYPE_L 'L'

#define FORM_N 'N'
#define FORM_T 'T'
#define FORM_C 'C'

#define MODE_S 'S'
#define MODE_B 'B'
#define MODE_C 'C'

#define DBUGWNDCLASS "WSDBUGWNDCLASS"

struct win_info {
  HWND hWnd;
  int nLineHeight;
  int nScreenRows;
  int nMemPtr;
  int nVpos;
  GLOBALHANDLE hGMem[100];
};

// **** function prototypes

int MakeLocalName(LPSTR,LPSTR);
void SaveHostName(LPSTR);
void LoadUserInfo(void);
void DoMainPaint(HWND);
void SaveUserInfo(void);
int StdInput(LPSTR,LPSTR,...);
int StdInputPassword(LPSTR,LPSTR,...);
int GPPS(LPSTR,LPSTR,LPSTR,int);
int WPPS(LPSTR,LPSTR);

// in ws_child.c
int CreateSubWindows(HWND,HWND);
int GetLocalDirForWnd(HWND);
LPSTR FindName(LPSTR);
int GetRemoteDirForWnd(HWND);
void ShowOurFlags(void);
int ReadProcessHelp(SOCKET);
void ScrollStatus(int);
void SetStatus(LPSTR);

// in ws_con.c
int getreply(SOCKET,LPSTR);
int command(SOCKET socket, char *fmt,...);
char *onoff(BOOL);
int DoSTAT(SOCKET);
int DoCHMOD(SOCKET,LPSTR,LPSTR);
int DoCWD(SOCKET,LPSTR);
```

```
int DoDirList(SOCKET,LPSTR);
int DoDELE(SOCKET,LPSTR);
int DoMKD(SOCKET,LPSTR);
int DoPWD(SOCKET);
int DoQUOTE(SOCKET,LPSTR);
int DoRMD(SOCKET,LPSTR);
SOCKET DoConnect(LPSTR);
int DoDirList(SOCKET,LPSTR);
int SendFile(SOCKET,LPSTR,LPSTR,char);
int RetrieveFile(SOCKET,LPSTR,LPSTR,char);
SOCKET DoClose(SOCKET sockfd);
int SendPacket(SOCKET,LPSTR);
int ReadDisplayLine(SOCKET);
int ReadLine(SOCKET);
SOCKET GetFTPListenSocket(SOCKET sockfd);
int SendMass(SOCKET,LPSTR filename,BOOL);
int ReadMass(SOCKET,LPSTR filename,BOOL);

// in ws_ip.c
SOCKET connectsock(char *host,char *service,char *protocol);
SOCKET connectTCP(char *host,char *service);
SOCKET connectUDP(char *host,char *service);
int sendstr(SOCKET sockfd,LPSTR ptr,int nbytes);

// in ws_debug.c
int CreateDebugWindow(HWND hMainWnd,HWND hInst);
LONG FAR PASCAL DebugWndProc(HWND hWnd,WORD Message,WORD wParam,LONG lParam);

// in ws_error.c
LPSTR ReturnWSError(UINT Err,LPSTR lpszBuf);
void ReportWSError(LPSTR lpszMsg,UINT Err);
VOID ReportWindowWSError(struct win_info *Window,LPSTR lpszMsg,UINT nErr);

// in ws_main.c
LONG FAR PASCAL WndProc(HWND, WORD, WORD, LONG);
BOOL FAR PASCAL WS_AboutMsgProc(HWND, WORD, WORD, LONG);
BOOL FAR PASCAL WS_HostMsgProc(HWND, WORD, WORD, LONG);
BOOL FAR PASCAL WS_InputMsgProc(HWND, WORD, WORD, LONG);
BOOL FAR PASCAL WS_StatMsgProc(HWND, WORD, WORD, LONG);
int nCwRegisterClasses(void);
void cwCenter(HWND, int);
void CwUnRegisterClasses(void);

// in ws_paint.c
int GetLocalInfo(void);
void ReleaseDisplayMem(VOID);
void ReleaseWindowMem(struct win_info *);
void DoAddLine(LPSTR);
void DoAddWindowLine(struct win_info *,LPSTR);
void DoPrintf(char *fmt,...);
void DoWindowPrintf(struct win_info *,char *,...);
void DoWindowPaint(struct win_info *);
```

```
#define DLG_HOST_NAME               105
#define DLG_HOST_ADDRESS            106
#define DLG_HOST_TYPE               107
#define DLG_HOST_USERID             108
#define DLG_HOST_PASSWORD           109
#define DLG_HOST_DIR                110
#define DLG_HOST_ANONY              111
#define DLG_HOST_SAVE               112
#define DLG_HOST_PWD                113
#define DLG_HOST_GATEWAY            114


#define HOST_TYPE_AUTO              6000
#define HOST_TYPE_CHAMELEON         6001
#define HOST_TYPE_PCTCP             6002
#define HOST_TYPE_IBM_TCP           6003
#define HOST_TYPE_IBM_VM            6004
#define HOST_TYPE_NOS               6005
#define HOST_TYPE_NCSA              6006
#define HOST_TYPE_SINTFTPD          6007
#define HOST_TYPE_SUPER             6008
#define HOST_TYPE_U5000             6009
#define HOST_TYPE_UNIX              6010
#define HOST_TYPE_VMS_MULTINET      6011
#define HOST_TYPE_VMS_UCX           6012
#define HOST_TYPE_QVT               6013


#define DLG_BTN_SAVE                101
#define DLG_BTN_DEL                 102
```

Listing 14.4 WS_GLOB.H

```
/*****************************************************************************

   Windows Sockets FTP Client Application Suport Module

   Written by:
      John A. Junod              Internet: <junodj@gordon-emh2.army.mil>
      267 Hillwood Street                   <zj8549@trotter.usma.edu>
      Martinez, GA 30907         Compuserve: 72321,366

   This program executable and all source code is released into the public
   domain.  It would be nice (but is not required) to give me a little
   credit for any use of this code.

   THE INFORMATION AND CODE PROVIDED IS PROVIDED AS IS WITHOUT WARRANTY
   OF ANY KIND, EITHER EXPRESS OR IMPLIED, INCLUDING BUT NOT LIMITED TO
   THE IMPLIED WARRANTIES OF MERCHANTABILITY AND FITNESS FOR A PARTICULAR
   PURPOSE. IN NO EVENT SHALL JOHN A. JUNOD BE LIABLE FOR ANY DAMAGES
   WHATSOEVER INCLUDING DIRECT, INDIRECT, INCIDENTAL, CONSEQUENTIAL, LOSS
   OF BUSINESS PROFITS OR SPECIAL DAMAGES, EVEN IF JOHN A. JUNOD HAS BEEN
   ADVISED OF THE POSSIBILITY OF SUCH DAMAGES.


*****************************************************************************/
```

```
/*
   MODULE: WS_GLOB.H   (global header file)
*/

#include <stdio.h>
#include <string.h>

#ifdef _MSC_
#include <direct.h>
#else
#include <dir.h>
#endif

#include "winsock.h"

#ifndef WS_GLOBHEADER

#define WS_GLOBHEADER

#ifndef INADDR_NONE
#define INADDR_NONE 0xffffffff
#endif

#ifndef MAXHOSTNAMELEN
#define MAXHOSTNAMELEN 64
#endif

#ifndef MAXPACKET
#define MAXPACKET 4096
#endif

// some miscellaneous definitions that we use

#define FTP_PRELIM     1
#define FTP_COMPLETE   2
#define FTP_CONTINUE   3
#define FTP_RETRY      4
#define FTP_ERROR      5

#ifndef IS_GLOBAL_C

extern BOOL bAutoStart;
extern BOOL bAborted;

extern u_int uiTimeOut;                  // 30 second timeout??

extern char szMsgBuf[MAXPACKET];      // main i/o buffer
extern u_char szSendPkt[MAXPACKET];   // output transfer buffer
extern char szString[512];            // temp string area
extern char szMailAddress[];
extern char szViewer[];
extern char szDlgPrompt[80];             // used by input dialog as prompt
```

```
extern char szDlgEdit[80];              // used by input dialog box for output
extern char szUserID[80];               // used by host dialog box for userid
extern char szPassWord[80];             // used by host dialog box for password
extern char szRemoteHost[80];            // remote host name/addr to connect to
extern char szGateUserID[80];           // used by host dialog box for gateway userid
extern char szGatePassWord[80];         // used by host dialog box for gateway password
extern char szGateHost[80];              // gateway host name/addr to connect to
extern char szAppName[20];               // this programs name "ws_ftp"
extern char szTmpFile[];                 // used for directory listings
extern char szTmp1File[];                // used for remote file displays
extern char szIniFile[];                // INI filename

extern char szFormName[10];             // ** not used in this version
extern char szModeName[10];             // ** not used in this version
extern char szStructName[10];           // ** not used in this version
extern char szTypeName[10];             // ** not used in this version

extern char fType;                      // file transfer type
extern char cType;                      // current transfer type
extern char cForm;                      // format (not used???)
extern char cMode;                      // mode (not used???)

extern GLOBALHANDLE hGMem[100];         // memory for debug window display

extern HCURSOR hStdCursor;             // cursors
extern HCURSOR hWaitCursor;            // cursors

extern HWND hInst;                      // handle of instance
extern HWND hWndMain;                   // handle of main window
// child window handles
extern HWND hLbxLDir,hLbxLFiles,hLbxRDir,hLbxRFiles;
extern HWND hBtnLCWD,hBtnLMKD,hBtnLRMD,hBtnLDisplay,hBtnLREN,hBtnLDEL;
extern HWND hBtnRCWD,hBtnRMKD,hBtnRRMD,hBtnRDisplay,hBtnRREN,hBtnRDEL;
extern HWND hBtnLtoR,hBtnRtoL;
extern HWND hBtnConnect,hBtnClose,hBtnLong,hBtnOption,hBtnAbout,hBtnExit;
extern HWND hTxtLDir,hTxtRHost,hTxtRDir,hTxtStatus,hTxtLBytes,hTxtRBytes;
extern HWND hRBascii,hRBbinary,hRB18,    hTxtStatus1;
extern HWND hScroll;
#define SCRLWND 7531

extern int bConnected;                  // connected flag
extern int bCmdInProgress;              // command in progress flag
extern int bSendPort;                   // use PORT commands (must be 1!!!)
extern int use_gateway ;

extern int nWndx;                       // the x axis multiplier
extern int nWndy;                       // the y axis multiplier

// options
extern int bBell;           // completion bell (not used in this version)
extern int bCRstrip;        // CRLF conversion (not used in this version)
extern int bDoGlob;         // globbing (not used in this version)
```

```
extern int bHash;              // show hash (not used in this version)
extern int bInteractive;    // prompting (not used in this version)
extern int bMCase;           // case conversion (not used in this version)
extern int bRecvUniq;        // unique name on receive (not used in this ver)
extern int bStorUniq;        // unique name on transmit (not used in this ver)
extern int bVerbose;         // maximum verbosity (turns extra debug msgs on)

extern int iCode;              // return code from last command(..)

extern int ptrhGMem;

extern SOCKET ctrl_socket;          // control channel socket
extern SOCKET data_socket;          // data channel socket
extern SOCKET listen_socket;        // data listen socket

extern struct sockaddr saDestAddr;
extern struct sockaddr_in saSockAddr;          // endpoint address
extern struct sockaddr_in saSockAddr1;         // used when bSendPort==0
extern struct sockaddr_in saCtrlAddr;

extern WORD sVPos;                      // scroll pos for debug window

extern WSADATA WSAData;                 // windows sockets dll information

#endif /* if IS_GLOBAL_C */

#endif /* if WS_GLOBHEADER */
```

References

It's a fact: network programming is a complex task. Don't undertake it alone! The following books and references can help you out.

Books

Comer, Douglas E. and David L. Stevens, *Internetworking with TCP/IP, Volumes I through III*, Prentice Hall, ISBN 0-13-468505-9. This is a great set of books for learning the details about TCP/IP. Volume I is a great introduction to TCP/IP. Volume II develops a complete TCP/IP implementation. Volume III presents network programming using the BSD Sockets API.

Stevens, W. Richard, and Gary R. Wright, *TCP/IP Illustrated, Volumes 1 and 2*, Addison-Wesley, ISBN 0-201-63346-9 (vol 1), ISBN 0-201-63354-X (vol 2). Volume 1 describes the TCP/IP protocol suite. Volume 2 examines the source code to the BSD Unix TCP/IP implementation.

Hafner, Katie and Matthew Lyon, *Where the Wizards Stay Up Late: A History of the Internet*, Simon & Schuster, to be published, 1996. This is shaping up as a great source for those interested in the origins of the Internet and the people who made it happen. Look for it in 1996.

ARPANET, the Defense Data Network, and Internet, from *The Froehlich/Kent Encyclopedia of Telecommunications, Volume 1*, Froehlich, Fritz E., Ph.D. editor-in-chief, Marcel Dekker, Inc., 1991. This contains a fairly thorough history of the Internet from the ARPANET beginnings through the conversion to TCP/IP and the development of NSFnet.

Specifications

The networking world is governed by specifications. Be sure to check out the set of RFCs available on the companion CD-ROM for the last word on all the protocols discussed in this book and many others. The companion CD-ROM also includes the Windows Sockets specification.

Information Online

There are many information sources on the Internet itself. Check these out:

Retrieving RFCs

Although the companion CD-ROM contains all the RFCs available at press time, new RFCs are released frequently. To see what is available and retrieve the new documents, FTP to *ds.internic.net* and look in the */rfc* directory. The latest RFC index is always named *rfc-index.txt*. Simply find the RFC's of interest and download them.

FTP and World Wide Web

Stardust Technologies maintains a great FTP server and World Wide Web server. You'll find the latest versions of the Windows Sockets specification, Winsock applications, and development information. Check out *ftp.stardust.com* and *www.stardust.com* using an FTP client or Web browser.

USENET

USENET can be a great source for network programming information. Check out *comp.os.ms-windows.programmer.networks* for discussions about Winsock.

Mailing Lists

Several mailing lists are available to support Winsock programmers and discuss aspects of the Winsock spec. Send mail to *majordomo@intel.com* with "help" in the body of the message (no subject needed). The majordomo account goes to an automated mail list robot that can add and remove you from mailing lists. When the server receives the "help" message, it will send back a complete set of instructions.

You can also place the "lists" in the body of a mail message to get information about the various mailing lists. The lists of interest are those beginning with "winsock". The "winsock-hackers" list discusses Winsock programming in particular, rather than Winsock specification issues.

When you send a note to the mailing list, it is sent to all the other members of the list. You can reply to the notes of others and discussions can be carried on very quickly. Be prepared to receive a lot of mail, however. Hot topics can result in an emailbox overflowing with messages.

Using the
Companion
CD-ROM

The companion CD-ROM contains over 125 megabytes of the best programs to help you get the most out of the Internet, especially if you're interested in creating your own applications to access the Net. A few of these shareware and freeware programs and resources are described here, but make sure you look at the CD-ROM directory for the complete list. And don't be afraid to experiment!

I've included all the source code from the book, as well as code modules for C and Pascal that will aid you in creating your own applications. The source code is located in the \SOURCE directory, and the code modules are located in the \WINSOCK directory.

As a bonus, we've also included the complete documentation of the Internet Request For Comments (RFCs). These documents contain all the information and specifications that have been used to create the Internet protocols we use today. If you want to learn the intricate details of a particular protocol, this is the place to look.

You've probably heard shareware described as "software on the honor system." Basically, if you try a program and decide to keep and use it, you should register and pay for it. Basic registration instructions are given for each of the shareware programs discussed here, but more details can be found in the programs themselves, usually in the form of a "readme" file or help screen.

Freeware is fully functional software that the author has generously made available to whomever wants it, no strings attached (although commercial versions, with more features, are sometimes available). Note, however, that the author almost always retains full rights to the program, and distribution policies vary, so read any copyright information carefully before you distribute your favorite freeware program to friends and business associates.

Enjoy!

Connecting to the Net

Trumpet Winsock

What: Trumpet Winsock is a TCP/IP dial-up client that facilitates Internet connections.
Where on the CD-ROM: \CONNECT\TRUMPET
Setup file: Read the INSTALL.DOC file

Trumpet Winsock is probably one of the most widely used shareware programs ever written. Why? Because it's simple and reliable. Trumpet can be used as a TCP/IP stack for internal or external use. In other words, it works over a LAN or a phone line. Trumpet is usually used over a phone line to connect to a service provider.

The documentation that comes with Trumpet tells you everything you need to know about using it, so we recommend looking at the INSTALL.DOC file for help setting it up.

Internet Chameleon with Instant Internet

What: Suite of applications to aid you in getting set up on the Net.
Where on the CD-ROM: \CONNECT\INSTINET\DISK1
Setup file: SETUP.EXE

Internet Chameleon is a complete Windows-based Internet connection suite. You can use it to get connected to just about every corner of the Internet. Supported protocols include FTP, Telnet, email, Ping, and the World Wide Web. If you haven't set yourself up with an access provider yet, this package or the NetCom package is a good way to start.

Before you run the install program, it's best to close all other running programs, because the program will make some minor changes to your AUTOEXEC.BAT file and will need to restart the computer for those changes to take effect.

To begin the installation, run SETUP.EXE in the \CONNECT\INSTINET\DISK1 directory. Then, when the install program asks for the next two disks, simply enter the path name that points to the appropriate disks.

We recommend registering the software to get the full benefit of the package, but do try it first to see whether you like it.

NetCom Netcrusier

What: Suite of applications to aid you in getting set up on the Net.
Where on the CD-ROM: \CONNECT\NETCRUIS
Setup file: SETUP.EXE

NetCom's Netcruiser is an easy way to get going on the Internet if you are starting from scratch. It allows you to get set up—providing you use NetCom's service. What you give up in connection options you gain back in ease of use. Netcruiser features a very complete, integrated environment that includes all the software you will need for Internet exploring.

Internet Documentation

What: Internet STDs, Request for Comments (RFCs), and FYIs.
Where on the CD-ROM: \DOCS

These are some pretty impressive documents. Basically, you get all the notes, memos, and specifications that have been used to document the growth and development of the Internet. This might sound too good to be true, but it's not! If you want to learn more about a certain Internet protocol or standard, the information is here. Since 1969, these memos have been written up and passed between colleagues so that everyone would have a common point of reference for developing new protocols or building applications that worked with older ones.

For instance, if you want to know exactly how the FTP protocol should be implemented, just look it up here! If you want to find out who was involved with a certain committee or project, that's here too.

Three different types of documents are listed. First, in the \DOCS\RFC directory, you'll find the Requests For Comments (RFCs). These documents contain the information about a new protocol so that it can get approved (or killed). These are the working notes of the committees that develop the protocols and standards for the Internet. Next are the FYIs (For Your Information). They're a subset of the RFCs and tend to be more informational and less technical. Finally, the STDs (Internet Activities Board standards) are what RFCs grow up to be. When an RFC becomes fully accepted and serves as a standard, it's designated as an STD—much like a bill becoming law.

In each of these directories, you'll find indexes to help you locate the specific document you need.

Internet Tools

HomePage Creator

What: Visual home page designer tool.
Where on the CD-ROM: \TOOLS\HTMLEDIT\HPC
Setup File: SETUP.EXE

HomePage Creator is a new tool designed to help you automatically create your own Web pages. It's not just another HTML editor, though. It allows you to insert a picture, text, and links to your favorite sites on the Web and then does the dirty work of generating HTML tags for you.

The installation procedure for HomePage Creator is easy: Just run the SETUP.EXE program in the directory \TOOLS\HTMLEDIT\HPC. You'll need to specify the directory where you want to install the HomePage Creator program. The developer of this program, Demetris Kafas, is currently developing a more feature-rich version of HomePage Creator that you'll be able to purchase in the future.

Microsoft Internet Assistant for Word 6.0

What: Word 6.0-based HTML editor.
Where on the CD-ROM: \TOOLS\HTMLEDIT\IA
Setup File: SETUP.EXE
Where on the Net: ftp://ftp.microsoft.com

Internet Assistant is both a powerful HTML document creator and an easy-to-use Web browser. The creation of documents is very easy, although a little slow. You simply type in your code, and format it by using styles and the extra toolbar that it creates while you are editing or browsing Web pages. You can move from document creating, to editing, to browsing with the click of a button.

The downside of this package is speed—or the lack of it. Because of the inherent overhead of the Word 6.0 environment, processing tends to be a little slow. However, if you're patient, the rewards are gratifying. Many of the Word tools still work with the Assistant, including spell-checking and grammar-checking. You won't find those features in very many standalone products.

HotMetal

What: HTML editor.
Where on the CD-ROM: \TOOLS\HTMLEDIT\HOTMETAL
Setup File: HMINST.EXE
Where on the Net: ftp://ftp.ncsa.uiuc.edu/Web/html/hotmetal/

HotMetal is a Windows-based freeware HTML editor from SoftQuad. An HTML editor is a standalone program used to write Web pages.

HotMetal has several elements that make it a good choice for beginning HTML publishers. It sticks to the basic, standard features of HTML, so you won't be overwhelmed by dozens of different tags. In fact, selecting Hide Tags from the View menu lets you ignore the tags altogether, so you can read just the text on the page that, for example, you saved to disk from someone else's Web site. Also, the **Structure** function (available from the View menu) creates an "outline" of your document, so you can keep track of its links without driving yourself crazy.

Best of all, HotMetal comes with 14 templates for typical documents like home pages, customer registration forms, and hotlists. Just choose File|Open Template, pick the appropriate one from the list, type your text between the tags, save your work as an HTM file, and *voila!*—instant HTML. Be sure to start with readme3.htm—a template that describes the other templates.

It's possible to run HotMetal straight from the CD, but installing it on your hard disk is more practical. It's not self-installing, so you'll have to copy the entire

\HOTMETAL branch from the CD to the root directory of your hard drive, and then make an icon for it. Here are the steps to follow:

1. In Program Manager, open (or create) the group in which you want HotMetal to be placed.

2. Choose File|New. The Program Item option should be selected. Click on OK to display the Program Item Properties dialog box.

3. Type HotMetal in the Description box.

4. Click on Browse and navigate through your hard disk until you find sqhm.exe. Click on that file to select it, then click on OK.

5. Click on OK again, and the HotMetal icon should appear in your group.

HotMetal takes up only about 5 MB of hard disk space, but is fairly greedy in its memory consumption. So, unless you have plenty of RAM to spare, it's a good idea to shut down other programs when you run HotMetal.

HTML Assistant

What: HTML editor.
Where on the CD-ROM: \TOOLS\HTMLEDIT\HTMLASST
Where on the Net: http://fox.nstn.ca/~harawitz/htmlpro1.html

HTML Assistant is an extremely popular freeware HTML editor for Windows. Like HotMetal, it's a standalone program for creating Web pages. The two differ, however, in their approach and specific feature sets. HTML Assistant doesn't come with a wide variety of pre-written templates like HotMetal does, but makes up for that with an elegant interface and an easy-to-use **Test** function that lets you see how your page will actually look on the Web.

The installation procedure for HTML Assistant is basically the same as for Hot Metal: Copy the directory and create a program icon. The file that runs HTML Assistant (step 4 in the installation instructions listed for HotMetal) is different from the one for HotMetal, of course; the one to browse for here is HTMLASST.EXE.

To create a page with HTML Assistant, start by choosing Command|Display Standard Document Template. This will bring up a skeleton Web page with basic codes. Add your text, and then add other elements by clicking on them from the toolbars or selecting them from the menus. When your page looks ready, choose Save and type in the filename, including the HTM extension. *Important: You have to explicitly type .HTM; it won't be added for you, and without it, your pages won't display properly.*

The real fun starts after you've saved a document. Click on the Test button. The first time you do this, you'll be asked for the test program name—the filename of the browser program you use. HTML Assistant will then run the browser, and your pages will appear just as they would on the Web! Note, however, that you have to close the browser yourself so HTML Assistant can restart it the next time you want to test a page. Once you've gotten the hang of basic HTML, dive into HTML Assistant's extensive support for URLs and start creating lots o' links.

HTMLed

What: Another HTML editor—very easy to use.
Where on the CD-ROM: \TOOLS\HTMLEDIT\HTMLED

This powerful HTML editor features a very well-laid-out interface. All the often-used tags are here, ready to use. The menus are also clear and intuitive. Unfortunately, HTMLed does not support any of the HTML3 tags (yet), but the author tells us that this omission will soon be corrected.

No installation instructions are provided, but you won't miss them. Just create a directory somewhere on your hard drive and copy all the files to that directory. Or you can just run the program off the CD. If you're already familiar with HTML, I highly recommend this program for its great interface and intuitive use of function keys and shortcuts.

Web Spinner

What: HTML editor (yes, another one).
Where on the CD-ROM: \TOOLS\HTMLEDIT\WEBSPIN
Setup File: SETUP.EXE

Web Spinner is the new kid on the block of HTML editors. It's a very powerful but easy-to-use editor for creating HTML documents. Web Spinner is a snap to install and to use. Just make sure you have Win32s installed on your computer if you're running Windows 3.1. If you're running Windows 95, you won't need Win32s to run Web Spinner.

This simple application uses multiple child windows to speed up page creation. The toolbars are some of the best designed I've seen anywhere. Adding images, horizontal rules, and special characters is simple to do. Web Spinner also lets you customize image placement to allow for formatted alignments.

Setting up links and anchors is painless also. Just highlight and click—Web Spinner displays a dialog box with all the available options. Even though this is a newer product, it does not support HTML3. Look for a slew of new editors that will make it a snap to create HTML3-compliant pages.

Win32s

What: Windows 32-bit API extension
Where on the CD-ROM: \TOOLS\WIN32S\DISK1
Setup File: SETUP.EXE
Where on the Net: ftp://ftp.microsoft.com

This Windows API (Application Programming Interface) is just about a prerequisite for modern Windows software. Win32s adds support for many 32-bit Windows calls, which many packages use to speed up programs—a huge difference when running complicated applications that perform a lot of file I/O (like Web browsers).

Webster

What: Custom control that contains a complete Web browser.
Where on the CD-ROM: \TOOLS\OCX\WEBSTER
Where on the Net: http://www.vpm.com/trafalmador/index.htm

Trafalmador has created a new way to travel the World Wide Web: Build your own browser, using the Webster HTML OCX. Available in both 16- and 32-bit versions, Webster provides a complete solution for both local and networked hypertext document retrieval and display.

This is one of the neatest custom controls we've ever seen! It's a complete HTML3 Web browser—all contained in a single control. Just drop the control on a form, run the program, and that's it—you've got a fully functional browser. If you want to customize it a little, or a lot, no problem—Webster gives you the ability to easily add features like security or your hotlists.

Internet Plug 'n' Play

What: 32-bit OCX custom controls that accesses the Internet.
Where on the CD-ROM: \TOOLS\OCX\INTERNET
Where on the Net: ftp://ftp.toupin.com/~etoupin

Here's another great way to use custom controls to get connected to the Net from within your own applications. In this directory, you'll find several 32-bit OCX controls that encompass many of the most popular Internet protocols. Supported protocols include FTP, GetHost, Ping, WHOIS, Finger, and SMTP (email).

These controls make it very easy to create some very powerful Internet-aware programs with a minimal amount of work.

Winsock Applications

If you look in the \WINSOCK directory, you'll see many applications that use Winsock to access the Internet. We could write an entire book about these programs, but we'll just highlight a couple here and let you experiment with the rest. Most of the applications have their own setup files and documentation, which we recommend you read first.

VRML Browsers

What: Three-dimensional interactive interfaces to the Internet.
Where on the CD-ROM: \APPS\VRML

The Virtual Reality Modeling Language (VRML) has received a tremendous amount of press in the past year, but what is it all about? VRML is being hailed as the best way to interact with other people and places. It gives the user a real-time 3D view of a simulated environment. However, at this point, the environments are very plain, and most connections are too slow to make VRML effective. That doesn't mean VRML serves no purpose. After all, we have to start somewhere.

Right now, VRML is mostly just a gimmick, but in a year or so it will be much more mainstream, especially as people move away from standard phone line modems to faster methods of data transfer like cable modems and ISDN.

Give these programs a try and see what you think.

NetSeeker

NetSeeker™ is a product created by The Coriolis Group that downloads programs from the Internet, uncompresses them, and installs them. Before you can use NetSeeker, you must make sure that you are connected to the Internet.

Running NetSeeker

To use NetSeeker, follow these steps:

1. Install NetSeeker by running the SETUP.EXE program located in the \NETSEEK directory on the CD-ROM.

2. Run your Internet connection software to connect to the Internet.

3. Once you are connected to the Internet, run the NetSeeker program (NETSEEK.EXE) by double clicking on its icon in the program group.

4. To continue, click on the Begin button. NetSeeker will then take over and access the Internet for you to obtain setup information. *This may take a few moments.*

While NetSeeker is accessing the Internet, status information will be displayed in a status box at the center of the screen and in the status panel at the bottom of the NetSeeker window. During these periods, NetSeeker will be automatically downloading files for you. The status bar tells you the percentage of the download that has been completed. You can cancel the process at any time by clicking the Cancel button.

When NetSeeker has finished its configuration, the message "NetSeeker Setup Complete! You may begin." is displayed at the bottom status panel, and the startup screen will change.

You are now ready to use NetSeeker to access new Internet applications or to update your old ones.

If NetSeeker can't configure itself, you will receive a message indicating that you are either not currently connected to the Internet or that the NetSeeker database cannot be accessed. For more information on what to do if problems occur, see the section "Troubleshooting NetSeeker" in this guide.

Using the NetSeeker Interface

The main NetSeeker window provides two groups of selectable options: *clickable tabs* and *buttons*. You click on one of the tabs to select a particular software program or a group of resources that you want to retrieve from the Internet. The buttons operate as follows:

Install	Starts the downloading and installation process. When this button is clicked, only the programs and resources that you've previously selected will be downloaded and installed.
Info	Displays information about NetSeeker including its version number.
Activity	Displays a log of the programs and resources that you've previously downloaded and installed with NetSeeker.
Help	Displays help information for using NetSeeker.
Options	Displays an Options dialog box so that you can select different installation options.
Exit	Quits NetSeeker.

Using NetSeeker to Download Resources and Software

To download and install a particular software program or set of resources, follow these steps:

1. Click on the tab that represents the software or group of resources that you want to retrieve from the Internet. (Some of the options may include Netscape, Helper Programs, Web Publishing, NCSA, Mosaic, and so on.)

2. When the new section appears, select the different options you want to download by clicking the appropriate check boxes.

3. Click on the Install button.

4. NetSeeker will then display a dialog box so that you can create a diretory to store the file(s) that NetSeeker will download. After you've selected or created a directory, click on OK.

   NetSeeker will then display the software you've selected from the Internet. As it downloads the file(s), a status indicator will be displayed at the center of the

NetSeeker window. If you are downloading a large file or if you have a slow connection to the Internet, this process could take a few minutes.

After NetSeeker finishes retrieving the file(s) for you, it will automatically decompress and install all of the programs and files that it has retrieved, if necessary. To decompress some files, NetSeeker may need to run a DOS program. If you desire, you can turn off the automatic installation feature by clicking on the Options button and deselecting the appropriate check box.

Selecting Installation Options

If you are downloading an application, NetSeeker offers a few options. Fr instance, NetSeeker will automatically uncompress files retrieved for you and install them on your hard drive. You can override any of these installation features at any time by clicking on the Options button.

Here is a description of these options:

Automatic Uncompress   When this option is selected, the files that are retrieved by NetSeeker will automatically be uncompressed for you. If you deselect this option, you'll need to uncompress the files that are retrieved manually.

Automatic Installation   When this option is selected, NetSeeker will both uncompress and install the files and programs that it retrieves. Installing programs typically involves running a special setup program and updating Windows configuration files.

Getting More Help and Information

You can view help information for NetSeeker at any time by clicking on the Help button. If you want more information about the software and resources that NetSeeker can retrieve for you, you can use the Info feature. To get more information:

1. Click on the tab that corresponds with the software or resource group you are interested in. For example, Helpers, Netscape, Internet Tools, and so on.

2. Click on the Info button.

Notice that the Information window displays a description and file sizes for the software that is available for you to retrieve.

When you are done viewing this window, click on its close button, on the Exit menu command, or anywhere on the form to make it disappear.

Getting a Report of Your Activity

NetSeeker allows you to view or print a log of your installation activity so that you can keep track of what you've retrieved from the Internet. To use this feature, click on the Activity button.

Notice that each entry listed contains a date, time, description, and version number. You can print a report by clicking on the Print menu. You can also delete an entry in the log by selecting the item with the mouse and then clicking on the Clear menu. NetSeeker will then display a confirmation dialog box to verify that you really want to delete the item you've selected.

Quitting NetSeeker

To quit NetSeeker, click on the Exit button. After NetSeeker shuts down, you may want to disconnect from the Internet if you no longer need to be connected.

Troubleshooting NetSeeker

In this section, we present some problems that you may encounter while you are using NetSeeker and the possible solutions to help you out.

When I first run NetSeeker, nothing happens.
In order for NetSeeker to run properly, you must restart your computer after running the installation program. If restarting your computer doesn't help, try reinstalling NetSeeker and restarting your computer.

You must also have TCP/IP Internet connection software running on your computer before you can start NetSeeker.

After I click on the Begin button, nothing happens or I get a timeout error.
This indicates that your computer is not currently connected to the Internet. You must quit NetSeeker, connect to the Internet, and then restart NetSeeker.

After I click on the Begin, button I get a "Busy-Try Again" warning.
This indicates that the NetSeeker Internet site is swamped with requests and that you should try again in a moment. If you continue to have problems logging in, you might want to wait a few minutes before trying again.

While I'm retrieving files with NetSeeker, I receive a download error message.
NetSeeker may encounter a problem while retrieving a file for you, but it will do its best to keep trying. If after trying a number of times it can't retrieve the file for you, you may want to cancel and try again in a few minutes.

Index

—G—

—X—

CORIOLIS GROUP BOOKS
Order Form

Name _____

Company _____

Address _____

City/State/Zip _____

Phone _____

VISA/MC # _____ Expires: _____

Signature for charge orders: _____

Quantity	Description	Unit price	Extension
	FAX, Phone, or **send this order form to:**	**TOTAL**	

The Coriolis Group
7339 E. Acoma Drive, Suite 7
Scottsdale, AZ 85260

FAX us your order at (602) 483-0193
Phone us your order at (800) 410-0192

Form: 24-X

Way More!
New Titles from Coriolis

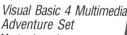